HOW TO THINK ABOUT ALGORITHMS

There are many algorithm texts that provide lots of well-polished code and proofs of correctness. Instead, this one presents insights, notations, and analogies to help the novice describe and think about algorithms like an expert. It is a bit like a carpenter studying hammers instead of houses. Jeff Edmonds provides both the big picture and easy step-by-step methods for developing algorithms, while avoiding the common pitfalls. Paradigms such as loop invariants and recursion help to unify a huge range of algorithms into a few meta-algorithms. Part of the goal is to teach students to think abstractly. Without getting bogged down in formal proofs, the book fosters deeper understanding so that how and why each algorithm works is transparent. These insights are presented in a slow and clear manner accessible to second- or third-year students of computer science, preparing them to find on their own innovative ways to solve problems.

Abstraction is when you translate the equations, the rules, and the underlying essences of the problem not only into a language that can be communicated to your friend standing with you on a streetcar, but also into a form that can percolate down and dwell in your subconscious. Because, remember, it is your subconscious that makes the miraculous leaps of inspiration, not your plodding perspiration and not your cocky logic. And remember, unlike you, your subconscious does not understand Java code.

HOW TO THINK ABOUT ALGORITHMS

JEFF EDMONDS

York University

CAMBRIDGE
UNIVERSITY PRESS

CAMBRIDGE UNIVERSITY PRESS
Cambridge, New York, Melbourne, Madrid, Cape Town, Singapore, Sao Paulo, Delhi

Cambridge University Press
32 Avenue of the Americas, New York, NY 10013-2473, USA

www.cambridge.org
Information on this title: www.cambridge.org/9780521614108

First published 2008

Printed in the United States of America

A catalog record for this publication is available from the British Library.

Library of Congress Cataloging in Publication data

Edmonds, Jeff, 1963–
How to think about algorithms / Jeff Edmonds.
    p.   cm.
Includes index.
ISBN 978-0-521-84931-9 (hardback) – ISBN 978-0-521-61410-8 (pbk.)
1. Algorithms – Study and teaching.   2. Loops (Group theory) – Study and teaching.
3. Invariants – Study and teaching.   4. Recursion theory – Study and teaching.   I. Title.
QA9.58.E36   2008
518′.1–dc22   2008001238

ISBN 978-0-521-84931-9 hardback
ISBN 978-0-521-61410-8 paperback

Dedicated to my father, Jack, and to my sons, Joshua and Micah.

May the love and the mathematics continue to flow between the generations.

Problem Solving
Out of the Box Leaping
Deep Thinking
Creative Abstracting
Logical Deducing
with Friends Working
Fun Having
Fumbling and Bumbling
Bravely Persevering
Joyfully Succeeding

CONTENTS

Contents

viii

Contents

x

PREFACE

To the Educator and the Student

This book is designed to be used in a twelve-week, third-year algorithms course. The goal is to teach students to think abstractly about algorithms and about the key algorithmic techniques used to develop them.

Meta-Algorithms: Students must learn so many algorithms that they are sometimes overwhelmed. In order to facilitate their understanding, most textbooks cover the standard themes of iterative algorithms, recursion, greedy algorithms, and dynamic programming. Generally, however, when it comes to presenting the algorithms themselves and their proofs of correctness, the concepts are hidden within optimized code and slick proofs. One goal of this book is to present a uniform and clean way of thinking about algorithms. We do this by focusing on the structure and proof of correctness of *iterative* and *recursive* meta-algorithms, and within these the *greedy* and *dynamic programming* meta-algorithms. By learning these and their proofs of correctness, most actual algorithms can be easily understood. The challenge is that thinking about meta-algorithms requires a great deal of abstract thinking.

Abstract Thinking: Students are very good at learning how to apply a concrete code to a concrete input instance. They tend, however, to find it difficult to think abstractly about the algorithms. I maintain that the more abstractions a person has from which to view the problem, the deeper his understanding of it will be, the more tools he will have at his disposal, and the better prepared he will be to design his own innovative ways to solve new problems. Hence, I present a number of different notations, analogies, and paradigms within which to develop and to think about algorithms.

Way of Thinking: People who develop algorithms have various ways of thinking and intuition that tend not to get taught. The assumption, I suppose, is that these cannot be taught but must be figured out on one's own. This text attempts to teach students to think like a designer of algorithms.

Not a Reference Book: My intention is not to teach a specific selection of algorithms for specific purposes. Hence, the book is not organized according to the application of the algorithms, but according to the techniques and abstractions used to develop them.

Developing Algorithms: The goal is not to present completed algorithms in a nice clean package, but to go slowly through every step of the development. Many false starts have been added. The hope is that this will help students learn to develop algorithms on their own. The difference is a bit like the difference between studying carpentry by looking at houses and by looking at hammers.

Proof of Correctness: Our philosophy is not to follow an algorithm with a formal proof that it is correct. Instead, this text is about learning how to think about, develop, and describe algorithms in such way that their correctness is transparent.

Big Picture vs. Small Steps: For each topic, I attempt both to give the big picture and to break it down into easily understood steps.

Level of Presentation: This material is difficult. There is no getting around that. I have tried to figure out where confusion may arise and to cover these points in more detail. I try to balance the succinct clarity that comes with mathematical formalism against the personified analogies and metaphors that help to provide both intuition and humor.

Point Form: The text is organized into blocks, each containing a title and a single thought. Hopefully, this will make the text easier to lecture and study from.

Prerequisites: The text assumes that the students have completed a first-year programming course and have a general mathematical maturity. The Appendix (Part Four) covers much of the mathematics that will be needed.

Homework Questions: A few homework questions are included. I am hoping to develop many more, along with their solutions. Contributions are welcome.

Read Ahead: The student is expected to read the material *before* the lecture. This will facilitate productive discussion during class.

Explaining: To be able to prove yourself on a test or on the job, you need to be able to explain the material well. In addition, explaining it to someone else is the best way to learn it yourself. Hence, I highly recommend spending a lot of time explaining the material over and over again out loud to yourself, to each other, and to your stuffed bear.

Dreaming: I would like to emphasis the importance of thinking, even daydreaming, about the material. This can be done while going through your day – while swimming, showering, cooking, or lying in bed. Ask questions. Why is it done this way and not that way? Invent other algorithms for solving a problem. Then look for input instances for which your algorithm gives the wrong answer. Mathematics is not all linear thinking.  If the essence of the material, what the questions are really asking, is allowed to seep down into your subconscious then with time little thoughts will begin to percolate up. Pursue these ideas. Sometimes even flashes of inspiration appear.

Acknowledgments

I would like to thank Andy Mirzaian, Franck van Breugel, James Elder, Suprakash Datta, Eric Ruppert, Russell Impagliazzo, Toniann Pitassi, and Kirk Pruhs, with whom I co-taught and co-researched algorithms for many years. I would like to thank Jennifer Wolfe and Lauren Cowles for their fantastic editing jobs. All of these people were a tremendous support for this work.

Introduction

From determining the cheapest way to make a hot dog to monitoring the workings of a factory, there are many complex *computational problems* to be solved. Before executable *code* can be produced, computer scientists need to be able to design the *algorithms* that lie behind the code, be able to understand and describe such algorithms abstractly, and be confident that they work correctly and efficiently. These are the goals of computer scientists.

A Computational Problem: A specification of a computational problem uses *preconditions* and *postconditions* to describe for each legal *input instance* that the computation might receive, what the required output or actions are. This may be a function mapping each input instance to the required output. It may be an optimization problem which requires a solution to be outputted that is "optimal" from among a huge set of possible solutions for the given input instance. It may also be an ongoing system or data structure that responds appropriately to a constant stream of input.

   Example: The *sorting* problem is defined as follows:

   Preconditions: The input is a list of n values, including possible repetitions.

   Postconditions: The output is a list consisting of the same n values in non-decreasing order.

An Algorithm: An *algorithm* is a step-by-step procedure which, starting with an input instance, produces a suitable output. It is described at the level of detail and abstraction best suited to the human audience that must understand it. In contrast, *code* is an implementation of an algorithm that can be executed by a computer. *Pseudocode* lies between these two.

An Abstract Data Type: Computers use zeros and ones, ANDs and ORs, IFs and GOTOs. This does not mean that *we* have to. The description of an algorithm may talk of *abstract objects* such as integers, reals, strings, sets, stacks, graphs, and trees;

abstract operations such as "sort the list," "pop the stack," or "trace a path"; and *abstract relationships* such as greater than, prefix, subset, connected, and child. To be useful, the nature of these objects and the effect of these operations need to be understood. However, in order to hide details that are tedious or irrelevant, the precise implementations of these data structure and algorithms do not need to be specified. For more on this see Chapter 3.

Correctness: An algorithm for the problem is *correct* if for every legal input instance, the required output is produced. Though a certain amount of logical thinking is requireds, the goal of this text is to teach how to think about, develop, and describe algorithms in such way that their correctness is transparent. See Chapter 28 for the formal steps required to prove correctness, and Chapter 22 for a discussion of *forall* and *exist* statements that are essential for making formal statements.

Running Time: It is not enough for a computation to eventually get the correct answer. It must also do so using a reasonable amount of time and memory space. The *running time* of an algorithm is a function from the *size n* of the input instance given to a bound on the number of *operations* the computation must do. (See Chapter 23.) The algorithm is said to be *feasible* if this function is a *polynomial* like $Time(n) = \Theta(n^2)$, and is said to be *infeasible* if this function is an *exponential* like $Time(n) = \Theta(2^n)$. (See Chapters 24 and 25 for more on the asymptotics of functions.) To be able to compute the running time, one needs to be able to add up the times taken in each iteration of a loop and to solve the recurrence relation defining the time of a recursive program. (See Chapter 26 for an understanding of $\sum_{i=1}^{n} i = \Theta(n^2)$, and Chapter 27 for an understanding of $T(n) = 2T(\frac{n}{2}) + n = \Theta(n \log n)$.)

Meta-algorithms: Most algorithms are best described as being either *iterative* or *recursive*. An iterative algorithm (Part One) takes one step at a time, ensuring that each step makes *progress* while maintaining the *loop invariant*. A recursive algorithm (Part Two) breaks its instance into smaller instances, which it gets a *friend* to solve, and then combines their solutions into one of its own.

Optimization problems (Part Three) form an important class of computational problems. The key algorithms for them are the following. *Greedy* algorithms (Chapter 16) keep grabbing the next object that looks best. *Recursive backtracking* algorithms (Chapter 17) try things and, if they don't work, backtrack and try something else. *Dynamic programming* (Chapter 18) solves a sequence of larger and larger instances, reusing the previously saved solutions for the smaller instances, until a solution is obtained for the given instance. *Reductions* (Chapter 20) use an algorithm for one problem to solve another. *Randomized* algorithms (Chapter 21) flip coins to help them decide what actions to take. Finally, *lower bounds* (Chapter 7) prove that there are no faster algorithms.

PART ONE

Iterative Algorithms and Loop Invariants

1 Iterative Algorithms: Measures of Progress and Loop Invariants

Using an *iterative algorithm* to solve a computational problem is a bit like following a road, possibly long and difficult, from your start location to your destination. With each iteration, you have a method that takes you a single step closer. To ensure that you move forward, you need to have a *measure of progress* telling you how far you are either from your starting location or from your destination. You cannot expect to know exactly where the algorithm will go, so you need to expect some weaving and winding. On the other hand, you do not want to have to know how to handle every ditch and dead end in the world. A compromise between these two is to have a *loop invariant*, which defines a road (or region) that you may not leave. As you travel, worry about one step

at a time. You must know how to get onto the road from any start location. From every place along the road, you must know what actions you will take in order to step forward while not leaving the road. Finally, when sufficient progress has been made along the road, you must know how to exit and reach your destination in a reasonable amount of time.

1.1 A Paradigm Shift: A Sequence of Actions vs. a Sequence of Assertions

Understanding iterative algorithms requires understanding the difference between a *loop invariant*, which is an *assertion* or picture of the computation at a particular point in time, and the actions that are required to maintain such a loop invariant. Hence, we will start with trying to understand this difference.

One of the first important paradigm shifts that programmers struggle to make is from viewing an algorithm as a sequence of actions to viewing it as a sequence of snapshots of the state of the computer. Programmers tend to fixate on the first view, because code is a sequence of instructions for action and a computation is a sequence of actions. Though this is an important view, there is another. Imagine stopping time at key points during the computation and taking still pictures of the state of the computer. Then a computation can equally be viewed as a sequence of such snapshots. Having two ways of viewing the same thing gives one both more tools to handle it and a deeper understanding of it. An example of viewing a computation as an alteration between assertions about the current state of the computation and blocks of actions that bring the state of the computation to the next state is shown here.

Max(a, b, c)

   PreCond: Input has 3 numbers.

   $m = a$

   assert: m is max in $\{a\}$.

   if$(b > m)$

      $m = b$

   end if

   assert: m is max in $\{a,b\}$.

   if$(c > m)$

      $m = c$

   end if

   assert: m is max in $\{a,b,c\}$.

   return(m)

   PostCond: return max in $\{a,b,c\}$.

end algorithm

The Challenge of the Sequence-of-Actions View: Suppose one is designing a new algorithm or explaining an algorithm to a friend. If one is thinking of it as sequence of actions, then one will likely start at the beginning: Do this. Do that. Do this. Shortly one can get lost and not know where one is. To handle this, one simultaneously needs to keep track of how the state of the computer changes with each new action. In order to know what action to take next, one needs to have a global plan of where the computation is to go. To make it worse, the computation has many IFS and LOOPS so one has to consider all the various paths that the computation may take.

The Advantages of the Sequence of Snapshots View: This new paradigm is useful one from which one can think about, explain, or develop an algorithm.

Pre- and Postconditions: Before one can consider an algorithm, one needs to carefully define the computational problem being solved by it. This is done with pre- and postconditions by providing the initial picture, or *assertion*, about the input instance and a corresponding picture or assertion about required output.

Start in the Middle: Instead of starting with the first line of code, an alternative way to design an algorithm is to jump into the middle of the computation and to draw a static picture, or assertion, about the state we would like the computation to be in at this time. This picture does not need to state the exact value of each variable.

Instead, it gives general properties and relationships between the various data structures that are key to understanding the algorithm. If this assertion is sufficiently general, it will capture not just this one point during the computation, but many similar points. Then it might become a part of a loop.

Sequence of Snapshots: Once one builds up a sequence of assertions in this way, one can see the entire path of the computation laid out before one.

Fill in the Actions: These assertions are just static snapshots of the computation with time stopped. No actions have been considered yet. The final step is to fill in actions (code) between consecutive assertions.

One Step at a Time: Each such block of actions can be executed completely independently of the others. It is much easier to consider them one at a time than to worry about the entire computation at once. In fact, one can complete these blocks in any order one wants and modify one block without worrying about the effect on the others.

Fly In from Mars: This is how you should fill in the code between the ith and the $i + 1$st assertions. Suppose you have just flown in from Mars, and absolutely the only thing you know about the current state of your computation is that the ith assertion holds. The computation might actually be in a state that is completely impossible to arrive at, given the algorithm that has been designed so far. It is allowing this that provides independence between these blocks of actions.

Take One Step: Being in a state in which the ith assertion holds, your task is simply to write some simple code to do a few simple actions, that change the state of the computation so that the $i + 1$st assertion holds.

Proof of Correctness of Each Step: The proof that your algorithm works can also be done one block at a time. You need to prove that if time is stopped and the state of the computation is such that the ith assertion holds and you start time again just long enough to execute the next block of code, then when you stop time again the state of the computation will be such that the $i + 1$st assertion holds. This proof might be a formal mathematical proof, or it might be informal handwaving. Either way, the formal statement of what needs to be proved is as follows:

$$\langle ith-assertion \rangle \,\&\, code_i \;\Rightarrow\; \langle i + 1st-assertion \rangle$$

Proof of Correctness of the Algorithm: All of these individual steps can be put together into a whole working algorithm. We assume that the input instance given meets the precondition. At some point, we proved that if the precondition holds and the first block of code is executed, then the state of the computation will be such that first assertion holds. At some other point, we proved that if the first assertion holds and the second block of code is executed then the state of the computation will be such that second assertion holds. This was done for each block. All of these independently proved statements can be put together to prove that if initially the input instance meets the precondition and the entire code is executed, then in the end the state of the computation will be such that the postcondition has been met. This is what is required to prove that algorithm works.

1.2 The Steps to Develop an Iterative Algorithm

Iterative Algorithms: A good way to structure many computer programs is to store the key information you currently know in some data structure and then have each iteration of the main loop take a step towards your destination by making a simple change to this data.

Loop Invariant: A *loop invariant* expresses important relationships among the variables that must be true at the start of every iteration and when the loop terminates. If it is true, then the computation is still on the road. If it is false, then the algorithm has failed.

The Code Structure: The basic structure of the code is as follows.

```
begin routine
    ⟨pre-cond⟩
    code_pre-loop   % Establish loop invariant
    loop
        ⟨loop-invariant⟩
        exit when ⟨exit-cond⟩
        code_loop   % Make progress while maintaining the loop invariant
    end loop
    code_post-loop   % Clean up loose ends
    ⟨post-cond⟩
end routine
```

Proof of Correctness: Naturally, you want to be sure your algorithm will work on all specified inputs and give the correct answer.

Running Time: You also want to be sure that your algorithm completes in a reasonable amount of time.

The Most Important Steps: If you need to design an algorithm, do not start by typing in code without really knowing how or why the algorithm works. Instead, I recommend first accomplishing the following tasks. See Figure 1.1. These tasks need to fit

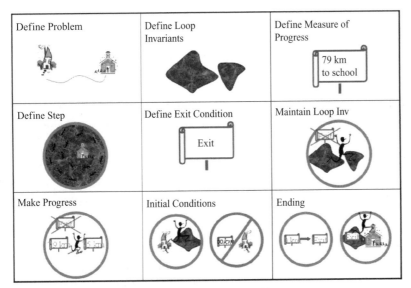

Define Problem	Define Loop Invariants	Define Measure of Progress
		79 km to school
Define Step	Define Exit Condition	Maintain Loop Inv
	Exit	
Make Progress	Initial Conditions	Ending

Figure 1.1: The requirements of an iterative algorithm.

together in very subtle ways. You may have to cycle through them a number of times, adjusting what you have done, until they all fit together as required.

1) Specifications: What problem are you solving? What are its pre- and postconditions—i.e., where are you starting and where is your destination?

2) Basic Steps: What basic steps will head you more or less in the correct direction?

3) Measure of Progress: You must define a measure of progress: where are the mile markers along the road?

4) The Loop Invariant: You must define a loop invariant that will give a picture of the state of your computation when it is at the top of the main loop, in other words, define the road that you will stay on.

5) Main Steps: For every location on the road, you must write the pseudocode $code_{loop}$ to take a single step. You do not need to start with the first location. I recommend first considering a typical step to be taken during the middle of the computation.

6) Make Progress: Each iteration of your main step must make progress according to your measure of progress.

7) Maintain Loop Invariant: Each iteration of your main step must ensure that the loop invariant is true again when the computation gets back to the top of the loop. (Induction will then prove that it remains true always.)

8) Establishing the Loop Invariant: Now that you have an idea of where you are going, you have a better idea about how to begin. You must write the pseudocode

$code_{pre\text{-}loop}$ to initially establish the loop invariant. How do you get from your house onto the correct road?

9) Exit Condition: You must write the condition ⟨*exit-cond*⟩ that causes the computation to break out of the loop.

10) Ending: How does the exit condition together with the invariant ensure that the problem is solved? When at the end of the road but still on it, how do you produce the required output? You must write the pseudocode $code_{post\text{-}loop}$ to clean up loose ends and to return the required output.

11) Termination and Running Time: How much progress do you need to make before you know you will reach this exit? This is an estimate of the running time of your algorithm.

12) Special Cases: When first attempting to design an algorithm, you should only consider one general type of input instances. Later, you must cycle through the steps again considering other types of instances and special cases. Similarly, test your algorithm by hand on a number of different examples.

13) Coding and Implementation Details: Now you are ready to put all the pieces together and produce pseudocode for the algorithm. It may be necessary at this point to provide extra implementation details.

14) Formal Proof: If the above pieces fit together as required, then your algorithm works.

EXAMPLE 1.2.1	**The Find-Max Two-Finger Algorithm** **to Illustrate These Ideas**

1) Specifications: An input instance consists of a list $L(1..n)$ of elements. The output consists of an index i such that $L(i)$ has maximum value. If there are multiple entries with this same value, then any one of them is returned.

2) Basic Steps: You decide on the two-finger method. Your right finger runs down the list.

3) Measure of Progress: The measure of progress is how far along the list your right finger is.

4) The Loop Invariant: The loop invariant states that your left finger points to one of the largest entries encountered so far by your right finger.

5) Main Steps: Each iteration, you move your right finger down one entry in the list. If your right finger is now pointing at an entry that is larger then the left finger's entry, then move your left finger to be with your right finger.

6) Make Progress: You make progress because your right finger moves one entry.

7) Maintain Loop Invariant: You know that the loop invariant has been maintained as follows. For each step, the new left finger element is Max(old left finger element, new element). By the loop invariant, this is Max(Max(shorter list), new element). Mathematically, this is Max(longer list).

8) Establishing the Loop Invariant: You initially establish the loop invariant by pointing both fingers to the first element.

9) Exit Condition: You are done when your right finger has finished traversing the list.

10) Ending: In the end, we know the problem is solved as follows. By the exit condition, your right finger has encountered all of the entries. By the loop invariant, your left finger points at the maximum of these. Return this entry.

11) Termination and Running Time: The time required is some constant times the length of the list.

12) Special Cases: Check what happens when there are multiple entries with the same value or when $n = 0$ or $n = 1$.

13) Coding and Implementation Details:

> **algorithm** $FindMax(L)$
>
> $\langle$ *pre-cond* $\rangle$: L is an array of n values.
> $\langle$ *post-cond* $\rangle$: Returns an index with maximum value.
>
> begin
> $i = 1$; $j = 1$
>   loop
> $\langle$*loop-invariant*$\rangle$: $L[i]$ is max in $L[1..j]$.
>   exit when $(j \geq n)$
>   % Make progress while maintaining the loop invariant
> $j = j + 1$
>   if($L[i] < L[j]$) then $i = j$
>   end loop
>   return(i)
> end algorithm

14) Formal Proof: The correctness of the algorithm follows from the above steps.

A New Way of Thinking: You may be tempted to believe that measures of progress and loop invariants are theoretical irrelevancies. But industry, after many expensive mistakes, has a deeper appreciation for the need for correctness. Our philosophy is to learn how to think about, develop, and describe algorithms in such a way that their correctness is transparent. For this, measures of progress and loop invariants are essential. The description of the preceding algorithms and their proofs of correctness are wrapped up into one.

Keeping Grounded: Loop invariants constitute a life philosophy. They lead to feeling grounded. Most of the code I mark as a teacher makes me feel ungrounded. It cycles, but I don't know what the variables mean, how they fit together, where the algorithm is going, or how to start thinking about it. Loop invariants mean starting my day at home, where I know what is true and what things mean. From there, I have enough confidence to venture out into the unknown. However, loop invariants also mean returning full circle to my safe home at the end of my day.

EXERCISE 1.2.1 *What are the formal mathematical things involving loop invariants that must be proved, to prove that if your program exits then it obtains the postcondition?*

1.3   More about the Steps

In this section I give more details about the steps for developing an iterative algorithm.

1) Specifications: Before we can design an iterative algorithm, we need to know precisely what it is supposed to do.

Preconditions: What are the legal input instances? Any assertions that are promised to be true about the input instance are referred to as *preconditions*.

Postconditions: What is the required output for each legal instance? Any assertions that must be true about the output are referred to as *postconditions*.

Correctness: An algorithm for the problem is *correct* if for every legal input instance, the required output is produced. If the input instance does not meet the preconditions, then all bets are off. Formally, we express this as

$$\langle pre\text{-}cond \rangle \ \& \ code_{alg} \ \Rightarrow \ \langle post\text{-}cond \rangle$$

This correctness is only with respect to the specifications.

Example: The *sorting* problem is defined as follows:

Preconditions: The input is a list of n values, including possible repeatations.

Postconditions: The output is a list consisting of the same n values in non-decreasing order.

The Contract: Pre- and postconditions are, in a sense, the contract between the implementer and the user (or invoker) of the coded algorithm.

Implementer: When you are writing a subroutine, you can assume the input comes to your program in the correct form, satisfying all the preconditions. You must write the subroutine so that it ensures that the postconditions hold after execution.

User: When you are using the subroutine, you must ensure that the input you provide meets the preconditions of the subroutine. Then you can trust that the output meets its postconditions.

2) Basic Steps: As a preliminary to designing the algorithm it can be helpful to consider what basic steps or operations might be performed in order to make progress towards solving this problem. Take a few of these steps on a simple input instance in order to get some intuition as to where the computation might go. How might the information gained narrow down the computation problem?

3) Measure of Progress: You need to define a function that, when given the current state of the computation, returns an integer value measuring either how much progress the computation has already made or how much progress still needs to be made. This is referred to either as a *measure of progress* or as a *potential function*. It must be such that the total progress required to solve the problem is not infinite and that at each iteration, the computation makes progress. Beyond this, you have complete freedom to define this measure as you like. For example, your measure might state the amount of the output produced, the amount of the input considered, the extent to which the search space has been narrowed, some more creative function of the work done so far, or how many cases have been tried. Section 1.4 outlines how these different measures lead to different types of iterative algorithms.

4) The Loop Invariant: Often, coming up with the loop invariant is the hardest part of designing an algorithm. It requires practice, perseverance, creativity, and insight. However, from it the rest of the algorithm often follows easily. Here are a few helpful pointers.

Definition: A *loop invariant* is an assertion that is placed at the top of a loop and that must hold true every time the computation returns to the top of the loop.

Assertions: More generally, an *assertion* is a statement made at some particular point during the execution of an algorithm about the current state of the computation's data structures that is either true or false. If it is false, then something has gone wrong in the logic of the algorithm. Pre- and postconditions are special cases of assertions that provide clean boundaries between systems, subsystems, routines, and subroutines. Within such a part, assertions can also provide checkpoints along the path of the computation to allow everyone to know what should have been accomplished so far. *Invariants* are the same, except they apply either to a loop that is executed many times or to an object-oriented data structure that has an ongoing life.

> **Designing, Understanding, and Proving Correct:** Generally, assertions are not tasks for the algorithm to perform, but are only comments that are added to assist the designer, the implementer, and the reader in understanding the algorithm and its correctness.

14

> **Debugging:** Some languages allow you to insert assertions as lines of code. If during the execution such an assertion is false, then the program automatically stops with a useful error message. This is helpful both when debugging and after the code is complete. It is what is occurring when an error box pops up during the execution of a program telling you to contact the vendor if the error persists. Not all interesting assertions, however, can be tested feasibly within the computation itself.

Picture from the Middle: A loop invariant should describe what you would like the data structure to look like when the computation is at the beginning of an iteration. Your description should leave your reader with a visual image. Draw a picture if you like.

Don't Be Frightened: A loop invariant need not consist of formal mathematical mumbo jumbo if an informal description gets the idea across better. On the other hand, English is sometimes misleading, and hence a more mathematical language sometimes helps. Say things twice if necessary. I recommend pretending that you are describing the algorithm to a first-year student.

On the Road: A loop invariant must ensure that the computation is still on the road towards the destination and has not fallen into a ditch or landed in a tree.

A Wide Road: Given a fixed algorithm on a fixed input, the computation will follow one fixed line. When the algorithm designer knows exactly where this line will go, he can use a very tight loop invariant to define a very narrow road. On the other hand, because your algorithm must work for an infinite number of input instances and because you may pass many obstacles along the way, it can be difficult to predict where the computation might be in the middle of its execution. In such cases, using a very loose loop invariant to define a very wide road is completely acceptable. The line actually followed by the computation might weave and wind, but as long as it stays within the boundaries of the road and continues to make progress, all is well. An advantage of a wide road is that it gives more flexibility in how the main loop is implemented. A disadvantage is that there are then more places where the computation might be, and for each the algorithm must define how to take a step.

> **Example:** As an example of a loose loop invariant, in the find-max two-finger algorithm, the loop invariant does not completely dictate which entry your

left finger should point at when there are a number of entries with the same maximum value.

Meaningful and Achievable: You want a loop invariant that is *meaningful*, meaning it is strong enough that, with an appropriate exit condition, it will guarantee the postcondition. You also want the loop invariant to be *achievable*, meaning you can establish and maintain it.

15

Know What a Loop Invariant Is: Be clear about what a loop invariant is. It is not code, a precondition, a postcondition, or some other inappropriate piece of information. For example, stating something that is always true, such as "$1 + 1 = 2$" or "The root is the max of any heap," may be useful information for the answer to the problem, but should not be a part of the loop invariant.

Flow Smoothly: The loop invariant should flow smoothly from the beginning to the end of the algorithm.

- At the beginning, it should follow easily from the preconditions.
- It should progress in small natural steps.
- Once the exit condition has been met, the postconditions should easily follow.

Ask for 100%: A good philosophy in life is to ask for 100% of what you want, but not to assume that you will get it.

> **Dream:** Do not be shy. What would you like to be true in the middle of your computation? This may be a reasonable loop invariant, and it may not be.

> **Pretend:** Pretend that a genie has granted your wish. You are now in the middle of your computation, and your dream loop invariant is true.

> **Maintain the Loop Invariant:** From here, are you able to take some computational steps that will make progress while maintaining the loop invariant? If so, great. If not, there are two common reasons.

>> *Too Weak:* If your loop invariant is too weak, then the genie has not provided you with everything you need to move on.

>> *Too Strong:* If your loop invariant is too strong, then you will not be able to establish it initially or maintain it.

No Unstated Assumptions: You don't want loop invariants that lack detail or are too weak to proceed to the next step. Don't make assumptions that you don't state. As a check, pretend that you are a Martian who has jumped into the top of the loop knowing *nothing* that is not stated in the loop invariant.

Example: In the find-max two-finger algorithm, the loop invariant does make some unstated assumptions. It assumes that the numbers above your right finger have been encountered by your right finger and those below it have not. Perhaps more importantly for, ±1 errors, is whether or not the number currently being pointed has been encountered already. The loop invariant also assumes that the numbers in the list have not changed from their original values.

A Starry Night: How did van Gogh come up with his famous painting, *A Starry Night*? There's no easy answer. In the same way, coming up with loop invariants and algorithms is an art form.

Use This Process: Don't come up with the loop invariant after the fact. Use it to design your algorithm.

5) Main Steps: The pseudocode *code*$_{loop}$ must be defined so that it can be taken not just from where you think the computation might be, but from any state of the data structure for which the loop invariant is true and the exit condition has not yet been met.

Worry about *one step at a time*. Don't get pulled into the strong desire to understand the entire computation at once. Generally, this only brings fear and unhappiness. I repeat the wisdom taught by both the Buddhists and the twelve-step programs: Today you may feel like like you were dropped off in a strange city without knowing how you got there. Do not worry about the past or the future. Be reassured that you are somewhere along the correct road. Your goal is only to take one step so that you make progress and stay on the road. Another analogy is to imagine you are part of a relay race. A teammate hands you the baton. Your job is only to carry it once around the track and hand it to the next teammate.

6) Make Progress: You must prove that progress of at least one unit of your measure is made every time the algorithm goes around the loop. Sometimes there are odd situations in which the algorithm can iterate without making any measurable progress. This is not acceptable. The danger is that the algorithm will loop forever. You must either define another measure that better shows how you are making progress during such iterations or change the step taken in the main loop so that progress is made. The formal proof of this is similar to that for maintaining the loop invariant.

7) Maintain the Loop Invariant: You must prove that the loop invariant is maintained in each iteration.

The Formal Statement: Whether or not you want to prove it formally, the formal statement that must be true is

$$\langle loop\text{-}invariant' \rangle \text{ \& } not \langle exit\text{-}cond \rangle \text{ \& } code_{loop} \Rightarrow \langle loop\text{-}invariant'' \rangle$$

Proof Technique:
- Assume that the computation is at the top of the loop.
- Assume that the loop invariant is satisfied; otherwise the program would have already failed. Refer back to the picture that you drew to see what this tells you about the current state of the data structure.
- You can also assume that the exit condition is not satisfied, because otherwise the loop would exit.
- Execute the pseudocode $code_{loop}$, in one iteration of the loop. How does this change the data structure?
- Prove that when you get back to the top of the loop again, the requirements set by the loop invariant are met once more.

Different Situations: Many subtleties can arise from the huge number of different input instances and the huge number of different places the computation might find itself in.
- I recommend first designing the pseudocode $code_{loop}$ to work for a general middle iteration when given a large and general input instance. Is the loop invariant maintained in this case?
- Then try the first and last couple of iterations.
- Also try special case input instances. Before writing separate code for these, check whether the code you already have happens to handle these cases. If you are forced to change the code, be sure to check that the previously handled cases still are handled.
- To prove that the loop invariant is true in all situations, pretend that you are at the top of the loop, but you do not know how you got there. You may have dropped in from Mars. Besides knowing that the loop invariant is true and the exit condition is not, you know nothing about the state of the data structure. Make no other assumptions. Then go around the loop and prove that the loop invariant is maintained.

Differentiating between Iterations: The assignment $x = x + 2$ is meaningful as a line of code, but not as a mathematical statement. Define x' to be the value of x at the beginning of the iteration and x'' that after going around the loop one more time. The effect of the code $x = x + 2$ is that $x'' = x' + 2$.

8) Establishing the Loop Invariant: You must prove that the initial code establishes the loop invariant.

The Formal Statement: The formal statement that must be true is

$$\langle pre\text{-}cond \rangle \text{ \& } code_{pre\text{-}loop} \Rightarrow \langle loop\text{-}invariant \rangle$$

17

Proof Technique:
- Assume that you are just beginning the computation.
- You can assume that the input instance satisfies the precondition; otherwise you are not expected to solve the problem.
- Execute the code $code_{pre\text{-}loop}$ before the loop.
- Prove that when you first get to the top of the loop, the requirements set by the loop invariant are met.

Easiest Way: Establish the loop invariant in the easiest way possible. For example, if you need to construct a set such that all the dragons within it are purple, the easiest way to do it is to construct the empty set. Note that all the dragons in this set are purple, because it contains no dragons that are not purple.

Careful: Sometimes it is difficult to know how to set the variables to make the loop invariant initially true. In such cases, try setting them to ensure that it is true after the first iteration. For example, what is the maximum value within an empty list of values? One might think 0 or ∞. However, a better answer is $-\infty$. When adding a new value, one uses the code $newMax = \max(oldMax, newValue)$. Starting with $oldMax = -\infty$, gives the correct answer when the first value is added.

9) Exit Condition: Generally you exit the loop when you have completed the task.

Stuck: Sometimes, however, though your intuition is that your algorithm designed so far is making progress each iteration, you have no clue whether, heading in this direction, the algorithm will ever solve the problem or how you would know it if it happens. Because the algorithm cannot make progress forever, there must be situations in which your algorithm gets stuck. For such situations, you must either think of other ways for your algorithm to make progress or have it exit. A good first step is to exit. In step 10, you will have to prove that when your algorithm exits, you actually are able to solve the problem. If you are unable to do this, then you will have to go back and redesign your algorithm.

Loop While vs Exit When: The following are equivalent:

```
while( A and B )         loop
    ...                      ⟨loop-invariant⟩
end while                    exit when (not A or not B)
                             ...
                         end loop
```

The second is more useful here because it focuses on the conditions needed to exit the loop, while the first focuses on the conditions needed to continue. Another advantage of the second is that it also allows you to slip in the loop invariant between the top of the loop and the exit condition.

10) Ending: In this step, you must ensure that once the loop has exited you will be able to solve the problem.

The Formal Statement: The formal statement that must be true is

$$\langle loop\text{-}invariant \rangle \ \& \ \langle exit\text{-}cond \rangle \ \& \ code_{post\text{-}loop} \ \Rightarrow \ \langle post\text{-}cond \rangle$$

19

Proof Technique:
- Assume that you have just broken out of the loop.
- You can assume that the loop invariant is true, because you have maintained that it is always true.
- You can also assume that the exit condition is true by the fact that the loop has exited.
- Execute the code $code_{post\text{-}loop}$ after the loop to give a few last touches towards solving the problem and to return the result.
- From these facts alone, you must be able to deduce that the problem has been solved correctly, namely, that the postcondition has been established.

11) Termination and Running Time: You must prove that the algorithm does not loop forever. This is done by proving that if the measure of progress meets some stated amount, then the exit condition has definitely been met. (If it exits earlier than this, all the better.) The number of iterations needed is then bounded by this stated amount of progress divided by the amount of progress made each iteration. The running time is estimated by adding up the time required for each of these iterations. For some applications, space bounds (i.e., the amount of memory used) may also be important. We discuss important concepts related to running time in Chapters 23–26: time and space complexity, the useful ideas of logarithms and exponentials, BigOh (O) and Theta (Θ) notation and several handy approximations.

12) Special Cases: When designing an algorithm, you do not want to worry about every possible type of input instance at the same time. Instead, first get the algorithm to work for one general type, then another and another. Though the next type of input instances may require separate code, start by tracing out what the algorithm that you have already designed would do given such an input. Often this algorithm will just happen to handle a lot of these cases automatically without requiring separate code. When adding code to handle a special case, be sure to check that the previously handled cases still are handled.

13) Coding and Implementation Details: Even after the basic algorithm is outlined, there can be many little details to consider. Many of these implementation details can be hidden in abstract data types (see Chapter 3). If a detail does not really make a difference to an algorithm, it is best to keep all possibilities open, giving extra flexibility to the implementer. For many details, it does not matter which choice you make, but bugs can be introduced if you are not consistent and clear as to what you have chosen. This text does not focus on coding details. This does not mean that they are not important.

14) Formal Proof: Steps 1–11 are enough to ensure that your iterative algorithm works, that is, that it gives the correct answer on all specified inputs. Consider some instance which meets the preconditions. By step 8 we establish the loop invariant the first time the computation is at the top of the loop, and by step 7 we maintain it each iteration. Hence by way of induction, we know that the loop invariant is true every time the computation is at the top of the loop. (See the following discussion.) Hence, by step 5, the step taken in the main loop is always defined and executes without crashing until the loop exits. Moreover, by step 6 each such iteration makes progress of at least one. Hence, by step 11, the exit condition is eventually met. Step 10 then gives that the postcondition is achieved, so that the algorithm works in this instance.

Mathematical Induction: Induction is an extremely important mathematical technique for proving universal statements and is the cornerstone of iterative algorithms. Hence, we will consider it in more detail.

Induction Hypothesis: For each $n \geq 0$, let $S(n)$ be the statement "If the loop has not yet exited, then the loop invariant is true when you are at the top of the loop after going around n times."

Goal: The goal is to prove that $\forall n \geq 0$, $S(n)$, namely, "As long as the loop has not yet exited, the loop invariant is always true when you are at the top of the loop."

Proof Outline: Proof by induction on n.

Base Case: Proving $S(0)$ involves proving that the loop invariant is true when the algorithm first gets to the top of the loop. This is achieved by proving the statement $\langle pre\text{-}cond \rangle$ & $code_{pre\text{-}loop} \Rightarrow \langle loop\text{-}invariant \rangle$.

Induction Step: Proving $S(n-1) \Rightarrow S(n)$ involves proving that the loop invariant is maintained. This is achieved by proving the statement $\langle loop\text{-}invariant' \rangle$ & not $\langle exit\text{-}cond \rangle$ & $code_{loop} \Rightarrow \langle loop\text{-}invariant'' \rangle$.

Conclusion: By way of induction, we can conclude that $\forall n \geq 0$, $S(n)$, i.e., that the loop invariant is always true when at the top of the loop.

The Process of Induction:

$$\begin{array}{ll} S(0) \text{ is true} & \text{(by base case)} \\ S(0) \Rightarrow S(1) & \text{(by induction step, } n=1) \end{array}$$

hence, $S(1)$ is true

$$S(1) \Rightarrow S(2) \quad \text{(by induction step, } n=2)$$

hence, $S(2)$ is true

$$S(2) \Rightarrow S(3) \quad \text{(by induction step, } n=3)$$

hence, $S(3)$ is true ...

Other Proof Techniques: Other formal steps for proving correctness are described in Chapter 28.

Faith in the Method: Convince yourself that these steps are sufficient to define an algorithm so that you do not have reconvince yourself every time you need to design an algorithm.

21

1.4 Different Types of Iterative Algorithms

To help you design a measure of progress and a loop invariant for your algorithm, here are a few classic types, followed by examples of each type.

More of the Output: If the solution is a structure composed of many pieces (e.g., an array of integers, a set, or a path), a natural thing to try is to construct the solution one piece at a time.

Measure of Progress: The amount of the output constructed.

Loop Invariant: The output constructed so far is correct.

More of the Input: Suppose the input consists of n objects (e.g., an array of n integers or a graph with n nodes). It would be reasonable for the algorithm to read them in one at a time.

Measure of Progress: The amount of the input considered.

Loop Invariant: Pretending that this prefix of the input is the entire input, I have a complete solution.

Examples: After i iterations of the preceding find-max two-finger algorithm, the left finger points at the highest score within the prefix of the list seen so far. After i iterations of one version of insertion sort, the first i elements of the input are sorted. See Figure 1.2.

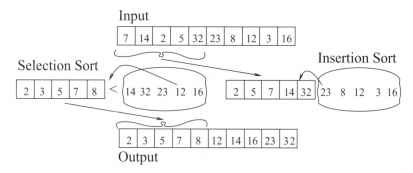

Figure 1.2: The loop invariants for insertion sort and selection sort are demonstrated.

Bad Loop Invariant: A common mistake is to give the loop invariant "I have handled and have a solution for each of the first i objects in the input." This is wrong because each object in the input does not need a separate solution; the input as a whole does. For example, in the find-max two-finger algorithm, one cannot know whether one element is the maximum by considering it in isolation from the other elements. An element is only the maximum in comparison with the other elements in the sublist.

Narrowing the Search Space: If you are searching for something, try narrowing the search space, maybe decreasing it by one or, even better, cutting it in half.

Measure of Progress: The size of the space in which you have narrowed the search.

Loop Invariant: If the thing being searched for is anywhere, then then it is in this narrowed sublist.

Example: Binary search.

Work Done: The measure of progress might also be some other more creative function of the work done so far.

Example: Bubble sort measures its progress by how many pairs of elements are out of order.

Case Analysis: Try the obvious thing. For which input instances does it work, and for which does it not work? Now you only need to find an algorithm that works for those later cases. An measure of progress might include which cases you have tried.

We will now give a simple examples of each of these. Though you likely know these algorithms already, use them to understand these different types of iterative algorithms and to review the required steps.

EXAMPLE 1.4.1   **More of the Output—Selection Sort**

1) Specifications: The goal is to rearrange a list of n values in nondecreasing order.

2) Basic Steps: We will repeatedly select the smallest unselected element.

3) Measure of Progress: The measure of progress is the number k of elements selected.

4) The Loop Invariant: The loop invariant states that the selected elements are the k smallest of the elements and that these have been sorted. The larger elements are in a set on the side.

5) Main Steps: The main step is to find the smallest element from among those in the remaining set of larger elements and to add this newly selected element to the end of the sorted list of elements.

6) Make Progress: Progress is made because k increases.

7) Maintain Loop Invariant: We must prove that $\langle loop\text{-}invariant'\rangle$ & not $\langle exit\text{-}cond\rangle$ & $code_{loop}$ $\Rightarrow$ $\langle loop\text{-}invariant''\rangle$. By the previous loop invariant, the newly selected element is at least the size of the previously selected elements. By the step, it is no bigger than the elements on the side. It follows that it must be the $k+1$st element in the list. Hence, moving this element from the set on the side to the end of the sorted list ensures that the selected elements in the new list are the $k+1$ smallest and are sorted.

8) Establishing the Loop Invariant: We must prove that $\langle pre\text{-}cond\rangle$ & $code_{pre\text{-}loop}$ $\Rightarrow$ $\langle loop\text{-}invariant\rangle$. Initially, $k=0$ are sorted and all the elements are set aside.

9) Exit Condition: Stop when $k=n$.

10) Ending: We must prove $\langle loop\text{-}invariant\rangle$ & $\langle exit\text{-}cond\rangle$ & $code_{post\text{-}loop}$ $\Rightarrow$ $\langle post\text{-}cond\rangle$. By the exit condition, all the elements have been selected, and by the loop invariant these selected elements have been sorted.

11) Termination and Running Time: We have not considered how long it takes to find the next smallest element or to handle the data structures.

EXAMPLE 1.4.2	**More of the Input—Insertion Sort**

1) Specifications: Again the goal is to rearrange a list of n values in nondecreasing order.

2) Basic Steps: This time we will repeatedly insert some element where it belongs.

3) Measure of Progress: The measure of progress is the number k of elements inserted.

4) The Loop Invariant: The loop invariant states that the k inserted elements are sorted within a list and that, as before, the remaining elements are off to the side somewhere.

5) Main Steps: The main step is to take any of the elements that are off to the side and *insert* it into the sorted list where it belongs.

6) Make Progress: Progress is made because k increases.

7) Maintain Loop Invariant: $\langle loop\text{-}invariant'\rangle$ & not $\langle exit\text{-}cond\rangle$ & $code_{loop}$ $\Rightarrow$ $\langle loop\text{-}invariant''\rangle$. You know that the loop invariant has been maintained because the new element is inserted in the correct place in the previously sorted list.

8) Establishing the Loop Invariant: Initially, with $k=1$, think of the first element in the array as a sorted list of length one.

9) Exit Condition: Stop when $k = n$.

10) Ending: $\langle loop\text{-}invariant \rangle$ & $\langle exit\text{-}cond \rangle$ & $code_{post\text{-}loop} \Rightarrow \langle post\text{-}cond \rangle$. By the exit condition, all the elements have been inserted, and by the loop invariant, these inserted elements have been sorted.

11) Termination and Running Time: We have not considered how long it takes to insert the element or to handle the data structures.

Example 1.4.3	**Narrowing the Search Space—Binary Search**

1) Specifications: An input instance consists of a sorted list $A[1..n]$ of elements and a key to be searched for. Elements may be repeated. If the key is in the list, then the output consists of an index i such that $A[i] = key$. If the key is not in the list, then the output reports this.

2) Basic Steps: Continue to cut the search space in which the key might be in half.

4) The Loop Invariant: The algorithm maintains a sublist $A[i..j]$ such that if the key is contained in the original list $A[1..n]$, then it is contained in this narrowed sublist. (If the element is repeated, then it might also be outside this sublist.)

3) Measure of Progress: The measure of progress is the number of elements in our sublist, namely $j - i + 1$.

5) Main Steps: Each iteration compares the key with the element at the center of the sublist. This determines which half of the sublist the key is not in and hence which half to keep. More formally, let mid index the element in the middle of our current sublist $A[i..j]$. If $key \leq A[mid]$, then the sublist is narrowed to $A[i..mid]$. Otherwise, it is narrowed to $A[mid + 1..j]$.

6) Make Progress: The size of the sublist decreases by a factor of two.

7) Maintain Loop Invariant: $\langle loop\text{-}invariant' \rangle$ & not $\langle exit\text{-}cond \rangle$ & $code_{loop} \Rightarrow$ $\langle loop\text{-}invariant'' \rangle$. The previous loop invariant gives that the search has been narrowed down to the sublist $A[i..j]$. If $key > A[mid]$, then because the list is sorted, we know that key is not in $A[1..mid]$ and hence these elements can be thrown away, narrowing the search to $A[mid + 1..j]$. Similarly if $key < A[mid]$. If $key = A[mid]$, then we could report that the key has been found. However, the loop invariant is also maintained by narrowing the search down to $A[i..mid]$.

8) Establishing the Loop Invariant: $\langle pre\text{-}cond \rangle$ & $code_{pre\text{-}loop} \Rightarrow \langle loop\text{-}invariant \rangle$. Initially, you obtain the loop invariant by considering the entire list as the sublist. It trivially follows that if the key is in the entire list, then it is also in this sublist.

9) Exit Condition: We exit when the sublist contains one (or zero) elements.

10) Ending: $\langle loop\text{-}invariant \rangle$ & $\langle exit\text{-}cond \rangle$ & $code_{post\text{-}loop} \Rightarrow \langle post\text{-}cond \rangle$. By the exit condition, our sublist contains at most one element, and by the loop invariant, if the key is contained in the original list, then the key is contained in this sublist, i.e., must be this one element. Hence, the final code tests to see if this one element is the key. If it is, then its index is returned. If it is not, then the algorithm reports that the key is not in the list.

11) Termination and Running Time: The sizes of the sublists are approximately $n, \frac{n}{2}, \frac{n}{4}, \frac{n}{8}, \frac{n}{16}, \ldots, 8, 4, 2, 1$. Hence, only $\Theta(\log n)$ splits are needed. Each split takes $O(1)$ time. Hence, the total time is $\Theta(\log n)$.

12) Special Cases: A special case to consider is when the key is not contained in the original list $A[1..n]$. Note that the loop invariant carefully takes this case into account. The algorithm will narrow the sublist down to one (or zero) elements. The counter positive of the loop invariant then gives that if the key is not contained in this narrowed sublist, then the key is not contained in the original list $A[1..n]$.

13) Coding and Implementation Details: In addition to testing whether $key \le A[mid]$, each iteration could test to see if $A[mid]$ is the key. Though finding the key in this way would allow you to stop early, extensive testing shows that this extra comparison slows down the computation.

EXAMPLE 1.4.4	**Work Done—Bubble Sort**

1) Specifications: The goal is to rearrange a list of n values in nondecreasing order.

2) Basic Steps: Swap elements that are out of order.

3) Measure of Progress: An *involution* is a pair of elements that are out of order, i.e., a pair i, j where $1 \le i < j \le n$, $A[i] > A[j]$. Our measure of progress will be the number of involutions in our current ordering of the elements. For example, in $[1, 2, 5, 4, 3, 6]$, there are three involutions.

4) The Loop Invariant: The loop invariant is relatively weak, stating only that we have a permutation of the original input elements.

5) Main Steps: The main step is to find two adjacent elements that are out of order and to swap them.

6) Make Progress: Such a step decreases the number of involutions by one.

7) Maintain Loop Invariant: $\langle loop\text{-}invariant' \rangle$ & not $\langle exit\text{-}cond \rangle$ & $code_{loop}$ $\Rightarrow$ $\langle loop\text{-}invariant'' \rangle$. By the previous loop invariant we had a permutation of the elements. Swapping a pair of elements does not change this.

8) Establishing the Loop Invariant: $\langle pre\text{-}cond \rangle$ & $code_{pre\text{-}loop}$ $\Rightarrow$ $\langle loop-invariant \rangle$. Initially, we have a permutation of the elements.

9) Exit Condition: Stop when we have a sorted list of elements.

10) Ending: $\langle loop\text{-}invariant \rangle$ & $\langle exit\text{-}cond \rangle$ & $code_{post\text{-}loop} \Rightarrow \langle post\text{-}cond \rangle$. By the loop invariant, we have a permutation of the original elements, and by the exit condition these are sorted.

11) Termination and Running Time: Initially, the measure of progress cannot be higher than $n(n-1)/2$ because this is the number of pairs of elements there are. In each iteration, this measure decreases by one. Hence, after at most $n(n-1)/2$ iterations, the measure of progress has decreased to zero. At this point the list has been sorted and the exit condition has been met. We have not considered how long it takes to find two adjacent elements that are out of order.

EXERCISE 1.4.1 *(See solution in Part Five.) Give the implementation details and the running times for selection sort.*

EXERCISE 1.4.2 *(See solution in Part Five.) Give the implementation details and the running times for insertion sort. Does using binary search to find the smallest element or to find where to insert help? Does it make a difference whether the elements are stored in an array or in a linked list?*

EXERCISE 1.4.3 *(See solution in Part Five.) Give the implementation details and the running times for bubble sort: Use another loop invariant to prove that the total number of comparisons needed is $O(n^2)$.*

1.5 Typical Errors

In a study, a group of experienced programmers was asked to code binary search. Easy, yes? 80% got it wrong! My guess is that if they had used loop invariants, they all would have got it correct.

Be Clear: The code specifies the current subinterval $A[i..j]$ with two integers i and j. Clearly document whether the sublist includes the end points i and j or not. It does not matter which, but you must be consistent. Confusion in details like this is the cause of many bugs.

Math Details: Small math operations like computing the index of the middle element of the subinterval $A(i..j)$ are prone to bugs. Check for yourself that the answer is $mid = \lfloor \frac{i+j}{2} \rfloor$.

6) Make Progress: Be sure that each iteration progress is made in every special case. For example, in binary search, when the current sublist has even length, it is reasonable (as done above) to let mid be the element just to the left of center. It is also reasonable to include the middle element in the right half of the sublist. However, together these cause a bug. Given the sublist $A[i..j] = A[3, 4]$, the middle will be the element indexed with 3, and the right sublist will be still be $A[mid..j] = A[3, 4]$. If this sublist is kept, no progress will be made, and the algorithm will loop forever.

7) Maintain Loop Invariant: Be sure that the loop invariant is maintained in every special case. For example, in binary search, it is reasonable to test whether $key < A[mid]$ or $key \geq A[mid]$. It is also reasonable for it to cut the sublist $A[i..j]$ into $A[i..mid]$ and $A[mid + 1..j]$. However, together these cause a bug. When key and $A[mid]$ are equal, the test $key < A[mid]$ will fail, causing the algorithm to think the key is bigger and to keep the right half $A[mid + 1..j]$. However, this skips over the key.

Simple Loop: Code like "$i = 1$; while$(i \leq n)$ $A[i] = 0$; $i = i + 1$; end while" is surprisingly prone to the error of being off by one. The loop invariant "When at the top of the loop, i indexes the next element to handle" helps a lot.

EXERCISE 1.5.1 *(See solution in Part Five.) You are now the professor. Which of the steps to develop an iterative algorithm did the student fail to do correctly in the following code? How? How would you fix it?*

    algorithm *Eg(I)*

    ⟨ **pre-cond**⟩: *I is an integer.*
    ⟨ **post-cond**⟩: *Outputs $\sum_{j=1}^{I} j$.*

    begin
        $s = 0$
        $i = 1$
        while$(i \leq I)$

                ⟨**loop-invariant**⟩: *Each iteration adds the next*
                    term giving that $s = \sum_{j=1}^{i} j$.

        $s = s + i$
        $i = i + 1$
    end loop
    return(s)
    end algorithm

1.6   Exercises

EXERCISE 1.6.1 *You are in the middle of a lake of radius 1. You can swim at a speed of 1 and can run infinitely fast. There is a smart monster on the shore who can't go in the water but can run at a speed of 4. Your goal is to swim to shore, arriving at a spot where the monster is not, and then run away. If you swim directly to shore, it will take you 1* *time unit. In this time, the monster will run the distance $\Pi < 4$ around to where you land and eat you. Your better strategy is to maintain the most obvious loop invariant while increasing the most obvious measure of progress for as long as possible and then swim for it. Describe how this works.*

EXERCISE 1.6.2 *Given an undirected graph G such that each node has at most $d + 1$ neighbors, color each node with one of $d + 1$ colors so that for each edge the two nodes have different colors. Hint: Don't think too hard. Just color the nodes. What loop invariant do you need?*

2 Examples Using More-of-the-Input Loop Invariants

We are now ready to look at more examples of iterative algorithms. For each example, look for the key steps of the loop invariant paradigm. What is the loop invariant? How is it obtained and maintained? What is the measure of progress? How is the correct final answer ensured?

In this chapter, we will encounter some of those algorithms that use the more-of-the-input type of loop invariant. The algorithm reads the n objects making up the input one at a time. After reading the first i of them, the algorithm temporarily pretends that this prefix of the input is in fact the entire input. The loop invariant is "I currently have a solution for the input consisting solely of these first i objects (and maybe some additional information)." In Section 2.3, we also encounter some algorithms that use the more-of-the-output type of loop invariant.

2.1 Coloring the Plane

See Figure 2.1.

1) Specifications: An input instance consists of a set of n (infinitely long) lines. These lines form a subdivision of the plane, that is, they partition the plane into a finite number of regions (some of them unbounded). The output consists of a coloring of each region with either black or white so that any two regions with a common boundary have different colors. An algorithm for this problem proves the theorem that such a coloring exists for any such subdivision of the plane.

2) Basic Steps: When an instance consists of a set of objects, a common technique is to consider them one at a time, incrementally solving the problem for those objects considered so far.

3) Measure of Progress: The measure of progress is the number of lines, i, that have been considered.

4) The Loop Invariant: We have considered the first i lines. C is a proper coloring of the plane subdivided by these lines.

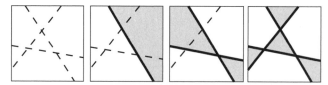

Figure 2.1: An example of coloring the plane.

5) Main Steps: We have a proper coloring C for the first i lines. Line $i + 1$ cuts the plane in half, cutting many regions in half. Each of these halves needs a different color. Then when we change the color of one region, its neighbors must change color too. We will accomplish this by keeping all the colors on one side of line $i + 1$ the same and flipping those on the other side from white to black and from black to white.

6) Make Progress: Each iteration increases i by one.

7) Maintain Loop Invariant: $\langle loop\text{-}invariant'\rangle$ & not$\langle exit\text{-}cond\rangle$ & $code_{loop} \Rightarrow \langle loop\text{-}invariant''\rangle$. We need to check each boundary to make sure that the regions on either side have opposite colors. Boundaries formed by one of the first i lines had opposite colors before the change. The colors of the regions on either side were either neither flipped or both flipped. Hence, they still have opposite colors. Boundaries formed by line $i + 1$ had the same colors before the change. One of these colors was flipped, the other not. Hence, they now have opposite colors.

8) Establishing the Loop Invariant: $\langle pre\text{-}cond\rangle$ & $code_{pre\text{-}loop} \Rightarrow \langle loop\text{-}invariant\rangle$. With $i = 0$ lines, the plane is all one region. The coloring that makes the entire plane white works.

9) Exit Condition: Exit when all n lines have been considered, i.e., $i = n$.

10) Ending: $\langle loop\text{-}invariant\rangle$ & $\langle exit\text{-}cond\rangle$ & $code_{post\text{-}loop} \Rightarrow \langle post\text{-}cond\rangle$). If C is a proper coloring given the first i lines and $i = n$, then clearly C is a proper coloring given all of the lines.

11) Termination and Running Time: Clearly, only n iterations are needed.

12) Special Cases: There are no special cases we need to consider.

13) Coding and Implementation Details:

    algorithm *ColoringPlane(lines)*

    ⟨ ***pre-cond***⟩: *lines* specifies n (infinitely long) lines.

    ⟨ ***post-cond***⟩: *C* is a proper coloring of the plane subdivided by the lines.

begin

    $C =$ "the coloring that colors the entire plane white."

    $i = 0$

    loop

        ⟨*loop-invariant*⟩: C is a proper coloring of the plane subdivided

        by the first i lines.

        exit when $(i = n)$

        % Make progress while maintaining the loop invariant

        Line $i + 1$ cuts the plane in half.

        On one half, the new coloring C' is the same as the old one C.

        On the other half, the new coloring C' is the same as the old one C,

            except white is switched to black and black to white.

        $i = i + 1 \,\&\, C = C'$

    end loop

    return(C)

end algorithm

2.2 Deterministic Finite Automaton

One large class of problems that can be solved using an iterative algorithm with the help of a loop invariant is the class of *regular languages*. You may have learned that this is the class of languages that can be decided by a deterministic finite automata (DFA) or described using a regular expression.

Applications: This class is useful for modeling

- simple iterative algorithms
- simple mechanical or electronic devices like elevators and calculators
- simple processes like the job queue of an operating system
- simple patterns within strings of characters.

Features: All of these have the following similar features.

    Input Stream: They receive a stream of information to which they must react. For example, the stream of input for a simple algorithm consists of the characters read from input; for a calculator, it is the sequence of buttons pushed; for the job queue, it is the stream of jobs arriving; and for the pattern within a string, one scans the string once from left to right.

    Read-Once Input: Once a token of the information has arrived, it cannot be requested for again.

    Bounded Memory: The algorithm, device, process, or pattern matcher has limited memory with which to remember the information that it has seen so far.

Though the amount of memory can be any fixed amount, this amount cannot grow even if the input instance becomes really big.

EXAMPLE 2.2.1   **A Simple DFA**

---

1) Specifications: Given a string α as the input instance, determine whether it is contained in the set (*language*)

$$L = \{\alpha \in \{0, 1\}^* \mid \alpha \text{ has length at most three and the number of 1's is odd}\}$$

In most, but not all, DFAs, the computation's task it to either accept or reject the input.

2) Basic Steps: The characters of the input instance are read one at a time. Because the computation will never be able to read a character again, it must remember what it needs about what it has read so far.

3) Measure of Progress: The measure of progress is the number of characters read so far.

4) The Loop Invariant: Let ω denote the prefix of the input instance read so far. The loop invariant states what information is remembered about it. Its length and the number of 1's read so far cannot be remembered with a bounded amount of memory, because these counts would grow arbitrarily large were the input instance to grow arbitrarily long. Luckily, the language is only concerned with this length up to three and whether the number of 1's is even or odd. This can be accomodated with two variables: length, $l \in \{0, 1, 2, 3, more\}$, and parity, $r \in \{even, odd\}$. This requires only a fixed amount of memory.

5) Main Steps: Read a character, and update what we know about the prefix.

6) Make Progress: Progress increases because the number of characters read so far increases by one.

7) Maintaining the Loop Invariant: After reading another character c, the prefix read is now ωc. We know that the length of ωc is one more than that of ω and that the number of 1's is either one more mod 2 or the same, depending on whether or not the new character c is a 1.

8) Establishing the Loop Invariant: At the beginning of the computation, the prefix that has been read so far is the empty string $\omega = \epsilon$, whose length is $l = 0$, and the number of 1's is $r = even$.

9) Exit Condition: We exit when the entire input instance has been read.

10) Ending: When the input instance has been completely read in, the knowledge that the loop invariant states what we know is sufficient for us to compute the final answer. We accept if the instance has length at most three and the number of 1's is odd.

11) Termination and Running Time: The number of iterations is clearly the length n of the input instance.

12) Special Cases: There are no special cases we need to consider.

13) Coding and Implementation Details:

algorithm $DFA()$

$\langle$ **pre-cond** $\rangle$: The input instance α will be read in one character at a time.

$\langle$ **post-cond** $\rangle$: The instance will be *accepted* if it has length at most three and the number of 1's is odd.

begin

    $l = 0$ and $r = even$

    loop

        $\langle$ **loop-invariant** $\rangle$: When the iterative program has read in some prefix ω of the input instance α, the bounded memory of the machine remembers the length $l \in \{0, 1, 2, 3, more\}$ of this prefix and whether the number of 1's in it is $r \in \{even, odd\}$.

        exit when end of input

        get(c)   % Reads next character of input

        if($l < 4$) then $l = l + 1$

        if($c = 1$) then $r = (r + 1) \bmod 2$

    end loop

    if($l < 4$ AND $r = odd$) then

        accept

    else

        reject

    end if

end algorithm

Mechanically Compiling an Iterative Program into a DFA: Any iterative program with bounded memory and an input stream can be mechanically compiled into a DFA that solves the same problem. This provides another model or notation for understanding the algorithm. A DFA is specified by $M = \langle \Sigma, Q, \delta, s, F \rangle$.

Alphabet Σ—**Precondition:** The precondition of the problem provides an alphabet Σ of characters and specifies that any string of these characters is a valid input instance. This may be $\{a, b\}$, $\{a, b, \dots, z\}$, ASCII, or any other finite set of tokens that the program may input. In Example 2.2.1, which we are continuing, $\Sigma = \{0, 1\}$.

Set of States, Q—The Loop Invariant: The loop invariant states what information is remembered about the prefix ω read so far. A discrete way of stating this loop invariant is by constructing the set Q of different states that this remembering iterative program might be in when at the top of the loop. In this example, these states are $Q = \{q_{\langle l=0, r=even \rangle}, q_{\langle l=0, r=odd \rangle}, \dots, q_{\langle l=more, r=odd \rangle}\}$, because at each point in time the computation remembers both the length $l \in \{0, 1, 2, 3, more\}$ and parity $r \in \{even, odd\}$ of the prefix read.

Recall that a restriction that we are imposing on DFAs is that the amount of memory that they use is fixed and cannot grow even if the input instance becomes really big. The consequence of this is that the number $|Q|$ of states that the DFA might be in is fixed to some finite number.

Each state $q \in Q$ of the DFA specifies a value for each of the program's variables. If the variables are allocated in total r bits of memory, then there are $|Q| = 2^r$ different states that these variable might be in. Conversely, with $|Q|$ states, a DFA can remember $r = \log_2 |Q|$ bits of information. If the algorithm has two variables, one with $|Q_1|$ different states and one with $|Q_2|$, then the algorithm can be in $|Q| = |Q_1| \times |Q_2|$ different states.

In our example, $|Q| = 5 \times 2 = 10$.

Be sure to assign meaningful names to the states, i.e., not $q_0, q_1, \ldots, q_{|Q|}$, as I have often seen.

Sometimes, when tightening up the algorithm, some of these states can be collapsed into one, if there is no need for the algorithm to differentiate between them. In our example, there are three states that can be collapsed into a dead state from which the final answer is known to be *reject*. Also, the state $q_{\langle l=0, r=odd \rangle}$ should be deleted because it is impossible to be in it.

Graphical Representation: Because the number of states that the computation might be in is fixed to some finite number, the DFA can be represented graphically by having one node for each state:

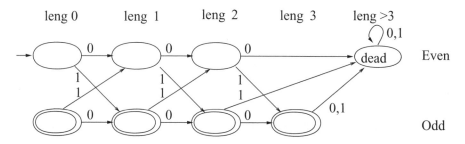

Transition Function δ—Maintain Loop Invariant: Suppose that the computation has read the prefix ω and is at top of the loop. By the loop invariant, the DFA will be remembering something about this prefix ω and a result will be in some state $q \in Q$. After reading another character c, the prefix read is now ωc. We maintain the loop invariant by putting the DFA into the state q' corresponding to what it is to remember about this new prefix ωc. Because the DFA does not know anything about the present prefix ω other than the fact that it is in state q, the next state that the DFA will be in can depend only on its present state q and on the next character c read.

The DFA's transition function δ defines how the machine transitions from state to state. Formally, it is a function $\delta : Q \times \Sigma \to Q$. If the DFA's current state is $q \in Q$ and the next input character is $c \in \Sigma$, then the next state of the DFA is given by $q' = \delta(q, c)$. Consider some state $q \in Q$ and some character $c \in \Sigma$. Set the program's variables to the values corresponding to state q, assume the character read is c, and execute the code once around the loop. The new state $q' = \delta(q, c)$ of the

DFA is defined to be the state corresponding to the values of the program's variables when the computation has reached the top of the loop again.

In a graph representation of a DFA, for each state q and character c, there is an edge labeled c from node q to node $q' = \delta(q, c)$.

The Start State s—Establishing the Loop Invariant: The start state s of the DFA M is the state in Q corresponding to the initial values that the program assigns to its variables before reading any input characters. In the graph representation, the corresponding node has an arrow to it.

Accept States F—Ending: When the input instance has been completely read in, the DFA might be in any one of the states $q \in Q$. Because the DFA does not know anything about the input instance other than the fact that it is in state q, the result of the computation can only depend on this state. If the task of the DFA is only to either accept or reject the input instance, then the set of states Q, must be partitioned into *accept* and *reject* states. If the DFA is in an accept state when the instance ends, then the instance is accepted. Otherwise, it is rejected. When the DFA is specified by $M = \langle \Sigma, Q, \delta, s, F \rangle$, F denotes the set of these accept states. In the graph representation these nodes are denoted by double circles.

EXAMPLE 2.2.2   **Addition**

In the standard elementary school algorithm for addition, the input consists of two integers x and y represented as strings of digits. The output is the sum z, also represented as a string of digits. The input can be viewed as a stream if the algorithm is first given the lowest digits of x and of y, then the second lowest, and so on. The algorithm outputs the characters of z as it proceeds. The only memory required is a single bit to store the carry bit. Because of these features, the algorithm can be modeled as a DFA.

algorithm *Adding( )*

⟨ **pre-cond** ⟩: The digits of two integers x and y are read in backwards in parallel.

⟨ **post-cond** ⟩: The digits of their sum will be outputted backwards.

```
begin
    allocate carry ∈ {0, 1}
    carry = 0
    loop
            ⟨loop-invariant⟩: If the low-order i digits of x and of y have been read,
                    then the low-order i digits of the sum z = x + y have been out-
                    putted. The bounded memory of the machine remembers the carry.
        exit when end of input
        get(⟨xᵢ, yᵢ⟩)
        s = xᵢ + yᵢ + carry
        zᵢ = low order digit of s
        carry = high order digit of s
        put(zᵢ)
```

```
        end loop
        if(carry = 1) then
              put(carry)
        end if
    end algorithm
```

The DFA is as follows.

Set of States: $Q = \{q_{\langle carry=0 \rangle}, q_{\langle carry=1 \rangle}\}$.

Alphabet: $\Sigma = \{\langle x_i, y_i \rangle \mid x_i, y_i \in [0..9]\}$.

Start State: $s = q_{\langle carry=0 \rangle}$.

Transition Function: $\delta(q_{\langle carry=c \rangle}, \langle x_i, y_i \rangle) = \langle q_{carry=c'}, z_i \rangle$

where c' is the high-order digit and z_i is the low order digit of $x_i + y_i + c$.

EXAMPLE 2.2.3 **Division**

Dividing an integer by seven requires a fairly complex algorithm. Surprisingly, it can be done by a DFA. The input consists of an integer x read in one digit at a time, starting with the high-order digit. Simultaneously, the digits of the output $\lfloor \frac{x}{7} \rfloor$ are outputted. In the end, the remainder is provided. Try computing $\lfloor \frac{39591}{7} \rfloor = 5655$. After the prefix $\omega = 395$ has been read, the loop invariant states that the answer $z = \lfloor \frac{395}{7} \rfloor = 56$ has been outputted and its remainder $r = 395 \bmod 7 = 3 \in \{0, 1, \ldots, 6\}$ has been remembered. When the next character $x_i = 9$ is read, we must do the same for $\omega 9 = 3959$. The new answer is

$$z' = \left\lfloor \frac{3959}{7} \right\rfloor = \left\lfloor \frac{395 \times 10 + 9}{7} \right\rfloor = \left\lfloor \frac{(\lfloor \frac{395}{7} \rfloor \times 7 + r) \times 10 + 9}{7} \right\rfloor$$

$$= \left\lfloor \frac{395}{7} \right\rfloor \times 10 + \left\lfloor \frac{r \times 10 + 9}{7} \right\rfloor = z \times 10 + \left\lfloor \frac{3 \times 10 + 9}{7} \right\rfloor = 56 \times 10 + 5 = 565.$$

In general, for $r \in \{0, 1, \ldots, 6\}$ and $x_i \in \{0, 1, \ldots, 9\}$, the value $z_i = \lfloor \frac{r \times 10 + x_i}{7} \rfloor$ is a single digit that is easy to compute. This gives that z' as a string is z concatenated with this new digit z_i. Given that z has already been outputted, what remains is to output z_i. Similarly, the new remainder $r' = 3959 \bmod 7 = (395 \times 10 + 9) \bmod 7 = ((395 \bmod 7) \times 10 + (9 \bmod 7)) \bmod 7 = ((3) \times 10 + (2)) \bmod 7 = 32 \bmod 7 = 4$. More generally, $r' = r \times 10 + c \bmod 7$. Initially, the prefix read so far is the empty string ω representing 0, giving $z = \lfloor \frac{0}{7} \rfloor = 0 =$ empty string and $r = 0 \bmod 7 = 0$. In the end, $z = \lfloor \frac{x}{7} \rfloor$ has been outputted, and what remains is to output its remainder r. The DFA to compute this will have seven states $q_0, \ldots, q_6$. The transition function is $\delta(q_r, c) = q_{\langle r \cdot 10 + c \bmod 7 \rangle}$.

EXAMPLE 2.2.4 **Calculator**

Invariants can be used to understand a computer system that, instead of simply computing one function, continues dynamically to take in inputs and produce outputs. In our simple calculator, the keys are limited to $\Sigma = \{0, 1, 2, \ldots, 9, +, clr\}$. You can enter a number. As you do so it appears on the screen. The + key adds the number on the screen to the accumulated sum and displays the sum on the screen. The clr key resets both the screen and the accumulator to zero. The machine only can store positive integers from zero to 99999999. Additions are done mod 10^8.

Set of States: $Q = \{q_{\langle acc, cur, scr \rangle} \mid acc, cur \in \{0..10^8 - 1\}$ and $scr \in \{showA, showC\}\}$.

There are $10^8 \times 10^8 \times 2$ states in this set, so you would not want to draw the diagram.

Alphabet: $\Sigma = \{0, 1, 2, \ldots, 9, +, clr\}$.

Start State: $s = q_{\langle 0,0,showC \rangle}$.

Transition Function:

- For $c \in \{0..9\}$, $\delta(q_{\langle acc,cur,scr \rangle}, c) = q_{\langle acc, 10 \times cur + c, showC \rangle}$.
- $\delta(q_{\langle acc,cur,scr \rangle}, +) = q_{\langle acc + cur, cur, showA \rangle}$.
- $\delta(q_{\langle acc,cur,scr \rangle}, clr) = q_{\langle 0,0,showC \rangle}$.

EXAMPLE 2.2.5	**Longest Block of Ones**

Suppose that the input consists of a sequence $A[1..n]$ of zeros and ones, and we want to find a longest contiguous block $A[p, q]$ of ones. For example, on input $A[1..n] = [1, 1, 0, 0, 1, 1, 1, 0, 0, 1, 1, 1, 0]$, the block $A[5..7]$ of length 3 is a suitable solution, and so is the block $A[10..12]$. Here are some things we must consider when designing the loop invariant.

Nonfinite Memory: Both the size of the longest block and the indices of its beginning and end are integers in $[1..n]$. These require $O(\log n)$ bits to remember. Hence, this algorithm will not be a deterministic *finite* automaton.

Remember the Solution for the Prefix: After reading the prefix $A[1..i]$, it is clear that you need to remember the longest block. Is this enough for a loop invariant? How would you maintain this loop invariant when reading in only the next character $A[i + 1]$? For example, if $A[1..i] = [0, 1, 1, 0, 0, 1, 1]$, then the loop invariant may give us only the block $A[2..3]$ of length 2. Then if we read $A[i + 1] = 1$, then the longest block of $A[1..i + 1] = [0, 1, 1, 0, 0, 1, 1, 1]$ becomes $A[6..8]$ of length 3. How would your program know about this block?

Remember the Longest Current Block: You also must keep a pointer to the beginning of the current block being worked on, i.e., the longest one ending in the value $A[i]$, and its size. With this the algorithm can know whether the current increasing contiguous subsequence gets to be longer than the previous one. This needs to be included in the loop invariant.

Maintaining the Loop Invariant: If you have this information about $A[1..i]$, then you can learn it about $A[1..i + 1]$ as follows. If $A[i + 1] = 1$, then the longest block of ones ending in the current value increases in length by one. Otherwise, it shrinks to being the empty string. If this block increases to be longer than our previous longest, then it replaces the previous longest. In the end, we know the longest block of ones.

Empty Blocks: $A[3..3]$ is a block of length 1, and $A[4..3]$ is a block of length zero ending in $A[3]$. This is why initially, with $i = 0$, the blocks are set to $A[1..0]$, and when the current block ending in $A[i + 1]$ becomes empty, it is set to $A[i + 2..i + 1]$.

Dynamic Programming: Dynamic programming, covered in Chapter 18, is a very powerful technique for solving optimization problems. Many of these amount to reading the elements of the input instance $A[1..n]$ one at a time and, when at $A[i]$, saving the optimal solution for the prefix $A[1..i]$ and its cost. This amounts to a deterministic nonfinite automaton. The maximum-block-of-ones problem is a trivial example of this. The solutions to the following two problems and more problems can be found in Chapter 19.2.

Longest Increasing Contiguous Subsequence: The input consists of a sequence $A[1..n]$ of integers, and we want to find the longest contiguous subsequence $A[k_1..k_2]$ such that the elements are monotonically increasing. For example, the optimal solution for $[5, 3, 1, 3, 7, 9, 8]$ is $[1, 3, 7, 9]$.

Longest Increasing Subsequence: This is a harder problem. Again the input consists of a sequence A of integers of size n. However, now we want to find the longest (not necessarily contiguous) subsequence $S \subseteq [1..n]$ such that the elements, in the order that they appear in A, are monotonically increasing. For example, an optimal solution for $[5, 1, 5, 7, 2, 4, 9, 8]$ is $[1, 5, 7, 9]$, and so is $[1, 2, 4, 8]$.

EXERCISE 2.2.1 *(See solution in Part Five.) Give the code for these examples:*
1. *Divide*
2. *Calculator*
3. *Longest block of ones*

EXERCISE 2.2.2 *For the longest block of ones, what are Σ, Q, δ, s, and F?*

EXERCISE 2.2.3 *For each of the following examples, give the code, and either give the DFA or, if necessary, give a deterministic nonfinite automaton as done in Example 2.2.5.*
1. $L = \{0^n 1^n \mid n \geq 0\} = \{\alpha \in \{0, 1\}^* \mid \alpha$ *has zero or more zeros followed by the same number of ones* $\}$.
2. $L = \{\alpha \in \{0, 1\}^* \mid$ *every third character of* α *is a* $1\}$. *e.g.,* $10\underline{1}00\underline{1}11\underline{1}01\underline{1}0 \in L, \epsilon \in L,$ $0 \in L,$ *and* $10\underline{0} \notin L$.
3. $L_{OR} = \{\alpha \in \{0, 1\}^* \mid \alpha$ *has length at most three* OR *the number of 1's is odd* $\}$.
4. $L = \{\alpha \in \{0, 1\}^* \mid \alpha$ *contains the substring* $0101\}$. *For example,* $\alpha = 1110101101 \in L$, *because it contains the substring, namely,* $\alpha = 111\ 0101\ 101$.

2.3   More of the Input vs. More of the Output

Sometimes it is not clear at first whether to use more-of-the-input or more-of-the-output loop invariants. This section gives two similar problems, of which the first works better for one and in which the second works better for the other.

EXAMPLE 2.3.1   **Tournament**

A *tournament* is a directed graph (see Section 3.1) formed by taking the complete undirected graph and assigning arbitrary directions to the edges, i.e., a graph $G = (V, E)$ such that for each $u, v \in V$, exactly one of $\langle u, v \rangle$ or $\langle v, u \rangle$ is in E. A *Hamiltonian path* is a path through a graph that can start and finish anywhere but must visit every node exactly once each. Design an algorithm that, given any tournament, finds a Hamiltonian path through it. Because it finds a Hamiltonian path for any tournament, this algorithm, in itself, acts as proof that every tournament has a Hamiltonian path.

More of the Output: It is natural to want to push forward and find the required path through a graph. The measure of progress would be the amount of the path outputted and the loop invariant would say "I have the first i nodes (or edges) in the final path." Maintaining this loop invariant would require extending the path constructed so far by one more node. The problem, however, is that the algorithm might get stuck when the path constructed so far has no edges from the last node to a node that has not yet been visited. This makes the loop invariant as stated false.

Recursive Backtracking: One is then tempted to have the algorithm *backtrack* when it gets stuck, trying a different direction for the path to go. This results in a fine algorithm. See the recursive backtracking algorithms in Chapter 17. However, unless one is really careful, such algorithms tend to require exponential time.

More of the Input: Instead, try solving this problem using a more-of-the-input loop invariant. Assume the nodes are numbered 1 to n in an arbitrary way. The algorithm temporarily pretends that the subgraph on the first i of the nodes is the entire input instance. The loop invariant is "I currently have a solution for this subinstance." Such a solution is a Hamiltonian path $u_1, \ldots, u_i$ that visits each of the first i nodes exactly once and that itself is simply a permutation the first i nodes. Maintaining this loop invariant requires constructing a path for the first $i + 1$ nodes. There is no requirement that this new path resemble the previous path. For this problem, however, it can be accomplished by finding a place to insert the $i + 1$st node within the permutation of the first i nodes. In this way, the algorithm looks a lot like insertion sort.

Case Analysis: When developing an algorithm, a good technique is to see for which input instances the obvious thing works and then try to design another algorithm for the remaining cases:

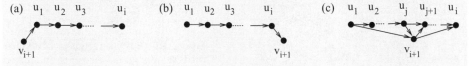

(a) If $\langle v_{i+1}, u_1 \rangle$ is an edge, then the extended path is easily $v_{i+1}, u_1, \ldots, u_i$.

(b) Similarly, if $\langle u_i, v_{i+1} \rangle$ is an edge, then the extended path is easily $u_1, \ldots, u_i, v_{i+1}$.

(c) Otherwise, because the graph is a tournament, both $\langle u_1, v_{i+1} \rangle$ and $\langle v_{i+1}, u_i \rangle$ are edges. Color each node u_j red if $\langle u_j, v_{i+1} \rangle$ is an edge, and blue if $\langle v_{i+1}, u_j \rangle$ is. Because u_1 is red and u_i is blue, there must be some place u_j to u_{j+i} in the path where it changes color from red to blue. Because both $\langle u_j, v_{i+1} \rangle$ and $\langle v_{i+1}, u_{j+i} \rangle$ are edges, we can form the extended path $u_1, \ldots, u_j, v_{i+1}, u_{j+i}, \ldots, u_i$.

EXAMPLE 2.3.2   Euler Cycle

An *Eulerian cycle* in an undirected graph is a cycle that passes through each edge exactly once. A graph contains an Eulerian cycle iff it is connected and the degree of each vertex is even. Given such a graph, find such a cycle.

More of the Output: We will again start by attempting to solve the problem using the more-of-the-output technique, namely, start at any node and build the output path one edge at a time. Not having any real insight into which edge should be taken next, we will choose them in a blind or greedy way (see Chapter 16). The loop invariant is that after i steps you have some path through i different edges from some node s to some node v.

Getting Stuck: The next step in designing this algorithm is to determine when, if ever, this simple blind algorithm gets stuck, and either to figure out how to avoid this situation or to fix it.

Making Progress: If $s \neq v$, then the end node v must be adjacent to an odd number of edges that are in the path. See Figure 2.2.a. This is because there is the last edge in the path, and for every edge in the path coming into the node there is one leaving. Hence, because v has even degree, it follows that v is adjacent to at least one edge that is not in the path. Follow this edge, extending the path by one edge. This maintains the loop invariant while making progress. This process can get stuck only when the path happens to cycle back to the starting node, giving $s = v$. In such a case, join the path here to form a cycle.

Ending: If the cycle created covers all of the edges, then we are done.

Getting Unstuck: If the cycle we have created from our chosen node s back to s does not cover all the edges, then we look for a node u within this cycle that is adjacent to an edge not in the cycle. See Figure 2.2.b. Change s to be this new node u. We break the cycle at u, giving us a path from u back to u. The difference with this path is that we can extend it past u along the unvisited edge. Again the loop invariant has been maintained while making progress.

(a)   (b)

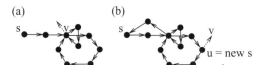

Figure 2.2: Path constructed thus far by the Euler algorithm within the undirected graph.

u **Exists:** The only thing remaining to prove is that when *v* comes around to meet *s* again and we are not done, then there is in fact a node *u* in the path that is adjacent to an edge not in the path. Because we are not done, there is an edge *e* in the graph that is not in our path. Because the graph is connected, there must be a path in the graph from *e* to our constructed path. The node *u* at which this connecting path meets our constructed path must be as required, because the last edge {*u*, *w*} in the connecting path is not in our constructed path.

Extended Loop Invariant: To avoid having to find such a node *u* when it is needed, we extend the loop invariant to state that in addition to the path, the algorithm remembers some node *u* other than *s* and *v* that is in the path and is adjacent to an edge not in the path.

EXERCISE 2.3.1 *(See solution in Part Five.) Iterative cake cutting: The famous algorithm for fairly cutting a cake in two is for one person to cut the cake in the place that he believes is half and for the other person to choose which "half" he likes. One player may value the icing and while the other the cake more, but it does not matter. The second player is guaranteed to get a piece that he considers to be worth at least a half, because he chooses between two pieces whose sum worth for him is at least one. Because the first person cut it in half according to his own criteria, he is happy which ever piece is left for him. Our goal is write an iterative algorithm that solves this same problem for n players.*

To make our life easier, we view a cake not as three-dimensional thing, but as the line from zero to one. Different players value different subintervals of the cake differently. To express this, each player assigns some numerical value to each subinterval. For example, if player p_i's name is written on the subinterval $[\frac{i-1}{2n}, \frac{i}{2n}]$ of cake, then he might allocate a higher value to it, say $\frac{1}{2}$. The only requirement is that the total value of the cake is one.

Your algorithm is only allowed the following two operations. In an evaluation query, $v = Eval(p, [a, b])$, the algorithm asks a player p how much (v) he values a particular subinterval $[a, b]$ of the whole cake $[0, 1]$. In a cut query, $b = Cut(p, a, v)$, the protocol asks the player p to identify the shortest subinterval $[a, b]$, starting at a given left endpoint a, with a given value v. In the above example, $Eval(p_i, [\frac{i-1}{2n}, \frac{i}{2n}])$ returns $\frac{1}{2}$ and $Cut(p_i, \frac{i-1}{2n}, \frac{1}{2})$ returns $\frac{i}{2n}$. Using these, the two-player algorithm is as follows:

algorithm *Partition2*({p_1, p_2}, [a, b])

⟨ **pre-cond**⟩: p_1 and p_2 are players.
　　[a, b] ⊆ [0, 1] is a subinterval of the whole cake.
⟨ **post-cond**⟩: Returns a partitioning of [a, b] into two disjoint pieces [a_1, b_1] and
　　[a_2, b_2] so that player p_i values [a_i, b_i] at least half as much as he values [a, b].

begin
　　$v_1 = Eval(p_1, [a, b])$
　　$c = Cut(p_1, a, \frac{v_1}{2})$

$$if(\ Eval(p_2, [a, c]) \leq Eval(p_2, [c, b]))\ then$$
$$[a_1, b_1] = [a, c]\ and\ [a_2, b_2] = [c, b]$$
$$else$$
$$[a_1, b_1] = [c, b]\ and\ [a_2, b_2] = [a, c]$$
$$end\ if$$
$$return([a_1, b_1]\ and\ [a_2, b_2])$$
end algorithm

The problem that you must solve is the following:

algorithm *Partition(n, P)*

⟨ **pre-cond**⟩: *P is a set of n players.*
   Each player in P values the whole cake [0, 1] by at least 1.
⟨ **post-cond**⟩: *Returns a partitioning of [0, 1] into n disjoint pieces $[a_i, b_i]$ so that*
   for each $i \in P$, the player p_i values $[a_i, b_i]$ by at least $\frac{1}{n}$.

begin
...
end algorithm

1. *Can you cut off n pieces of cake, each of size strictly bigger than $\frac{1}{n}$, and have cake left over? Is it sometimes possible to have allocated a disjoint piece to each player, each worth much more than $\frac{1}{n}$, to the receiving player, and for there to still be cake left? Explain.*

2. *As a big hint to designing an iterative algorithm, I will tell you what the first iteration accomplishes. (Later iterations may do slightly modified things.) Each player specifies where he would cut if he were to cut off the first fraction $\frac{1}{n}$ of the [a, b] cake. The player who wants the smaller amount of this first part of the cake is given this piece of the cake. The code for this is as follows:*

   $$loop\ i \in P$$
   $$c_i = Cut(p_i, 0, \tfrac{1}{n})$$
   $$end\ loop$$
   $$i_{min} = the\ i \in P\ that\ minimizes\ c_i$$
   $$[a_{i_{min}}, b_{i_{min}}] = [0, c_{i_{min}}]$$

   As your first step in designing the algorithm, what is your loop invariant? It should include:
   (a) how the cake has been cut so far
   (b) who has been given cake, and how he feels about it
   (c) how the remaining players feel about the remaining cake.

3. *Give the iterative pseudocode.*
4. *Formally prove that the loop invariant is established.*
5. *Formally prove that the loop invariant is maintained.*
6. *Formally prove that the postcondition is established.*
7. *What is the running time of this algorithm?*
8. *Is this a more-of-the-input or a more-of-the-output loop invariant?*

3 Abstract Data Types

Abstract data types (ADTs) provide both a language for talking about and tools for operating on complex data structures. Each is defined by the types of objects that it can store and the operations that can be performed. Unlike a function that takes an input and produces an output, an ADT is more dynamic, periodically receiving information and commands to which it must react in a way that reflects its history. In an object-oriented language, these are implemented with objects, each of which has its own internal variables and operations. A user of an ADT has no access to its internal structure except through the operations provided. This is referred to as *information hiding* and provides a clean boundary between the user and the ADT. One person can use the ADT to develop other algorithms without being concerned with how it is implemented or worrying about accidentally messing up the data structure. Another can implement and modify the ADT without knowing how it is used or worrying about unexpected effects on the rest of the code. A general purpose ADT—not just the code, but also the understanding and the mathematical theory—can be reused in many applications. Having a limited set of operations guides the implementer to use techniques that are efficient for these operations yet may be slow for the operations excluded. Conversely, using an ADT such as a stack in your algorithm automatically tells someone attempting to understand your algorithm a great deal about the purpose of this data structure. Generally, the running time of an operation is not a part of the description of an ADT, but is tied to a particular implementation. However, it is useful for the user to know the relative expense of using operations so that he can make his own choices about which ADTs and which operations to use.

This chapter will treat the following ADTs: lists, stacks, queues, priority queues, graphs, trees, and sets. From the user's perspective, these consist of a data structure and a set of operations with which to access the data. From the perspective of the data structure itself, it is a ongoing system that continues to receive a stream of commands to which it must react dynamically. ADTs have a set of invariants or integrity constraints (both public and hidden) that must be true every time the system is entered or left. Imagining a big loop around the system allows us to regard them as a kind of loop invariant.

3.1 Specifications and Hints at Implementations

The following are examples frequently used ADTs.

Simple Types: Integers, floating point numbers, strings, arrays, and records are abstract data types provided by all programming languages.

The List ADT:

Specification: A list consists of an ordered sequence of elements. Unlike arrays, they contain no empty positions. Elements can be *inserted, deleted, read, modified*, and *searched* for.

Array Implementations: There are different implementations that have tradeoffs in the running time, memory requirements, and difficulty of implementing. The obvious implementation of a list is to put the elements in an array. If the elements are packed one after the other, then the ith element can be accessed in $\Theta(1)$ time, but inserting or deleting an element requires $\Theta(n)$ time because all the elements need to be shifted. Alternatively, blank spaces could be left between the elements. This leaves room to insert or delete elements in $\Theta(1)$ time, but finding the ith element might now take $\Theta(n)$ time.

Linked List Implementations: A problem with the array implementation is that the array needs to be allocated some fixed size of memory when initialized. An alternative implementation, which can be expanded or shrunk in size as needed, uses a linked list. This implementation has the disadvantage of requiring $\Theta(n)$ time to access a particular element. See Section 3.2.

Tree Implementations: A nice balance between the advantages of array and the linked list implementations is data structure called a *heap*. Heaps can do every operation in $\Theta(\log n)$ time. See Section 10.4. Adelson-Velsky–Landis (AVL) trees and red–black trees have similar properties.

The Stack ADT:

Specification: A stack ADT is the same as a list ADT, except its operations are limited. It is analogous to a stack of plates. A *push* is the operation of adding a new element to the top of the stack. A *pop* is the operation of removing the top element from the stack. The rest of the stack is hidden from view. This order is referred to as *last in, first out* (LIFO).

Use: Stacks are the key data structure for recursion and parsing. Having the operations limited means that all operations can implemented easily and be performed in constant time.

Array Implementation: The hidden invariants in an array implementation of a stack are that the elements in the stack are stored in an array starting with the bottom of the stack and that a variable *top* indexes the entry of the array containing the top element. It is not difficult to implement push and pop so that they maintain these invariants. The stack grows to the right as elements are pushed and shrinks to the left as elements are popped. For the code, see Exercise 3.1.1.

```
                                          top
                                           ↓
 | 1 | 2 | 3 | 4 | 5 | 6 | 7 | 8 | / | / | / | / |
```

Linked List Implementation: As with lists, stacks are often implemented using linked lists. See Section 3.2.

The Queue ADT:

Specification: The queue ADT is also the same as a list ADT, except with a different limited set of operations. A queue is analogous to a line-up for movie tickets. One is able to *insert* an element at the *rear* and *remove* the element that is at the *front*. This order is *first in first out* (FIFO).

Queue Use: An operating system will have a queue of jobs to run and a *network hub* will have a queue of packets to transmit. Again all operations can be implement easily to run in constant time.

Array Implementation:

Trying Small Steps: If the front element is always stored at index 1 of the array, then when the current front is removed, all the remaining elements would need to shift by one to take its place. To save time, once an element is placed in the array, we do not want to move it until it is removed. The effect is that the rear moves to the right as elements arrive, and the front moves to the right as elements are removed. We use two different variables, *front* and *rear*, to index their locations. As the queue migrates to the right, eventually it will reach the end of the array. To avoid getting stuck, we will treat the array as a circle, indexing modulo the size of the array. This allows the queue to migrate around and around as elements arrive and leave.

Hidden Invariants: The elements are stored in order from the entry indexed by *front* to that indexed by *rear* possibly wrapping around the end of the array.

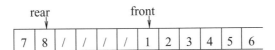

```
         rear              front
          ↓                 ↓
 | 7 | 8 | / | / | / | / | 1 | 2 | 3 | 4 | 5 | 6 |
```

Extremes: It turns out that the cases of a completely empty and a completely full queue are indistinguishable, because with both *front* will be one to the left of *rear*. The easiest solution is not to let the queue get completely full.

Code: See Exercises 3.1.2 and 3.1.3.

Linked List Implementation: Again see Section 3.2.

The Priority Queue ADT:

Specification: A priority queue is still analogous to a line-up for movie tickets. However, in these queues the more important elements are allowed to move to the front of the line. When *inserting* an element, its priority must be specified. This priority can later be changed. When *removing*, the element with the highest priority in the queue is removed and returned. Ties are broken arbitrarily.

Tree Implementations: Heaps, AVL trees, and red–black trees can do each operation in $\Theta(\log n)$ time. See Sections 4.1, 10.2, and 10.4.

The Set ADT:

Specification: A *set* is basically a bag within which you can put any elements that you like. It is the same as a list, except that the elements cannot be repeated or ordered.

Indicator Vector Implementation: If the universe of possible elements is sufficiently small, then a good data structure is to have a Boolean array indexed with each of these possible elements. An entry being true will indicate that the corresponding element is in the set. All set operations can be done in constant time, i.e., in a time independent of the number of items in the set.

Hash Table Implementation: Surprisingly, even if the universe of possible elements is infinite, a similar trick can be done, using a data structure called a *hash table*. A pseudorandom function H is chosen that maps possible elements of the set to the entries $[1, N]$ in the table. It is a deterministic function in that it is easy to compute and always maps an element to the same entry. It is pseudorandom in that it appears to map each element into a random place. Hopefully, all the elements that are in your set happen to be placed into different entries in the table. In this case, one can determine whether or not an element is contained in the set, ask for an arbitrary element from the set, determine the number of elements in the set, iterate through all the elements, and add and delete elements— all in constant time, i.e., independently of the number of items in the set. If collisions occur, meaning that two of your set elements get mapped to the same entry, then there are a number of possible methods to rehash them somewhere else.

The Set System ADT:

Specification: A set system allows you to have a set (or list) of sets. Operations allow the *creation, union, intersection, complementation,* and *subtraction* of sets. The *find* operator determines which set a given element is contained in.

List-of-Indicator-Vectors or Hash-Table Implementations: One way to implement these is to have a list of elements implemented using an array or a linked list where each of these elements is an implementation of a set. What remains is to implement operations that operate on multiple sets. Generally, these operations take $\Theta(n)$ time.

Union–Find Set System Implementation: Another quite surprising result is that on disjoint sets, the union and find operations can be done on average in a constant amount of time for all practical purposes. See the end of this section.

The Dictionary ADT: A dictionary associates a meaning with each word. Similarly, a dictionary ADT associates data with each *key*.

Graphs:

Specification: A *graph* is set of nodes with edges between them. They can represent networks of roads between cities or friendships between people. The key information stored is which pairs of nodes are connected by an edge. Sometimes data, such as weight, cost, or length, can be associated with each edge or with each node. Though a drawing implicitly places each node at some location on the page, a key abstraction of a graph is that the location of a node is not specified. The basic operations are to determine whether an edge is in a graph, to add or delete an edge, and to iterate through the neighbors of a node. There is a huge literature of more complex operations that one might want to do. For example, one might want to determine which nodes have paths between them or to find the shortest path between two nodes. See Chapter 14.

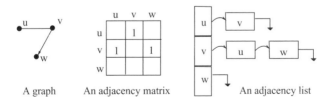

A graph   An adjacency matrix   An adjacency list

Adjacency Matrix Implementation: This consists of an $n \times n$ matrix with $M(u, v) = 1$ if $\langle u, v \rangle$ is an edge. It requires $\Theta(n^2)$ space (corresponding to the number of potential edges) and $\Theta(1)$ time to access a given edge, but $\Theta(n)$ time to find the edges adjacent to a given node, and $\Theta(n^2)$ to iterate through all the nodes. This is only a problem when the graph is large and sparse.

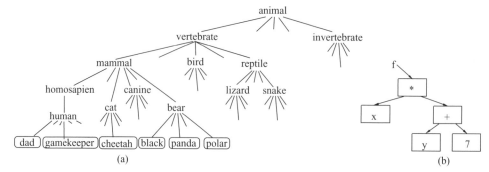

Figure 3.1: Classification tree of animals and a tree representing the expression $f = x \times (y + 7)$.

Adjacency List Implementation: It lists for each node the nodes adjacent to it. It requires $\Theta(E)$ space (corresponding to the number of actual edges) and can iterate quickly through the edges adjacent to a give node, but requires time proportional to the degree of a node to access a specific edge.

Trees:

Specification: Data is often organized into a hierarchy. A person has children, who have children of their own. The boss has people under her, who have people under them. The abstract data type for organizing this data is a *tree*.

Uses: There is a surprisingly large list of applications for trees. For two examples see Figure 3.1 and Section 10.5.

Pointer Implementation: Trees are generally implemented by having each node point to each of its children:

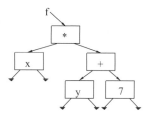

Orders: Imposing rules on how the nodes can be ordered speeds up certain operations.

Binary Search Tree: A binary search tree is a data structure used to store keys along with associated data. The nodes are ordered so that for each node, all the keys in its left subtree are smaller than its key, and all those in the right subtree are larger. Elements can be found in such a tree, using binary search, in $O(height)$ instead of $O(n)$ time. See Sections 4.1 and 10.2.

Heaps: A heap requires that the key of each node be bigger than those of both its children. This allows one to find the maximum key in $O(1)$ time. All updates can be done in $O(\log n)$ time. Heaps are useful for a sorting algorithm known as heap sort and for the implementation of priority queues. See Section 10.4.

Balanced Trees: If a binary tree is balanced, it takes less time to traverse down it, because it has height at most $\log_2 n$. It is too much work to maintain a perfectly balanced tree as nodes are added and deleted. There are, however, a number of data structures that are able to add and delete in $O(\log_2 n)$ time while ensuring that the tree remains almost balanced. Here are two.

AVL Trees: Every node has a *balance factor* of -1, 0, or 1, defined as the difference between the heights of its left and right subtrees. As nodes are added or deleted, this invariant is maintained using rotations like the following (see Exercise 3.1.5):

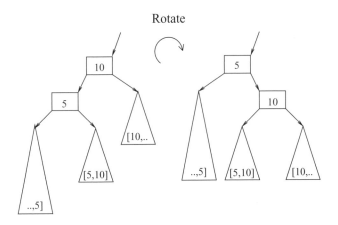

Red–Black Trees: Every node is either red or black. If a node is red, then both its children are black. Every path from the root to a leaf contains the same number of black nodes. See Exercise 3.1.6.

Balanced Binary Search Tree: By storing the elements in a balanced binary search tree, insertions, deletions, and searches can be done in $\Theta(\log n)$ time.

Union–Find Set System: This data structure maintains a number of disjoint sets of elements.

Operations: (1) *Makeset(v)*, which creates a new set containing the specified element v; (2) *Find(v)*, which determines the *name* of the set containing a specified element (each set is given a distinct but arbitrary name); and (3) *Union(u, v)*, which merges the sets containing the specified elements u and v.

Use: One application of this is in the minimum-spanning-tree algorithm in Section 16.2.3.

Running Time: On average, for all practical purposes, each of these operations can be completed in a constant amount of time. More formally, the total time to do m of these operations on n elements is $\Theta(m\alpha(n))$, where α is the *inverse Ackermann's function*. This function is so slow growing that even if n equals the number of atoms in the universe, then $\alpha(n) \leq 4$. See Section 9.3.

Implementation: The data structure used is a rooted tree for each set, containing a node for each element in the set. The difference is that each node points to its parent instead of to its children. The name of the set is the contents of the root node. *Find(w)* is accomplished by tracing up the tree from w to the root u. *Union(u, v)* is accomplished by having node u point to node v. From then on, *Find(w)* for a node w in u's tree will trace up and find v instead. What makes this fast on average is that whenever a *Find* operation is done, all nodes that are encountered during the find are changed to point directly to the root of the tree, collapsing the tree into a shorter tree.

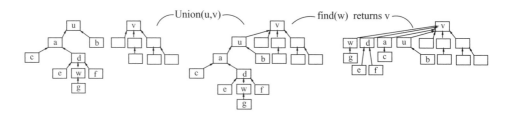

EXERCISE 3.1.1 *Implement the push and pop operations on a stack using an array as described in Section 3.1.*

EXERCISE 3.1.2 *Implement the insert and remove operations on a queue using an array as described in Section 3.1.*

EXERCISE 3.1.3 *When working with arrays, as in Section 3.1, what is the difference between "rear = (rear + 1) mod MAX" and "rear = (rear mod MAX) + 1," and when should each be used?*

Figure: The top row shows three famous graphs: the complete graph on four nodes, the cube, and the Peterson graph. The bottom row shows the same three graphs with their nodes laid out differently.

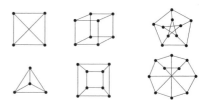

EXERCISE 3.1.4 *For each of the three pairs of graphs, number the nodes in such the way that $\langle i, j \rangle$ is an edge in one if and only if it is an edge in the other.*

EXERCISE 3.1.5 *(See solution in Part Five.) Prove that the height of an AVL tree with n nodes is $\Theta(\log n)$.*

EXERCISE 3.1.6 *Prove that the height of a red–black tree with n nodes is $\Theta(\log n)$.*

3.2　Link List Implementation

As said, a problem with the array implementation of the list ADT is that the array needs to be allocated some fixed size of memory when it is initialized. A solution to this is to implement these operations using a linked list, which can be expanded in size as needed. This implementation is particularly efficient when the operations are restricted to those of a stack or a queue.

List ADT Specification: A list consists of an ordered sequence of elements. Unlike arrays, it has no empty positions. Elements can be *inserted, deleted, read, modified,* and *searched* for. There are tradeoffs in the running time. Arrays can access the ith element in $\Theta(1)$ time, but require $\Theta(n)$ time to insert an element. A *linked list* is an alternative implementation in which the memory allocated can grow and shrink dynamically with the needs of the program. Linked lists allow insertions in $\Theta(1)$ time, but require $\Theta(n)$ time to access the ith element. Heaps can do both in $\Theta(\log n)$ time.

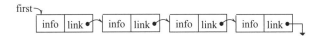

Hidden Invariants: In a linked list, each node contains the information for one element and a pointer to the next. The variable *first* points to the first node, and *last* to the last. The last node has its pointer variable contain the value *nil*. When the list contains no nodes, *first* and *last* also point to nil.

Notation: A pointer, such as *first*, is a variable that is used to store the address of a block of memory. The information stored in the *info* field of such a block is denoted by *first.info* in Java and *first–> info* in C. We will adopt the first notation. Similarly, *first.link* denotes the pointer field of the node. Being a pointer itself, *first.link.info* denotes the information stored in the second node of the linked list, and *first.link.link.info* in the third.

Adding a Node to the Front: Given a list ADT and new *Info* to store in an element, this operation is to insert an element with this information into the front the list.

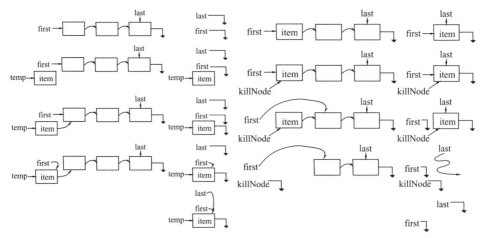

Figure 3.2: Adding and removing a node from the front of a linked list.

General Case: We need the following steps (with pseudocode given to the right) for a large and general linked list. See Figure 3.2.

- Allocate space for the new node.   New *temp*
- Store the information for the new element.   *temp.info = Info*
- Point the new node at the rest of the list.   *temp.link = first*
- Point *first* at the new node.   *first = temp*

Special Case: The main special case is an empty list. Sometimes we are lucky and the code written for the general case also works for such special cases. Inserting a node starting with both *first* and *last* pointing to *nil*, everything works except for *last*. Add the following to the bottom of the code.

- Point *last* to the new and only node.   if(*last = nil*) then
         last = temp
         end if

Whenever adding code to handle a special case, be sure to check that the previously handled cases still are handled correctly.

Removing Node from Front: Given a list ADT, this operation is to remove the element in the front the list and to return the information *Info* stored within it.

General Case:

- Point a temporary variable *kill Node* to point to the node to be removed.   *kill Node = first*
- Move *first* to point to the second node.   *first = first.link*
- Save the value to be returned.   *Info = kill Node.info*
- Deallocate the memory for the first node.   free *kill Node*
- Return the value.   return(*item*)

Special Cases: If the list is already empty, a node cannot be removed. The only other special case occurs when there is one node pointed to by both *first* and *last*. At the end of the code, *first* points to nil, which is correct for an empty list. However, *last* still points to the node that has been deleted. This can be solved by adding the following to the bottom of the code:

- The list becomes empty.

$$
\text{if}(\, first = nil\,) \text{ then}
$$
$$
last = nil
$$
$$
\text{end if}
$$

Note that the value of *first* and *last* change. If the routine *Pop* passes these parameters in by value, the routine needs to be written to allow this to happen.

Testing Whether Empty: A routine that returns whether the list is empty returns *true* if *first* = *nil* and *false* otherwise. It does not look like this routine does much, but it serves two purposes. It hides these implementation details from the user, and by calling this routine instead of doing the test directly, the user's code becomes more readable. See Exercise 3.2.1.

Adding Node to End: See Exercise 3.2.2.

Removing Node from End: It is easy to access the last node and delete it, because *last* is pointing at it. However, in order to maintain this invariant, *last* must be pointed at the node that had been the second-to-last node. It takes $\Theta(n)$ time to *walk* down the list from the first node to find this second-to-last node. Luckily, neither stacks nor queues need this operation. For a faster implementation see Exercise 3.2.3.

Walking Down the Linked List: Now suppose that the elements in the linked lists are sorted by the field *info*. When given an *info* value *newElement*, our task is to point the pointer *next* at the first element in the list with that value. The pointer *prev* is to point to the previous element in the list. This needs to be saved, because if it is needed, there is no back pointer to back up to it. If such an element does not exist, then *prev* and *next* are to sandwich the location where this element would go. For example, if *newElement* had either the value 6 or the value 8, the result of the search would be

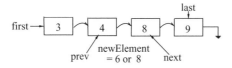

- Walk down the list
- maintaining the two pointers

loop
    ⟨*loop-inv*⟩: *prev* and *next* point to consecutive nodes before or at our desired location.

- until the desired location is found

    exit when *next* = *nil*
    or *next.info* ≥ *newElement*

- pointing *prev* where *next* is pointing
- and pointing *next* to the next node.

    prev = *next*
    next = *next.link*
    end loop

Running Time: This can require $O(n)$ time, where n is the length of the list.

Initialize the Walk: To initially establish the loop invariant, *prev* and *next* must sandwich the location before the first node. We do this as follows:

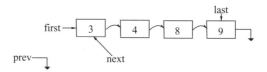

- Sandwich the location before the first node.

    prev = *nil*
    next = *first*

Adding a Node:

Into the Middle: The general case to consider first is adding the node into the middle of the list.

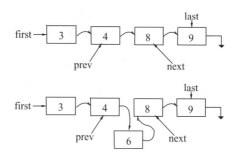

- Allocate space for the new node.

    new *temp*

- Store the information for the new element.

    temp.info = *item*

- Point the previous node to the new node.

    prev.link = *temp*

- Point the new node to the next node.

    temp.link = *next*

At the Beginning: If the new node belongs at the beginning of the list (say value 2), then *prev.link* = *temp* would not work, because *prev* is not pointing at a node. We will replace this line with the following:

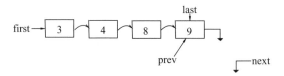

- If the new node is to be the first node,
- point *first* at the new node
- else
- point the previous node to the new node.

if *prev* = *nil* then
    first = *temp*
else
    prev.link = *temp*
end if

55

At the End: Now what if the new node is to be added on the end (e.g. value 12)? The variable *last* will no longer point at the last node. Adding the following code to the bottom will solve the problem:

- If the new node will be the last node,
- point *last* at the new node.

if *prev* = *last* then
    last = *temp*
end if

To an Empty List: Another case to consider is when the initial list is empty. In this case, all the variables, *first, last, prev,* and *next,* will be nil. The new code works in this case as is.

Compete Code for Adding a Node: One needs to put all of these pieces together into one *insert* routine. See Exercise 3.2.5.

Deleting a Node:

From the Middle: Again the general case to consider first is deleting the node from the middle of the list. We must maintain the linked list *before* destroying the node. Otherwise, we will drop the list.

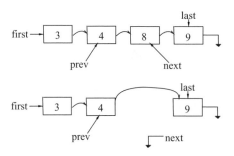

- Bypass the node being deleted. $prev.link = next.link$
- Deallocate the memory pointed to by   free *next*
  next.

From the Beginning or the End: As before, you need to consider all the potential special cases. See Exercise 3.2.6.

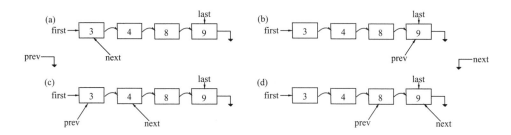

EXERCISE 3.2.1 *Implement testing whether a linked list is empty.*

EXERCISE 3.2.2 *Implement adding a node to the end of a linked list.*

EXERCISE 3.2.3 *Double pointers: Describe how this operation can be done in $\Theta(1)$ time if there are pointers in each node to both the previous and the next node.*

EXERCISE 3.2.4 *(See solution in Part Five.) In the code for walking down the linked list, what effect, if any, would it have if the order of the exit conditions were switched to "exit when next.info $\geq$ newElement or next $=$ nil"?*

EXERCISE 3.2.5 *Implement the complete code insert that, when given an info value newElement, inserts a new element where it belongs into a sorted linked list. This involves only putting together the pieces just provided.*

EXERCISE 3.2.6 *Implement the complete code Delete that, when given an info value newElement, finds and deletes the first element with this value, if it exists. This involves also considering the four special cases listed for deleting a node from the beginning or the end of a linked list.*

3.3 Merging with a Queue

Merging consists of combining two sorted lists, A and B, into one completely sorted list, C. Here A, B, and C are each implemented as queues. The loop invariant maintained is that the k smallest of the elements are sorted in C. (This is a classic more-of-the-output loop invariant. It is identical to that for selection sort.) The larger elements are still in their original lists A and B. The next smallest element will be either first element in A or the first element in B. Progress is made by removing the smaller of these two first elements and adding it to the back of C. In this way, the algorithm proceeds like two lanes of traffic merging into one. At each iteration, the first car from one of the incoming lanes is chosen to move into the merged lane. This increases k by one. Initially, with $k = 0$, we simply have the given two lists. We stop when $k = n$. At this point, all the elements will be sorted in C. Merging is a key step in the merge sort algorithm presented in Section 9.1.

algorithm *Merge(list : A, B)*

⟨ *pre-cond*⟩*:* A and B are two sorted lists.

⟨ *post-cond*⟩*:* C is the sorted list containing the elements of the other two.

begin
    loop
        ⟨*loop-invariant*⟩*:* The k smallest of the elements are sorted in C.
            The larger elements are still in their original lists A and B.

        exit when A and B are both empty
        if(the first in A is smaller than the first in B or B is empty) then
            next Element = Remove first from A
        else
            next Element = Remove first from B
        end if
        Add *next Element* to C
    end loop
    return(C)
end algorithm

3.4   Parsing with a Stack

One important use of stack is for parsing.

Specifications:

Preconditions: An input instance consists of a string of brackets.

Postconditions: The output indicates whether the brackets match. Moreover, each left bracket is allocated an integer $1, 2, 3, \ldots$, and each right bracket is allocated the integer from its matching left bracket.

Example:

Input:	(	[	{	}	(	)	]	(	)	{	(	)	}	)
Output:	1	2	3	3	4	4	2	5	5	6	7	7	6	1

The Loop Invariant: Some prefix of the input instance has been read, and the correct integer allocated to each of these brackets. (Thus, it is a more-of-the-input loop invariant.) The left brackets that have been read and not matched are stored along with their integers in left-to-right order in a stack, with the rightmost on top. The variable c indicates the next integer to be allocated to a left bracket.

Maintaining the Loop Invariant: If the next bracket read is a left bracket, then it is allocated the integer c. Not being matched, it is pushed onto the stack. c is incremented. If the next bracket read is a right bracket, then it must match the rightmost left bracket that has been read in. This will be on the top of the stack. The top bracket on the stack is popped. If it matches the right bracket, i.e., we have ( ), {}, or [], then the right bracket is allocated the integer for this left bracket. If not, then an error message is printed.

Initial Conditions: Initially, nothing has been read and the stack is empty.

Ending: If the stack is empty after the last bracket has been read, then the string has been parsed.

Code:

```
algorithm  Parsing (s)

⟨ pre-cond⟩: s is a string of brackets.
⟨ post-cond⟩: Prints out a string of integers that indicate how the brackets
     match.
begin
     i = 0, c = 1
     loop
          ⟨loop-invariant⟩: Prefix s[1, i] has been allocated integers, and
               its left brackets are on the stack.
          exit when i = n
          if(s[i + 1] is a left bracket) then
               print(c)
               push(⟨s[i + 1], c⟩)
               c = c + 1
          elseif(s[i + 1] = right bracket) then
               if( stackempty( ) ) return("Cannot parse")
               ⟨left, d⟩ = pop( )
               if(left matches s[i + 1]) then print(d)
               else return("Cannot parse")
```

```
            else
                  return("Invalid input character")
            end if
            i = i + 1
      end loop
      if( stackempty( ) ) return("Parsed") else return("Cannot parse")
end algorithm
```

Parsing only "( )"**:** If you only need to parse one type of brackets and you only want to know whether or not the brackets match, then you do not need the stack in the above algorithm, only an integer storing the number of left brackets in the stack.

Parsing with Context-Free Grammars: To parse more complex sentences see Chapter 12 and Section 19.8.

4 Narrowing the Search Space: Binary Search

In this chapter, we will consider more binary search algorithms, which use the narrowing-the-search-space type of loop invariant. In this case, if the thing being searched for is anywhere, then it is in the narrowed sublist. We first look at general binary search trees, which are often used in recursive algorithms (see Section 10.2) and then look at another example of an algorithm that incorporates binary search.

4.1 Binary Search Trees

Section 3.1 defines a *binary search tree* to be a binary tree data structure in which each node stores an element (and some associated data). The nodes are ordered so that for each node all the elements in its left subtree are smaller than that node's element and all those in its right subtree are larger. I will show here how to search quickly for a element with a given tree.

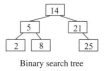
Binary search tree

1) Specifications: Given a binary search tree and a key, find a node whose element is this key or report that there is no such node.

2) Basic Steps: The restricted search space will be a subtree. Just as in binary search, our goal is to cut the size of this search space in half.

3) Measure of Progress: For binary search Example 1.4.3, the measure of progress was the number of elements in the current sublist. With binary search trees this number is not as predictable when the tree is not balanced. Hence, the measure of progress will be the number of edges in the path from the root of the entire subtree to the root of the current subtree.

4) The Loop Invariant: The loop invariant states that if the key is contained somewhere in the entire binary search tree, then it is contained in our current subtree.

5) Main Steps: In binary search, we compared the key with the element in the middle of the current search space. With an unbalanced binary search tree, we do not know which node is at the exact middle. Instead, we compare the key with the element at the root of the current subtree. If it contains the key, then we are done. If the key is smaller than it, then we know that if the key is anywhere, then it is in the left subtree of our current tree, else we know that it is in the right subtree.

6) Make Progress: As the root of our current subtree moves down to either its left or its right subtree, the measure of progress increases by one.

7) Maintain Loop Invariant: $\langle loop\text{-}invariant' \rangle$ & *not* $\langle exit\text{-}cond \rangle$ & $code_{loop} \Rightarrow \langle loop\text{-}invariant'' \rangle$. The previous loop invariant gives that the search has been narrowed down to the current subtree. The property of binary search trees is that all the elements within this subtree that are smaller than the root of this subtree are in this subtree's left subtree, and all those larger in its right. Hence, the main steps narrow the search space to the subtree, that would contain the key.

8) Establishing the Loop Invariant: $\langle pre\text{-}cond \rangle$ & $code_{pre\text{-}loop} \Rightarrow \langle loop\text{-}invariant \rangle$. Initially, you obtain the loop invariant by considering the entire tree of elements as the current subtree.

9) Exit Condition: We exit either when the key is found or when the current subtree becomes empty.

10) Ending: $\langle loop\text{-}invariant \rangle$ & $\langle exit\text{-}cond \rangle$ & $code_{post\text{-}loop} \Rightarrow \langle post\text{-}cond \rangle$. By the exit condition, either we have found the key, in which case we are done, or we have narrowed the search space to an empty subtree. The loop invariant says that if the key is contained in the original list, then the key is contained in this empty subtree, which it is not, and hence the algorithm can safely report that the key is not in the original list.

11) Termination and Running Time: The number of iterations of this algorithm is at most the height of the binary search tree, which (if the tree more or less balanced) is $\Theta(\log n)$.

12) Special Cases: There are no special cases here: any input is either equal to, larger than, or smaller than the root of the current subtree.

13) Coding and Implementation Details:

algorithm *SearchBST(tree, keyToFind)*

$\langle$ ***pre-cond***$\rangle$*: tree* is a binary tree whose nodes contain key and data fields. *keyToFind* is a key.

⟨ **post-cond**⟩**:** If there is a node with this key in the tree, then the associated data is returned.

```
begin
    subtree = tree
    loop
        ⟨loop-invariant⟩: If the key is contained in tree, then the key is
            contained in subtree.
        if( subtree = emptyTree ) then
            result( "key not in tree" )
        else if( keyToFind < rootKey(subtree) ) then
            subtree = leftSub(subtree)
        else if( keyToFind = rootKey(subtree) ) then
            result( rootData(subtree) )
        else if( keyToFind > rootKey(subtree) ) then
            subtree = rightSub(subtree)
        end if
    end loop
end algorithm
```

4.2 Magic Sevens

My mom gave my son Joshua a book of magic tricks. The book says, "This trick really is magic. It comes right every time you do it, but there is no explanation why." As it turns out, there is a bug in the way that they explain the trick. Our task is to fix the bug and to counter "there is no explanation why." The only magic is that of loop invariants. The algorithm is a variant on binary search.

1) Specifications:

- Let c, an odd integer, be the number of *columns*. The book uses $c = 3$.
- Let r, an odd integer, be the number of *rows*. The book uses $r = 7$.
- Let $n = c \cdot r$ be the number of cards. The book uses $n = 21$.
- Let t be the number of iterations. The book uses $t = 2$.
- Let f be the final index of the selected card. The book uses $f = 11$.
- Ask someone to select one of the n cards and then shuffle the deck.

- Repeat t times:
  - Spread the cards out as follows. Put c cards in a row left to right face up. Put a second row on top, but shifted down slightly so that you can see what both the first and second row of cards are. Repeat for r rows. This forms c columns of r cards each.
  - Ask which column the selected card is in.
  - Stack the cards in each column. Put the selected column in the middle. (This is why c is odd.)
- Output the fth card.

Our task is to determine for which values c, r, n, t, and f this trick finds the selected card.

Easier Version: Analyzing this trick turns out to be harder than I initially thought. Hence, we'll consider the following easier trick first. Instead of putting the selected column in the middle of the other columns, we put it in front.

2) Basic Steps: At each iteration we gain some information about which card had been selected. The trick seems to be similar to binary search. A difference is that binary search splits the current sublist into two parts, whereas this trick splits the entire pile into c parts. In both algorithms, at each iteration we learn which of these piles the sought-after element is in.

4) Loop Invariant: A good first guess for a loop invariant would be that used by binary search. The loop invariant will state that some subset S_i of the cards contains the selected card. In this easier version, the column containing the card is continually moved to the front of the stack. Hence, let us guess that $S_i = \{1, 2, \ldots, s_i\}$ indexes the first s_i cards in the deck. We will later solve a recurrence relation to determine that $s_i = \lceil n/c^i \rceil$.

7) Maintain Loop Invariant: $\langle \textit{loop-invariant}' \rangle$ & *not* $\langle \textit{exit-cond} \rangle$ & $code_{loop} \Rightarrow$ $\langle \textit{loop-invariant}'' \rangle$. By the previous loop invariant, the selected card is one of the first s_{i-1} in the deck. When the cards are laid out, the first s_{i-1} cards will be spread on the tops of the c columns. Some columns will get $\lceil s_{i-1}/c \rceil$ of these cards, and some will get $\lfloor s_{i-1}/c \rfloor$ of them. When we are told which column the selected card is in, we will know that the selected card is one of the first $\lceil s_{i-1}/c \rceil$ cards in this column. In conclusion,

$$s_i = \left\lceil \frac{s_{i-1}}{c} \right\rceil = \left\lceil \frac{\left\lceil \frac{n}{c^{i-1}} \right\rceil}{c} \right\rceil = \left\lceil \frac{n}{c^i} \right\rceil .$$

8) Establishing the Loop Invariant: Again, as done in binary search, we initially obtain the loop invariant by considering the entire stack of cards, giving $s_0 = \lceil n/c^0 \rceil = n$.

9) Exit Condition: When sufficient rounds have occurred so that $s_t = 1$, the search space has narrowed down to containing only the first card. Hence, the algorithm is able to select card $f = 1$.

11) Running Time: After $t = \lceil \log_c n \rceil$ rounds, $s_t = \lceil n/c^t \rceil = 1$.

For a matching lower bound on the number of iterations needed see Chapter 7.

The book has $n = 21$, $c = 3$, and $t = 2$. Because $21 = n \not\leq c^t = 3^2 = 9$, the trick in the book does not work. Two rounds is not enough. There must be three.

Original Trick: Consider again the original trick where the selected column is put into the middle.

4) The Loop Invariant: Because the selected column is put into the middle, let us guess that S_i consists of the middle s_i cards. More formally, let $d_i = (n - s_i)/2$. Neither the first nor the last d_i cards will be the selected card. Instead it will be one of $S_i = \{d_i + 1, \ldots, d_i + s_i\}$. Note that both n and s_i need to be odd.

8) Establishing the Loop Invariant: For $i = 0$, we have $s_0 = n$, $d_0 = 0$, and the selected card can be any card in the deck.

7) Maintain Loop Invariant: Suppose that before the ith iteration, the selected card is not one of the first d_{i-1} cards, but is one of the middle s_{i-1} in the deck. Then when the cards are laid out, the first d_{i-1} cards will be spread on the tops of the c columns. Some columns will get $\lceil d_{i-1}/c \rceil$ of these cards, and some will get $\lfloor d_{i-1}/c \rfloor$ of them. In general, however, we can say that the first $\lfloor d_{i-1}/c \rfloor$ cards of each column are not the selected card. We use the floor instead of the ceiling here, because this is the worst case. By symmetry, we also know that the selected card is not one of the last $\lfloor d_{i-1}/c \rfloor$ cards in each column. When the person points at a column, we learn that the selected card is somewhere in that column. However, from before we knew that the selected card is not one of the first or last $\lfloor d_{i-1}/c \rfloor$ cards in this column. There are only r cards in the column. Hence, the selected card must be one of the middle $r - 2\lfloor d_{i-1}/c \rfloor$ cards in the column. Define s_i to be this value. The new deck is formed by stacking the columns together with these cards in the middle.

9) Exit Condition: When sufficient rounds have occurred so that $s_t = 1$, then the selected card will be in the middle indexed by $f = \lceil \frac{n}{2} \rceil$.

Trick in Book: The book has $n = 21$, $c = 3$, and $r = 7$. Thus

$$s_i = r - 2\lfloor \tfrac{d_{i-1}}{c} \rfloor \qquad d_i = \tfrac{n-s_i}{2} \qquad S_i = \{d_i + 1, \ldots, d_i + s_i\}$$

$$s_0 = n = 21 \qquad\qquad d_0 = \tfrac{21-21}{2} = 0 \qquad S_0 = \{1, 2, \ldots, 21\}$$

$$s_1 = 7 - 2\lfloor \tfrac{0}{3} \rfloor = 7 \qquad d_1 = \tfrac{21-7}{2} = 7 \qquad S_1 = \{8, 9, \ldots, 14\}$$

$$s_2 = 7 - 2\lfloor \tfrac{7}{3} \rfloor = 3 \qquad d_2 = \tfrac{21-3}{2} = 9 \qquad S_2 = \{10, 11, 12\}$$

$$s_3 = 7 - 2\lfloor \tfrac{9}{3} \rfloor = 1 \qquad d_3 = \tfrac{21-1}{2} = 10 \qquad S_3 = \{11\}$$

Again three and not two rounds are needed.

11) Running Time: Temporarily ignoring the floor in the equation for s_i makes the analysis easier. We have

$$s_i = r - 2\left\lfloor \frac{d_{i-1}}{c} \right\rfloor \approx r - 2\frac{d_{i-1}}{c} = \frac{n}{c} - 2\frac{(n - s_{i-1})/2}{c} = \frac{s_{i-1}}{c}.$$

Again, this recurrence relation gives that $s_i = n/c^i$. If we include the floor, challenging manipulations give that $s_i = 2\lfloor s_{i-1}/2c - \tfrac{1}{2} \rfloor + 1$. More calculations give that s_i is always n/c^i rounded up to the next odd integer.

EXERCISE 4.2.1 *Give code for the original Magic Sevens trick.*

EXERCISE 4.2.2 *Suppose S and T are sorted arrays, each containing n elements. Find the nth smallest of the 2n numbers.*

4.3 VLSI Chip Testing

The following is a strange problem with strange rules. However, it is no stranger than the problems that you will need to solve in the world. We will use this as an example of how to develop a strange loop invariant with which the algorithm and its correctness become transparent.

Specification: Our boss has n supposedly identical VLSI chips that are potentially capable of testing each other. His test jig accommodates two chips at a time. The result is either that they are the same (that is, both are good or both are bad), or that they are different (that is at least one is bad). The professor hires us to design an algorithm to distinguish good chips from bad ones.

Impossible? Some computational problems have exponential-time algorithms, but no polynomial time algorithms. Because we are limited in what we are able to do, this problem may not have an algorithm at all. It is often hard to know. A good thing to do with a new problem is to alternate between author and critic. The author does his best to design an algorithm for the problem. The critic does his best to prove that the author's algorithm does not work or, even better, prove that no algorithm works.

Suppose that the professor happened to have one good chip and one bad chip. The single test that he has tells him that these chips are different, but does not tell him which is which. There is no algorithm using only this single test that accomplishes the task. The professor may not be happy with our findings, but he will not be able to blame us.

Though we have shown that there is no algorithm that distinguishes these two chips, perhaps we can find an algorithm that can be of some use for the professor.

A Data Structure: It is useful to have a good data structure with which to store the information that has been collected. Here we can have a graph with a node for each chip. After testing a pair of chips, we put a solid edge between the corresponding nodes if they are reportedly the same and a dotted edge if they are different.

The Brute Force Algorithm: One way of understanding a problem better is to initially pretend that you have unbounded time and energy. With this, what tasks can you accomplish? With $\Theta(n^2)$ tests we can test every pair of chips. We assume that the test is tensitive, meaning that if chip a tests to be the same as b, which tests to be the same as c, then a will test to be the same as c. Given this, we can conclude that the tests will partition the chips into sets of chips that are the same. (In graph theory we call these sets *cliques*, as in a clique of friends in which everyone in the group is friends with everyone else in the group.) There is, however, no test available to determine which of these sets contain the good chips.

Change the Problem: When you get stuck, a useful thing to do is to go back to your boss or to the application at hand and see if you can change the problem to make it easier. There are three ways of doing this.

> **More Tools:** One option is to allow the algorithm more powerful tools. A test that told you whether a chip was good would solve the problem. On the other hand, if the professor had such a test, you would be out of a job.

> **Change the Preconditions:** You can change the preconditions to require additional information about the input instance or to disallow particularly difficult instances. You need some way of distinguishing between the good chips and the various forms of bad chips. Perhaps you can get the professor to assure you that more than half of the chips are good. With this, you can solve the problem. Test all pairs of chips and partition the chips into the sets of equivalent chips. The largest of these sets will be the good chips.

> **Change the Postconditions:** Another option is to change the postconditions by not requiring so much in the output. Instead of needing to distinguish completely between good and bad chips, an easier task would be to find a single good chip.

A Faster Algorithm: Once we have our brute force algorithm, we will want to attempt to find a faster algorithm. Let us attempt to find a single good chip from among n chips, assuming that more than $n/2$ of the chips are good, using an iterative algorithm. Hopefully, it will be faster than $\Theta(n^2)$ time.

Designing the Loop Invariant: In designing an iterative algorithm for this problem, the most creative step is designing the loop invariant.

> **Start with Small Steps:** What basic steps might we follow to make some kind of progress? Certainly the first step is to test two chips. There are two cases.
>
> > **Different:** Suppose that we determine that the two chips are different. One way to make progress is to narrow down the input instance while maintaining what we know about it. What we know is that more than half of the chips are good. Because we know that at least one of the two tested chips is bad, we can throw both of them away. We know that we do not go wrong by doing this, because we maintain the loop invariant that more than half of the chips are good. From this we know that there is still at least one good chip remaining, which we can return as the answer.
> >
> > **Same:** If the two chips test the same, we cannot throw them away, because they might both be good. However, this too seems like we are making progress, because, as in the brute force algorithm, we are building up a set of chips that are the same.
>
> **Picture from the Middle:** From our single step, we saw two forms of progress. First, we saw that some chips will have been set aside. Let S denote the subset containing all the chips that we have not set aside. Second, we saw that we were building up sets of chips that we know to be the same. It may turn out that we will need to maintain a number of these sets. To begin, however, let's start with the simplest picture and build only one such set.
>
> **The Loop Invariant:** We maintain two sets. The set S contains the chips that we have not set aside. We maintain that more than half of the chips in S are good. The set C is a subset of S. We maintain that all of the chips in C are the same, though we do not know whether they are all good or all bad.
>
> **Type of Loop Invariant:** This is a strange loop invariant, but it has a number of familiar aspects.
>
> > **More of the Input:** We do consider the chips one at a time in order.
> >
> > **More of the Output:** The set C is our first guess at what the outputted good chips will be (but this may change).
> >
> > **Narrow the Search Space:** The narrowed set S contains at least one good chip.

Case Analysis: We check different cases as to whether the chips are the same or different.

Work Done: The sets S and C keep track of the work done so that it need not be redone.

Maintaining the Loop Invariant: $\langle loop\text{-}invariant' \rangle \& \text{not}\langle exit\text{-}cond \rangle \& code_{loop} \Rightarrow$ $\langle loop\text{-}invariant'' \rangle$. Assume that all we know is that the loop invariant is true. It being the only thing that we know how to do, we must test two chips. Testing two from C is not useful, because we already know that they are the same. Testing two that are not in C is dangerous, because if we learn that they are same, then we will have to start a second set of alike chips, yet we previously decided to maintain only one. The remaining possibility is to choose any chip from C and any from $S - C$ and test them. Let us denote these chips by c and s.

Same: If the conclusion is that the chips are the same, then add chip s to C. We have not changed S, so its loop invariant still holds. From our test, we know that s has the same characteristic as c. From the loop invariant, we know that c is that same as all the other chips in C. Hence, we know that s is the same as all the other chips in C, and the loop invariant follows.

Different: If the conclusion is that at least one is bad, then delete both c and s from C and S. Now S has lost two chips, at least one of which is bad. Hence, we have maintained the fact that more than half of the chips in S are good. Also, C has only become smaller, and hence we have maintained the fact that its chips are all the same.

Either way, we maintain the loop invariant while making some (yet undefined) progress.

Handle All Cases: We can only test one chip from C and one from $S - C$ if both are nonempty. We need to consider the cases in which they are not.

S **Is Empty:** If S is empty, then we are in trouble, because we have no more chips to return as the answer. We must stop before this.

$S - C$ **Is Empty:** If $S - C$ is empty, then we know that all the chips in $S = C$ are the same. Because more than half of them must be good, we know that all of them are good. Hence, we are done.

C **Is Empty:** If C is empty, take any chip from S and add it to C. We have not changed S, so its loop invariant still holds. The single chip in C is the same as itself.

The Measure of Progress: The measure cannot be $|S|$, because this does not decrease when the chips are the same. Instead, let the measure be $|S - C|$. In two of our cases, we remove a chip from $S-C$ and add it to C. In another case, we remove a chip from $S-C$ and one from C. Therefore, in all cases this measure decreases by 1.

Initial Code: $\langle pre\text{-}cond \rangle$ & $code_{pre\text{-}loop} \Rightarrow \langle loop\text{-}invariant \rangle$. The initial code sets S to be all the chips and C to be empty. More than half of the chips in S are good according to the precondition. Because there are no chips in C, all the chips that are in it are the same.

Exiting Loop: $\langle loop\text{-}invariant \rangle$ & $\langle exit\text{-}cond \rangle$ & $code_{post\text{-}loop} \Rightarrow \langle post\text{-}cond \rangle$. $|S - C| = 0$ is a good halting condition, but not the first. Halt when $|C| > |S|/2$, and return any chip from C. According to the loop invariant, the chips in C are either all good or all bad. The chips in C constitute more than half the chips, so if they were all bad, more than half of the chips in S would also be bad. This contradicts the loop invariant. Hence, the chips in C are all good.

Running Time: Initially, the measure of progress $|S-C|$ is n. We showed that it decreases by at least 1 each iteration. Hence, there are at most n steps before $S-C$ is empty. We are guaranteed to exit the loop by this point, because $|S-C| = 0$ assures us that the exit condition $|C| = |S| > |S|/2$ is met. S must contain at least one chip, because by the loop invariant more than half of them are good.

Additional Observations: C can flip back and forth between being all bad and being all good many times. Suppose it is all bad. If s from $S-C$ happens to be bad, then C gets bigger. If s from $S-C$ happens to be good, then C gets smaller. If C ever becomes empty during this process, then a new chip is added to C. This chip may be good or bad. The process repeats.

Extending the Algorithm: The algorithm finds one good chip. This good chip will tell you which of the other chips are good in $O(n)$ time.

Randomized Algorithm: Chapter 21 provides a much easier randomized algorithm for this problem.

4.4 Exercises

EXERCISE 4.4.1 *(See solution in Part Five.) Search a sorted matrix: The input consists of a real number x and a matrix A[1..n, 1..m] of nm real numbers such that each row A[i, 1..m] is sorted and each column A[1..n, j] is sorted. The goal is to find the maximum array entry A[i, j] that is less than or equal to x, or report that all elements of A are larger than x. Design and analyze an iterative algorithm for this problem that examines as few matrix entries as possible. Be careful if you believe that a simple binary search solves the problem. Exercise 7.0.7 asks for a lower bound, and Exercise 9.1.3 for a recursive algorithm.*

EXERCISE 4.4.2 *Suppose a train was supposed to start at station A, pause at stations B, C, D, . . . , Y, and finish at station Z. However, it did not arrive at Z. Suppose in your factory the piece of equipment or process labeled A makes part B work, which in turn makes C, D, . . . , and Z work. However, Z is not working. You want to find out why. What algorithm do you use? Think of other applications of this technique.*

EXERCISE 4.4.3 *The following question is not about narrowing the search space. If anything, it is about doubling the size of the search space. But it still has a binary search feel. This question finds the length $D_{\min}(u, v)$ of the shortest path between any pair of nodes in a directed (or undirected) graph. The input provides the length $d(u, v) \geq 0$ of each edge $\langle u, v \rangle$ in the complete graph. It is not necessary that $d(u, v) = d(v, u)$, and these lengths may be ∞. The distance along a path is the sum of the $d(u, v)$ values along its edges. Let $d_i(u, v)$ denote the length of the shortest path from u to v with at most 2^i edges. Do steps 7, 8, 10, and 11, proving that the loop invariant is established and maintained, proving that on exiting the postcondition is established, and bounding the running time. As a hint, trace the algorithm on a graph consisting of a single path, namely, for $j \in [1, n-1]$, $d(u_j, u_{j+1}) = 1$ and all other edges have $d(u, v) = \infty$.*

algorithm *Alg(d)*

$\langle$ **pre-cond** $\rangle$: $d(u, v) \in [0, \infty]$ is the length of edge $\langle u, v \rangle$ in the complete graph.
$\langle$ **post-cond** $\rangle$: *Returned is the length $D_{\min}(u, v)$ of the shortest path from u to v for each pair of nodes.*

begin
    for each edge $\langle u, v \rangle$, $D(u, v) = d(u, v)$
    loop $\log_2(n)$ times
        $\langle$ **loop-invariant** $\rangle$: *After i iterations, $D_{\min}(u, v) \leq D(u, v) \leq d_i(u, v)$*
        for each edge $\langle u, v \rangle$ (iteratively or in parallel)
            % $D_i(u, v) = Min(D_{i-1}(u, v), Min_w[D_{i-1}(u, w) + D_{i-1}(w, v)])$
            loop over nodes w
                if($D(u, v) \geq D(u, w) + D(w, v)$) then
                    $D(u, v) = D(u, w) + D(w, v)$
                end if
            end loop
        end loop
    end loop
    return (D)
end algorithm

One can find more about this in Exercise 19.6.2.

5 Iterative Sorting Algorithms

Sorting is a classic computational problem. During the first few decades of computers, almost all computer time was devoted to sorting. Many sorting algorithms have been developed. It is useful to know a number of them, because sorting needs to be done in many different situations. Some depend on low time complexity, other on small memory, others on simplicity. Throughout the book, we consider a number of sorting algorithms because they are simple yet provide a rich selection of examples for demonstrating different algorithmic techniques. We have already looked at selection, insertion, and bubble sort in Section 1.4. In this chapter we start with a simple version of bucket sort and then look at counting sort. Radix sort, which is another surprising sort, is considered. Finally, counting and radix sort are combined to give radix counting sort.

Most sorting algorithms are said to be *comparison-based*, because the only way of accessing the input values is by comparing pairs of them, i.e., $a_i \leq a_j$. Radix counting sort manipulates the elements in other ways. Another strange thing about this algorithm is that its loop invariants are rather unexpected.

In Section 9.1, we consider merge sort and quick sort, which is a recursive and randomized version of bucket sort. We look at heap sort in Section 10.4.

5.1 Bucket Sort by Hand

Specifications: As a professor, I often have to sort a large stack of students' papers by last name. The algorithm that I use is an iterative version of quick sort and bucket sort. See Section 9.1.

Basic Steps:

Partitioning into Five Buckets: Computers are good at using a single comparison to determine whether an element is greater than the pivot value or not. Humans, on the other hand, tend to be good at quickly determining which of five buckets an element belongs in. I first partition the papers based on which of the following ranges the first letter of the name is within: [A–E], [F–K], [L–O], [P–T], or [U–Z]. Then I partition the [A–E] bucket into the subbuckets [A], [B], [C], [D], and [E]. Then I partition the [A] bucket based on the second letter of the name. This works for this application because the list to be sorted consists of names whose first letters are fairly predictably distributed through the alphabet.

A Stack of Buckets: One difficulty with this algorithm is keeping track of all the buckets. For example, after the second partition, we will have nine buckets: [A], [B], [C], [D], [E], [F–K], [L–O], [P–T], and [U–Z]. After the third, we will have 13. On a computer, the recursion of the algorithm is implemented with a stack of stack frames. Correspondingly, when I sort the student's papers, I have a stack of buckets.

The Loop Invariant: I use the following loop invariant to keep track of what I am doing. The papers are split between a pile of already sorted papers and a stack of piles of partially sorted papers. The papers in the sorted pile (initially empty) come before all the partially sorted papers. Within the partially sorted stack of piles, the papers within each pile are out of order. However, each paper in a pile belongs before each paper in a later pile. For example, at some point in the algorithm, the papers starting with [A–C] will be sorted, and the piles in my stack will consist of [D], [E], [F–K], [L–O], [P–T], and [U–Z].

Maintain Loop Invariant: I make progress while maintaining this loop invariant as follows. I take the top pile off the stack, here the [D]. If it only contains a half dozen or so papers, I sort them using insertion sort. These are then added to the top of the sorted pile, [A–C], giving [A–D]. On the other hand, if the pile [D] taken off the stack is larger then this, I partition it into five piles, [DA–DE], [DF–DK], [DL–DO], [DP–DT], and [DU-DZ], which I push back onto the stack. Either way, my loop invariant is maintained.

Exit Condition: When the last bucket has been removed from the stack, the papers are sorted.

EXERCISE 5.1.1 *Try sorting a deck of cards using this algorithm.*

EXERCISE 5.1.2 *Give code for this algorithm.*

5.2 Counting Sort (a Stable Sort)

The counting sort algorithm is only useful in the special case where the elements to be sorted have very few possible values.

Specifications:

Preconditions: The input is a list of N values $a_0, \ldots, a_{N-1}$, each within the range $0, \ldots, k - 1$.

Postconditions: The output is a list consisting of the same N values in nondecreasing order. The sort is *stable*, meaning that if two elements have the same value, then they must appear in the same order in the output as in the input. (This is important when extra data is carried with each element.)

Basic Steps:

Where an Element Goes: Consider any element of the input. By counting, we will determine where this element belongs in the output, and then we simply put it there. Where it belongs is determined by the number of elements that must appear before it. To simplify the argument, let's index the locations with $[0, N-1]$. This way, the element in the location indexed by 0 has no elements before it, and the element in location $\hat{c}$ has $\hat{c}$ elements before it.

Suppose that the element a_i has the value v. Every element that has a strictly smaller value must go before it. Let's denote this count with $\hat{c}_v$, that is, $\hat{c}_v = |\{j \mid a_j < v\}|$. The only other elements that go before a_i are elements with exactly the same value. Because the sort must be stable, the number of these that go before it is the same as the number that appear before it in the input. If this number happens to be q_{a_i}, then element a_i belongs in location $\hat{c}_v + q_{a_i}$. In particular, the first element in the input with value v goes in location $\hat{c}_v + 0$.

Example:

$$
\begin{array}{ll}
\text{Input:} & 1\,0\,1\,0\,2\,0\,0\,1\,2\,0 \\
\text{Output:} & 0\,0\,0\,0\,0\,1\,1\,1\,2\,2 \\
\text{Index:} & 0\,1\,2\,3\,4\,5\,6\,7\,8\,9
\end{array}
$$

The first element to appear in the input with value 0 goes into location 0, because there are $\hat{c}_0 = 0$ elements with smaller values. The next such element goes into location 1, the next into 2, and so on.

The first element to appear in the input with value 1 goes into location 5, because there are $\hat{c}_1 = 5$ elements with smaller values. The next such element goes into location 6, and the next into 7.

Similarly, the first element with value 2 goes into location $\hat{c}_2 = 8$.

Computing $\hat{c}_v$: We could compute $\hat{c}_v$ by making a pass through the input, counting the number of elements that have values smaller than v. Doing this separately for each value $v \in [0..k-1]$, however, would take $O(kN)$ time, which is too much.

Instead, let's first count how many times each value occurs in the input. For each $v \in [0..k-1]$, let $c_v = |\{i \mid a_i = v\}|$. This count can be computed with one pass through the input. For each element, if the element has value v, increment the counter c_v. This requires only $O(N)$ addition and indexing operations.

Given the c_v values, we could compute $\hat{c}_v = \sum_{v'=0}^{v-1} c_v$. Computing one such $\hat{c}_v$ would require $O(k)$ additions, and computing all of them would take $O(k^2)$ additions, which is too much.

Alternatively, note that $\widehat{c}_0 = 0$ and $\widehat{c}_v = \widehat{c}_{v-1} + c_{v-1}$. Of course, we must have computed the previous values before computing the next. Now computing one such $\widehat{c}_v$ takes $O(1)$ additions, and computing all of them takes only $O(k)$ additions.

Put in Place: The main loop in the algorithm considers the input elements one at a time in the order $a_0, \ldots, a_{N-1}$ that they appear in the input and places them in the output array where they belong.

The Loop Invariant:

1. The input elements that have already been considered have been put in their correct places in the output.

2. For each $v \in [0..k-1]$, $\widehat{c}_v$ gives the index in the output array where the next input element with value v goes.

Establishing the Loop Invariant: Compute the counts $\widehat{c}_v$ as described above. This establishes the loop invariant before any input elements are considered, because this $\widehat{c}_v$ value gives the location where the first element with value v goes.

Main Step: Take the next input element. If it has value v, place it in the output location indexed by $\widehat{c}_v$. Then increment $\widehat{c}_v$.

Maintain Loop Invariant: $\langle loop\text{-}invariant' \rangle$ & not $\langle exit\text{-}cond \rangle$ & $code_{loop}$ $\Rightarrow$ $\langle loop\text{-}invariant'' \rangle$. By the loop invariant, we know that if the next input element has value v, then it belongs in the output location indexed by $\widehat{c}_v$. Hence, it is being put in the correct place. The next input element with value v will then go immediately after this current one in the output, i.e., into location $\widehat{c}_v + 1$. Hence, incrementing $\widehat{c}_v$ maintains the second part of the loop invariant.

Exit Condition: Once all the input elements have been considered, the first loop invariant establishes that the list has been sorted.

Code:
```
∀v ∈ [0..k − 1],  c_v = 0
loop i = 0 to N − 1
      + + c_{a[i]}
ĉ_0 = 0
loop v = 1 to k − 1
      ĉ_v = ĉ_{v−1} + c_{v−1}
loop i = 0 to N − 1
      b[ĉ_{a[i]}] = a[i]
      + + ĉ_{a[i]}
```

Running Time: The total time is $O(N + k)$ addition and indexing operations. If the input can only contain $k = O(N)$ possible values, then this algorithm works in linear time. It does not work well if the number of possible values is much higher.

5.3   Radix Sort

The radix sort is a useful algorithm that dates back to the days of card-sorting machines, now found only in computer museums.

Specifications:

> *Preconditions:* The input is a list of N values. Each value is an integer with d digits. Each digit is a value from 0 to $k - 1$, i.e., the value is viewed as an integer base k.

> *Postconditions:* The output is a list consisting of the same N values in nondecreasing order.

Basic Steps: For some digit $i \in [1..d]$, sort the input according to the ith digit, ignoring the other digits. Use a stable sort, such as counting sort.

> **Examples:** Old computer punch cards were organized into $d = 80$ columns, and in each column a hole could be punched in one of $k = 12$ places. A card-sorting machine could mechanically examine each card in a deck and distribute the card into one of 12 bins, depending on which hole had been punched in a specified column.
>
> A "value" might consist of a year, a month, and a day. You could then sort the elements by the year, by the month, or by the day.

> **Order in Which to Consider the Digits:** It is most natural to sort with respect to the most significant digit first. The final sort, after all, has all the elements with a 0 as the first digit at the beginning, followed by those with a 1.
>
> If the operator of the card-sorting machine sorted first by the most significant digit, he would get 12 piles. Each of these piles would then have to be sorted separately, according to the remaining digits. Sorting the first pile according to the second digit would produce 12 more piles. Sorting the first of those piles according to the third digit would produce 12 more piles. The whole process would be a nightmare.
>
> Sorting with respect to the least significant digit seems silly at first. Sorting ⟨79, 94, 25⟩ gives ⟨94, 25, 79⟩, which is completely wrong. Even so, this is what the algorithm does.

> **The Algorithm:** Loop through the digits from low to high order. For each, use a stable sort to sort the elements according to the current digit, ignoring the other digits.

Example:

Sorted by first 3 digits	Considering 4th digit	Stably sorted by 4th digit
184	3184	1195
192	5192	1243
195	1195	1311
243	1243	3184
271	3271	3271
311	1311	5192

The result is sorted by the first four digits.

Loop Invariant: After sorting with respect to (wrt) the first i low-order digits, the elements are sorted wrt the value formed from these i digits.

Establishing the Loop Invariant: The loop invariant is initially trivially true, because initially no digits have been considered.

Maintain Loop Invariant: $\langle loop\text{-}invariant' \rangle$ & *not* $\langle exit\text{-}cond \rangle$ & $code_{loop}$ $\Rightarrow$ $\langle loop\text{-}invariant'' \rangle$. Suppose that the elements are sorted wrt the value formed from the lowest $i - 1$ digits. For the elements to be sorted wrt the value formed from the lowest i digits, all the elements with a 0 in the ith digit must come first, followed by those with a 1, and so on. This can be accomplished by sorting the elements wrt the ith digit while ignoring the other digits. Moreover, the block of elements with a 0 in the ith digit must be sorted wrt the lowest $i - 1$ digits. By the loop invariant, they were in this order, and because the sorting wrt the ith digit was stable, these elements will remain in the same relative order. The same is true for the block of elements with a 1 or 2 or ... in the ith digit.

Ending: $\langle loop\text{-}invariant \rangle$ & $\langle exit\text{-}cond \rangle$ & $code_{post\text{-}loop}$ $\Rightarrow$ $\langle post-cond \rangle$. When $i = d$, they are sorted wrt the value formed from all d digits, and hence are sorted.

5.4   Radix Counting Sort

I will now combine the radix and counting sorts. The resulting algorithm is said to run in linear $\Theta(n)$ time, whereas merge, quick, and heap sort are said to run in $\Theta(n \log n)$ time. This makes radix counting appear to be faster, but this is confusing and misleading. Radix counting requires $\Theta(n)$ bit operations, where n is the total number of bits in the input instance. Merge, quick, and heap sort require $\Theta(N \log N)$ comparisons, where N is the number of numbers in the list. Assuming that the N numbers to be sorted are distinct, each needs $\Theta(\log N)$ bits to be represented, for a total of $n = \Theta(N \log N)$ bits. Hence, merge, quick, and heap sort are also linear time in that they require $\Theta(n)$ bit operations, where n is the total number of bits in the input instance.

In practice, the radix counting algorithm may be a little faster than the other algorithms. However, quick and heap sort have the advantage of being done "in place" in memory, while the radix counting sort requires an auxiliary array of memory to transfer the data to.

Specifications:

Preconditions: The input is a list of N values. Each value is an l-bit integer.

Postconditions: The output is a list consisting of the same N values in nondecreasing order.

The Algorithm: The algorithm is to use radix sort with counting sort to sort each digit. To do this, we need to view each l-bit value as an integer with d digits, where each digit is a value from 0 to $k - 1$. This is done by splitting the l bits into d blocks of $\frac{l}{d}$ bits each and treating each such block as a digit between 0 and $k - 1$, where $k = 2^{l/d}$. Here d is a parameter to be set later.

Example: Consider sorting the numbers $30, 41, 28, 40, 31, 26, 47, 45$. Here $N = 8$ and $l = 6$. Let's set $d = 2$ and split the $l = 6$ bits into $d = 2$ blocks of $\frac{l}{d} = 3$ bits each. Treat each of these blocks as a digit between 0 and $k - 1$, where $k = 2^3 = 8$. For example, $30 = 011110_2$ gives the blocks $011_2 = 3$ and $110_2 = 6$.

For all the numbers:	Stable sorting wrt the first digit:	Stable sorting wrt the second digit:
$30 = 36_8 = 011\ 110_2$		
$41 = 51_8 = 101\ 001_2$	$40 = 50_8 = 101\ 000_2$	$26 = 32_8 = 011\ 010_2$
$28 = 34_8 = 011\ 100_2$	$41 = 51_8 = 101\ 001_2$	$28 = 34_8 = 011\ 100_2$
$40 = 50_8 = 101\ 000_2$	$26 = 32_8 = 011\ 010_2$	$30 = 36_8 = 011\ 110_2$
$31 = 37_8 = 011\ 111_2$	$28 = 34_8 = 011\ 100_2$	$31 = 37_8 = 011\ 111_2$
$26 = 32_8 = 011\ 010_2$	$45 = 55_8 = 101\ 101_2$	$40 = 50_8 = 101\ 000_2$
$47 = 57_8 = 101\ 111_2$	$30 = 36_8 = 011\ 110_2$	$41 = 51_8 = 101\ 001_2$
$45 = 55_8 = 101\ 101_2$	$31 = 37_8 = 011\ 111_2$	$45 = 55_8 = 101\ 101_2$
	$47 = 57_8 = 101\ 111_2$	$47 = 57_8 = 101\ 111_2$

This is sorted.

Running Time: Using the counting sort to sort with respect to one of the d digits takes $\Theta(N + k)$ *operations.* Hence, the entire algorithm takes $\Theta(d \cdot (N + k))$ operations. We have $d = \frac{l}{\log k}$, giving $T = \Theta(\frac{l}{\log k} \cdot (N + k))$ operations.

The parameter k (like l) is not dictated by the specifications of the problem, but can be chosen freely by the algorithm. Exercise 23.1.4 sets $k = O(N)$ in order to minimize the running time to $T = \Theta(\frac{l}{\log N} N)$ operations.

Formally, time complexity measures the number of bit operations performed as a function of the number of bits to represent the input. When we say that counting sort takes $\Theta(N+k)$ operations, a single operation must be able to add two values with magnitude $\Theta(N)$ or to index into arrays of size N (or k). Each of these takes $\Theta(\log N)$ bit operations. Hence, the total time to sort is $T = \Theta(\frac{l}{\log N}N)$ operations $\times \log N$ (bit operations)/operation $= \Theta(l \cdot N)$ bit operations. The input, consisting of N l-bit values, requires $n = l \cdot N$ bits to represent it. Hence, the running time $\Theta(l \cdot N) = \Theta(n)$ is linear in the size of the input.

One example is when you are sorting N values in the range 0 to N^r. Each value requires $l = \log N^r = r \log N$ bits to represent it, for a total of $n = N\log(N^r) = rN$ bits. Our settings would then be $k = N$, $d = \frac{l}{\log N} = r$, and $T = \Theta(d \cdot N) = \Theta(rN) = \Theta(n)$.

6 Euclid's GCD Algorithm

More-of-the-input iterative algorithms extend a solution for a smaller input instance into a larger one. We will see in Chapter 9 that recursive algorithms do this too. The following is an amazing algorithm that does this. It finds the greatest common divisor (GCD) of two integers. For example, $GCD(18, 12) = 6$. It was first done by Euclid, an ancient Greek. Without the use of loop invariants, you would never be able to understand what the algorithm does; with their help, it is easy.

Specifications: An input instance consists of two positive integers, a and b. The output is $GCD(a, b)$.

The Loop Invariant: Like many loop invariants, designing this one required creativity. The algorithm maintains two variables x and y whose values change with each iteration of the loop under the invariant that their GCD, $GCD(x, y)$, does not change, but remains equal to the required output $GCD(a, b)$.

> **Type of Loop Invariant:** This is a strange loop invariant. The algorithm is more like recursion. A solution to a smaller instance of the problem gives the solution to the original.

Establishing the Loop Invariant: The easiest way of establishing the loop invariant that $GCD(x, y) = GCD(a, b)$ is by setting x to a and y to b.

Measure of Progress: Progress is made by making x or y smaller.

Ending: We will exit when x or y is small enough that we can compute their GCD easily. By the loop invariant, this will be the required answer.

A Middle Iteration on a General Instance: Let us first consider a general situation in which x is bigger than y and both are positive.

Main Steps: Our goal is to make x or y smaller without changing their GCD. A useful fact is that $GCD(x, y) = GCD(x - y, y)$, e.g., $GCD(52, 10) = GCD(42, 10) = 2$, because any value that divides x and y also divides $x - y$, and similarly any value that divides $x - y$ and y also divides x. Hence, replacing x with $x - y$ would make progress while maintaining the loop invariant.

Exponential Running Time? A good idea when you are considering a loop invariant and iterations is to jump ahead in designing the algorithm and estimate its running time. A loop executing only $x = x - y$ will iterate $\frac{a}{b}$ times. However, even if $b = 1$, this is only a iterations. This looks like it is linear time. However, you should express the running time of an algorithm as a function of input size. See Section 23.1. The number of bits needed to represent the instance $\langle a, b \rangle$ is $n = \log a + \log b$. Expressed in these terms, the running time is $Time(n) = \Theta(a) = \Theta(2^n)$. This is exponential time. If $a = 1,000,000,000,000,000$ and $b = 1$, I would not want to wait for it.

Faster Main Steps: One thing to try when faced with exponential running time is to look for a way to speed up the main steps. Instead of subtracting one y from x each iteration, why not speed up the process by subtracting a multiple of y all at once? We could set $x_{new} = x - d \cdot y$ for some integer value of d. Our goal is to make x_{new} as small as possible without making it negative. Clearly, d should be $\lfloor \frac{x}{y} \rfloor$. This gives $x_{new} = x - \lfloor \frac{x}{y} \rfloor \cdot y = x \bmod y$, which is within the range $[0..y - 1]$ and is the remainder when dividing y into x. For example, $52 \bmod 10 = 2$.

Maintaining the Loop Invariant: The step $x_{new} = x \bmod y$ maintains the loop invariant because $GCD(x, y) = GCD(x \bmod y, y)$, e.g., $GCD(52, 10) = GCD(2, 10) = 2$.

Making Progress: The step $x_{new} = x \bmod y$ makes progress by making x smaller only if $x \bmod y$ is smaller than x. This is only true if x is greater than or equal to y. Suppose that initially this is true because a is greater than b. After one iteration, $x_{new} = x \bmod y$ becomes smaller than y. Then the next iteration will do nothing. A solution is to then swap x and y.

New Main Steps: Combining $x_{new} = x \bmod y$ with a swap gives the main steps of $x_{new} = y$ and $y_{new} = x \bmod y$.

Maintaining the Loop Invariant: This maintains our original loop invariant because $GCD(x, y) = GCD(y, x \bmod y)$, e.g., $GCD(52, 10) = GCD(10, 2) = 2$. It also maintains the new loop invariant that $0 \leq y \leq x$.

Making Progress: Because $y_{new} = x \bmod y \in [0..y - 1]$ is smaller than y, we make progress by making y smaller.

Special Cases: Setting $x = a$ and $y = b$ does not establish the loop invariant, which says that x is at least y if a is smaller than b. An obvious solution is to initially test for this and to swap x and y if necessary. However, as advised in Section 1.2, it is sometimes fruitful to try tracing out what the algorithm that you have already designed would do given such an input. Suppose $a = 10$ and $b = 52$. The first iteration would set $x_{new} = 52$ and $y_{new} = 10$ *mod* 52. This last value is a number within the range $[0..51]$ that is the remainder when dividing 10 by 52. Clearly this is 10. Hence, the code automatically swaps the values by setting $x_{new} = 52$ and $y_{new} = 10$. Hence, no new code is needed. Similarly, if a and b happen to be negative, the initial iteration will make y positive, and the next will make both x and y positive.

Exit Condition: We are making progress by making y smaller. We should stop when y is small enough that we can compute the GCD easily. Let's try small values of y. Using $GCD(x, 1) = 1$, the GCD is easy to compute when $y = 1$; however, we will never get this unless $GCD(a, b) = 1$. How about $GCD(x, 0)$? This turns out to be x, because x divides evenly into both x, and 0. Let's try an exit condition of $y = 0$.

Termination: We know that the program will eventually stop as follows: $y_{new} = x$ *mod* $y \in [0..y - 1]$ ensures that each step y gets strictly smaller and does not go negative. Hence, eventually y must be zero.

Ending: Formally we prove that $\langle$*loop-invariant*$\rangle$ & $\langle$*exit-cond*$\rangle$ & *code*$_{post\text{-}loop}$ $\Rightarrow$ $\langle$*post-cond*$\rangle$. We see that $\langle$*loop-invariant*$\rangle$ gives $GCD(x, y) = GCD(a, b)$ and $\langle$*exit-cond*$\rangle$ gives $y = 0$. Hence, $GCD(a, b) = GCD(x, 0) = x$. The final code will return the value of x. This establishes the $\langle$*post-cond*$\rangle$ that $GCD(a, b)$ is returned.

Code:

```
algorithm  GCD(a, b)

⟨ pre-cond⟩: a and b are integers.
⟨ post-cond⟩: Returns GCD(a, b).

begin
     int x,y
     x = a
     y = b
     loop
          ⟨loop-invariant⟩: GCD(x,y) = GCD(a,b).
          if(y = 0) exit
          x_new = y,  y_new = x mod y
          x = x_new
          y = y_new
     end loop
     return( x )
end algorithm
```

Example: The following traces the algorithm given two input instances, $\langle a, b \rangle = \langle 22, 33 \rangle$ and $\langle a, b \rangle = \langle 1,000,000,005, 999,999,999 \rangle$.

Iteration	Value of x	Value of y
1st	22	32
2nd	32	22
3rd	22	10
4th	10	2
5th	2	0

$GCD(22, 32) = 2$.

Iteration	Value of x	Value of y
1st	1,000,000,005	999,999,999
2nd	999,999,999	6
3rd	6	3
4th	3	0

$GCD(1,000,000,005, 999,999,999) = 3$

Running Time: For the running time to be linear in the size of the input, the number of bits ($\log y$) to represent y must decrease by at least one in each iteration. This means that the value of y must decrease by at least a factor of two. Consider the example of $x = 19$ and $y = 10$. Then y_{new} becomes $19 \bmod 10 = 9$, which is only a decrease of one. However, the next value of y will be $10 \bmod 9 = 1$, which is a huge drop.

We will be able to prove that every two iterations, y drops by a factor of 2, namely, that $y_{k+2} < y_k/2$. There are two cases. In the first case, $y_{k+1} \le y_k/2$. Then we are done, because, as stated above, $y_{k+2} < y_{k+1}$. In the second case, $y_{k+1} \in [y_k/2 + 1, y_k - 1]$. Unwinding the algorithm gives that $y_{k+2} = x_{k+1} \bmod y_{k+1} = y_k \bmod y_{k+1}$. One algorithm for computing $y_k \bmod y_{k+1}$ is to continually subtract y_{k+1} from y_k until the amount is less than y_{k+1}. Because y_k is more than y_{k+1}, this y_{k+1} is subtracted at least once. It follows that $y_k \bmod y_{k+1} \le y_k - y_{k+1}$. By the case, $y_{k+1} > y_k/2$. In conclusion, $y_{k+2} = y_k \bmod y_{k+1} \le y_k - y_{k+1} < y_k/2$.

We prove that the number of times that the loop iterates is $O(\log(\min(a, b))) = O(n)$, as follows. After the first or second iteration, y is $\min(a, b)$. Every iteration y goes down by at least a factor of 2. Hence, after k iterations, y_k is at most $\min(a, b)/2^k$, and after $O(\log(\min(a, b)))$ iterations it is at most one.

The algorithm iterates a linear number $O(n)$ of times. Each iteration must do a *mod* operation. Poor Euclid had to compute these by hand, which must have gotten very tedious. A computer may be able to do *mod*s in one operation; however, the number of bit operations needed for two n-bit inputs is $O(n \log n)$. Hence, the time complexity of this GCD algorithm is $O(n^2 \log n)$.

Lower Bound: We will prove a lower bound, not of the minimum time for any algorithm to find the GCD, but of this particular algorithm, by finding a family of input values $\langle a, b \rangle$ for which the program loops $\Theta(\log(\min(a, b)))$ times. Unwinding the code gives $y_{k+2} = x_{k+1} \bmod y_{k+1} = y_k \bmod y_{k+1}$. As stated, $y_k \bmod y_{k+1}$ is computed by subtracting y_{k+1} from y_k a number of times. We want the y's to shrink as slowly as possible. Hence, let us say that it is subtracted only once. This gives $y_{k+2} = y_k - y_{k+1}$ or $y_k = y_{k+1} + y_{k+2}$. This is the definition of Fibonacci numbers, only backwards, i.e., $Fib(0) = 0$, $Fib(1) = 1$, and $Fib(n) = Fib(n-1) + Fib(n-2)$. (See Exercise 27.2.1.) On input $a = Fib(n + 1)$ and $b = Fib(n)$, the program iterates n times. This is $\Theta(\log(\min(a, b)))$, because $Fib(n) = 2^{\Theta(n)}$.

EXERCISE 6.0.1

algorithm *Converge($x_{original}$)*

⟨ *pre-cond* ⟩: $x_{original} \in [0, \ldots, 1]$.
⟨ *post-cond* ⟩: *This algorithm returns the converged value ???*
or runs forever

begin
    $x = x_{original}$
    loop
        ⟨*loop-invariant*⟩: $x \in [0, \ldots, 1]$
        exit when $(x = f(x))$
        $x = f(x)$
    end loop
    return(x)
end algorithm

This is the function f being used.

1. *Prove that the algorithm correctly establishes the loop invariant.*
2. *Prove that the loop invariant is maintained.*
3. *Fill in the rest of the postcondition by giving as specifically as possible which value is returned by this algorithm when it does converge. Prove that if the algorithm halts, then this postcondition is met.*
4. *Change the algorithm so that also has an integer input N and it halts after N iterations. What is the running time (time complexity) of this algorithm as a function of the size of the input?*
5. *Change the algorithm so that it halts after a billion iterations. What is the running time (time complexity) of this algorithm as a function of the size of the input?*

EXERCISE 6.0.2 *(See solution in Part Five.) The ancient Egyptians and Ethiopians had advanced mathematics. Merely by halving and doubling, they could multiply any two numbers correctly. Say they wanted to buy 15 sheep at 13 Ethiopian dollars each. Here is how they figured out the product. Put 13 in a left column, 15 on the right. Halve the left value; you get $6\frac{1}{2}$. Ignore the $\frac{1}{2}$. Double the right value. Repeat this (keeping all intermediate values) until the left value is 1. What you have is*

13	15
6	30
3	60
1	120

Even numbers in the left column are evil and, according to the story, must be destroyed, along with their guilty partners. So scratch out the 6 and its partner 30. Now add the right column, giving $15 + 60 + 120 = 195$, which is the correct answer.

1. *Write pseudocode that, given two positive integers x and y, follows this procedure and outputs the resulting value. Part of the loop invariant is that the variable ℓ holds the current left value, r the current right value, and s the sum of all previous right values that will be included in the final answer. Break the algorithm within the loop into two steps. In the first step, if ℓ is odd, it decreases by one. In the second step ℓ (now even) is divided by two. These steps must update r and s as needed.*

2. *Give a meaningful loop invariant relating the current values of ℓ, r, s, x, and y. (Hint: Look at the GCD loop invariant.) In addition to this invariant being true every time the computation is at the top of the loop, it will also be true every time the computation is between the first and the second step of each iteration. Prove that your algorithm establishes and maintains the loop invariant as stated.*

3. *Draw pictures to give a geometric explanation for the steps.*

4. *What is the Ethiopian exit condition? How might you improve on this? How do the exit condition, the loop invariant, and perhaps some extra code establish the postcondition?*

5. *Suppose that the input instances x and y are each n-bit numbers. How many bit operations are used by your algorithm, as a function of n? (Adding two n'-bit numbers requires $O(n')$ time.) Suppose the Ethiopians counted with pebbles. How many pebble operations did their algorithm require? How do these times compare? How do these times compare with the high school algorithm for multiplying? How do they compare with laying out a rectangle of x by y pebbles and then counting them?*

6. *This algorithm seems very strange. Compare it with using the high school algorithm for multiplying in binary.*

Time Complexity: The time complexity of a computational problem P is the minimum time needed by an algorithm to solve it:

$$\exists A, \ \forall I, \ \left[A(I) = P(I) \text{ and } Time(A, I) \leq T_{upper}(|I|) \right]$$

$$\forall A, \ \exists I, \ \left[A(I) \neq P(I) \text{ or } Time(A, I) \geq T_{lower}(|I|) \right]$$

Asymptotic Notation: When we want to bound the running time of an algorithm while ignoring multiplicative constants, we use the following notation.

Name	Standard Notation	My Notation	Meaning
Theta	$f(n) = \Theta(g(n))$	$f(n) \in \Theta(g(n))$	$f(n) \approx c \cdot g(n)$
BigOh	$f(n) = O(g(n))$	$f(n) \leq O(g(n))$	$f(n) \leq c \cdot g(n)$
Omega	$f(n) = \Omega(g(n))$	$f(n) \geq \Omega(g(n))$	$f(n) \geq c \cdot g(n)$

See Chapter 25.

An Upper Bound Is an Algorithm: An upper bound for P is obtained by constructing an algorithm A that outputs the correct answer, namely $A(I) = P(I)$, within the bounded time, i.e., $Time(A, I) \leq T_{upper}(|I|)$, on every input instance I.

A Lower Bound Is an Algorithm: Amusingly enough, a lower bound, proving that there is no faster algorithm for the problem P, is also obtained by constructing an algorithm, but it is an algorithm for a different problem. The input to this problem is an algorithm A claiming to solve P in the required time. The output, as proof that this is false, is an input instance I on which the given algorithm A either does not give the correct answer, namely, $A(I) \neq P(I)$, or uses too much time, namely, $Time(A, I) \geq T_{lower}(|I|)$.

Read the Appendix: To understand this better you may have to read two discussions in the appendix (Part Four): Chapter 22 on how to think of statements with existential and universal quantifiers as a game between two players, and Section 23.2 on time complexity.

Circular Argument: Proving lower bounds can lead to the following circular argument. Given an arbitrary algorithm A, we must find an input instance I for which A gives the wrong answer. The problem is that you do not know for which input instance the algorithm will give the wrong answer until you know what the algorithm does. But you do not know what the algorithm does until you give it an input instance and run it. This paradox is avoided by stepping through the computation on A one time step at a time, at each step narrowing the search space for I. This makes your algorithm for solving the lower bound problem an iterative algorithm. As such, it needs a loop invariant.

The Loop Invariant Argument:

> **Knowledge:** At each time step, the actions taken by algorithm A depend on the *knowledge* that it has collected already. For example, if the input is $\langle x_1, \ldots, x_n \rangle$ and during the first time step A tests if $x_5 < x_6$, then A can base what it does during the second time step on whether or not $x_5 < x_6$, but it does not yet *know* anything else about the input instance. We define A's knowledge, or *state*, to be determined by the values of its variables (except for the variables storing the input instance) and which line of code it is on.

> **The Loop Invariant:** The loop invariant will be a classic narrowing-the-search-space type. It states that we have a set S of input instances on which algorithm A's knowledge and actions for its first t time steps are identical.

> **Establishing the Loop Invariant:** Initially the set S is some large set of instances that we want to focus on. The loop invariant is trivially established for $t = 0$, because initially the algorithm knows nothing and has done nothing.

> **Maintaining the Loop Invariant:** The loop invariant is maintained as follows. Assume that it is true at time $t - 1$. Though we do not know which input instance I from S will ultimately be given to algorithm A, we do know that what A learns during its first $t - 1$ time steps is independent of this choice. A, knowing what it has learned during these first $t - 1$ steps, but unaware that it has not been given a specific input instance, will then state what action it will do during time step t. What A learns at time t from this action will depend on which instance $I \in S$ is given to A. We then partition S based on what A learns and narrow S down to one such part. This maintains the loop invariant, i.e., that we have a set S of input instances on which the algorithm A's knowledge and actions for its first t time steps are identical.

> **Measure of Progress:** The measure of progress for our lower bound algorithm is that S does not get too much smaller.

Exit Condition: The exit condition is then $t = T_{lower}(|I|)$.

Ending: From the loop invariant and the exit condition, we obtain the post-condition by finding two input instances I and I' in S for which the computational problem P requires different outputs: $P(I) \neq P(I')$. If, on instance I, algorithm A either does not give the correct answer, so that $A(I) \neq P(I)$, or uses too much time, so that $Time(A, I) \geq T_{lower}(|I|)$, then the postcondition is met. Otherwise, we turn our attention to instance I'. By the loop invariant and the exit condition, the computation of A is identical on the two instances I and I' for the first $T_{lower}(|I|)$ time steps, because both I and I' are in S. Hence, their outputs must be identical: $A(I) = A(I')$. By our choice of instances, $P(I) \neq P(I')$. Because $A(I) = P(I)$, it follows that $A(I') \neq P(I')$. Again we have found an instance on which A does not give the correct answer, and the postcondition is met.

87

EXAMPLE 7.1	**Sorting**

We have seen a number of algorithms that can sort N numbers using $O(N \log N)$ comparisons between the elements, such as merge, quick, and heap sort. We will prove that no algorithm can sort faster.

Information Theory: The lower bounds technique just described does not consider the amount of work that must get done to solve the problem, but the amount of *information* that must be transferred from the input to the output. The problem with these lower bounds is that they are not bigger than linear with respect to the bit size of the input and the output.

$n = \Theta(N \log N)$: At first it may appear that this is a superlinear lower bound. However, N is the number of elements in the list. Assuming that the N numbers to be sorted are distinct, each needs $\Theta(\log N)$ bits to be represented, for a total of $n = \Theta(N \log N)$ bits. Hence, the lower bound does not in fact say that more than $\Theta(n)$ bit operations are required when n is the total number of bits in the input instance.

Definition of Binary Operation: Before we can prove that no algorithm exists that quickly sorts, we need to first be very clear about what an algorithm is and what its running time is. This is referred to as a *model of computation*. For this sorting lower bound, we will be very generous. We will allow the algorithm to perform any binary operation. This operation can use any information about the input or about what has already been computed by the algorithm, but the result of the operation is restricted to a yes–no answer. For example, as is done in merge sort, it could ask whether the ith element is less than the jth element. For a stranger example, it could ask with one operation whether the number of odd elements is odd.

Definition of the Sorting Problem P: The standard sorting problem, given N elements, is to output the same N elements in sorted order. To make our life easier, we will define the problem P to sort pointers to the elements instead of sorting the elements themselves. Note this is often done when elements are too large to move easily. For example, if the input is $I = \langle 19, 5, 81 \rangle$ pointers to these elements are $\langle 1, 2, 3 \rangle$, the output will be $\langle 2, 1, 3 \rangle$, because the first element in the sorted order $\langle 5, 19, 81 \rangle$ was second in I, the second was the first, and the third element was the third. Similarly, the output for $I' = \langle 19, 81, 5 \rangle$ will be $\langle 3, 1, 2 \rangle$. What makes our lives easier in this version of the sorting problem is that the instances $I = \langle 19, 5, 81 \rangle$ and $I' = \langle 19, 81, 5 \rangle$ have different outputs, while in the standard problem definition, they would both have the output $\langle 5, 19, 81 \rangle$. This change is reasonable because any sorting algorithm needs to learn the order that the elements should be in.

The Initial Set of Instances: Because of the way we modified the sorting problem, the nature of the elements being sorted does not matter, only their initial order. Hence, we may as well assume that we are sorting the numbers 1 to N. Let the initial set S of input instances being considered consist of every permutation of these numbers.

$P(I) \neq P(I')$: Note that each pair of instances $I, I' \in S$ have different outputs for the sorting problem P, i.e., $P(I) \neq P(I')$. This is good because our search is supposed to end by finding two input instances I and I' in S for which this is the case.

The Measure of Progress: Our measure of progress, as we search for an instance I on which algorithm A does not work, will be the number $|S|$ of instances still being considered. Initially, because S consists of all permutations of N elements, $|S| = N!$. We will prove that each iteration, S does not decrease by more than a factor of 2. Hence, after t iterations, $|S| \geq N!/2^t$. By setting $T_{lower}(|I|)$ to be $\log_2(N!) - 1$, we know that in the end we have at least two input instances remaining to be our I and I'.

Math: In $N! = 1 \times 2 \times 3 \times \cdots \times N$, $\frac{N}{2}$ of the factors are at least $\frac{N}{2}$, and all N of the factors are at most N. Hence, $N!$ is in the range $[N/2^{N/2}, N^N]$. Hence, $\log N!$ is in the range $[\frac{N}{2} \log \frac{N}{2}, N \log N]$.

Maintaining the Loop Invariant: Assume that the loop invariant is true at time $t - 1$ and that S is the set of input instances on which algorithm A's knowledge and actions for its first $t - 1$ time steps are identical. Given this, the action A will perform during time step t is fixed. The model of computation dictates that the result of A's actions is restricted to a yes–no answer. We then partition S into two sets based on whether this answer on this instance I is yes or no. We simply narrow S down to the part of S that is larger of the two. Restricting the algorithm to learning only this one answer maintains the loop invariant. Clearly, the larger of the two parts has size at least a half.

The Lower Bound: This completes the lower bound that any algorithm requires at least $\Omega(N \log N)$ binary operations to correctly solve the sorting problem.

EXAMPLE 7.2   Binary Search Returning Index

Consider the problem of searching a sorted list of N elements where the output states the index of the key in the list. Binary search solves the problem with $\log_2(N)$ comparisons. We will now prove a matching lower bound.

The Initial Set of Instances: To follow the same technique that we did for sorting, we need a set of legal input instances each of which has a unique output. Now, however, there are now only N possible outputs. Let the initial set of instances be $S = \{I_j \mid j \in [1, N]\}$, where I_j is the input instance searching for the key 5 within the list that has the first $j - 1$ elements zero, the jth element 5, and the last $n - j$ elements 10.

The Measure of Progress: Initially, $|S| = N$. As before, S does not decrease by more than a factor of 2 at each iteration. Hence, after t iterations, $|S| \geq N/2^t$. By setting $T_{lower}(|I|)$ to be $\log_2(N) - 1$, we know that in the end we have at least two input instances remaining to be our I and I'.

The Lower Bound: The rest of the lower bound is the same, proving that any algorithm requires at least $\Omega(\log N)$ binary operations to correctly solve the problem of searching a sorted list.

You Have to Look at the Data Lower Bounds: The following lower bounds do not really belong in the iterative algorithms part of this book, because in these cases we do not find the instances I and I' iteratively. However, the basic idea is the same. These lower bounds say that at least $N' \leq N$ operations are required on an input of size N, because you must look at at least N' of the input values.

EXAMPLE 7.3   Parity

The easiest example is for the problem of computing *parity*. The input consists of n bits, and the output simply states whether the number of ones is even or odd.

The Information-Theoretic Approach Does Not Work: The information-theoretic approach given above allows the model of computation to charge only one time step for any yes–no operation about the input instance, because it counts only the bits of information learned. However, this does not work for the parity problem. If any yes–no operation about the input instance is allowed, then the algorithm can simply ask for the parity. This solves the problem in one time step.

Reading the Input: Suppose, on the other hand, the model of computation charges one time step for reading a single bit of the input. (We could even give any additional operations for free.) Clearly, an algorithm cannot know the parity of the input until it has read all of the bits. This proves the lower bound that any algorithm solving the problem requires at least n time. We will see, however, that there is a bug in this argument.

EXAMPLE 7.4   Multiplexer

The *multiplexer* computational problem has two inputs: an n-bit string x, and a $\log_2(n)$-bit index i, which has the range 1 to n. The output is simply the ith bit of x. As we did for parity, we might give a lower bound of n for this problem as follows: If the algorithm does not read a particular bit of x, then it will give the wrong answer when this bit is the required output. This argument is clearly wrong, because the following is a correct algorithm that has running time $\log_2(n) + 1$: It reads i and then learns the answer by reading the ith bit of x.

Dynamic Algorithms: Proving a lower bound based on how many bits need to be read is a little harder, because an algorithm is allowed to change which bits it reads based on what it has read before. Given any single instance, the algorithm might read only $n - 1$ of the bits, but which bit is not read depends on the input instance.

Fixing One Instance and Flipping a Bit: Before we can know what the algorithm A does, we must give it a specific input instance I. We must choose one. Then we determine the set $J \subseteq [1, n]$ of bits of this instance that are critical, meaning for each $j \in J$, if you flip just the jth bit of I but leave the rest of the instance alone, then the answer to the computation problem on this instance changes. We then obtain a lower bound of $n' = |J|$ on the time required to solve the problem as follows. We run the algorithm on I and see which bits of this instance it reads. If it reads $n' = |J|$ bits, then we are done. Otherwise, there is some bit $j \in J$ that the algorithm does not read on this instance. Because the algorithm does not read it, we can flip this bit of the instance without affecting the answer the algorithm gives. We are not allowed to change any of the bits that the algorithm does read, because not only may this change the answer that it gives, it may also change which bits it reads. We have made sure, however, that the flipping of this single bit changes the answer to the computation question. Hence, on one of the two input instances, the algorithm must give the wrong answer.

EXAMPLE 7.3′   Parity

We now obtain a formal lower bound of n for the parity problem, as follows. Let I be the all-zero instance. Let $J = [1, n]$ be the set of all bits of the input. For each $j \in J$, changing the jth bit of I changes the answer from even parity to odd parity. Hence, if the algorithm does not read the jth bit when given instance I, it gives the wrong answer either on instance I or on the instance with this bit flipped.

EXAMPLE 7.4′   Multiplexer

We have obtained a $\log_2(n) + 1$-time algorithm for solving the multiplexer problem. Now we obtain a matching lower bound. Let I be the instance with $x = 100,000$, i.e., one in its first bit and zero in the rest, and with $j = 1$. Let J consist of the $\log_2(n)$ bits of j and the first bit of x. The output of the multiplexer on I is one, because this is the jth bit of x. But if you flip any bit of j, then a different bit of x is indexed and the answer changes to zero. If you flip the first bit of x from being a one, then the answer also changes. Hence, if the algorithm does not read one of these bits when given instance I, it either gives the wrong answer on instance I or does so on the instance with this bit flipped.

EXAMPLE 7.2′   **Binary Search Returning Yes or No:**

In Example 7.2 we proved a $\log_2(N)$ lower bound for searching a sorted list of N elements. We are to do the same again. The difference now is that if the key is in the list, the problem returns only the output yes, and if not then no.

The Approach:

The Information-Theoretic Approach Does Not Work: Again the information-theoretic approach does not work, because if any yes–no operation on the input instance is allowed, then the algorithm can simply ask whether the key is in the list, solving the problem in one time step.

The Set-J-of-Bits-to-Flip-Approach Does Not Work: The initial instance I needs to consist of the key being searched for and some sorted list. Given this, there are not many elements J that can be changed in order to change the output of the searching problem.

Some Combination: Instead, we will use a combination of the two lower bound approaches.

The Initial Set of Instances: As we did when we proved the lower bound for this problem in Example 7.2, we consider the input instance I_j, which is to search for the key 5 within the list with the first $j - 1$ elements zero, the jth element 5, and the last $n - j$ elements 10. Unlike before, however, these instances all have the same outputs: yes. As in the set-J-of-bits-to-flip approach, let I'_j be the same instance, except the jth element is changed to from 5 to 6 so that I_j and I'_j have opposite answers. Considering these, let the initial set of instances be $S = \{I_j \mid j \in [1, n]\} \cup \{I'_j \mid j \in [1, n]\}$.

The Standard Loop Invariant: As before, the loop invariant states that we have a set S of input instances on which algorithm A's knowledge and actions for its first t time steps are identical.

Another Loop Invariant: We have additional loop invariants stating that the current structure of S is $S = \{I_j \mid j \in [j_1, j_2]\} \cup \{I'_j \mid j \in [j_1, j_2]\}$, where $[j_1, j_2]$ is a subinterval of the sorted list of size. Moreover, $|[j_1, j_2]| \geq N/2^t$.

Maintaining the Loop Invariant: We maintain the loop invariant as follows. Assume that the loop invariant is true for time $t - 1$. Let m be the index of the element read at time t by the algorithm on all inputs instances in S.

$m \notin [j_1, j_2]$: If the algorithm reads an element m before our subrange $[j_1, j_2]$, then for all instances in S, this mth element is zero. Similarly, if m is after, then this element is definitely 10. In either case, the algorithm learns nothing that has not already been fixed. The loop invariant is maintained trivially without changing anything.

$m \in [j_1, j_{mid}]$: Let $[j_1, j_{mid}]$ and $[j_{mid} + 1, j_2]$ split our subrange in half. If m is in the first half $[j_1, j_{mid}]$, then we set our new subinterval to be the second half $[j_{mid} + 1, j_2]$. This narrows our set of instances down to $S = \{I_j \mid j \in [j_{mid} + 1, j_2]\} \cup \{I'_j \mid j \in [j_{mid} + 1, j_2]\}$. For all instances in this new S, the mth element is zero. The algorithm reads and learns the value zero and proceeds. The loop invariant is maintained.

$m \in [j_{mid} + 1, j_2]$: If m is in the second half $[j_{mid} + 1, j_2]$, then we set our new subinterval to be the first half, and for all instances in the new S, the mth element is 10.

Ending: The exit condition is then $t = T_{lower}(|I|) = \log_2(N)$. From the loop invariant, when we exit our subinterval $[j_1, j_2]$, its size is at least $N/2^t = 1$. Let $j = j_1 = j_2$. Our set S still contains the two instances I_j and I'_j. By the definition of these instances, the first requires the answer $P(I_j) = $ yes and the second $P(I'_j) = $ no. From the loop invariant, the computation of A is identical on these instances for the first $T_{lower}(|I|)$ time steps, and hence their outputs must be identical: $A(I_j) = A(I'_j)$. Hence, the computation must give a wrong answer on at least one of them.

The Lower Bound: The rest of the lower bound is the same, proving that any algorithm requires at least $\Omega(\log N)$ binary operations to correctly solve the problem of searching a sorted list.

Current State of the Art in Proving Lower Bounds: Lower bounds are hard to prove, because you must consider *every* algorithm, no matter how strange or complex. After all, there are examples of algorithms that start out doing very strange things and then in the end magically produce the required output.

Information Theory: The technique used here to prove lower bounds does not consider the amount of work that must get done to solve the problem, but the amount of *information* that must be transferred from the input to the output. The problem with these lower bounds is that they are not bigger than linear with respect to the bit size of the input and the output.

Restricted Model: A common method of proving lower bounds is to consider only algorithms that have a restricted structure. My PhD thesis proved lower bounds on the tradeoffs between the time and space needed to check $(s - t)$-connectivity of a graph in a model that only allows pebbles to slide along edges and jump between each other.

General Model: The theory community is just now managing to prove the first nonlinear lower bounds on a general model of computation. This is quite exciting for those of us in the field.

EXERCISE 7.0.1 *How would the lower bound change if a single operation, instead of being only a yes–no question, could be a question with at most r different answers? Here r is some fixed parameter.*

EXERCISE 7.0.2 *(See solution in Part Five.) Recall the Magic Sevens card trick introduced in Section 4.2. Someone selects one of n cards, and the magician must determine what it is by asking questions. Each round, the magician rearranges the cards into rows and asks which of the r rows the card is in. Give an information-theoretic argument to prove a lower bound on the number of rounds, t, that are needed.*

EXERCISE 7.0.3 *(See solution in Part Five.) Suppose that you have n objects that are completely identical except that one is slightly heavier. The problem P is to find the heavier object. You have a scale. A single operation consists of placing any two disjoint sets of the objects the two sides of the scale. If one side is heavier, then the scale tips over. Give matching upper and lower bounds for this problem.*

EXERCISE 7.0.4 *Communication complexity: Consider the following problem: Alice has some object from the M objects $\{I_1, \ldots, I_M\}$, and she must communicate which object she has to Bob by sending a string of bits. The string sent will be an* identifier *for the object. The goal is to assign each object a unique identifier so that the longest one has as few bits as possible.*

EXERCISE 7.0.5 *State and prove a lower bound when instead of bits Alice can send Bob letters from some fixed alphabet Σ.*

EXERCISE 7.0.6 *(See solution in Part Five.) The* AND *computational problem given n bits determines whether at least one of the bits is a one. This is the same as the game show problem mentioned in Chapter 21, which requires finding which of the n doors conceals a prize. The way this differs from the parity problem is that the algorithm can stop as soon as it finds a prize. Give a tight lower bound for this problem. In the lower bound for the parity problem, which initial instances I work? Which ones work for the AND problem?*

EXERCISE 7.0.7 *Search a sorted matrix: The input consists of a real number x and a matrix $A[1..n, 1..m]$ of nm real numbers such that each row $A[i, 1..n]$ is sorted and each* column $A[1..n, j]$ is sorted. The goal is to find the maximum array entry $A[i, j]$ that is less than or equal to x, or report that all elements of A are larger than x.

1. Exercise 4.4.1 gives an iterative algorithm that accesses $T(n, n) = m + n - 1 = 2n - 1$ entries when $n = m$. Prove a matching lower bound of $T(n, n) = 2n - 1$ for this case. (Start with a lower bound of n if you like.)

2. Exercise 9.1.3 gives a recursive algorithm that accesses $T(n, m) = n \log_2(\frac{m}{n})$ elements when $m \gg n$. Prove a matching lower bound.

EXERCISE 7.0.8 Consider the problem of determining the smallest element in a max heap. The smallest elements of a max heap must be one of the $\lceil n/2 \rceil$ leaves. (Otherwise, there must be a nonleaf that is smaller than one of its descendants, which means the tree is not a max heap.) Thus, it is sufficient to search all leaves. Prove a lower bound that searching all the leaves is necessary.

PART TWO

Recursion

Iterative algorithms start at the beginning and take one step at a time towards the final destination. Another technique used in many algorithms is to slice the given task into a number of disjoint pieces, solve each of these separately, and then combine these answers into an answer for the original task. This is the *divide-and-conquer* method. When the subtasks are different, it leads to different subroutines. When they are instances of the original problem, it leads to recursive algorithms.

People often find recursive algorithms very difficult. To understand them, it is important to have a good solid understanding of the theory and techniques presented in this chapter.

8.1   Thinking about Recursion

There are a number of ways to view a recursive algorithm. Though the resulting algorithm is the same, having the different paradigms at your disposal can be helpful.

Code: Code is useful for implementing an algorithm on a computer. It is precise and succinct. However, code is prone to bugs, is language-dependent, and often lacks higher levels of intuition.

Stack of Stack Frames: Recursive algorithms are executed using a stack of stack frames. See Section 8.6. Though this should be understood, tracing out such an execution is painful.

Tree of Stack Frames: This is a useful way of viewing the entire computation at once. It is particularly useful when computing the running time of the algorithm. However, the structure of the computation tree may be very complex and difficult to understand all at once.

Friends, on Strong Induction: The easiest method is to focus on one step at a time. Suppose that someone gives you an instance of the computational problem. You solve it as follows. If it is sufficiently small, solve it yourself. Otherwise, you have a number of friends to help you. You construct for each friend an instance of the same computational problem that is *smaller* then your own. We refer to these  as *subinstances*. Your friends magically provide you with the solutions to these. You then combine these *subsolutions* into a solution for your original instance.

I refer to this as the *friends* level of abstraction. If you prefer, you can call it the *strong induction* level of abstraction and use the word "recursion" instead of "friend." Either way, the key is that you concern yourself only about your task. Do not worry about how your friends solve the subinstances that you assigned them. Similarly, do not worry about whoever gave you your instance and what he does with your answer. Leave these things up to him. Trust your friends.

Use It: I strongly recommend using this method when designing, understanding, and describing a recursive algorithm.

Faith in the Method: As with the loop invariant method, you do not want to be rethinking the issue of whether or not you should steal every time you walk into a store. It is better to have some general principles with which to work. You do not want to be rethinking the issue of whether or not you believe in recursion every time you consider a hard algorithm. Understanding the algorithm itself will be hard enough. While reading this chapter you should once and for all come to understand and believe how the following steps are sufficient to describing a recursive algorithm. Doing this can be difficult. It requires a whole new way of looking at algorithms. However, at least for now, adopt this as something that you believe in.

8.2 Looking Forward vs. Backward

Circular Argument? Recursion involves designing an algorithm by using it as if it already exists. At first this looks paradoxical. Suppose, for example, the key to the house that you want to get into is in that same house. If you could get in, you could get the key. Then you could open the door, so that you could get in. This is a circular argument. It is not a legal recursive program because the subinstance is not smaller.

One Problem and a Row of Instances:
Consider a row of houses. Each house is bigger than the next. Your task is to get into the biggest one. You are locked out of all the houses. The key to each house is locked in the house of the next smaller size. The recursive problem consists in getting into any specified house. Each house in the row is a separate instance of this problem.

To get into my house
I must get the key from a smaller house

The Algorithm: The smallest house is small enough that one can use brute force to get in. For example, one could simply lift off the roof. Once in this house, we can get the key to the next house, which is then easily opened. Within this house, we can get the key to the house after that, and so on. Eventually, we are in the largest house as required.

Focus on One Step: Though this algorithm is quite simple to understand, more complex algorithms are harder to understand all at once. Instead we focus on one step at a time. Here, one step consists in opening house i. We ask a friend to open house $i - 1$, out of which we take the key with which we open house i. We do not worry about how to open house $i - 1$.

Working Forward vs. Backward: An iterative algorithm works forward. It knows about house $i - 1$. It uses a loop invariant to show that this house has been opened. It searches this house and learns that the key within it is that for house i. Because of this, it decides that house i would be a good one to go to next.

A recursion algorithm works backward. It knows about house i. It wants to get it open. It determines that the key for house i is contained in house $i - 1$. Hence, opening house $i - 1$ is a subtask that needs to be accomplished.

There are two advantages of recursive algorithms over iterative ones. The first is that sometimes it is easier to work backward than forward. The second is that a recursive algorithm is allowed to have more than one subtask to be solved. This forms a tree of houses to open instead of a row of houses.

Do Not Trace: When designing a recursive algorithm it is tempting to trace out the entire computation. "I must open house n, so I must open house $n - 1, \ldots$. The smallest house I rip the roof off. I get the key for house 1 and open it. I get the key for house 2 and open it. . . . I get the key for house n and open it." Such an explanation is complicated and unnecessary.

Solving Only Your Instance: An important quality of any leader is knowing how to delegate. Your job is to open house i. Delegate to a friend the task of opening house $i - 1$. Trust him, and leave the responsibility to him.

8.3 With a Little Help from Your Friends

The following are the steps to follow when developing a recursive algorithm within the friends level of abstraction.

Specifications: Carefully write the specifications for the problem.

Preconditions: The preconditions state any assumptions that must be true about the input instance for the algorithm to operate correctly.

Postconditions: The postconditions are statements about the output that must be true when the algorithm returns.

This step is even more important for recursive algorithms than for other algorithms, because there must be tight agreement between what is expected from you in terms of pre- and postconditions and what is expected from your friends.

Size: Devise a measure of the *size* of each instance. This measure can be anything you like and corresponds to the measure of progress within the loop invariant level of abstraction.

General Input: Consider a large and general instance of the problem.

Magic: Assume that by magic a friend is able to provide the solution to any instance of your problem as long as the instance is strictly smaller than the current instance (according to your measure of size). More specifically, if the instance that you give the friend meets the stated preconditions, then her solution will meet the stated postconditions. Do *not*, however, expect your friend to accomplish more than this. (In reality, the friend is simply a mirror image of yourself.)

Subinstances: From the original instance, construct one or more *subinstances*, which are smaller instances of the same problem. Be sure that the preconditions are met for these smaller instances. Do not refer to these as "subproblems." The problem does not change, just the input instance to the problem.

Subsolutions: Ask your friend to (recursively) provide solutions for each of these subinstances. We refer to these as *subsolutions* even though it is not the solution, but the instance, that is smaller.

Solution: Combine these subsolutions into a solution for the original instance.

Generalizing the Problem: Sometimes a subinstance you would like your friend to solve is not a legal instance according to the preconditions. In such a case, start over, redefining the preconditions in order to allow such instances. Note, however, that now you too must be able to handle these extra instances. Similarly, the solution provided by your friend may not provide enough information about the subinstance for you to be able to solve the original problem. In such a case, start over, redefining the postcondition by increasing the amount of information that your friend provides. Again, you must now also provide this extra information. See Section 10.3.

> **Natural Pre- and Postconditions:** On the other hand, have the more generalized problem still be a natural problem. Do not attempt to pass it lots of extra information about your instance. For the very first call (or stack frame) of the computation to pass a value through the chain of recursive calls is a type of global-variable "cheat." It also makes it look like you are micromanaging your friends. Similarly, a stack frame (friend) should not know what level of recursion it is on.

> **Both the Pre- and the Postconditions Act as Loop Invariants:** The *loop invariant* in an iterative algorithm states what is maintained as the control gets passed from iteration to iteration. It provides a picture of what you want to be true in the middle of this computation. With recursion, however, there are two directions. The *precondition* states what you want to be true halfway down the recursion tree. The postcondition states what you want to be true halfway back up the recursion tree.

Minimizing the Number of Cases: You must ensure that the algorithm that you develop works for *every* valid input instance. To achieve this, the algorithm will often require many separate pieces of code to handle inputs of different types. Ideally, the algorithm developed has as few such cases as possible. One way to help you minimize the number of cases needed is as follows. Initially, consider an instance that is as large and as general as possible. If there are a number of different types of instances, choose one whose type is as general as possible. Design an algorithm that works for this instance. Afterwards, if there is another type of instance that you have not yet considered, consider a general instance of this type. Before designing a separate algorithm for this new instance, try executing your existing algorithm on it. You may be surprised to find that it works. If, on the other hand, it fails to work for this instance, then repeat the above steps to develop a separate algorithm for this case. You may need to repeat this process a number of times.

For example, suppose that the input consists of a binary tree. You may well find that the algorithm designed for a tree with a full left child and a full right child also works for a tree with a missing child and even for a child consisting of only a single node. The only remaining case may be the empty tree.

Base Cases: When all the remaining unsolved instances are sufficiently small, solve them in a brute force way.

Running Time: Use a recurrence relation or a tree of stack frames to estimate the running time.

A Link to the Techniques for Iterative Algorithms: The techniques that often arise in iterative algorithms also arise in recursive algorithms, though sometimes in a slightly different form.

More of the Input: When the input includes n objects, this technique for iterative algorithms extends (for $i = 1, \ldots, n - 1$) a solution for the first $i - 1$ objects into a solution for the first i. This same technique also can be used for recursive algorithms. Your friend provides you a solution for the first $n - 1$ objects in your instance, and then you extend this to a solution to your entire instance. This iterative algorithm and this recursive algorithm would be two implementations of the same algorithm. The recursion is more interesting when one friend can provide you a solution for the first $\lfloor \frac{n}{2} \rfloor$ objects in your instance, another friend can provide a solution for the next $\lceil \frac{n}{2} \rceil$ objects, and you combine them into a solution for the whole.

More of the Output: This technique for iterative algorithms builds the output one piece at a time. Again a recursive algorithm could have a friend build all but the last piece and have you add the last piece. However, it is better to have one friend build the first half of the output, another the second half, and you combine them somehow.

Narrowing the Search Space: Some iterative algorithms repeatedly narrow the search space in which to look for something. Instead, a recursive algorithm may split the search space in half and have a friend search each half.

Case Analysis: Instead of trying each of the cases oneself, one could give one case to each friend.

Work Done: Work does not accumulate in recursive algorithms as it does in iterative algorithms. We get each friend to do some work, and then we do some work, ourselves to combine these solution.

8.4 The Towers of Hanoi

The towers of Hanoi is a classic puzzle for which the only possible way of solving it is to think recursively.

Specification: The puzzle consists of three poles and a stack of N disks of different sizes.

Precondition: All the disks are on the first of the three poles.

Figure 8.1: The towers of Hanoi problem.

> *Postcondition:* The goal is to move the stack over to the last pole. See the first and the last parts of Figure 8.1.

You are only allowed to take one disk from the top of the stack on one pole and place it on the top of the stack on another pole. Another rule is that no disk can be placed on top of a smaller disk.

Lost with First Step: The first step must be to move the smallest disk. But it is by no means clear whether to move it to the middle or to the last pole.

Divide: Jump into the middle of the computation. One thing that is clear is that at some point, you must move the biggest disk from the first pole to the last. In order to do this, there can be no other disks on either the first or the last pole. Hence, all the other disks need to be stacked on the middle pole. See the second and the third parts of Figure 8.1. This point in the computation splits the problem into two subproblems that must be solved. The first is how to move all the disks except the largest from the first pole to the middle. See the first and second parts of Figure 8.1. The second is how to move these same disks from the middle pole to the last. See the third and fourth parts of Figure 8.1.

Conquer: Together these steps solve the entire problem. Starting with all disks on the first pole, somehow move all but the largest to the second pole. Then, in one step, move the largest from the first to the third pole. Finally, somehow move all but the largest from the second to the third pole.

Magic: In order to make a clear separation between task of solving the entire problem and that of solving each of the subproblems, I like to say that we delegate to one friend the task of solving one of the subproblems and delegate to another friend the other.

More General Specification: The subproblem of moving all but the largest disk from the first to the middle pole is very similar to original towers of Hanoi problem. However, it is an instance of a slightly more general problem, because not all of the disks are moved. To include this as an instance of our problem, we generalize the problem as follows.

> *Precondition:* The input specifies the number n of disks to be moved and the roles of the three poles. These three roles for poles are $pole_{source}$, $pole_{destination}$, and $pole_{spare}$. The precondition requires that the smallest n disks be currently on $pole_{source}$. It does not care where the larger disks are.

Postcondition: The goal is to move these smallest n disks to $pole_{destination}$. Pole $pole_{spare}$ is available to be used temporarily. The larger disks are not moved.

Subinstance: Our task is to move all the disks from the first to the last pole. This is specified by giving $n = N$, $pole_{source} = first$, $pole_{destination} = last$, and $pole_{spare} = middle$. We will get one friend to move all but the largest disk from the first to the middle pole. This is specified by giving $n = N - 1$, $pole_{source} = first$, $pole_{destination} = middle$, and $pole_{spare} = last$. On our own, we move the largest disk from the first to the last disk. Finally, we will get another friend to move all but the largest disk from the middle to the last pole. This is specified by giving $n = N - 1$, $pole_{source} = middle$, $pole_{destination} = last$, and $pole_{spare} = first$.

Code:

```
algorithm TowersOfHanoi(n, source, destination, spare)
    ⟨ pre-cond⟩: The n smallest disks are on pole_source.
    ⟨ post-cond⟩: They are moved to pole_destination.
    begin
        if(n ≤ 0)
            Nothing to do
        else
            TowersOfHanoi(n − 1, source, spare, destination)
            Move the nth disk from pole_source to pole_destination.
            TowersOfHanoi(n − 1, spare, destination, source)
        end if
    end algorithm
```

Running Time: Let $T(n)$ be the time to move n disks. Clearly, $T(1) = 1$ and $T(n) = 2 \cdot T(n-1) + 1$. Solving this gives $T(n) = 2^n - 1$.

8.5 Checklist for Recursive Algorithms

Writing a recursive algorithm is surprisingly hard when you are first starting out and surprisingly easy when you get it. This section contains a list of things to think about to make sure that you do not make any of the common mistakes.

0) The Code Structure: The code does not need to be much more complex than the following.

```
algorithm Alg(a, b, c)
    ⟨ pre-cond⟩: Here a is a tuple, b an integer, and c a binary tree.
    ⟨ post-cond⟩: Outputs x, y, and z, which are useful objects.
```

```
begin
    if( ⟨a, b, c⟩ is a sufficiently small instance) return( ⟨0, 0, 0⟩ )
    ⟨a_sub1, b_sub1, c_sub1⟩ = a part of ⟨a, b, c⟩
    ⟨x_sub1, y_sub1, z_sub1⟩ = Alg(⟨a_sub1, b_sub1, c_sub1⟩)
    ⟨a_sub2, b_sub2, c_sub2⟩ = a different part of ⟨a, b, c⟩
    ⟨x_sub2, y_sub2, z_sub2⟩ = Alg(⟨a_sub2, b_sub2, c_sub2⟩)
    ⟨x, y, z⟩ = combine ⟨x_sub1, y_sub1, z_sub1⟩ and ⟨x_sub2, y_sub2, z_sub2⟩
    return( ⟨x, y, z⟩ )
end algorithm
```

1) Specifications: You must clearly define what the algorithm is supposed to do.

2) Variables: A great deal is understood about an algorithm by understanding its variables. As in any algorithm, you want variables to be well documented and to have meaningful names. It is also important to carefully check that you give variables values of the correct type, e.g., k is an integer, G is a graph, and so on. Moreover, with recursive programs there are variables that play specific roles and should be used in specific ways. This can be a source of many confusions and mistakes. Hence, I outline these carefully here.

2.1.) Your Input: Your mission, if you are to accept it, is received through your inputs. The first line of your code, algorithm $Alg(a, b, c)$, specifies both the name Alg of the routine and the names of its inputs. Here $⟨a, b, c⟩$ is the input instance that you need to find a solution for. I sometimes use $Alg(⟨a, b, c⟩)$ because it emphasizes the viewpoint that we are receiving one instance, even if that instance might be composed of a tuple of things. Your preconditions must clearly specify what each of these components a, b, and c are and any restrictions on their values. You must be able to handle any instance that meets these conditions.

2.2.) Your Output: You must return a solution $⟨x, y, z⟩$ to your instance $⟨a, b, c⟩$ through a return statement $return(⟨x, y, z⟩)$. Your postconditions must clearly specify what each of the components x, y, and z of your solution are and their required relation to the input instance $⟨a, b, c⟩$.

2.2.1.) Every Path: Given any instance meeting the precondition, you must return a correct solution. Hence, if your code has *if* or *loop* statements, then every path through the code must end with a return statement.

2.2.2.) Type of Output: Each return statement must return a solution $⟨x, y, z⟩$ of the right type. The one partial exception to this is: if the postcondition leaves open the possibility that a solution does not exist, then some paths through the code may end with the statement *return*("no solution exists").

2.3.) Your Friend's Input: To get help from friends, you must create a subinstance $\langle a_{sub}, b_{sub}, c_{sub} \rangle$ for each friend. You pass this to a friend by recursing with $Alg(\langle a_{sub}, b_{sub}, c_{sub} \rangle)$. To be able to give a subinstance to a friend, it needs to meet the preconditions of your problem. Do not recurse with $Alg(a_{sub}, b_{sub})$.

2.4.) Your Friend's Output: You can trust that each friend will give you a correct solution $\langle x_{sub}, y_{sub}, z_{sub} \rangle$ to the subinstance $\langle a_{sub}, b_{sub}, c_{sub} \rangle$ that you give her. Be sure to save her result in variables of the correct type, using the code $\langle x_{sub}, y_{sub}, z_{sub} \rangle = Alg(\langle a_{sub}, b_{sub}, c_{sub} \rangle)$. In contrast, the code $Alg(\langle a_{sub}, b_{sub}, c_{sub} \rangle)$ as a line by itself is insulting to your friend, because you got her to do all of this work and then you dropped her result in the garbage.

2.5.) Rarely Need New Inputs or Outputs: I did speak of the need to generalize the problem by adding new inputs and/or outputs. This, however, is needed far less often than people think. Try hard to solve the problem using the friend analogy without extra variables. Only add them if absolutely necessary. If you do add extra inputs or outputs, clearly specify in the pre- and postconditions what they are for. Do not have inputs or outputs that are not explained.

2.6.) No Global Variables or Global Effects: When you recurse with the line $\langle x_{sub}, y_{sub}, z_{sub} \rangle = Alg(\langle a_{sub}, b_{sub}, c_{sub} \rangle)$, the only thing that should happen is that your friend passes back a correct solution $\langle x_{sub}, y_{sub}, z_{sub} \rangle$ to the subinstance $\langle a_{sub}, b_{sub}, c_{sub} \rangle$ that you gave her. If the code has a local variable n, then your variable n is completely different than your friend's. (They are stored in different stack frames. See Section 8.6.) If you set your variable n to 5 and then recurse, your friend's variable n will not have this value. If you want him to have a 5, you must pass it in as part of his subinstance $\langle a_{sub}, 5, c_{sub} \rangle$. Similarly, if your friend sets his variable n to 6 and then returns, your variable n will not have this value, but will still have the value 5. If you want him to give you a 6, he must return it as part of his solution $\langle x_{sub}, 6, z_{sub} \rangle$.

I often suspect that people intend for a parameter in their algorithm's arguments to both pass a value in and pass a value out. Though I know there are programming languages that allow this, I strongly recommend not doing this. The code $\langle x_{sub}, y_{sub}, z_{sub} \rangle = Alg(\langle a_{sub}, b_{sub}, c_{sub} \rangle)$ does not change the values of a_{sub}, b_{sub}, or c_{sub}.

I have seen lots of code that loops n times recursing $Alg(\langle a_{sub}, b_{sub}, c_{sub} \rangle)$ on the exact same subinstance $\langle a_{sub}, b_{sub}, c_{sub} \rangle$. One definition of insanity is repeating the same thing over and over and expecting to get a different result. Your friend on the same subinstance will give you the same solution. Do not waste her time.

It is tempting to use a global variable that everyone has access too. However, this is very bad form, mainly because it is very prone to errors and side effects that you did not expect.

Similarly, you can have no global returns. For example, suppose your friend's friend's friend's friend finds something that you are looking for. It needs to be passed back friend to friend, because things returned by your friends do not get returned to your boss unless you do the returning.

2.7.) Few Local Variables: An iterative algorithm consists of a big loop with a set of local variables holding the current state. Each iteration these variables get updated. Because thinking iteratively comes more naturally to people, they want to do this with recursive algorithms. Don't. Generally there is no need for a loop in a recursive algorithm unless you require the immediate help of many friends and you loop through them, creating subinstances for each and considering their subsolutions. In fact, despite the name "variable," rarely is there a need to change the value of a variable once initially set. For example, the variables $\langle a, b, c \rangle$ storing your instance are sacred. This is the instance you must solve. Why ever change it? You must construct a solution $\langle x, y, z \rangle$. Create it and return it. Why ever change it? Similarly for what you give $\langle a_{sub}, b_{sub}, c_{sub} \rangle$ and receive $\langle x_{sub}, y_{sub}, z_{sub} \rangle$ from each friend. Other local variables are rarely needed. If you do need them, be sure to document what they are for.

3) Tasks to Complete: Your mission, given an arbitrary instance $\langle a, b, c \rangle$ meeting the preconditions, is to construct and return a solution $\langle x, y, z \rangle$ that meets the postcondition. The following are the only steps that you should be following towards this goal.

3.1.) Accept Your Mission: Imagine that you have an $\langle a, b, c \rangle$ meeting the preconditions. Know the range of things that your instance might be. For example, if the input instance is a binary tree, make sure that your program works for a general tree with big left and right subtrees, a tree with big left and empty right, a tree with empty left and big right, and the empty tree. Also know what is require of your output.

3.2.) Construct Subinstances: For each friend, construct from your instance $\langle a, b, c \rangle$ a subinstance $\langle a_{sub}, b_{sub}, c_{sub} \rangle$ to give this friend. Sometimes this requires a block of code. Sometimes it happens right in place. For example, if your instance is $\langle \langle a_1, a_2, \ldots, a_n \rangle, b, c \rangle$, you might construct the subinstance $\langle \langle a_1, a_2, \ldots, a_{n-1} \rangle, b - 5, leftSub(c) \rangle$ for your friend by stripping the last object off the tuple a, subtracting 5 from the integer b, and taking the left subtree of the tree c. This subinstance can be constructed and passed to your friend in the one line

$$\langle x_{sub}, y_{sub}, z_{sub} \rangle = Alg(\langle \langle a_1, a_2, \ldots, a_{n-1} \rangle, b - 5, leftSub(c) \rangle)$$

3.2.1.) Valid Subinstance: Be sure that the subinstance $\langle a_{sub}, b_{sub}, c_{sub} \rangle$ that you give your friend meets the preconditions.

3.2.2.) Smaller Subinstance: Be sure that the subinstance $\langle a_{sub}, b_{sub}, c_{sub} \rangle$ that you give your friend is smaller in some way than your own subinstance $\langle a, b, c \rangle$.

3.3.) Trust Your Friend: Focus on only your mission. Trust your friend to give you a correct solution $\langle x_{sub}, y_{sub}, z_{sub} \rangle$ to the instance $\langle a_{sub}, b_{sub}, c_{sub} \rangle$ that you give her. Do not worry about how she gets her answer. Do not trace through the entire computation. Do not talk of your friends' friends' friends. I cannot emphasize this enough. Time and time again, I see students not trusting. It causes them no end of trouble until they finally see the light and let go.

3.4.) Construct Your Solution: Using the solutions $\langle x_{sub}, y_{sub}, z_{sub} \rangle$ provided by your friends for your subinstances $\langle a_{sub}, b_{sub}, c_{sub} \rangle$, your next task is to construct a solution $\langle x, y, z \rangle$ for your subinstance $\langle a, b, c \rangle$. This generally requires a block of code, but sometimes it can be contained in a single line. For example, if the only output is a single integer x, then the one line of code $return(Alg(a_{sub1}, b_{sub1}, c_{sub1}) + Alg(a_{sub2}, b_{sub2}, c_{sub2}))$ combines the friends' solutions x_{sub1} and x_{sub2} to give your solution $x = x_{sub1} + x_{sub2}$ and returns it.

3.5.) Base Cases: Consider which instance get solved by your program. For those that don't, either add more cases to solve them recursively or add base cases to solve them in a brute force way. If your input instance is sufficiently small according to *your* definition of size then you must solve it yourself as a base case.

This is all that you need to do. Do not do more.

EXERCISE 8.5.1 *You are now the professor. Which of the above steps to develop a recursive algorithm did the students fail to do correctly in the following code? How? How would you fix it? See Exercise 10.3.1 for corrrect code for this problem.*

algorithm *Smallest(tree, k, num, v)*

$\langle$ ***pre-cond*** $\rangle$: *tree is a binary search tree and $k > 0$ is an integer.*

$\langle$ ***post-cond*** $\rangle$: *Outputs the kth smallest element s.*

begin

    if(k = 0) return(0)

    if(v = k) return(element)

    n = 0

    Smallest(leftSub(tree))

    + + n

```
    if( n = k )
        return( root(tree) )
    end if
    Smallest(rightSub(tree))
    end if
end algorithm
```

algorithm *Smallest(tree, k, num, v)*

$\langle$ ***pre-cond*** $\rangle$***:*** *tree is a binary search tree and $k > 0$ is an integer.*
$\langle$ ***post-cond*** $\rangle$***:*** *Outputs the kth smallest element s.*

```
begin
    n = 0
    while( n < k )
        Smallest(leftSub(tree))
        + + n
        Smallest(rightSub(tree))
    end while
    return( element )
end algorithm
```

EXERCISE 8.5.2 *(See solution in Part Five.) In the friends level of abstracting recursion, you can give your friend any legal instance that is smaller than yours according to some measure as long as you solve in your own any instance that is sufficiently small. For which of these algorithms has this been done? If so, what is your measure of the size of the instance? On input instance $\langle n, m \rangle$, either bound the depth to which the algorithm recurses as a function of n and m, or prove that there is at least one path down the recursion tree that is infinite.*

algorithm $R_a(n, m)$	**algorithm** $R_b(n, m)$
$\langle$ ***pre-cond*** $\rangle$***:*** *n & m ints.*	$\langle$ ***pre-cond*** $\rangle$***:*** *n & m ints.*
$\langle$ ***post-cond*** $\rangle$***:*** *Say Hi*	$\langle$ ***post-cond*** $\rangle$***:*** *Say Hi*
begin	*begin*
$\quad$ *if(n $\leq$ 0)*	$\quad$ *if(n $\leq$ 0)*
$\quad\quad$ *Print("Hi")*	$\quad\quad$ *Print("Hi")*
$\quad$ *else*	$\quad$ *else*
$\quad\quad$ $R_a(n - 1, 2m)$	$\quad\quad$ $R_b(n - 1, m)$
$\quad$ *end if*	$\quad\quad$ $R_b(n, m - 1)$
end algorithm	$\quad$ *end if*
	end algorithm

algorithm $R_c(n, m)$

⟨ *pre-cond* ⟩: *n & m ints.*

⟨ *post-cond* ⟩: *Say Hi*

begin

    if(n ≤ 0 or m ≤ 0)

        Print("Hi")

    else

        $R_c(n - 1, m)$

        $R_c(n, m - 1)$

    end if

end algorithm

(d) Replace recursive lines with

    $R_d(n - 1, m + 2)$

    $R_e(n + 6, m - 3)$

(e) Replace recursive lines with

    $R_e(n - 4, m + 2)$

    $R_e(n + 6, m - 3)$

8.6   The Stack Frame

Tree of Stack Frames: Tracing out the entire computation of a recursive algorithm, one line of code at a time, can get incredibly complex. This is why the friends level of abstraction, which considers one stack frame at a time, is the best way to understand, explain, and design a recursive algorithm. However, it is also useful to have some picture of the entire computation. For this, the tree-of-stack-frames level of abstraction is best.

The key thing to understand is the difference between a particular routine and a particular execution of a routine on a particular input instance. A single routine can at one moment in time have many executions going on. Each such execution is referred to as a *stack frame*. You can think of each as the task given to a separate friend. Even though each friend may be executing exactly the same routine, each execution may currently be on a different line of code and have different values for the local variables.

If each routine makes a number of subroutine calls (recursive or not), then the stack frames that get executed form a tree. In the example in Figure 8.2, instance A is called first. It executes for a while and at some point recursively calls B. When B returns, A then executes for a while longer before calling H. When H returns, A executes for a while before completing. We have skipped over the details of the execution of B. Let's go back to when instance A calls B. Then B calls C, which calls D. D completes; then C calls E. After E, C completes. Then B calls F, which calls G. Then G completes, F completes, B completes, and A goes on to call H. It does get complicated.

Stack of Stack Frames: The algorithm is actually implemented on a computer by a stack of stack frames. What is stored in the computer memory at any given point in time is only a single path down the tree. The tree represents what occurs throughout time. In Figure 8.2, when instance G is active, A, B, F, and G are in the stack. C, D, and E have been removed from memory as these have completed. H, I, J, and K have

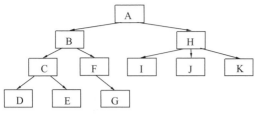

Figure 8.2: Tree of stack frames.

not been started yet. Although we speak of many separate stack frames executing on the computer, the computer is not a parallel machine. Only the top stack frame G is actively being executed. The other instances are on hold, waiting for the return of a subroutine call that it made.

Memory: Here is how memory is managed for the simultaneous execution of many instances of the same routine. The routine itself is described only once, by a block of code that appears in static memory. This code declares a set of variables. On the other hand, each instance of this routine that is currently being executed may be storing different values in these variables and hence needs to have its own separate copy of these variables. The memory requirements of each of these instances are stored in a separate *stack frame*. These frames are stacked on top of each other within stack memory.

Using a Stack Frame: Recall that a stack is a data structure in which either a new element is *pushed* onto the top or the last element to have been added is *popped* off (Section 3.1). Let us denote the top stack frame by A. When the execution of A makes a subroutine call to a routine with some input values, a stack frame is created for this new instance. This frame denoted B is pushed onto the stack after that for A. In addition to a separate copy of the local variables for the routine, it contains a pointer to the next line of code that A must execute when B returns. When B returns, its stack frame is popped, and A continues to execute at the line of code that had been indicated within B. When A completes, it too is popped off the stack.

Silly Example: This example demonstrates how difficult it is to trace out the full stack-frame tree, yet how easy it is to determine the output using the friends (strong-induction) method:

algorithm *Fun*(*n*)

⟨ *pre-cond*⟩*:* *n* is an integer.

⟨ *post-cond*⟩*:* Outputs a silly string.

begin

    if($n > 0$) then

```
            if( n = 1 ) then
                  put "X"
            else if( n = 2 ) then
                  put "Y"
            else
                  put "A"
                  Fun(n − 1)
                  Put "B"
                  Fun(n − 2)
                  Put "C"
            end if
      end if
end algorithm
```

EXERCISE 8.6.1 *Attempt to trace out the tree of stack frames for the silly example* $Fun(5)$.

EXERCISE 8.6.2 *(See solution in Part Five.) Now try the following simpler approach. What is the output of $Fun(1)$? What is the output of $Fun(2)$? Trust the answers to all previous questions; do not recalculate them. (Assume a trusted friend gave you the answer.) Now, what is the output of $Fun(3)$? Repeat this approach for $n = 4, 5,$ and 6.*

8.7 Proving Correctness with Strong Induction

Whether you give your subinstances to friends or you recurse on them, this level of abstraction considers only the algorithm for the top stack frame. We must now prove that this suffices to produce an algorithm that successfully solves the problem for every input instance. When proving this, it is tempting to talk about stack frames. This stack frame calls this one, which calls that one, until you hit the base case. Then the solutions bubble back up to the surface. These proofs tend to make little sense. Instead, we use strong induction to prove formally that the friends level of abstraction works.

Strong Induction: Strong induction is similar to induction, except that instead of assuming only $S(n − 1)$ to prove $S(n)$, you must assume all of $S(0), S(1), S(2), \ldots, S(n − 1)$.

> **A Statement for Each n:** For each value of $n \geq 0$, let $S(n)$ represent a Boolean statement. For some values of n this statement may be true, and for others it may be false.

> **Goal:** Our goal is to prove that it is true for every value of n, namely that $\forall n \geq 0, \ S(n)$.

Proof Outline: Proof by strong induction on n.

> **Induction Hypothesis:** For each $n \geq 0$, let $S(n)$ be the statement that .... (It is important to state this clearly.)
>
> **Base Case:** Prove that the statement $S(0)$ is true.
>
> **Induction Step:** For each $n \geq 0$, prove $S(0)$, $S(1)$, $S(2)$, ..., $S(n-1) \Rightarrow S(n)$.
>
> **Conclusion:** By way of induction, we can conclude that $\forall n \geq 0$, $S(n)$.

See Exercises 8.7.1 and 8.7.2.

Proving the Recursive Algorithm Works:

Induction Hypothesis: For each $n \geq 0$, let $S(n)$ be the statement "The recursive algorithm works for *every* instance of size n."

Goal: Our goal is to prove that $\forall n \geq 0$, $S(n)$, i.e. that the recursive algorithm works for *every* instance.

Proof Outline: The proof is by strong induction on n.

> **Base Case:** Proving $S(0)$ involves showing that the algorithm works for the base cases of size $n = 0$.
>
> **Induction Step:** The statement $S(0)$, $S(1)$, $S(2)$, ..., $S(n-1) \Rightarrow S(n)$ is proved as follows. First assume that the algorithm works for every instance of size strictly smaller than n, and then prove that it works for every instance of size n. This mirrors exactly what we do on the friends level of abstraction. To prove that the algorithm works for every instance of size n, consider an arbitrary instance of size n. The algorithm constructs subinstances that are strictly smaller. By our induction hypothesis we know that our algorithm works for these. Hence, the recursive calls return the correct solutions. On the friends level of abstraction, we proved that the algorithm constructs the correct solutions to our instance from the correct solutions to the subinstances. Hence, the algorithm works for this arbitrary instance of size n. The $S(n)$ follows.
>
> **Conclusion:** By way of strong induction, we can conclude that $\forall n \geq 0$, $S(n)$, i.e., the recursive algorithm works for every instance.

EXERCISE 8.7.1 *Give the process of strong induction as we did for regular induction.*

EXERCISE 8.7.2 *(See solution in Part Five.) As a formal statement, the base case can be eliminated in strong induction because it is included in the formal induction step. How is this? (In practice, the base cases are still proved separately.)*

9 Some Simple Examples of Recursive Algorithms

I will now give some simple examples of recursive algorithms. Even if you have seen them before, study them again, keeping the techniques and theory from Chapter 8 in mind. For each example, look for the key steps of the friend paradigm. What are the subinstances given to the friend? What is the size of an instance? Does it get smaller? How are the friend's solutions combined to give your solution? What does the tree of stack frames look like? What is the time complexity of the algorithm?

9.1 Sorting and Selecting Algorithms

The classic divide-and-conquer algorithms are merge sort and quick sort. They both have the following basic structure.

General Recursive Sorting Algorithm:
- Take the given list of objects to be sorted (numbers, strings, student records, etc.).
- Split the list into two sublists.
- Recursively have friends sort each of the two sublists.
- Combine the two sorted sublists into one entirely sorted list.

This process leads to four different algorithms, depending on the following factors (see Exercise 9.1.1):

Sizes: Do you split the list into two sublists each of size $\frac{n}{2}$, or one of size $n - 1$ and one of size one?

Work: Do you put minimal effort into splitting the list but put lots of effort into recombining the sublists, or put lots of effort into splitting the list but put minimal effort into recombining the sublists?

EXAMPLE 9.1.1	**Merge Sort (Minimal Work to Split in Half)**

This is the classic recursive algorithm.

Friend's Level of Abstraction: Recursively give one friend the first half of the input to sort and another friend the second half to sort. Then combine these two sorted sublists into one completely sorted list. This combining process is referred to as *merging*. A simple linear-time algorithm for it can be found in Section 3.3.

Size: The size of an instance is the number of elements in the list. If this is at least two, then the sublists are smaller than the whole list. Hence, it is valid to recurse on them with the reassurance that your friends will do their parts correctly. On the other hand, if the list contains only one element, then by default it is already sorted and nothing needs to be done.

Generalizing the Problem: If the input is assumed to be received in an array indexed from 1 to n, then the second half of the list is not a valid instance, because it is not indexed from 1. Hence, we redefine the preconditions of the sorting problem to require as input both an array A and a subrange $[i, j]$. The postcondition is that the specified sublist is to be sorted in place.

Running Time: Let $T(n)$ be the total time required to sort a list of n elements. This total time consists of the time for two subinstances of half the size to be sorted, plus $\Theta(n)$ time for merging the two sublists together. This gives the recurrence relation $T(n) = 2T(n/2) + \Theta(n)$. See Chapter 27 to learn how to solve recurrence relations like these. In this example, $\frac{\log a}{\log b} = \frac{\log 2}{\log 2} = 1$ and $f(n) = \Theta(n^1)$, so $c = 1$. Because $\frac{\log a}{\log b} = c$, the technique concludes that the time is dominated by all levels and $T(n) = \Theta(f(n) \log n) = \Theta(n \log n)$.

Tree of Stack Frames: The following is a tree of stack frames for a concrete example:

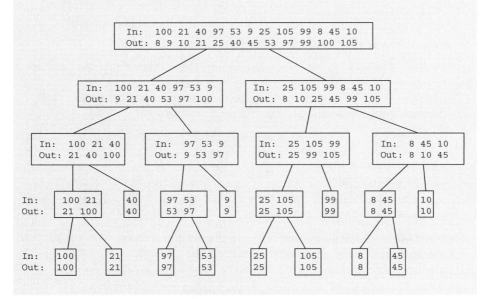

EXAMPLE 9.1.2 **Quick Sort (Minimal Work to Recombine the Halves)**

The following is one of the fastest sorting algorithms. Hence the name.

Friend's Level of Abstraction: The algorithm partitions the list into two sublists where all the elements that are less than or equal to a chosen *pivot element* are to the left of the pivot element and all the elements that are greater than it are to the right of it. (There are no requirements on the order of the elements in the sublists.) Next, recursively have a friend sort those elements before the pivot and those after it. Finally, (without effort) put the sublists together, forming one completely sorted list.

The first step in the algorithm is to choose one of the elements to be the pivot element. How this is to be done is discussed below.

Tree of Stack Frames: The following is a tree of stack frames for a specific input:

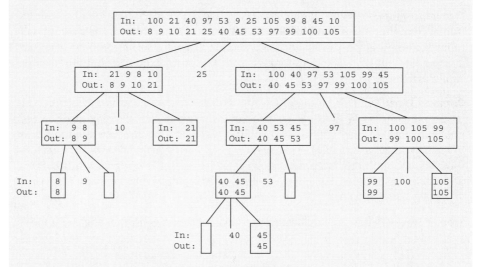

Running Time: The computation time depends on the choice of the pivot element.

Median: If we are lucky and the pivot element is close to having the median value, then the list will be split into two sublists of size approximately $n/2$. We will see that partitioning the array according to the pivot element can be done in time $\Theta(n)$. In this case, the timing is $T(n) = 2T(n/2) + \Theta(n) = \Theta(n \log n)$.

Reasonable Split: The above timing is quite robust with respect to the choice of the pivot. For example, suppose that the pivot always partitions the list into one sublist of one-fifth the original size and one of four-fifths the original size. The total time is then the time to partition plus the time to sort the sublists of these sizes. This gives $T(n) = T(\frac{1}{5}n) + T(\frac{4}{5}n) + \Theta(n)$. Because $\frac{1}{5} + \frac{4}{5} = 1$, this evaluates to $T(n) = \Theta(n \log n)$. (See Chapter 27.)

Worst Case: On the other hand, suppose that the pivot always splits the list into one of size $n - 1$ and one of size 1. In this case, $T(n) = T(n-1) + T(1) + \Theta(n)$, which evaluates to $T(n) = \Theta(n^2)$. This is the worst case scenario.

We will return to quick sort after considering the following related problem.

EXAMPLE 9.1.3   Finding the kth Smallest Element

Given an unsorted list and an integer k, this example finds the kth smallest element from the list. It is not clear at first that there is an algorithm for doing this that is any faster than sorting the entire list. However, it can be done in linear time using the subroutine *Pivot*.

Friend's Level of Abstraction: The algorithm is like that for binary search. Ignoring input k, it proceeds just like quick sort. A pivot element is chosen randomly, and the list is split into two sublists, the first containing all elements that are all less than or equal to the pivot element and the second those that are greater than it. Let ℓ be the number of elements in the first sublist. If $\ell \geq k$, then we know that the kth smallest element from the entire list is also the kth smallest element from the first sublist. Hence, we can give this first sublist and this k to a friend and ask him to find it. On the other hand, if $\ell < k$, then we know that the kth smallest element from the entire list is the $(k - \ell)$th smallest element from the second sublist. Hence, on giving the second sublist and $k - \ell$ to a friend, he can find it.

Tree of Stack Frames: The following is a tree of stack frames for our input.

```
In:      100 21 40 97 53 9 25 105 99 8 45 10
Sorted: 8 9 10 21 25 40 45 53 97 99 100 105)
k = 7
Pivot = 25
Left:    21 9 25 8 10
Right:   100 40 97 53 105 99 45
Left Size = 5 < k
Out = 45
```

```
In:      100 40 97 53 105 99 45
Sorted: 40 45 53 97 99 100 105)
k = 7-5 = 2
Pivot = 97
Left:    40 97 53 45
Right:   100 105 99
Left Size = 4 >= k
Out = 45
```

```
In:     40 97 53 45
Sorted: 40 45 53 97)
k = 2
Pivot = 45
Left:    40 45
Right:   97 53
Left Size = 2 >= k
Out = 45
```

```
In:     40 45
Sorted: 40 45)
k = 2
Pivot = 40
Left:    40
Right:   45
Left Size = 1 < k
Out = 45
```

```
In:       45
Sorted: 45)
k=2-1=1 Out:45
```

EXAMPLE 9.1.3 **Finding the kth Smallest Element** (cont.)

Running Time: Again, the computation time depends on the choice of the pivot element.

> **Median:** If we are lucky and the pivot element is close to the median value, then the list will be split into two sublists of size approximately $n/2$. Because the routine recurses on only one of the halves, the timing is $T(n) = T(n/2) + \Theta(n) = \Theta(n)$.

> **Reasonable Split:** If the pivot always partitions the list so that the larger half is at most $\frac{4}{5}n$, then the total time is at most $T(n) = T(\frac{4}{5}n) + \Theta(n)$, which is still linear time, $T(n) = \Theta(n)$.

> **Worst Case:** In the worst case, the pivot splits the list into one of size $n-1$ and one of size 1. In this case, $T(n) = T(n-1) + \Theta(n)$, which is $T(n) = \Theta(n^2)$.

Choosing the Pivot: In Examples 9.1.2 and 9.1.3, the timing depends on choosing a good pivot element quickly.

> **Fixed Value:** If you know that you are sorting elements that are numbers within the range [1..100], then it is reasonable to partition these elements based on whether they are smaller or larger than 50. This is often referred to as *bucket sort*. See Section 5.1. However, there are two problems with this technique. The first is that in general we do not know what range the input elements will lie in. The second is that at every level of recursion another pivot value is needed with which to partition the elements. The solution is to use the input itself to choose the pivot value.

> **Use $A[1]$ as the Pivot:** The first thing one might try is to let the pivot be the element that happens to be first in the input array. The problem with this is that if the input happens to be sorted (or almost sorted) already, then this first element will split the list into one of size zero and one of size $n - 1$. This gives a worst case time of $\Theta(n^2)$. Given random data, the algorithm will execute quickly. On the other hand, if you forget that you sorted the data and you run it a second time, then the second run will take a long time to complete.

> **Use $A[\frac{n}{2}]$ as the Pivot:** Motivated by the last attempt, one might use the element that happens to be located in the middle of the input array. For all practical purposes, this would likely work well. It would work exceptionally well when the list is already sorted. However, there are some strange inputs cooked up for the sole purpose of being nasty to this particular implementation of the algorithm, on which the algorithm runs in $\Theta(n^2)$ time. The adversary will provide such an input, giving a worst case time complexity of $\Theta(n^2)$.

> **A Randomly Chosen Element:** In practice, what is often done is to choose the pivot element randomly from the input elements. See Section 21.1. The advantage of this is that the adversary who is choosing the worst case input instance

knows the algorithm, but does not know the random coin tosses. Hence, all input instances are equally good and equally bad.

We will prove that the expected computation time is $\Theta(n \log n)$. What this means is that if you ran the algorithm 1,000,000 times on the same input, then the average running time would be $\Theta(n \log n)$.

> **Intuition:** One often gains good intuition by assuming that what we expect to happen happens reasonably often. If the pivot always partitions the list into one sublist of one-fifth the original size and one of four-fifths the original size, then the total time is $T(n) = T(\frac{1}{5}n) + T(\frac{4}{5}n) + \Theta(n) = \Theta(n \log n)$. When a pivot is chosen randomly, the probability that it partitions the list at least this well is $\frac{3}{5}$. When a partition is worse than this, it is not a big problem. We just say that no significant progress is made, and we try again. After all, we expect to make progress in approximately three of every five partitions.

> **More Formal:** Formally, we set up and solve a difficult recurrence relation. Suppose that the randomly chosen pivot element happens to be the ith smallest element. This splits the list into one of size i and one of size $n - i$, in which case the running time is $T(i) + T(n - i) + \Theta(n)$. Averaging this over all possible values of i gives the recursive relation $T(n) = \text{Avg}_{i \in [0..n]} \left[T(i) + T(n - i) + \Theta(n) \right]$. With a fair bit of work, this evaluates to $\Theta(n \log n)$.

Randomly Choose Three Elements: Another option is to randomly select three elements from the input list and use the middle one as the pivot. Doing this greatly increases the probability that the pivot is close to the middle and hence decreases the probability of the worst case occurring. However, it so also takes time. All in all, the expected running time is worse.

A Deterministic Algorithm: Though in practice such a probabilistic algorithm is easy to code and works well, theoretical computer scientists like to find a deterministic algorithm that is guaranteed to run quickly.

The following is a deterministic method of choosing the pivot that leads to a worst case running time of $\Theta(n)$ for finding the kth smallest element. First group the n elements into $\frac{n}{5}$ groups of five elements each. Within each group of five elements, do $\Theta(1)$ work to find the median of the group. Let S_{median} be the set of $\frac{n}{5}$ elements containing the median from each group. Recursively ask a friend to find the median element from the set S_{median}. This element will be used as our pivot.

I claim that this pivot element has at least $\frac{3}{10}n$ elements that are less than or equal to it and another $\frac{3}{10}n$ elements that are greater or equal to it. The proof of the claim is as follows. Because the pivot is the median within S_{median}, there are $\frac{1}{10}n = \frac{1}{2}|S_{median}|$ elements within S_{median} that are less than or equal to the pivot. Consider any such element $x_i \in S_{median}$. Because x_i is the median within its group of five elements, there are three elements within this group (including x_i itself) that are less than or equal to x_i and hence in turn less than or equal to the pivot.

Counting all these gives $3 \times \frac{1}{10}n$ elements. A similar argument counts this many that are greater than or equal to the pivot.

The algorithm to find the kth largest element proceeds as stated originally. A friend is asked to find either the kth smallest element within all elements that are less than or equal to the pivot or the $(k - \ell)$th smallest element from all those that are greater than it. The claim ensures that the size of the sublist given to the friend is at most $\frac{7}{10}n$.

Unlike the first algorithm for the finding kth smallest element, this algorithm recurses twice. Hence, one would naively assume that the running time is $\Theta(n \log n)$. However, careful analysis shows that it is only $\Theta(n)$. Let $T(n)$ denote the running time. Finding the median of each of the $\frac{1}{5}n$ groups takes $\Theta(n)$ time. Recursively finding the median of S_{median} takes $T(\frac{1}{5}n)$ time. Recursing on the remaining at most $\frac{7}{10}n$ elements takes at most $T(\frac{7}{10}n)$ time. This gives a total of $T(n) = T(\frac{1}{5}n) + T(\frac{7}{10}n) + \Theta(n)$ time. Because $\frac{1}{5} + \frac{7}{10} < 1$, this evaluates to $T(n) = \Theta(n)$. (See Chapter 27.)

A deterministic quick sort algorithm can use this deterministic $\Theta(n)$-time algorithm for the finding kth smallest element, to find the median of the list to be the pivot. Because partitioning the elements according to the pivot already takes $\Theta(n)$ time, the timing is still $T(n) = 2T(\frac{n}{2}) + \Theta(n) = \Theta(n \log n)$.

Partitioning According to the Pivot Element: This is an iterative step. The input consists of a list of elements $A[I], \ldots, A[J]$ and a pivot element. The output consists of the rearranged elements and an index i, such that the elements $A[I], \ldots, A[i-1]$ are all less than or equal to the pivot element, $A[i]$ is the pivot element, and the elements $A[i+1], \ldots, A[J]$ are all greater than it.

The loop invariant is that there are indices $I \le i \le j \le J$ for which:

1. The values in $A[I], \ldots, A[i-1]$ are less than or equal to the pivot element.

2. The values in $A[j+1], \ldots, A[J]$ are greater than the pivot element.

3. The pivot element has been removed and is on the side, leaving an empty entry either at $A[i]$ or at $A[j]$.

4. The other elements in $A[i], \ldots, A[j]$ have not been considered.

The loop invariant is established by setting $i = I$ and $j = J$, making $A[i]$ empty by putting the element in $A[i]$ where the pivot element is and putting the pivot element aside.

If the loop invariant is true and $i < j$, then there are four possible cases (see Figure 9.1):

Case A. $A[i]$ is empty and $A[j] \le$ pivot: $A[j]$ belongs on the left, so move it to the empty $A[i]$. Now $A[j]$ is empty. Increase the left side by increasing i by one.

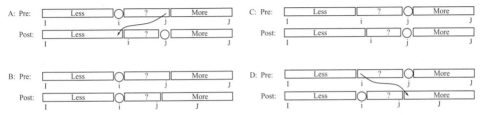

Figure 9.1: The four cases of how to iterate are shown.

Case B. *A[i] is empty and A[j] > pivot:* $A[j]$ belongs on the right and is already there. Increase the right side by decreasing j by one.

Case C. *A[j] is empty and A[i] ≤ pivot:* $A[i]$ belongs on the left and is already there. Increase the left side by increasing i by one.

Case D. *A[j] is empty and A[i] > pivot:* $A[i]$ belongs on the right, so move it to the empty $A[j]$. Now $A[i]$ is empty. Increase the right side by decreasing j by one.

In each case, the loop invariant is maintained. Progress is made because $j - i$ decreases.

When $i = j$, the list is split as needed, leaving $A[i]$ empty. Put the pivot there. The postcondition follows.

EXERCISE 9.1.1 *(See solution in Part Five.) Consider the algorithm that puts minimal effort into splitting the list into one of size $n - 1$ and one of size one, but puts lots of effort into recombining the sublists. Also consider the algorithm that puts lots of effort into splitting the list into one of size $n - 1$ and one of size one, but puts minimal effort into recombining the sublists. What are these two algorithms?*

EXERCISE 9.1.2 *(See solution in Part Five.) One-friend recursion vs iteration.*

1. *Your task is to accept a tuple $\langle a_1, a_2, \ldots, a_n \rangle$ and return the reversed tuple $\langle a_n, a_{n-1}, \ldots, a_1 \rangle$. Being lazy, you will only strip off an element from one end or add an element back onto one end. But you have recursive friends to help you. Provide both a paragraph containing the friend's explanation of the algorithm, and the recursive code.*

2. *Now suppose that you have a stack, but no friends. (See Chapter 3). Quickly sketch an iterative program that solves this same problem. Be sure to include loop invariants and other the key steps required for describing an iterative algorithm.*

3. *Trace each of these two programs. Step by step, compare and contrast their computations on a computer.*

EXERCISE 9.1.3 *Exercise 4.4.1 asks for an iterative algorithm for searching within a matrix $A[1..n, 1..m]$ in which each row is sorted and each column is sorted. This requires that $T(n, m) = n + m - 1$ of the matrix entries be examined. Exercise 7.0.7* *proves that this is tight when $n = m$. But it is clearly too big when $m >> n$, given one can do binary search in each row in time $n \log m << n + m - 1$. The goal now is to design a recursive algorithm that accesses $T(n, m) \approx n \log_2(\frac{m}{n})$ entries. As a huge hint, the recurrence relation will be $T(n, m) = \max_{n' \in [1,n]} T(n', \frac{m}{2}) + T(n - n', \frac{m}{2}) + \log_2 n$. You must look at the recursive tree in order to get some intuition to why the time is $T(n, m) \approx n \log_2(\frac{m}{n})$. You can also plug $T(n, m) = n \log_2(\frac{m}{n}) + 2n - \log(n) - 2$ into this recurrence relation and see that it satisfies it.*

9.2 Operations on Integers

Raising an integer to a power b^N, multiplying $x \times y$, and matrix multiplication each have surprising divide-and-conquer algorithms.

EXAMPLE 9.2.1 b^N

Suppose that you are given two integers b and N and want to compute b^N.

The Iterative Algorithm: The obvious iterative algorithm simply multiplies b together N times. The obvious recursive algorithm recurses with $Power(b, N) = b \times Power(b, N - 1)$. This requires the same N multiplications.

The Straightforward Divide-and-Conquer Algorithm: The obvious divide-and-conquer technique cuts the problem into two halves using the property that $b^{\lceil \frac{N}{2} \rceil} \times b^{\lfloor \frac{N}{2} \rfloor} = b^{\lceil \frac{N}{2} \rceil + \lfloor \frac{N}{2} \rfloor} = b^N$. This leads to the recursive algorithm $Power(b, N) = Power(b, \lceil \frac{N}{2} \rceil) \times Power(b, \lfloor \frac{N}{2} \rfloor)$. Its recurrence relation gives $T(N) = 2T(\frac{N}{2}) + 1$ multiplications. The technique in Chapter 27 notes that $\frac{\log a}{\log b} = \frac{\log 2}{\log 2} = 1$ and $f(N) = \Theta(N^0)$, so $c = 0$. Because $\frac{\log a}{\log b} > c$, the technique concludes that time is dominated by the base cases and $T(N) = \Theta(N^{(\log a)/(\log b)}) = \Theta(N)$. This is no faster than the standard iterative algorithm.

Reducing the Number of Recursions: This algorithm can be improved by noting that the two recursive calls are almost the same and hence need only to be made once. The new recurrence relation gives $T(N) = 1T(\frac{N}{2}) + 1$ multiplications. Here $\frac{\log a}{\log b} = \frac{\log 1}{\log 2} = 0$ and $f(N) = \Theta(N^0)$, so $c = 0$. Because $\frac{\log a}{\log b} = c$, we conclude that the time is dominated by all levels and $T(N) = \Theta(f(N) \log N) = \Theta(\log N)$ multiplications.

Code:

```
algorithm Power(b, N)

⟨ pre-cond⟩: N ≥ 0 (N and b not both 0)
⟨ post-cond⟩: Outputs bⁿ.

begin
    if( N = 0 ) then
        return(1)
    else
        half = ⌊ N/2 ⌋
        p = Power(b, half)
```

$$\text{if}(\,2 \cdot half = N\,) \text{ then}$$
$$\quad \text{return}(\,p \cdot p\,) \ \% \text{ if } N \text{ is even, } b^N = b^{\lfloor N/2 \rfloor} \cdot b^{\lfloor N/2 \rfloor}$$
$$\text{else}$$
$$\quad \text{return}(\,p \cdot p \cdot b\,) \ \% \text{ if } N \text{ is odd, } b^N = b \cdot b^{\lfloor N/2 \rfloor} \cdot b^{\lfloor N/2 \rfloor}$$
$$\text{end if}$$
$$\text{end if}$$
$$\text{end algorithm}$$

Tree of Stack Frames:

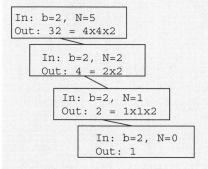

```
In: b=2, N=5
Out: 32 = 4x4x2

    In: b=2, N=2
    Out: 4 = 2x2

        In: b=2, N=1
        Out: 2 = 1x1x2

            In: b=2, N=0
            Out: 1
```

Running Time:

Input Size: One is tempted to say that the first two $\Theta(N)$ algorithms require a linear number of multiplications and that the last $\Theta(\log N)$ one requires a logarithmic number. However, in fact the first two require exponential $\Theta(2^n)$ number and the last a linear $\Theta(n)$ number in the size of the input, which is typically taken as the number of bits, $n = \log N$, needed to represent the number.

Operation: Is it fair to count the multiplications and not the bit operations in this case? I say not. The output b^N contains $\Theta(N \log b) = 2^{\Theta(n)}$ bits, and hence it will take this many bit operations to simply output the answer. Given this, it is not really fair to say that the time complexity is only $\Theta(n)$.

EXAMPLE 9.2.2 $x \times y$

The time complexity of Example 9.2.1 was measured in terms of the number of multiplications. This ignores the question of how quickly one can multiply.

The input for the next problem consists of two strings of n digits each. These are viewed as two integers x and y, either in binary or in decimal notation. The problem is to multiply them.

The Iterative Algorithm: The standard elementary school algorithm considers each pair of digits, one from x and the other from y, and multiplies them together. These n^2 products are shifted appropriately and summed. The total time is $\Theta(n^2)$. It is hard to believe that one could do it faster.

EXAMPLE 9.2.2	$x \times y$ (cont.)

```
          8   2   7
          5   9   6
        ─────────────
                  4   2
              1   2
          4   8
              6   3
          1   8
      7   2
      3   5
      1   0
  4   0
  ───────────────────
  4   9   2   8   9   2
```

The Straightforward Divide-and-Conquer Algorithm: Let us see how well the divide-and-conquer technique can work. Split each sequence of digits in half, and consider each half as an integer. This gives $x = x_1 \times 10^{n/2} + x_0$ and $y = y_1 \times 10^{n/2} + y_0$. Multiplying these symbolically gives

$$x \times y = \left(x_1 \times 10^{\frac{n}{2}} + x_0 \right) \times \left(y_1 \times 10^{\frac{n}{2}} + y_0 \right)$$
$$= (x_1 y_1) \times 10^n + (x_1 y_0 + x_0 y_1) \times 10^{\frac{n}{2}} + (x_0 y_0).$$

The obvious divide-and-conquer algorithm would recursively compute the four subproblems $x_1 y_1$, $x_1 y_0$, $x_0 y_1$, and $x_0 y_0$, each of $\frac{n}{2}$ digits. This would take $4T(\frac{n}{2})$ time. Then these four products are shifted appropriately and summed. Note that additions can be done in $\Theta(n)$ time. See Section 2.2. Hence, the total time is $T(n) = 4T(\frac{n}{2}) + \Theta(n)$. Here $\frac{\log a}{\log b} = \frac{\log 4}{\log 2} = 2$ and $f(n) = \Theta(n^1)$, so $c = 1$. Because $\frac{\log a}{\log b} > c$, the technique concludes that the time is dominated by the base cases and $T(n) = \Theta(n^{(\log a)/(\log b)}) = \Theta(n^2)$. This is no improvement in time.

Reducing the Number of Recursions: Suppose that we could find a trick so that we only needed to recurse three times instead of four. One's intuition might be that this would only provide a linear time saving, but in fact the saving is much more. $T(n) = 3T(\frac{n}{2}) + \Theta(n)$. Now $\frac{\log a}{\log b} = \frac{\log 3}{\log 2} = 1.58\ldots$, which is still bigger than c. Hence, time is still dominated by the base cases, but now this is $T(n) = \Theta(n^{\frac{\log a}{\log b}}) = \Theta(n^{1.58\ldots})$. This is a significant improvement over $\Theta(n^2)$.

The Trick: The first step is to multiply $x_1 y_1$ and $x_0 y_0$ recursively as required. This leaves us only one more recursive multiplication.

If you review the symbolic expansion for $x \times y$, you will see that we do not actually need to know the values of $x_1 y_0$ and $x_0 y_1$. We only need to know their sum. Symbolically, we can observe the following:

$$x_1 y_0 + x_0 y_1 = \left[x_1 y_1 + x_1 y_0 + x_0 y_1 + x_0 y_0 \right] - x_1 y_1 - x_0 y_0$$
$$= \left[(x_1 + x_0)(y_1 + y_0) \right] - x_1 y_1 - x_0 y_0$$

Hence, the sum $x_1 y_0 + x_0 y_1$ that we need can be computed by adding x_1 to x_0 and y_1 to y_0; multiplying these sums; and subtracting off the values $x_1 y_1$ and $x_0 y_0$ that we know from before. This requires only one additional recursive multiplication. Again we use the fact that additions are fast, requiring only $\Theta(n)$ time.

Code:

    algorithm *Multiply*(x, y)

    ⟨ *pre-cond*⟩: x and y are two integers represented as an array of n digits

    ⟨ *post-cond*⟩: The output consists of their product represented as an array of $n + 1$ digits

    begin

        if$(n = 1)$ then

            result$(\,x \times y\,)$ % product of single digits

        else

            $\langle x_1, x_0 \rangle = $ high- and low-order $\frac{n}{2}$ digits of x

            $\langle y_1, y_0 \rangle = $ high- and low-order $\frac{n}{2}$ digits of y

            $A = Multiply(x_1, y_1)$

            $C = Multiply(x_0, y_0)$

            $B = Multiply(x_1 + x_0, y_1 + y_0) - A - C$

            result$(\,A \times 10^n + B \times 10^{\frac{n}{2}} + C\,)$

        end if

    end algorithm

It is surprising that this trick reduces the time from $\Theta(n^2)$ to $\Theta(n^{1.58})$.

Dividing into More Parts: The next question is whether the same trick can be extended to improve the time even further. Instead of splitting each of x and y into two pieces, let's split them each into d pieces. The straightforward method recursively multiplies each of the d^2 pairs of pieces together, one from x and one from y. The total time is $T(n) = d^2 T(\frac{n}{d}) + \Theta(n)$. Here $a = d^2$, $b = d$, $c = 1$, and $\frac{\log d^2}{\log d} = 2 > c$. This gives $T(n) = \Theta(n^2)$. Again, we are back where we began.

Reducing the Number of Recursions: The trick now is to do the same with fewer recursive multiplications. It turns out it can be done with only $2d - 1$ of them. This gives time of only $T(n) = (2d - 1)T(\frac{n}{d}) + \Theta(n)$. Here $a = 2d - 1$, $b = d$, $c = 1$, and $\frac{\log(2d-1)}{\log(d)} \approx \frac{\log(d)+1}{\log(d)} = 1 + \frac{1}{\log(d)} \approx c$. By increasing d, the times for the top stack frame and for the base cases become closer and closer to being equal. Recall that when this happens, we must add an extra $\Theta(\log n)$ factor to allow for the $\Theta(\log n)$ levels of recursion. This gives $T(n) = \Theta(n \log n)$, which is a surprising running time for multiplication.

Fast Fourier Transformation: I will not describe the trick for reducing the number of recursive multiplications from d^2 to only $2d - 1$. Let it suffice to say that it involves thinking of the problem as the evaluation and interpolation of polynomials. When d becomes large, other complications arise. These are solved by using the $2d$th roots of unity over a finite field. Performing operations over this finite field requires $\Theta(\log \log n)$ time. This increases the total time from $\Theta(n \log n)$ to $\Theta(n \log n \log \log n)$. This algorithm is used often for multiplication and many other applications such as signal processing. It is referred to as *fast Fourier transformation*.

EXAMPLE 9.2.3   **Strassen's Matrix Multiplication**

The next problem is to multiply two $n \times n$ matrices.

The Iterative Algorithm: The obvious iterative algorithm computes the $\langle i, j \rangle$ entry of the product matrix by multiplying the ith row of the first matrix with the jth column of the second. This requires $\Theta(n)$ scalar multiplications. Because there are n^2 such entries, the total time is $\Theta(n^3)$.

The Straightforward Divide-and-Conquer Algorithm: When designing a divide-and-conquer algorithm, the first step is to divide these two matrices into four submatrices each. Multiplying these symbolically gives the following:

$$\begin{pmatrix} a & b \\ c & d \end{pmatrix} \begin{pmatrix} e & g \\ f & h \end{pmatrix} = \begin{pmatrix} ae+bf & ag+bh \\ ce+df & cg+dh \end{pmatrix}$$

Computing the four $\frac{n}{2} \times \frac{n}{2}$ submatrices in this product in this way requires recursively multiplying eight pairs of $\frac{n}{2} \times \frac{n}{2}$ matrices. The total computation time is given by the recurrence relation $T(n) = 8T(n/2) + \Theta(n^2) = \Theta(n^{(\log 8)}(\log 2)) = \Theta(n^3)$. This is no faster than the standard iterative algorithm.

Reducing the Number of Recursions: Strassen found a way of computing the four $\frac{n}{2} \times \frac{n}{2}$ submatrices in this product using only seven such recursive calls. This gives $T(n) = 7T(n/2) + \Theta(n^2) = \Theta(n^{(\log 7)}(\log 2)) = \Theta(n^{2.8073})$. I will not include the details of the algorithm.

EXERCISE 9.2.1   *(See solution in Part Five) Recursive GCD.*

1. *Write a recursive program to find the GCD of two numbers. The program should mirror the iterative algorithm found in Chapter 6.*

2. *Rewrite this recursive algorithm to solve the following more general problem. The input still consists of two integers a and b. The output consists of three integers g, u, and v, such that ua + vb = g = GCD(a, b). For example, on a = 25 and b = 15 the algorithm outputs $\langle 5, 2, -3 \rangle$, because $2 \times 25 - 3 \times 15 = 50 - 45 = 5 = GCD(25, 15)$. Provide both a paragraph containing the friend's explanation of the algorithm, and the recursive code.*

3. *Write an algorithm for the following problem. The input consist of three integers a, b, and w. Assume that you live in a country that has two types of coins, one worth a dollars and the other b dollars. Both you and the storekeeper have a pocket full of each. You must pay him w dollars. You can give him any number of coins, and he may give you change with any number of coins. Your algorithm must determine whether or not this is possible and, if so, describe some way of doing it (not necessarily the optimal way). [Hint: Compute GCD(a, b), and use the three values g, u, and v. Consider the two cases when g divides w and when it does not. (If you want to find the optimal number of coins, basically you change a solution by using the fact that $(\frac{b}{g}) \cdot a - (\frac{a}{g}) \cdot b = 0$.)]*

4. *Designing an algorithm that, when given a prime p and an integer $x \in [1, p-1]$, outputs an inverse y such that $x \cdot y \equiv_{mod\ p} 1$. [Hint: First show that GCD(p, x) = 1.]*

Then compute GCD(p, x) and use the values u, and v. Proving that every x has such an inverse proves that the integers modulo a prime form a field.]

9.3 Ackermann's Function

If you are wondering just how slowly a program can run, consider the algorithm below. Assume the input parameters n and k are natural numbers.

Algorithm:
```
algorithm A(k, n)
    if( k = 0) then
        return( n +1 + 1 )
    else
        if( n = 0) then
            if( k = 1) then
                return( 0 )
            else
                return( 1 )
        else
            return( A(k − 1, A(k, n − 1)))
        end if
    end if
end algorithm
```

Recurrence Relation: Let $T_k(n)$ denote the value returned by $A(k, n)$. This gives $T_0(n) = 2 + n$, $T_1(0) = 0$, $T_k(0) = 1$ for $k \geq 2$, and $T_k(n) = T_{k-1}(T_k(n-1))$ for $k > 0$ and $n > 0$.

Solving:

$$T_0(n) = 2 + n$$

$$T_1(n) = T_0(T_1(n-1)) = 2 + T_1(n-1) = 4 + T_1(n-2)$$
$$= 2i + T_1(n-i) = 2n + T_1(0) = 2n$$

$$T_2(n) = T_1(T_2(n-1)) = 2 \cdot T_2(n-1) = 2^2 \cdot T_2(n-2) = 2^i \cdot T_2(n-i) = 2^n \cdot T_2(0) = 2^n$$

$$T_3(n) = T_2(T_3(n-1)) = 2^{T_3(n-1)} = 2^{2^{T_3(n-2)}} = \underbrace{\left[2^{2^{2^{\cdot^{\cdot^{\cdot^2}}}}} \right]}_{i}^{T_3(n-i)} = \underbrace{\left[2^{2^{2^{\cdot^{\cdot^{\cdot^2}}}}} \right]}_{n}^{T_3(0)} = \underbrace{2^{2^{2^{\cdot^{\cdot^{\cdot^2}}}}}}_{n}$$

$$T_4(0) = 1. \ T_4(1) = T_3(T_4(0)) = T_3(1) = \underbrace{2^{2^{2^{\cdot^{\cdot^{\cdot^2}}}}}}_{1} = 2.$$

$$T_4(2) = T_3(T_4(1)) = T_3(2) = \underbrace{2^{2^{2^{\cdot^{\cdot^{\cdot^2}}}}}}_{2} = 2^2 = 4.$$

$$T_4(3) = T_3(T_4(2)) = T_3(4) = \underbrace{2^{2^{2^{...^2}}}}_{4} = 2^{2^{2^2}} = 2^{2^4} = 2^{16} = 65,536.$$

Note that

$$\underbrace{2^{2^{2^{...^2}}}}_{5} = 2^{65,536} \approx 10^{21,706}$$

while the number of atoms in the universe is less than 10^{100}. We have

$$T_4(4) = T_3(T_4(3)) = T_3(65,536) = \underbrace{2^{2^{2^{...^2}}}}_{65,536}$$

Ackermann's function is defined to be $A(n) = T_n(n)$. We see that $A(4)$ is bigger than any number in the natural world. $A(5)$ is unimaginable.

Running Time: The only way that the program builds up a big number is by continually incrementing it by one. Hence, the number of times one is added is at least as huge as the value $T_k(n)$ returned.

Crashing: Programs can stop at run time because of (1) overflow in an integer value; (2) running out of memory; (3) running out of time. Which is likely to happen first? If the machine's integers are 32 bits, then they hold a value that is about 10^{10}. Incrementing up to this value will take a long time. However, much worse than this, each two increments need another recursive call creating a stack of about this many recursive stack frames. The machine is bound to run out of memory first.

EXERCISE 9.3.1 *Design the algorithm and compute the running time when $d = 3$.*

9.4 Exercises

EXERCISE 9.4.1 *Review the problem of iterative cake cutting (Section 2.3). You are now to write a recursive algorithm for the same problem. You will, of course, need to make the pre- and postconditions more general so that when you recurse, your subinstances meet the preconditions. As in moving from insertion sort to merge sort, you need to make the algorithm faster by cutting the problem in half.*

1. *You will need to generalize the problem so that the subinstance you would like your friend to solve is a legal instance according to the preconditions and so that the postconditions state the task you would like him to solve. Make the new problem, however, natural. Do not, for example, pass the number n of players in the original problem or the level of recursion. The input should simply be a set of players and a subinterval of cake. The postcondition should state the requirements on how this subinterval is to be divided among these players. To make the problem easier, assume that the number of players is $n = 2^i$ for some integer i.*

2. *Give recursive pseudocode for this algorithm. As a big hint, towards designing a recursive algorithm, I will tell you the first things that the algorithm does. Each*

player specifies where he would cut if he were to cut the cake in half. Then one of these spots is chosen. You need to decide which one and how to create two subinstances from this.

3. Prove that if your instance meets the preconditions, then your two subinstances also meet the preconditions.

4. Prove that if your friend's solutions meet the postconditions, then your solution meets the postcondition.

129

5. Prove that your solution for the base case meets the postconditions.

6. Give and solve the recurrence relation for the running time of this algorithm.

7. Now suppose that n is not 2^i for any integer i. How would we change the algorithm so that it handles the case when n is odd? I have two solutions: one that modifies the recursive algorithm directly, and one that combines the iterative algorithm and the recursive algorithm. You only need to do one of the two (as long as it works and does not increase the BigOh of the running time.)

10 Recursion on Trees

One key application of recursive algorithms is to perform actions on trees, because trees themselves have a recursive definition. Terminology for trees is summarized in the following table:

Term	Definition
Root	Node at the top
RootInfo(*tree*)	The information stored at the root node
Child of node u	One of the nodes just under node u
Parent of node u	The unique node immediately above node u
Siblings	Nodes with same parent
Ancestors of node u	The nodes on the unique path from the root to the node u
Descendants of node u	All the nodes below node u
Leaf	A node with no children
Height of tree	The maximum level. Some definitions say that a tree with a single node has height 0, others say height 1. It depends on whether you count nodes or edges.
Depth of node u	The number of nodes (or edges) on the path from the root to u.
Binary tree	Each node has at most two children. Each of these is designated as either the right child or the left child.
leftSub(*tree*)	Left subtree of root
rightSub(*tree*)	Right subtree of root

Recursive Definition of Tree: A tree is either:
- an empty tree (zero nodes) or
- a root node with some subtrees as children.

A *binary tree* is a special kind of tree where each node has a right and a left subtree.

Binary Tree

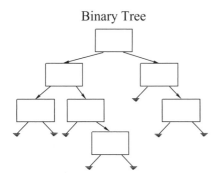

Tree representing (x + y) * z

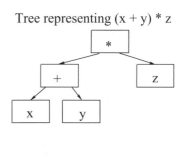

EXAMPLE 10.1	**Number of Nodes in a Binary Tree**

We will now develop a recursive algorithm that will compute the number of nodes in a binary tree.

Specifications:

Preconditions: The input is any binary tree. Trees with an empty subtree are valid trees. So are trees consisting of a single node and the empty tree.

Postconditions: The output is the number of nodes in the tree.

Size: The *size* of an instance is the number of nodes in it.

General Input: Consider a large binary tree with two complete subtrees.

Magic: We assume that by *magic* a friend is able to count the nodes in any tree that is strictly smaller than ours.

Subinstances: The subinstances of our instance tree will be the tree's left and its right subtree. These are valid instances that are strictly smaller than ours because the root (and the other subtree) have been removed.

Subsolutions: We ask one friend to recursively count the number of nodes in the left subtree and another friend to do so in the right subtree.

Solution: The number of nodes in our tree is the number in its left subtree plus the number in its right subtree plus one for the root.

Other Instances: Suppose the instance is a tree with the right subtree missing. Surprisingly, the algorithm still works. The number of nodes in our tree's right subtree is zero. This is the answer that our friend will return. Hence, the algorithm returns the number in the left subtree plus zero plus one for the root. This is the correct answer. Similarly, the algorithm works when the left subtree is empty or when the instance consists of a single leaf node.

The remaining instance is the empty tree. The algorithm does not work in this case, because it does not have any subtrees. Hence, the algorithm can handle all trees except the empty tree with one piece of code.

EXAMPLE 10.1   **Number of Nodes in a Binary Tree** (cont.)

Base Cases: The empty tree is sufficiently small that we can solve it in a brute force way. The number of nodes in it is zero.

The Tree of Stack Frames: There is one recursive stack frame for each node in the tree, and the tree of stack frames directly mirrors the structure of the tree.

Running Time: Because there is one recursive stack frame for each node in the tree and each stack frame does a constant amount of work, the total time is linear in the number of nodes in the input tree, i.e., $T(n) = \Theta(n)$. Proved another way, the recurrence relation is $T(n) = T(n_{left}) + T(n_{right}) + \Theta(1)$. Plugging the guess $T(n) = cn$ gives $cn = cn_{left} + cn_{right} + \Theta(1)$, which is correct because $n = n_{left} + n_{right} + 1$.

Code:

```
algorithm NumberNodes(tree)

    ⟨ pre-cond⟩: tree is a binary tree.
    ⟨ post-cond⟩: Returns the number of nodes in the tree.

    begin
        if( tree = emptyTree ) then
            result( 0 )
        else
            result( NumberNodes(leftSub(tree))
                    +NumberNodes(rightSub(tree)) + 1 )
        end if
    end algorithm
```

We have ensured that the algorithm developed works for every valid input instance.

Problem with the Single-Node Base Case: Many people are tempted to use trees with a single node as the base case. A minor problem with this is that it means that the routine no longer works for the empty tree, i.e., the tree with zero nodes. A bigger problem is that the routine no longer works for trees that contain a node with a left child but no right child, or vice versa. This tree is not a base case, because it has more than one node. However, when the routine recurses on the right subtree, the new subinstance consists of the empty tree. The routine, however, no longer works for this tree. See Exercise 10.2.1 for more on this.

Answer for the Empty Tree: A common mistake is to provide the wrong answer for the empty tree. When in doubt as to what answer should be given for the empty tree, consider an instance with the left or right subtree empty. What answer do you need to receive from the empty tree to make this tree's answer correct?

> **Height:** For example, a tree with one node can either be defined to have height 0 or height 1. It is your choice. However, if you say that it has height 0, then be careful when defining the height of the empty tree.

Definition of Binary Search Tree: Another example is that people often say that the empty tree is not a binary search tree (Section 3.1). However, it is. A binary tree fails to be a binary search tree when certain relationships between the nodes exist. Because the empty tree has no nodes, none of these violating conditions exist. Hence, by default it is a binary search tree.

Max: What is the maximum value within an empty list of values? One might think 0 or ∞. However, a better answer is $-\infty$. When adding a new value, one uses the code $newMax = \max(oldMax, newValue)$. Starting with $oldMax = -\infty$ gives the correct answer when the first value is added.

10.1 Tree Traversals

A task one needs to be able to perform on a binary tree is to traverse it, visiting each node once, in one of three defined orders. Before one becomes familiar with recursive programs, one tends to think about computation iteratively, "I visit this node first, then this one, then this one, and so on." Each iteration, the program says "I just visited this node, so now let me find the next node to visit." Surprisingly, such a computation is hard to code. The reason is that binary trees by their very nature have a recursive structure. At the end of this section, I include code that traverses a binary tree in an iterative way, but only to convince you that this is much harder than doing it recursively and should be avoided.

Recursion, on the other hand, provides a very easy and slick algorithm for traversing a binary tree. Such a tree is composed of three parts. There is the root node, its left subtree, and its right subtree. You, being lazy, get one friend to traverse the left and another to traverse the right. You, feeling that you need to do some work yourself, visit the root. The order in which the three of you preform your tasks dictates the order in which the nodes get visited. The three classic orders to visit the nodes of a binary tree are *prefix*, *infix*, and *postfix*, in which the root is visited before, between, or after its left and right subtrees are visited.

algorithm *PreFix* (*tree*))

⟨ **pre-cond**⟩**:** *tree* is a binary tree.
⟨ **post-cond**⟩**:** Visits the nodes in prefix order.

```
begin
    if(tree ≠ emptyTree) then
        put rootInfo(tree)
        PreFix(leftSub(tree))
        PreFix(rightSub(tree))
    end if
end algorithm
```

algorithm *InFix* (*tree*))

⟨ **pre-cond**⟩**:** *tree* is a binary tree.
⟨ **post-cond**⟩**:** Visits the nodes in infix order.

```
begin
    if(tree ≠ emptyTree) then
        InFix(leftSub(tree))
        put rootInfo(tree)
        InFix(rightSub(tree))
    end if
end algorithm
```

algorithm *PostFix* (*tree*))

⟨ ***pre-cond*** ⟩***:*** *tree* is a binary tree.
⟨ ***post-cond*** ⟩***:*** Visits the nodes
in postfix order.

begin
    if(*tree* ≠ *emptyTree*) then
        PostFix(*leftSub*(*tree*))
        PostFix(*rightSub*(*tree*))
        put *rootInfo*(*tree*)
    end if
end algorithm

The following order is produced if you tracing out these computations on the two trees displayed below:

PreFix	InFix	PostFix
5 3 1 2 4 6	1 2 3 4 5 6	2 1 4 3 6 5
* + 3 4 7	3 + 4 * 7	3 4 + 7 *

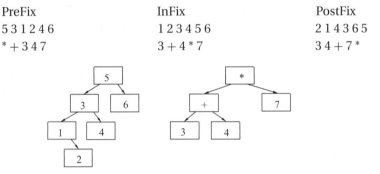

These three orders have different applications. In math the typical order to put operators is infix notation as in $3 + 4 * 7$. However, printed like this produces the wrong order of operations. What is required is $(3 + 4) * 7$. Using pre- and postfix order, the precedence of the operators is correctly determined even without brackets. For this reason, Hewlett Packard's first calculator used postfix notations $3\,4 + 7\,*$. It was called reverse Polish notation after Jan Łukasiewicz, who developed it in the 1920s. These were a bit of a pain, but luckily for me, the technology improved enough by the time I was starting high school in 1977 so that I did not need to use one. However, such calculators still have their partisans, and Hewlett Packard still makes them.

    PreFix visits the nodes in the same order that a depth-first search finds the nodes. See Section 14.4 for the iterative algorithm for doing depth-first search of a more general graph, and Section 14.5 for the recursive version of the algorithm.

    Below is the iterative program for visiting the nodes in infix order. As said, it is needlessly complex and is included only to show you what to avoid.

algorithm *IterativeTraversal*(*tree*)

⟨ ***pre-cond*** ⟩***:*** *tree* is a binary tree. As usual, each node has a value and pointers to the roots of its left and right subtrees. In addition, each node has a pointer to its parent.
⟨ ***post-cond*** ⟩***:*** Does an infix traversal of tree.

begin
    element = *root*(*tree*)   % Current node in traversal
    count = zero   % Current count of nodes
    loop
        ⟨***loop-invariant***⟩***:*** *element* is some node in the tree, and some nodes
        have been visited.
        if(*element* has a left child and it has not been visited) then
                element = leftChild(element)
        elseif(*element* has no left child or its left child have been visited
           and *element* has not been visited) then
                visit *element*
        elseif(*element*'s left subtree and *element* itself has been visited
           and *element* has a right child and it has not been visited) then
                element = *rightChild*(*element*)
        elseif(*element*'s left subtree, *element* itself, and right subtree have been
           visited and *element* has a parent) then
                element = *parent*(*element*)
        elseif(Everything has been visited and *element* is the root of the global
           tree) then
                exit
        end if
    end loop
end algorithm

10.2 Simple Examples

Here is a list of problems involving binary trees.

1.   Return the maximum of data fields of nodes.

2.   Return the height of the tree.

3.   Return the number of leaves in the tree. (A harder one.)

4.   Copy the tree.

Try them first on your own. See Figure 10.1.

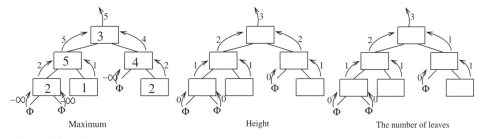

Figure 10.1: The result returned on each subtree is provided.

Maximum: Given a binary tree, your task is to determine its maximum value. The first step is to decide how to create subinstances for your friends. As said, when the input instance is a binary trees, the most natural subinstances are its left and right subtrees. Your friends must solve the same problem that you do. Hence, assume that they provide you with the maximum value within each of these trees. Luckily, the maximum value within a tree is either the maximum on the left, the maximum on the right, or the value at the root. Our only job then is to determine which of these three is the maximum. As described in the beginning of Chapter 10, the maximum of the empty list is $-\infty$.

> **algorithm** *Max(tree)*
>
> ⟨ **pre-cond** ⟩**:** *tree* is a binary tree.
> ⟨ **post-cond** ⟩**:** Returns the maximum of data fields of nodes.
>
> begin
>   if(*tree* = *emptyTree*) then
>   result($-\infty$)
>   else
>   result(*max(Max(leftSub(tree)), Max(rightSub(tree)), rootData(tree))*)
>   end if
> end algorithm

Height: In this problem, your task it to find the height of your binary tree. Again, your friends can easily give you the height of your left and right subtrees. The height of your tree is determined by the deeper of its subtrees. Given their heights, you determine which is deeper and add one to take the root into account. The height of the empty tree is discussed in the beginning of this chapter.

> **algorithm** *Height(tree)*
>
> ⟨ **pre-cond** ⟩**:** *tree* is a binary tree.
> ⟨ **post-cond** ⟩**:** Returns the height of the tree measured in nodes, e.g., a tree with one node has height 1.
>
> begin
>   if(*tree* = *emptyTree*) then
>   result(0)
>   else
>   result(*max(Height(leftSub(tree)), Height(rightSub(tree)))* + 1)
>   end if
> end algorithm

Exercise 10.2.3 considers another version of this algorithm.

Number of Leaves: This problem is harder than the previous ones. We start by considering a tree with both a left an a right subtree. For this, the number of leaves in the entire tree is the sum of the numbers in the left and right subtrees. If the tree has one subtree, but the other is empty, then this same algorithm still works. If the tree is empty, then it has zero leaves. However, if this were all of the code, then the answer returned would always be zero. The case that still needs to be considered is the tree consisting of a root with no children. This root is a leaf. We need to count it.

algorithm *NumberLeaves*(*tree*)

⟨ ***pre-cond***⟩***:*** *tree* is a binary tree.
⟨ ***post-cond***⟩***:*** Returns the number of leaves in the tree.

begin
    if(*tree = emptyTree*) then
        result(0)
    else if(*leftSub*(*tree*) = *emptyTree* and *rightSub*(*tree*) = *emptyTree*) then
        result(1)
    else
        result(*NumberLeaves*(*leftSub*(*tree*)) + *NumberLeaves*(*rightSub*(*tree*)))
    end if
end algorithm

Copy Tree: If you want to make a copy of a tree, you might be tempted to use the code *treeCopy = tree*. However, the effect of this will only be that both the variables *treeCopy* and *tree* refer to the same tree data structure that *tree* originally did. This would be sufficient if you only want to have read access to the data structure from both variables. However, if you want to modify one of the copies, then you need a completely separate copy. To obtain this, the copy routine must allocate memory for each of the nodes in the tree, copy over the information in each node, and link the nodes together in the appropriate way. The following simple recursive algorithm, *treeCopy = Copy*(*tree*), accomplishes this.

algorithm *Copy*(*tree*)

⟨ ***pre-cond***⟩***:*** *tree* is a binary tree.
⟨ ***post-cond***⟩***:*** Returns a copy of the tree.

begin
    if(*tree = emptyTree*) then
        result(*emptyTree*)
    else
        treeCopy = allocate memory for one node
        rootInfo(*treeCopy*) = *rootInfo*(*tree*)   % copy overall data in root node
        leftSub(*treeCopy*) = *Copy*(*leftSub*(*tree*))   % copy left subtree
        rightSub(*treeCopy*) = *Copy*(*rightSub*(*tree*))   % copy right subtree
        result(*treeCopy*)
    end if
end algorithm

EXERCISE 10.2.1 *Many texts that present recursive algorithms for trees do not consider the empty tree to be a valid input instance, but by not considering empty trees the algorithm requires many more cases. Redesign the algorithm of Example 10.1 to return the number of nodes in the input tree without considering the empty tree.*

EXERCISE 10.2.2 *Develop an algorithm that returns the sum of the values within the nodes of a binary tree.*

EXERCISE 10.2.3 *We have given a recursive algorithm for finding the height of a binary tree measured in nodes, e.g., a tree with one node has height 1. Rewrite this algorithm so that the height is measured in edges, e.g., a tree with one node has height 0.*

EXERCISE 10.2.4 *If the computer system does not have garbage collection, then it is the responsibility of the programmer to deallocate the memory used by all the nodes of a tree when the tree is discarded. Develop a recursive algorithm, Deallocate(tree), that accomplishes this. How much freedom is there in the order of the lines of the code?*

EXERCISE 10.2.5 *Develop an algorithm that searches for a key within a binary search tree.*

10.3 Generalizing the Problem Solved

Sometimes when writing a recursive algorithm for a problem it is easier to solve a more general version of the problem, providing more information about the original instance or asking for more information about subinstances. Remember, however, that anything that you ask your friend to do, you must be able to do yourself.

EXAMPLE 10.3.1   **Is the Tree a Binary Search Tree?**

The required algorithm returns whether or not the given tree is a binary search tree (BST).

An Inefficient Algorithm:

    algorithm *IsBSTtree* (*tree*)

    ⟨ *pre-cond* ⟩*:* *tree* is a binary tree.
    ⟨ *post-cond* ⟩*:* The output indicates whether it is a binary search tree.

    begin
        if(*tree* = *emptyTree*) then
            return *Yes*
        else if(*IsBSTtree*(*leftSub*(*tree*)) and *IsBSTtree*(*rightSub*(*tree*))
            and *Max*(*leftSub*(*tree*)) ≤ *rootKey*(*tree*) ≤ *Min*(*rightSub*(*tree*)))then
            return *Yes*

        else

             return *No*

       end if

    end algorithm

Running Time: For each node in the input tree, the above algorithm computes the minimum or the maximum value in the node's left and right subtrees. Though these operations are relatively fast for binary search trees, performing them for each node increases the time complexity of the algorithm, because each node may be traversed by either the *Min* or the *Max* routine many times. Suppose, for example, that the input tree is completely unbalanced, i.e., a single path. For node i, computing the max of its subtree involves traversing to the bottom of the path and takes time $n - i$. Hence, the total running time is $T(n) = \sum_{i=1..n}(n - i) = \Theta(n^2)$. This is far too slow.

Ask for More Information about the Subinstance: It is better to combine the *IsBSTtree* and the *Min* and *Max* routines into one routine so that the tree only needs to be traversed once.

In addition to whether or not the tree is a BST, the routine will return the minimum and the maximum value in the tree. If our instance tree is the empty tree, then we return that it is a BST with minimum value ∞ and with maximum value $-\infty$. (See Section 8.5.) Otherwise, we ask one friend about the left subtree and another about the right. They tell us the minimum and the maximum values of these and whether they are BST. If both subtrees are BSTs and $leftMax \le rootKey(tree) \le rightMin$, then our tree is a BST. Our minimum value is $min(leftMin, rightMin, rootKey(tree))$, and our maximum value is $max(leftMax, rightMax, rootKey(tree))$.

    algorithm *IsBSTtree* (*tree*)

    ⟨ **pre-cond**⟩*: tree* is a binary tree.

    ⟨ **post-cond**⟩*:* The output indicates whether it is a BST. It also gives the minimum and the maximum values in the tree.

    begin

        if(*tree* = *emptyTree*) then

            return ⟨*Yes*, ∞, $-\infty$⟩

        else

            ⟨*leftIs,leftMin,leftMax*⟩ = *IsBSTtree*(*leftSub*(*tree*))

            ⟨*rightIs,rightMin,rightMax*⟩ = *IsBSTtree*(*rightSub*(*tree*))

            min = min(*leftMin, rightMin, rootKey*(*tree*))

            max = max(*leftMax, rightMax, rootKey*(*tree*))

            if(*leftIs* and *rightIs* and *leftMax* $\le$ *rootKey*(*tree*) $\le$ *rightMin*) then

                isBST = Yes

            else

                isBST = No

```
                end if
                return ⟨isBST, min, max⟩
            end if
        end algorithm
```

You might ask why the left friend provides the minimum of the left subtree even though it is not used. There are two related reasons. First, the postconditions require her to do so. You can change the postconditions if you like, but whatever contract is made, everyone needs to keep it. Second, the left friend does not know that she is the left friend. All she knows is that she is given a tree as input. The algorithm designer must not assume that the friend knows anything about the context in which she is solving her problem other than what she is passed within the input instance.

Provide More Information about the Original Instance: Another elegant algorithm for the *IsBST* problem generalizes the problem in order to provide your friend more information about your subinstance. Here the more general problem, in addition to the tree, will provide a range of values [*min,max*] and ask whether the tree is a BST with values within this range. The original problem is solved using *IsBSTtree*(*tree*, $[-\infty, \infty]$).

algorithm *IsBSTtree* (*tree*, [*min,max*])

⟨ *pre-cond*⟩: *tree* is a binary tree. In addition, [*min, max*] is a range of values.
⟨ *post-cond*⟩: The output indicates whether it is a BST with values within this range.

```
begin
    if(tree = emptyTree) then
        return Yes
    else if(   rootKey(tree) ∈ [min, max] and
               IsBSTtree( leftSub(tree), [min,rootKey(tree)]) and
               IsBSTtree( rightSub(tree),[rootKey(tree),max]) then
        return Yes
    else
        return No
    end if
end algorithm
```

EXERCISE 10.3.1 *(See solution in Part Five.) Write a recursive program that takes a BST and an integer k as input and returns the kth smallest element in the tree. Recall that all the nodes in the left subtree are smaller than the root and all those in the right are larger.*

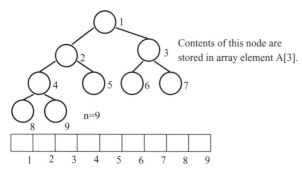

Contents of this node are
stored in array element A[3].

Figure 10.2: The mapping between the nodes in a balanced binary tree and the elements of an array.

10.4 Heap Sort and Priority Queues

Heap sort is a fast sorting algorithm that is easy to implement. Like quick sort, it has the advantage of being done in place in memory, whereas merge and radix–counting sorts require an auxiliary array of memory to transfer the data to. I include heap sort in this chapter because it is implemented using recursion within a tree data structure.

Completely Balanced Binary Tree: We will visualize the values being sorted as stored in a binary tree that is completely balanced, i.e., every level of the tree is completely full except for the bottom level, which is filled in from the left.

Array Implementation of a Balanced Binary Tree: Because the tree always has this balanced shape, we do not have to bother with the overhead of having nodes with pointers. In actuality, the values are stored in a simple array $A[1, n]$. See Figure 10.2. The mapping between the visualized tree structure and the actual array structure is done by indexing the nodes of the tree $1, 2, 3, \ldots, n$, starting with the root of the tree and filling each level in from left to right.

- The root is stored in $A[1]$.
- The parent of $A[i]$ is $A[\lfloor \frac{i}{2} \rfloor]$.
- The left child of $A[i]$ is $A[2 \cdot i]$.
- The right child of $A[i]$ is $A[2 \cdot i + 1]$.
- The node in the far right of the bottom level is stored in $A[n]$.
- If $2i + 1 > n$, then the node does not have a right child.

Definition of a Heap: A heap imposes a partial order (see Section 14.6) on the set of values, requiring that the value of each node be greater than or equal to that of each of the node's children. There are no rules about whether the left or the right child is larger. See Figure 10.3.

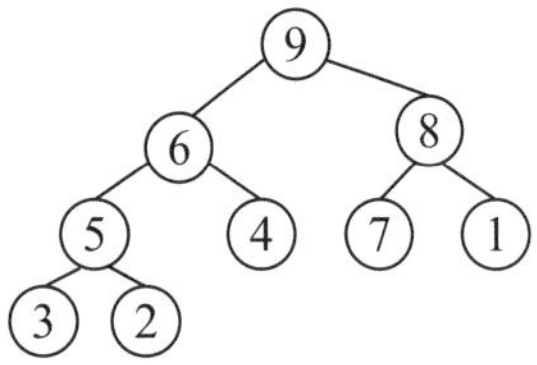

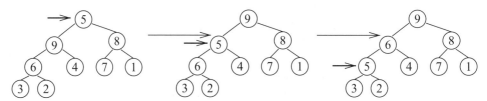

Figure 10.3: *An example of nodes ordered into a heap.*

142

Maximum at Root: An implication of the heap rules is that the root contains the maximum value. The maximum may appear repeatedly in other places as well.

Exercise 10.4.1 gives you more practice understanding this definition.

The Heapify Problem:

Specifications:

Precondition: The input is a balanced binary tree such that its left and right subtrees are heaps. (That is, it is a heap except that its root might not be larger than that of its children.)

Postcondition: Its values are rearranged in place to make it complete heap.

Recursive Algorithm: The first task in making this tree into a heap is to put its maximum value at the root. See Figure 10.4. Because the left and right subtrees are heaps, the maxima of these trees are at their roots. Hence, the maximum of the entire tree is either at the root, at its left child node, or at its right child node. You find the maximum among these three. If the maximum is at the root, then you are finished. Otherwise, for the purpose of discussion, assume that the maximum is in the root's left child. Swap this maximum value with that of the root. The root and the right subtree now form a heap, but the left subtree might not. You will give the subtask of making your left subtree into a heap to a recursive friend. Before you can do this, you need to make sure that this subinstance meets the preconditions of the problem. By our precondition, our left subtree was a heap when we received it. We changed its root. After this change, it still has the property that its left and right subtrees are heaps. Hence, the preconditions of our problem are met and you can give your left subtree to your friend. By the postcondition, the friend makes this subtree into a heap. Your entire tree is now a heap.

Figure 10.4: *An example computation of* Heapify.

Code:

algorithm *Heapify(r)*

⟨ *pre-cond* ⟩*:* The balanced binary tree rooted at $A[r]$ is such that its left and right subtrees are heaps.

⟨ *post-cond* ⟩*:* Its values are rearranged in place to make it complete heap.

begin
    if($A[rightchild(r)]$ is max of $\{A[r], A[rightchild(r)],$
    $A[leftchild(r)]\}$) then
        swap($A[r], A[rightchild(r)]$)
        Heapify(rightchild(r))
    elseif($A[leftchild(r)]$ is max of $\{A[r], A[rightchild(r)],$
    $A[leftchild(r)]\}$) then
        swap($A[r], A[leftchild(r)]$)
        Heapify(leftchild(r))
    else % $A[r]$ is max of $\{A[r], A[rightchild(r)], A[leftchild(r)]\}$
        exit
    end if
end algorithm

Running Time: $T(n) = 1 \cdot T(n/2) + \Theta(1)$. From Chapter 27 we know that $\frac{\log a}{\log b} = \frac{\log 1}{\log 2} = 0$ and $f(n) = \Theta(n^0)$, so $c = 0$. Because $\frac{\log a}{\log b} = c$, we conclude that time is dominated by all levels and $T(n) = \Theta(f(n) \log n) = \Theta(\log n)$.

Because this algorithm recurses only once per call, it can easily be made into an iterative algorithm.

Iterative Algorithm: A good loop invariant would be "The entire tree is a heap except that node i might not be greater or equal to both of its children. As well, the value of i's parent is at least the value of i and of i's children." When i is the root, this is the precondition. The algorithm proceeds as in the recursive algorithm. Node i follows one path down the tree to a leaf. When i is a leaf, the whole tree is a heap.

Code:

algorithm *Heapify(r)*

⟨ *pre-cond* ⟩*:* The balanced binary tree rooted at $A[r]$ is such that its left and right subtrees are heaps.

⟨ *post-cond* ⟩*:* Its values are rearranged in place to make it complete heap.

begin
    $i = r$
    loop

⟨*loop-invariant*⟩*:* The entire tree rooted at $A[r]$ is a heap except that node i might not be greater or equal to both of its children. As well, the value of i's parent is at least the value of i and of i's children.

exit when i is a leaf
if($A[rightchild(i)]$ is max of $\{A[i], A[rightchild(i)]$,)
$A[leftchild(i)]\}$ then
 swap($A[i], A[rightchild(i)]$)
 $i = rightchild(i)$
elseif($A[leftchild(i)]$ is max of $\{A[i], A[rightchild(i)]$,
$A[leftchild(i)]\}$) then
 swap($A[i], A[leftchild(i)]$)
 $i = leftchild(i)$
else % $A[i]$ is max of $\{A[i], A[rightchild(i)], A[leftchild(i)]\}$
 exit
end if
 end loop
end algorithm

Running Time: $T(n) = \Theta(\text{height of tree}) = \Theta(\log n)$.

The MakeHeap Problem:

Specifications:

Precondition: The input is an array of numbers, which can be viewed as a balanced binary tree of numbers.

Postcondition: Its values are rearranged in place to make it heap.

Recursive Algorithm: The obvious recursive algorithm is to recursively make $\lceil \frac{n-1}{2} \rceil$ of the numbers into a heap, make another $\lfloor \frac{n-1}{2} \rfloor$ into a heap, and put the remaining number at the root of a tree with these two heaps as children. This now meets the precondition for *Heapify*, which turns the whole thing into a heap.

Running Time: $T(n) = 2T(\frac{n}{2}) + \Theta(\log n)$. Again from Chapter 27, $\frac{\log a}{\log b} = \frac{\log 2}{\log 2} = 1$ and $f(n) = \Theta(n^0 \log n)$, so $c = 0$. Because $\frac{\log a}{\log b} > c$, we conclude that time is dominated the base cases and $T(n) = \Theta(n^{\log a/\log b}) = \Theta(n)$.

The structure of the recursive tree for this algorithm is very predictable, so it can easily be made into an iterative algorithm, which calls *Heapify* on exactly the same nodes though in a slightly different order.

Iterative Algorithm: See Figure 10.5. The loop invariant is that all subtrees of height i are heaps. Initially, the leaves of height $i = 1$ are already heaps. Suppose that all subtrees of height i are heaps. The subtrees of height $i + 1$ have the

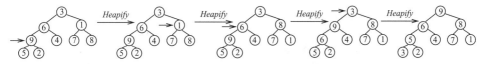

Figure 10.5: An example of the iterative version of *MakeHeap*.

property that their left and right subtrees are heaps. Hence, we can use *Heapify* to make them into heaps. This maintains the loop invariant while increasing i by one. The postcondition clearly follows from the loop invariant and the exit condition that $i = \log n$.

Code:

algorithm *MakeHeap*( )

⟨ **pre-cond**⟩: The input is an array of numbers, which can be viewed as a balanced binary tree of numbers.

⟨ **post-cond**⟩: Its values are rearranged in place to make it a heap.

begin
    loop $k = \lfloor \frac{n}{2} \rfloor, \lfloor \frac{n}{2} \rfloor - 1, \lfloor \frac{n}{2} \rfloor - 2, \ldots, 2, 1$
        Heapify(k)
    end loop
end algorithm

Running Time: The number of subtrees of height i is $2^{(\log n)-i}$, because each such tree has its root at level $(\log n) - i$ in the tree. Each take $\Theta(i)$ to heapify. This gives a total time of $T(n) = \sum_{i=1}^{\log n}(2^{(\log n)-i})i$. This sum is geometric. Hence, its total is theta of its maximum term. The first term with $i = 1$ is $(2^{(\log n)-i})i = \Theta(2^{\log n}) = \Theta(n)$. The last term with $i = \log n$ is $(2^{(\log n)-i})i = (2^0)\log n = \log n$. The first term is the biggest, giving a total time of $\Theta(n)$. See Chapter 26 for more on approximation summations.

The HeapSort Problem:

Specifications:

Precondition: The input is an array of numbers.

Postcondition: Its values are rearranged in place to be in sorted order.

Algorithm: The loop invariant is that for some $i \in [0, n]$, the $n - i$ largest elements have been removed and are sorted on the side, and the remaining i elements form a heap. See Figures 10.6 and 10.7. The loop invariant is established for $i = n$ by forming a heap from the numbers using the *MakeHeap* algorithm. When $i = 0$, the values are sorted.

Suppose that the loop invariant is true for i. The maximum of the remaining values is at the root of the heap. Remove it and put it in its sorted place on the left

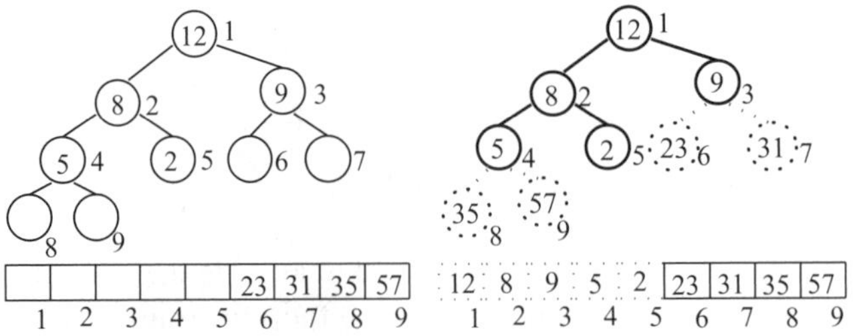

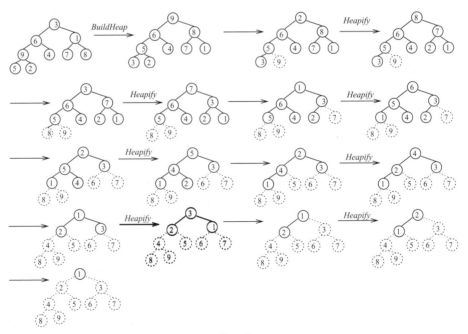

Figure 10.6: The left diagram shows the loop invariant with $n - i = 9 - 5 = 4$ of the largest elements in the array and the remaining $i = 5$ elements forming a heap. The right diagram emphasizes the fact that though a heap is viewed as being stored in a tree, it is actually implemented in an array. When some of the elements are in still in the tree and some are in the array, these views overlap.

end of the sorted list. Take the bottom right-hand element of the heap, and fill the newly created hole at the root. This maintains the correct shape of the tree. The tree now has the property that its left and right subtrees are heaps. Hence, you can use *Heapify* to make it into a heap. This maintains the loop invariant while decreasing i by one.

Array Implementation: The heap sort can occur in place within the array. As the heap gets smaller, the array entries on the right become empty. These can be used to store the sorted list that is on the side. Putting the root element where it

Figure 10.7: An example computation of *HeapSort*.

belongs, putting the bottom left element at the root, and decreasing the size of the heap can be accomplished by swapping the elements at $A[1]$ and at $A[i]$ and decrementing i.

Code:

```
algorithm HeapSort( )
```

⟨ *pre-cond*⟩: The input is an array of numbers.
⟨ *post-cond*⟩: Its values are rearranged in place to be in sorted order.

```
begin
    MakeHeap( )
    i = n
    loop
        ⟨loop-invariant⟩: The n − i largest elements have been re-
        moved and are sorted in A[i + 1, n], and the remaining i ele-
        ments form a heap in A[1, i].
        exit when i = 1
        swap(A[root], A[i])
        i = i − 1
        Heapify(root)      % On a heap of size i.
    end loop
end algorithm
```

Running Time: *MakeHeap* takes $\Theta(n)$ time, heapifying a tree of size i takes time $\log(i)$, for a total of $T(n) = \Theta(n) + \sum_{i=n}^{1} \log i$. This sum behaves like an arithmetic sum. Hence, its total is n times its maximum value, i.e., $\Theta(n \log n)$.

Common Mistakes When Describing These Algorithms: Statements that are *always* true, such as "The root is the max of any heap," give no information about the state of the program within the loop. For *Heapify*, "The left subtree and the right subtree of the current node are heaps" is useful. However, in the end the subtree becomes a leaf, at which point this loop invariant does not tell you that the whole tree is a heap. For *HeapSort*, "The tree is a heap" is good, but how do you get a sorted list from this in the end? Do not run routines without making sure that their preconditions are met, such as having *HeapSort* call *Heapify* without being sure that the left and right subtrees of the given node are heaps.

Priority Queues: Like stacks and queues, priority queues are an important ADT.

Definition: A *priority queue* consists of:

Data: A set of elements, each of which is associated with an integer that is referred to as the *priority* of the element.

Operations:

Insert an Element: An element, along with its priority, is added to the queue. Coding this is left for Exercise 10.4.2.

Change Priority: The priority of an element already in the queue is changed. The routine is passed a pointer to the element within the priority queue and its new priority. Coding this is left for Exercise 10.4.3.

Remove an Element: Removes and returns an element of the highest priority from the queue.

Implementations:

Implementation	Insert Time	Change Time	Remove Time
Sorted in an array or linked list by priority	$O(n)$	$O(n)$	$O(1)$
Unsorted in an array or linked list separate queue for each priority level	$O(1)$	$O(1)$	$O(n)$
(To add, go to correct queue; to delete, find first nonempty queue)	$O(1)$	$O(1)$	$O(\text{No. of priorities})$
Heaps	$O(\log n)$	$O(\log n)$	$O(\log n)$

Heap Implementation: The elements of a priority queue are stored in a heap ordered according to the priority of the elements.

Operations:

Remove an Element: The element of the highest priority is at the top of the heap. It can be removed, and the heap then should be reheapified as done in *HeapSort*.

Insert an Element: Place the new element in the lower right corner of the heap, and then bubble it up the heap until it finds the correct place according to its priority.

Change Priority: The routine is passed a pointer to the element whose priority is changing. After making the change, this element is bubbled either up or down the heap, depending on whether the priority has increased or decreased.

EXERCISE 10.4.1 *(See solution in Part Five.)* *Consider a heap storing the values* $1, 2, 3, \ldots, 15$.

1. *Where in the heap can the value* 1 *go?*
2. *Which values can be stored in entry* $A[2]$?
3. *Where in the heap can the value* 15 *go?*
4. *Where in the heap can the value* 6 *go?*

EXERCISE 10.4.2 *Design an algorithm to insert a new element into the heap implementation of the priority queue.*

EXERCISE 10.4.3 *Design an algorithm to change the priority of an element in the heap implementation of the priority queue.*

10.5 Representing Expressions with Trees

We will now consider how to represent multivariate expressions using binary trees. We will develop the algorithms to evaluate, copy, differentiate, simplify, and print such an expression. Though these are seemingly complex problems, they have simple recursive solutions.

Recursive Definition of an Expression:
- Single variables x, y, and z and single real values are themselves expressions.
- If f and g are expressions, then $f + g$, $f - g$, $f * g$, and f/g are also expressions.

Tree Data Structure: The recursive definition of an expression directly mirrors that of a binary tree. Because of this, a binary tree is a natural data structure for storing an expression. (Conversely, you can use an expression to represent a binary tree.)

EXAMPLE 10.5.1 **Evaluate Expression**

This routine evaluates an expression that is represented by a tree. For example, it can evaluate $f = x * (y + 7)$, with $xvalue = 2$, $yvalue = 3$, and $zvalue = 5$, and return $2 * (3 + 7) = 20$.

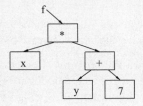

EXAMPLE 10.5.1   **Evaluate Expression** (cont.)

Code:

    algorithm *Eval*(*f, xvalue, yvalue, zvalue*)

    ⟨ *pre-cond* ⟩: *f* is an expression whose only variables are *x*, *y*, and *z*, and *xvalue*, *yvalue*, and *zvalue* are the three real values to assign to these variables.
    ⟨ *post-cond* ⟩: The returned value is the evaluation of the expression at these values for *x*, *y*, and *z*. The expression is unchanged.

    begin
        if(*f* = a real value) then
            result(*f*)
        else if(*f* = "*x*") then
            result(*xvalue*)
        else if(*f* = "*y*") then
            result(*yvalue*)
        else if(*f* = "*z*") then
            result(*zvalue*)
        else if(*rootOp*(*f*) = "+") then
            result(*Eval*(*leftSub*(*tree*), *xvalue, yvalue, zvalue*)
                + *Eval*(*rightSub*(*tree*), *xvalue, yvalue, zvalue*))
        else if(*rootOp*(*f*) = "−") then
            result(*Eval*(*leftSub*(*tree*), *xvalue, yvalue, zvalue*)
               − *Eval*(*rightSub*(*tree*), *xvalue, yvalue, zvalue*))
        else if(*rootOp*(*f*) = "*") then
            result(*Eval*(*leftSub*(*tree*), *xvalue, yvalue, zvalue*)
               × *Eval*(*rightSub*(*tree*), *xvalue, yvalue, zvalue*))
        else if(*rootOp*(*f*) = "/") then
            result(*Eval*(*leftSub*(*tree*), *xvalue, yvalue, zvalue*)
               / *Eval*(*rightSub*(*tree*), *xvalue, yvalue, zvalue*))
        end if
    end algorithm

EXAMPLE 10.5.2   **Differentiate Expression**

This routine computes the derivative of a given expression with respect to an indicated variable.

Specification:

Preconditions: The input consists of ⟨*f*, *x*⟩, where *f* is an expression represented by a tree and *x* is a string giving the name of a variable.

Postconditions: The output is the derivative $f' = df/dx$. This derivative should be an expression represented by a tree whose nodes are separate from those of *f*. The data structure *f* should remain unchanged. See Figure 10.8.

Coding this is left for Exercise 10.5.1, and tracing it for Exercise 10.5.2.

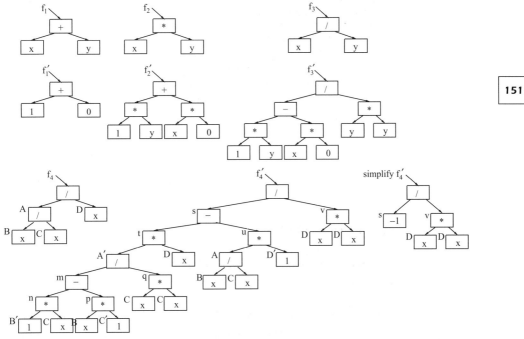

Figure 10.8: Four functions and their derivatives. The fourth derivative has been simplified.

EXAMPLE 10.5.3   Simplify Expression

This routine simplifies a given expression. For example, the derivative of $x * y$ with respect to x will be computed to be $1 * y + x * 0$. This should be simplified to y.

Specification:

Preconditions: The input consists of an expression f represented by a tree.

Postconditions: The output is another expression that is a simplification of f. Its nodes should be separate from those of f, and f should remain unchanged.

Code:

algorithm *Simplify*(f)

⟨ *pre-cond*⟩: f is an expression.
⟨ *post-cond*⟩: The output is a simplification of this expression.

begin
    if(f = a real value or a single variable) then
        result(*Copy*(f))
    else % f is of the form (g' op h')
        g = *Simplify*(*leftSub*(f))
        h = *Simplify*(*rightSub*(f))

EXAMPLE 10.5.3 **Simplify Expression** (cont.)

        if(one of the following forms applies:

$1 * h = h$	$g * 1 = g$	$0 * h = 0$	$g * 0 = 0$
$0 + h = h$	$g + 0 = g$	$g - 0 = g$	$x - x = 0$
$0/h = 0$	$g/1 = g$	$g/0 = \infty$	$x/x = 1$
$6 * 2 = 12$	$6/2 = 3$	$6 + 2 = 8$	$6 - 2 = 4$

) then

            result(the simplified form)

      else

            result(g op h)

      end if

    end if

  end algorithm

This is traced out in Exercise 10.5.3.

EXERCISE 10.5.1 *(See solution in Part Five.) Describe the algorithm for the derivative. Do not give the complete code. Only give the key ideas.*

EXERCISE 10.5.2 *Trace out the execution of the derivative algorithm on the instance $f = (x/x)/x$ given above. In other words, draw a tree with a box for each time a routine is called. For each box, include only the function f passed and derivative returned.*

EXERCISE 10.5.3 *(See solution in Part Five.) Trace out the execution of Simplify on the derivative f' obtained in Exercise 10.5.1, where $f = (x/x)/x$. In other words, draw a tree with a box for each time a routine is called. For each box, include only the function f passed and the simplified expression returned.*

11 Recursive Images

Recursion can be used to construct very complex and beautiful pictures. We begin by combining the same two fixed images recursively over and over again. This produces fractal-like images whose substructures are identical to the whole. Next we will generate random mazes by using randomness to slightly modify these two images so that the substructures are not identical.

11.1 Drawing a Recursive Image from a Fixed Recursive and a Base Case Image

Drawing an Image: An image is specified by a set of lines, circles, and arcs and by two points A and B that are referred to as the *handles*. Before such an image can be drawn on the screen, its location, size, and orientation on the screen need to be specified. We will do this by specifying two points A and B on the screen. Then a simple program can translate, rotate, scale, and draw the image on the screen in such a way that the two handle points of the image land on these two specified points on the screen.

Specifying a Recursive Image: A recursive image is specified by the following:

1. a *base case* image

2. a *recurse* image

3. a set of places within the recurse image to recurse

4. the two points A and B on the screen at which the recursive image should be drawn.

5. an integer n.

The Base Case: If $n = 1$, then the base case image is drawn.

(a)   (b)

Figure 11.1: (a) Man recursively framed; (b) rotating square.

Recursing: If $n > 1$, then the recursive image is drawn on the screen at the location specified. Included in the recursive image are a number of *places to recurse*. These are each depicted by an arrow, —> >—. When the recursive image is translated, rotated, scaled, and drawn on the screen, these arrows are located somewhere on the screen. The arrows themselves are not drawn. Instead, the same picture is drawn recursively at these locations, but with the value $n - 1$.

Examples:

Man Recursively Framed: See Figure 11.1.a. The base case for this construction consists of a happy face. When $n = 1$, this face is drawn. The recursive image consists of a man holding a frame. There is one place to recurse within the frame. Hence, when $n = 2$, this man is drawn with the $n = 1$ happy face inside it. For $n = 3$, the man is holding a frame containing the $n = 2$ image of a man holding a framed $n = 1$ happy face. The recursive image provided is with $n = 5$. It consists of a man holding a picture of a man holding a picture of a man holding a picture of ... a face. In general, the recursive image for n contains $R(n) = R(n - 1) + 1 = n - 1$ men and $B(n) = B(n - 1) = 1$ happy faces.

Rotating Square: See Figure 11.1.b. This image is constructed similarly to the previous one. Here, however, the $n = 1$ base case consists of a circle. The recursive image consists of a single square with the $n - 1$ image shrunk and rotated within it. The squares continue to spiral inward until the base case is reached.

Birthday Cake: See Figure 11.2. The birthday cake recursive image is different in that it recurses in two places. The $n = 1$ base case consists of a single circle. The recursive image consists of a single line with two smaller copies of the $n - 1$ image drawn above it. In general, the recursive image for n contains $R(n) =$

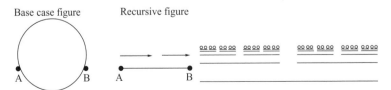

Figure 11.2: Birthday cake.

Leaf Figure

Base case figure   Non-base-case figure

Figure 11.3: Leaf.

$2R(n-1) + 1 = 2^{n-1} - 1$ lines from the recursive image and $B(n) = 2B(n-1) = 2^{n-1}$ circles from the base case image.

Leaf: See Figure 11.3. A leaf consists of a single stem plus eight subleaves along it. Each subleaf is an $n-1$ leaf. The base case image is empty, and the recursive image consists of the stem plus the eight places to recurse. Hence, the $n = 1$ image is blank. The $n = 2$ image consists of a lone stem. The $n = 3$ image is a stem with eight stems for leaves, and so on. In general, the recursive image for n contains $R(n) = 8R(n-1) + 1 = \frac{1}{7}(8^{n-1} - 1)$ stems from the recursive image.

Fractal: See Figure 11.4. This recursive image is a classic. The base case is a single line. The recursive image is empty except for four places to recurse. Hence, $n = 1$ consists of the line. $n = 2$ consists of four lines, forming a line with an equilateral triangle jutting out of it. As n becomes large, the image becomes a snowflake. It is a fractal in that every piece of it looks like a copy of the whole.

The classic way to construct it is slightly different than done here. In the classical method, we are allowed the following operation. Given a line, divide it into three equal parts. Replace the middle part with the two equal-length lines forming an equilateral triangle. Starting with a single line, construct the fractal by repeatedly applying this operation to all the lines that appear.

In general, the recursive image for n contains $B(n) = 4B(n-1) = 4^{n-1}$ base case lines. The length of each of these lines is $L(n) = \frac{1}{3}L(n-1) = \left(\frac{1}{3}\right)^{n-1}$. The total length of all these lines is $B(n) \cdot L(n) = \left(\frac{4}{3}\right)^{n-1}$. As n approaches infinity, the fractal becomes a curve of infinite length.

Three–four figure

Base case figure   Non-base-case figure

Figure 11.4: Fractal.

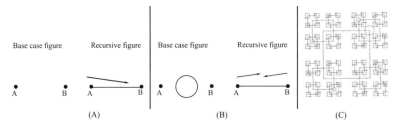

Figure 11.5: Three more examples.

EXERCISE 11.1.1 *(See solution in Part Five.) See Figure 11.5.a. Construct the recursive image that arises from the base case and recursive image for some large n. Describe what is happening.*

EXERCISE 11.1.2 *(See solution in Part Five.) See Figure 11.5.b. Construct the recursive image that arises from the base case and recursive image for some large n. Note that one of the places to recurse is pointing opposite the other. To line the image up with these arrows, the image must be rotated 180°. The image cannot be flipped.*

EXERCISE 11.1.3 *See Figure 11.5.c. This construction looks simple enough. The difficulty is keeping track of at which corners the circle is. Construct the base case and the recursive image from which the given recursive image arises. Describe what is happening.*

11.2 Randomly Generating a Maze

We will use similar methods to generate a random maze. The maze M will be represented by an $n \times m$ two-dimensional array with entries from {*brick, floor, cheese*}. Walls consist of lines of bricks. A mouse will be able to move along floor squares in any of the eight directions. The maze generated will not contain corridors as such, but only many small rectangular rooms. Each room will either have one door in one corner of the room or two doors in opposite corners. The *cheese* will be placed in a room that is chosen randomly from among the rooms that are far enough from the start location.

Precondition: The routine *AddWalls* is passed a matrix representing the maze as constructed so far and the coordinates of a room within it. The room will have a surrounding wall except for one door in one of its corners. The room will be empty of walls. The routine is also passed a flag indicating whether or not cheese should be added somewhere in the room.

Postcondition: The output is the same maze with a randomly chosen submaze added within the indicated room and cheese added as appropriate.

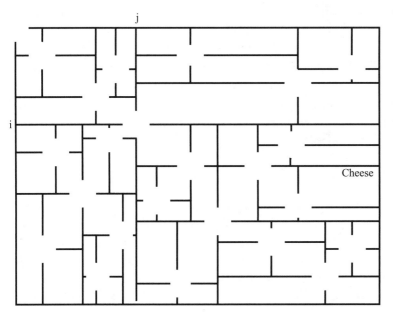

Figure 11.6: A maze containing cheese.

Initial Conditions: To meet the preconditions of *AddWalls*, the main routine first constructs the four outer walls with the top right corner square left as a floor tile to act as a door into the maze and as the start square for the mouse. Calling *AddWalls* on this single room completes the maze.

Subinstances: If the indicated room has height and width of at least 3, then the routine *AddWalls* will choose a single location (i, j) uniformly at random from all those in the room that are not right next to one of its outer walls. (The (i, j) chosen by the top stack frame in Figure 11.6 is indicated.) A wall is added within the room all the way across row i and all the way down column j, subdividing the room into four smaller rooms. To act as a door connecting these four rooms, the square at location (i, j) remains a floor tile. See Figure 11.7. Then four friends are asked to fill a maze into each of these four smaller rooms. If our room is to have cheese, then one of the three rooms not containing the door to our room is selected to contain the cheese.

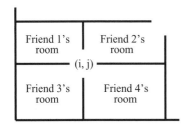

Figure 11.7: Partitioning a room of the maze.

Running Time: The time required to construct an $n \times n$ maze is $\Theta(n^2)$. This can be seen two ways. For the easy way, note that a brick is added at most once to any entry of the matrix and that there are $\Theta(n^2)$ entries. The hard way solves the recurrence relation $T(n) = 4T(n/2) + \Theta(n) = \Theta(n^2)$.

Searching the Maze: One way of representing a maze is by a graph. Chapter 14 presents a number of iterative algorithms for searching a graph. Section 14.5 presents the recursive version of the depth-first search algorithm. All of these could be used by a mouse to find the cheese.

EXERCISE 11.2.1 *Write the code for generating a maze of rooms.*

EXERCISE 11.2.2 *Tiling: The precondition to the problem is that you are given three integers $\langle n, i, j \rangle$, where i and j are in the range 1 to 2^n. You have a 2^n by 2^n square board of squares. You have a sufficient number of tiles each with the shape⌐. Your goal is to place nonoverlapping tiles on the board to cover each of the $2^n \times 2^n$ tiles except for the single square at location $\langle i, j \rangle$. Give a recursive algorithm for this problem in which you place one tile yourself and then have four friends help you. What is your base case?*

12 Parsing with Context-Free Grammars

An important computer science problem is parsing a string according a given context-free grammar. A *context-free grammar* is a means of describing which strings of characters are contained within a particular language. It consists of a set of rules and a start *nonterminal* symbol. Each rule specifies one way of replacing a nonterminal symbol in the current string with a string of terminal and nonterminal symbols. When the resulting string consists only of terminal symbols, we stop. We say that any such resulting string has been *generated* by the grammar.

Context-free grammars are used to understand both the syntax and the semantics of many very useful languages, such as mathematical expressions, Java, and English. The *syntax* of a language indicates which strings of tokens are valid sentences in that language. The *semantics* of a language involves the meaning associated with strings. In order for a compiler or natural-language recognizers to determine what a string means, it must *parse* the string. This involves deriving the string from the grammar and, in doing so, determining which parts of the string are noun phrases, verb phrases, expressions, and terms.

Some context-free grammars have a property called *look ahead one*. Strings from such grammars can be parsed in linear time by what I consider to be one of the most amazing and magical recursive algorithms. This algorithm is presented in this chapter. It demonstrates very clearly the importance of working within the friends level of abstraction instead of tracing out the stack frames: Carefully write the specifications for each program, believe by magic that the programs work, write the programs calling themselves as if they already work, and make sure that as you recurse, the instance being input gets smaller.

In Section 19.8 we will analyze an elegant dynamic programming algorithm that parses a string from any context-free grammar, not just look ahead one, in $\Theta(n^3)$ time.

The Grammar: We will look at a very simple grammar that considers expressions over $\times$ and $+$. In this grammar, a *factor* is either a simple integer or a more complex expression within brackets; a *term* is one or more factors multiplied together; and an *expression* is one or more terms added together. More precisely:

$$\text{exp} \Rightarrow \text{term}$$
$$\Rightarrow \text{term} + \text{term} + \ldots + \text{term}$$

$$\text{term} \Rightarrow \text{fact}$$
$$\Rightarrow \text{fact} * \text{fact} * \cdots * \text{fact}$$

$$\text{fact} \Rightarrow \text{int}$$
$$\Rightarrow (\text{exp})$$

Nonterminals, Terminals, and Rules: More generally, a grammar is defined by a set of *nonterminals*, a set of *terminals*, a *start nonterminal*, and a set of rules. Here the nonterminals are 'exp,' 'term,' and 'fact.' The terminals are integers, the character '+,' and the character '*'. The start nonterminal is 'exp.' The preceding display gives the list of rules for this grammar.

A Derivation of a String: A grammar defines a *language* of strings that can be derived in the following way. A derivation of a string starts with the start symbol (a nonterminal). Then each rule, like those just given, says that you can replace the nonterminal on the left with the string of terminals and nonterminals on the right.

A Parsing of an Expression: Let s be a string consisting of terminals. A parsing of this string is a tree. Each internal node of the tree is labeled with a nonterminal symbol, and the root with the start nonterminal. Each internal node must correspond to a rule of the grammar. For example, for rule $A \Rightarrow BC$, the node is labeled A and its two children are labeled B and C. The leaves of the tree, read left to right, give the input string s of terminals. Figure 12.1 is an example.

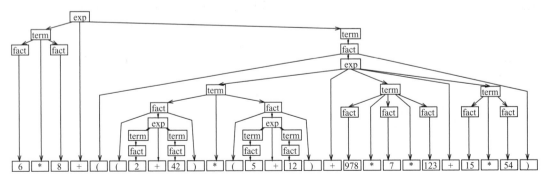

Figure 12.1: A parse tree for the string $s = 6 * 8 + ((2 + 42) * (5 + 12) + 987 * 7 * 123 + 15 * 54)$.

The Parsing Abstract Data Type: The following is an example where it is useful not to give the full implementation details of an abstract data type. If fact, we will even leave the specification of parsing structure open for the implementer to decide.

For our purposes, we will only say the following: When p is a variable of type parsing, we will use "$p = 5$" to indicate that it is assigned a parsing of the expression '5.' We will go on to *overload* the operations $*$ and $+$ as operations that join two parsings into one. For example, if p_1 is a parsing of the expression '$2 * 3$' and p_2 of '$5 * 7$', then we will use $p = p_1 + p_2$ to denote a parsing of the expression '$2 * 3$' $+ 5 * 7$.

The implementer defines the structure of a parsing by specifying in more detail what these operations do. For example, if the implementer wants a parsing to be a binary tree representing the expression, then $p_1 + p_2$ would be the operation of constructing a binary tree with the root being a new '$+$' node, the left subtree being the binary tree p_1, and the right subtree being the binary tree p_2. On the other hand, if the implementer wants a parsing to be simply an integer evaluation of the expression, then $p_1 + p_2$ would be the integer sum of the integers p_1 and p_2.

Specifications for the Parsing Algorithm:

Precondition: The input consists of a string of tokens s. The possible tokens are the characters '$*$' and '$+$' and arbitrary integers. The tokens are indexed as $s[1], s[2], s[3], \ldots, s[n]$.

Postcondition: If the input is a valid *expression* generated by the grammar, then the output is a *parsing* of the expression. Otherwise, an error message is output.

The algorithm consists of one routine for each nonterminal of the grammar: *GetExp*, *GetTerm*, and *GetFact*.

Specifications for *GetExp*:

Precondition: The input of *GetExp* consists of a string s of tokens and an index i that indicates a starting point within s.

Postcondition: The output consists of a parsing of the longest substring $s[i]$, $s[i + 1], \ldots, s[j - 1]$ of s that starts at index i and is a valid expression. The output also includes the index j of the token that comes immediately after the parsed expression.

If there is no valid expression starting at $s[i]$, then an error message is output.

The specifications for *GetTerm* and *GetFact* are the same as for *GetExp*, except that they return the parsing of the longest term or factor starting at $s[i]$ and ending at $s[j - 1]$.

Examples of *GetExp*, *GetTerm*, and *GetFact*: See Figure 12.2

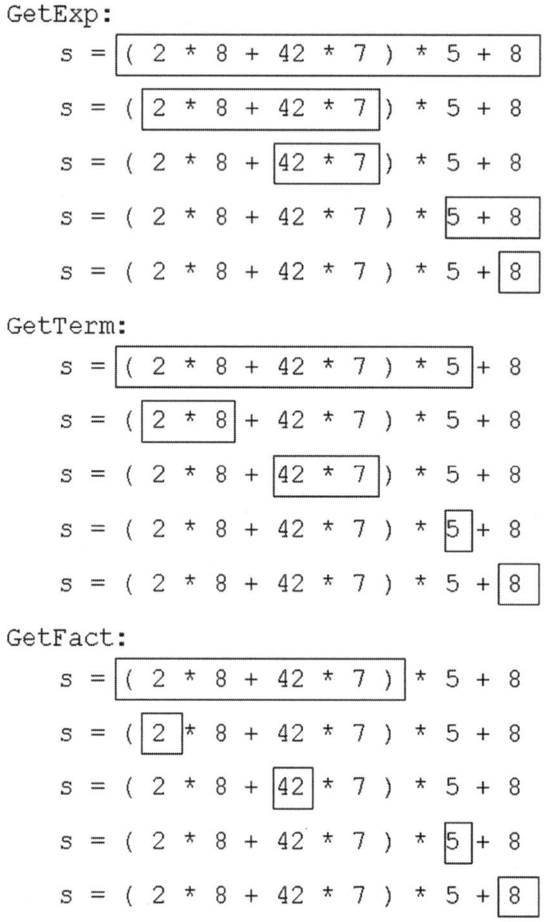

```
GetExp:
    s = |( 2 * 8 + 42 * 7 ) * 5 + 8|
    s = ( |2 * 8 + 42 * 7| ) * 5 + 8
    s = ( 2 * 8 + |42 * 7| ) * 5 + 8
    s = ( 2 * 8 + 42 * 7 ) * |5 + 8|
    s = ( 2 * 8 + 42 * 7 ) * 5 + |8|

GetTerm:
    s = |( 2 * 8 + 42 * 7 ) * 5| + 8
    s = ( |2 * 8| + 42 * 7 ) * 5 + 8
    s = ( 2 * 8 + |42 * 7| ) * 5 + 8
    s = ( 2 * 8 + 42 * 7 ) * |5| + 8
    s = ( 2 * 8 + 42 * 7 ) * 5 + |8|

GetFact:
    s = |( 2 * 8 + 42 * 7 )| * 5 + 8
    s = ( |2| * 8 + 42 * 7 ) * 5 + 8
    s = ( 2 * 8 + |42| * 7 ) * 5 + 8
    s = ( 2 * 8 + 42 * 7 ) * |5| + 8
    s = ( 2 * 8 + 42 * 7 ) * 5 + |8|
```

Figure 12.2: Example input instances are given for *Get Exp, Get Term,* and *Get Fact*. The string *s* is the same for all examples. The beginning of the rectangle indicates the input index *i* at which the parsing should begin. The contents of the rectangle indicates resulting parsing. The end of the rectangle indicates the output index *j* at which the parsing ends.

Reasoning for *GetExp*: Consider some input string s and some index i. The longest substring $s[i], \ldots, s[j-1]$ that is a valid expression consists of some number of terms added together. In all of these cases, it begins with a term. By magic, assume that the *GetTerm* routine already works. Calling *GetTerm(s, i)* will return p_{term} and j_{term}, where p_{term} is the parsing of this first term and j_{term} indexes the token immediately after this term. Specifically, if the expression has another term then j_{term} indexes the '+' that is between these terms. Hence, we can determine whether there is another term by checking $s[j_{term}]$. If $s[j_{term}] = '+,'$ then *GetExp* will call *GetTerm* again to get the next term. If $s[j_{term}]$ is not a '+' but some other character, then *GetExp* is finished reading in all the terms. *GetExp* then constructs the parsing consisting of all of these terms added together.

The reasoning for *GetTerm* is the same.

GetExp **Code:**

algorithm *GetExp* (s, i)

⟨ *pre-cond*⟩: s is a string of tokens, and i is an index that indicates a starting point within s.

⟨ *post-cond*⟩: The output consists of a parsing p of the longest substring $s[i]$, $s[i+1], \ldots, s[j-1]$ of s that starts at index i and is a valid expression. The output also includes the index j of the token that comes immediately after the parsed expression.

begin

    if $(i > |s|)$ return "Error: Expected characters past end of string." **end if**

    $\langle p_{\langle term,1 \rangle}, j_{\langle term,1 \rangle} \rangle = GetTerm(s, i)$

    $k = 1$

    loop

        ⟨*loop-invariant*⟩: The first k terms of the expression have been read.

        exit when $s[j_{\langle term,k \rangle}] \neq '+'$

        $\langle p_{\langle term,k+1 \rangle}, j_{\langle term,k+1 \rangle} \rangle = GetTerm(s, j_{\langle term,k \rangle} + 1)$

        $k = k + 1$

    end loop

    $p_{exp} = p_{\langle term,1 \rangle} + p_{\langle term,2 \rangle} + \ldots + p_{\langle term,k \rangle}$

    $j_{exp} = j_{\langle term,k \rangle}$

    return $\langle p_{exp}, j_{exp} \rangle$

end algorithm

GetTerm **Code:**

algorithm *GetTerm* (s, i)

⟨ *pre-cond*⟩: s is a string of tokens, and i is an index that indicates a starting point within s.

⟨ *post-cond*⟩: The output consists of a parsing p of the longest substring $s[i]$, $s[i+1], \ldots, s[j-1]$ of s that starts at index i and is a valid term. The output also includes the index j of the token that comes immediately after the parsed term.

begin
    if $(i > |s|)$ return "Error: Expected characters past end of string." end if
    $\langle p_{\langle fact,1 \rangle}, j_{\langle fact,1 \rangle} \rangle = GetFact(s, i)$
    $k = 1$
    loop
        $\langle$*loop-invariant*$\rangle$: The first k facts of the term have been read.
        exit when $s[j_{\langle fact,k \rangle}] \neq$ '*'
        $\langle p_{\langle fact,k+1 \rangle}, j_{\langle fact,k+1 \rangle} \rangle = GetFact(s, j_{\langle fact,k \rangle} + 1)$
        $k = k + 1$
    end loop
    $p_{term} = p_{\langle fact,1 \rangle} * p_{\langle fact,2 \rangle} * \cdots * p_{\langle fact,k \rangle}$
    $j_{term} = j_{\langle fact,k \rangle}$
    return $\langle p_{term}, j_{term} \rangle$
end algorithm

Reasoning for *GetFact*: The longest substring $s[i], \ldots, s[j-1]$ that is a valid factor has one of the following two forms:

$$\text{fact} \Rightarrow \text{int}$$

$$\text{fact} \Rightarrow (\text{exp})$$

Hence, we can determine which form the factor has by testing $s[i]$.

If $s[i]$ is an integer, then we are finished. p_{fact} is a parsing of this single integer $s[i]$, and $j_{fact} = i + 1$. The $+1$ moves the index past the integer.

If $s[i] =$ '(', then for s to be a valid factor there must be a valid expression starting at $j_{term} + 1$, followed by a closing bracket ')'. We can parse this expression with *GetExp*$(s, j_{term} + 1)$, which returns p_{exp} and j_{exp}. The closing bracket after the expression must be in $s[j_{exp}]$. Our parsed factor will be $p_{fact} = (p_{exp})$ and $j_{fact} = j_{exp} + 1$. The $+1$ moves the index past the ')'.

If $s[i]$ is neither an integer nor a '(', then it cannot be a valid factor. Give a meaningful error message.

GetFact Code:

algorithm *GetFact* (s, i)

$\langle$ *pre-cond*$\rangle$: s is a string of tokens and i is an index that indicates a starting point within s.

$\langle$ *post-cond*$\rangle$: The output consists of a parsing p of the longest substring $s[i], s[i+1], \ldots, s[j-1]$ of s that starts at index i and is a valid factor. The output also includes the index j of the token that comes immediately after the parsed factor.

begin
    if $(i > |s|)$ return "Error: Expected characters past end of string." end if
    if $(s[i]$ is an int)
        $p_{fact} = s[i]$
        $j_{fact} = i + 1$
        return $\langle p_{fact}, j_{fact} \rangle$

```
        else if (s[i] = '(')
            ⟨p_exp, j_exp⟩ = GetExp(s, i + 1)
            if (s[j_exp] = ')')
                p_fact = (p_exp)
                j_fact = j_exp + 1
                return ⟨p_fact, j_fact⟩
            else
                Output "Error: Expected ')' at index j_exp"
            end if
        else
            Output "Error: Expected integer or '(' at index i"
        end if
    end algorithm
```

Tree of Stack Frames: *GetExp* calls *GetTerm*, which calls *GetFact*, which may call *GetExp*, and so on. If one were to draw out the entire tree of stack frames showing who calls whom, this would exactly mirror the parse tree that it created. See Exercise 12.0.1.

Running Time: We prove that the running time of this entire computation is linear in the size of the parse tree produced, which in turn is linear in the size $\Theta(n)$ of the input string.

To prove the first, it is sufficient to prove that the running time of each stack frame either is constant or is linear in the number of children of the node in the parse tree that this stack frame produces. For example, if the stack frame for *GetFact* finds an integer, then its node in the parse tree has no children, but *GetFact* uses only a constant amount of time. In contrast, if a stack frame for *GetExp* reads in t terms, then its running time will be some constant times t, and its node in the parse tree will have t children.

We now prove that the size to the parse tree produced is linear in the size $\Theta(n)$ of the input string. If the grammar is such that every nonterminal goes to at least one terminal or at least two nonterminals, then each node in the parse tree either is a leaf or has at least two children. It follows that the number of nodes in the parse tree will be at most some constant times the number of leaves, which is the size of the input string. In our grammar, however, an expression might go to a single term, which can go to a single factor. This creates a little path of outdegree one. It cannot, however, be longer than this, because a factor either is a leaf or has three children: one is '(', the second an expression, and the third ')'. Such little paths can only increase the size of the parse tree by a factor of 3.

In conclusion, the running time is $\Theta(n)$.

Proof of Correctness: To prove that a recursive program works, we must consider the *size* of an instance. The routine need only consider the postfix $s[i], s[i + 1], \ldots,$ which contains $|s| - i + 1$ characters. Hence, we will define the size of the instance

$\langle s, i \rangle$ to be $|\langle s, i \rangle| = |s| - i + 1$. Let $H(n)$ be the statement "Each of *GetFac*, *GetTerm*, and *GetExp* works on the instance $\langle s, i \rangle$ when $|\langle s, i \rangle| = |s| - i + 1 \le n$." We prove by induction that $\forall n \ge 0$, $H(n)$.

If $|\langle s, i \rangle| = 0$, then $i > |s|$: There is no valid expression, term, or factor starting at $s[i]$, and all three routines return an error message. It follows that $H(0)$ is true.

If $|\langle s, i \rangle| = 1$, then there is one remaining token: For this to be a factor, term, or expression, it must be a single integer. *GetFac* is written to give the correct answer in this situation. *GetTerm* gives the correct answer, because it calls *GetFac*. *GetExp* gives the correct answer, because it calls *GetTerm*, which in turn calls *GetFac*. It follows that $H(1)$ is true.

Assume $H(n-1)$ is true, that is, that each of *GetFac*, *GetTerm*, and *GetExp* works on instances of size at most $n - 1$.

Consider *GetFac*(s, i) on an instance of size $|s| - i + 1 = n$. It makes at most one subroutine call, *GetExp*$(s, i+1)$. The size of this instance is $|s| - (i+1) + 1 = n - 1$. Hence, by assumption, this subroutine call returns the correct answer. Because all of *GetFac*(s, i)'s subroutine calls return the correct answer, it follows that *GetFac*(s, i) works on all instances of size n.

Now consider *GetTerm*(s, i) on an instance of size $|s| - i + 1 = n$. It calls *GetFac* some number of times. The input instance for the first call *GetFac*(s, i) still has size n. Hence, the induction hypothesis $H(n-1)$ does *not* claim that it works. However, the previous paragraph proves that this routine does in fact work on instances of size n. The remaining calls are on smaller instances.

Finally, consider *GetExp*(s, i) on an instance $\langle s, i \rangle$ of size $|s| - i + 1 = n$. We use the previous paragraph to prove that is first subroutine call *GetTerm*(s, i) works.

In conclusion, all three work on all instances of size n and hence on $H(n)$. This completes the induction step.

Look Ahead One: A grammar is said to be *look ahead one* if, given any two rules for the same nonterminal, the first place that the rules differ is a difference in a terminal. (Equivalently, the rules can be viewed as paths down a tree.) This feature allows our parsing algorithm to look only at the next token in order to decide what to do next. Thus the algorithm runs in linear time. An example of a good set of rules would be

$$A \Rightarrow B \text{ 'u' } C \text{ 'w' } E$$
$$A \Rightarrow B \text{ 'u' } C \text{ 'x' } F$$
$$A \Rightarrow B \text{ 'u' } C$$
$$A \Rightarrow B \text{ 'v' } G H$$

(Actually, even this grammar could also be problematic if when $s = $ '*bbbucccweee*,' B could either be parsed as '*bbb*' or as '*bbbu*.' Having B *eat* the '*u*' would be a problem.)

An example of a bad set of rules would be

$$A \Rightarrow BC$$
$$A \Rightarrow DE$$

With such a grammar, you would not know whether to start parsing the string as a B or a D. If you made the wrong choice, you would have to back up and repeat the process.

EXERCISE 12.0.1 *(See solution in Part Five.) Consider* $s = (((1) * 2 + 3) * 5 * 6 + 7)$.

1. *Give a derivation of the expression* s.
2. *Draw the tree structure of the expression* s.
3. *Trace out the execution of your program on GetExp(s, 1). In other words, draw a tree with a box for each time a routine is called. For each box, include only whether it is an expression, term, or factor and the string* $s[i], \ldots, s[j-1]$ *that is parsed.*

EXERCISE 12.0.2 *Consider a grammar G that includes the four lookahead rules for A. Give the code for GetA (s, i) that is similar to that for GetExp (s, i). We can assume that it can be parsed, so do not bother with error detection.*

EXERCISE 12.0.3 *If you are feeling bold, try to write a recursive program for a generic parsing algorithm. The input is $\langle G, T, s, i \rangle$, where G is a look-ahead-one grammar, T is a nonterminal of G, s is a string of terminals, and i is an index. The output consists of a parsing of the longest substring $s[i], s[i+1], \ldots, s[j-1]$ of s that starts at index i and is a valid T according to the grammar G. In other words, the parsing starts with nonterminal T and ends with the string $s[i], s[i+1], \ldots, s[j-1]$. The output also includes the index j of the token that comes immediately after the parsed expression. For example, GetExp(s, i) is the same as calling this algorithm on $\langle G, exp, s, i \rangle$ where G is the grammar given above.*

The loop invariant is that you have parsed a prefix $s[i], s[i+1], \ldots, s[j'-1]$ of s, producing a partial parsing, p and the rest of the string, $s[j'], s[j'+1], \ldots, s[j-1]$, will be parsed using one of the partial rules in the set R. For example, suppose the grammar G includes the four lookahead rules for A given above, we are starting with the non-terminal T = A, and we are parsing the string s = 'bbbucccwee'. Initially, we have parsed nothing, and R contains all of each of the four rules, namely R = {BuCwE, BuCxF, BuC, BvGH}. After two iterations, we have parsed 'bbbu' using a parsing p_B for 'bbb' followed by the character 'u'. We must parse the rest of the string cccwee using one of the rules in R = {CwE, CxF, C}. Note that the used-up prefix Bu from the consistent rules and the inconsistent rules were deleted. Because the grammar is look ahead one, we know that either the first token in each rule of R is the same nonterminal B, or each rule of R begins with a terminal or is the empty rule. These are the two cases your iteration needs to deal with.

PART THREE

Optimization Problems

13 Definition of Optimization Problems

Many important and practical problems can be expressed as *optimization problems*. Such problems involve finding the best of an exponentially large set of solutions. It can be like finding a needle in a haystack. The obvious algorithm, considering each of the solutions, takes too much time because there are so many solutions. Some of these problems can be solved in polynomial time using network flow, linear programming, greedy algorithms, or dynamic programming. When not, recursive backtracking can sometimes find an optimal solution for some instances in some practical applications. Approximately optimal solutions can sometimes be found more easily. Random algorithms, which flip coins, sometimes have better luck. However, for the most optimization problems, the best known algorithm require $2^{\Theta(n)}$ time on the worst case input instances. The commonly held belief is that there are no polynomial-time algorithms for them (though we may be wrong). NP-completeness helps to justify this belief by showing that some of these problems are universally hard amongst this class of problems. I now formally define this class of problems.

Ingredients: An optimization problem is specified by defining instances, solutions, and costs.

> **Instances:** The *instances* are the possible inputs to the problem.

> **Solutions for Instance:** Each instance has an exponentially large set of *solutions*. A solution is *valid* if it meets a set of criteria determined by the instance at hand.

> **Measure of Success:** Each solution has an easy-to-compute *cost, value,* or *measure of success* that is to be minimized or maximized.

Specification of an Optimization Problem:

> *Preconditions:* The input is one instance.

> *Postconditions:* The output is one of the valid solutions for this instance with optimal (minimum or maximum as the case may be) measure of success. (The solution to be outputted need not be unique.)

Examples:

Longest Common Subsequence: This is an example for which we have a polynomial-time algorithm.

Instances: An instance consists of two sequences, e.g., $X = \langle A, B, C, B, D, A, B \rangle$ and $Y = \langle B, D, C, A, B, A \rangle$.

Solutions: A subsequence of a sequence is a subset of the elements taken in the same order. For example, $Z = \langle B, C, A \rangle$ is a subsequence of $X = \langle A, \underline{B}, \underline{C}, B, D, \underline{A}, B \rangle$. A solution is a sequence Z that is a subsequence of both X and Y. For example, $Z = \langle B, C, A \rangle$ is solution, because it is a subsequence common to both X and Y ($Y = \langle \underline{B}, D, \underline{C}, \underline{A}, B, A \rangle$).

Measure of Success: The value of a solution is the length of the common subsequence, e.g., $|Z| = 3$.

Goal: Given two sequences X and Y, the goal is to find the longest common subsequence (LCS for short). For the example given above, $Z = \langle B, C, B, A \rangle$ is a longest common subsequence.

Course Scheduling: This is an example for which we do not have a polynomial-time algorithm.

Instances: An instance consists of the set of courses specified by a university, the set of courses that each student requests, and the set of time slots in that courses can be offered.

Solutions: A solution for an instance is a schedule that assigns each course a time slot.

Measure of Success: A conflict occurs when two courses are scheduled at the same time even though a student requests them both. The cost of a schedule is the number of conflicts that it has.

Goal: Given the course and student information, the goal is to find the schedule with the fewest conflicts.

Airplane: The following is an example of a practical problem.

Instances: An instance specifies the requirements of a plane: size, speed, fuel efficiency, etc.

Solutions: A solution for an instance is a specification of a plane, right down to every curve and nut and bolt.

Measure of Success: The company has a way of measuring how well the specification meets the requirements.

Goal: Given plane requirements, the goal is to find a specification that meets them in an optimal way.

14 Graph Search Algorithms

An optimization problem requires finding the best of a large number of solutions. This can be compared to a mouse finding cheese in a maze. Graph search algorithms provide a way of systematically searching through this maze of possible solutions.

Another example of an optimization problem is finding the shortest path between two nodes in a graph. There may be an exponential number of paths between these two nodes. It would take too much time to consider each such path. The algorithms used to find a shortest one demonstrate many of the principles that will arise when solving harder optimization problems.

A surprisingly large number of problems in computer science can be expressed as graph theory problems. In this chapter, we will first learn a generic search algorithm that finds more and more of the graph by following arbitrary edges from nodes that have already been found. We also consider the more specific orders of depth-first and breadth-first search to traverse the graph.

Using these ideas, we are able to solve the optimization problem of discovering shortest paths between pairs of nodes and to learn about the structure of the graph.

14.1 A Generic Search Algorithm

The Reachability Problem:

Preconditions: The input is a graph G (either directed or undirected) and a source node s.

Postconditions: The output consists of all the nodes u that are reachable by a path in G from s.

Basic Steps: Suppose you know that node u is reachable from s (denoted as $s \longrightarrow u$) and that there is an edge from u to v. Then you can conclude that v is reachable from s (i.e., $s \longrightarrow u \to v$). You can use such steps to build up a set of reachable nodes.
- s has an edge to v_4 and v_9. Hence, v_4 and v_9 are reachable.
- v_4 has an edge to v_7 and v_3. Hence, v_7 and v_3 are reachable.
- v_7 has an edge to v_2 and v_8. . . .

Difficulties:

Data Structure: How do you keep track of all this?

Exit Condition: How do you know that you have found all the nodes?

Halting: How do you avoid cycling, as in $s \to v_4 \to v_7 \to v_2 \to v_4 \to v_7 \to v_2 \to v_4 \to v_7 \to v_2 \to v_4 \to \cdots$, forever?

Ingredients of the Loop Invariant:

Found: If you trace a path from s to a node, then we will say that the node has been *found.*

Handled: At some point in time after node u has been found, you will want to follow all the edges from u and find all the nodes v that have edges from u. When you have done that for node u, we say that it has been *handled.*

Data Structure: You must maintain (1) the set of nodes *foundHandled* that have been found and handled and (2) the set of nodes *foundNotHandled* that have been found but not handled. See Figure 14.1.

The Loop Invariant:

LI1: For each found node v, we know that v is reachable from s, because we have traced out a path $s \longrightarrow v$ from s to it.

LI2: If a node has been handled, then all of its neighbors have been found.

These loop invariants are simple enough that establishing and maintaining them should be easy. But do they suffice to prove the postcondition? We will see.

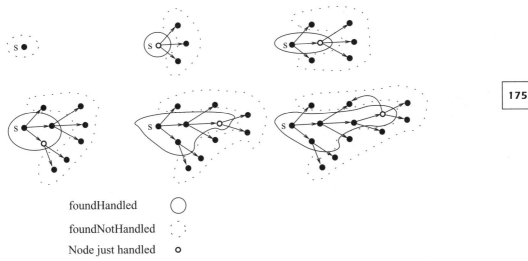

foundHandled   ◯

foundNotHandled   ⋰⋱

Node just handled   ○

Figure 14.1: The generic search algorithm *handles* one found node at a time by *finding* its neighbors.

Body of the Loop: A reasonable step would be:

- Choose some node *u* from *foundNotHandled*, and handle it. This involves following all the edges from *u*.
- Newly found nodes are now added to the set *foundNotHandled* (if they have not been found already).
- *u* is moved from *foundNotHandled* to *foundHandled*.

Code:

> **algorithm** *GenericSearch (G, s)*
>
> ⟨ *pre-cond*⟩: *G* is a (directed or undirected) graph, and *s* is one of its nodes.
> ⟨ *post-cond*⟩: The output consists of all the nodes *u* that are reachable by a path in *G* from *s*.
>
> begin
>   *foundHandled* = ∅
>   *foundNotHandled* = {*s*}
>   loop
>   ⟨*loop-invariant*⟩: See LI1, LI2.
>   exit when *foundNotHandled* = ∅
>   let *u* be some node from *foundNotHandled*
>   for each *v* connected to *u*
>   if *v* has not previously been found then
>   add *v* to *foundNotHandled*
>   end if
>   end for

> move *u* from *foundNotHandled* to *foundHandled*
> end loop
> return *foundHandled*
> end algorithm

Maintaining the Loop Invariant ($\langle LI' \rangle$ & not $\langle exit \rangle$ & $code_{loop} \to \langle LI'' \rangle$):
Suppose that LI' (the statement of the loop invariant before the iteration) is true, the exit condition $\langle exit \rangle$ is not, and we have executed another iteration of the algorithm.

Maintaining LI1: After the iteration, the node v is considered found. Hence, in order to maintain the loop invariant, we must be sure that v is reachable from s. Because u was in *foundNotHandled*, the loop invariant assures us that we have traced out a path $s \longrightarrow u$ to it. Now that we have traced the edge $u \to v$, we have traced a path $s \longrightarrow u \to v$ to v.

Maintaining LI2: Node u is designated handled only after ensuring that all its neighbors have been found.

The Measure of Progress: The measure of progress requires the following three properties:

Progress: We must guarantee that our measure of progress increases by at least one every time around the loop. Otherwise, we may loop forever, making no progress.

Bounded: There must be an upper bound on the progress required before the loop exits. Otherwise, we may loop forever, increasing the measure of progress to infinity.

Conclusion: When sufficient progress has been made to exit, we must be able to conclude that the problem is solved.

An obvious measure would be the number of found nodes. The problem is that when handling a node, you may only find nodes that have already been found. In such a case, no progress is actually made.

A better measure of progress is the number of nodes that have been handled. We can make progress simply by handling a node that has not yet been handled. We also know that if the graph G has only n nodes, then this measure cannot increase past n.

Exit Condition: Given our measure of progress, when are we finished? We can only handle nodes that have been found and not handled. Hence, when all the nodes that have been found have also been handled, we can make no more progress. At this point, we must stop.

Initial Code ($\langle pre\text{-}cond \rangle$ & $code_{pre\text{-}loop} \Rightarrow \langle loop\text{-}invariant \rangle$): Initially, we know only that s is reachable from s. Hence, let's start by saying that s is found but not handled and that all other nodes have not yet been found.

Exiting Loop (⟨LI⟩ & ⟨exit⟩ → ⟨post⟩): Our output will be the set of found nodes. The postcondition requires the following two claims to be true.

> **Claim:** Found nodes are reachable from s.
>   This is clearly stated in the loop invariant.

> **Claim:** Every reachable node has been found. A logically equivalent statement is that every node that has not been found is not reachable.

> **One Proof:** Draw a circle around the nodes of the graph G that have been found. If there are no edges going from the inside of the circle to the outside of the circle, then there are no paths from s to the nodes outside the circle. Hence, we can claim we have found all the nodes reachable from s. How do we know that this circle has no edges leaving it? Consider a node u in the circle. Because u has been found and *foundNotHandled* = ∅, we know that u has also been handled. By the loop invariant LI2, if $\langle u, v \rangle$ is an edge, then v has been found and thus is in the circle as well. Hence, if u is in the circle and $\langle u, v \rangle$ is an edge, then v is in the circle as well (i.e., no edges leave the circle).

> **Closure Property:** This is known as a *closure property*. See Section 18.3.3 for more information on this property.

> **Another Proof:** Proof by contradiction.
>   Suppose that w is reachable from s and that w has not been found. Consider a path from s to w. Because s has been found and w has not, the path starts in the set of found nodes and at some point leaves it. Let $\langle u, v \rangle$ be the first edge in the path for which u but not v has been found. Because u has been found and *foundNotHandled* = ∅, it follows that u has been handled. Because u has been handled, v must be found. This contradicts the definition of v.

Running Time:

> **A Simple but False Argument:** For every iteration of the loop, one node is handled, and no node is handled more than once. Hence, the measure of progress (the number of nodes handled) increases by one with every loop. G only has $|V| = n$ nodes. Hence, the algorithm loops at most n times. Thus, the running time is $O(n)$.
>   This argument is false, because while handling u we must consider v for every edge coming out of u.

> **Overestimation:** Each node has at most n edges coming out of it. Hence, the running time is $O(n^2)$.

> **Correct Complexity:** Each edge of G is looked at exactly twice, once from each direction. The algorithm's time is dominated by this fact. Hence, the running time is $O(|E|)$, where E is the set of edges in G.

The Order of Handling Nodes: This algorithm specifically did not indicate which node u to select from *foundNotHandled*. It did not need to, because the algorithm works no matter how this choice is made. We will now consider specific orders in which to handle the nodes and specific applications of these orders.

Queue (Breadth-First Search): One option is to handle nodes in the order they are found in. This treats *foundNotHandled* as a queue: "first in, first out." The effect is that the search is *breadth first*, meaning that all nodes at distance 1 from s are handled first, then all those at distance 2, and so on. A byproduct of this is that we find for each node v a shortest path from s to v. See Section 14.2.

Priority Queue (Shortest (Weighted) Paths): Another option calculates for each node v in *foundNotHandled* the minimum weighted distance from s to v along any path seen so far. It then handles the node that is closest to s according to this approximation. Because these approximations change throughout time, *foundNotHandled* is implemented using a priority queue: "highest current priority out first." Like breadth-first search, the search handles nodes that are closest to s first, but now the length of a path is the sum of its edge weights. A byproduct of this method is that we find for each node v the shortest weighted path from s to v. See Section 14.3.

Stack (Depth-First Search): Another option is to handle the node that was found most recently. This method treats *foundNotHandled* as a stack: "last in, first out." The effect is that the search is *depth first*, meaning that a particular path is followed as deeply as possible into the graph until a dead end is reached, forcing the algorithm to backtrack. See Section 14.4.

EXERCISE 14.1.1 *Try searching the following graph using queue (breadth-first search), priority queue (shortest (weighted) paths), and stack (depth-first search).*

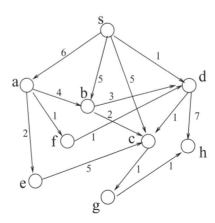

14.2 Breadth-First Search for Shortest Paths

We will now develop an algorithm for an optimization problem called the *shortest-path problem.* The algorithm uses a breadth-first search. This algorithm is a less generic version of the algorithm in Section 14.1, because the order in which the nodes are handled is now specified more precisely. The loop invariants are strengthened in order to solve the shortest-path problem.

The Shortest-Path Problem (Multiple Sink): Generally, the shortest-path problem finds a shortest path between a source node s and a sink node t in a graph G. Here, however, we will consider the case where we simultaneously consider all nodes v to be the sink.

> *Precondition:* $\langle G, s \rangle$ consists of a graph G and a source node s. The graph G can be directed or undirected.

> *Postconditions:* The output consists of a $d(v)$ and a $\pi(v)$ for each node of G. It has the following properties:

> 1. For each node v, $d(v)$ gives the length $\delta(s, v)$ of the shortest path from s to v.

> 2. The *shortest-path* or *breadth-first search tree* is defined using a function π as follows: s is the root of the tree. $\pi(v)$ is the parent of v in the tree. For each node v, one of the shortest paths from s to v is given backward, with $v, \pi(v), \pi(\pi(v)), \pi(\pi(\pi(v))), \ldots, s$. A recursive definition is that this shortest path from s to v is the given shortest path from s to $\pi(v)$, followed by the edge $\langle \pi(v), v \rangle$.

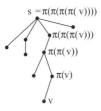

An Optimization Problem: The single-source, single-sink version of the shortest-path problem can be viewed as an optimization problem. See Chapter 13.

> **Instances:** An instance $\langle G, s, t \rangle$ consists of a graph and two nodes s and t.

> **Solutions for Instance:** A solution for the instance $\langle G, s, t \rangle$ is a path π from s to t.

> **Measure of Success:** The length (or cost) of a path π is the number of edges in the path.

> **Goal:** Given an instance $\langle G, s, t \rangle$, the goal is to find an optimal solution, i.e., a shortest path from s to t in G.

> **Brute Force Algorithm:** As is often the case with optimization problems, the number of solutions for an instance may well be exponential. We do not want to check them all.

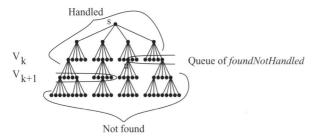

Figure 14.2: Breadth-first search tree: We cannot assume that the graph is a tree. Here I have presented only the tree edges given by π. The figure helps to explain the loop invariant, showing which nodes have been found, which found but not handled, and which handled.

Prove Path Is Shortest: In order to claim that the shortest path from s to v is of some length $d(v)$, you must do two things:

Not Further: You must produce a suitable path of this length. We call this path a *witness* of the fact that the distance from s to v is at most $d(v)$. In finding a node, we trace out a path from s to it. If we have already traced out a shortest path from s to u with $d(u)$ edges in it and we trace an edge from u to v, then we have traced a path from s to v with $d(v) = d(u) + 1$ edges in it. In this path from s to v, the node preceding v is $\pi(v) = u$.

Not Closer: You must prove that there are no shorter paths. This is harder. Other than checking an exponential number of paths, how can you prove that there are no shorter paths? We will do it using the following trick: Suppose we can ensure that the order in which we find the nodes is according to the length of the shortest path from s to them. Then, when we find v, we know that there isn't a shorter path to it, or else we would have found it already.

Definition of V_j: Let V_j denote the set of nodes at distance j from s.

The Loop Invariant: See Figure 14.2.

LI1: For each found node v, the values of $d(v)$ and $\pi(v)$ are as required, that is, they give the shortest length and a shortest path from s to the node.

LI2: If a node has been handled, then all of its neighbors have been found.

LI3: So far, the order in which the nodes have been found is according to the length of the shortest path from s to it, that is, the nodes in V_j before those in V_{j+1}.

Order in Which to Handle Nodes: The only way in which we are changing the generic search algorithm of Section 14.1 is being more careful in our choice of which

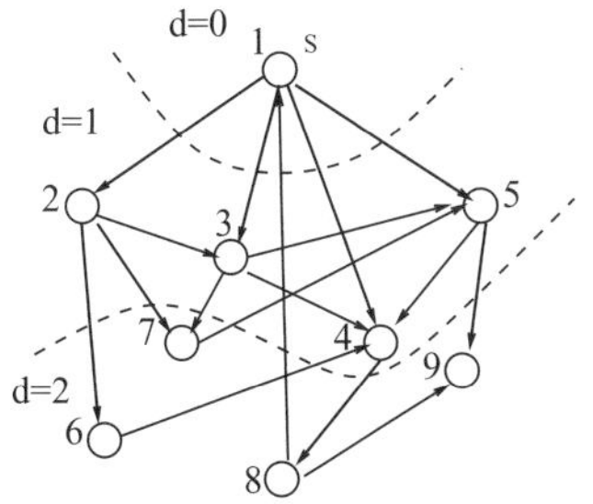

Figure 14.3: Breadth-first search of a graph. The numbers show the order in which the nodes were found. The contents of the queue are given at each step. The tree edges are darkened.

Handled	{Queue}
1	{1}
1,2	{2,3,4,5}
1,2,3	{3,4,5,6,7}
1,2,3,4	{4,5,6,7}
1,2,3,4,5	{5,6,7,8}
1,2,3,4,5,6,7,8,9	{6,7,8,9}

node from *foundNotHandled* to handle next. According to LI3, the nodes that were found earlier are closer to s than those that are found later. The closer a node is to s, the closer are its neighbors. Hence, in an attempt to find close nodes, the algorithm will next handle the earliest found node. This is accomplished by treating the set *foundNotHandled* as a queue, "first in, first out."

Example: See Figure 14.3.

Body of the Loop: Remove the first node u from the *foundNotHandled* queue and handle it as follows. For every neighbor v of u that has not been found,
- add the node to the queue,
- let $d(v) = d(u) + 1$,
- let $\pi(v) = u$, and
- consider u to be handled and v to be in *foundNotHandled*.

Code:

```
algorithm ShortestPath (G, s)

⟨ pre-cond⟩: G is a (directed or undirected) graph, and s is one of its nodes.
⟨ post-cond⟩: π specifies a shortest path from s to each node of G, and d specifies
their lengths.

begin
    foundHandled = Ø
    foundNotHandled = {s}
    d(s) = 0, π(s) = ε
    loop
        ⟨loop-invariant⟩: See above.
        exit when foundNotHandled = Ø
        let u be the node in the front of the queue foundNotHandled
        for each v connected to u
            if v has not previously been found then
                add v to foundNotHandled
```

$$d(v) = d(u) + 1$$
$$\pi(v) = u$$
   end if
  end for
  move u from *foundNotHandled* to *foundHandled*
 end loop
 (for unfound v, $d(v) = \infty$)
 return $\langle d, \pi \rangle$
end algorithm

Maintaining the Loop Invariant ($\langle LI' \rangle$ & not $\langle exit \rangle$ & $code_{loop} \rightarrow \langle LI'' \rangle$): Suppose that LI′ (the statement of the loop invariant before the iteration) is true, the exit condition $\langle exit \rangle$ is not, and we have executed another iteration of the algorithm.

 Closer Nodes Have Already Been Found: We will need the following claim twice.

 Claim: If the first node in the queue *foundNotHandled*, that is, u, is in V_k, then

  1. all the nodes in $V_0, V_1, V_2, \ldots, V_{k-1}$ have already been found and handled, and

  2. all the nodes in V_k have already been found.

 Proof of Part 1 of Claim: Let u' denote any node in $V_0, V_1, V_2, \ldots, V_{k-1}$. Because LI3′ ensures that nodes have been found in the order of their distance and because u' is closer to s than u, u' must have been found earlier than u. Hence, u' cannot be in the queue *foundNotHandled*, or else it would be earlier in the queue than u, yet u is first. This proves that u' has been handled.

 Proof of Part 2 of Claim: Consider any node v in V_k and any path of length k to it. Let u' be the previous node in this path. Because the subpath to u' is of length $k-1$, u' is in V_{k-1}, and hence by claim 1 has already been handled. Therefore, by LI2′, the neighbors of u', of which v is one, must have been found.

Maintaining LI1: During this iteration, all the neighbors v of node u that had not been found are now considered found. Hence, their $d(v)$ and $\pi(v)$ must now give the shortest length and a shortest path from s. The code sets $d(v)$ to $d(u) + 1$ and $\pi(v)$ to u. Hence, we must prove that the neighbors v are in V_{k+1}.

 Not Further: There is a path from s to v of length $k + 1$: follow the path of length k to u, and then take the edge to v. Hence, the shortest path to v can be no longer then this.

> **Not Closer:** We know that there isn't a shorter path to v, or it would have been found already. More formally, the claim states that all the nodes in V_0, V_1, V_2, ..., V_k have already been found. Because v has not already been found, it cannot be one of these.

> **Maintaining LI2:** Node u is designated handled only after ensuring that all its neighbors have been found.

> **Maintaining LI3:** By the claim, all the nodes in V_0, V_1, V_2, ..., V_k have already been found and hence have already been added to the queue. We have also already proved that the node v being found is in V_{k+1}. It follows that the order in which the nodes are found continues to be according to their distance from s.

Initial Code ($\langle pre \rangle \to \langle LI \rangle$): The initial code puts the source s into *foundNotHandled* and sets $d(s) = 0$ and $\pi(s) = \epsilon$. This is correct, given that initially s has been found but not handled. The other nodes have not been found, and hence their $d(v)$ and $\pi(v)$ are irrelevant. The loop invariants follow easily.

Exiting Loop ($\langle LI \rangle$ & $\langle exit \rangle \to \langle post \rangle$): The general-search postconditions from Section 14.1 prove that all reachable nodes have been found. LI1 states that for these nodes the values of $d(v)$ and $\pi(v)$ are as required.

For the nodes that are unreachable from s, you can set $d(v) = \infty$ or you can leave them undefined. In some applications (such as the World Wide Web), you have no access to unreachable nodes. An advantage of this algorithm is that it never needs to know about a node unless it has been found.

EXERCISE 14.2.1 *(See solution in Part Five.) Suppose u is being handled, $u \in V_k$, and v is a neighbor of u. For each of the following cases, explain which $V_{k'}$ v might be in:*
- *$\langle u, v \rangle$ is an undirected edge, and v has been found before.*
- *$\langle u, v \rangle$ is an undirected edge, and v has not been found before.*
- *$\langle u, v \rangle$ is a directed edge, and v has been found before.*
- *$\langle u, v \rangle$ is a directed edge, and v has not been found before.*

EXERCISE 14.2.2 *(See solution in Part Five.) Estimate the time required to find the shortest path between two given nodes s and t.*

14.3 Dijkstra's Shortest-Weighted-Path Algorithm

We will now make the shortest-path problem more general by allowing each edge to have a different weight (length). The length of a path from s to v will be the sum of the weights on the edges of the path. This makes the problem harder, because the shortest path to a node may wind deep into the graph along many short edges instead of along a few long edges. Despite this, only small changes need to be made to the algorithm. The new algorithm is called *Dijkstra's algorithm*.

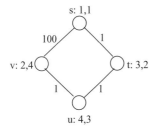

Figure 14.4: *The shortest paths algorithm handles the nodes in the order of length of the shortest path to them.*

Node: order found, order handled

Specifications of the Shortest-Weighted-Path Problem:

Preconditions: The input is a graph G (either directed or undirected) and a source node s. Each edge $\langle u, v \rangle$ is allocated a nonnegative weight $w_{\langle u,v \rangle}$.

Postconditions: The output consists of d and π, where for each node v of G, $d(v)$ gives the length $\delta(s, v)$ of the shortest weighted path from s to v, and π defines a *shortest-weighted-path tree*. (See Section 14.2.)

Prove Path Is Shortest: As before, proving that the shortest path from s to v is of some length $d(v)$ involves producing a suitable path of this length and proving that there are no shorter paths.

Not Further: As before, a witness that there is such a path is produced by tracing it out. The only change is that when we find a path $s \longrightarrow u \to v$, we compute its length to be $d(v) = d(u) + w_{\langle u,v \rangle}$ instead of only $d(v) = d(u) + 1$.

Not Closer: Unlike the breadth-first search shortest-path algorithm from Section 14.2, the algorithm does not find the nodes in the order of length of the shortest path to them from s. It does, however, *handle* the nodes in this order. See Figure 14.4. Because of this, when we handle a node, we know that there is no shorter path to it, because otherwise we would have handled it already.

The Next Node To Handle: The algorithm must choose which of the unhandled nodes to handle next. The difficulty is that initially we do not know the length of the shortest path. Instead, we choose the node closest to s according to our current approximation. In Figure 14.4, after handling s our best approximation of the distance to v is 100 and to t is only 1. Hence, we handle t next.

An Adaptive Greedy Criterion: This choice amounts to an *adaptive greedy criterion*. See Chapter 16 for more on greedy algorithms.

Growing a Tree One Node at a Time: It turns out that the next node to be handled will always be only one edge from a previously handled node. Hence, the tree of handled nodes expands out, one node at a time.

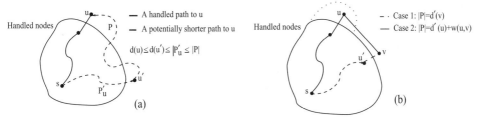

Figure 14.5: (a) shows a handled path to node u and is used to maintain LI1. (b) is used to maintain LI2.

Approximation of Shortest Distances: For every node v, before getting its shortest overall distance, we will maintain $d(v)$ and $\pi(v)$ as the shortest length and path from s to v from among those paths that we have *handled* so far.

Updating: This information is continuously updated as we find shorter paths to v. For example, if we find v when handling u, then we update these values as follows:

> $foundPathLength = d(u) + w_{\langle u,v \rangle}$
> if $d(v) > foundPathLength$ then
> $d(v) = foundPathLength$
> $\pi(v) = u$
> end if

When handling s in our example, $d(v)$ is set to $d(s) + w_{\langle s,v \rangle} = 0 + 100 = 100$. Later, when handling u, it is updated to $d(u) + w_{\langle u,v \rangle} = 2 + 1 = 3$.

Definition of a Handled Path: We say that a path has been handled if it contains only handled edges. Such paths start at s, visit as any number of handled nodes, and then follow one last edge to a node that may or may not be handled. (See the solid path to u in Figure 14.5.a.)

Priority Queue: The next node to be handled is the one with the smallest $d(u)$ value. Searching the set of unhandled nodes for this node during each iteration would be too time-consuming. Re-sorting the nodes each iteration as the $d(u)$ values change would also be too time-consuming. A more efficient implementation uses a priority queue to hold the unhandled nodes prioritized according to their current $d(u)$ value. This can be implemented using a heap. (See Section 10.4.) We will denote this priority queue by *notHandled*.

Consider All Nodes "Found": No path has yet been handled to any node that has not yet been found, and hence $d(v) = \infty$. If we add these nodes to the queue, they will be selected last. Therefore, there is no harm in adding them. Hence, we will distinguish only between those nodes that have been handled and those that have not.

The Loop Invariant:

LI1: For each handled node v, the values of $d(v)$ and $\pi(v)$ give the shortest length and a shortest path from s (and this path contains only handled nodes).

LI2: For each of the unhandled nodes v, the values of $d(v)$ and $\pi(v)$ give the shortest length and path from among those paths that have been handled.

Body of the Loop: Take the next node u from the priority queue *notHandled*, and handle it. This involves handling all edges $\langle u, v \rangle$ out of u. Handling the edge $\langle u, v \rangle$ involves updating the $d(v)$ and $\pi(v)$ values. The priorities of these nodes are changed in the priority queue as necessary.

Example: See Figure 14.6.

Code:

```
algorithm DijkstraShortestWeightedPath(G, s)
```

⟨ *pre-cond*⟩: G is a weighted (directed or undirected) graph, and s is one of its nodes.

⟨ *post-cond*⟩: π specifies a shortest weighted path from s to each node of G, and d specifies their lengths.

```
begin
    d(s) = 0, π(s) = ε
    for other v, d(v) = ∞ and π(v) = nil
    handled = ∅
    notHandled = priority queue containing all nodes. Priorities given by d(v).
    loop
        ⟨loop-invariant⟩: See above.
        exit when notHandled = ∅
        let u be a node from notHandled with smallest d(u)
        for each v connected to u
            foundPathLength = d(u) + w⟨u,v⟩
            if d(v) > foundPathLength then
                d(v) = foundPathLength
                π(v) = u
                (update the notHandled priority queue)
            end if
        end for
        move u from notHandled to handled
    end loop
    return ⟨d, π⟩
end algorithm
```

Maintaining LI1 (⟨*LI1′*, *LI2′*⟩ **& not** ⟨*exit*⟩ **&** *code_{loop}* → ⟨*LI1″*⟩**):** The loop handles a node u with smallest $d(u)$ from *notHandled*. Hence to maintain LI1, we must ensure that its $d(u)$ and $\pi(u)$ values give an overall shortest path to u. Consider some other path P to u. We will see that it is no shorter. See Figure 14.5.a. Because the path P starts at the handled node s and ends at the previously unhandled node u, there has to be some node u' that is the first previously unhandled node along P. (It is possible that $u' = u$.) By the choice of u, u has the smallest $d(u)$ from *notHandled*. Hence, $d(u) \leq d(u')$. Let $P_{u'}$ be the part the path that goes from s to u'. This is a previously handled path. Hence, by LI2', $d(u') \leq |P_{u'}|$. Since $|P_{u'}|$ is a subpath and there are no negative weights, $|P_{u'}| \leq |P|$. Combining these gives $d(u) \leq |P|$. In conclusion, $d(u)$ is the length of the shortest path to u, and hence LI1 has been maintained.

187

Maintaining LI2 ($\langle LI1', LI2' \rangle$ & not $\langle exit \rangle$ & $code_{loop} \to \langle LI2'' \rangle$): Setting $d''(v)$ to $\min\{d'(v), d'(u) + w_{\langle u,v \rangle}\}$ ensures that there is a handled path with this length to v. To maintain LI2, we must prove that there does not exist a shorter one from among those paths that now are considered handled. Such paths can now include the newly handled node u. Let P be a shortest one. See Figure 14.5.b. Let u' be the second last node in P. Because P is a handled path, u' must be a handled node. There are two cases:

> $u \neq u'$: If u' is a previously handled node, then by the second part of LI1', the shortest path to it does not need to contain the newly handled node u. It follows that this path P to v is a previously handed path. Hence, its length is at least the length of the shortest previously handed path to v, which by LI2', is $d'(v)$. This in turn is at least $\min\{d'(v), d'(u) + w_{\langle u,v \rangle}\} = d''(v)$.

> $u = u'$: If the second last node in P is the newly handled node u, then its length is the length of the shortest path to u, which we now know is $d'(u)$, plus the weight of the edge $\langle u, v \rangle$. It follows that $|P| \geq \min\{d'(v), d'(u) + w_{\langle u,v \rangle}\} = d''(v)$.

Either way, the shortest path P to v that is now considered to be handled has length at least $d''(v)$. Hence, LI2 is maintained.

Initial Code ($\langle pre \rangle \to \langle LI \rangle$): The initial code is the same as that for the breadth-first search shortest-path algorithm from Section 14.2, that is, s is found but not handled with $d(s) = 0$, $\pi(s) = \epsilon$. Initially no paths to v have been handled, and hence the

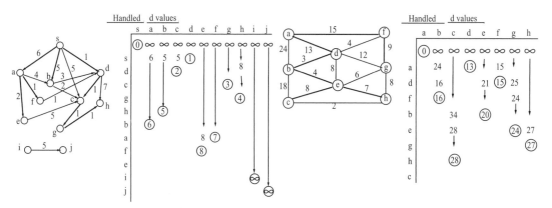

Figure 14.6: Dijkstra's algorithm. The d value at each step is given for each node. The tree edges are darkened.

length of the shortest handled path to v is $d(v) = \infty$. This satisfies all three loop invariants.

Exiting Loop ($\langle LI \rangle$ & $\langle exit \rangle \to \langle post \rangle$): See the shortest-path algorithm.

188

EXERCISE 14.3.1 *Estimate the running time of Dijkstra's shortest-weighted-path algorithm.*

EXERCISE 14.3.2 *(See solution in Part Five.) Given a graph where each edge weight is one, compare and contrast the computation of the breadth-first search shortest-path algorithm from Section 14.2 and that of Dijkstra's shortest-weighted-path algorithm. How do their choices of the next node to handle and their loop invariants compare?*

EXERCISE 14.3.3 *Dijkstra's algorithm:*

1. *Give the full loop invariant for Dijkstra's algorithm. Include the definition of any terms you use.*
2. *What is the exit condition for Dijkstra's algorithm?*
3. *Prove that the postcondition is obtained.*
4. *Consider a computation of Dijkstra's algorithm on the following graph when the circled nodes have been handled. The start node is a. On the left, give the current values of d.*

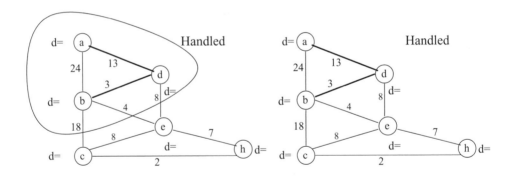

5. *On the right, change the figure to take one step in Dijkstra's algorithm. Include as well any π's that change.*

EXERCISE 14.3.4 *Give a simple graph with an edge with a negative weight, and show that Dijkstra's algorithm gives the wrong answer.*

14.4 Depth-First Search

We have considered breadth-first search, which first visits nodes at distance 1 from s, then those at distance 2, and so on. We will now consider a *depth-first search*, which

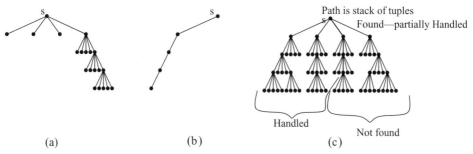

Figure 14.7: If the next node in the stack was completely handled, then the initial order in which nodes are found is given in (a). If the next node is only partially handled, then this initial order is given in (b). (c) presents more of the order in which the nodes are found. Though the input graph may not be a tree, the figure only shows the tree edges given by π.

continues to follow some path as deeply as possible into the graph before it is forced to backtrack. I give an iterative algorithm in this section and a recursive one in Section 14.5.

Changes to the Generic Search Algorithm in Section 14.1: The next node u we handle is the one most recently found. *foundNotHandled* will be implemented as a stack of tuples $\langle v, i_v \rangle$. At each iteration, we pop the most recently pushed tuple $\langle u, i_u \rangle$ and handle the $(i_u + 1)$st edge from u. Try this out on a graph (or on a tree). The pattern in which nodes are found consists of a single path with single edges hanging off it. See Figure 14.7.

In order to prevent the single edges hanging off the path from being searched, we make a second change to the original searching algorithm: We no longer completely handle one node before we start handling edges from other nodes. From s, an edge is followed to one of its neighbors v_1. Before visiting the other neighbors of s, the current path to v_1 is extended to $v_2, v_3, \ldots$. (See Figure 14.7.b.) We keep track of what has been handled by storing an integer i_u for each node u. We maintain that for each u, the first i_u edges of u have already been handled.

Loop Invariants:

LI1: The nodes in the stack *foundNotHandled* are ordered so that they define a path starting at s.

LI2: *foundNotHandled* is a stack of tuples $\langle v, i_v \rangle$ such that for each v, the first i_v edges of v have been handled. Each node v appears no more than once.

Code:

algorithm *DepthFirstSearch* (G, s)

$\langle$ *pre-cond* $\rangle$: G is a (directed or undirected), graph, and s is one of its nodes.

$\langle$ *post-cond* $\rangle$: The output is a depth-first search tree of G rooted at s.

```
begin
    foundHandled = ∅
    foundNotHandled = {⟨s, 0⟩}
    time = 0 % Used for time stamping. See following discussion.
    loop
        ⟨loop-invariant⟩: See preceding list.
        exit when foundNotHandled = ∅
        pop ⟨u, i⟩ off the stack foundNotHandled
        if u has an (i+1)st edge ⟨u, v⟩
            push ⟨u, i + 1⟩ onto foundNotHandled
            if v has not previously been found then
                π(v) = u
                ⟨u, v⟩ is a tree edge
                push ⟨v, 0⟩ onto foundNotHandled
                s(v) = time; time = time + 1
            else if v has been found but not completely handled then
                ⟨u, v⟩ is a back edge
            else (v has been completely handled)
                ⟨u, v⟩ is a forward or cross edge
            end if
        else
            move u to foundHandled
            f(v) = time; time = time + 1
        end if
    end loop
    return foundHandled
end algorithm
```

Example: See Figure 14.8.

Establishing and Maintaining the Loop Invariant: It is easy to see that with $foundNotHandled = \{\langle s, 0 \rangle\}$, the loop invariant is established. If the stack does contain a path from s to u and u has an unhandled edge to v, then u is kept on the stack and v is pushed on top. This extends the path from u onward to v. If u does not have an unhandled edge, then u is popped off the stack. This decreases the path from s by one.

Classification of Edges: The depth-first search algorithm can be used to classify edges:

Tree Edges: Tree edges are the edges $\langle u, v \rangle$ in the depth-first search tree. When such edges are handled, v has not yet been found.

Back Edges: Back edges are the edges $\langle u, v \rangle$ such that v is an ancestor of u in the depth-first search tree. When such edges are handled, v is in the stack, that is, found but not completely handled.

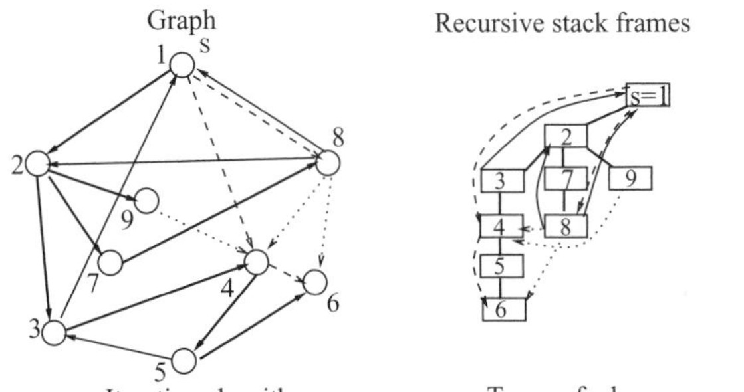

Graph Recursive stack frames

Iterative algorithm Types of edges

Stack	Handled
{s=1}	
{1,2,3,4,5,6}	
{1,2}	6,5,4,3
{1,2,7,8}	6,5,4,3
{1,2}	6,5,4,3,8,7
{1,2,9}	6,5,4,3,8,7
	6,5, 4,3,8, 7,9,2,1

Tree edges →
Back edges →
Forward edges ---►
Cross edges ·····►

Figure 14.8: Depth-first search of a graph. The numbers give the order in which the nodes are found. The contents of the stack are given at each step.

Cyclic: A graph is cyclic if and only if it has a back edge.

Proof ($\Leftarrow$): The loop invariant of the depth-first search algorithm ensures that the contents of the stack form a path from s through v and onward to u. Adding on the edge $\langle u, v \rangle$ creates a cycle back to v.

Proof ($\Rightarrow$): Later we prove that if the graph has no back edges, then there is a total ordering of the nodes respecting the edges and hence the graph has no cycles.

Bipartite: A graph is bipartite if and only if there is no back edge between any two nodes with the same level parity, that is, iff it has no odd-length cycles.

Forward Edges and Cross Edges: Forward edges are edges $\langle u, v \rangle$ such that v is a descendant of u in the depth-first search tree.

Cross edges $\langle u, v \rangle$ are such that u and v are in different branches of the depth-first search tree (that is, are neither ancestors nor descendants of each other) and v's branch is traversed before (to the left of) u's branch.

When forward edges and cross edges are handled, v has been completely handled. The depth-first search algorithm does not distinguish between forward edges and cross edges.

Time Stamping: Some implementations of depth-first search time-stamp each node u with a start time $s(u)$ and a finish time $f(u)$. Here *time* is measured by starting a counter at zero and incrementing it every time a node is found for the first time or a node is completely handled. $s(u)$ is the time at which node u is first found, and $f(u)$ is the time at which it is completely handled. The time stamps are useful in the following way:

- v is a descendant of u if and only if the time interval $[s(v), f(v)]$ is completely contained in $[s(u), f(u)]$.

- If u and v are neither ancestor or descendant of each other, then the time intervals $[s(u), f(u)]$ and $[s(v), f(v)]$ are completely disjoint.

Using the time stamps, this can be determined in constant time.

EXERCISE 14.4.1 *Prove that when doing depth-first search on undirected graphs there are never any forward or cross edges.*

14.5 Recursive Depth-First Search

I now present a recursive implementation of a depth-first search algorithm, which directly mirrors the iterative version. The only difference is that the iterative version uses a stack to keep track of the route back to the start node, while the recursive version uses the stack of recursive stack frames. The advantage of the recursive algorithm is that it is easier to code and easier to understand. The iterative algorithm might run slightly faster, but a good compiler will convert the recursive algorithm into an iterative one.

Code:

```
algorithm DepthFirstSearch (s)

⟨pre-cond⟩: An input instance consists of a (directed or undirected) graph G
with some of its nodes marked found and a source node s.
⟨post-cond⟩: The output is the same graph G, except all nodes v reachable from
s without passing through a previously found node are now also marked as being
found. The graph G is a global variable ADT, which is assumed to be both input
and output to the routine.

begin
    if s is marked as found then
        do nothing
    else
        mark s as found
        for each v connected to s
            DepthFirstSearch (v)
        end for
    end if
end algorithm
```

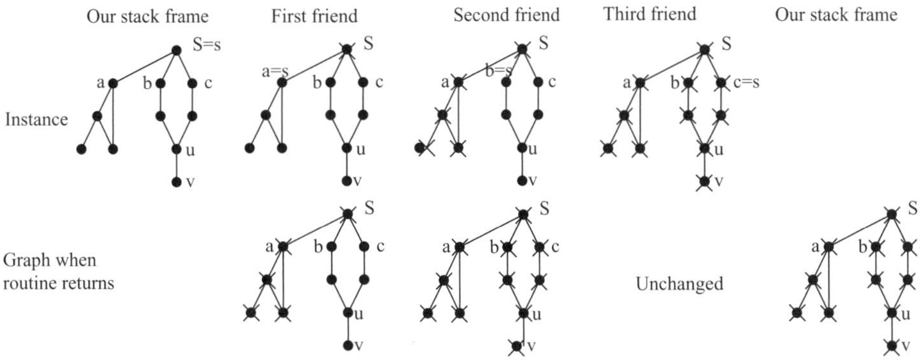

Figure 14.9: An example instance graph.

Pruning Paths: Consider the instance graph in Figure 14.9. There are two obvious paths from node S to node v. However, there are actually an infinite number of such paths. One path of interest is the one that starts at S, and traverses around past u up to c and then down to v. All of these equally valued paths will be pruned from consideration, except the one that goes from S through b and u directly to v.

Three Friends: Given this instance, we first mark our source node S with an x, and then we recurse three times, once from each of a, b, and c.

> ***Friend a***: Our first friend marks all nodes that are reachable from its source node $a = s$ without passing through a previously marked node. This includes only the nodes in the leftmost branch, because when we marked our source S, we blocked his route to the rest of the graph.

> ***Friend b***: Our second friend does the same. He finds, for example, the path that goes from b through u directly to v. He also finds and marks the nodes back around to c.

> ***Friend c***: Our third friend is of particular interest. He finds that his source node, c, has already been marked. Hence, he returns without doing anything. This prunes off this entire branch of the recursion tree. The reason that he can do this is that for any path to a node that he would consider, another path to the same node has already been considered.

Achieving the Postcondition: Consider the component of the graph reachable from our source s without passing through a previously marked nodes. (Because our instance has no marked nodes, this includes all the nodes.) To mark the nodes within this component, we do the following. First, we mark our source s. This partitions our component of reachable nodes into subcomponents that are still reachable from each other. Each such subcomponent has at least one edge from s into it. When we traverse the first such edge, the friend marks all the nodes within this subcomponent.

Running Time: Marking a node before it is recursed from ensures that each node is recursed from at most once. Recursing from a node involves traversing each edge from it. Hence, each edge is traversed at most twice: once from each direction. Hence, the running time is linear in the number of edges.

EXERCISE 14.5.1 *Trace out the iterative and the recursive algorithm on the same graph, and see how they compare. Do they have the same running time?*

14.6 Linear Ordering of a Partial Order

Finding a linear order consistent with a given partial order is one of many applications of a depth-first search. (Hint: If a question ever mentions that a graph is directed acyclic, always start by running this algorithm.)

Definition of Total Order: A *total order* of a set of objects V specifies for each pair of objects $u, v \in V$ either (1) that u is before v or (2) that v is before u. It must be *transitive*, in that if u is before v and v is before w, then u is before w.

Definition of Partial Order: A *partial order* of a set of objects V supplies only some of the information of a total order. For each pair of objects $u, v \in V$, it specifies either that u is before v, that v is before u, or that the order of u and v is undefined. It must also be transitive.

For example, you must put on your underwear before your pants, and you must put on your shoes after both your pants and your socks. According to transitivity, this means you must put your underwear on before your shoes. However, you do have the freedom to put your underwear and your socks on in either order. My son, Josh, when six, mistook this partial order for a total order and refused to put on his socks before his underwear. When he was eight, he explained to me that the reason that he could get dressed faster than I was that he had a "shortcut," consisting in putting his socks on before his pants. I was thrilled that he had at least partially understood the idea of a partial order:

```
underwear
    \
  pants    socks
      \   /
      shoes
```

A partial order can be represented by a directed acyclic graph (DAG) G. The vertices consist of the objects V, and the directed edge $\langle u, v \rangle$ indicates that u is before v. It follows from transitivity that if there is a directed path in G from u to v, then we know that u is before v. A cycle in G from u to v and back to u presents a contradiction, because u cannot be both before and after v.

Specifications of the Topological Sort Problem:

Preconditions: The input is a directed acyclic graph G representing a partial order.

Postconditions: The output is a total order consistent with the partial order given by G, that is, for all edges $\langle u, v \rangle \in G$, u appears before v in the total order.

An Easy but Slow Algorithm:

The Algorithm: Start at any node v of G. If v has an outgoing edge, walk along it to one of its neighbors. Continue walking until you find a node t that has no outgoing edges. Such a node is called a *sink*. This process cannot continue forever, because the graph has no cycles.

The sink t can go after every node in G. Hence, you should put t last in the total order, delete t from G, and recursively repeat the process on $G - v$.

Running Time: It takes up to n time to find the first sink, $n - 1$ to find the second, and so on. The total time is $\Theta(n^2)$.

Algorithm Using a Depth-First Search: Start at any node s of G. Do a depth-first search starting at node s. After this search completes, nodes that are considered found will continue to be considered found, and so should not be considered again. Let s' be any unfound node of G. Do a depth-first search starting at node s'. Repeat the process until all nodes have been found.

Use the time stamp $f(u)$ to keep track of the order in which nodes are *completely handled*, that is, removed from the stack. Output the nodes in reverse order.

If you ever find a back edge, then stop and report that the graph has a cycle.

Proof of Correctness:

Lemma: For every edge $\langle u, v \rangle$ of G, node v is completely handled before u.

Proof of Lemma: Consider some edge $\langle u, v \rangle$ of G. Before u is completely handled, it must be put onto the stack *foundNotHandled*. At this point in time, there are three cases:

Tree Edge: v has not yet been found. Because u has an edge to v, v is put onto the top of the stack above u before u has been completely handled. No more progress will be made towards handling u until v has been completely handled and removed from the stack.

Back Edge: v has been found, but not completely handled, and hence is on the stack somewhere below u. Such an edge is a back edge. This contradicts the fact that G is acyclic.

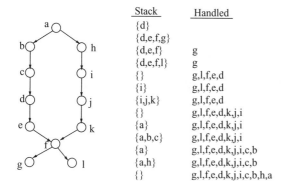

Stack	Handled
{d}	
{d,e,f,g}	
{d,e,f}	g
{d,e,f,l}	g
{}	g,l,f,e,d
{i}	g,l,f,e,d
{i,j,k}	g,l,f,e,d
{}	g,l,f,e,d,k,j,i
{a}	g,l,f,e,d,k,j,i
{a,b,c}	g,l,f,e,d,k,j,i
{a}	g,l,f,e,d,k,j,i,c,b
{a,h}	g,l,f,e,d,k,j,i,c,b
{}	g,l,f,e,d,k,j,i,c,b,h,a

(Toplogical sort) = a,h,b,c,i,j,k,d,e,f,l,g

Figure 14.10: *A topological sort is found using a depth-first search.*

Forward or Cross Edge: v has already been completely handled and re-moved from the stack. In this case, we are done: v was completely handled before u.

Topologically Sorted: Exercise 14.6.1 asks to show that this lemma is sufficient to prove that the reverse order in which the nodes were completely handled is a correct topological sort.

Example: See the example instance in Figure 14.10.

Running Time: As with the depth-first search, no edge is followed more than once. Hence, the total time is $\Theta(|E|)$.

Shortest-Weighted Path on a DAG: Suppose you want to find the shortest-weighted path for a directed graph G that you know is acyclic. You could use Dijkstra's algorithm from Section 14.3. However, as hinted above, whenever a question mentions that a graph is acyclic, it is always fastest to start by finding a linear order consistent with the edges of the graph. Once this has been completed, you can handle the nodes (as done in Dijkstra's algorithm) in this linear order. Exercise 14.6.2 asks you to prove the correctness of this algorithm.

EXERCISE 14.6.1 *Show that in order to prove that the reverse order in which the nodes were completely handled is a correct topological sort, it is sufficient to prove that for every edge $\langle u, v \rangle$ of G, node v is completely handled before u.*

EXERCISE 14.6.2 *(See solution in Part Five.) Prove the correctness and estimate the running time of this algorithm for shortest weighted paths for DAGs.*

14.7 Exercise

EXERCISE 14.7.1 *Trace breadth-first and depth-first searches on the following two graphs. For each do the following:*

1. *Start at node s, and when there is a choice, follow edges from left to right. Number the nodes 1, 2, 3, ... in the order that they are found, starting with node s = 1.*
2. *Darken the edges of the tree specified by the predecessor array π.*
3. *What is the data structure used by each search to store nodes that are found but not yet handled?*
4. *Circle the nodes that are in this data structure when node 8 is first found.*

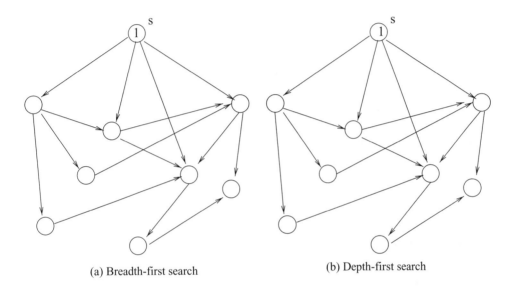

(a) Breadth-first search   (b) Depth-first search

15 Network Flows and Linear Programming

Network flow is a classic computational problem with a surprisingly large number of applications, such as routing trucks and matching happy couples. Think of a given directed graph as a network of pipes starting at a source node s and ending at a sink node t. Through each pipe water can flow in one direction at some rate up to some maximum capacity. The goal is to find the maximum total rate at which water can flow from the source node s to the sink node t. If this were a physical system of pipes, you could determine the answer simply by pushing as much water through as you could. However, achieving this algorithmically is more difficult than you might at first think, because the exponentially many paths from s to t overlap, winding forward and backward in complicated ways.

An Optimization Problem: Network flow is another example of an optimization problem, which involves searching for a best solution from some large set of solutions. The formal specifications are described in Chapter 13.

Network Flow Specification: Given an instance $\langle G, s, t \rangle$, the goal is to find a maximum rate of flow through graph G from node s to node t.

> *Precondition:* We are given one of the following instances.
>
> > **Instances:** An *instance* $\langle G, s, t \rangle$ consists of a directed graph G and specific nodes s and t. Each edge $\langle u, v \rangle$ is associated with a positive capacity $c_{\langle u,v \rangle}$. For example, see Figure 15.1.a.
>
> *Postcondition:* The output is a solution with maximum value and the value of that solution.
>
> > **Solutions for Instance:** A solution for the instance is a *flow* F, which specifies the flow $F_{\langle u,v \rangle}$ through each edge of the graph. The requirements of a flow are as follows. For example, see Figure 15.1.b.
> >
> > > *Unidirectional Flow:* For any pair of nodes, it is easiest to assume that flow does not go in both directions between them. Hence, we will require that at least one of $F_{\langle u,v \rangle}$ and $F_{\langle v,u \rangle}$ be zero and that neither be negative.

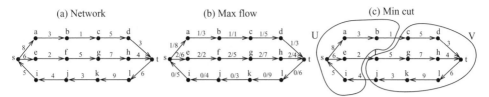

Figure 15.1: (a) A network with its edge capacities labeled. (b) A maximum flow in this network. The first value associated with each edge is its flow, and the second is its capacity. The total rate of the flow is $3 = 1 + 2 - 0$. Note that no more flow can be pushed along the top path, because the edge $\langle b, c \rangle$ is at capacity. Similarly for the edge $\langle e, f \rangle$. Note also that no flow is pushed along the bottom path, because this would decrease the total from s to t. (c) A minimum cut in this network. The capacity of this min cut is $3 = 1 + 2$. Note that the capacity of the edge $\langle j, i \rangle$ is not included in the capacity of the cut, because it is going in the wrong direction. (b) vs (c): The rate of the maximum flow is the same as the capacity of the min cut. The edges crossing forward across the cut are at capacity in the flow, while those crossing backward have zero flow. These things are not coincidences.

> *Edge Capacity:* The flow through any edge cannot exceed the capacity of the edge, namely $F_{\langle u,v \rangle} \le c_{\langle u,v \rangle}$.
>
> *No Leaks:* No water can be added at any node other than the source s, and no water can be drained at any node other than the sink t. At each other node the total flow into the node equals the total flow out, i.e., for all nodes $u \notin \{s, t\}$, $\sum_v F_{\langle v,u \rangle} = \sum_v F_{\langle u,v \rangle}$.

Measure of Success: The value of a flow F, denoted $rate(F)$, is the total rate of flow from the source s to the sink t. We will define this to be the total that leaves s without coming back, $rate(F) = \sum_v [F_{\langle s,v \rangle} - F_{\langle v,s \rangle}]$. Agreeing with our intuition, we will later prove that because no flow leaks or is created in between s and t, this flow equals that flowing into t without leaving it, namely $\sum_v [F_{\langle v,t \rangle} - F_{\langle t,v \rangle}]$.

Min Cut Specification: Another interesting and perhaps surprisingly related optimization problem is *min cut*. Given an instance $\langle G, s, t \rangle$, the goal is to find a *cut* between s and t that has the possible minimum capacity crossing it from the s side to the t side.

> *Precondition:* We are given one of the following instances.
>
> **Instances:** An *instance* $\langle G, s, t \rangle$ consists of a directed graph G and specific nodes s and t. Each edge $\langle u, v \rangle$ is associated with a positive capacity $c_{\langle u,v \rangle}$. Note that the network flow and min cut Problems have the same instances. For example, see Figure 15.1.a.
>
> *Postcondition:* The output is a solution with minimum value and the value of that solution.
>
> **Solutions for the Instance:** A solution for the instance is a *cut* $C = \langle U, V \rangle$, which is a partitioning of the nodes of the graph into two sets U and V such that the source s is in U and the sink t is in V. For example, see Figure 15.1.c.

For example, if G gives the roads, s is Toronto, and t is Berkeley, a cut could be the Canadian–US border. Because the nodes in a graph do not have a location as cities do, there is no reason for the partition of the nodes to be geographically contiguous. Anyone of the exponential number of partitions will do.

Measure of Success: The capacity of a cut is the sum of the capacities of all edges from U to V, namely, $cap(C) = \sum_{u \in U} \sum_{v \in V} c_{\langle u,v \rangle}$. Note that this does not include the capacities $c_{\langle v,u \rangle}$ of the edges going back from V to U.

In Section 15.1, we will design an algorithm for the network flow problem. We will see that this algorithm is an example of a *hill-climbing algorithm* and that it does not necessarily work, because it may get stuck in a small local maximum. In Section 15.2, we will modify the algorithm and use the *primal–dual* method, which uses a min cut to guarantee that it has found a global maximum. This algorithm, however, may have exponential running time. In Section 15.3, we prove that the steepest-ascent version of this hill climbing algorithm runs in polynomial time. Finally, Section 15.4 relates these ideas to another, more general problem called *linear programming*.

EXERCISE 15.0.1 *Suppose we ensured that flow goes in only one direction between any two nodes, not by requiring that the flow in one direction $F_{\langle v,u \rangle}$ be zero, but by requiring that $F_{\langle v,u \rangle} = -F_{\langle u,v \rangle}$. This is less consistent with intuition and obscures some subtleties. The change does, however have the advantage of simplifying many of the equations. For example, the no-leak requirement simplifies to $\sum_v F_{\langle u,v \rangle} = 0$. How does this change all of the other equations in this section?*

15.1 A Hill-Climbing Algorithm with a Small Local Maximum

Hiking at the age of seven, my son Josh stated that the way to find the top of the hill is simply to keep walking in a direction that takes you up, and you know you are there when you cannot go up any more. Little did he know that this is also a common technique for finding the best solution for many optimization problems. The algorithm maintains one solution for the problem and repeatedly makes one of a small set of prescribed changes to this solution in a way that makes it a better solution. It stops when none of these changes seems able to make a better solution.

There are two problems with this technique. First, it is not necessarily clear how long it will take until the algorithm stops. Second, sometimes it finds a small local maximum, i.e., the

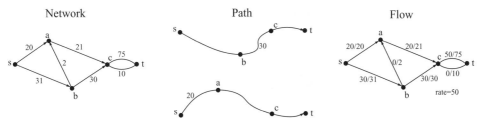

Figure 15.2: *A network, with its edge capacities labeled, is given on the left. In the middle are two paths through which flow can be pushed, with the resulting flow on the right. The first value associated with each edge is its flow, and the second is its capacity. The total rate of the flow is 50.*

201

top of a small hill, instead of the overall global maximum. Many hill-climbing algorithms, however, are used extensively even though they are not guaranteed to work, because in practice they seem to work well. In this section, we describe a hill-climbing algorithm that is guaranteed to quickly solve its problem.

Basic Ideas: I will start by giving some ideas that do not work.

Push from Source: The first obvious thing to try is to simply start pushing water out of s. If the capacities of the edges near s are large, then they can take lots of flow. Further down the network, however, the capacities may be smaller, in which case the flow that we started will get stuck. To avoid causing capacity violation or leaks, we will have to back off the flow that we started. Even further down the network, an edge may fork into edges with larger capacities, in which case we will need to decide in which direction to route the flow. Keeping track of this could be a headache.

Plan Path for a Drop of Water: A solution to both the problem of flow getting stuck and the problem of routing flow along the way is to first find an entire path from s to t through which flow can take place. In the example in Figure 15.2, water can flow along the path $\langle s, b, c, t \rangle$: see the top middle path. We then can push as much as possible through this path. It is easy to see that the bottleneck is the edge $\langle b, c \rangle$ with capacity 30. Hence, we add a flow of 30 to each edge along this path. That working well, we can try adding more water through another path. Let us try the path $\langle s, a, c, t \rangle$. The first interesting thing to note is that the edge $\langle c, t \rangle$ in this path already has flow 30 through it. Because this edge has a capacity of 75, the maximum flow that can be added to it is $75 - 30 = 45$. This, however, turns out not to be the bottleneck, because the edge $\langle s, a \rangle$ has capacity 20. Adding a flow of 20 to each edge along this path gives the flow shown on the right in Figure 15.2. For each edge, the left value gives its flow and the right gives its capacity. There being no more paths forward from s to t, we are now stuck. Is this the maximum flow?

A Winding Path: Water has a funny way of seeping from one place to another. It does not need to only go forward. Though the path $\langle s, b, a, c, t \rangle$ winds backward,

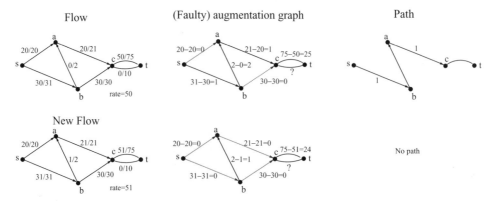

Flow   (Faulty) augmentation graph   Path

New Flow

Figure 15.3: The top left is the same flow given in Figure 15.2, the first value associated with each edge being its flow, and the second being its capacity. The top middle is a first attempt at an augmentation graph for this flow. Each edge is labeled with the amount of more flow that it can handle, namely $c_{(u,v)} - F_{(u,v)}$. The top right is the path in this augmentation graph through which flow is augmented. The bottom left is the resulting flow. The bottom middle is its (faulty) augmentation graph. No more flow can be added through it.

more flow can be pushed through it. Another way to see that the concept of "forward" is not relevant to this problem. The bottleneck in adding flow through this path is the edge $\langle a, c \rangle$. Already having a flow 20, its flow can only increase by 1. Adding a flow of 1 along this path gives the flow shown on the bottom left in Figure 15.3. Though this example reminds us that we need to consider all possible paths from s to t, we know that finding paths through a graph is easy using either breadth-first or depth-first search (Sections 14.2 and 14.4). However, in addition, we want to make sure that the path we find is such that we can add a nonzero amount of flow through it. For this, we introduce the idea of an *augmentation graph*.

The (Faulty) Augmentation Graph: Before we can find a path through which more flow can be added, we need to compute for each edge the amount of flow that can be added through it. To keep track of this information, we construct from the current flow F a graph denoted by G_F and called an *augmentation graph*. (Augment means to add on. The augmentation is the amount you add on.) This graph initially will have the same directed edges as our network, G. Each of these edges is labeled with the amount by which its flow can be increase. We will call this the edge's *augmentation capacity*. Assuming that the current flow through the edge is $F_{(u,v)}$ and its capacity is $c_{(u,v)}$, this augmentation capacity is given by $c_{(u,v)} - F_{(u,v)}$. Any edge for which this capacity is zero is deleted from the augmentation graph. Because of this, nonzero flow can be added along any path found from s to t within this augmentation graph. The path chosen will be called the *augmentation path*. The minimum augmentation capacity of any of its edges is the amount by which the flow in each of its edges is augmented. For an example, see Figure 15.3. In this case, the only path happens to be $\langle s, b, a, c, t \rangle$, which is the path that we used. Its path is augmented by a flow of 1.

The (Faulty) Algorithm: We have now defined the basic steps and can easily fill in the remaining detail of the algorithm.

The Loop Invariant: The most obvious loop invariant is that at the top of the main loop we have a legal flow. It is possible that some more complex invariant will be needed, but for the time being this seems to be enough.

The Measure of Progress: The obvious measure of progress is how much flow the algorithm has managed to get between s and t, that is, the rate $rate(F)$ of the current flow.

The Main Steps: Given some current legal flow F through the network G, the algorithm improves the flow as follows: It constructs the augmentation graph G_F for the flow; finds an augmentation path from s to t through this graph using breadth-first or depth-first search; finds the edge in the path whose augmentation capacity is the smallest; and increases the flow by this amount through each edge in the path.

Maintaining the Loop Invariant: We must prove that the newly created flow is a legal flow in order to prove that $\langle loop\text{-}invariant' \rangle \,\&\, \text{not}\langle exit\text{-}cond \rangle \& code_{loop} \Rightarrow \langle loop\text{-}invariant'' \rangle$.

Edge Capacity: We are careful never to increase the flow of any edge by more than the amount $c_{\langle u,v \rangle} - F_{\langle u,v \rangle}$. Hence, its flow never increases beyond its capacity $c_{\langle u,v \rangle}$.

No Leaks: We are careful to add the same amount to every edge along a path from s to t. Hence, for any node u along the path, there is one edge $\langle v, u \rangle$ into the node whose flow changes and one edge $\langle u, v' \rangle$ out of the node whose flow changes. Because these change by the same amount, the flow into the node remains equal to that out, so that for all nodes $u \notin \{s, t\}$, we have $\sum_v F_{\langle v,u \rangle} = \sum_v F_{\langle u,v \rangle}$. In this way, we maintain the fact that the current flow has no leaks.

Making Progress: Because the edges whose flows could not change were deleted from the augmenting graph, we know that the flow through the path that was found can be increase by a positive amount. This increases the total flow. Because the capacities of the edges are integers, we can prove inductively that the flows are always integers and hence the flow increases by at least one. (Having fractions as capacities is fine, but having irrationals as capacities can cause the algorithm to run forever.)

Initial Code: We can start with a flow of zero through each edge. This establishes the loop invariant, because it is a legal flow.

Exit Condition: At the moment, it is hard to imagine how we will know whether or not we have found the maximum flow. However, it is easy to see what will cause our algorithm to get stuck. If the augmenting graph for our current flow is such that there is no path in it from s to t, then unless we can think of something better to do, we must exit.

Termination: As usual, we prove that this iterative algorithm eventually terminates because at every iteration the rate of flow increases by at least one and because the total flow certainly cannot exceed the sum of the capacities of all the edges.

This completely defines an algorithm.

Getting Stuck at a Local Maximum: Hill-climbing algorithms move up until they cannot go up any more. The reason that they are not allowed to go down is the same reason that iterative algorithms need to make progress every iteration, namely, to ensure that the algorithm eventually stops.

A major problem with this is that sometimes they find a small *local maximum*, that is, the top of a small hill, instead of the overall global maximum. Because a hill-climbing algorithm is not allowed to move down, it gets stuck at such a local maximum.

This is similar to the class of algorithms known as *greedy algorithms*, described in Chapter 16. In these, no decision that is made is revoked. Our network flow algorithm could be considered to be greedy in that once the algorithm decides to put flow through an edge, it may later add more, but it never removes flow. Given that our goal is to get as much flow from s to t as possible and that it does not matter how that flow gets there, it makes sense that such a greedy approach would work. However, we will see that it does not work.

A Counterexample: Proving that a given algorithm works for every input instance can be a major challenge. However, in order to prove that it does not work, we only need to give one input instance in which it fails. Figure 15.4 gives such an example. It traces out the algorithm on the same instance from Figure 15.2 that we did before. However, this time the algorithm happens to choose different paths. First it puts a flow of 2 through the path $\langle s, b, a, c, t \rangle$, followed by a flow of 19 through $\langle s, a, c, t \rangle$, followed by a flow of 29 through $\langle s, b, c, t \rangle$. At this point, we are stuck because the augmenting graph does not contain a path from s to t. This is a problem because the current flow is only 50, whereas we have already seen that the flow for this network can be 51. In hill-climbing terminology, this flow is a small local maximum, because we cannot improve it using the steps that we have allowed; but it is not a global maximum, because there is a better solution.

Where We Went Wrong: From a hill-climbing perspective, we took a step in an arbitrary direction that takes us up, but with our first attempt we happened to head up the big hill and in the second we happened to head up the small hill.

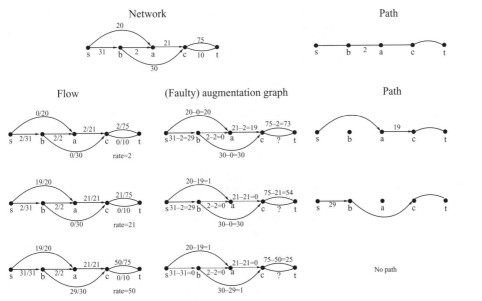

Figure 15.4: The faulty algorithm is traced on the instance from Figure 15.2. The nodes in this graph are laid out differently to emphasize the first path chosen. The current flow is given on the left, the corresponding augmentation graph in the middle, the augmenting path on the right, and the resulting flow on the next line. The algorithm gets stuck at a suboptimal local maximum.

The flow of 51 that we obtained first turns out to be the unique maximum solution (often there are more than one possible maximum solutions). Hence, we can compare it with our present solution to see where we went wrong. In the first step, we put a flow of 2 through the edge $\langle b, a \rangle$; however, in the end it turns out that putting more than 1 through it is a mistake.

Fixing the Algorithm: The following are possible ways of fixing the kind of bugs we found.

Make Better Decisions: If we start by putting flow through the path $\langle s, b, c, t \rangle$, then the algorithm works, but if we start with the path $\langle s, b, a, c, t \rangle$, it does not. One way of fixing the bug is to find some way to choose which path to add flow to next so that we do not get stuck in this way. From the greedy algorithm's perspective, if we are going to commit to a choice, then we had better make a good one. I know of no way to fix the network flow algorithm in this way.

Backtrack: Chapter 17 describes another class of algorithms, known as recursive backtracking algorithms, that continually notice when they have made a mistake and that backtrack, trying other options, until a correct sequence of choices is made. In this example, we need to find a way of decreasing the flow through the edge $\langle b, a \rangle$ from 2 to 1. A general danger of backtracking algorithms in comparison with greedy algorithms is that the algorithm will have a much longer running time if it keeps changing its mind.

Take Bigger Steps: One way of avoiding getting stuck at the top of a small hill is to take a step that is big enough so that you step over the valley onto the slope of the bigger hill and a little higher up. Doing this requires redefine your definition of a step. This is the approach that we will take. We need to find a way of decreasing the flow through the edge $\langle b, a \rangle$ from 2 to 1 while maintaining the loop invariant that we have a legal flow and increasing the overall flow from s to t. The place in the algorithm at which we consider how the flow through an edge is allowed to change is where we define the augmenting graph. In the next section we reconsider this definition.

15.2 The Primal–Dual Hill-Climbing Method

We will now define a larger step that the hill-climbing algorithm may take in hopes of avoiding a local maximum.

The (Correct) Algorithm:

The Augmentation Graph: As before, the augmentation graph expresses how the flow in each edge is able to change.

Forward Edges: As before, when an edge $\langle u, v \rangle$ has flow $F_{\langle u,v \rangle}$ and capacity $c_{\langle u,v \rangle}$, we put the corresponding edge $\langle u, v \rangle$ in the augmentation graph with augmentation capacity $c_{\langle u,v \rangle} - F_{\langle u,v \rangle}$ to indicate that we are allowed to add this much flow from u to v.

Reverse Edges: Now we see that there is a possibility that we might want to decrease the flow from u to v. Given that its current flow is $F_{\langle u,v \rangle}$, this is the amount that it can be decreased by. Effectively, it is the same as increasing the flow from v to u by this same amount. Moreover, if the reverse edge $\langle v, u \rangle$ is also in the graph and has capacity $c_{\langle v,u \rangle}$, then we are able to increase the flow from v to u by this second amount $c_{\langle v,u \rangle}$ as well. Therefore, when the edge $\langle u, v \rangle$ has flow $F_{\langle u,v \rangle}$ and the reverse edge $\langle v, u \rangle$ has capacity $c_{\langle v,u \rangle}$, we

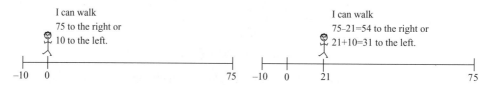

Figure 15.5: Suppose that from my home, I can walk 75 km to the right or 10 to the left. If I am already 21 km to the right, then I can walk $75 - 21 = 54$ km to the right or $21 + 10 = 31$ to the left. More over, walking 31 to the left and -31 to the right are the same. Similarly, suppose that my bank account can only hold \$75 or go into overdraft of up to \$10. If I already have \$21 in the account, then I am able to add $75 - 21 = \$54$ or remove $21 + 10 = \$31$. Removing \$31 and adding $-\$31$ are also the same.

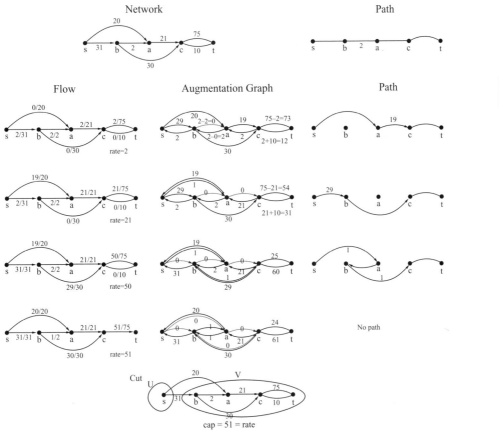

Figure 15.6: A trace of the correct algorithm on the instance from Figure 15.4. The current flow is given on the left, the corresponding augmentation graph in the middle, the augmentation path on the right, and the resulting flow on the next line. The optimal flow is obtained. The bottom diagram shows a minimum cut $C = \langle U, V \rangle$.

also put the reverse edge $\langle v, u \rangle$ in the augmentation graph with augmentation capacity $F_{\langle u,v \rangle} + c_{\langle v,u \rangle}$. For more intuition see Figure 15.5, and for an example see edge $\langle c, t \rangle$ in the second augmentation graph in Figure 15.6.

The Main Steps: Little else changes in the algorithm. Given some current legal flow F through the network G, the algorithm improves the flow as follows: It constructs the augmentation graph G_F for the flow; finds an augmentation path from s to t through this graph using breadth-first or depth-first search; finds the edge in the path whose augmentation capacity is the smallest; and increases the flow by this amount through each edge in the path. If the edge in the augmenting graph is in the opposite direction to that in the flow graph, then this involves decreasing its flow by this amount. This is because increasing flow from v to u is effectively the same as decreasing it from u to v.

Does It Work on the Counterexample?: Figure 15.6 traces this new algorithm on the same example as in Figure 15.4. The new augmenting graphs include edges in the reverse direction. Each step is the same as that in Figure 15.4, until the last step, in which these reverse edges provide the path $\langle s, a, b, c, t \rangle$ from s to t. The bottleneck in this path is 1. Hence, we increase the flow by 1 in each edge in the path. The effect is that the flow through the edge $\langle b, a \rangle$ decreases from 2 to 1, giving the optimal flow that we had obtained before.

Bigger Step: The reverse edges that have been added to the augmentation graph may well not be needed. They do, after all, undo flow that has already been added through an edge. On the other hand, having more edges in the augmentation graph can only increase the possibility of there being a path from s to t through it.

Maintaining the Loop Invariant and Making Progress: See Exercise 15.2.1.

Exit Condition: As before the algorithm exits when it gets stuck because the augmenting graph for our current flow is such that there is no path in it from s to t. However, with more edges in our augmenting graph this may not occur as soon.

Code:

```
algorithm NetworkFlow (G, s, t)

⟨ pre-cond⟩: G is a network given by a directed graph with capacities on the
edges. s is the source node. t is the sink.
⟨ post-cond⟩: F specifies a maximum flow through G, and C specifies a min-
imum cut.

begin
    F = the zero flow
    loop
        ⟨loop-invariant⟩: F is a legal flow.

        G_F = the augmentation graph for F, where
            edge ⟨u, v⟩ has augmentation capacity c_⟨u,v⟩ − F_⟨u,v⟩ and
            edge ⟨v, u⟩ has augmentation capacity c_⟨v,u⟩ + F_⟨u,v⟩.
        exit when s is not connected to t in G_F
        P = a path from s to t in G_F
        w = the minimum augmentation capacity in P
        Add w to the flow F in every edge in P
    end loop
    U = nodes reachable from s in G_F
    V = nodes not reachable from s in G_F
    C = ⟨U, V⟩
    return( F,C)
end algorithm
```

Ending: The next step is to prove that this improved algorithm always finds a global maximum without getting stuck at a small local maximum. Using the notation of iterative algorithms, we must prove that $\langle loop\text{-}invariant \rangle$ & $\langle exit\text{-}cond \rangle$ & $code_{post\text{-}loop} \Rightarrow \langle post\text{-}cond \rangle$. From the loop invariant we know that the algorithm has a legal flow. Because we have exited, we know that the augmenting graph does not contain a path from s to t and hence we are at a local maxima. We must prove that there are no small local maxima and hence we must be at a global maximum and hence have an optimal flow. The method used is called the *primal–dual method*.

> **Primal–Dual Hill Climbing:** Suppose that over the hills on which we are climbing there are an exponential number of roofs, one on top of the other. As before, our problem is to find a place to stand on the hills that has maximum height. We call this the *primal* optimization problem. An equally challenging problem is to find the lowest roof. We call this the *dual* optimization problem. The situation is such that each roof is above each place to stand. It follows trivially that the lowest and hence optimal roof is above the highest and hence optimal place to stand, but offhand we do not know how far above it is.
>
> We say that a hill-climbing algorithm gets stuck when it is unable to step in a way that moves it to a higher place to stand. A primal–dual hill-climbing algorithm is able to prove that the only reason for getting stuck is that the place it is standing is pressed up against a roof. This is proved by proving that from any location, it can either step to a higher location or specify a roof to which this location is adjacent. We will now see how these conditions are sufficient for proving what we want.
>
>> **Lemma: Finds Optimal.** A primal–dual hill-climbing algorithm is guaranteed to find an optimal solution to both the primal and the dual optimization problems.
>>
>> **Proof:** By the design of the algorithm, it only stops when it has a location L and a roof R with matching heights $height(L) = height(R)$. This location must be optimal, because every other location L' must be below this roof and hence cannot be higher than this location, that is, $\forall L', \; height(L') \leq height(R) = height(L)$. We say that this dual solution R *witnesses* the fact that the primal solution L is optimal. Similarly, L witnesses the fact that R is optimal, that is, $\forall R', \; height(R') \geq height(L) = height(R)$. This is called the *duality principle*.

Cuts as Upper Bounds: In order to apply these ideas to the network flow problem, we must find some upper bounds on the flow between s and t. Through a single path, the capacity of each edge acts as an upper bound, because the flow through the path cannot exceed the capacity of any of its edges. The edge with the smallest capacity, being the lowest upper bound, is the bottleneck. In a general network (see Figure 15.1), a single edge cannot act as a bottleneck, because the flow might be able to go around this edge via other edges. A similar approach, however, works. Suppose that we wanted to bound the traffic between Toronto and Berkeley. We know that any such flow must cross the Canadian–US border. Hence, there is no need to worry about what the flow might do within Canada or within the US. We can safely say that the flow from Toronto to Berkeley is bounded above by the sum of the capacities of all the border crossings. Of course, this does not mean that that flow can be achieved. Other upper bounds can be obtained by summing the border crossing for other regions. For example, you could bound the traffic leaving Toronto, leaving Ontario, entering California, or entering Berkeley. This brings us to the following definition.

Cut of a Graph: A cut $C = \langle U, V \rangle$ of a graph is a partitioning of the nodes of the graph into two sets U and V such that the source s is in U and the sink t is in V. The capacity of a cut is the sum of the capacities of all edges from U to V, namely, $cap(C) = \sum_{u \in U} \sum_{v \in V} c_{\langle u,v \rangle}$.

Because the nodes in a graph do not have a location as cities do, there is no reason for the partition of the nodes to be geographically contiguous. Any one of the exponential number of partitions will do.

Flow across a Cut: To be able to compare the rate of flow from s to t with the capacity of a cut, we will first need to define the flow across a cut.

rate(F, C): Define $rate(F, C)$ to be the current flow F across the cut C, which is the total of all the flow in edges that cross from U to V minus the total of all the flow that comes back, i.e., $rate(F, C) = \sum_{u \in U} \sum_{v \in V} [F_{\langle u,v \rangle} - F_{\langle v,u \rangle}]$.

rate(F) = rate(F, ⟨{s}, G − {s}⟩): We defined the flow from s to t to be the total flow that leaves s without coming back, namely, $rate(F) = \sum_v [F_{\langle s,v \rangle} - F_{\langle v,s \rangle}]$. This is precisely the equation for the flow across the cut that puts s all by itself, namely, $rate(F) = rate(F, \langle \{s\}, G - \{s\} \rangle)$.

Lemma: rate(F, C) = rate(F). Intuitively this makes sense. Because no water leaks or is created between the source s and the sink t, the flow out of s equals the flow across any cut between s and t, which in turn equals the flow into t. It is because these are the same that we simply call this the flow from s to t. Since the flow into a node is the same as that out of the node, if you move the node from one side of the cut to the other this does not change the total flow across the cut. Hence we can change the cut one node at a time from being the one containing only s to being the cut that we are interested in.

More formally this is done by induction on the size of U. For the base case, $rate(F) = rate(F, \langle \{s\}, G - \{s\} \rangle)$ gives us that our hypothesis $rate(F, C) = rate(F)$ is true for every cut that has only one node in U. Now suppose that, by way of induction, we assume that it is true for every cut that has i nodes in U. We will now prove it for those cuts that have $i + 1$ nodes in it. Let $C = \langle U, V \rangle$ be any such cut. Choose one node

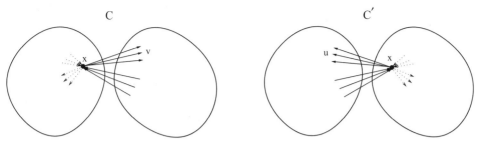

Figure 15.7: The edges across the cut that do not cancel in rate(F, C) − rate(F, C′).

x (other then s) from U and move it across the border. This gives us a new cut $C' = \langle U - \{x\}, V \cup \{x\} \rangle$, where the side $U - \{x\}$ contains only i nodes. Our assumption then gives us that the flow across this cut is equal to the flow of F: $rate(F, C') = rate(F)$. Hence, in order to prove that $rate(F, C) = rate(F)$, we only need to prove that $rate(F, C) = rate(F, C')$. We will do this by proving that the difference between these is zero. By definition,

$$rate(F, C) - rate(F, C')$$

$$= \left[\sum_{u \in U} \sum_{v \in V} F_{\langle u, v \rangle} - F_{\langle v, u \rangle} \right] - \left[\sum_{u \in U - \{x\},} \sum_{v \in V \cup \{x\}} F_{\langle u, v \rangle} - F_{\langle v, u \rangle} \right]$$

(Figure 15.7 shows the terms that do not cancel)

$$= \left[\sum_{v \in V} F_{\langle x, v \rangle} - F_{\langle v, x \rangle} \right] - \left[\sum_{u \in U} F_{\langle u, x \rangle} - F_{\langle x, u \rangle} \right]$$

$$= \left[\sum_{v \in V} F_{\langle x, v \rangle} - F_{\langle v, x \rangle} \right] + \left[\sum_{v \in U} F_{\langle x, v \rangle} - F_{\langle v, x \rangle} \right]$$

$$= \left[\sum_{v} F_{\langle x, v \rangle} - F_{\langle v, x \rangle} \right] = 0$$

This is the total flow out of the node, x minus the total flow into the node, which is zero by the requirement that no node leaks. This proves that $rate(F, C) = rate(F)$ for every cut that has $i + 1$ nodes in U. By induction, it then is true for all cuts for every size of U. This formally proves that the rate of any given flow F is the same across any cut C.

Lemma: $rate(F) \leq cap(C)$: It is now easy to prove that $rate(F)$ of any flow F is at most the capacity of any cut C. In the primal–dual analogy, this proves that each roof is above each place to stand. Given $rate(F) = rate(F, C)$, it is sufficient to prove that the flow across a cut is at most the capacity of the cut. This follows easily from the definition $rate(F, C) = \sum_{u \in U} \sum_{v \in V} [F_{\langle u, v \rangle} - F_{\langle v, u \rangle}] \leq \sum_{u \in U} \sum_{v \in V} [F_{\langle u, v \rangle}]$, because having positive flow backwards across the cut from V to U only decreases the flow. Then this sum is at most

$\sum_{u \in U} \sum_{v \in V}[c_{\langle u,v \rangle}]$, because no edge can have flow exceeding its capacity. This is the definition of the capacity $cap(C)$ of the cut. This proves the required $rate(F) \le cap(C)$.

Take a Step or Find a Cut: The primal–dual method requires that from any location, you can either step to a higher location or specify a roof to which this location is adjacent. In the network flow problem, this translates to: given any legal flow F, either find a better flow or find a cut whose capacity is equal to the rate of the current flow. The augmentation graph G_F includes those edges through which the flow rate can be increased. Hence, the nodes reachable from s in this graph are the nodes to which more flow could be pushed. Let U denote this set of nodes. In contrast, the remaining set of nodes, which we will denote by V, are those to which more flow cannot be pushed. See the cut at the bottom of Figure 15.6. No flow can be pushed across the border between U and V, because all the edges crossing over are at capacity. If t is in U, then there is a path from s to t through which the flow can be increased. On the other hand, if t is in V, then $C = \langle U, V \rangle$ is a cut separating s and t. What remains is to formalize the proof that the capacity of this cut is equal to rate of the current flow. (For another example, see the cut in Figure 15.1.c. Although $cap(C) = rate(F)$, this cut was not formed as described here because the node i is not reachable from s in the augmentation graph.)

Since we know $rate(F, C) = rate(F)$, it remains only to prove $rate(F, C) = cap(C)$, that is, that the current flow across the cut C is equal to the capacity of the cut.

Lemma: $rate(F, C) = cap(C)$: To prove this, it is sufficient to prove that every edge $\langle u, v \rangle$ crossing from U to V has flow in F at capacity ($F_{\langle u,v \rangle} = c_{\langle u,v \rangle}$) and every edge $\langle v, u \rangle$ crossing back from V to U has zero flow in F. These give that $rate(F, C) = \sum_{u \in U} \sum_{v \in V}[F_{\langle u,v \rangle} - F_{\langle v,u \rangle}] = \sum_{u \in U} \sum_{v \in V}[c_{\langle u,v \rangle} - 0] = cap(C)$.

$F_{\langle u,v \rangle} = c_{\langle u,v \rangle}$: Consider any edge $\langle u, v \rangle$ crossing from U to V. If $F_{\langle u,v \rangle} < c_{\langle u,v \rangle}$, then the edge $\langle u, v \rangle$ with augmentation capacity $c_{\langle u,v \rangle} - F_{\langle u,v \rangle}$ would be added to the augmentation graph. However, having such an edge in the augmentation graph contradicts the fact that u is reachable from s in the augmentation graph and v is not.

$F_{\langle v,u \rangle} = 0$: If $F_{\langle v,u \rangle} > 0$, then the edge $\langle u, v \rangle$ with augmentation capacity $c_{\langle u,v \rangle} + F_{\langle v,u \rangle}$ would be added to the augmentation graph. Again, having such an edge is a contradiction.

This proves that $rate(F, C) = cap(C)$.

Lemma: $cap(C) = rate(F)$: $cap(C) = rate(F, C) = rate(F)$, that is, the flow we have found equals the capacity of the cut, as required.

Ending: This improved network flow algorithm always finds a global maximum without getting stuck at a small local maximum. In each iteration it either finds a path in the augmenting graph through which it can improve the current flow or finds a cut that witnesses the fact that there are no better flows.

Max-Flow–Min-Cut Duality Principle: The max flow and min cut problems were defined at the beginning of this chapter, both being interesting problems in their own right. Now we see that cuts can be used as the ceilings on the flows.

Max Flow = Min Cut: We have proved that, given any network as input, the network flow algorithm finds a maximum flow and—almost as an accident—finds a minimum cut as well. This proves that the maximum flow through any network equals its minimum cut.

Dual Problems: We say that the *dual* of the max flow problem is the min cut problem, and conversely that the *dual* of the min cut problem is the max flow problem.

Credits: This algorithm was developed by Ford and Fulkerson in 1962.

Running Time Exponential? Suppose that the network graph has m edges, each with a capacity that is represented by an $O(\ell)$ bit number. Each capacity could be as large as $O(2^\ell)$, and the total maximum flow could be as large as $O(m \cdot 2^\ell)$. Starting out as zero and increasing by about one each iteration, the algorithm would need $O(m \cdot 2^\ell)$ iterations until the maximum flow is found. This running time is polynomial in the number of edges, m. However, the size of the input instance, which in this case is the number of bits (or digits) needed to represent all of the values, is $O(m \cdot \ell)$. If ℓ is large, then the number of iterations, $O(m \cdot 2^\ell)$, is exponential in this size. This is a common problem with hill-climbing algorithms.

EXERCISE 15.2.1 *Prove that the network flow algorithm presented in this section maintains the loop invariant that it always holds a legal flow. Do this by proving that the changes to the flow do not violate any edge capacities or create leaks at nodes. Also prove that progress is made because the total flow increases. You need to be careful with your plus and minus signs.*

EXERCISE 15.2.2 *Starting with the flow given below, complete the network flow algorithm.*

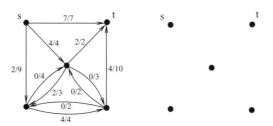

EXERCISE 15.2.3 *In hill-climbing algorithms there are steps that make lots of progress and steps that make very little progress. For example, the first iteration on the input given in Figure 15.2 might find a path through the augmentation graph through which a flow of 30 can be added. It might, however, find the path through which only a flow of 2 can be added. How bad might the running time be when the computation is unlucky enough to always take the worst legal step allowed by the algorithm? Start by taking the step that increases the flow by 2 for the input given in Figure 15.2. Then continue to take the worst possible step. You could draw out each and every step, but it is better to use this opportunity to use loop invariants. What does the flow look like after i iterations? Repeat this process on the same graph except that the four edges forming the square now have capacities 1,000,000,000,000,000 and the crossover edge has capacity 1. (Also move t to c or give that last edge a large capacity.)*

1. *What is the worst case number of iterations of this network flow algorithm as a function of the number of edges m in the input network?*
2. *What is the official "size" of a network?*
3. *What is the worst case number of iterations of this network flow algorithm as a function of the size of the input network?*

EXERCISE 15.2.4 *If all the capacities in the given network are integers, prove that the algorithm always returns a solution in which the flow through each edge is an integer. For some applications, this fact is crucial.*

EXERCISE 15.2.5 *(See solution in Part Five.) Give an algorithm for solving the* min cut *problem. Given a network $\langle G, s, t \rangle$ with capacities on the edges, find a minimum cut $C = \langle U, V \rangle$ where $s \in U$ and $t \in V$. The cost of the cut is its capacity $cap(C) = \sum_{u \in U} \sum_{v \in V} c_{\langle u, v \rangle}$. (Hint: you have already been told how to do this.)*

15.3 The Steepest-Ascent Hill-Climbing Algorithm

We have all experienced that climbing a hill can take a long time if you wind back and forth, barely increasing your height at all. In contrast, you get there much faster if you head energetically straight up the hill. This method, which is call the method of *steepest ascent*, is to always take the step that increases your height the most. If you already know that the hill-climbing algorithm in which you take any step up the hill works, then this new, more specific algorithm also works. However, if you are lucky, it finds the optimal solution faster.

In our network flow algorithm, the choice of what step to take next involves choosing which path in the augmentation graph to take. The amount the flow increases is the smallest augmentation capacity of any edge in this path. It follows that the choice that would give us the biggest improvement is the path whose smallest edge is the largest for any path from s to t. Our steepest-ascent network flow algorithm will augment such a best path each iteration. What remains to be done is to give an algorithm that finds such a path and to prove that this finds a maximum flow within a polynomial number of iterations.

Finding the Augmentation Path with the Biggest Smallest Edge: The input consists of a directed graph with positive edge weights and with special nodes s and t. The output consists of a path from s to t through this graph whose smallest weighted edge is as big as possible.

Easier Problem: Before attempting to develop an algorithm for this, let us consider an easier but related problem. In addition to the directed graph, the input to the easier problem provides a weight, denoted w_{min}. It either outputs a path from s to t whose smallest weighted edge is at least as big as w_{min}, or states that no such path exists.

Using the Easier Problem: Assuming that we can solve this easier problem, we solve the original problem by running the first algorithm with w_{min} being every edge weight in the graph, until we find the weight for which there is a path with such a smallest weight, but there is no path with a bigger smallest weight. This is our answer. (See Exercise 15.3.1.)

Solving the Easier Problem: A path whose smallest weighted edge is at least as big as w_{min} will obviously not contain any edge whose weight is smaller than w_{min}. Hence, the answer to this easier problem will not change if we delete from the graph all edges whose weight is smaller. Any path from s to t in the remaining graph will meet our needs. If there is no such path, then we also know there is no such path in our original graph. This solves the problem.

Implementation Details: In order to find a path from s to t in a graph, the algorithm branches out from s using breadth-first or depth-first search, marking every node reachable from s with the predecessor of the node in the path to it from s. If in the process t is marked, then we have our path. (See Section 14.1.) It seems a waste of time to have to redo this work for each w_{min}, so let's use an iterative algorithm. The loop invariant will be that the work for the previous w_{min} has been done and is stored in a useful way. The main loop will then complete the work for the current w_{min}, reusing as much of the previous work as possible. This can be implemented as follows. Sort the edges from biggest to smallest (breaking ties arbitrarily). Consider them one at a time. When considering w_i, we must construct the graph formed by deleting all the edges with weights smaller than w_i. Denote this by G_{w_i}. We must mark every node reachable from s in this graph. Suppose that we have already done these things in the graph $G_{w_{i-1}}$. We form G_{w_i} from $G_{w_{i-1}}$ by adding the single edge with weight w_i. Let $\langle u, v \rangle$ denote this edge. Nodes are reachable from s in G_{w_i} that were not reachable in $G_{w_{i-1}}$ only if u was reachable and v was not. This new edge then allows v to be reachable. Unmarked nodes now reachable from s via v can all be marked reachable by starting a depth-first search from v. The algorithm will stop at the first edge that allows t to be reached. The edge with the smallest weight in this path to t

will be the edge with weight w_i added during this iteration. There is no path from s to t in the input graph with a larger smallest weighted edge, because t was not reachable when only the larger edges were added. Hence, this path is a path to t in the graph whose smallest weighted edge is the largest. This is the required output of this subroutine.

Running Time: Even though the algorithm for finding the path with the largest smallest edge runs depth-first search for each weight w_i, because the work done before is reused, no node in the process is marked reached more than once, and hence no edge is traversed more than once. It follows that this process requires only $O(m)$ time, where m is the number of edges. This time, however, is dominated by the time $O(m \log m)$ to sort the edges.

Code:

```
algorithm LargestShortestWeight(G, s, t)
```

⟨ **pre-cond**⟩: G is a weighted directed (augmenting) graph. s is the source node. t is the sink.

⟨ **post-cond**⟩: P specifies a path from s to t whose smallest edge weight is as large as possible. $\langle u, v \rangle$ is its smallest weighted edge.

```
begin
    Sort the edges by weight from largest to smallest
    G' = graph with no edges
    mark s reachable
    loop
```

⟨**loop-invariant**⟩: Every node reachable from s in G' is marked reachable.

```
        exit when t is reachable
        ⟨u, v⟩ = the next largest weighted edge in G
        Add ⟨u, v⟩ to G'
        if( u is marked reachable and v is not ) then
            Do a depth-first search from v, marking all reachable nodes
            not marked before.
        end if
    end loop
    P = path from s to t in G'
    return( P, ⟨u, v⟩ )
end algorithm
```

Running Time of Steepest Ascent: How many times must the network flow algorithm augment the flow in a path when the path chosen is that whose augmentation capacity is the largest possible?

Decreasing the Remaining Distance by a Constant Factor: The flow starts out as zero and may need to increase to be as large as $O(m \cdot 2^{\ell})$ when there are m edges with ℓ bit capacities. We would like the number of steps to be not exponential but linear in ℓ. One way to achieve this is to ensure that the current flow doubles each iteration. This, however, is likely not to happen. Another possibility is to turn the measure of progress around. After the ith iteration, let R_i denote the remaining amount that the flow must increase. More formally, suppose that the maximum flow is $rate_{max}$ and that the rate of the current flow is $rate(F)$. The remaining distance is then $R_i = rate_{max} - rate(F)$. We will show that the amount w_{min} by which the flow increases is at least some constant fraction of R_i.

Bounding the Remaining Distance: The funny thing about this measure of progress is that the algorithm does not know what the maximum flow $rate_{max}$ is. It is only needed as part of the analysis. We must bound how big the remaining distance, $R_i = rate_{max} - rate(F)$, is. Recall that the augmentation graph for the current flow is constructed so that the augmentation capacity of each edge gives the amount that the flow through this edge can be increased by. Hence, just as the sum of the capacities of the edges across any cut $C = \langle U, V \rangle$ in the network acts as an upper bound to the total flow possible, the sum of the augmentation capacities of the edges across any cut $C = \langle U, V \rangle$ in the augmentation graph acts as an upper bound to the total amount that the current flow can be increased.

Choosing a Cut: We need to choose which cut we will use. (This is not part of the algorithm.) As before, the natural cut to use comes out of the algorithm that finds the path from s to t. Let $w_{min} = w_i$ denote the smallest augmentation capacity in the path whose smallest augmentation capacity is largest. Let $G_{w_{i-1}}$ be the graph created from the augmenting graph by deleting all edges whose augmentation capacities are smaller than or equal to w_{min}. This is the last graph that the algorithm that finds the augmenting path considers before adding the edge with weight w_{min} that connects s and t. We know that there is not a path from s to t in $G_{w_{i-1}}$, or else there would be an path in the augmenting graph whose smallest augmenting capacity was larger then w_{min}. Form the cut $C = \langle U, V \rangle$ by letting U be the set of all the nodes reachable from s in $G_{w_{i-1}}$ and letting V be those that are not. Now consider any edge in the augmenting graph that crosses this cut. This edge cannot be in the graph $G_{w_{i-1}}$, or else it would be crossing from a node in U that is reachable from s to a node that is not reachable from s, which is a contradiction. Because this edge has been deleted in $G_{w_{i-1}}$, we know that its augmentation capacity is at most w_{min}. The number of edges across this cut is at most the number of edges in the network, which has been denoted by m. It follows that the sum of the augmentation capacities of the edges across this cut $C = \langle U, V \rangle$ is at most $m \cdot w_{min}$.

Bounding the Increase, $w_{min} \geq \frac{1}{m} R_i$: We have determined that the remaining amount that the flow needs to be increased, $R_i = rate_{max} - rate(F)$, is at most the sum of the augmentation capacities across the cut C, which is at most $m \cdot w_{min}$, that is, $R_i \leq m \cdot w_{min}$. Rearranging this gives that $w_{min} \geq \frac{1}{m} R_i$.

The Number of Iterations: If the flow increases each iteration by at least $\frac{1}{m}$ times the remaining amount R_i, it decreases the remaining amount, giving that $R_{i+1} \leq R_i - \frac{1}{m} R_i$. You might think that it follows that the maximum flow is obtained in only m iterations. This would be true if $R_{i+1} \leq R_i - \frac{1}{m} R_0$. However, it is not, because the smaller R_i gets, the smaller the amount it decreases by. One way to bound the number of iterations needed is to note that $R_i \leq (1 - \frac{1}{m})^i R_0$ and then either to bound logarithms to base $1 - \frac{1}{m}$ or to note that $\lim_{m \to \infty} (1 - \frac{1}{m})^m = \frac{1}{e} \approx \frac{1}{2.17}$. However, I prefer the following method. As long as R_i is big, we know that it decreases by a lot. After some Ith iteration, say that R_i is still big when it is still at least $\frac{1}{2} R_I$. As long as this is the case, R_i decreases by at least $\frac{1}{m} R_i \geq \frac{1}{2m} R_I$. After m such iterations, R_i would decrease from R_I to $\frac{1}{2} R_I$. The only reason that it would not continue to decrease this fast would be that it already had decreased that much. Either way, we know that every m iterations, R_i decreases by a factor of two. This process may make you think of Zeno's paradoxes. If you cut the remaining distance in half and then in half again and so on, then though you get very close very fast, you never actually get there. However, if all the capacities are integers, then all values will be integers, and hence when R_i decreases to less than one, it must in fact be zero, giving us the maximum flow.

Initially, the remaining amount $R_i = rate_{max} - rate(F)$ is at most $O(m \cdot 2^\ell)$. Hence, if it decreases by at least a factor of 2 each m iterations, then after mj iterations, this amount is at most $O(m \cdot 2^\ell / 2^j)$. This reaches one when $j = O(\log_2(m \cdot 2^\ell)) = O(\ell + \log m)$, or in $O(m\ell + m \log m)$ iterations. If your capacities are real numbers, then you will be able to approximate the maximum flow to within ℓ' bits of accuracy in another $m\ell'$ iterations.

Bounding the Running Time: We have determined that each iteration takes $m \log m$ time and that only $O(m\ell + m \log m)$ iterations are required. It follows that this steepest-ascent network flow algorithm runs in time $O(\ell m^2 \log m + m^2 \log^2 m)$.

Fully Polynomial Time: A lot of work has been done finding an algorithm that is what is known as *fully polynomial*. This requires that the number of iterations be polynomial in the number of values and not depend at all on the values themselves. Hence, if you charge only one time step for addition and subtraction, even if the capacities are strange things like $\sqrt{2}$, then the algorithm gives the exact answer (at least symbolically) in polynomial time. My father, Jack Edmonds, and a colleague, Richard Karp, developed such an algorithm in 1972. It is a version of the original Ford–Fulkerson algorithm. In it, however, in each iteration, the path from s to t in the augmentation graph with the smallest number of edges is augmented. This algorithm iterates at most $O(nm)$ times, where n is the number of nodes and m the number of edges. In practice, this is slower than the $O(m\ell)$-time steepest-ascent algorithm.

EXERCISE 15.3.1 *Could we use binary search on the weights w_{min} to find the critical weight (see Section 1.4), and if so, would that be faster? Why?*

15.4 Linear Programming

When I was an undergraduate, I had a summer job with a food company. Our goal was to make cheap hot dogs. Every morning we got the prices of thousands of ingredients: pig hearts, sawdust, etc. Each ingredient had an associated variable indicating how much of it to add to the hot dogs. There are thousands of linear constraints on these variables: so much meat, so much moisture, and so on. Together these constraints specify which combinations of ingredients constitute a hot dog. The cost of the hot dog is a linear function of the quantities you put into it and their prices. The goal is to determine what to put into the hot dogs that day to minimize the cost. This is an example of a general class of problems referred to as *linear programs.*

Formal Specification: A linear program is an optimization problem whose constraints and objective functions are linear functions. The goal is to find a setting of variables that optimizes the objective function, while respecting all of the constraints.

Precondition: We are given one of the following instances.

> **Instances:** An input instance consists of (1) a set of linear constraints on a set of variables and (2) a linear objective function.

Postcondition: The output is a solution with minimum cost and the cost of that solution.

> **Solutions for Instance:** A solution for the instance is a setting of all the variables that satisfies the constraints.

> **Measure of Success:** The cost or value of a solutions is given by the objective function.

Example 15.4.1: Instance Example

$$\text{maximize}$$
$$7x_1 - 6x_2 + 5x_3 + 7x_4$$
$$\text{subject to}$$
$$3x_1 + 7x_2 + 2x_3 + 9x_4 \leq 258$$
$$6x_1 + 3x_2 + 9x_3 - 6x_4 \leq 721$$
$$2x_1 + 1x_2 + 5x_3 + 5x_4 \leq 524$$
$$3x_1 + 6x_2 + 2x_3 + 3x_4 \leq 411$$
$$4x_1 - 8x_2 - 4x_3 + 4x_4 \leq 685$$

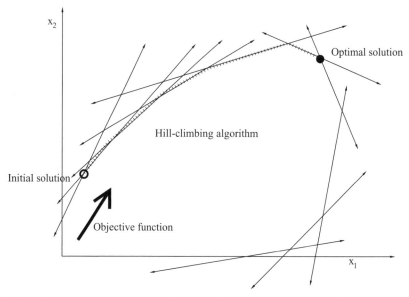

Figure 15.8: *The Euclidean space representation of a linear program with $n = 2$.*

Matrix Representation: A linear program can be expressed very compactly using matrix algebra. Let n denote the number of variables and m the number of constraints. Let a denote the row of n coefficients in the objective function, let M denote the matrix with m rows and n columns of coefficients on the left-hand side of the constraints, let b denote the column of m coefficients on the right-hand side of the constraints, and finally let x denote the column of n variables. Then the goal of the linear program is to maximize $a \cdot x$ subject to $M \cdot x \leq b$.

Network Flows: The network flows problem can be expressed as instances of linear programming. See Exercise 15.4.1.

The Euclidean Space Interpretation: Each possible solution, giving values to the variables $x_1, \ldots, x_n$, can be viewed as a point in n-dimensional space. This space is easiest to view when there are only two or three dimensions, but the same ideas hold for any number of variables.

    Constraints: Each constraint specifies a boundary in space, on one side of which a valid solution must lie. When $n = 2$, this constraint is a one-dimensional line. See Figure 15.8. When $n = 3$, it is a two-dimensional plane, like the side of a box. In general, it is an $(n - 1)$-dimensional space. The space bounded by all of the constraints is called a *polyhedral*.

    Vertices: The boundary of the polyhedral is defined by *vertices* where a number of constraints intersect. When $n = 2$, pairs of line constraints intersect at a vertex. See Figure 15.8. For $n = 3$, three sides of a box define a vertex (corner). In general, it requires n constraints to intersect to define a single vertex. This is because saying that the solution is on the constraint is saying that the linear equation holds with equality and not with "less than or equal to." Then recall that n linear equations with n unknowns are sufficient to specify a unique solution.

The Objective Function: The objective function gives a direction in Euclidean space. The goal is to find a point in the bounded polyhedral that is the furthest in this direction. The best way to visualize this is to rotate the Euclidean space so that the objective function points straight up. The goal is to find a point in the bounded polyhedral that is as high as possible.

A Vertex Is an Optimal Solution: As you can imagine from looking at Figure 15.8, if there is a unique solution, it will be at a vertex where n constraints meet. If there is a whole region of equivalently optimal solutions, then at least one of them will be a vertex. Our search for an optimal solution will focus on these vertices.

The Hill-Climbing Algorithm: The obvious algorithm simply climbs the hill formed by the outside of the bounded polyhedral until the top is reached. In defining a hill-climbing algorithm for linear programming we just need to devise a way to find an initial valid solution and to define what constitutes a step to a better solution.

A Step: Suppose, by the loop invariant, we have a solution that, in addition to being valid, is also a vertex of the bounding polyhedral. More formally, the solution satisfies all of the constraints and meets n of the constraints with equality. A step will involve climbing along the edge (one-dimensional line) between two adjacent vertices. This involves *relaxing* one of the constraints that is met with equality, so that it no longer is met with equality, and *tightening* one of the constraints that was not met with equality so that it now is met with equality. This is called is called *pivoting* out one equation and in another. The new solution will be the unique solution that satisfies with equality the n presently selected equations. Of course, at each iteration such a step can be taken only if it continues to satisfy all of the constraints and improves the objective function. There are fast ways of finding a good step to take. However, even if you do not know these, there are only $n \cdot m$ choices of steps to try, when there are n variables and m equations.

Finding an Initial Valid Solution: If we are lucky, the origin will be a valid solution. However, in general finding some valid solution is itself a challenging problem. Our algorithm to do so will be an iterative algorithm that includes the constraints one at a time. Suppose we have a vertex solution that satisfies all of the constraints in Example 15.4.1 except the last one. We will then treat the negative of this next constraint as the objective function, namely $-4x_1 + 8x_2 + 4x_3 - 4x_4$. We will run our hill-climbing algorithm, starting with the vertex we have, until we have a vertex solution that maximizes this new objective function subject to the first i equations. This is equivalent to minimizing the objective $4x_1 - 8x_2 - 4x_3 + 4x_4$. If its minimum is less that 685, then we have found a vertex solution that satisfies the first $i+1$ equations. If not, then we have determined that no such solution exists.

No Small Local Maximum: To prove that the algorithm eventually finds a global maximum, we must prove that it will not get stuck in a small local maximum.

Convex: Because the bounded polyhedral is the intersection of straight cuts, it is what we call *convex*. More formally, this means that the line between any two points in the polyhedral is also in the polyhedral. This means that there cannot be two local maximum points, because between these two hills there would need to be a valley and a line between two points across this valley would be outside the polyhedral.

The Primal–Dual Method: The primal–dual method formally proves that a global maximum will be found. Given any linear program, defined by an optimization function and a set of constraints, there is a way of forming its *dual* minimization linear program. Each solution to this dual acts as a roof or upper bound on how high the primal solution can be. Then each iteration either finds a better solution for the primal or provides a solution for the dual linear program with a matching value. This dual solution witnesses the fact that no primal solution is bigger.

Forming the Dual: If the primal linear program is to maximize $a \cdot x$ subject to $Mx \le b$, then the dual is to minimize $b^T \cdot y$ subject to $M^T \cdot y \ge a^T$, where b^T, M^T, and a^T are the transposes formed by interchanging rows and columns. The dual of Example 15.4.1 is

minimize
$$258 + 721y_2 + 524y_3 + 411y_4 + 685y_5$$
subject to
$$3y_1 + 6y_2 + 2y_3 + 3y_4 + 4y_5 \ge 7$$
$$7y_1 + 3y_2 + 1y_3 + 6y_4 - 8y_5 \ge -6$$
$$2y_1 + 9y_2 + 5y_3 + 2y_4 - 4y_5 \ge 5$$
$$9y_1 - 6y_2 + 5y_3 + 3y_4 + 4y_5 \ge 7$$

The dual will have a variable for each constraint in the primal and a constraint for each of its variables. The coefficients of the objective function become the numbers on the right-hand sides of the inequalities, and the numbers on the right-hand sides of the inequalities become the coefficients of the objective function. Finally, "maximize" becomes "minimize." The dual is the same as the original primal.

Upper Bound: We prove that the value of any solution to the primal linear program is at most the value of any solution to the dual linear program. The value of the primal solution x is $a \cdot x$. The constraints $M^T \cdot y \ge a^T$ can be turned around to give $a \leq y^T \cdot M$. This gives that $a \cdot x \leq y^T \cdot M \cdot x$. Using the constraints $Mx \leq b$, this is at most $y^T \cdot b$. This can be turned around to give $b^T \cdot y$, which is the value of the dual solution y.

Running Time: The primal–dual hill-climbing algorithm is guaranteed to find the optimal solution. In practice, it works quickly (though for my summer job, the computers would crank for hours). However, there is no known hill-climbing algorithm that is guaranteed to run in polynomial time.

There is another algorithm that solves this problem, called the *ellipsoid method*. Practically, it is not as fast, but theoretically it provably runs in polynomial time.

EXERCISE 15.4.1 *Express the network flow instance in Figure 15.2 as a linear program.*

15.5 Exercises

EXERCISE 15.5.1 *(See solution in Part Five.) Let $G = (L \cup R, E)$ be a bipartite graph with nodes L on the left and R on the right. A matching is a subset of the edges such that each node appears at most once. For any $A \subseteq L$, let $N(A)$ be the neighborhood set of A, namely $N(A) = \{v \in R \mid \exists u \in A \text{ such that } (u, v) \in E\}$. Prove Hall's theorem, which states that there exists a matching in which every node in L is matched if and only if $\forall A \subseteq L, |A| \leq |N(A)|$.*

1. *For each of the following two bipartite graphs, give a short witness either to the fact that it has a perfect matching or to the fact that it does not. Use Hall's theorem in your explanation why a graph does not have a matching. No need to mention flows or cuts.*

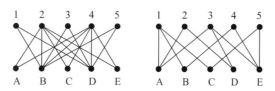

2. *$\Rightarrow$: Suppose there exists a matching in which every node in L is matched. For $u \in L$, let $M(u) \in R$ specify one such matching. Prove that $\forall A \subseteq L, |A| \leq |N(A)|$.*
3. *Section 20.4 describes a network with nodes $\{s\} \cup L \cup R \cup \{t\}$ with a directed edge from s to each node in L, the edges E from L to R in the bipartite graph directed from L to R, and a directed edge from each node in R to t. The notes give each edge capacity 1. However, the edges $\langle u, v \rangle$ across the bipartite graph could just as well be given capacity ∞. Consider some cut (U, V) in this network. Note that U contains s, some nodes of L, and some nodes of R, whereas V contains the remaining nodes*

of L, the remaining nodes of R, and t. Assume that $\forall A \subseteq L,\ |A| \leq |N(A)|$. Prove that the capacity of this cut, i.e., $cap(U, V) = \sum_{u \in U} \sum_{v \in V} c_{\langle u,v \rangle}$, is at least $|L|$.

4. *$\Leftarrow$: Assume that $\forall A \subseteq L,\ |A| \leq |N(A)|$ is true. Prove that there exists a matching in which every node in L is matched. (Hint: Use everything you know about network flows.)*

5. *Suppose that there is some integer $k \geq 1$ such that every node in L has degree at least k and every node in R has degree at most k. Prove that there exists a matching in which every node in L is matched.*

16 Greedy Algorithms

Every two-year-old knows the greedy algorithm. In order to get what you want, just start grabbing what looks best.

16.1 Abstractions, Techniques, and Theory

Specifications: A very select number of optimization problems can be solved using a greedy algorithm. Most of these have the following form.

> *Precondition:* We are given one of the following instances.
>
> > **Instances:** An instance consists of a set of objects and a relationship between them. Think of the objects as being prizes that you must choose among.
>
> *Postcondition:* Given an instance, the goal is to find one of the valid solutions for this instance with optimal (minimum or maximum as the case may be) measure of success. (The solution to be outputted need not be unique.)
>
> > **Solutions for Instance:** A solution requires the algorithm to make a choice about each of the objects in the instance. Sometimes, this choice is complex, but usually it is simply whether or not to keep it. In this case, a solution is the subset of the objects that you have kept. The catch is that some subsets are not allowed because these objects conflict somehow with each other.
> >
> > **Measure of Success:** Each solution is assigned a cost or measure of success. Often, when a solution consists of a nonconflicting subset of the objects, this

measure is the number of objects in the subset or the sum of the costs of its individual objects. Sometimes the measure is a more complex function.

The Brute Force Algorithm (Exponential Time): The brute force algorithm for an optimization problem considers each possible solution for the given instance, computes its cost, and outputs the cheapest. Because each instance has an exponential number of solutions, this algorithm takes exponential time.

226

The Greedy Choice: The greedy step is the first that would come to mind when designing an algorithm for a problem. Given the set of objects specified in the input instance, the greedy step chooses and commits to one of these objects because, according to some simple criterion, it seems to be the best. When proving that the algorithm works, we must be able to prove that this locally greedy choice does not have negative global consequences.

EXAMPLE 16.1.1   The Game Show

Suppose the instance specifies a set of prizes and an integer m and allows you to choose m of the prizes. The criterion, according to which some of these prizes appear to be better than others, may be its dollar price, the amount of joy it would bring you, how practical it is, or how much it would impress the neighbors. At first it seems obvious that you should choose your first prize using the greedy approach. However, some of these prizes conflict with each other, and (as is often the case in life) compromises need to be made. For example, if you take the pool, then your yard is too full to be able to take many of the other prizes. A lion might impress your neighbors, but it might eat your dog. As is also true in life, it is sometimes hard to look into the future and predict the ramifications of the choices made today.

EXAMPLE 16.1.2   Making Change

The goal of this optimization problem is to find the minimum number of quarters, dimes, nickels, and pennies that total to a given amount. An instance consists of a set of objects and a relationship between them. Here, the set is a huge pile of coins, and the relationship is that the chosen coins must total to the given amount. The cost of a solution, which is to be minimized, is the number of coins in the solution.

EXAMPLE 16.1.2	**Making Change** (cont.)

The Greedy Choice: The coin that appears to be best to take is a quarter, because it makes the most progress towards making our required amount while only incurring a cost of one.

A Valid Choice: Before committing to a quarter, we must make sure that it does not conflict with the possibility of arriving at a valid solution. If the sum to be obtained happens to be less than $0.25, then this quarter should be rejected, even though it appears at first to be best. On the other hand, if the amount is at least $0.25, then we can commit to the quarter without invalidating the solution we are building.

Leading to an Optimal Solution: A much more difficult and subtle question is whether or not committing to a quarter leads us towards obtaining an optimal solution. In this case, it happens that it does, though this not at all obvious.

Going Wrong: Suppose that the problem is generalized to include as part of the input the set of coin denominations available. Then greedy algorithm does not work. For example, suppose we have 4-, 3-, and 1-cent coins. If the given amount is 6, than the optimal solution contains two 3-cent coins. We go wrong by greedily committing to a 4-cent coin.

Proof of Correctness Using Loop Invariants: Committing to the pool, to the lion, or to the 4-cent coin, though they locally appear to be the best objects, does not lead to an optimal solution. However, for some problems and for some definitions of "best," the greedy algorithm does work. When it does not work, we will prove it using one simple counterexample as we did above. When it does work, we will prove it using the same method with which we prove all iterative algorithms correct: loop invariants.

> **Main Steps:** Each iteration the algorithm chooses the best object from among those not considered so far and either commits to it or rejects it.
>
> **Make Progress:** One more object has been considered.
>
> **Exit Condition:** All objects have been considered.
>
> **Loop Invariant:** Recall that a loop invariant makes a statement each time the algorithm is at the top of the loop about what it has accomplished. So far the algorithm has made one iteration, during which it has committed to one of the objects. What statement do we want to make about this action?

Types of Loop Invariants: In order to find a good loop invariants, let us start by considering the types of loop invariants considered in Section 1.4. It turns out that our chosen loop invariant will be of the narrowing-the-search-space type.

> **More of the Output:** Recall that the more-of-the-output loop invariant states that the first i items of the output have been produced and the output

constructed so far is correct. In the case of greedy algorithms, the output is a decision about each object, and the algorithm makes another decision each iteration. Hence, the first part of the loop invariant is easily maintained. However, what does it even mean for the output constructed so far to be correct?

No Conflict Yet: If our goal is to obtain a solution that has no conflicts, a good loop invariant might be that within the commitments made so far, there are no conflicts. The problem with this is that the commitments made so far may have backed the algorithm into a corner so that future conflicts are inevitable. See Exercise 16.1.3.

The Postcondition as a Loop Invariant: The postcondition is that the algorithm has committed to an optimal solution. However, at this point we cannot talk about the algorithm's "solution," because before the algorithm completes it may have made some commitments already, but this partial work does not yet constitute a valid solution.

Optimal So Far: The loop invariant might be "What the algorithm has done so far is optimal." However, being optimal is a property of full solutions, and we don't have one yet.

More of the Input: Recall that the more-of-the-input loop invariant states that if we pretend that the prefix of the input read so far by the algorithm is the entire input, then the algorithm has an optimal solution. Though this is tempting, it does not work. That what you have is optimal within this part of the instance is only a *local* property. It won't necessarily guarantee global optimality. For example, if the input of the game show problem consisted of only a lion, then the optimal solution would be to take the lion. However, when there are also more objects, the lion is not part of the solution. Similarly, in the make change problem with 4-, 3-, and 1-cent coins, if the input is to make the amount 4, then one should take a 4; but not if the input is to make the amount 6.

Narrowing the Search Space: Recall the narrowing-the-search-space type of loop invariant. While searching for something, the algorithm narrows the search space. The loop invariant is "If the thing being searched for is anywhere, then it is in this narrowed search space." Greedy algorithms are in fact searching for an optimal solution from the search space of all possible solutions. Every time the algorithm commits to something, the set of possible solutions that it might still output narrows to those that are consistent with the decisions made so far. A natural loop invariant would then be "If the optimal solution being searched for is anywhere, then it is consistent with the decisions made so far."

"The" Optimal Solution Contains the "Best" Object: Before committing to the seemingly best object or making the first decision, we need to prove that we do not go wrong by doing so. As a first attempt, we might try to prove that for every set of objects that might be given as an instance, the "best" of these objects is definitely in its optimal solution. The problem with this is that there may be more than one optimal solution. It might not be the case that all of them contain the chosen object.

At Least One Optimal Solution Remaining: Instead of requiring all optimal solutions to contain the "best" object, what we need to prove is that at least one does. The effect of this is that though committing to the "best" object may eliminate the possibility of some of the optimal solutions, it does not eliminate all of them. There is the saying, "Do not burn your bridges behind you." The message here is slightly different. It is o.k. to burn a few of your bridges as long as you do not burn all of them.

If There Is an Optimal Solution: For most problems, it is clear that an instance has at least one solution (maybe a trivial solution) and hence there is a best solution. Hence, this first conditional part of the loop invariant is usually dropped. Be aware, however, that it is sometimes needed. See Exercise 16.1.3.

The Chosen Loop Invariant: To recap, the loop invariant is that we have not gone wrong. If there is a solution, then there is at least one optimal solution consistent with the choices made so far.

The Second Step: After the "best" object has been chosen and committed to, the algorithm must continue and choose the remaining objects for the solution. You can think about this process within either the iterative or the recursive paradigm. Though the resulting algorithm is (usually) the same, having the different paradigms at your disposal can be helpful.

Iterative: In the iterative version, there is a main loop. At each iteration, you choose the best from amongst the objects that have not yet been considered. The algorithm then commits to some choice about this object. Usually, this involves deciding whether to commit to putting this chosen object in the solution or to commit to rejecting it.

A Valid Choice: The most common reason is that it conflicts with the objects committed to previously. Another reason is that the object fills no requirements that are not already filled by the objects already committed to.

Cannot Predict the Future: At each step, the choice that is made can depend on the choices that were made in the past, but it cannot depend on the choices that will be made in the future. Because of this, no backtracking is required.

Making Change Example: The greedy algorithm for finding the minimum number of coins summing to a given amount is as follows. Commit to quarters until the next quarter increases your current sum above the required amount. Then reject the remaining quarters. Then do the same with the dimes, the nickels, and the pennies.

Recursive: A recursive greedy algorithm makes a greedy first choice and then recurses once or twice in order to solve the remaining subinstance.

> **Making Change Example:** After committing to a quarter, we could subtract $0.25 from the required amount and ask a friend to find the minimum number of coins to make this new amount. Our solution will be his solution plus our original quarter.

> **Binary Search Tree Example:** The recursive version of a greedy algorithm is more useful when you need to recurse more than once. For example, suppose you want to construct a binary search tree for a set of keys that minimizes the total height of the tree, i.e., a balanced tree. The greedy algorithm will commit to the middle key being at the root. Then it will recurse once for the left subtree and once for the right.

To learn more about how to recurse after the greedy choice has been made, see the recursive backtracking algorithms in Chapter 17.

Proof of Correctness: Greedy algorithms themselves are very easy to understand and to code. If your intuition is that they should not work, then your intuition is correct. For most optimization search problems, no greedy algorithms that are tried work. By some miracle, however, for some problems there is a greedy algorithm that works. The proof that they work, however, is very subtle and difficult. As with all iterative algorithms, we prove that they work using loop invariants.

> **A Formal Proof:** Chapter 1 proves that an iterative algorithm works if the loop invariant can be established and maintained and from it the postcondition can be proved. The loop invariant here is that the algorithm has not gone wrong: there is at least one optimal solution consistent with the choices made so far. This is established ($\langle pre \rangle \rightarrow \langle LI \rangle$) by noting that initially no choices have been made and hence all optimal solutions are consistent with these choices. The loop invariant is maintained ($\langle LI' \rangle$ & not $\langle exit \rangle$ & $code_{loop} \rightarrow \langle LI'' \rangle$) as follows. If it is true when at the top of the loop, then let $optS_{LI}$ denote one such solution. $code_{loop}$ during the next iteration either commits to or rejects the next best object. The proof describes a method for modifying $optS_{LI}$ into $optS_{ours}$ and proves that this is a valid solution, is consistent both with the choices made previously by the algorithm and with this new choice, and is optimal. The existence of such a $optS_{ours}$ proves that the loop invariant has been maintained. The last step is to prove that in the end, the algorithm has a concrete optimal solution ($\langle LI \rangle$ & $\langle exit \rangle \rightarrow \langle post \rangle$). Progress is made at each step by committing to or rejecting another object. When each object has been considered, the algorithm exits. These choices specify a

solution. The loop invariant states there is an optimal solution consistent with these choices. Hence, the solution obtained must be optimal.

We will now redo the proof in a more intuitive, fun, and detailed way.

The Loop Invariant: The loop invariant maintained is that we have not gone wrong. There is at least one optimal solution consistent with the choices made so far, that is, containing the objects committed to so far and not containing the objects rejected so far.

Three Players: To help understand this proof, we will tell a story involving three characters: the algorithm, the prover, and a fairy godmother.

The Algorithm: At each iteration, the algorithm chooses the best object from amongst those not considered so far and either commits to it or rejects it.

The Prover: The prover's task is to prove that the loop invariant is maintained. Having a separate prover emphasizes that fact that his actions are not a part of the algorithm and hence do not need to be coded or executed.

The Fairy Godmother: Instead of the prover pretending that he has and is manipulating a hypothetical optimal solution $optS_{LI}$, he can pretend that he has a fairy godmother who holds and manipulates one for him. We say that this solution *witnesses* the fact such a solution exists. Having a separate fairy godmother emphasizes that neither the algorithm nor the prover actually knows the solution.

Initially ($\langle pre \rangle \rightarrow \langle LI \rangle$): Initially, the algorithm has made no choices, neither committing to nor rejecting any objects. The prover then establishes the loop invariant as follows. Assuming that there is at least one legal solution, he knows that there must be an optimal solution. He goes on to note that this optimal solution by default is consistent with the choices made so far, because no choices have been made so far. Knowing that such a solution exists, the prover kindly asks his fairy godmother to find one. She, being all-powerful, has no problem doing this. If there are more than one equally good optimal solutions, then she chooses one arbitrarily.

Maintaining the Loop Invariant ($\langle LI' \rangle$ & not $\langle exit \rangle$ & $code_{loop} \rightarrow \langle LI'' \rangle$): Now consider an arbitrary iteration.

What We Know: At the beginning of this iteration, the algorithm has a set *Commit* of objects committed to so far, and a set *Reject* of objects rejected so far. The prover knows that the loop invariant is true, that is, that there is at least one optimal solution consistent with these choices made so far; however, he does not know one. Witnessing that there is one, the fairy godmother is holding one such optimal solution. We will use $optS_{LI}$ to denote the solution that she holds. In addition to containing those objects in *Commit* and not those in *Reject*, this solution may contain objects that the algorithm has not considered yet.

Taking a Step: During the iteration, the algorithm proceeds to choose the best object from amongst those not considered so far and either commits to it or rejects it. In order to prove that the loop invariant has been maintained, the prover must prove that there is at least one optimal solution consistent with both the choices made previously and this new choice. He is going to accomplish this by getting his fairy godmother to witness this fact by switching to such an optimal solution.

Weakness in Communication: It would be great if the prover could simply ask the fairy godmother whether such a solution exists. However, he cannot ask her to find such a solution if he is not already confident that it exists, because he does not want to ask her to do anything that is impossible.

Modify Instructions: The prover accomplishes his task by giving his fairy godmother detailed instructions. He starts by saying, "If it happens to be the case that the optimal solution that you hold is consistent with this new choice that was made, then we are done, because this will witness the fact that there is at least one optimal solution consistent with both the choices made previously and this new choice." "Otherwise," he says, "you must modify the optimal solution that you have in the following ways." The fairy godmother follows the detailed instructions that he gives her, but gives him no feedback as to how they go. We will use $optS_{ours}$ to denote what she constructs.

Making Change Example: If the remaining amount required is at least $0.25, then the algorithm commits to another quarter. Excluding the committed-to coins, the fairy godmother's optimal solution $optS_{LI}$ must be making up the same remaining amount. This amount must contain either an additional quarter, three dimes, two dimes and a nickel, one dime and three nickels, five nickels, or combinations with at least five pennies. The prover tells her to replace the three dimes with the newly committed-to quarter and nickel, and the other options with just the quarter. If the algorithm, on the other hand, rejects the next (and later all remaining) quarters because the remaining amount required is less than $0.25, then the prover is confident that optimal solution held by his fairy godmother cannot contain additional quarters either.

Proving That She Has a Witness: It is the job of the prover to prove that the thing $optS_{ours}$ that his fairy godmother now holds is a valid, consistent, and optimal solution.

Proving a Valid Solution: Because he knows that what she had been holding, $optS_{LI}$, at the beginning of the iteration was a valid solution, he knows that the objects in it did not conflict in any way. Hence, all he needs to do is to prove that he did not introduce any conflicts that he did not fix.

Making Change Example: The prover was careful that the changes he made did not change the total amount that she was holding.

Proving Consistency: He must also prove that the solution she is now holding is consistent both with the choices made previously by the algorithm and with this new choice. Because he knows that what she had been holding was consistent with the previous choices, he only needs to prove that he modified it to be consistent with the new choices without messing up earlier ones.

Making Change Example: Though the prover may have removed some of the coins that the algorithm has not considered yet, he was sure not to have her remove any of the previously committed-to coins. He also managed to add the newly committed-to quarter.

Proving Optimal: You might think that proving that the solution $optS_{ours}$ is optimal would be hard, given that we do not even know the cost of an optimal solution. However, the prover can be assured that it is optimal as long as its cost is the same as the optimal solution, $optS_{LI}$, from which it was derived. If there were a case in which the prover managed to improve the solution, then this would contradict the fact that $optS_{LI}$ is optimal. This contradiction only proves that such a case will not occur. However, the prover does not need to concern himself with this problem.

Making Change Example: Each change that the prover instructs his fairy godmother to make either keeps the number of coins the same or decreases the number. Hence, because $optS_{LI}$ is optimal, $optS_{ours}$ is as well.

This completes the prover's proof that his fairy godmother now has an optimal solution consistent both with the previous choices and with the latest choice. This witnesses the fact that such a solution exists.

This proves that the loop invariant has been maintained.

Continuing: This completes everybody's requirements for this iteration. The process is repeated over and over again. Each iteration, the algorithm commits to more about the solution, and the fairy godmother's solution is changed to be consistent with these commitments.

Exiting Loop ($\langle LI \rangle$ & $\langle exit \rangle \rightarrow \langle post \rangle$): After the algorithm has considered every object in the instance and each has either been committed to or rejected, the algorithm exits. We still know that the loop invariant is true. Hence, the prover knows that there is an optimal schedule $optS_{LI}$ consistent with all of these choices. Previously, this optimal solution was only imagined. However, now we concretely know that this imagined solution consists of those objects committed to. Hence, the algorithm can return this set as the solution.

Running Time: Greedy algorithms are very fast, because they take only a small amount of time per object in the instance.

Fixed vs. Adaptive Priority: Iterative greedy algorithms come in two flavors, *fixed priority* and *adaptive priority*.

Fixed Priority: A fixed-priority greedy algorithm begins by sorting the objects in the input instance from best to worst according to a fixed greedy criterion. For example, it might sort the objects based on the cost of the object or the arrival time of the object. The algorithm then considers the objects one at a time in this order.

Adaptive Priority: In an adaptive priority greedy algorithm, the greedy criterion is not fixed, but depends on which objects have been committed to so far. At each step, the next-best object is chosen according to the current greedy criterion. Blindly searching the remaining list of objects each iteration for the next-best object would be too time-consuming. So would re-sorting the objects each iteration according to the new greedy criterion. A more efficient implementation uses a priority queue to hold the remaining objects prioritized according to the current greedy criteria. This can be implemented using a heap. (See Section 10.4.)

Code:

```
algorithm AdaptiveGreedy( set of objects )
    ⟨ pre-cond⟩: The input consists of a set of objects.
    ⟨ post-cond⟩: The output consists of an optimal subset of them.
```

```
begin
        Put objects in a priority queue according to the initial greedy
        criterion
        Commit = Ø  % set of objects previously committed to
        loop
                ⟨loop-invariant⟩: There is at least one optimal solution
                consistent with the choices made so far

                exit when the priority queue is empty
                Remove "best" object from priority queue
                If this object does not conflict with those in Commit and is
                needed, then
                        Add object to Commit
                end if
                Update the priority queue to reflect the new greedy criterion
                This is done by changing the priorities of the objects effected.
        end loop
        return (Commit)
end algorithm
```

Example: Dijkstra's shortest-weighted-path algorithm (Section 14.3) can be considered to be a greedy algorithm with an adaptive priority criteria. It chooses the next edge to include in the optimal shortest-weighted-path tree based on which node currently seems to be the closest to s. Those yet to be chosen are organized in a priority queue. Even breadth-first and depth-first search can be considered to be adaptive greedy algorithms. In fact, they very closely resemble Prim's minimal-spanning-tree algorithm (Section 16.2.3), in how a tree is grown from a source node. They are adaptive in that as the algorithm proceeds, the set from which the next edge is chosen changes.

EXERCISE 16.1.1 *We proved that the greedy algorithm does not work for the making change problem when the denominations of the coins are 4, 3, and 1 cent, but it does work when the denominations are 25, 10, 5, and 1. Does it work when the denominations are 25, 10, and 1, with no nickels?*

EXERCISE 16.1.2 *Suppose the coin denominations are $c_1 > c_2 > \cdots > c_r$ in the order taken by the greedy algorithm. An interesting problem is determining whether the greedy algorithm works. A complete answer to this question is too hard. However, what restrictions on the coin denominations are sufficient to ensure that the greedy algorithm works?*

- *Suppose, for each i, each coin c_i is an integer multiple of the next smaller c_{i+1}, e.g., 120, 60, 12, 3, 1. If this is true, do we know that the greedy algorithm works? If it is not true, do we know that the greedy algorithm does not work?*

- *Suppose, for each i, each coin is more than twice the previous, that is, $c_i \geq 2c_{i+1}$. Do we know that the greedy algorithm works? If this is not true, do we know that the greedy algorithm does not work?*
- *Other interesting characteristics?*

EXERCISE 16.1.3 *The 2-coloring problem is as follows: Given any undirected n-node graph, color the nodes with two colors so that no edge connects two nodes of the same color (i.e., adjacent nodes always have different colors), or report that it is impossible.*

1. *A tempting loop invariant is "There are no adjacent nodes of the same color in my partial solution." In order for this to be a good loop invariant, one needs to be able to arrive from Mars, knowing nothing about what the algorithm has done so far except that the loop invariant is true. From here that algorithm must be able to continue until the postcondition is obtained. Prove that this is a bad loop invariant as follows:*
   (a) *Provide a graph that has a valid 2-coloring.*
   (b) *Provide a valid partial coloring that a (faulty) algorithm may provide for which the loop invariant holds.*
   (c) *Prove that the algorithm has gone wrong because there are no valid colorings consistent with this partial solution.*
2. *This is an example in which an instance might not have any valid solution. One possible algorithmic technique is to check the validity of the solution after all the nodes have been colored. Another is to check as it proceeds, to make sure that the coloring being created has no mistakes. (Which technique is used in the binary search algorithm?) For each of these two techniques, give a loop invariant and then prove $\langle$pre-cond$\rangle$ & $code_{alg}$ $\Rightarrow$ $\langle$post-cond$\rangle$.*
3. *Briefly describe a greedy algorithm. The algorithm should be able to handle graphs that are not connected.*
4. *Is the greedy criterion used adaptive or nonadaptive? Does it need to be?*
5. *Prove that the loop invariant is maintained. ($\langle$loop-invariant$'\rangle$ & not$\langle$exit-cond$\rangle$ & $code_{loop}$ $\Rightarrow$ $\langle$loop-invariant$''\rangle$). Be sure to handle boundary conditions, e.g., the first iteration, and graphs that are not connected.*
6. *What is the running time of your algorithm?*

16.2 Examples of Greedy Algorithms

16.2.1 Example: The Job/Event Scheduling Problem

Suppose that many people want to use your conference room for events and you must schedule as many of these as possible. (The version in which some events are given a higher priority is considered in Section 19.3.) We examine a fixed-priority greedy algorithm.

Specifications:

Precondition: We are given one of the following instances.

Instances: An instance is $\langle \langle s_1, f_1 \rangle, \langle s_2, f_2 \rangle, \ldots, \langle s_n, f_n \rangle \rangle$, where $0 \le s_i \le f_i$ are the starting and finishing times for the ith event.

Postcondition: The output is a solution with maximum number of events scheduled.

Solutions: A solution for an instance is a schedule S. This consists of a subset $S \subseteq [1..n]$ of the events that don't conflict by overlapping in time.

Measure of Success: The success of a solution S is the number of events scheduled, that is, $|S|$.

Possible Criteria for Defining "Best":

The Shortest Event $f_i - s_i$: It seems that it would be best to schedule short events first, because they increase the number of events scheduled without booking the room for a long period of time. This greedy approach does not work.

Counterexample: Suppose that the following lines indicate the starting and completing times of three events to schedule.

We would be going wrong to schedule the short event in the middle, because the only optimal schedule does not include it.

The Earliest Starting Time s_i or the Latest Finishing Time f_i: First come first served, which is a common scheduling algorithm, does not work either.

Counterexample:

The long event is both the earliest and the latest. Committing to scheduling it would be a mistake.

Event Conflicting with the Fewest Other Events: Scheduling an event that conflicts with other events prevents you from scheduling these events. Hence a reasonable criterion would be to first schedule the event with the fewest conflicts.

Counterexample: In the following example, the middle event would be committed to first. This eliminates the possibility of scheduling four events.

Figure 16.1: A set of events and those committed to by the earliest-finishing-time-first Greedy algorithm.

Earliest Finishing Time f_i: This criterion may seem a little odd at first, but it makes sense. It says to schedule the event that will free up your room for someone else as soon as possible. We will see that this criterion works for every set of events.

Example: You can trace out this algorithm on the example shown in Figure 16.1.

Code: A greedy algorithm for the event scheduling problem.

>**algorithm** *Scheduling*$((\langle s_1, f_1 \rangle, \langle s_2, f_2 \rangle, \ldots, \langle s_n, f_n \rangle))$
>
>⟨*pre-cond*⟩: The input consists of a set of events.
>⟨*post-cond*⟩: The output consists of a schedule that maximizes the number of events scheduled.
>
>begin
>   Sort the events based on their finishing times f_i
>   *Commit* $= \emptyset$ % The set of events committed to be in the schedule
>   loop $i = 1 \ldots n$ % Consider the events in sorted order.
>   if(event i does not conflict with an event in *Commit*) then
>   *Commit* $=$ *Commit* $\cup \{i\}$
>   end loop
>   return(*Commit*)
>end algorithm

The Loop Invariant: The loop invariant is that we have not gone wrong: There is at least one optimal solution consistent with the choices made so far, that is, containing the objects committed to so far and not containing the objects rejected so far.

Initial Code (⟨*pre*⟩ → ⟨*LI*⟩): Initially, no choices have been made, and hence trivially all optimal solutions are consistent with these choices.

Figure 16.2: A set of events, those committed to at the current point in time, those rejected, those in the optimal solution assumed to exist, and the next event to be considered.

Maintaining the Loop Invariant (⟨*LI'*⟩ & not ⟨*exit*⟩ & *code_loop* → ⟨*LI''*⟩): We are at the top of the loop of the algorithm. Consider the example in Figure 16.2.

Hypothetical Optimal Solution: Let $optS_{LI}$ denote one of the hypothetical optimal schedules assumed to exist by the loop invariant.

Algorithm's Actions: If event i conflicts with an event in *Commit*, then the algorithm rejects it. $optS_{LI}$ contains all the events in *Commit* and hence cannot contain event i either. Hence, the loop invariant is maintained. From here on, let us assume that i does not conflict with any event in *Commit* and hence will be added to it.

Modifying Optimal Solutions: If we are lucky, the schedule $optS_{LI}$ already contains event i. In this case, we are done. Otherwise, we will modify the schedule $optS_{LI}$ into another schedule $optS_{ours}$ by adding i and removing any events that conflict with it. This modifying is not part of the algorithm, as we do not actually have an optimal schedule yet.

A Valid Solution: Our modified set $optS_{ours}$ contains no conflicts, because $optS_{LI}$ contained none and we were careful to introduce none.

Consistent with Choices Made: $optS_{LI}$ was consistent with the previous choices. We added event i to make $optS_{ours}$ consistent with these choices. We did not remove any events from *Commit*, because these do not conflict with event i.

Optimal: To prove that $optS_{ours}$ has the optimal number of events in it, we need only to prove that it has at least as many as $optS_{LI}$. We added one event to the schedule. Hence, we must prove that we have not removed more than one. Let j denote a deleted event. Being in $optS_{LI}$ and not in *Commit*, it must be an event not yet considered. Because the events are sorted based on their finishing time, $j > i$ implies that event j finishes after event i finishes, that is, $f_j \geq f_i$. If event j conflicts with event i, it follows that it also starts before it finishes, i.e., $s_j \leq f_i$. (In Figure 16.2, there are three future events conflicting with i.) Combining $f_j \geq f_i$ and $s_j \leq f_i$ gives that such an event j is running at the finishing time f_i of event i. Hence, any two such events j conflict with each other. Therefore, they cannot both be in the schedule $optS_{LI}$, because it contains conflicts.

Loop Invariant Has Been Maintained: In conclusion, we have constructed a valid optimal schedule $optS_{ours}$ that contains the events in *Commit* ∪ {i} and no rejected events. This proves that the loop invariant is maintained.

Exiting Loop (⟨*LI*⟩ & ⟨*exit*⟩ → ⟨*post*⟩): By LI, there is an optimal schedule $optS_{LI}$ containing the events in *Commit* and not containing the previous events not in *Commit*. Because all events are previous events, it follows that *Commit* = $optS_{LI}$ is in an optimal schedule for our instance.

Figure 16.3: *An example instance of the interval cover problem. The intervals in one optimal solution are highlighted.*

Running Time: The loop is iterated once for each of the n events. The only work is determining whether event i conflicts with a event within *Commit*. Because of the ordering of the events, event i finishes after all the events in *Commit*. Hence, it conflicts with an event in *Commit* if and only if it starts before the last finishing time of an event in it. It is easy to remember this last finishing time, because it is simply the finishing time of the last event to be added to *Commit*. Hence, the main loop runs in $\Theta(n)$ time. The total time of the algorithm then is dominated by the time to sort the events.

16.2.2 Example: The Interval Cover Problem

For this problem, we will develop an adaptive priority greedy algorithm.

Specifications: Given a set of points and intervals, the goal is to find an *optimal cover*, that is, a subset of the intervals that covers all the points and that contains the minimum number of intervals.

Precondition: We are given one of the following instances.

Instances: An instance consists a set P of points and a set I of intervals on the real line. An interval consists of a starting and a finishing time $\langle s_i, f_i \rangle$. See the example in Figure 16.3.

Postcondition: The output is a solution with minimum cost and the cost of that solution.

Solutions: A solution for an instance is a subset S of the intervals that covers all the points. It is fine if the intervals overlap.

Measure of Success: The cost of a solution S is $|S|$, the number of intervals required. Having longer or shorter intervals does not matter. Covering the points more than once does not matter. Covering parts of the line without points does not matter. Only the number of intervals matters.

The Adaptive Greedy Criterion: The algorithm sorts the points and covers them in order from left to right. If the intervals committed to so far cover all of the points in P, then the algorithm stops. Otherwise, let P_i denote the leftmost point in P that is not covered by *Commit*. The next interval committed to must cover this next uncovered point, P_i. Of the intervals that start to the left of the point, the algorithm greedily takes the one that extends as far to the right as possible. The hope in doing so is that the chosen interval, in addition to covering P_i, will cover as many other points as possible. Let I_j denote this interval. If there is no such interval I_j or it does not extend to the right far enough to cover the point, P_i, then no interval covers this point, and the algorithm reports that no subset of the intervals covers all of the points. Otherwise, the algorithm commits to this interval by adding it to *Commit*. This greedy criterion with which to select the next interval changes as the point P_i to be covered changes.

The Loop Invariant: The loop invariant is that we have not gone wrong: There is at least one optimal solution consistent with the choices made so far, that is, containing the objects committed to so far and not containing the objects rejected so far.

Maintaining the Loop Invariant ($\langle LI' \rangle$ & not $\langle exit \rangle$ & $code_{loop} \rightarrow \langle LI'' \rangle$): Assume that we are at the top of the loop and that the loop invariant is true, so that there exists an optimal cover that contains all of the intervals in *Commit*. Let $optS_{LI}$ denote such a cover that is assumed to exist. If we are lucky and $optS_{LI}$ already contains the interval I_j being committed to in this iteration, then we automatically know that there exists an optimal cover that contains all of the intervals in $Commit \cup \{I_j\}$ and hence the loop invariant has been maintained. If, on the other hand, the interval I_j being committed to is not in $optS_{LI}$, then we must modify this optimal solution into another optimal solution that does contain it.

> **Modifying $optS_{LI}$ into $optS_{ours}$:** The optimal solution $optS_{LI}$ must cover the point P_i. Let $I_{j'}$ denote one of the intervals in $optS_{LI}$ that covers P_i. Our solution $optS_{ours}$ is the same as $optS_{LI}$ except that $I_{j'}$ is removed and I_j is added. We know that $I_{j'}$ is not in *Commit*, because the point P_i is not covered by *Commit*. Hence, as constructed, $optS_{ours}$ contains all the intervals in $Commit \cup \{I_j\}$.
>
> **$optS_{ours}$ Is an Optimal Solution:** Because $optS_{LI}$ is an optimal cover, we can prove that $optS_{ours}$ in an optimal cover, by proving that it covers all of the points covered by $optS_{LI}$ and that it contains the same number of intervals.
>
> The algorithm considered the point P_i because it was the leftmost uncovered point. It follows that the intervals in *Commit* cover all the points to the left of P_i.
>
> The interval $I_{j'}$, because it covers P_i, must start to the left of P_i. Hence, the algorithm must have considered it when it chose I_j. Now I_j, being the interval that extends as far to the right as possible of those that start to the left of P_i, must extend at least as far to the right as $I_{j'}$, and hence I_j covers as many points to the right as $I_{j'}$ covers. It follows that $optS_{ours}$ covers all of the points covered by $optS_{LI}$.
>
> Because $optS_{ours}$ is an optimal solution containing $Commit \cup \{I_j\}$, we have proved such a solution exists. Hence, the loop invariant has been maintained.

Maintaining the Greedy Criterion: As the point P_i to be covered changes, the greedy criterion according to which the next interval is chosen changes. Blindly searching for the interval that is best according to the current greedy criterion would be too time-consuming. The following data structures help to make the algorithm more efficient.

An Event Queue: The progress of the algorithm can be viewed as an *event marker* moving along the real line. An *event* in the algorithm occurs when this marker reaches either the start of an interval or a point to be covered. This is implemented not with an actual marker, but with an *event queue*. The queue is constructed initially by sorting the intervals according to their start time and the points according to their position, and merging these two lists together. The algorithm removes and processes these events one at a time.

Additional Loop Invariants: The following additional loop invariants relate the current position event marker with to current greedy criterion.

> **LI1, Points Covered:** All the points to the left of the event marker have been covered by the intervals in *Commit*.

> **LI2, the Priority Queue:** A priority queue contains all intervals (except possibly those in *Commit*) that start to the left of the event marker. The priority according to which they are organized is how far f_j to the right the interval extends. This priority queue can be implemented using a heap. (See Section 10.4.)

> **LI3, Last Place Covered:** A variable *last* indicates the rightmost place covered by an interval in *Commit*.

Maintaining the Additional Loop Invariants:

> **A Start Interval Event:** When the event marker passes the starting time s_j of an interval I_j, this interval from then on will start to the left of the event marker and hence is added to the priority queue, its priority being its finishing time f_j.

> **An End Interval Event:** When the event marker passes the finishing time f_j of an interval I_j, we learn that this interval will not be able to cover future points P_i. Though the algorithm no longer wants to consider this interval, the algorithm will be lazy and leave it in the priority queue. Its priority will be lower than those actually covering P_i. The algorithm does not consider these events, there being nothing useful to do with them.

> **A Point Event:** When the event marker reaches a point P_i in P, the algorithm uses $last \geq P_i$ to check whether the point is already covered by an interval in *Commit*. If it is covered, then nothing needs to be done. If not, then LI1 assures us that this point is the leftmost uncovered point. LI2 ensures that the priority queue is organizing the intervals according to the current greedy criterion, namely, it contains all intervals that start to the left of the point P_i, sorted according to how far to the right the interval extends. Let I_j denote the highest-priority interval in the priority queue. Assuming that it covers P_i, the algorithm commits to it. As well, if it covers P_i, then it must extend further to the right than other intervals in *Commit*, and hence *last* is updated to f_j. (The

algorithm can either remove the interval I_j committed to from the priority queue or not. That interval will not extend far enough to the right to cover the next uncovered point, and hence its priority will be low in the queue.)

Code: Interval point cover.

algorithm *IntervalPointCover*(P, I)

⟨ **pre-cond**⟩: P is a set of points, and I is a set of intervals on a line.
⟨ **post-cond**⟩: The output consists of the smallest set of intervals that covers all of the points.

```
begin
    Sort P = {P₁, ..., Pₙ} in ascending order of pᵢ's.
    Sort I = {⟨s₁, f₁⟩, ..., ⟨sₘ, fₘ⟩} in ascending order of sⱼ's.
    Events = Merge(P, I)         % sorted in ascending order
    consideredI = ∅              % the priority queue of intervals being considered
    Commit = ∅                   % solution set: covering subset of intervals
    last = −∞                    % rightmost point covered by intervals in Commit
    for each event e ∈ Events, in ascending order do
        if(e = ⟨sⱼ, fⱼ⟩) then
            Insert interval ⟨sⱼ, fⱼ⟩ into the priority queue consideredI with
            priority fⱼ
        else (e = Pᵢ)
            if(Pᵢ > last) then % Pᵢ is not covered by Commit
                ⟨sⱼ, fⱼ⟩ = ExtractMax(consideredI) % fⱼ is max in consideredI
                if(consideredI was empty or Pᵢ > fⱼ) then
                    return (Pᵢ cannot be covered)
                else
                    Commit = Commit ∪ {j}
                    last = fⱼ
                end if
            end if
        end if
    end for
    return (Commit)
end algorithm
```

Running Time: The initial sorting takes $O((n + m)\log(n + m))$ time. The main loop iterates $n + m$ times, once per event. Since H contains a subset of I, the priority queue operations *Insert* and *ExtractMax* each take $O(\log m)$ time. The remaining operations of the loop take $O(1)$ time per iteration. Hence, the loop takes a total of $O((n + m)\log m)$ time. Therefore, the running time of the algorithm is $O((n + m)\log(n + m))$.

16.2.3 Example: The Minimum-Spanning-Tree Problem

Suppose that you are building a network of computers. You need to decide which pairs of computers to run a communication line between. You want all of the computers to be connected via the network. You want to do it in a way that minimizes your costs. This is an example of the minimum-spanning-tree problem.

Definitions: Consider a subset S of the edges of an undirected graph G.

A Tree: S is said to be *tree* if it contains no cycles and is connected.

Spanning Set: S is said to *span* the graph iff every pair of nodes is connected by a path through edges in S.

Spanning Tree: S is said to be a *spanning tree* of G iff it is a tree that spans the graph. Cycles will cause redundant paths between pairs of nodes.

Minimal Spanning Tree: S is said to be a *minimal spanning tree* of G iff it is a spanning tree with minimal total edge weight.

Spanning Forest: If the graph G is not connected, then it cannot have a spanning tree. S is said to be a *spanning forest* of G iff it is a collection of trees that spans each of the connected components of the graph. In other words, pairs of nodes that are connected by a path in G are still connected by a path if we consider only the edges in S.

Specification: The goal of the *minimum-spanning-tree (-forest) problem* is to find a minimum spanning tree (forest) for a given graph.

Precondition: We are given one of the following instances.

Instances: An instance consists of an undirected graph G. Each edge $\{u, v\}$ is labeled with a real-valued (possibly negative) weight $w_{\{u,v\}}$.

Postcondition: The output is a solution with minimum cost and the cost of that solution.

Solutions: A solution for an instance is a spanning tree (forest) S of the graph G.

Measure of Success: The cost of a solution S is the sum of its edge weights.

Possible Criteria for Defining "Best":

Cheapest Edge (Kruskal's Algorithm): The obvious greedy algorithm simply commits to the cheapest edge that does not create a cycle with the edges committed to already. See the example in Figure 16.4.

Checking for a Cycle: One task that this algorithm must be able to do quickly is to determine whether the new edge i creates a cycle with the edges in *Commit*. As a task in itself, this would take a while. However, if we maintain an extra data structure, this task can be done very quickly.

Connected Components of **Commit:** We partition the nodes in the graph into sets so that between any two nodes in the same set, *Commit* provides a path between them, and between any two nodes in different sets, *Commit* does not connect them. These sets are referred to as *components* of the subgraph induced by the edges in *Commit*. The algorithm can determine whether the new edge i creates a cycle with its edges in *Commit* by checking whether the end points of the edge $i = \{u, v\}$ are contained in the same component. The required operations on components are handled by the following *union–find* data structure.

Union–Find Set System: This data structure maintains a number of disjoint sets of elements and allows three operations: (1) *Makeset(v)*, which creates a new set containing the specified element v; (2) *Find(v)*, which determines the *name* of the set containing a specified element; and (3) *Union(u, v)*, which merges the sets containing the specified elements u and v. On average, for all practical purposes, each of these operations can be competed in a constant amount of time. See Section 3.1.

Code: Kruskal's algorithm with the union–find data structure incorporated is as follows.

algorithm *KruskalMST(G)*

⟨ *pre-cond*⟩*:* G is an undirected graph.
⟨ *post-cond*⟩*:* The output consists of a minimal spanning tree.

begin
    Sort the edges based on their weights $w_{\{u,v\}}$.
    Commit = ∅ % The set of edges committed to
    loop for each v
        % With no edges in *Commit*, each node is in a component
        by itself.
        MakeSet(v)
    end for
    loop $i = 1 \ldots m$ % Consider the edges in sorted order.
        u and v are end points of edge i.
        if(*Find(u)* ≠ *Find(v)*) then
            % The end points of edge i are in different components
            and hence do not create a cycle with edges in *Commit*.
            Commit = *Commit* ∪ {i}

$Union(u, v)$ % Edge i connects the two components: hence they are merged into one component.

       end if
      end loop
      return($Commit$)
  end algorithm

Running Time: The initial sorting takes $O(m \log m)$ time when G has m edges. The main loop iterates m times, once per edge. Checking for a cycle takes time $\alpha(n) \leq 4$ on average. Therefore, the running time of the algorithm is $O(m \log m)$.

Cheapest Connected Edge (Prim's Algorithm): The following greedy algorithm expands out a tree of edges from a source node as done in the generic search algorithm of Section 14.1. At each iteration it commits to the cheapest edge of those that expand this tree, that is, the cheapest from amongst those edges that are connected to the tree $Commit$ and yet do not create a cycle with it. See the example in Figure 16.4.

Advantage: If you are, for example, trying to find a minimum spanning tree of the World Wide Web, then you may not know about an edge until you have expanded out to it.

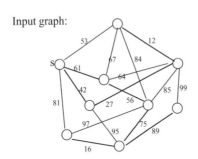

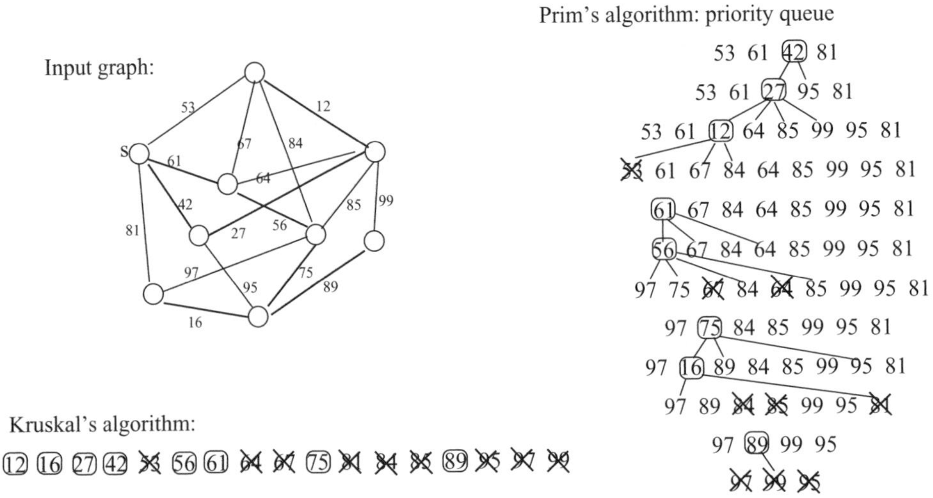

Prim's algorithm: priority queue

53 61 ⑷ 81
53 61 ㉗ 95 81
53 61 ⑿ 64 85 99 95 81
⨯ 61 67 84 64 85 99 95 81
�61㉘ 67 84 64 85 99 95 81
㊻ 67 84 64 85 99 95 81
97 75 ⨯ 84 ⨯ 85 99 95 81
97 ㊙ 84 85 99 95 81
97 ⑯ 89 84 85 99 95 81
97 89 ⨯ ⨯ 99 95 ⨯
97 ㊙ 99 95
⨯ ⨯ ⨯

Input graph:

Kruskal's algorithm:

⑿ ⑯ ㉗ ㊷ ⨯ ㊶ �61 ⨯ ⨯ ㊆ ⨯ ⨯ ⨯ ㊥ ⨯ ⨯ ⨯

Figure 16.4: Both Kruskal's and Prim's algorithms are run on the given graph. For Kruskal's algorithm the sorted order of the edges is shown. For Prim's algorithm the running content of the priority queue is shown (edges are in no particular order). Each iteration, the best edge is considered. If it does not create a cycle, it is added to the minimum spanning tree. This is shown by circling the edge weight and darkening the graph edge. For Prim's algorithm, the lines out of the circles indicate how the priority queue is updated. If the best edge does create a cycle, then the edge weight is crossed out.

Adaptive: This is an adaptive greedy algorithm, because which edges are considered changes as the algorithm proceeds. A priority queue is maintained with the allowed edges, with priorities given by their weights $w_{\{u,v\}}$. Because the allowed edges are those that are connected to the tree *Commit*, when a new edge i is added to *Commit*, the edges connected to i are added to the queue.

Code: Prim's MST algorithm.

```
algorithm PrimMST (G)

⟨ pre-cond⟩: G is an undirected graph.
⟨ post-cond⟩: The output consists of a minimum spanning tree.

begin
    Let s be the start node in G.
    Commit = ∅                          % The set of edges committed to
    Queue = edges adjacent to s   % Priority queue
    Loop until Queue = ∅
        i = cheapest edge in Queue
        if( edge i does not create a cycle with the edges in Commit) then
            Commit = Commit ∪ {i}
            Add to Queue edges adjacent to edge i that have not been
            added before
        end if
    end loop
    return(Commit)
end algorithm
```

Checking for a Cycle: As in the generic search algorithm of Section 14.1, because one tree is grown, one end of the edge i will have been found already. It will create a cycle iff the other end has also been found already.

Running Time: The main loop iterates m times, once per edge. The priority queue operations *Insert* and *ExtractMax* each takes $O(\log m)$ time. Therefore, the running time of the algorithm is $O(m \log m)$.

A More General Algorithm: When designing an algorithm it is best to leave as many implementation details unspecified as possible. This gives more freedom to anyone who may want to implement or to modify your algorithm. Also, it provides better intuition as to why the algorithm works. The following is a greedy criterion that is quite general.

Cheapest Connected Edge of Some Component: Partition the nodes of the graph G into connected *components* of nodes that are reachable from each other only through the edges in *Commit*. Nodes with no adjacent edges will be in a component by themselves. Each iteration, the algorithm is free to choose one of these components for any reason it likes. Denote this component by C. (C can be the union of a number of different components.) Then the algorithm greedily commits to the cheapest edge of those that expand this component, that is, the cheapest from amongst those edges that are connected to the component and yet do not create a cycle with it. Whenever it likes, the algorithm also has the freedom to throw away uncommitted edges that create a cycle with the edges in *Commit*.

Generalizing: This greedy criterion is general enough to include both Kruskal's and Prim's algorithms. Therefore, if we prove that this greedy algorithm works no matter how it is implemented, then we automatically prove that both Kruskal's and Prim's algorithms work.

> *Cheapest Edge (Kruskal's Algorithm):* This general algorithm may choose the component that is connected to the cheapest uncommitted edge that does not create a cycle. Then when it chooses the cheapest edge out of this component, it gets the overall cheapest edge.

> *Cheapest Connected Edge (Prim's Algorithm):* This general algorithm may always choose the component that contains the source node s. This amounts to Prim's algorithm.

The Loop Invariant: The loop invariant is that we have not gone wrong. There is at least one optimal solution consistent with the choices made so far.

Maintaining the Loop Invariant ($\langle LI' \rangle$ & not $\langle exit \rangle$ & $code_{loop} \rightarrow \langle LI'' \rangle$): See the example in Figure 16.5. If we are unlucky and the optimal minimum spanning tree $optS_{LI}$ that is assumed to exist by the loop invariant does not contain the edge i being committed to this iteration, then we must modify this optimal solution $optS_{LI}$ into another one $optS_{ours}$ that contains all of the edges in $Commit \cup \{i\}$. This proves that the loop invariant has been maintained.

> **Modifying $optS_{LI}$ into $optS_{ours}$:** To the optimal solution $optS_{LI}$ we add the edge $i = \{u, v\}$ being committed to this iteration. Because $optS_{LI}$ spans the graph G, there is some path P within it from node u to node v. This path along with the edge $i = \{u, v\}$ creates a cycle, which must be broken by removing one edge from P. Let C denote the component of *Commit* that the general greedy algorithm chooses the edge i from. Because i expands the component without creating a cycle with it, one and only one of the edge i's nodes u and v is within the component. Hence, this path P starts within C and ends outside of C. Hence, there must be some edge j in the path that leaves C. We will delete this edge from our optimal minimum spanning tree: $optS_{ours} = optS_{LI} \cup \{i\} - \{j\}$.

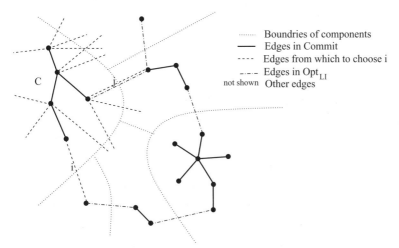

Boundries of components
—— Edges in Commit
---- Edges from which to choose i
---·--- Edges in Opt$_{LI}$
not shown   Other edges

Figure 16.5: C is one of the components of the graph induced by the edges in *Commit*. Edge i is the cheapest out of C. Edge j is an edge in $optS_{LI}$ that is out of C. Finally, $optS_{ours}$ is formed by removing j and adding i.

$optS_{ours}$ is an Optimal Solution:

$optS_{ours}$ **Has No Cycles:** Because $optS_{LI}$ has no cycles, we create only one cycle by adding edge i, and we destroy this cycle by deleting edge j.

$optS_{ours}$ **Spans G:** Because $optS_{LI}$ spans G, $optS_{ours}$ spans it as well. Any path between two nodes that goes through edge j in $optS_{LI}$ will now follow the remaining edges of path P together with edge i in $optS_{ours}$.

$optS_{ours}$ **Has Minimum Weight:** Because $optS_{LI}$ has minimum weight, it is sufficient to prove that edge i is at least as cheap as edge j. Note that by construction edge j leaves component C and does not create a cycle with it. Because edge i was chosen because it was the cheapest such edges, (or at least one of the cheapest) it is true that edge i is at least as cheap as edge j.

EXERCISE 16.2.1 *Show how the earliest-finishing-time criterion works on the three counterexamples in Section 16.2.1 and on the example in Figure 16.1.*

EXERCISE 16.2.2 *(See solution in Part Five.) For the example in Section 16.2.2, consider the greedy criterion that selects the interval that covers the largest number of uncovered points. Does this work? If not, give a counterexample.*

EXERCISE 16.2.3 *In Figure 16.4, suppose we decide to change the weight 56 to some other real number from $-\infty$ to $+\infty$. What is the interval of values that it could be changed to for which the minimum spanning tree remains the same? Explain your answer. Similarly for the weight 85.*

EXERCISE 16.2.4 *Give a simple graph with edge weights for which the tree of shortest weighted paths from node s is not a minimum spanning tree.*

16.3 Exercises

EXERCISE 16.3.1 *One aspect of the game called magic (or jugio) is as follows. You have n defense cards, the ith of which, denoted D_i, has worth w_i and defense ability d_i. Your opponent has n attack cards, the jth of which, denoted A_j, has attack ability a_j. You can see all of the cards. Your task is to define a one-to-one matching between the attacking cards and the defending cards, that is, each attack card is allocated to a unique defense card. If card D_i is defending against A_j and $d_i < a_j$, then d_i dies. Your goal is to maximize the sum of the worths w_i of your cards that live. Give your algorithm. Then prove that it works.*

EXERCISE 16.3.2 *(See solution in Part Five.) Review the job/event scheduling problem from Section 16.2.1. This problem is the same except you have r rooms/processors within which to schedule that the set of jobs/events in two rooms or on two processors. An instance is $\langle r, \langle s_1, f_1 \rangle, \langle s_2, f_2 \rangle, \ldots, \langle s_n, f_n \rangle \rangle$, where, as before, $0 \leq s_i \leq f_i$ are the starting and finishing times for the ith event. But now the input also specifies the number of rooms, r. A solution for an instance is a schedule $S = \langle S_1, \ldots, S_r \rangle$ for each of the rooms. Each of these consists of a subset $S_j \subseteq [1..n]$ of the events that don't conflict by overlapping in time. The success of a solution S is the number of events scheduled, that is, $|\cup_{j \in [r]} S|$. Consider the following four algorithms:*

1. *Find the greedy solution for the first room. Then find the greedy solution for the second room from the remaining events. Then for the third room, and so on.*
2. *The algorithm starts by sorting the events by their finishing times, just as in the one-room case. Then, it looks at each event in turn, scheduling it if possible. If it can be scheduled in more than one room, we assign it in the first room in which it fits, i.e., first try room 1, then room 2, and so on, until it fits. If it cannot be scheduled in any room, then it is not scheduled.*
3. *The same, except that the next event is scheduled in the room with the latest last-scheduled finishing time. For example, if the last event scheduled in room 5 finishes at time 10 and the last event scheduled in room 12 finishes at time 15 and the next event starts at time 17, then the next event could be scheduled into either of these rooms. This algorithm would schedule it, however, in room 12.*
4. *The same except that the next event is scheduled in the room with the earliest last-scheduled finishing time.*

Prove that three of these algorithms do not lead to an optimal schedule, and the remaining one does.

17 Recursive Backtracking

The brute force algorithm for an optimization problem is to simply compute the cost or value of each of the exponential number of possible solutions and return the best. A key problem with this algorithm is that it takes exponential time. Another (not obviously trivial) problem is how to write code that enumerates over all possible solutions. Often the easiest way to do this is *recursive backtracking*. The idea is to design a recurrence relation that says how to find an optimal solution for one instance of the problem from optimal solutions for some number of smaller instances of the same problem. The optimal solutions for these smaller instances are found by recursing. After unwinding the recursion tree, one sees that recursive backtracking effectively enumerates all options. Though the technique may seem confusing at first, once you get the hang of recursion, it really is the simplest way of writing code to accomplish this task. Moreover, with a little insight one can significantly improve the running time by pruning off entire branches of the recursion tree. In practice, if the instance that one needs to solve is sufficiently small and has enough structure that a lot of pruning is possible, then an optimal solution can be found for the instance reasonably quickly. For some problems, the set of subinstances that get solved in the recursion tree is sufficiently small and predictable that the recursive backtracking algorithm can be mechanically converted into a quick dynamic programming algorithm. See Chapter 18. In general, however, for most optimization problems, for large worst case instances, the running time is still exponential.

17.1 Recursive Backtracking Algorithms

An Algorithm as a Sequence of Decisions: An algorithm for finding an optimal solution for your instance must make a sequence of small decisions about the solution: "Do we include the first object in the solution or not?" "Do we include the second?" "The third?" . . . , or "At the first fork in the road, do we go left or right?" "At the second fork which direction do we go?" "At the third?" . . . . As one stack frame in the recursive algorithm, our task is to deal only with the first of these decisions. A recursive friend will deal with the rest. We saw in Chapter 16 that greedy algorithms make decisions simply by committing to the option that looks best at the moment. However, this usually does not work. Often, in fact, we have no inspirational technique to know how to make each decision in a way that leads to an optimal (or even a sufficiently good) solution. The difficulty is that it is hard to see the global consequences of the local choices that we make. Sometimes a local initial sacrifice can globally lead to a better overall solution. Instead, we use perspiration. We try all options.

EXAMPLE 17.1.1   Searching a Maze

When we come to a fork in the road, all possible directions need to be tried. For each, we get a friend to search exhaustively, backtrack to the fork, and report the highlights. Our task is to determine which of these answers is best overall. Our friends will have their own forks to deal with. However, it is best not to worry about this, since their path is their responsibility, not ours.

High-Level Code: The following is the basic structure that the code will take.

algorithm *Alg* (*I*)

⟨ *pre-cond*⟩: *I* is an instance of the problem.
⟨ *post-cond*⟩: *optSol* is one of the optimal solutions for the instance *I*, and *optCost* is its cost.
begin
    if(*I* is small) then
        return(brute force answer)
    else
        % Deal with the first decision by trying each of the *K* possibilities.

for $k = 1$ to K

  % Temporarily, commit to making the first decision in the kth way.

  $\langle optSol_k, optCost_k \rangle$ = Recursively deal with all the remaining decisions, and in doing so find the best solution $optSol_k$ for our instance I from among those consistent with this kth way of making the first decision. $optCost_k$ is its cost.

end for

% Having the best, $optSol_k$, for each possibility k, we keep the best of these best.

k_{min} = "a k that minimizes $optCost_k$"

$optSol = optSol_{k_{min}}$

$optCost = optCost_{k_{min}}$

return $\langle optSol, optCost \rangle$

end if

end algorithm

EXAMPLE 17.1.2   *Searching for the Best Animal*

Suppose, instead of searching through a structured maze, we are searching through a large set of objects, say for the best animal at the zoo. See Figure 17.1. Again we break the search into smaller searches, each of which we delegate to a friend. We might ask one friend for the best vertebrate and another for the best invertebrate. We will take the better of these best as our answer. This algorithm is recursive. The friend with the vertebrate task asks a friend to find the best mammal, another for the best bird, and another for the best reptile.

A Classification Tree of Solutions: This algorithm unwinds into the tree of stack frames that directly mirrors the taxonomy tree that classifies animals. Each solution is identified with a leaf.

Iterating through the Solutions to Find the Optimal One: This algorithm amounts to using depth-first search (Section 14.4) to traverse this classification tree, iterating through all the solutions associated with the leaves. Though this algorithm may seem complex, it is often the easiest way to iterate through all solutions.

Speeding Up the Algorithm: This algorithm is not any faster than the brute force algorithm that simply compares each animal with every other. However, the structure that the recursive backtracking adds can possibly be exploited to speed up the algorithm. A branch of the tree can be pruned off when we know that this does not eliminate all optimal solutions. Greedy algorithms (Chapter 16) prune off all branches except one path down the tree. In Section 18.2, we will see how dynamic programming reuses the optimal solution from one subtree within another subtree.

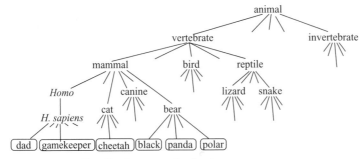

Figure 17.1: Classification tree of animals.

The Little Bird Abstraction: I like to use a *little bird* abstraction to help focus on two of the most difficult and creative parts of designing a recursive backtracking algorithm.

What Question to Ask: The key difference between searching a maze and searching for the best animal is that in the first the forks are fixed by the problem, but in the second the algorithm designer is able to choose them. Instead of forking on vertebrates vs invertebrates, we could fork on brown animals vs green animals. This choice is a difficult and creative part of the algorithm design process. It dictates the entire structure of the algorithm, which in turns dictates how well the algorithm can be sped up. I like to view this process of forking as asking a *little bird* a question, "Is the best animal a vertebrate or an invertebrate?" or "Is the best vertebrate, a mammal, a bird, a reptile, or a fish?" The classification tree becomes a strategy for the game of twenty questions. Each sequence of possible answers (for example, vertebrate–mammal–cat–cheetah) uniquely specifies an animal. Worrying only about the top level of recursion, the algorithm designer must formulate one small question about the optimal solution that is being searched for. The question should be such that having a correct answer greatly reduces your search.

Constructing a Subinstance for a Friend: The second creative part of designing a recursive backtracking algorithm is how to express the problem "Find the best mammal" as a smaller instance of the same search problem. The little bird helps again. We pretend that she answered "mammal." Trusting (at least temporarily) in her answer helps us focus on the fact that we are now only considering mammals, and this helps us to design a subinstance that asks for the best one. A solution to this subinstance needs to be translated before it is in the correct form to be a solution to our instance.

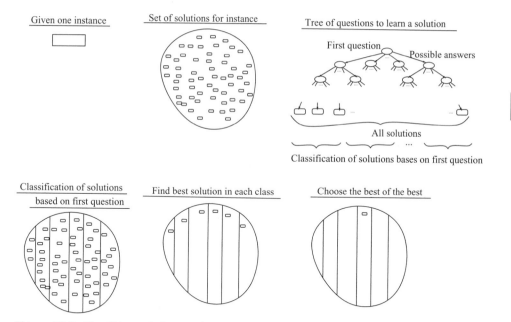

Figure 17.2: *Classifying solutions and taking the best of the best.*

A Flock of Stupid Birds vs. a Wise Little Bird: The following two ways of thinking about the algorithm are equivalent.

> **A Flock of Stupid Birds:** Suppose that our question about whether the optimal solution is a mammal, a bird, or a reptile has K different answers. For each, we pretend that a bird gave us this answer. Giving her the benefit of doubt, we ask a friend to give us the optimal solution from among those that are consistent with this answer. At least one of these birds must have been telling us the truth. We find it by taking the best of the optimal solutions obtained in this way. See Figure 17.2 for an illustration of these ideas.

> **A Wise Little Bird:** If we had a little bird who would answer our questions correctly, designing an algorithm would be a lot easier: We ask the little bird "Is the best animal a bird, a mammal, a reptile, or a fish?" She tells us a mammal. We ask our friend for the best mammal. Trusting the little bird and the friend, we give this as the best animal. Just as nondeterministic finite automata (NFAs) and nondeterministic Turing machines can be viewed as higher powers that provide help, our little bird can be viewed as a limited higher power. She is limited in that we can only ask her questions that do not have too many possible answers, because in reality we must try all these possible answers.

17.2 The Steps in Developing a Recursive Backtracking

This section presents the steps that I recommend using when developing a recursive backtracking algorithm. To demonstrate them, we will develop an algorithm for the *queens problem.*

EXAMPLE 17.2.1 The Queens Problem

Physically get yourself (or make on paper) a chessboard and eight tokens to act as queens. More generally, you could consider an $n \times n$ board and n queens. A queen can move as far as she pleases, horizontally, vertically, or diagonally. The goal is to place all the queens on the board in a way such that no queen is able to capture any other.

Try It: Before reading on, try yourself to place the queens on an 8-by-8 board. How would you do it?

1) Specification: The first step is to be very clear about what problem needs to be solved. For an optimization problem, we need to be clear about what the set of instances is; for each instance, what its set of solutions is; and for each solution, what its cost or value is.

> **Queens:** The set of possible solutions is the set of ways placing the queens on the board. We do not value one solution over another as long as it is valid, i.e., no queen is able to capture any other queen. Hence, the value of a solution can simply be one if it is a valid solution and zero if not. What is not clear is what an input instance for this problem is, beyond the dimension n. We will need to generalize the problem to include more instances in order to be able to recurse. However, we will get back to that later.

2) Design a Question and Its Answers for the Little Bird: Suppose the little bird knows one of the optimal solutions for our instance. You, the algorithm designer, must formulate a small question about this solution and the list of its possible answers.

> **Question about the Solution:** The question should be such that having a correct answer greatly reduces the search. Generally, we ask for the first *part* of the solution.

>> **Queens:** We might ask the bird, "Where should I place the first queen?"

> **The Possible Bird Answers:** Together with your question, you provide the little bird with a list $A_1, A_2, \ldots, A_K$ of possible answers, and she simply returns the index $k \in [1..K]$ of her answer. To be consistent, we will always use the letter k to index the bird answers. In order for the final algorithm to be efficient, it is important that the number K of different answers be small.

Queens: Given that there are n queens and n rows and that two queens cannot be placed in the same row, the first observation is that the first queen must be in the first row. Hence, there are $K = n$ different answers the bird might give.

3) Constructing Subinstances: Suppose that the bird gives us the kth of her answers. This giving us some of the solution; we want to ask a recursive friend for the rest of the solution. The friend must be given a smaller instance of the same search problem. You must formulate subinstance *subI* for the friend so that he returns to us the information that we desire.

Queens: I start by (at least temporarily) trusting the bird, and I place a queen where she says in the first row. In order to give an instance to the friend, we need to go back to step 1 and generalize the problem. An input instance will specify the locations of queens in the first r rows. A solution is a valid way of putting the queens in the remaining rows. Given such an instance, the question for the bird is "Where does the queen in the next row go?" Trusting the bird, we place a queen where she says. The instance, *subI*, we give the friend is the board with these $r + 1$ queens placed.

Trust the Friend: We proved in Section 8.7 that we can trust the friend to provide an optimal solution to the subinstance *subI*, because he is really a smaller recursive version of ourselves.

4) Constructing a Solution for My Instance: Suppose that the friend gives you an optimal solution *optSubSol* for his instance *subI*. How do you produce an optimal solution *optSol* for your instance *I* from the bird's answer k and the friend's solution *optSubSol*?

Queens: The bird tells you where on the $r + 1$st row the queen should go and your friend tells you where on the rows $r + 2$ to n the queens should go. Your solution combines these to tell where the on the rows $r + 1$ to n the queens should go.

We can trust the friend to give provide an optimal solution to the subinstance *subI*, because he is really a smaller recursive version of ourselves. Recall, in Section 8.7, we used strong induction to prove that we can trust our recursive friends.

5) Costs of Solutions and Subsolutions: We must also return the cost *optCost* of our solution *optSol*.

Queens: The solutions in this case, don't have costs.

6) Best of the Best: Try all the bird's answers, and take best of the best.

Queens: If we trust both the bird and the friend, we conclude that this process finds us a best placement of the queens. If, however, our little bird gave us the wrong placement of the queen in the $r + 1$st row, then this might not be the best placement. However, our work was not wasted, because we did succeed in finding the best placement from amongst those consistent with this bird's answer.

Not trusting the little bird, we repeat this process, finding a best placement starting with each of the possible bird answers. Because at least one of the bird answers must be correct, one of these placements must be an overall best. We return the best of these best as the overall best placement.

To find the best of these best placements, let $optSol_k$ and $optCost_k$ denote the optimal solution for our instance I and its cost that we formed when temporarily trusting the kth bird's answer. Search through this list of costs $optCost_1$, $optCost_2, \ldots, optCost_K$, finding the best one. Denote the index of the chosen one by k_{max}. The optimal solution that we will return is then $optSol = optSol_{k_{max}}$ and its cost is $optCost = optCost_{k_{max}}$.

7) Base Cases: The base case instances are instances of your problem that are small enough that they cannot be solved using steps 2–6, but they can be solved easily in a brute force way. What are these base cases, and what are their solutions?

Queens: If all n queens have been placed, then there is nothing to be done.

8) Code: The following code might be made slightly simpler, but in order to be consistent we will always use this same basic structure.

algorithm $Queens\ (C, n, r)$

$\langle$ **pre-cond** $\rangle$: $C = \langle \langle 1, c_1 \rangle, \langle 2, c_2 \rangle, \ldots, \langle r, c_r \rangle \rangle$ places the jth queen in the jth row and the c_jth column. The remaining rows have no queen.

$\langle$ **post-cond** $\rangle$: Returned if possible is a placement $optSol$ of the n queens consistent with this initial placement of the first r queens. A placement is legal if no two queens can capture each other. Whether this is possible is flagged with $optCost$ equal to one or zero.

begin
    % Base case: If all the queens have been already been placed, then the
    problem is easy to solve.
    if($r = n$) then
        if(C is legal) then $optSol = C$ & $optCost = 1$ else $optCost = 0$
        return $\langle optSol, optCost \rangle$
    else
    % General case:
        % Try each possible bird answer.
        loop $k = 1 \ldots n$
            % The bird-and-friend algorithm: The bird tells us the column k
            in which to put the $r + 1$st queen. We ask the friend to place the
            remaining queens. This will be our best solution $optSol_k$ amongst
            those consistent with this bird's answer.
            $C' = C \cup \langle r + 1, k \rangle$ % Place a queen at this location.
            $\langle optSol_k, optCost_k \rangle = Queens\ (C', n, r + 1)$
        end for

% Having the best, $optSol_k$, for each bird's answer k, we keep the
best of these best.
$k_{max} = $ a k that maximizes $optCost_k$,
% i.e., if possible k for which $optCost_k = 1$
$optSol = optSol_{k_{max}}$
$optCost = optCost_{k_{max}}$

         return $\langle optSol, optCost \rangle$
   end if
end algorithm

9) Recurrence Relations: At the core of every recursive backtracking and dynamic programming algorithm is a *recurrence relation*. These define one element of a sequence as a function of previous elements in the same sequence. The following are examples.

The Fibonacci Sequence: If $Fib(i)$ is the ith element in the famous Fibonacci sequence, then $Fib(n) = Fib(n-1) + Fib(n-2)$. The base cases $Fib(0) = 0$ and $Fib(1) = 1$ are also needed.

Running Time: If $T(n)$ is the running time of merge sort on an input of n numbers, then we have $T(n) = 2T(\frac{n}{2}) + n$. The base case $T(1) = 1$ is also needed.

Optimal Solution: Suppose $Solution[I]$ is defined to be an optimal solution for instance I of a problem, and $Cost[I]$ is its cost. This is not a sequence of elements like the previous examples, because I is not in integer. However, in Chapter 18 the instances will be indexed by integers i so that $Solution[i]$ and $Cost[i]$ are sequences. But even when I is an arbitrary input instance, a *recurrence relation* can be developed as follows from the bird – friend algorithm.

$Solution$[my instance]

    $= \text{Min}_{k \in [K]}$[An optimal solution to my instance from those that
                  are consistent with the kth bird's answer]

    $= \text{Min}_{k \in [K]}$[combine bird's answer and friend's answer]

    $= \text{Min}_{k \in [K]}$[combine bird's answer and $Solution$[friend's instance]]

$Cost$[my instance]

    $= \text{Min}_{k \in [K]}$[cost of optimal solution to my instance from those that
                  are consistent with the kth bird's answer]

    $= \text{Min}_{k \in [K]}$[combine bird's cost and friend's cost]

    $= \text{Min}_{k \in [K]}$[combine bird's cost and $Cost$[friend's instance]]

Base cases " $Solution$[small instance] = solution" are also needed.

Queens: For our queens example this becomes

$$Queens\,(C, n, r) = \text{Min}_{k \in [n]}\,Queens\,(C \cup \langle r + 1, k \rangle, n, r + 1)$$

This is bit of a silly example, because here all the work is done in the base cases.

Running Time: A recursive backtracking algorithm faithfully enumerates all solutions for your instance and hence requires exponential time. We will see that this time can be reduced by pruning off branches of the recursion tree.

17.3 Pruning Branches

The following are typical reasons why an entire branch of the solution classification tree can be pruned off.

Invalid Solutions: Recall that in a recursive backtracking algorithm, the little bird tells the algorithm something about the solution and then the algorithm recurses by asking a friend a question. Then this friend gets more information about the solution from his little bird, and so on. Hence, following a path down the recursive tree specifies more and more about a solution until a leaf of the tree fully specifies one particular solution. Sometimes it happens that partway down the tree, the algorithm has already received enough information about the solution to determine that it contains a conflict or defect making any such solution invalid. The algorithm can stop recursing at this point and backtrack. This effectively prunes off the entire subtree of solutions rooted at this node in the tree.

> **Queens:** Before we try placing a queen on the square $\langle r + 1, k \rangle$, we should check to make sure that this does not conflict with the locations of any of the queens on $\langle \langle 1, c_1 \rangle, \langle 2, c_2 \rangle, \ldots, \langle r, c_r \rangle \rangle$. If it does, we do not need to ask for help from this friend. Exercise 17.5.4 bounds the resulting running time.
>
> **Time Saved:** The time savings can be huge. Recall that for Example 9.2.1 in Section 9.2, reducing the number of recursive calls from two to one decreased the running time from $\Theta(N)$ to $\Theta(\log N)$, and how in Example 9.2.2 reducing the number of recursive calls from four to three decreased the running time from $\Theta(n^2)$ to $\Theta(n^{1.58\cdots})$.

No Highly Valued Solutions: Similarly, when the algorithm arrives at the root of a subtree, it might realize that no solutions within this subtree are rated sufficiently high to be optimal—perhaps because the algorithm has already found a solution provably better than all of these. Again, the algorithm can prune this entire subtree from its search.

Greedy Algorithms: Greedy algorithms are effectively recursive backtracking algorithms with extreme pruning. Whenever the algorithm has a choice as to which little bird's answer to take, i.e., which path down the recursive tree to take, instead of iterating through all of the options, it goes only for the one that looks best according to some greedy criterion. In this way the algorithm follows only one path down the recursive tree. Greedy algorithms are covered in Chapter 16.

Modifying Solutions: Let us recall why greedy algorithms are able to prune, so that we can use the same reasoning with recursive backtracking algorithms. In each step in a greedy algorithm, the algorithm commits to some decision about the solution. This effectively burns some of its bridges, because it eliminates some solutions from consideration. However, this is fine as long as it does not burn all its bridges. The prover proves that there is an optimal solution consistent with the choices made by modifying any possible solution that is not consistent with the latest choice into one that has at least as good value and is consistent with this choice. Similarly, a recursive backtracking algorithm can prune of branches in its tree when it knows that this does not eliminate all remaining optimal solutions.

> **Queens:** By symmetry, any solution that has the queen in the second half of the first row can be modified into one that has the this queen in the first half, simply by flipping the solution left to right. Hence, when placing a queen in the first row, there is no need to try placing it in the second half of the row.

> **Depth-First Search:** Recursive depth-first search (Section 14.5) is a recursive backtracking algorithm. A solution to the optimization problem of searching a maze for cheese is a path in the graph starting from s. The value of a solution is the weight of the node at the end of the path. The algorithm marks nodes that it has visited. Then, when the algorithm revisits a node, it knows that it can prune this subtree in this recursive search, because it knows that any node reachable from the current node has already been reached. In Figure 14.9, the path $\langle s, c, u, v \rangle$ is pruned because it can be modified into the path $\langle s, b, u, v \rangle$, which is just as good.

17.4 Satisfiability

A famous optimization problem is called *satisfiability*, or SAT for short. It is one of the basic problems arising in many fields. The recursive backtracking algorithm given here is referred to as the *Davis–Putnam* algorithm. It is an example of an algorithm whose running time is exponential for worst case inputs, yet in many practical situations can work well. This algorithm is one of the basic algorithms underlying automated theorem proving and robot path planning, among other things.

The Satisfiability Problem:

> **Instances:** An instance (input) consists of a set of constraints on the assignment to the binary variables $x_1, x_2, \ldots, x_n$. A typical constraint might be $\langle x_1 \text{ or } \overline{x_3} \text{ or } x_8 \rangle$,

meaning ($x_1 = 1$ or $x_3 = 0$ or $x_8 = 1$) or equivalently that either x_1 is true, x_3 is false, or x_8 is true. More generally an instance could be a more general circuit built with *AND*, *OR*, and *NOT* gates, but we leave this until Section 20.1.

Solutions: Each of the 2^n assignments is a possible solution. An assignment is valid for the given instance if it satisfies all of the constraints.

Measure of Success: An assignment is assigned the value one if it satisfies all of the constraints, and the value zero otherwise.

Goal: Given the constraints, the goal is to find a satisfying assignment.

Iterating through the Solutions: The brute force algorithm simply tries each of the 2^n assignments of the variables. Before reading on, think about how you would nonrecursively iterate through all of these solutions. Even this simplest of examples is surprisingly hard.

Nested Loops: The obvious algorithm is to have n nested loops each going from 0 to 1. However, this requires knowing the value of n before compile time, which is not likely.

Incrementing Binary Numbers: Another option is to treat the assignment as an n-bit binary number and then loop through the 2^n assignments by incrementing this binary number each iteration.

Recursive Algorithm: The recursive backtracking technique is able to iterate through the solutions with much less effort in coding. First the algorithm commits to assigning $x_1 = 0$ and recursively iterates through the 2^{n-1} assignments of the remaining variables. Then the algorithm backtracks, repeating these steps with the choice $x_1 = 1$. Viewed another way, the first little bird question about the solutions is whether the first variable x_1 is set to zero or one, the second question asks about the second variable x_2, and so on. The 2^n assignments of the variables $x_1, x_2, \ldots, x_n$ are associated with the 2^n leaves of the complete binary tree with depth n. A given path from the root to a leaf commits each variable x_i to being either zero or one by having the path turn to either the left or to the right when reaching the ith level.

Instances and Subinstances: Given an instance, the recursive algorithm must construct two subinstances for its friends' to recurse with. There are two techniques for doing this.

Narrowing the Class of Solutions: Associated with each node of the classification tree is a subinstance defined as follows: The set of constraints remains unchanged except that the solutions considered must be consistent in the variables $x_1, x_2, \ldots, x_r$ with the assignment given by the path to the node. Traversing a step further down the classification tree further narrows the set of solutions.

Reducing the Instance: Given an instance consisting of a number of constraints on n variables, we first try assigning $x_1 = 0$. The subinstance to be given to the first friend will be the constraints on remaining variables given that $x_1 = 0$. For example, if one of our original constraints is $\langle x_1 \text{ OR } \overline{x_3} \text{ OR } x_8 \rangle$, then after assigning $x_1 = 0$, the reduced constraint will be $\langle \overline{x_3} \text{ OR } x_8 \rangle$. This is because it is no longer possible for x_1 to be true, given that one of $\overline{x_3}$ or x_8 must be true. On the other hand, after assigning $x_1 = 1$, the original constraint is satisfied independently of the values of the other variables, and hence this constraint can be removed.

Pruning: This recursive backtracking algorithm for SAT can be sped up. This can either be viewed globally as a pruning off of entire branches of the classification tree or be viewed locally as seeing that some subinstances, after they have been sufficiently reduced, are trivial to solve.

Pruning Branches Off the Tree: Consider the node of the classification tree arrived at down the subpath $x_1 = 0$, $x_2 = 1$, $x_3 = 1$, $x_4 = 0, \ldots,$ $x_8 = 0$. All of the assignment solutions consistent with this partial assignment fail to satisfy the constraint $\langle x_1 \text{ OR } \overline{x_3} \text{ OR } x_8 \rangle$. Hence, this entire subtree can be pruned off.

Trivial Subinstances: When the algorithm tries to assign $x_1 = 0$, the constraint $\langle x_1 \text{ OR } \overline{x_3} \text{ OR } x_8 \rangle$ is reduced to $\langle \overline{x_3} \text{ or } x_8 \rangle$. Assigning $x_2 = 1$ does not change this particular constraint. Assigning $x_3 = 1$ reduces this constraint further to simply $\langle x_8 \rangle$, stating that x_8 must be true. Finally, when the algorithm is considering the value for x_8, it sees from this constraint that x_8 is *forced* to be one. Hence, the $x_8 = 1$ friend is called, but the $x_8 = 0$ friend is not.

Stop When an Assignment is Found: The problem specification only asks for one satisfying assignment. Hence, the algorithm can stop when one is found.

Davis–Putnam: The above algorithm branches on the values of each variable, $x_1, x_2, \ldots, x_n$, in order. However, there is no particular reason that this order needs to be fixed. Each branch of the recursive algorithm can dynamically use some heuristic to decide which variable to branch on next. For example, if there is a variable, like x_8 in the preceding example, whose assignment is forced by some constraint, then clearly this assignment should be done immediately. Doing so removes this variable from all the other constraints, simplifying the instance. Moreover, if the algorithm branched on $x_4, \ldots, x_7$ before the forcing of x_8, then this same forcing would need to be repeated within all 2^4 of these branches.

If there are no variables to force, a common strategy is to branch on the variable that appears in the largest number of constraints. The thinking is that the removal of this variable may lead to the most simplification of the instance.

An example of how different branches may set the variables in a different order is the following. Suppose that $\langle x_1 \text{ OR } x_2 \rangle$ and $\langle \overline{x_1} \text{ OR } x_3 \rangle$ are two of the constraints.

Assigning $x_1 = 0$ will simplify the first constraint to $\langle x_2 \rangle$ and remove the second constraint. The next step would be to force $x_2 = 1$. On the other hand, assigning $x_1 = 1$ will simplify the second constraint to forcing $x_3 = 1$.

Code:

```
algorithm DavisPutnam(c)

    ⟨ pre-cond⟩: c is a set of constraints on the assignment to x⃗.
    ⟨ post-cond⟩: If possible, optSol is a satisfying assignment and optCost is also one.
    Otherwise optCost is zero.

    begin
        if( c has no constraints or no variables ) then
            % c is trivially satisfiable.
            return ⟨∅, 1⟩
        else if( c has both a constraint forcing a variable xᵢ to 0
                and one forcing the same variable to 1) then
            % c is trivially not satisfiable.
            return ⟨∅, 0⟩
        else
            for any variable forced by a constraint to some value
                substitute this value into c.
            let xᵢ be the variable that appears the most often in c
            % Loop over the possible bird answers.
            for k = 0 to 1 (unless a satisfying solution has been found)
                % Get help from friend.
                let c′ be the constraints c with k substituted in for xᵢ
                ⟨optSubSol, optSubCost⟩ = DavisPutnam(c′)
                optSolₖ = ⟨forced values, xᵢ = k, optSubSol⟩
                optCostₖ = optSubCost
            end for
            % Take the best bird answer.
            kₘₐₓ = a k that maximizes optCostₖ
            optSol = optSolₖₘₐₓ
            optCost = optCostₖₘₐₓ
            return ⟨optSol, optCost⟩
        end if
    end algorithm
```

Running Time: If no pruning is done, then clearly the running time is $\Omega(2^n)$, as all 2^n assignments are tried. Considerable pruning needs to occur to make the algorithm polynomial-time. Certainly in the worst case, the running time is $2^{\Theta(n)}$. In practice, however, the algorithm can be quite fast. For example, suppose that the instance is chosen randomly by choosing m constraints, each of which is the OR of three variables or their negations, e.g., $\langle x_1 \ OR \ \overline{x_3} \ OR \ x_8 \rangle$. If few constraints are chosen (say m is less than about $3n$), then with very high probability there are many satisfying assignments and the algorithm quickly finds one of these assignments. If a lot of constraints are chosen, (say m is at least n^2), then with very high probability there are many conflicting constraints, preventing there from being any satisfying assignments, and the algorithm quickly finds one of these contradictions. On the other hand, if the number of constraints chosen is between these thresholds, then it has been proven that the Davis–Putnam algorithm takes exponential time.

17.5 Exercises

EXERCISE 17.5.1 *(See solution in Part Five.) In one version of the game Scrabble, an input instance consists of a set of letters and a board, and the goal is to find a word that returns the most points. A student described the following recursive backtracking algorithm for it. The bird provides the best word out of the list of letters. The friend provides the best place on the board to put the word. Why are these bad questions?*

EXERCISE 17.5.2 *(See solution in Part Five.) Consider the following Scrabble problem. An instance consists of a set of letters and a dictionary. A solution consists of a permutation of a subset of the given letters. A solution is valid if it is in the dictionary. The value of a solution depends on its placement on the board. The goal is to find a highest-value word that is in the dictionary.*

EXERCISE 17.5.3 *(See solution in Part Five.) Trace the queens algorithm (Section 17.2.1) on the standard 8-by-8 board. What are the first dozen legal outputs for the algorithm? To save time note that the first two or three queens do not move so fast. Hence, it might be worth it to draw a board with all squares conflicting with these crossed out.*

EXERCISE 17.5.4 *(See solution in Part Five.) What is the running time of the queens algorithm (Section 17.2.1) for the n-by-n board when there is no pruning? Give reasonable upper and lower bounds on the running time of this algorithm after all the pruning occurs.*

EXERCISE 17.5.5 *(See solution in Part Five.) An instance may have many optimal solutions with exactly the same cost. The postcondition of the problem allows any one of these to become output. In any recursive backtracking algorithm, which line of code chooses which of these optimal solutions will be selected?*

EXERCISE 17.5.6 *Suppose you are solving SAT from Section 17.4. Suppose your instance is x AND y, and the little bird tells you to set x to one. What is the instance that you give to your friend? Do the same for instances ¬x AND y, x OR y, and ¬x OR y.*

EXERCISE 17.5.7 *Independent set: Given a graph, find a largest subset of the nodes for which there are no edges between any pair in the set. Give the bird-and-friend abstraction of a recursive backtracking algorithm for this problem. What do you ask the bird, and what do give your friend?*

EXERCISE 17.5.8 *Graph 3-coloring (3-COL): Given a graph, determine whether its nodes can be colored with three colors so that two nodes do not have the same color if they have an edge between them. What difficulty arises when attempting to design a recursive backtracking algorithm for it? Redefine the problem so that the input consists of a graph and a partial coloring of the nodes. The new goal is to determine whether there is a coloring of the graph consistent with the partial coloring given. Give the bird-and-friend abstraction of a recursive backtracking algorithm for this problem. What do you ask the bird, and what do give your friend?*

18 Dynamic Programming Algorithms

Dynamic programming is another powerful tool for solving optimization problems. Just like recursive backtracking, it has as a key component a recurrence relation that says how to find an optimal solution for one instance of the problem from optimal solutions for some number of smaller instances of the same problem. Instead of recursing on these subinstances, dynamic programming iteratively fills in a table with an optimal solution for each, so that each only needs to be solved once. Dynamic programming provides polynomial-time algorithms for many important and practical problem.

Personally, I do not like the name "dynamic programming." It is true that dynamic programming algorithms have a program of subinstances to solve. But these subinstances are chosen in a fixed prescheduled order, not *dynamically*. In contrast, in recursive backtracking algorithms, the subinstances are constructed dynamically.

One way to design a dynamic programming algorithm is to start by guessing the set of subinstances that need to be solved. However, I feel that it is easier to start by designing the recurrence relation, and the easiest way to do this is to first design a recursive backtracking algorithm for the problem. Once you have done this, you can use a technique referred to as *memoization* to mechanically convert this recursive backtracking algorithm into a dynamic programming algorithm.

18.1 Start by Developing a Recursive Backtracking

This section reviews the recommended steps for developing a recursive backtracking algorithm.

EXAMPLE 18.1.1   *Shortest Weighted Path within a Directed Leveled Graph*

To demonstrate the steps, we will develop an algorithm for a version of the shortest-weighted-path problem from Chapter 14. We generalize the problem by allowing negative weights on the edges and simplify it by requiring the input graph to be leveled.

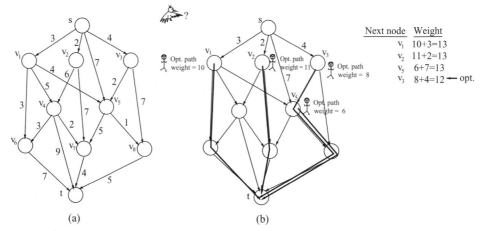

Figure 18.1: (a) The directed layered weighted graph G for Example 18.1.1. (b) The recursive backtracking algorithm.

1) Specification: The first step is to be very clear about what problem needs to be solved. For an optimization problem, we need to be clear about what the set of instances is, for each instance what its set of solutions is, and for each solution what its cost is.

Precondition: We are given one of the following instances.

Instances: An instance consists of $\langle G, s, t \rangle$, where G is a weighted directed layered graph, s is a specified source node and t is a specified destination node. See Figure 18.1.a. The graph G has n nodes. Each node has maximum in- and outdegree d. Each edge $\langle v_i, v_j \rangle$ is labeled with a real-valued (possibly negative) weight $w_{\langle v_i, v_j \rangle}$. The nodes are partitioned into levels so that each edge is directed from some node to a node in a lower level to prevent cycles. It is easiest to assume that the nodes are ordered so that an edge can go from node v_i to node v_j only if $i < j$.

Postcondition: The output is a solution with minimum cost and the cost of that solution.

Solutions: A solution for an instance is a path from source node s to destination node t.

Cost of Solution: The cost of a solution is the sum of the weights of the edges within the path.

Brute Force Algorithm: The problem with simply trying all paths is that there may be an exponential number of them.

2) Design a Question and Its Answers for the Little Bird: Suppose the little bird knows one of the optimal solutions for our instance. You, the algorithm designer, must formulate a small question about this solution and the list of its possible answers. The question should be such that having a correct answer greatly reduces the search.

Question about the End of the Solution: When designing recursive backtracking algorithms, one generally asks about the *first part* of the solution. We will later see that if our ultimate goal is a dynamic programming algorithm, then it is best to turn this around and ask for the *last part* of the solution (see Section 18.3.1).

Leveled Graph: Not knowing yet why we ask about the last part of the solution, we will design this algorithm by asking instead about the first part. Given a graph and nodes s and t, I ask, "Which edge should we take first to form an optimal path to t?" She assures me that taking edge $\langle s, v_1 \rangle$ is good. The specification of the problem gives that there are at most d edges out of any node. Hence, this is a bound on the number K of different answers.

To be consistent, we will always use the letter k to index the bird answers. In order for the final algorithm to be efficient, it is important that the number K of different answers be small.

3) Constructing Subinstances: Suppose that the bird gives us the kth of her answers. This gives us some of the solution, and we want to ask a recursive friend for the rest of the solution. The friend must be given a smaller instance of the same search problem. You must formulate subinstance *subI* for the friend so that he returns to us the information that we desire.

Leveled Graph: I start by (at least temporarily) trusting the bird and take a step along the edge $\langle s, v_1 \rangle$. Standing at v_1, the natural question to ask my friend is "Which is the best path from v_1 to t?" Expressed as $\langle G, v_1, t \rangle$, this is a subinstance of the same computational problem.

4) Constructing a Solution for My Instance: Suppose that the friend gives us an optimal solution *optSubSol* for his instance *subI*. How do we produce an optimal solution *optSol* for your instance I from the bird's answer k and the friend's solution *optSubSol*?

Leveled Graph: My friend will faithfully give me the path $optSubSol = \langle v_1, v_6, t \rangle$, this being a best path from v_1 to t. The difficulty is that this is not a solution for my instance $\langle G, s, t \rangle$, because it is not, in itself, a path from s to t. The path from s is formed by first taking the step from s to v_i and then following the best path from there to t, namely $optSol = \langle \text{bird answer} \rangle + optSubSol = \langle s, v_1 \rangle + \langle v_1, v_6, t \rangle = \langle s, v_1, v_6, t \rangle$.

We proved in Section 8.7 that we can trust the friend to give provide an optimal solution to the subinstance *subI*, because he is really a smaller recursive version of ourselves.

5) Costs of Solutions and Subsolutions: We must also return the cost *optCost* of our solution *optSol*. How do we determine it from the bird's k and the cost *optSubCost* of the friend's *optSubSol*?

Leveled Graph: The cost of the entire path from s to t is the cost of the edge $\langle s, v_1 \rangle$ plus the cost of the path from v_1 to t. Luckily, our friend gives the latter: $optCost_k = w_{\langle s, v_1 \rangle} + optSubCost = 3 + 10 = 13$.

6) Best of the Best: Try all the bird's answers, and take best of the best.

Leveled Graph: If we trust both the bird and the friend, we conclude that this path from s to t is a best path. It turns out that because our little bird gave us the wrong first edge, this might not be the best path from s to t. However, our work was not wasted, because we did succeed in finding the best path from among those that start with the edge $\langle s, v_1 \rangle$. Not trusting the little bird, we repeat this process, finding a best path starting with each of $\langle s, v_2 \rangle$, $\langle s, v_5 \rangle$, and $\langle s, v_3 \rangle$. At least one of these four paths must be an overall best path. We give the best of these best as the overall best path.

7) Base Cases: The base case instances are instances of your problem that are small enough that they cannot be solved using steps 2–6, but they can be solved easily in a brute force way. What are these base cases, and what are their solutions?

Leveled Graph: The only base case is finding a best path from s to t when s and t are the very same node. In this case, the bird would be unable to give the first edge in the best path, because it contains no edges. The optimal solution is the empty path, and its cost is zero.

8) Code: From steps 1–7, the code can always be put together using the same basic structure.

algorithm *LeveledGraph* (G, s, t)

$\langle$ *pre-cond* $\rangle$: G is a weighted directed layered graph, and s and t are nodes.
$\langle$ *post-cond* $\rangle$: *optSol* is a path with minimum total weight from s to t, and *optCost* is its weight.

begin
    % Base case: The only base case is for the best path from t to t. Its solution
    is the empty path with cost zero.
    if($s = t$) then
        return $\langle \emptyset, 0 \rangle$
    else
        % General case:
        % Try each possible bird answer.
        for each of the d edges $\langle s, v_k \rangle$

% The bird-and-friend algorithm: The bird tells us that the first
edge in an optimal path from s to t is $\langle s, v_k \rangle$. We ask the friend
for an optimal path from v_k to t. He solves this recursively giving
us *optSubSol*. To this, we add the bird's edge, giving us $optSol_k$.
This $optSol_k$ is a best path from s to t from amongst those paths
consistent with the bird's answer.

271

$\langle optSubSol, optSubCost \rangle = LeveledGraph(\langle G, v_k, t \rangle)$
$optSol_k = \langle s, v_k \rangle + optSubSol$
$optCost_k = w_{\langle s, v_k \rangle} + optSubCost$

    end for
% Having the best, $optSol_k$, for each bird's answer k, we keep the
best of these best.
$k_{min} =$ "a k that minimizes $optCost_k$"
$optSol = optSol_{k_{min}}$
$optCost = optCost_{k_{min}}$
    return $\langle optSol, optCost \rangle$
  end if
end algorithm

9) Recurrence Relations: The recurrence relation at the core of this recursive backtracking algorithm is the following.

$$LeveledGraphSolution(G, s, t) = \text{Min}_{v_k \in N(s)} \langle s, v_k \rangle$$
$$+ LeveledGraphSolution(\langle G, v_k, t \rangle)$$
$$LeveledGraphCost(G, s, t) = \text{Min}_{v_k \in N(s)} \ w_{\langle s, v_k \rangle} + LeveledGraphCost(\langle G, v_k, t \rangle)$$

where $N(s)$ is the set of nodes v_k with edge $\langle s, v_k \rangle$.

Running Time: The recursive backtracking algorithm faithfully enumerates all solutions for your instance and hence requires exponential time.

EXERCISE 18.1.1 *Give a directed leveled graph on n nodes that has a small number of
edges and as many paths from s to t as possible.*

18.2 The Steps in Developing a Dynamic Programming Algorithm

Though the recursive backtracking algorithm for Example 18.1.1 may seem complex,
how else would you iterate through all paths? We will now use *memoization* techniques to mechanically convert this algorithm into a dynamic programming algorithm that runs in polynomial time. The word "memoization" comes from "memo."
This technique speeds up a recursive algorithm by saving the result for each subinstance it encounters so that it does not need to be recomputed. Dynamic programming takes the idea of memoization one step further. Instead of traversing the tree of

recursive stack frames, keeping track of which friends are waiting for answers from which friends, it first determines the complete set of subinstances for which solutions are needed and then computes them in an order such that no friend must wait. As it goes, it fills out a table containing an optimal solution for each subinstance. The technique for finding an optimal solution for a given subinstance is identical to the technique used in the recursive backtracking algorithm. The only difference is that instead of recursing to solve a sub-subinstance, the algorithm looks up in the table an optimal solution found earlier. When the entire table has been completed, the last entry will contain an optimal solution for the original instance.

1) The Set of Subinstances: We obtain the set of subinstances that need to be solved by the dynamic programming algorithm by tracing the recursive backtracking algorithm through the tree of stack frames starting with the given instance I. The set consists of the initial instance I, its subinstances, their subinstances, and so on. We ensure that this set contains all the required subinstances by making sure that is closed under this *sub* operation, or equivalently that no subinstance is lonely, because if it's included then so are all its friends. See Section 18.3.3. Also ensure that all (or at least most) of these subinstances are needed.

Leveled Graph:

Include $\langle G, v_7, t \rangle$: On $\langle G, s, t \rangle$, the little bird, among other things, suggests taking the edge $\langle s, v_1 \rangle$ leading to the subinstance $\langle G, v_1, t \rangle$. On this subinstance, the little bird, among other things, suggests taking the edge $\langle v_1, v_4 \rangle$ leading to the subinstance $\langle G, v_4, t \rangle$. On this subinstance, the little bird, among other things, suggests taking the edge $\langle v_4, v_7 \rangle$ leading, as said, to the subinstance $\langle G, v_7, t \rangle$. Hence, this subinstance must be considered by the dynamic programming algorithm. See Figure 18.2.a, $\langle G, v_7, t \rangle$.

Exclude $\langle G, v_{81}, t \rangle$: Given the same instance I, $\langle G, v_{81}, t \rangle$ is not a subinstance, because node v_{81} is not a node in the graph, so it never arises.

Exclude $\langle G, v_1, v_8 \rangle$: Neither is $\langle G, v_1, v_8 \rangle$ a required subinstance, because each subinstance that arises is looking for a path that ends in the node t.

Guess the Set: Starting with the instance $\langle G, s, t \rangle$, the complete set of subinstances called will be $\{\langle G, v_i, t \rangle \mid v_i \text{ above } t\}$. See Figure 18.2.b.

Redundancy: We can speed up the recursive backtracking algorithm only when it solves the same subinstance many times.

Leveled Graph: The recursive backtracking algorithm of Section 18.1 traverses each of the exponentially many paths from s to t. Within this exponential amount of work, there is a great deal of redundancy. Different friends are assigned the

(a) (b) (c)

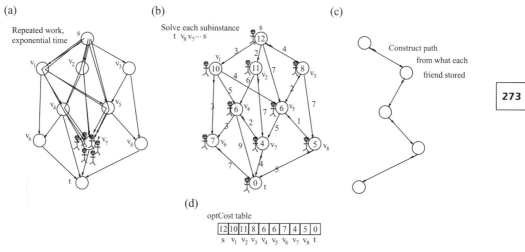

(d)

optCost table

12	10	11	8	6	6	7	4	5	0
s	v_1	v_2	v_3	v_4	v_5	v_6	v_7	v_8	t

Figure 18.2: (a) The recursive algorithm. (b) The dynamic programming algorithm: The little arrow out of node v_i indicates the first edge in an optimal path from v_i to t, and the value within the circle on the node gives the cost of this path. (c) The optimal path from s to t. (d) The contents of the optCost table. It is filled in backwards.

exact same task. In fact, for each path from s to v_i, some friend is asked to solve the subinstance $\langle G, v_i, t \rangle$. See Figure 18.2.a.

One Friend per Subinstance: To save time, the dynamic programming algorithm solves each of these subinstances only once. We allocate one friend to each of these subinstances, whose job it is to find an optimal solution for it and to provide this solution to any other friend who needs it.

2) Count the Subinstances: The running time of the dynamic programming algorithm is proportional to the number of subinstances. At this point in the design of the algorithm, you should count how many subinstances an instance I has as a function of the size $n = |I|$ of the instance. If there are too many of them, then start at the very beginning, designing a new recursive backtracking algorithm with a different question for the little bird.

Leveled Graph: The number of subinstances in the set $\{\langle G, v_i, t \rangle \mid v_i$ above $t\}$ is n, the number of nodes in the graph G.

3) Construct a Table Indexed by Subinstances: The algorithm designer constructs a table. It must have one entry for each subinstance. Generally, the table will have one dimension for each parameter used to specify a particular subinstance. To be consistent, we will always use the letter i and if necessary j to index the subinstances. Each entry in the table is used to store an optimal solution for the subinstance along with its cost. Often we split this table into two tables: one for the solution and one for the cost.

Leveled Graph: The single parameter used to specify a particular subinstance is i. Hence, suitable tables would be $optSol[0..n]$ and $optCost[0..n]$, where $optSol[i]$ will store the best path from node v_i to node t and $optCost[i]$ will store its cost. See Figure 18.2.d.

4) Solution from Subsolutions: The dynamic programming algorithm for finding an optimal solution to a given instance from an optimal solution to a subinstance is identical to that within the recursive backtracking algorithm, except that instead of recursing to solve a subinstance, the algorithm finds its optimal solution in the table.

Leveled Graph: The task of $Friend_i$ in the dynamic programming algorithm is not to solve $\langle G, s, t \rangle$ but $\langle G, v_i, t \rangle$, looking for a best path from v_i to t. He does this as follows. He asks the little bird for the first edge in his path and tries each of her possible answers. When the bird suggests the edge $\langle v_i, v_k \rangle$, he asks a friend for a best path from v_k to t. This task is the subinstance $\langle G, v_k, t \rangle$, which has been allocated to $Friend_k$ and whose solution has been stored in $optSol[k]$. The recursive backtracking code

$$\langle optSubSol, optSubCost \rangle = LeveledGraph\,(\langle G, v_k, t \rangle)$$
$$optSol_k = \langle s, v_k \rangle + optSubSol$$
$$optCost_k = w_{\langle s, v_k \rangle} + optSubCost$$

is changed to simply

$$optSol_k = \langle v_i, v_k \rangle + optSol[k]$$
$$optCost_k = w_{\langle v_i, v_k \rangle} + optCost[k]$$

$Friend_i$ tacks the bird's edge $\langle v_i, v_k \rangle$ onto this path from v_k to t, giving a path that is the best path from v_i to t amongst those consistent with the bird's answer $\langle v_i, v_k \rangle$. After trying each bird's answer, $Friend_i$ saves the best of these best paths in the table.

5) Base Cases: The base case instances are exactly the same as with the recursive backtracking algorithm. The dynamic programming algorithm starts its computation by storing in the table an optimal solution for each of these and their costs.

Leveled Graph: The only base case is finding a best path from s to t when s and t are the very same node. This only occurs with the subinstance $\langle G, v_n, t \rangle$, where v_n is another name for t. The recursive backtracking code

```
if(s = t) then
    return ⟨∅, 0⟩
```

is changed to

> % Base Case:
> $optSol[n] = \emptyset$
> $optCost[n] = 0$

6) The Order in Which to Fill the Table: When a friend in the recursive backtracking algorithm needs help from a friend, the algorithm recurses, and the stack frame for the first friend waits until the stack frame for the second friend returns. This forms a tree of recursive stack frames, keeping track of which friends are waiting for answers from which friends. In contrast, in a dynamic programming algorithm, the friends solve their subinstances in an order such that nobody has to wait. Every recursive algorithm must guarantee that it recurses only on *smaller* instances. Hence, if the dynamic programming algorithm fills in the table from smaller to larger instances, then when an instance is being solved, the solution for each of its subinstances is already available. Alternatively, the algorithm designer can simply choose any order to fill the table that respects the dependences between the instances and their subinstances. The table must be indexed by subinstances. When allocating the table, be clear what subinstance each entry of the table represents.

> **Leveled Graph:** $Friend_i$, with instance $\langle G, v_i, t \rangle$, depends on $Friend_k$ when there is an edge $\langle v_i, v_k \rangle$. From the precondition of the problem, we know that each edge must go from a higher level to a lower one, and hence we know that $k > i$. Filling the table in the order $t = v_n, v_{n-1}, v_{n-2}, \ldots, v_2, v_1, v_0 = s$ ensures that when $Friend_i$ does his work, $Friend_k$ has already stored his answer in the table. The subinstance $\langle G, v_n, t \rangle$ has been solved already. The following loop is put around the general case code of the recursive backtracking algorithm:

> % General Cases: Loop over subinstances in the table.
> for $i = n - 1$ to 0
> > % Solve instance $\langle G, v_i, t \rangle$ and fill in table entry $\langle i \rangle$.

Viewing the dynamic programming algorithm as an iterative algorithm, the loop invariant when working on a particular subinstance is that all *smaller* subinstances that will be needed have been solved. Each iteration maintains the loop invariant while making progress by solving this next subinstance.

7) The Final Solution: The original instance will be the last subinstance to be solved. When complete the dynamic program simply returns this answer.

> **Leveled Graph:** The original instance $\langle G, s, t \rangle$ is the same as the subinstance $\langle G, v_0, t \rangle$, where v_0 is another name for s. The dynamic program ends with the code

> return $\langle optSol[0], optCost[0] \rangle$

8) Code: From steps 1–7, the code can always be put together using the same basic structure:

> **algorithm** *LeveledGraph* (G, s, t)
>
> ⟨ **pre-cond**⟩: G is a weighted directed layered graph, and s and t are nodes.
> ⟨ **post-cond**⟩: *optSol* is a path with minimum total weight from s to t, and *optCost* is its weight.

begin

    % Table: *optSol*[i] stores an optimal path from v_i to t, and *optCost*[i] its cost.
    table[$0..n$] *optSol*, *optCost*

    % Base case: The only base case is for the best path from t to t.
    Its solution is the empty path with cost zero.
    optSol[n] = ∅
    optCost[n] = 0

    % General cases: Loop over subinstances in the table.
    for $i = n - 1$ to 0
        % Solve instance ⟨G, v_i, t⟩ and fill in table entry ⟨i⟩.
        % Try each possible bird answer.
        for each of the d edges ⟨v_i, v_k⟩
            % The bird-and-friend Algorithm: The bird tells us that the first edge in an optimal path from v_i to t is ⟨v_i, v_k⟩. We ask the friend for an optimal path from v_k to t. He gives us *optSol*[k], which he had stored in the table. To this we add the bird's edge. This gives us *optSol*$_k$ which is a best path from v_i to t from among those paths consistent with the bird's answer.
            optSol$_k$ = ⟨v_i, v_k⟩ + *optSol*[k]
            optCost$_k$ = $w_{⟨v_i,v_k⟩}$ + *optCost*[k]
        end for
        % Having the best, *optSol*$_k$, for each bird's answer k, we keep the best of these best.
        k_{min} = a k that minimizes *optCost*$_k$
        optSol[i] = *optSol*$_{k_{min}}$
        optCost[i] = *optCost*$_{k_{min}}$
    end for
    return ⟨*optSol*[0], *optCost*[0]⟩
end algorithm

Consistent Structure: To be consistent, we will always use this same structure for all dynamic programming code. Even when there are small ways that the code could be optimized, we stick to this same structure. Even when different variable names would be more meaningful, we stick to i and if necessary j to index the subinstances, and k to index the bird answers. I believe that this consistency will make it easier for you (and for the marker) to understand the many dynamic programming algorithms.

9) Running Time: We can see that the code loops over each subinstance and, for each, loops over each bird answer. From this, the running time seems to be the number of subinstances in the table times the number K of answers to the bird's question. We will see in Section 18.3.4 that actually the running time of this version of the algorithm is a factor of n bigger than this. The same section will tell how to remove this extra factor of n.

> **Leveled Graph:** The running time of this algorithm is now polynomial. There are only n friends, one for each node in the graph. For the instance $\langle G, v_i, t \rangle$, there is a bird answer for each edge out of its source node v_i. There are at most d of these. The running time is then only $O(n \cdot d)$ times this extra factor of n.

18.3 Subtle Points

Before listing a few of the more subtle points in developing recursive backtracking and a dynamic programming algorithms, I give another example problem.

EXAMPLE 18.3.1 Printing Neatly

Consider the problem of printing a paragraph neatly on a printer. The input text is a sequence of n words with lengths $l_1, l_2, \ldots, l_n$, measured in characters. Each printer line can hold a maximum of M characters. Our criterion for neatness is for there to be as few spaces on the ends of the lines as possible.

Preconditions: An instance $\langle M; l_1, \ldots, l_n \rangle$ consists of the line length and the word lengths. Generally, M will be thought of as a constant, so we will leave it out when it is clear from the context.

Postconditions: The goal is to split the text into lines in a way that minimizes the cost.

> **Solutions:** A solution for an instances is a list giving the number of words for each line, $\langle k_1, \ldots, k_r \rangle$.

> **Cost of Solution:** Given the number of words in each line, the cost of this solution is the sum of the cubes of the numbers of blanks on the end of each line (including for now the last line).

> **Example:** Suppose that one way of breaking the text into lines gives 10 blanks on the end of one of the lines, while another way gives 5 blanks on the end of one line and 5 on the end of another. Our sense of esthetics dictates that the second way is "neater." Our cost heavily penalizes having a large number of blanks on a single line by cubing the number. The cost of the first solution is $10^3 = 1,000$ whereas the cost of the second is only $5^3 + 5^3 = 250$.

EXAMPLE 18.3.1 **Printing Neatly (cont.)**

Example: Consider printing neatly the silly text "This week has seven dates in it ok" in column with width $M = 11$. This is represented as the printing neatly instance $\langle M; l_1, \ldots, l_n \rangle = \langle 11; 4, 4, 3, 5, 5, 2, 2, 2 \rangle$. Three of the possible ways to print this text are as follows:

$\langle k_1, k_2, \ldots, k_r \rangle = \langle 2,2,2,2 \rangle$		$\langle k_1, k_2, \ldots, k_r \rangle = \langle 1,2,2,3 \rangle$		$\langle k_1, k_2, \ldots, k_r \rangle = \langle 2,2,1,3 \rangle$	
This.week..	2^3	This.......	7^3	This.week..	2^3
has.seven..	2^3	week.has...	3^3	has.seven..	2^3
dates.in...	3^3	seven.dates	0^3	dates......	6^3
it.ok......	6^3	in.it.ok...	3^3	in.it.ok...	3^3
Cost	$= 259$	Cost	$= 397$	Cost	$= 259$

Of these three, the first and the last are the cheapest and are likely the cheapest of all the possible solutions.

18.3.1 The Question for the Little Bird

The designer of a recursive backtracking algorithm, a dynamic programming algorithm, or a greedy algorithm must decide which question to ask the little bird. That is, the algorithm designer must decide which sequence of decisions will specify the solution constructed by the algorithm: which things will the algorithm try before backtracking to try something else? This is one of the main creative steps in designing the algorithm.

Local vs. Global Considerations: One of the reasons that optimization problems are difficult is that we are able to make what we call *local* observations and decisions but it is hard to see the *global* consequences of these decisions.

> **Leveled Graph:** Which edge out of s is cheapest is a local question. Which path is the overall cheapest is a global question. We were tempted to follow the cheapest edge out of the source s. However, sometimes one can arrive at a better overall path by starting with a first edge that is not the cheapest.

> **Printing Neatly:** If we follow a greedy algorithm, we will put as many words on the first line as possible. However, a local *sacrifice* of putting fewer words on this line may lead globally to a better overall solution.

Ask about a Local Property: The question that we ask the bird is about some *local* property of the solution:

> **First Object:** If the solution is a sequence of objects, a good question would be "What is the first object in the sequence?"

Leveled Graph: If the solution is a path though a graph, we might ask, "What is the first edge in the path?"

Printing Neatly: If the solution is a sequence of how many words to put on each line, we ask, "How many words k do we put on the first line?"

Yes or No: If the instance is a sequence of objects and a solution is a subset of these object, a good question would be "Is the first object of the instance included in the optimal solution?"

Event Scheduling: If the solution states which events to schedule, we will ask, "Do we schedule the first event?"

Which Root: If a solution is a binary tree of objects, a good question would be "What object is at the root of the tree?"

The Best Binary Search Tree: Note that the first question is not whether to take the left or right branch of the given binary search tree, but what the root should be when constructing the binary search tree.

In contrast, asking the bird for the number of edges in the best path in the leveled graph is a global, not a local, question.

The Number K of Different Bird Answers: You can only ask the bird a little question. (It is only a *little* bird.) In a little question, the number K of different answers $A_1, A_2, \ldots, A_K$ that the bird might give must be small. The smaller K is, the more efficient the final algorithm will be.

Leveled Graph: When asking for an edge out of s, the number K of answers is the degree of the node. This gives a bound on K.

Printing Neatly: K is the maximum number of the first words of the text that would fit on the first line.

Event Scheduling: "Do we schedule the first event?" has $K = 2$ answers, yes and no.

Brute Force: The obvious question to ask the little bird is for her to tell you an entire optimal solution. However, the number of solutions for your instance I is likely exponential; each solution is a possible answer. Hence, K would be exponential. After getting rid of the bird, the resulting algorithm would be the usual brute force algorithm.

Repeated Questions: Although you want to avoid thinking about it, each of your recursive friends will have to ask his little bird a similar question. Hence, you should

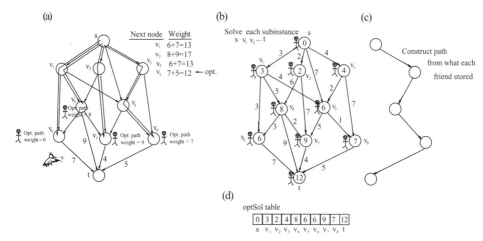

(a)
(b)
(c)

Next node   Weight
v_1 6+7=13
v_2 8+9=17
v_3 6+7=13
v_3 7+5=12 ← opt.

Solve each subinstance   s
s v_1 v_2 ··· t

Construct path
from what each
friend stored

(d)

optSol table

0	3	2	4	8	6	6	9	7	12
s	v_1	v_2	v_3	v_4	v_5	v_6	v_7	v_8	t

Figure 18.3: (a) The recursive algorithm. (b) The dynamic programming algorithm: The little arrow out of node v_i indicates the last edge in an optimal path from s to v_i, and the value within the circle at a node gives the cost of this path. (c) The optimal path from s to t. (d) The contents of the optCost table. In contrast with that in Figure 18.2, it is filled in forwards.

choose a question that provides a reasonable follow-up question of a similar form. For example:

- "What is the second object in the sequence?"
- "Is the second object of the instance included in the optimal solution?"
- "What is the root in the left (the right) subtree?"

In contrast, asking the bird for the number of edges in the best path in the leveled graph does not have a good follow-up question.

Reversing the Order: This change is purely for aesthetic reasons. The dynamic program loops backwards through the nodes of the graph, $t = v_n, v_{n-1}, v_{n-2}, \ldots, v_2, v_1, v_0 = s$. The standard way to do it is to work forward. The recursive backtracking algorithm worked forward from s. The dynamic programming technique reverses the recursive backtracking algorithm by completing the subinstances from smallest to largest. In order to have the final algorithm move forward, the recursive backtracking algorithm needs to go backwards. To do this, the little bird should ask something about the end of the solution and not about the beginning. Compare Figure 18.2 and Figure 18.3, and see the final code in Section 18.3.6.

Last Object: "What is the last object in the sequence?" What is the last edge in the optimal path, and how many words do we put on the last line?

Yes or No: "Is the last object of the instance included in the optimal solution?" Do we schedule the last event?

Which Root: We still ask about the root. It is not useful to ask about the leaves.

EXERCISE 18.3.1 *Start over and redevelop the leveled graph dynamic programming algorithm with this new question for the little bird, so that the work is completed starting at the top of the graph.*

18.3.2 Subinstances and Subsolutions

Getting a trustworthy answer from the little bird narrows our search problem down to the task of finding the best solution from among those solutions consistent with this answer. It would be great if we could simply ask a friend to find us such a solution; however, we are only allowed to ask our friend to solve subinstances of the original computational problem. Our task within this subsection is to formulate a subinstance to our computational problem such that the search for its optimal solutions some how parallels our narrowed search task.

The Recursive Structure of the Problem: In order for us to be able to design a recursive backtracking algorithm for an optimization problem, the problem needs to have a recursive structure. For a solution of the instance to be optimal, some part of the solution must itself be optimal. The computational problem has a recursive structure if the task of finding an optimal way to construct this part of the solution is a subinstance of the same computational problem.

> **Leveled Graph:** For a path from s to t to be optimal, the subpath from some v_i to some v_j along the path must itself be an optimal path between these nodes. The computational problem has a recursive structure because the task of finding an optimal way to construct this part of the path is a subinstance of the same computational problem.

> **Printing Neatly:** In order for all the words to be printed neatly, the words that are on the last ten lines need to be printed neatly on these ten lines.

Question from Answer: Sometimes it is a challenge to know what subinstance to ask our friend. It turns out that it is easier to know what answer (subsolution) we want from him. Knowing the answer we want will be a huge hint as to what the question should be.

> **Each Solution as a Sequence of Answers:** One task that you as the algorithm designer must do is to organize the information needed to specify a solution into a sequence of fields, $sol = \langle field_1, field_2, \ldots, field_m \rangle$.

> > **Best Animal:** In the zoo problem, each solution consists of an animal, which we will identify with the sequence of answers to the little bird's questions, $sol = \langle vertebrate, mammal, cat, cheetah \rangle$.

Leveled Graph: In the leveled graph problem, a solution consists of a path, $\langle s, v_1, v_6, t \rangle$, which we will identify with the sequence of edges $sol = \langle \langle s, v_1 \rangle, \langle v_1, v_6 \rangle, \langle v_6, t \rangle \rangle$.

Printing Neatly: A solution for the printing neatly problem gives the number of words for each line, $\langle k_1, \ldots, k_r \rangle$.

Bird's Question and Remaining Task: The algorithm asks the little bird for the last field $field_m$ of one of the instance's optimal solutions and asks the friend for the remaining fields $\langle field_1, \ldots, field_{m-1} \rangle$. We will let k denote the answer provided by the bird, and $optSubSol$ the one provided by the friend. Given both, the algorithm constructs the final solution by simply concatenating these two parts together, namely, $optSol = \langle optSubSol, k \rangle = \langle \langle field_1, \ldots, field_{m-1} \rangle, field_m \rangle$.

Leveled Graph: Asking for the last field of an optimal solution $optSol = \langle \langle s, v_1 \rangle, \langle v_1, v_6 \rangle, \langle v_6, t \rangle \rangle$ amounts to asking for the last edge that the path should take. The bird answers $\langle v_6, t \rangle$. The friend provides $optSubSol = \langle \langle s, v_1 \rangle, \langle v_1, v_6 \rangle \rangle$. Concatenating these forms our solution.

Printing Neatly: Asking for the last field of an optimal solution $optSol = \langle k_1, \ldots, k_r \rangle$ amounts to asking how many words should go on the last line.

Formulating the Subinstance: We need to find an instance of the computational problem whose optimal solution is $optSubSol = \langle field_1, \ldots, field_{m-1} \rangle$. The instance is that whose set of valid solutions is $setSubSol = \{subSol \mid \langle subSol, k \rangle \in setSol\}$.

Leveled Graph: The instance whose solution is $optSubSol = \langle \langle s, v_1 \rangle, \langle v_1, v_6 \rangle \rangle$ is $\langle G, s, v_6 \rangle$, asking for the optimal path from s to v_6.

Printing Neatly: If the bird told you that an optimal number of words to put on the last line is k, then an optimal printing of the words is an optimal printing of the first $n - k$ words followed by the remaining k words on a line by themselves. Your friend can find an optimal way of printing these first words by solving the subinstance $\langle M; l_1, \ldots, l_{n-k} \rangle$. All you need to do then is to add the last k words, i.e., $optSol = \langle optSubSol, k \rangle$.

Costs of Solutions: In addition to finding an optimal solution for the instance I, the algorithm must also produce the cost of this solution. To be helpful, the friend provides the cost of his solution, $optSubSol$. Due to the recursive structure of the problem, the costs of these solutions $optSol = \langle \langle field_1, \ldots, field_{m-1} \rangle, field_m \rangle$ and $optSubSol = \langle field_1, \ldots, field_{m-1} \rangle$ usually differ in some uniform way. For example, often the cost is the sum of the costs of the fields, that is, $cost(optSol) = \sum_{i=1}^{m} cost(field_i)$. In this case we have that $cost(optSol) = cost(optSubSol) + cost(field_m)$.

Leveled Graph: The cost of a path from s to t is the cost of the last edge plus the cost of the rest of the path.

Printing Neatly: The total cost of an optimal solution for the given instance $\langle M; l_1, \ldots, l_n \rangle$ is the cost of the optimal solution for the subinstance $\langle M; l_1, \ldots, l_{n-k} \rangle$ plus the cube of the number of blanks on the end of the line that contains the last k words, i.e., $optCost = optSubCost + (M - k + 1 - \sum_{j=n-k+1}^{n} l_j)^3$.

283

Formal Proof of Correctness:

Recursive Structure of Costs: In order for this recursive backtracking method to solve an optimization problem, the costs that the problem allocates to the solutions must have the following recursive structure. Consider two solutions $sol = \langle subSol, k \rangle$ and $sol' = \langle subSol', k \rangle$ both consistent with the same bird's answer k. If the given cost function dictates that the solution sol is better than the solution sol', then the subsolution $subSol$ of sol will also be better than the subsolution $subSol'$ of sol'. This ensures that any optimal subsolution of the subinstance leads to an optimal solution of the original instance.

Theorem 18.3.1: The solution $optSol$ returned is a best solution for I from amongst those that are consistent with the information k provided by the bird.

Proof: By way of contradiction, assume not. Then there must be another solution $betterSol$ consistent with k whose cost is strictly better then that for $optSol$. From the way we constructed our friend's subinstance $subI$, this better solution must have the form $betterSol = \langle betterSubSol, k \rangle$ where $betterSubSol$ is a solution for $subI$. We proved in Section 8.7, using strong induction, that we can trust the friend to provide an optimal solution to the subinstance $subI$. Because the cost of $betterSol$ is better than that of $optSol$, it follows that the cost of $betterSubSol$ is better than that of $optSubSol$. This contradicts the statement that $optSubSol$ is an optimal solution for the subinstance $subI$.

Size of an Instance: In order to avoid recursing indefinitely, the subinstance that you give your friend must be *smaller* than your own instance according to some measure of size. By the way that we formulated the subinstance, we know that its valid solutions $subSol = \langle field_2, \ldots, field_m \rangle$ are shorter than the valid solutions $sol = \langle field_1, field_2, \ldots, field_m \rangle$ of the instance. Hence, a reasonable measure of the size of an instance is the length of its longest valid solution. This measure only fails to work when an instance has valid solutions that are infinitely long.

Leveled Graph: The size of the instance $\langle G, s, t \rangle$ is the length of the longest path, or simply the number of levels, between s and t. Given this, the size of the subinstance $\langle G, s, v_k \rangle$, which is the number of levels between s and v_k, is smaller.

Each Solution as a Tree of Answers: A few recursive backtracking, dynamic programming, and greedy algorithms have the following more complex structure than in the previous sections. In these, the fields specifying a solution are organized into a tree instead of a sequence. For example, if the problem is to find the best binary search tree, then it is quite reasonable that the fields are the nodes of the tree and these fields should be organized as the tree itself. The algorithm asks the little bird to tell it the field at the root of one of the instance's optimal solutions. One friend is asked to fill in the left subtree, and another the right. See Sections 19.5 and 19.6.

18.3.3 The Set of Subinstances

Can Be Difficult: When using the memoization technique to mechanically convert a recursive algorithm into an iterative algorithm, the most difficult step is determining for each input instance the complete set of subinstances that will get called by the recursive algorithm, starting with this instance.

> **Leveled Graph:** We speculated that a subinstance for the leveled graph problem consists of $\{\langle G, v_i, v_j \rangle \mid \text{pair } v_i, v_j\}$, namely, the task of finding the best path between each pair of nodes. Later, by tracing the recursive algorithm, we saw that these subinstances are not all needed, because the subinstances called always search for a path ending in the same fixed node t. After changing the bird question to ask about the last edge, all subinstances called always search for a path beginning with the fixed node s.

Guess and Check: The technique to find the set of subinstances is to first try to trace out the recursive algorithm on a small example and guess what the set of subinstances will be. Then Lemma 18.3.2 can be used to check if this set is big enough and not too big.

A Set Being Closed under an Operation: We say that the set of even integers is *closed under* addition and multiplication because the sum and the product of any two even numbers is even. In general, we say a set is closed under an operation if applying the operation to any elements in the set results in an element that is also in the set.

The Construction Game: Consider the following game: I give you the integer 2. You are allowed to construct new objects by taking objects you already have and either adding them or multiplying them. What is the complete set of numbers that you are able to construct?

> **Guess a Set:** You might guess that you are able to construct the set of positive even integers. How do you know that this set is big enough and not too big?

Big Enough: Because the set of positive even integers is closed under addition and multiplication, I claim you will never construct an object that is not a positive even number.

> **Proof:** We prove by induction on $t \geq 0$ that after t steps you only have positive even numbers. This is true for $t = 0$, because initially you only have the positive even integer 2. If it is true for t, the object constructed in step $t + 1$ is either the sum or the product of previously constructed objects, which are all positive even integers. Because the set of positive even integers is closed under these operations, the resulting object must also be positive even. This completes the inductive step.

Not Too Big: Every positive even integer can be generated by this game.

> **Proof:** Consider some positive even number $i = 2j$. Initially, we have only 2. We construct i by adding $2 + 2 + 2 + \cdots + 2$ a total of j times.

Conclusion: The set of positive even integers accurately characterizes which numbers can be generated by this game, no less and no more.

Lemma 18.3.2: The set S will be the complete set of subinstances called starting from our initial instance I_{start} iff

1. $I_{start} \in S$.

2. S is closed under the sub operator. (S is big enough.) The sub operator is defined as follows: Given a particular instance of the problem, applying the sub operator produces all the subinstances constructed from it by a single stack frame of the recursive algorithm.

3. Every subinstance $I \in S$ can be generated from I_{start} using the sub operator. (S is not too big.) This ensures that there are not any instances in S that are not needed. The dynamic programming algorithm will work fine if your set of subinstances contains subinstances that are not called. However, you do not want the set too much larger than necessary, because the running time depends on its size.

Examples:

The Wedding Invitation List: One of the nightmares when getting married is deciding upon the invitation list. The goal is to make everyone there happy while keeping the number of people small. The three rules in the lemma also apply here.

> $I_{start} \in S$: Clearly the bride and groom need to be invited.

Closure Ensures That Everyone Is Happy: If you invite aunt Hilda, then in order to keep her happy, you need to invite her obnoxious son. Similarly, you need to keep all of your subinstances happy, by being sure that for every subinstance included, its immediate friends are also included. In the wedding list problem, you will quickly invite the entire world. The six-degrees-of-separation principle states that the set consisting of your friends' friends' friends' friends' friends' friends includes everyone. Similarly, for most optimization problems the number of subinstances needed tends to be exponential in the size of the instance. A problem has a good dynamic programming algorithm when the number of subinstances is small.

Everyone Needed: We see that everyone on the list must be invited. Even the obnoxious son must come. Because the bride must come, her mother must come. Because her mother must come, aunt Hilda must come, and hence the son.

Leveled Graph:

Guess a Set: The guessed set is $\{\langle G, s, v_i\rangle \mid v_i \ below\ s\}$.

Closed: Consider an arbitrary subinstance $\langle G, s, v_i\rangle$ from this set. The sub operator considers some edge $\langle v_k, v_i\rangle$ and forms the subinstance $\langle G, s, v_k\rangle$. This is contained in the stated set of subinstances.

Generating: Consider an arbitrary subinstance $\langle G, s, v_i\rangle$. It will be called by the recursive algorithm if and only if there is a path $\langle v_i, v_{k_1}, v_{k_2}, \ldots, v_{k_r}, t\rangle$ from v_i to the original destination t. The initial stack frame on the instance $\langle G, s, t\rangle$, among other things, recurses on $\langle G, s, v_{k_r}\rangle$, which recurses on $\langle G, s, v_{k_{r-1}}\rangle, \ldots$, which recurses on $\langle G, s, v_{k_1}\rangle$, which recurses on $\langle G, s, v_i\rangle$.

If the node v_i cannot be reached from node s, then the subinstance $\langle G, s, v_i\rangle$ will never be called by the recursive algorithm. Despite this, we will include it in our dynamic program, because this is not known about v_i until after the algorithm has run.

Printing Neatly: By tracing the recursive algorithm, we see that the set of subinstance used consists only of prefixes of the words, namely, $\{\langle M; l_1, \ldots, l_i\rangle \mid i \in [0, n]\}$.

Closed: We know that this set contains all subinstances generated by the recursive algorithm, because it contains the initial instance and is closed under the sub operator. Consider an arbitrary subinstance $\langle M; l_1, \ldots, l_i\rangle$ from this set. Applying the sub operator constructs the subinstances $\langle M; l_1, \ldots, l_{i-w}\rangle$ for $1 \leq w \leq i$, which are contained in the stated set of subinstances.

Generating: Consider the arbitrary subinstance $\langle M; l_1, \ldots, l_i\rangle$. We demonstrate that it is called by the recursive algorithm as follows: The initial stack frame on the instance $\langle M; l_1, \ldots, l_n\rangle$, among other things, sets w to 1 and recurses on $\langle M; l_1, \ldots, l_{n-1}\rangle$. This stack frame also sets w to 1 and recurses on

$\langle M; l_1, \ldots, l_{n-2}\rangle$. This continues $n - i$ times, until the desired $\langle M; l_1, \ldots, l_i\rangle$ is called.

The Number of Subinstances: A dynamic programming algorithm is fast only if the given instance does not have many subinstances.

Subinstance is a Subsequence: A common reason for the number of subinstances of a given instance being polynomial is that the instance consists of a *sequence* of things rather than a *set* of things. In such a case, each subinstance can be a contiguous (continuous) subsequence of the things rather than an arbitrary subset of them. There are only $O(n^2)$ contiguous subsequences of a sequence of length n, because one can be specified by specifying the two end points. Even better, there are even fewer subinstances if they are defined to be a prefix of the sequence. There are only n prefixes, because one can be specified by specifying the one end point. On the other hand, there are 2^n subsets of a set, because for each object you must decide whether or not to include it.

Leveled Graph: As stated in the definition of the problem, it is easiest to assume that the nodes are ordered so that an edge can go from node v_i to node v_j only if $i < j$. We initially guessed that three were $O(n^2)$ subinstances consisting of subsequences between two nodes v_i and v_j. We then decreased this to only the $O(n)$ postfixes from the fixed source s to some node v_i. Note that subinstances cannot be subsequences of the instance if the input graph is not required to be leveled.

Printing Neatly: Because the subinstance used consists only of prefixes of the words, namely $\{\langle M; l_1, \ldots, l_i\rangle \mid i \in [0, n]\}$, the number of them is $O(n)$. The single parameter used to specify a particular subinstance is i. Hence, suitable tables would be *birdAdvice*$[0..n]$ and *cost*$[0..n]$. The *size* of subinstance is simply the number of words, i. Hence, the table is filled in by looping with i from 0 to n.

Reusing the Table: Sometimes you can solve many related instances of the same problem using the same table.

Leveled Graph: The algorithm gives you for free the shortest path from s to each of the nodes.

Printing Neatly: When actually printing text neatly, it does not matter how many spaces are on the end of the very last line. Hence, the cube of this number should not be included in the cost. We could use the original algorithm to find for $k = 1, 2, 3, \ldots$ how to print all but the last k words and then put these last k on the last line. However, this would take a total of $O(n \cdot n^2)$ time. Instead, time can be saved by filling in the table only once. One can get the costs for these different instances off this single table. After determining which is best, call *PrintingNeatlyWithAdvice* once to construct the solution for this instance. The total time is reduced to only $O(n^2)$.

18.3.4 Decreasing Time and Space

Recap of a Dynamic Programming Algorithm: A dynamic programming algorithm has two nested loops (or sets of loops). The first iterates through all the subinstances represented in the table, finding an optimal solution for each. When finding an optimal solution for the current subinstance, the second loop iterates through the K possible answers to the little bird's question, trying each of them. Within this inner loop, the algorithm must find a best solution for the current subinstance from amongst those consistent with the current bird's answer. This step seems to require only a constant amount of work. It involves looking up in the table an optimal solution for a sub-subinstance of the current subinstance and using this to construct a solution for the current subinstance.

Running Time? The running time is clearly the number of subinstances in the table times the number K of answers to the bird's question times what appears (falsely) to be constant time.

Friend-to-Friend Information Transfer: In both a recursive backtracking and a dynamic programming algorithm, information is transferred from subfriend to friend. In recursive backtracking, this information is transferred by returning it from a subroutine call. In dynamic programming, this information is transferred by having the subfriend store the information in the table entry associated with his subinstance and having the friend look this information up from the table. The information transferred is an optimal solution and its cost. The cost, being only an integer, is not a big deal. However, an optimal solution generally requires $\Theta(n)$ characters to write down. Hence, transferring this information requires this much time.

> **Leveled Graph:** In the line of code "$optSol_k = optSol[k] + \langle v_k, v_i \rangle$," *Friend$_i$* asks *Friend$_k$* for his best path. This path may contain n nodes. Hence, it could take *Friend$_i$* $O(n)$ time steps simply to transfer the answer from *Friend$_k$*.

Time and Space Bottleneck: Being within these two nested loops, this information transfer is the bottleneck on the running time of the algorithm. In a dynamic programming algorithm, this information for each subinstance is stored in the table for the duration of the algorithm. Hence, this is a bottleneck on the memory space requirements of the algorithm.

> **Leveled Graph:** The total time is $O(n \cdot d \cdot n)$. The total space is $\Theta(n \cdot n)$, being $O(n)$ for each of the n table entries.

A Faster Dynamic Programming Algorithm: We will now modify the dynamic programming algorithm to decrease its time and space requirements. The key idea is to reduce the amount of information transferred.

Cost from Subcost: The subfriends do not need to provide an optimal subsolution in order to find the cost of an optimal solution to the current subinstance. The subfriends need only provide the cost of this optimal subsolution. Transferring only the costs speeds up the algorithm.

> **Leveled Graph:** In order for *Friend$_i$* to find the cost of a best path from s to v_i, he need receive only the best *subcost* from his friends. (See the numbers within the circles in Figure 18.3.b.) For each of the edges $\langle v_k, v_i \rangle$ from his destination node v_i, he learns from *Friend$_k$* the cost of a best path from s to v_k. He adds the cost of the edge $\langle v_k, v_i \rangle$ to this to determine the cost of a best path from s to v_i from amongst those that take this edge. Then he determines the cost of an overall best path from s to v_i by taking the best of these best costs.
>
> Note that this algorithm requires $O(n \cdot d)$—not $O(n \cdot d \cdot n)$—time, because this best cost can be transferred from *Friend$_k$* to *Friend$_i$* in constant time. However, this algorithm finds only the cost of the best path; it does not find a best path.

The Little Bird's Advice:

> **Definition of Advice:** A friend trying to find an optimal solution to his subinstance asks the little bird a question about this optimal solution. The answer, usually denoted k, to this question classifies the solutions. If this friend had an all-powerful little bird, then she could advise him which class of solutions to search in to find an optimal solution. Given that he does not have such a bird, he must simply try all K of the possible answers and determine himself which answer is best. Either way, we will refer to this best answer as *the little bird's advice*.
>
> > **Leveled Graph:** The bird's advice to *Friend$_i$*, who is trying to find a best path from s to v_i, is which edge to take last. This edge for each friend is indicated by the little arrows in Figure 18.3.b.
>
> **Advice from Cost:** Within the algorithm that transfers only the cost of an optimal solution, each friend is able to determine the little bird's advice to him.
>
> > **Leveled Graph:** *Friend$_i$* determines, for each of the edges $\langle v_k, v_i \rangle$ into his node, the cost of a best path from s to v_i from amongst those that take this edge, and then determines which of these is best. Hence, though this *Friend$_i$* never learns a best path from s to v_i in its entirety, he does learn which edge is taken last. In other words, he does determine, even without help from the little bird, what the little bird's advice would be.

Transferring the Bird's Advice: The bird's advice does not need to be transferred from $Friend_k$ to $Friend_i$, because $Friend_i$ does not need it. However, $Friend_k$ will store this advice in the table so that it can be used at the end of the algorithm. This advice can usually be stored in constant space. Hence, it can be stored along with the best cost in constant time without slowing down the algorithm.

Leveled Graph: The advice indicates a single edge. Theoretically, taking $O(\log n)$ bits, this takes more than constant space; practically, however, it can be stored using two integers.

Information Stored in Table: In order to make the dynamic programming algorithm faster, the information stored in the table will no longer be an optimal solution and its cost. Instead, only the cost of an optimal solution and the little bird's advice k are stored.

Leveled Graph: The dynamic programming code in Section 18.2 for *Leveled-Graph* has only two small changes. The line "$optSol_k = optSol[k] + \langle v_k, v_i \rangle$" within the inner loop and the line "$optSol[i] = optSol_{k_{min}}$," which stores the optimal solution, are commented out (I recommend leaving them in as comments to add clarity for the reader). The second of these is replaced with the line "$birdAdvice[i] = k_{min}$," which stores the bird's advice. See Section 18.3.6 for the new code.

Time and Space Requirements: The running time of the algorithm computing the costs and the bird's advice is

Time = (the number of subinstances indexing your table)

$\times$ (the number of different answers K to the bird's question)

The space requirement is

Space = the number of subinstances indexing your table

Leveled Graph: As said, there are n subinstances and a bird answer for each edge out of his source node v_i. Hence, the running time is $O(n \cdot d)$.

Printing Neatly: There are $\Theta(n)$ subinstances in the table, and the number of possible answers for the bird is $\Theta(n)$, because she has the option of telling you pretty well any number of words to put on the last line. Hence, the total running time is $\Theta(n) \cdot \Theta(n) = \Theta(n^2)$, and the space requirement is $\Theta(n)$.

Constructing an Optimal Solution: With these modifications, the algorithm no longer constructs an optimal solution. An optimal solution for the original instance is required, but not for the subinstances. We construct an optimal solution for the instance using a separate algorithm that is run after the faster dynamic programming algorithm fills the table in with costs and bird's advice. This new algorithm starts over from the beginning, solving the optimization problem. However, now we know what answer the little bird would give for every subinstance considered. Hence, we can simply run the bird–friend algorithm.

A Recursive Bird–Friend Algorithm: The second run of the algorithm will be identical to the recursive algorithm, except now we only need to follow one path down the recursion tree. Each stack frame, instead of branching for each of the K answers that the bird might give, recurses only on the single answer given by the bird. This algorithm runs very quickly. Its running time is proportional to the number of fields needed to represent the optimal solution.

Leveled Graph: A best path from $s = v_0$ to $t = v_n$ is found as follows. Each friend knows which edge is the last edge taken to get to his node. What remains is to put these pieces together by walking backwards through the graph, following the indicated directions. See Figure 18.3.c. $Friend_t$ knows that the last edge is $\langle v_8, t \rangle$. $Friend_8$ knows that the previous one is $\langle v_5, v_8 \rangle$. $Friend_5$ knows the edge $\langle v_3, v_5 \rangle$. Finally, $Friend_3$ knows the edge $\langle s, v_3 \rangle$. This completes the path.

algorithm *LeveledGraphWithAdvice($\langle G, s, v_i \rangle$, birdAdvice)*

⟨ **pre- & post-cond** ⟩**:** Same as *LeveledGraph* except with advice.

begin
    if$(s = v_i)$ then return$(\emptyset)$
    $k_{min} = birdAdvice[i]$
    $optSubSol = LeveledGraphWithAdvice(\langle G, s, v_{k_{min}} \rangle, \ birdAdvice)$
    $optSol = optSubSol + \langle v_k, v_i \rangle$
    return *optSol*
end algorithm

EXERCISE 18.3.2 *Because the algorithm for leveled graphs with advice only recurses once per stack frame, it is easy to turn it into an iterative algorithm. The algorithm is a lot like a greedy algorithm. In that it always knows which greedy choice to make. Design this iterative algorithm.*

18.3.5 Counting the Number of Solutions

The dynamic programming algorithms we have considered so far return one of the possibly many optimal solutions for the given instance. There may be an exponential number of solutions. In this section, we see how to change the algorithms so that they also output the number of possible optimal solutions.

Counting Fruit: If I want to count the number of pieces of fruit in a bowl, I can ask one friend to count for me the red fruit and another the green fruit and another the orange. My answer is the sum of these three. If all the orange fruit is rotten, then I might not include the number of orange fruits in my sum.

Double Counting: To be sure that we do not double-count some optimal solutions, we need the set of solutions consistent with one bird answer to be disjoint from those consistent with another bird answer.

> **Fruit:** If some fruits are half red and half green, these might get double counted. We want to make sure that color disjointly partitions the fruit according to the answer given.

> **Leveled Graph:** If the bird's answer tells us the first edge of the optimal path, then those paths beginning in the first edge are clearly different than the paths ending in the second.

Computing the Count: In the new dynamic programming algorithm, each friend stores the number of optimal solutions for the subinstance, in addition to the cost of the optimal solution for his subinstance and the bird's advice. This is computed as follows. A friend with one of these subinstances tries each of the K possible bird's answers. When trying k, he finds the best solution to his instance from amongst its solutions that are consistent with this bird's answer k by asking a friend of his to solve some subinstance. This friend tells him the number of optimal solutions to this subinstance. Let num_k be this number. Generally, there is a one-to-one mapping between our friend's optimal solutions and solutions to his instance that are consistent with this bird's answer k. Hence, he knows that there are num_k of these. As before, let $optCost_k$ be the cost of the best solution to my instance from among its solutions that are consistent with this bird's answer k. The friend computes the cost of his optimal solution simply by $optCost = \max_{k \in [K]} optCost_k$. There may be a number of bird's answers that lead to this same optimal cost $optCost$. Each of these lead to optimal solutions. We were careful that the set of solutions consistent with one bird answer is disjoint from that consistent with another bird answer. Hence, the total number of optimal solutions to my instance is $num = \sum_{k \in \{k \mid optCost_k = optCost\}} num_k$. See Section 18.3.6 for the new leveled graph code.

Bounding the Number of Solutions: Let $Num(n)$ denote the maximum number of possible optimal solutions that any dynamic program as described above might output, given an instance of size n. The number num_k of optimal solutions reported by our friend's friend is at most $Num(n-1)$, because his subinstance has size at most $n-1$. There are at most K bird answers. Hence, $num = \sum_{k \in \{k \mid optCost_k = optCost\}} num_k$ can be at most $Num(n) = \sum_{k \in [1..K]} Num(n-1) = K \times Num(n-1) = K^n$. Note that it would take exponential time to output these optimal solutions. However, the number of bits to represent this number is only $\log_2(K^n) = \log_2(K) \times n = \Theta(n)$. Hence, this number can be outputted.

18.3.6 The New Code

Three Changes: The dynamic programming algorithm for the leveled graph problem developed in Section 18.2 has been changed in three ways.

Reversing the Order: As described in Section 18.3.1, the algorithm was redeveloped with the little bird being asked for the last edge in the path instead of for the first edge. This has the aesthetic advantage of having the algorithm now branch out forward from s instead of backward from t.

Storing Bird's Advice Instead of Solution: As described in Section 18.3.4, the algorithm now stores the little bird's advice instead of the optimal solution. This is done to decrease the time and space used by the algorithm by a factor of n.

Counting the Number of Solutions: As described in Section 18.3.5, the algorithm, in addition to one of the many optimal solutions for the given instance, now also outputs the number of possible optimal solutions.

Code:

algorithm *LeveledGraph* (G, s, t)

⟨ *pre-cond* ⟩*:* G is a weighted directed layered graph, and s and t are nodes.
⟨ *post-cond* ⟩*:* *optSol* is a path with minimum total weight from s to t, and *optCost* is its weight, and *optNum* is the number of possible optimal solutions.

begin
    % Table: *optSol*[i] would store an optimal path from s to v_i,
    but actually we store only the bird's advice for the subinstance
    and the cost of its solution.
    table[0..n] *birdAdvice, optCost, optNum*

    % Base case: The only base case is for the best path from s to s.
    It only has one optimal solution, which is the empty path with cost zero.
    % *optSol*[0] = ∅
    optCost[0] = 0
    birdAdvice[0] = ∅
    optNum[0] = 1
    % General cases: Loop over subinstances in the table.
    for $i = 1$ to n
        % Solve instance ⟨G, s, v_i⟩ and fill in table entry ⟨i⟩.
        % Try each possible bird answer.
        for each of the d edges ⟨v_k, v_i⟩
            % The bird-and-friend algorithm: The bird tells us that the last
            edge in an optimal path from s to v_i is ⟨v_k, v_i⟩. We ask the friend
            for an optimal path from s to v_k. He gives us *optSol*[k], which he
            has stored in the table. To this we add the bird's edge. This gives
            us *optSol*$_k$, which is a best path from s to v_i from amongst those
            paths consistent with the bird's answer.
            % *optSol*$_k$ = *optSol*[k] + ⟨v_k, v_i⟩
            optCost$_k$ = *optCost*[k] + $w_{⟨v_k,v_i⟩}$
        end for

% Having the best, $optSol_k$, for each bird's answer k, we keep the best of these best.

k_{min} = a k that minimizes $optCost_k$

% $optSol[i] = optSol_{k_{min}}$

$optCost[i] = optCost_{k_{min}}$

$birdAdvice[i] = k_{min}$

$optNum[i] = \sum_{k \in \{k \mid optCost_k = optCost_{k_{min}}\}} optNum[k]$.

end for

$optSol = LeveledGraphWithAdvice(\langle G, s, v_n \rangle, birdAdvice)$

return $\langle optSol, optCost[n], optNum[n] \rangle$

end algorithm

EXERCISE 18.3.3 *(See solution in Part Five.) Give the code for printing neatly.*

EXERCISE 18.3.4 *Consider printing neatly the silly text "This week has seven dates in it ok" in a column with width $M = 11$. This is represented as the printing neatly instance $\langle M; l_1, \ldots, l_n \rangle = \langle 11; 4, 4, 3, 5, 5, 2, 2, 2 \rangle$. (a) Fill in the $birdAdvice[0..n]$ and $cost[0..n]$ tables for this example. The original instance, its solution, and its cost are in the bottom row. (b) When filling in this last row, give solutions and costs associated with each of the possible bird answers.*

EXERCISE 18.3.5 *I saw this puzzle on a Toronto subway. The question is how many times the word "TRAINS" appears in the accompanying diagram. Each occurence of the word must follow a connected path so that each of its letters are adjacent to its previous letter. In order to learn the number of such occurences, we could count them, but this might be exponential in the number of squares. Instead, for each box do a constant amount of work and write one integer. In the end, the answer should appear in the box with a "T." You should give a few sentences explaining the order in which you fill the boxes, how you do it, and how much work it is.*

This completes the presentation of the general techniques and the theory behind dynamic programming algorithms. We will now develop algorithms for other optimization problems.

19 Examples of Dynamic Programs

19.1 The Longest-Common-Subsequence Problem

There is a big demand for algorithms that find patterns in strings, for example, DNA. The following optimization problem is called the *longest common subsequence* (LCS).

Longest Common Subsequence:

> **Instances:** An instance consists of two sequences $X = \langle x_1, \ldots, x_n \rangle$ and $Y = \langle y_1, \ldots, y_m \rangle$ For example, $X = \langle B, D, C, A, B, A \rangle$ and $Y = \langle A, B, C, B, D, A, B \rangle$.
>
> **Solutions:** A subsequence of a sequence is a subset of the elements taken in the same order. A solution is a subsequence $Z = \langle z_1, \ldots, z_l \rangle$ that is common to both X and Y.
>
> **Measure of Success:** The cost (or success) of a solution is the length of the common subsequence.
>
> **Goal:** Given two sequences X and Y, the goal is to find the LCS.
>
> **Example:** $Z = \langle B, C, A \rangle$ is a solution because it is a subsequence of $X = \langle \underline{B}, D, \underline{C}, \underline{A}, B, A \rangle$ and Y ($Y = \langle A, \underline{B}, \underline{C}, B, D, \underline{A}, B \rangle$). The cost (success) of this subsequence is $|Z| = 3$. Here $Z = \langle B, C, B, A \rangle$ would be a longer common subsequence with cost 4.

Greedy Algorithm: Suppose $X = \langle A, B, C, D \rangle$ and $Y = \langle B, C, D, A \rangle$. A greedy algorithm might commit to matching the two A's. However, this would be a mistake, because the optimal answer is $Z = \langle B, C, D \rangle$.

Possible Little Bird Answers: Typically, the question asked of the little bird is for some detail about the end of an optimal solution.

> **Case $x_n \neq z_l$:** Suppose that the bird assures us that the last character of X is not the last character of at least one LCS Z of X and Y. We could then simply

ignore this last character of X. We could ask a friend to give us a LCS of $X' = \langle x_1, \ldots, x_{n-1}\rangle$ and Y, and this would be a LCS of X and Y.

Case $y_m \neq z_l$: Similarly, if we are told that the last character of Y is not used, then we can ignore it.

Case $x_n = y_m = z_l$: Suppose that the little bird tells us that the last character of both X and Y is the last character of an optimal Z. This, of course, implies that the last characters of X and Y are the same. In this case, we could simply ignore this last character of both X and Y. We could ask a friend to give us a longest common subsequence of $X' = \langle x_1, \ldots, x_{n-1}\rangle$ and $Y' = \langle y_1, \ldots, y_{m-1}\rangle$. A LCS of X and Y would be the same, except with the character $x_n = y_m$ tacked on to the end, that is, $Z = Z'x_n$. On the other hand, if the little bird answers this case with $x_n = y_m = z_l$ and we on our own observe that $x_n \neq y_n$, then we know that the little bird is wrong.

Case $z_l = ?$: Even more extreme, suppose that the little bird goes as far as to tell us the last character of a LCS Z. We could then delete the last characters of X and Y up to and including the last occurrence of this character. A friend could give us a LCS of the remaining X and Y, and then we could add on the known character to give us Z.

Case $x_n = z_l \neq y_m$: Suppose that the bird assures us that the last character of X is the last character of an optimal Z. This will tell us the last character of Z, and hence the last case will apply.

The Question for the Little Bird: We have a number of different answers that the little bird might give, each of which would help us find an optimal Z. We could add even more possible answers to the list. However, the larger the number K of possible answers is, the more work our algorithm will have to do. Hence, we want to narrow this list of possibilities down as far as possible. We will consider only the first three bird answers. This is sufficient because for every possible solution at least one of these is true, namely, either (1) $x_n \neq z_l$, (2) $y_m \neq z_l$, or (3) $x_n = y_m = z_l$. Of course, it may be the case that $x_n \neq z_l$ and $y_m \neq z_l$, but if this is true, than the bird has a choice whether to answer (1) or (2).

The Set of Subinstances: We guess that the set of subinstances of the instance $\langle\langle x_1, \ldots, x_n\rangle, \langle y_1, \ldots, y_m\rangle\rangle$ is $\{\langle\langle x_1, \ldots, x_i\rangle, \langle y_1, \ldots, y_j\rangle\rangle \mid i \leq n, \ j \leq m\}$.

Closed: We know that this set contains all subinstances generated by the recursive algorithm, because it contains the initial instance and is closed under the sub operation. Consider an arbitrary subinstance, $\langle\langle x_1, \ldots, x_i\rangle, \langle y_1, \ldots, y_j\rangle\rangle$. Applying the sub operator constructs the subinstances $\langle\langle x_1, \ldots, x_{i-1}\rangle, \langle y_1, \ldots, y_{j-1}\rangle\rangle$, $\langle\langle x_1, \ldots, x_{i-1}\rangle, \langle y_1, \ldots, y_j\rangle\rangle$, and $\langle\langle x_1, \ldots, x_i\rangle, \langle y_1, \ldots, y_{j-1}\rangle\rangle$, which are all contained in the stated set of subinstances.

Generating: We know that the specified set of subinstances does not contain subinstances not called by the recursive program, because we can construct any arbitrary subinstance from the set with the sub operator. Consider an arbitrary subinstance $\langle\langle x_1, \ldots, x_i \rangle, \langle y_1, \ldots, y_j \rangle\rangle$. The recursive program on the instance $\langle\langle x_1, \ldots, x_n \rangle, \langle y_1, \ldots, y_m \rangle\rangle$ can recurse on the first option $n - i$ times and then on the second option $m - j$ times. This results in the subinstance $\langle\langle x_1, \ldots, x_i \rangle, \langle y_1, \ldots, y_j \rangle\rangle$.

Constructing a Table Indexed by Subinstances: We now construct a table having one entry for each subinstance. It will have a dimension for each of the parameters i and j used to specify a particular subinstance. The tables will be $cost[0..n, 0..m]$ and $birdAdvice[0..n, 0..m]$.

Base Cases: The subinstance represented by $cost[0, j]$ is $\langle \emptyset, \langle y_1, \ldots, y_m \rangle\rangle$ and has no characters in X. Hence, it is not reasonable to ask the bird about the last character of X. Besides, this is an easy case to handle as a base case. The only subsequence of the empty string is the empty string. Hence, the LCS is the empty string. The cost of this solution is $cost[0, j] = 0$.

Order in Which to Fill the Table: The official order in which to fill the table with subinstances is from smaller to larger. Here the size of the subinstance $\langle\langle x_1, \ldots, x_i \rangle, \langle y_1, \ldots, y_j \rangle\rangle$ is $i + j$. Thus, you would fill in the table along the diagonals. However, the obvious order of looping, for $i = 0$ to n and from $j = 0$ to m, also respects the dependences between the instances and thus could be used instead.

Code:

```
algorithm LCS(⟨⟨x₁, . . . , xₙ⟩, ⟨y₁, . . . , yₘ⟩⟩)

⟨ pre-cond⟩: An instance consists of two sequences.
⟨ post-cond⟩: optSol is a LCS, and optCost is its length.

begin
    % Table: optSol[i, j] would store an optimal LCS for ⟨⟨x₁, . . . , xᵢ⟩,
    ⟨y₁, . . . , yⱼ⟩⟩, but actually we store only the bird's advice for the
    subinstance and the cost of its solution.
    table[0..n, 0..m] birdAdvice, cost

    % Base cases: The base cases consist of when one string or the other is
    empty, i.e., when i = 0 or when j = 0.
    For each, the solution is the empty string with cost zero.
    for j = 0 to m
        % optSol[0, j] = ∅
        cost[0, j] = 0
        birdAdvice[0, j] = ∅
```

```
end for
for i = 0 to n
% optSol[i, 0] = ∅
    cost[i, 0] = 0
    birdAdvice[i, 0] = ∅
end for
```

% General cases: Loop over subinstances in the table.
for $i = 1$ to n

    for $j = 1$ to m

        % Solve instance $\langle\langle x_1, \ldots, x_i\rangle, \langle y_1, \ldots, y_j\rangle\rangle$, and fill in table entry $\langle i, j\rangle$.

        % The bird-and-friend algorithm: The bird tells us either (1) $x_i \neq z_{l'}$, (2) $y_j \neq z_{l'}$, or (3) $x_i = y_j = z_{l'}$. We remove this last letter (1) x_i, (2) y_j, or (3) both and ask the friend for an optimal LCS for the remaining words. He gives us (1) $optSol[i - 1, j]$, (2) $optSol[i, j - 1]$, or (3) $optSol[i - 1, j - 1]$, which he has stored in the table. For cases 1 and 2, we leave this the same. For case 3, we add on the bird's letter, assuming that $x_i = y_j$. This gives us $optSol_k$ which is a LCS for $\langle i, j\rangle$ from amongst those printings consistent with the bird's answer.

        % Try each possible bird answers.

        % Case $k = 1$): $x_i \neq z_{l'}$

            % $optSol_1 = optSol[i - 1, j]$

            $cost_1 = cost[i - 1, j]$

        % Case $k = 2$): $y_j \neq z_{l'}$

            % $optSol_2 = optSol[i, j - 1]$

            $cost_2 = cost[i, j - 1]$

        % Case $k = 3$): $x_i = y_j = z_{l'}$

            if $x_i = y_j$ then

                % $optSol_3 = optSol[i - 1, j - 1] + x_i$

                $cost_3 = cost[i - 1, j - 1] + 1$

            else

                % Bird was wrong.

                % $optSol_3 =?$

                $cost_3 = -\infty$

            end if

        % end cases

        % Having the best, $optSol_k$, for each bird's answer k, we keep the best of these best.

        $k_{max} =$ a $k \in [1, 2, 3]$ that maximizes $cost_k$

        % $optSol[i, j] = optSol_{k_{max}}$

$$cost[i, j] = cost_{k_{max}}$$
$$birdAdvice[i, j] = k_{max}$$
        end for
      end for
      $optSol = LCSWithAdvice(\langle\langle x_1, \ldots, x_n\rangle, \langle y_1, \ldots, y_m\rangle\rangle, birdAdvice)$
      return $\langle optSol, cost[n, m]\rangle$
    end algorithm

Using Information about the Subinstance: This algorithm only has three different bird answers. Surely, this is good enough. However, the number of the possible answers can be narrowed even further. We know the instance is $\langle\langle x_1, \ldots, x_i\rangle,$ $\langle y_1, \ldots, y_j\rangle\rangle$; hence, without asking the bird, we know whether or not the last characters are the same, that is, whether or not $x_i = y_j$. If $x_i \neq y_j$, the third case with $x_i = y_j = z_{l'}$ is clearly not possible. Conversely, when $x_i = y_j$, one might also wonder whether the case $x_i \neq z_{l'}$ could ever lead to an optimal solution. Exercise 19.1.1 shows that in this case we only need to consider $x_i = y_j = z_{l'}$. As in a greedy algorithm, we know the answer even before asking the question.

Constructing an Optimal Solution:
    algorithm $LCSWithAdvice(\langle\langle x_1, \ldots, x_i\rangle, \langle y_1, \ldots, y_j\rangle\rangle, birdAdvice)$
    ⟨ *pre- & post-cond*⟩: Same as LCS except with advice.
    begin
        if $(i = 0$ or $j = 0)$ then
            $optSol = \emptyset$
            return $optSol$
        end if
        $k_{max} = birdAdvice[i, j]$
        if $k_{max} = 1$ then
            $optSubSol = LCSWithAdvice(\langle\langle x_1, \ldots, x_{i-1}\rangle, \langle y_1, \ldots, y_j\rangle\rangle, birdAdvice)$
            $optSol = optSubSol$
        else if $k_{max} = 2$ then
            $optSubSol = LCSWithAdvice(\langle\langle x_1, \ldots, x_i\rangle, \langle y_1, \ldots, y_{j-1}\rangle\rangle, birdAdvice)$
            $optSol = optSubSol$
        else if $k_{max} = 3$ then
            $optSubSol = LCSWithAdvice(\langle\langle x_1, \ldots, x_{i-1}\rangle, \langle y_1, \ldots, y_{j-1}\rangle\rangle, birdAdvice)$
            $optSol = \langle optSubSol, x_i\rangle$
        end if
        return $optSol$
    end algorithm

Time and Space Requirements: See Exercise 19.1.2.

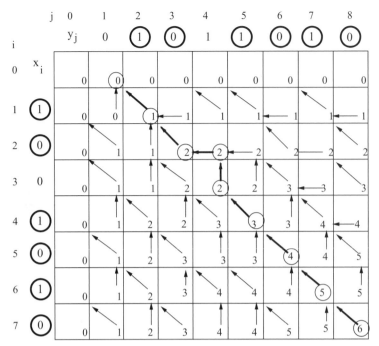

Figure 19.1: The tables generated for the instance $X = 1001010$ and $Y = 01011010$. Each number is $cost[i, j]$, which is the length of the longest common subsequence of the first i characters of X and the first j characters of Y. The arrow indicates whether the bird's advice is to include $x_i = y_j$, to exclude x_i, or to exclude y_j. The circled digits of X and Y give an optimal solution.

Example: See Figure 19.1.

EXERCISE 19.1.1 *(See solution in Part Five.) (a) Prove that if $x_i = y_j$, then we only need to consider the third case, and if $x_i \neq y_j$, then we only need to consider the first two cases. (b) Show how this changes the code.*

EXERCISE 19.1.2 *(See solution in Part Five.) Calculate the running time of this algorithm.*

19.2 Dynamic Programs as More-of-the-Input Iterative Loop Invariant Algorithms

A dynamic program can be thought of from two very different perspectives: as an optimized recursive backtracking algorithm and as an iterative loop invariant algorithm that fills in a table. From the perspective of an iterative algorithm, the loop invariant maintained is that the previous table entries have been filled in correctly. Progress is made while maintaining this loop invariant by filling in the next entry. This is accomplished using the solutions stored in the previous entries.

In *more-of-the-input* iterative algorithms (see Section 1.2), the subinstances are prefixes of the instance, and hence the algorithm iterates through the subinstances by iterating in some way through the elements of the instance.

SIMPLE EXAMPLE 19.2.1 **Longest Increasing Contiguous Subsequence**

Suppose that the input consists of a sequence $A[1..n]$ of integers and we want to find the longest contiguous subsequence $A[k_1, k_2]$ such that the elements are monotonically increasing. For example, the optimal solution for $[5, 3, 1, 3, 7, 9, 8]$ is $[1, 3, 7, 9]$.

Longest Block of Ones: The problem is very similar to the longest-block-of-ones problem given in Section 2.2.

Deterministic Nonfinite Automation: The algorithm will read the input characters one at a time. Let $A[1..i]$ denote the subsequence read so far. The loop invariant will be that some information about this prefix $A[1..i]$ is stored. From this information about $A[1..i]$ and the element $A[i + 1]$, the algorithm must be able to determine the required information about the prefix $A[1..i + 1]$. In the end, the algorithm must be able to determine the solution from this information about the entire sequence $A[1..n]$. Such an algorithm is a deterministic finite automaton (DFA) if only a constant amount of information is stored at each point in time. (See Section 2.2.) However, in this chapter more memory will be required.

The Algorithm: After reading $A[1..i]$, remember the longest increasing contiguous subsequence $A[k_1..k_2]$ read so far and its size. In addition, so that you know whether the current increasing contiguous subsequence gets to be longer than the previous one, save the longest one ending in the value $A[i]$, and its size.

If you have this information about $A[1..i - 1]$, then you can learn it about $A[1..i]$ as follows. If $A[i - 1] \leq A[i]$, then the longest increasing contiguous subsequence ending in the current value increases in length by one. Otherwise, it shrinks to being only the one element $A[i]$. If this subsequence increases to be longer than our previous longest, then it replaces the previous longest. In the end, we know the longest increasing contiguous subsequence.

The running time is $\Theta(n)$. This is not a DFA, because the amount of space to remember an index and a count (amounting to $\Theta(n)$ values) is $\Theta(\log n)$ bits.

HARDER EXAMPLE 19.2.2 **Longest Increasing Subsequence**

Again the input consists of a sequence A of integers of size n. However, now we want to find the longest (not necessarily contiguous) subsequence $S \subseteq [1..n]$ such that the elements, in the order that they appear in A, are monotonically increasing. For example, an optimal solution for $[5, 1, 5, 7, 2, 4, 9, 8]$ is $[1, 5, 7, 9]$, and so is $[1, 2, 4, 8]$.

Dynamic Programming Deterministic Nonfinite Automation: Again the algorithm will read the input characters one at a time. But now the algorithm will store suitable

302

HARDER EXAMPLE 19.2.2	**Longest Increasing Subsequence** (cont.)

information, not only about the current subsequence $A[1..i]$, but also about each previous subsequence $\forall j \leq i$, $A[1..j]$. Each of these subsequences $A[1..j]$ will be referred to as a *subinstance* of the original instance $A[1..n]$.

The Algorithm: As before, we will store both the longest increasing sequence seen so far and the longest one(s) that we are currently growing.

The Loop Invariant: Suppose that the subsequence read so far is 10, 20, 1, 30, 40, 2, 50. Then 10, 20, 30, 40, 50 is the longest increasing subsequence so far. A shorter one is 1, 2, 50. The problem is that these end in a relatively large number, so we may not be able to extend them further. If the rest of the string is 3, 4, 5, 6, 7, 8, we will have to have remembered that 1, 2 is the longest increasing subsequence that ends in the value 2. In fact, for many values v, we need to remember the longest increasing subsequence ending in this value v (or a smaller one), because in the end, it may be that many of the remaining elements increase starting from this value. We only need to do this for values v that have been seen so far in the array. Hence, one possibility is to store, for each $j \leq i$, the longest increasing subsequence in $A[1..j]$ that ends with the value $A[j]$.

Maintaining the Loop Invariant: If we have this information for each $j \leq i - 1$, then we learn it about $A[i]$ as follows. For each $j \leq i - 1$, if $A[j] \leq A[i]$, then $A[i]$ can extend the subsequence ending with $A[j]$. Given this construction, the maximum length for i will then be one more than that for j. We get the longest one for i by taking the best of these overall such j. If there is no such j, then the count for i will be 1, namely, simply $A[i]$ itself.

Final Solution: In the end, the solution is the increasing subsequence ending in $A[j]$, where $j \in [1..n]$ is that for which this count is the largest.

Running Time: The time for finding this best subsequence ending in $A[j]$ from which to extend to $A[i]$ would be $\Theta(i)$ if each $j \in [1..i-1]$ needed to be checked. However, by storing this information in a heap, the best j can be found in $\Theta(\log i)$ time. This gives a total time of $\Theta(\sum_{i=1}^{n} \log i) = \Theta(n \log n)$ for this algorithm.

Recursive Backtracking: We can also understand this same algorithm from the recursive backtracking perspective. Given the goal of finding the longest increasing subsequence of $A[1..i]$, we might ask the little bird whether or not the last element $A[i]$ should be included. Both options need to be tried. If $A[i]$ is not to be included, then the remaining subtask is to find the longest increasing subsequence of $A[1..i-1]$. This is clearly a subinstance of the same problem. However, if $A[i]$ is to be included, then the remaining subtask is to find the longest increasing subsequence of $A[1..i-1]$ that ends in a value that is smaller than or equal to this last value $A[i]$. This is another way of seeing that we need to learn both the longest increasing sequence of the prefix $A[1..i]$ and the longest one ending in $A[i]$.

19.3 A Greedy Dynamic Program: The Weighted Job/Event Scheduling Problem

We revisit the event scheduling problem from Section 16.2.1, now prioritizing the events. Our original greedy algorithm won't work, but dynamic programming will.

The Weighted Event Scheduling Problem: Suppose that many events want to use your conference room. Some of these events are given a higher priority than others. Your goal is to schedule the room in the optimal way.

> **Instances:** An instance is $\langle\langle s_1, f_1, w_1\rangle, \langle s_2, f_2, w_2\rangle, \ldots, \langle s_n, f_n, w_n\rangle\rangle$, where $0 \le s_i \le f_i$ are the starting and finishing times and w_i the priority weight for n events.

> **Solutions:** A solution for an instance is a schedule S. This consists of a subset $S \subseteq [1..n]$ of the events that don't conflict by overlapping in time.

> **Measure of Success:** The cost (or success) $C(S)$ of a solution S is the sum of the weights of the events scheduled, i.e., $\sum_{i \in S} w_i$.

> **Goal:** The goal of the algorithm is to find the *optimal solution*, that is, that maximizes the total scheduled weight.

Failed Algorithms:

> **Greedy Earliest Finishing Time:** The greedy algorithm used in Section 16.2.1 for the unweighted version greedily selects the event with the earliest finishing time f_i. This algorithm fails when the events have weights. The following is a counterexample:

$$\frac{1}{\underline{1000}}$$

> The specified algorithm schedules the top event for a total weight of 1. The optimal schedule schedules the bottom event for a total weight of 1000.

> **Greedy Largest Weight:** Another greedy algorithm selects the first event using the criterion of the largest weight w_i. The following is a counterexample for this:

$$\frac{2}{\overline{1}\ \overline{1}\ \overline{1}\ \overline{1}\ \overline{1}\ \overline{1}\ \overline{1}\ \overline{1}\ \overline{1}}$$

> The top event has weight 2 and the bottom ones each have weight 1. The specified algorithm schedules the top event for a total weight of 2. The optimal schedule schedules the bottom events for a total weight of 9.

> **Dynamic Programming:** The obvious dynamic programming algorithm is for the little bird to tell you whether or not to schedule event J_n.

Bird-and-Friend Algorithm: Consider an instance $J = \langle \langle s_1, f_1, w_1 \rangle, \langle s_2, f_2, w_2 \rangle, \ldots, \langle s_n, f_n, w_n \rangle \rangle$. The little bird considers an optimal schedule. We ask the little bird whether or not to schedule event J_n. If she says yes, then the remaining possible events to schedule are those in J, excluding event J_n and excluding all events that conflict with event J_n. We ask a friend to schedule these. Our schedule is his with event J_n added. If instead the bird tells us not to schedule event J_n, then the remaining possible events to schedule are those in J excluding event J_n.

The Set of Subinstances: When tracing the recursive algorithm on small examples, we see that the set of subinstance used can be exponentially large. See the left side of Figure 19.2 for an example. The events in the instance are paired so that for $i \in [1..\frac{n}{2}]$, job J_i conflicts with job $J_{\frac{n}{2}+i}$, but jobs between pairs do not conflict. After the little bird tells you whether or not to schedule jobs $J_{\frac{n}{2}+i}$ for $i \in [1..\frac{n}{2}]$, job J_i will remain in the subinstance if and only if job $J_{\frac{n}{2}+i}$ was not scheduled. This results in at least $2^{n/2}$ different paths down the tree of stack frames in the recursive backtracking algorithm, each leading to a different subinstance.

In contrast, look at the instance on the right in Figure 19.2. It only has a linear number of subinstances, because each subinstance is a prefix of the events. The only difference between these examples is the order of the events.

Greedy Dynamic Programming: First sort the events in increasing order of their finishing times f_i (a greedy thing to do). Then run the same dynamic programming algorithm in which the little bird tells you whether or not to schedule event J_n.

The Set of Subinstances: When tracing the recursive algorithm on small examples, it looks hopeful that the set of subinstance used is $\{\langle \langle s_1, f_1, w_1 \rangle, \langle s_2, f_2, w_2 \rangle, \ldots, \langle s_i, f_i, w_i \rangle \rangle \mid i \in [0..n]\}$. If so, the algorithm is polynomial time. The danger is that when excluding those events that conflict with event J_n, the subinstance created will no longer have a contiguous prefix of the events. For example, if event J_2 conflicts with J_n but event J_3 does not, then the new subinstance will need to be $\langle \langle s_1, f_1, w_1 \rangle, \langle s_3, f_3, w_3 \rangle, \ldots, ?? \rangle$, which is not included. Needing to solve this subinstance as well may make the running time exponential.

Closed: For this algorithm, more than those previous, we must be careful to show that this set contains all subinstances generated by the recursive algorithm by showing that it is closed under the sub operation. Consider an arbitrary subinstance $\langle \langle s_1, f_1, w_1 \rangle, \langle s_2, f_2, w_2 \rangle, \ldots, \langle s_i, f_i, w_i \rangle \rangle$ in the set. If we delete from this event J_i and all events that conflict with it, we must show that this new subinstance is again in our set. Let $i' \in [0..i-1]$ be the largest index such that $f_{i'} \leq s_i$. Because the events have been sorted by

Job numbers

1	2	3	4	5	6	7	8	9
10	11	12	13	14	15	16	17	18

1	3	5	7	9	11	13	15	17
2	4	6	8	10	12	14	16	18

Subinstance after committing to keeping 18

1	2	3	4	5	6	7	8
10	11	12	13	14	15	16	17

Subinstance after committing to keeping 18

1	3	5	7	9	11	13	15
2	4	6	8	10	12	14	16

Subinstance after committing to rejecting 17

1	2	3	4	5	6	7	8
10	11	12	13	14	15	16	

Subinstance after committing to rejecting 16

1	3	5	7	9	11	13	15
2	4	6	8	10	12	14	

Subinstance after committing to keeping 16

1	2	3	4	5	6		8
10	11	12	13	14	15		

Subinstance after committing to keeping 15

1	3	5	7	9	11	13
2	4	6	8	10	12	14

Subinstance after committing to rejecting 15

1	2	3	4	5	6		8
10	11	12	13	14			

Subinstance after committing to rejecting 14

1	3	5	7	9	11	13
2	4	6	8	10	12	

Subinstance after committing to keeping 14

1	2	3	4		6		8
10	11	12	13				

Subinstance after committing to rejecting 13

1	3	5	7	9	11
2	4	6	8	10	12

Subinstance after committing to keeping 13

1	2	3			6		8
10	11	12					

Subinstance after committing to keeping 12

1	3	5	7	9
2	4	6	8	10

and so on

Figure 19.2: Two examples of the subinstances formed from the recursive backtracking algorithm.

their finishing time, we know that all events J_k in $\langle\langle s_1, f_1, w_1\rangle, \langle s_2, f_2, w_2\rangle, \ldots, \langle s_{i'}, f_{i'}, w_{i'}\rangle\rangle$ also have $f_k \leq s_i$ and hence do not conflict with J_i. All events J_k in $\langle\langle s_{i'+1}, f_{i'+1}, w_{i'+1}\rangle, \ldots, \langle s_i, f_i, w_i\rangle\rangle$ have $s_i < f_k \leq f_i$ and hence conflict with J_i. It follows that the resulting subinstance is $\langle\langle s_1, f_1, w_1\rangle, \langle s_2, f_2, w_2\rangle, \ldots, \langle s_{i'}, f_{i'}, w_{i'}\rangle\rangle$, which is our set of subinstances. If, on the other hand, only event J_i is deleted, then the resulting subinstance is $\langle\langle s_1, f_1, w_1\rangle, \ldots, \langle s_{i-1}, f_{i-1}, w_{i-1}\rangle\rangle$, which is obviously in our set of subinstances. It is because this works out that the algorithm is polynomial-time.

Generating: Consider the arbitrary subinstance $\langle\langle s_1, f_1, w_1\rangle, \langle s_2, f_2, w_2\rangle, \ldots, \langle s_i, f_i, w_i\rangle\rangle$. It is generated by the recursive algorithm when the little bird states that none of the later events are included in the solution.

The Table: The dynamic programming table is a one-dimensional array indexed by $i \in [0..n]$. The order to fill it in is with increasing i. As in the greedy algorithm, the events are considered to be ordered by earliest finishing time first. The i entry is filled in by trying each of the two answers the bird might give.

Time and Space Requirements: Generally, the running time is the number of subinstances times the number of possible bird answers, and the space is the number of subinstances. This would give $T = \Theta(n \times 2)$ and $S = \Theta(n)$. In this case, however, the running time is larger than that. The reason is that when the event J_i is to be included, it takes $O(\log n)$ time to do a binary search to find which earlier events conflict with it and hence need to be deleted. This gives a running time of $O(n \log n)$, apart from the initial $O(n \log n)$ time for sorting of the activities by finishing time.

EXERCISE 19.3.1 *Write out the pseudocode for this algorithm.*

19.4 The Solution Viewed as a Tree: Chains of Matrix Multiplications

We now look at an example in which the fields of information specifying a solution are organized into a tree instead of into a sequence (see Section 18.3.2). The algorithm asks the little bird to tell it the field at the root of one of the instance's optimal solutions, and then a separate friend will be asked for each of the solution's subtrees.

The optimization problem determines how to optimally multiply together a chain of matrices. Multiplying an $a_1 \times a_2$ matrix by a $a_2 \times a_3$ matrix requires $a_1 \cdot a_2 \cdot a_3$ scalar multiplications. Matrix multiplication is associative, meaning that $(M_1 \cdot M_2) \cdot M_3 = M_1 \cdot (M_2 \cdot M_3)$. Sometimes different bracketing of a sequence of matrix multiplications can lead to the total number of scalar multiplications being very different. For example,

$$((\langle 5 \times 1{,}000 \rangle \cdot \langle 1{,}000 \times 2 \rangle) \cdot \langle 2 \times 2{,}000 \rangle = \langle 5 \times 2 \rangle \cdot \langle 2 \times 2{,}000 \rangle = \langle 5 \times 2{,}000 \rangle$$

requires $5 \times 1{,}000 \times 2 + 5 \times 2 \times 2{,}000 = 10{,}000 + 20{,}000 = 30{,}000$ scalar multiplications. However,

$$\langle 5 \times 1{,}000 \rangle \cdot (\langle 1{,}000 \times 2 \rangle \cdot \langle 2 \times 2{,}000 \rangle) = \langle 5 \times 1{,}000 \rangle \cdot \langle 1{,}000 \times 2{,}000 \rangle$$
$$= \langle 5 \times 2{,}000 \rangle$$

requires $1{,}000 \times 2 \times 2{,}000 + 5 \times 1{,}000 \times 2{,}000 = 4{,}000{,}000 + 10{,}000{,}000 = 14{,}000{,}000$. The problem considered here is to find how to bracket a sequence of matrix multiplications in order to minimize the number of scalar multiplications.

Chains of Matrix Multiplications:

Instances: An instance is a sequence of n matrices $\langle A_1, A_2, \ldots, A_n \rangle$. (A precondition is that for each $k \in [1..n-1]$, $width(A_k) = height(A_{k+1})$.)

Solutions: A solution is a way of bracketing the matrices, e.g., $((A_1 A_2)(A_3(A_4 A_5)))$. A solution can equivalently be viewed as a binary tree with the matrices $A_1, \ldots, A_n$ at the leaves. The binary tree would give the order in which to multiply the matrices:

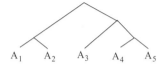

$A_1 \quad A_2 \quad A_3 \quad A_4 \quad A_5$

Measure of Success: The cost of a solution is the number of scalar multiplications needed to multiply the matrices according to the bracketing.

Goal: Given a sequence of matrices, the goal is to find a bracketing that requires
the fewest multiplications.

A Failed Greedy Algorithm: An obvious greedy algorithm selects where the last
multiplication will occur according to which is cheapest. We can prove that any such
simple greedy algorithm will fail, even when the instance contains only three ma-
trices. Let the matrices A_1, A_2, and A_3 have height and width $\langle a_0, a_1 \rangle$, $\langle a_1, a_2 \rangle$, and
$\langle a_2, a_3 \rangle$. There are two orders in which these can be multiplied. Their costs are as
follows:

$$cost((A_1 \cdot A_2) \cdot A_3) = a_0 a_1 a_2 + a_0 a_2 a_3$$
$$cost(A_1 \cdot (A_2 \cdot A_3)) = a_1 a_2 a_3 + a_0 a_1 a_3$$

Consider the algorithm that chooses so that the last multiplication is the cheapest.
Let us assume that the algorithm uses the first order. This gives that $a_0 a_2 a_3 < a_0 a_1 a_3$,
that is, $a_2 < a_1$. However, the second order will be cheaper if $a_0 a_1 a_2 + a_0 a_2 a_3 >
a_1 a_2 a_3 + a_0 a_1 a_3$, that is, if $a_0 >> a_3$. Let us now assign simple values meeting $a_2 < a_1$
and $a_0 >> a_3$. Say $a_0 = 1000$, $a_1 = 2$, $a_2 = 1$, and $a_3 = 1$. Plugging these in gives

$$cost((A_1 \cdot A_2) \cdot A_3) = 1000 \times 2 \times 1 + 1000 \times 1 \times 1 = 2000 + 1000 = 3000$$
$$cost(A_1 \cdot (A_2 \cdot A_3)) = 2 \times 1 \times 1 + 1000 \times 2 \times 1 = 2 + 2000 = 2002$$

This is an instance in which the algorithm gives the wrong answer. Because $1000 <
2000$, it uses the first order. However, the second order is cheaper.

A Failed Dynamic Programming Algorithm: An obvious question to ask the little
bird would be which pair of consecutive matrices to multiply together last. Though
this algorithm works, it has exponential running time. The problem is that there are
an exponential number of different subinstances. Consider paths down the tree of
stack frames in which for each pair A_{2i} and A_{2i+1}, the bird either gets us to multiply them together or does not. This results in $2^{n/2}$ different paths down the tree
of stack frames in the recursive backtracking algorithm, each leading to a different
subinstance.

The Question to Ask the Little Bird: A better question is to ask the little bird
to give us the splitting k so that the last multiplication multiplies the product

of $\langle A_1, A_2, \ldots, A_k \rangle$ and of $\langle A_{k+1}, \ldots, A_n \rangle$. This is equivalent to asking for the root of the binary tree. For each of the possible answers, the best solution is found that is consistent with this answer, and then the best of these best solutions is returned.

Reduced to Subinstance: With this advice, our search for an optimal bracketing is simplified. We need only solve two subinstances: finding an optimal bracketing of $\langle A_1, A_2, \ldots, A_k \rangle$ and of $\langle A_{k+1}, \ldots, A_n \rangle$. In the example with $\langle A_1, A_2, \ldots, A_5 \rangle$ above, the bird splits the problem into subinstances $\langle A_1, A_2 \rangle$ and $\langle A_3, A_4, A_5 \rangle$.

Recursive Structure: An optimal bracketing of the matrices $\langle A_1, A_2, \ldots, A_n \rangle$ multiplies the sequence $\langle A_1, \ldots, A_k \rangle$ with its optimal bracketing, and $\langle A_{k+1}, \ldots, A_n \rangle$ with its optimal bracketing, and then multiplies these two resulting matrices together, that is, $optSol = (optLeft)(optRight)$.

The Cost of the Optimal Solution Derived from the Cost for Subinstances: The total number of scalar multiplications used in this optimal bracketing is the number used to multiply $\langle A_1, \ldots, A_k \rangle$, plus the number for $\langle A_{k+1}, \ldots, A_n \rangle$, plus the number to multiply the final two matrices. $\langle A_1, \ldots, A_k \rangle$ evaluates to a matrix whose height is the same as that of A_1 and whose width is that of A_k. Similarly, $\langle A_{k+1}, \ldots, A_n \rangle$ becomes a $height(A_{k+1}) \times width(A_n)$ matrix. Multiplying these requires a number $height(A_1) \times width(A_k) \times width(A_n)$ scalar multiplications. Hence, in total, $cost = costLeft + costRight + height(A_1) \times width(A_k) \times width(A_n)$.

The Set of Subinstances Called: The set of subinstances of the instance $\langle A_1, A_2, \ldots, A_n \rangle$ is $\langle A_i, A_{i+1}, \ldots, A_j \rangle$ for every choice of end points $1 \leq i \leq j \leq n$. This set of subinstances contains all the subinstances called, because it is closed under the sub operation. Applying the sub operator to an arbitrary subinstance $\langle A_i, A_{i+1}, \ldots, A_j \rangle$ from this set constructs subinstances $\langle A_i, \ldots, A_k \rangle$ and $\langle A_{k+1}, \ldots, A_j \rangle$ for $i \leq k < j$, which are contained in the stated set of subinstances. Similarly, the set does not contain subinstances *not* called by the recursive program, because we easily can construct any arbitrary subinstance in the set with the sub operator. For example, $\langle A_1, \ldots, A_n \rangle$ sets $k = j$ and calls $\langle A_1, \ldots, A_j \rangle$, which sets $k = i + 1$ and calls $\langle A_i, \ldots, A_j \rangle$.

Constructing a Table Indexed by Subinstances: The table indexed by the set of subinstances will have a dimension for each of the parameters i and j used to specify a particular subinstance. The tables will be $cost[1..n, 1..n]$ and $birdAdvice[1..n, 1..n]$. See Figure 19.3.

Order in Which to Fill the Table: The size of a subinstance is the number of matrices in it. We will fill the table in this order.

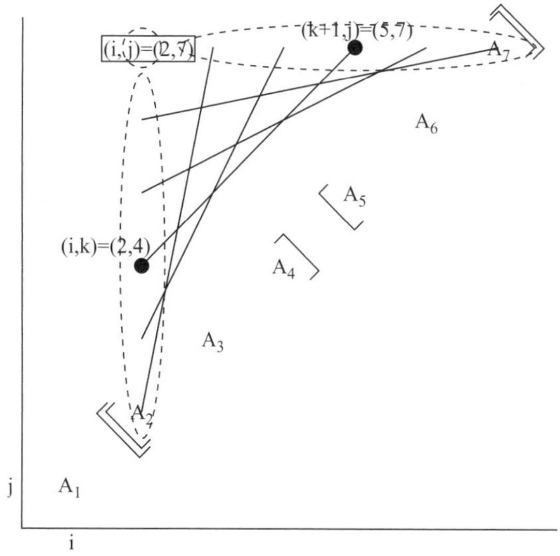

Figure 19.3: The table produced by the dynamic programming solution for Matrix Multiplication. When searching for the optimal bracketing of $A_2, \ldots, A_7$, one of the methods to consider is $[A_2, \ldots, A_4][A_5, \ldots, A_7]$.

algorithm *MatrixMultiplication* $(\langle A_1, A_2, \ldots, A_n \rangle)$

⟨ **pre-cond**⟩*:* An instance is a sequence of n matrices.

⟨ **post-cond**⟩*: optSol* is a bracketing that requires the fewest multiplications, and *optCost* is the resulting number of multiplications.

begin

    % Table: *optSol*[i, j] would store an optimal way of bracketing the matrices $\langle A_i, A_{i+1}, \ldots, A_j \rangle$,

    but actually we store only the bird's advice for the subinstance

    and the cost of its solution.

    table[$1..n$, $1..n$] *birdAdvice, cost*

    % Base cases: The base cases are when there is only one matrix, i.e., $\langle A_i \rangle$.

    For each, the solution is the empty bracketing with cost zero.

    for $i = 1$ to n

        % *optSol*[i, i] = A_i

        cost[i, i] = 0

        birdAdvice[i, i] = $\emptyset$

    end for

    % General cases: Loop over subinstances in the table.

    for *size* = 2 to n

        for $i = 1$ to $n - size + 1$

            $j = i + size - 1$

            % Solve instance $\langle i, j \rangle$ and fill in the table.

% Try each possible bird answers.

for $k = i$ to $j - 1$

  % The bird-and-friend algorithm: The bird gives us the splitting k, so that the last multiplication multiplies the product of $\langle A_i, A_{i+1}, \ldots, A_k \rangle$ and that of $\langle A_{k+1}, \ldots, A_j \rangle$. One friend gives us $optSol[i, k]$, an optimal bracketing $\langle A_i, \ldots, A_k \rangle$, and another gives us $optSol[k + 1, j]$, an optimal bracketing of $\langle A_{k+1}, \ldots, A_j \rangle$. We combine these friends' and the bird's information, obtaining $optSol_k$, which is a best bracketing for $\langle i, j \rangle$ from amongst those consistent with the bird's answer.

  % Get help from friend

  % $optSol_k = (optLeft)(optRight)$

  $cost_k = cost[i, k] + cost[k + 1, j] + height(A_i)$
    $\times\ width(A_k) \times width(A_j)$

end for

% Having the best, $optSol_k$, for each bird's answer k, we keep the best of these best.

  $k_{min} =$ a k that minimizes $cost_k$

% $optSol[i, j] = optSol_{k_{min}}$

  $cost[i, j] = cost_{k_{min}}$

  $birdAdvice[i, j] = k_{min}$

end for

end for

$optSol = MatrixMultiplicationWithAdvice(\langle A_1, A_2, \ldots, A_n \rangle, birdAdvice)$

return $\langle optSol, cost[1, n] \rangle$

end algorithm

Constructing an Optimal Solution:

algorithm *MatrixMultiplicationWithAdvice*$(\langle A_i, A_2, \ldots, A_j \rangle, birdAdvice)$

$\langle$ *pre- & post-cond* $\rangle$*:* Same as *MatrixMultiplication* except with advice.

begin

 if $(i = j)$ then

  $optSol = A_i$

  return $optSol$

 end if

 $k_{min} = birdAdvice[i, j]$

 $optLeft = MatrixMultiplicationWithAdvice(\langle A_1, \ldots, A_{k_{min}} \rangle, birdAdvice)$

 $optRight = MatrixMultiplicationWithAdvice(\langle A_{k_{min}+1}, \ldots, A_j \rangle, birdAdvice)$

 $optSol = (optLeft)(optRight)$

 return $optSol$

end algorithm

Time and Space Requirements: The running time is the number of subinstances times the number of possible bird answers, and the space is the number of subinstances. The number of subinstances is $\Theta(n^2)$, and the bird chooses one of $\Theta(n)$ places to split the sequence of matrices. Hence, the running time is $\Theta(n^3)$, and the space requirements are $\Theta(n^2)$.

EXERCISE 19.4.1 *Give the steps to find a counterexample for the greedy algorithm that multiplies the cheapest pair together first.*

EXERCISE 19.4.2 *(See solution in Part Five.) Use a picture to make sure that when $\langle i, j \rangle$ is filled, $\langle i, k \rangle$ and $\langle k + 1, j \rangle$ are already filled for all $i \leq k < j$. Give two other orders that work.*

19.5 Generalizing the Problem Solved: Best AVL Tree

As discussed in Section 8.3, it is sometimes useful to generalize the problem solved so that you can either give or receive more information from your friend in a recursive algorithm. This was demonstrated in Chapter 10 with a recursive algorithm for determining whether or not a tree is an AVL tree. This same idea is useful for dynamic programming. I will now demonstrate this by giving an algorithm for finding the best AVL tree. To begin, we will develop an algorithm for the best binary search tree.

The Best Binary Search Tree:

Instances: An instance consists of n probabilities $p_1, \ldots, p_n$ to be associated with the n keys $a_1 < a_2 < \cdots < a_n$. The values of the keys themselves do not matter. Hence, we can assume that $a_i = i$.

Solutions: A solution for an instance is a binary search tree containing the keys. A binary search tree is a binary tree such that the nodes are labeled with the keys and for each node all the keys in its left subtree are smaller and all those in the right are larger.

Measure of Success: The cost of a solution is the expected depth of a key when choosing a key according to the given probabilities, namely $\sum_{i \in [1..n]}$ [$p_i \cdot$ depth of a_i in tree].

Goal: Given the keys and the probabilities, the goal is to find a binary search tree with minimum expected depth.

Expected Depth: The time required to search for a key is proportional to the depth of the key in the binary search tree. Finding the root is fast. Finding a deep leaf takes much longer. The goal is to design the search tree so that the keys that are searched for often are closer to the root. The probabilities $p_1, \ldots, p_n$, given as part of the input, specify the frequency with which each key is searched for; e.g., $p_3 = \frac{1}{8}$ means that key a_3 is search for on average one out of every eight times.

One minimizes the depth of a binary search tree by making it completely balanced. Having it balanced, however, dictates the location of each key. Although having the tree partially unbalanced increases its overall height, it may allow for the keys that are searched for often to be placed closer to the top.

We will manage to put some of the nodes close to the root, and others we will not. The standard mathematical way of measuring the overall success of putting more likely keys closer to the top is the expected depth of a key when the key is chosen randomly according to the given probability distribution. It is calculated by $\sum_{i \in [1..n]} p_i \cdot d_i$, where d_i is the depth of a_i in the search tree.

One way to understand this is to suppose that we needed to search for a billion keys. If $p_3 = \frac{1}{8}$, then a_3 is searched for on average one out of every eight times. Because we are searching for so many keys, it is almost certain that the number of times we search for this key is very close to $\frac{1}{8}$ billion. In general, the number of times we search for a_i is p_i billion. To compute the average depth of these billion searches, we sum their depths and divide by a billion, namely $\frac{1}{10^9} \sum_{k \in [1..10^9]}$ [depth of kth search] $= \frac{1}{10^9} \sum_{i \in [1..n]} (p_i \times 10^9) \cdot d_i = \sum_{i \in [1..n]} p_i \cdot d_i$.

Bird-and-Friend Algorithm: I am given an instance consisting of n probabilities $p_1, \ldots, p_n$. I ask the bird which key to put at the root. She answers a_k. I ask one friend for the best binary search tree for the keys $a_1, \ldots, a_{k-1}$ and its expected depth. I ask another friend for the best tree of the specified height for $a_{k+1}, \ldots, a_n$ and its expected depth. I build the tree with a_k at the root and these as the left and right subtrees.

Generalizing the Problem Solved: A set of probabilities $p_1, \ldots, p_n$ defining a probability distribution should have the property that $\sum_{i \in [1..n]} p_i = 1$. However, we will generalize the problem by removing this restriction. This will allow us to ask our friend to solve subinstances that are not officially legal. Note that the probabilities given to the friends in the above algorithm do not sum to 1.

The Cost of an Optimal Solution Derived from the Costs for the Subinstances:
The expected depth of my tree is computed from that given by my friend as follows.

$$Cost = \sum_{i \in [1..n]} [p_i \cdot \text{depth of } a_i \text{ in tree}] \qquad (19.1)$$

$$= \sum_{i \in [1..k-1]} [p_i \cdot (\text{depth of } a_i \text{ in left subtree}) + 1] + [p_k \cdot 1] \qquad (19.2)$$

$$+ \sum_{i \in [k+1..n]} [p_i \cdot (\text{depth of } a_i \text{ in right subtree}) + 1] \qquad (19.3)$$

$$= Cost_{left} + \left[\sum_{i \in [1..k-1]} p_i\right] + p_k + Cost_{right} + \left[\sum_{i \in [k+1..n]} p_i\right] \qquad (19.4)$$

$$= Cost_{left} + \left[\sum_{i \in [1..n]} p_i\right] + Cost_{right} \qquad (19.5)$$

$$= Cost_{left} + Cost_{right} + 1 \qquad (19.6)$$

The Complete Set of Subinstances That Will Get Called: The complete set of subinstances is $S = \{\langle a_i, \ldots, a_j; p_i, \ldots, p_j \rangle \mid 1 \leq i \leq j \leq n\}$. The table is two-dimensional with size $\Theta(n \times n)$.

Running Time: The table has size $\Theta(n \times n)$. The bird can give n different answers. Hence, the time is $\Theta(n^3)$.

We now change the problem so that it is looking for the best AVL search tree.

The Best-AVL-Tree Problem:

> **Instances:** An instance consists of n probabilities $p_1, \ldots, p_n$ to be associated with the n keys $a_1 < a_2 < \cdots < a_n$.

> **Solutions:** A solution for an instance is an AVL tree containing the keys. An AVL tree is a binary search tree with the property that every node has a balance factor of -1, 0, or 1. Its *balance factor* is the difference between the heights of its left and its right subtrees.

> **Measure of Success:** The cost of a solution is the expected depth of a key, $\sum_{i \in [1..n]} [p_i \cdot \text{depth of } a_i \text{ in } T]$.

> **Goal:** Given the keys and the probabilities, the goal is to find an AVL tree with minimum expected depth.

> **Cannot Coordinate Friends:** We could simply ask friends to build the left and right sub-AVL-trees, but then what would we do if the difference in their heights were greater than one? We cannot expect friends to coordinate their answers.

> **The New Generalized Problem:** An instance consists of the keys, the probabilities, and a required height. The goal is to find the best AVL tree with the given height.

EXERCISE 19.5.1 *(See solution in Part Five.)*

1. *What are the possible heights for the left and the right subtrees of an AVL tree of height h?*
2. *What question would you ask the bird? It is O.K. to ask two questions. What subinstance would you give your friend?*
3. *How would you ensure the balance between the heights of the left and right subtrees?*
4. *What is the complete set of subinstances that will get called?*
5. *What is the running time of your algorithm?*
6. *In the original problem, the height was not fixed. How would you use the table to solve this problem?*

19.6 All Pairs Using Matrix Multiplication

There is another dynamic programming algorithm that also finds the shortest path between every pair of nodes. It is similar in some ways to the Floyd-Warshall–Johnson algorithm, but it is fun because it can be viewed as matrix multiplication.

EXERCISE 19.6.1 *Let $G = (V, E)$ be a (directed or undirected) graph, and $k \leq n$ some integer. Let M^k be a matrix with a both a row and a column for each node in the graph, such that for each pair of nodes $u, v \in V$ the element $M^k[u, v]$ gives the number of distinct paths from u to v that contain exactly k edges. Here a path may visit a node more than once. $M^1[u, v]$ is one if there is an edge $\langle u, v \rangle$ and zero otherwise, and $M^1[u, u] = 1$ because there is a path of length zero from u to u. Prove that $M^{i+j} = M^i M^j$, where $\times$ is standard matrix multiplication, i.e., $M^{i+j}[u, v] = \sum_w [M^i[u, w] \cdot M^j[w, v]]$.*

EXERCISE 19.6.2 *Now let the graph $G = (V, E)$ have weights $w_{u,v}$ (positive or negative) on each edge. Redefine $\widehat{M}^k[u, v]$ to give the weight of the shortest path from u to v with the smallest total weight from amongst these paths that contains exactly k edges. Note that $\widehat{M}^1[u, v]$ is the weight of the edge $w_{u,v}$ (or infinity), and $\widehat{M}^1[u, u] = 0$ because there is a path of length zero from u to u. Prove that $\widehat{M}^{i+j} = \widehat{M}^i \times \widehat{M}^j$, where $\times$ is standard matrix multiplication except that scalar multiplication is changed to $+$ and that $+$ is changed to Min, i.e., $\widehat{M}^{i+j}[u, v] = Min_w[\widehat{M}^i[u, w] + \widehat{M}^j[w, v]]$. Compare this exercise with Exercise 4.4.3.*

EXERCISE 19.6.3 *If all the edge weights are positive, then the shortest weighted path contains at most $n - 1$ edges. Hence, $\widehat{M}^N[u, v]$ for $N \geq n - 1$ gives the overall shortest weighted path from u to v. Given $\widehat{M}^1$, what is the fastest way of computing $\widehat{M}^N$ for some $N \geq n$?*

EXERCISE 19.6.4 *If there is a path from u to v containing a negative weighted cycle, then this cycle can be repeated infinitely often, giving a path with negative infinite weight and infinitely many edges. To detect this, compute $\widehat{M}^N[u, v]$ and $\widehat{M}^{2N}[u, v]$ for some large N and see if they are different. The questions is how large N needs to be. You would think that $N = n - 1$ would be sufficient, but it is not. Give a graph with n edges, each with positive or negative ℓ-bit integer weights, for which $\widehat{M}^k[u, v] = \widehat{M}^1[u, v]$ for $k \in [1, N]$ for some very large N, but $\widehat{M}^{N+1}[u, v]$ is smaller.*

EXERCISE 19.6.5 *The standard algorithm for standard matrix multiplication takes $\Theta(n^3)$ time. Strassen's algorithm (Section 9.2) is able to do it in $\Theta(n^{2.8073})$ time. Does this same algorithm work for this strange multiplication? The equations $x \cdot (y + z) = x \cdot y + x \cdot z$ and $(x - y) + y = x$ are true for all real numbers. Are they true on replacing $\cdot$ with $+$ and replacing $+$ with Min?*

19.7 Parsing with Context-Free Grammars

In Chapter 12 we developed an elegant recursive algorithm for parsing a string according to a given context-free grammar that works only for look-ahead-one grammars. We now develop a dynamic programming algorithm that works for any context-free grammar.

Given a grammar G and a string s, the first step in parsing is to convert the grammar into one in *Chomsky normal form,* which is defined below. Although a dynamic program could be written to work directly for any context-free grammar, it runs much faster if the grammar is converted first.

The Parsing Problem:

Instance: An instance consists of $\langle G, T_{start}, s \rangle$, where G is a grammar in Chomsky normal form, T_{start} is the nonterminal of G designated as the start symbol, and s is the string $\langle a_1, \ldots, a_n \rangle$ of terminal symbols to be generated. The grammar G consists of a set of nonterminal symbols $V = \langle T_1, \ldots, T_{|V|} \rangle$ and a set of rules $\langle r_1, \ldots, r_m \rangle$. The definition of Chomsky normal form is that each rule r_q has one of the following three forms:

- $A_q \Rightarrow B_q C_q$, where A_q, B_q, and C_q are nonterminal symbols.
- $A_q \Rightarrow b_q$, where b_q is a terminal symbol.
- $T_{start} \Rightarrow \epsilon$, where T_{start} is the start symbol and ϵ is the empty string. This rule may only be used to parse the string $s = \epsilon$. It may not be used within the parsing of a larger string.

Solution: A solution is a partial parsing P, consisting of a tree. Each internal node of the tree is labeled with a nonterminal symbol; the root is labeled with the specified symbol T_{start}. Each internal node must correspond to a rule of the grammar G. For example, for the rule $A \Rightarrow BC$, the node is labeled A and its two children are labeled B and C. In a complete parsing, each leaf of the tree is labeled with a terminal symbol. In a partial parsing, some leaves may still be labeled with nonterminals.

Measure of Success: A parsing P is said to generate the string s if the leaves of the parsing in order form s. The cost of P will be one if it generates the string s, and will be zero otherwise.

Goal: The goal of the problem is, given an instance $\langle G, T_{start}, s \rangle$, to find a parsing P that generates s.

Not Look Ahead One: The grammar G might not be look-ahead-one. For example, in

$$A \Rightarrow B\,C$$
$$A \Rightarrow D\,E$$

you do not know whether to start parsing the string as a B or a D. If you make the wrong choice, you have to back up and repeat the process. However, this problem is a perfect candidate for a dynamic programming algorithm.

The Parsing Abstract Data Type: We will use the following abstract data type to represent parsings. Suppose that there is a rule $r_q = \text{“}A_q \Rightarrow B_q C_q\text{”}$ that generates B_q and C_q from A_q. Suppose as well that the string $s_1 = \langle a_1, \ldots, a_k \rangle$ is generated starting with the symbol B_q using the parsing P_1 (B_q is the root of P_1) and that $s_2 = \langle a_{k+1}, \ldots, a_n \rangle$ is generated from C_q using P_2. Then we say that the string $s = s_1 \circ s_2 = \langle a_1, \ldots, a_n \rangle$ is generated from A_q using the parsing $P = \langle A_q, P_1, P_2 \rangle$.

The Number of Parsings: Usually, the first algorithmic attempts at parsing are some form of brute force algorithm. The problem is that there are an exponential number of parsings to try. This number can be estimated roughly as follows. When parsing, the string of symbols needs to increase from being of size 1 (consisting only of the start symbols) to being of size n (consisting of s). Applying a rule adds only one more symbol to this string. Hence, rules need to be applied $n-1$ times. Each time you apply a rule, you have to choose which of the m rules to apply. Hence, the total number of choices may be $\Theta(m^n)$.

The Question to Ask the Little Bird: Given an instance $\langle G, T_{start}, s \rangle$, we will ask the little bird a question that contains two subquestions about a parsing P that generates s from T_{start}.

The first subquestion is the index q of the rule $r_q = \text{“}T_{start} \Rightarrow B_q C_q\text{”}$ that is applied first to our start symbol T_{start}. Although this is useful information, I don't see how it alone could lead to a subinstance.

We don't know P, but we do know that P generates $s = \langle a_1, \ldots, a_n \rangle$. It follows that, for some $k \in [1..n]$, after P applies its first rule $r_q = \text{“}T_{start} \Rightarrow B_q C_q\text{”}$, it then generates the string $s_1 = \langle a_1, \ldots, a_k \rangle$ from B_q and the string $s_2 = \langle a_{k+1}, \ldots, a_n \rangle$ from C_q, so that overall it generates $s = s_1 \circ s_2 = \langle a_1, \ldots, a_n \rangle$. Our second subquestion asked of the bird is to tell us this k that splits the string s.

Help from Friend: What we do not know about the parsing tree P is how B_q generates $s_1 = \langle a_1, \ldots, a_k \rangle$ and how C_q generates $s_2 = \langle a_{k+1}, \ldots, a_n \rangle$. Hence, we ask our friends for optimal parsings for the subinstances $\langle G, B_q, s_1 \rangle$ and $\langle G, C_q, s_2 \rangle$. They respond with the parsings P_1 and P_2. We conclude that $P = \langle T_{start}, P_1, P_2 \rangle$ generates $s = s_1 \circ s_2 = \langle a_1, \ldots, a_n \rangle$ from T_{start}. If either friend gives us a parsing with zero cost, then we know that no parsing consistent with the information provided by the bird is possible. The cost of our parsings in this case is zero as well. This can be achieved by setting the cost of the new parsing to be the minimum of those for P_1 and for P_2. The line of code will be $cost_{\langle q,k \rangle} = \min(cost[B_q, 1, k], cost[C_q, k+1, n])$.

The Set of Subinstances: The set of subinstances that get called by the recursive program consisting of you, your friends, and their friends is $\{\langle G, T_h, a_i, \ldots, a_j \rangle \mid h \in V, 1 \le i \le j \le n\}$.

> **Closed:** We know that this set contains all subinstances generated by the recursive algorithm because it contains the initial instance and is closed under the sub operation. Consider an arbitrary subinstance $\langle G, T_h, a_i, \ldots, a_j \rangle$ in the set. Its subinstances are $\langle G, B_q, a_i, \ldots, a_k \rangle$ and $\langle G, C_q, a_{k+1}, \ldots, a_j \rangle$, which are both in the set.

317

> **Generating:** Some of these subinstances will not be generated. However, most of our instances will.

Constructing a Table Indexed by Subinstances: The table will be three-dimensional. The solution for the subinstance $\langle G, T_h, a_i, \ldots, a_j \rangle$ will be stored in the entry $Table[h, i, j]$ for $h \in V$ and $1 \le i \le j \le n$. See Figure 19.4.

The Order in Which to Fill the Table: The size of the subinstance $\langle G, T_h, a_i, \ldots, a_j \rangle$ is the length of the string to be generated, i.e., $j - i + 1$. We will start with smaller strings and then move to longer and longer strings.

Base Cases: One base case is the subinstance $\langle G, T_{start}, \epsilon \rangle$. This empty string ϵ is parsed with the rule $T_{start} \Rightarrow \epsilon$, assuming that this is a legal rule. The other base cases are the subinstances $\langle G, A_q, b_q \rangle$. This string, consisting of the single character b_q, is parsed with the rule $A_q \Rightarrow b_q$, assuming that this is a legal rule.

Constructing an Optimal Solution:

    algorithm *ParsingWithAdvice*($\langle G, T_h, a_i, \ldots, a_j \rangle$, *birdAdvice*)

    ⟨ *pre-* & *post-cond*⟩*:* Same as *Parsing* except with advice.

    begin

        $\langle q, k \rangle = birdAdvice[h, i, j]$

        if($i = j$) then

            Rule r_q must have the form "$A_q \Rightarrow b_q$", where A_q is T_h and b_q is a_i

            Parsing $P = \langle T_h, a_i \rangle$

        else

            Rule r_q must have the form "$A_q \Rightarrow C_q B_q$", where A_q is T_h.

            $P_1 = ParsingWithAdvice(\langle G, B_q, a_i, \ldots, a_k \rangle,\ birdAdvice)$

            $P_2 = ParsingWithAdvice(\langle G, C_q, a_{k+1}, \ldots, a_j \rangle,\ birdAdvice)$

            Parsing $P = \langle T_h, P_1, P_2 \rangle$

        end if

        return(P)

    end algorithm

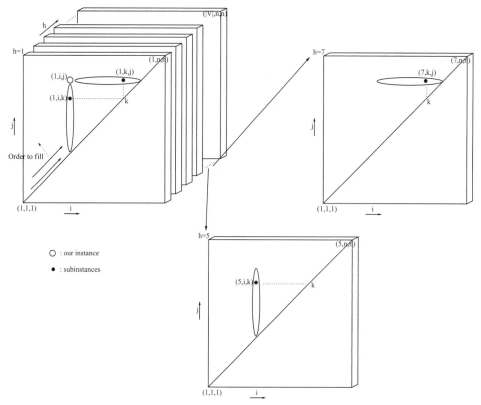

Figure 19.4: The dynamic programming table for parsing. The table entry corresponding to the instance $\langle G, T_1, a_i, \ldots, a_j \rangle$ is represented by the little circle. Using the rule $T_1 \Rightarrow T_1 T_1$, the subinstances $\langle G, T_1, a_i, \ldots, a_k \rangle$ and $\langle G, T_1, a_{k+1}, \ldots, a_j \rangle$ are formed. Using the rule $T_1 \Rightarrow T_5 T_7$, the subinstances $\langle G, T_5, a_i, \ldots, a_k \rangle$ and $\langle G, T_7, a_{k+1}, \ldots, a_j \rangle$ are formed. The table entries corresponding to these subinstances are represented by the dots within the ovals.

EXERCISE 19.7.1 *(See solution in Part Five.) (a) Give the code for the parsing algorithm. (b) Give the running time for this algorithm.*

19.8 Designing Dynamic Programming Algorithms via Reductions

Sometimes, when trying to develop an algorithm for a new problem, it is easier to look for the similarities between your new problem and a problem that you already have an algorithm for. With these insights you can make the new algorithm similar to the old. When done formally, this is called doing a *reduction* from the one problem to the another. Chapter 20 covers these ideas in depth. Here we will be looking for similarities between problems more informally. We will start by using this technique to developing a dynamic programming algorithm for a harder version of the event scheduling problem.

Event Scheduling Problem: The problem is to schedule a tour trying to attend the greatest worth of events possible. Unlike the version from Section 19.3, the events occur at different locations. An instance is $\langle E, d \rangle$. Here $E = \{E_1, E_2, \ldots, E_n\}$ is a set of n events. For $j \in [n]$, event E_j is specified by $\langle s_j, f_j, w_j \rangle$, where s_j its start time, f_j its finishing time, and w_j its worth in dollars. The events occur at different locations. For each pair of events E_j and $E_{j'}$, $d_{j,j'}$ is the time required to travel between the locations of these events. Note that the second parameter d is an n-by-n matrix.

A solution is a schedule of events to attend. This includes which events you attend and the order that you attend them, (e.g., $S = \langle E_5, E_{32}, E_{16}, \ldots, E_{21} \rangle$. The restriction is that to attend an event, you must get to the location of the event before it starts and you must stay until it completes. More formally, suppose after you attend event E_j, you next attend event $E_{j'}$. Now E_j finishes at time f_j, and $E_{j'}$ starts at time $s_{j'}$. Hence, you have $s_{j'} - f_j$ time to travel the distance $d_{j,j'}$ between them. This requires $d_{j,j'} \le s_{j'} - f_j$. (Note that we assume that the distances $d_{j,j'}$ meet the triangle inequality, so that if from event E_j you can reach $E_{j'}$ and from event $E_{j'}$ you can reach $E_{j''}$, then by transitivity from event E_j you can reach $E_{j''}$.)

The worth of a solution is the total of the worths w_j of the events attended. The goal is to maximize the worth of the schedule.

Dynamic Programming: Start by attempting to design a dynamic programming algorithm for this problem. Do not be surprised if you find it hard. This is why we are going to compare this problem with a previously known problem.

Similarity to Best Path: The solution to this problem is a schedule of events, which effectively is a path through a subset of the events. We have looked at many algorithms for finding a best path within graphs, so let us try to model this problem with a graph.

Reduction: Given an instance of $\langle E, d \rangle$ of the scheduling problem, we solve it as follows. We first map it to an instance of the graph problem. Our graph algorithm finds the best path with in this graph. Then we map this best path to a solution of the scheduling problem.

Forming a Graph Instance: We now consider how to form a graph representing a given set of events.

> **Nodes:** A solution to the scheduling problem is a *path* of events, and to the graph problem is a *path* of nodes. This indicates a link between events and nodes. Hence, in the graph, we construct a node for each event e_j.

Edges: In the graph problem, whether or not there is an edge between two nodes indicates whether or not the path can travel from the one node to the other. Hence, for each pair of events e_j and $e_{j'}$, we add the directed edge $\langle e_j, e_{j'} \rangle$ if e_j can proceed $e_{j'}$ in the schedule. More formally, $\langle e_j, e_{j'} \rangle$ is an edge if and only if $d_{j,j'} \le s_{j'} - f_j$. So far the correspondence between these problems is good, because every path through this graph corresponds to a legal schedule of events and vice versa.

Nodes s and t: The standard problems for finding paths in a graph assume that the input specifies a start node s and a finishing node t, whereas the scheduling algorithm does not specify a first or last event to attend. The standard way to get around this problem is to simply add an extra *start* event e_s and *final* event e_t. Giving event e_s finishing time $f_s = -\infty$ means that imposing the constraint that the schedule starts with e_s does not affect which schedules are legal, because one can get from event e_s to any other event. Giving event e_s worth $w_s = 0$ means that including event s does not change the worth of the final solution. Similarly, let $s_t = \infty$ and $w_t = 0$. From the graph perspective, we add two new nodes s and t and a directed edge from s to every other node and from every node to t.

Costs and Weights: The worth or cost of a path is also different in the two problems. The worth of a schedule is the sum of the worths of the events, which becomes the sum of the weights of the nodes, while the worth or cost of a path through a graph tends to be defined as the sum of the weights of the edges. This difference, however, should not be too significant. One option is to go back to the graph path algorithms and try to get them to work where the nodes and not the edges have weights. Another option is to simply shift the weight of each event onto the outgoing edges. The edges $\langle e_i, e_j \rangle$ and $\langle e_i, t \rangle$ will have the value v_i of the first event e_i. The edges $\langle s, e_j \rangle$ will have the value zero.

Minimize or Maximize: Another difference between these problems is that the scheduling problem is looking for the schedule of maximum value, whereas the graph problem is looking for the path of minimum value. It turns out that finding the maximum weighted path in a general directed graph is a hard problem. This motivates looking at other structures related to the graph that we know.

The Longest Weighted Path within a Directed Level Graph: Recall the dynamic programming algorithm for finding the shortest weighted path within a directed level graph that is given in Sections 18.1 and 18.2. Here the nodes can be leveled so that all the edges go forward. In turns out that minimal changes are needed to this algorithm so that it instead finds the longest weighted path within a directed level graph, i.e., solves the same problem but finds a path from s to t with the largest weight. When taking the best of the best, we simply take the max and not the min path. Because there are no cycles, we don't have to worry about paths that cycle in order to have longer weight. Hence, the proof of correctness goes through just as it did before.

Leveled: In order to use this leveled graph algorithm, we need to make sure that the graph that arises from the scheduling problem is in fact leveled. The level of a node e_j can be the start time s_j of the corresponding event. The rules for when edges are added ensure that each edge is directed from some node to a node in a lower level.

Mapping Back the Algorithm: Given this similarity between these two problems, let us recall the dynamic programming algorithm given in Section 18.2 for finding the shortest weighted path within a directed level graph, and let us use it to find a dynamic programming algorithm for the event scheduling problem.

Set of Instances: A key part of a dynamic programming algorithm is the set of subinstances solved. Starting with the instance $\langle G, s, t \rangle$ and looking for the shortest path from s to t, the algorithm finds the shortest path from s to each node v_i, so that the complete set of subinstances solved by the dynamic programming algorithm will be $\{\langle G, s, v_i \rangle | v_i\}$. Similarly, for the scheduling problem, given the instance $\langle E, d \rangle$, the set of subinstances will be $\{\langle E, d, i \rangle | e_i\}$, where the instance $\langle E, d, i \rangle$ asks for the best schedule of events $S = \langle e_5, e_{32}, e_{16}, \ldots, e_{21}, e_i \rangle$ that ends in event e_i. Note that there may be events that occur after event e_i, but the solution schedule is not allowed to attend them.

The Bird–Friend Algorithm: Given an instance $\langle E, d, i \rangle$, we know that the second to last event before e_i in the optimal solution must be an event e_k for which $d_{k,i} \leq s_i - f_k$. We ask the bird to tell us this k. We get the friend to solve the instance $\langle E, d, k \rangle$. Our solution is the same with e_i added on the end. The value of our solution is the same with v_k added in.

The Code: The final code to solve the event scheduling problem is almost identical to that for finding the shortest weighted path within a directed level graph.

algorithm *Schedule*(E, d)

$\langle$ *pre-cond* $\rangle$: An instance consists of a set of events $E = \{e_j\}$, with start time s_j, finishing time f_j, worth w_j, and distances $d_{j,j'}$ between them.

$\langle$ *post-cond* $\rangle$: *optSol* is an optimal valid schedule of events that ends with event e_n.

begin
    Add an imaginary start event $s = e_0$ with $s_0 = f_0 = -\infty$.
    Add an imaginary finishing event $s = e_{n+1}$ with $s_{n+1} = f_{n+1} = \infty$.
    Sort the events by starting time.
    % Table: *optSol*[i] stores an optimal schedule of events ending with e_i and *costSol*[i] its cost.
    table[$0..n + 1$] *optCost, birdAdvice*

% Base case: The only base case is for the optimal set ending in e_0. Its solution consists of the empty set with cost zero.

% $optSol[0] = \emptyset$

$optCost[0] = 0$

$birdAdvice[0] = \emptyset$

% General cases: Loop over subinstances in the table.

for $i = 1$ to $n + 1$

    % Solve instance $\langle E, d, i \rangle$, and fill in table entry $\langle i \rangle$.

    % Try each possible bird answer.

    for each k for which $d_{k,i} \leq s_i - f_k$

        % The bird–friend algorithm: The last event must be e_i. The bird tells us that the second to last event is e_k. We ask the friend for an optimal set ending in e_k. He gives us $optSol[k]$, which he has stored in the table. To this we add e_i. This gives us $optSol_k$ which is a best solution ending in e_i from amongst those paths consistent with the bird's answer.

        % $optSol_k = optSol[k] + e_i$

        $optCost_k = optCost[k] + v_i$

    end for

    % Having the best, $optSol_k$, for each bird's answer k, we keep the best of these best.

    $k_{min} =$ a k that maximizes $optCost_k$

    % $optSol[i] = optSol_{k_{max}}$

    $optCost[i] = optCost_{k_{max}}$

    $birdAdvice[i] = k_{max}$

end for

$optSol = SchedulingWithAdvice(\langle E, d \rangle, birdAdvice)$

return $\langle optSol, optCost[n + 1] \rangle$

end algorithm

Running Time: The number of subinstances is $n + 1$, and the number of bird answers is at most $n + 1$. Hence, the running time is $O(n^2)$.

Bigger-Is-Smarter Elephant Problem: We will now consider another problem.

Instances: A set of elephants $E = \{e_1, e_2, ..., e_n\}$, where $e_i = \langle w_i, s_i, v_i \rangle$ represents the ith elephant, w_i its weight, s_i its intelligence, and v_i its value. (To make life easier, assume that the weights and intelligences are unique values, i.e., $w_i \neq w_j$ and $s_i \neq s_j$.)

Solutions: A subset of elephants $S \subseteq E$ for which bigger is smarter.

Formally, $\forall i, j \in S$, $[[w_i < w_j]$ iff $[s_i < s_j]]$. An equivalent way of looking at it is that if you were to sort the elephants in S in increasing order of their weight, then this same order would sort them with respect to intelligence. (Hint: It is useful to assume that the elephants in the solution are sorted in this way.)

Measure of Success: The cost of the solution is the sum of the values of the elephants, $\sum_{i \in S} v_i$.

Goal: We should find a maximum-valued solution.

EXERCISE 19.8.1 *Design a dynamic programming algorithm for the bigger-is-smarter elephant problem by comparing it, as done previously, with the problem of finding the longest weighted path within a directed level graph problem.*

EXERCISE 19.8.2 *(See solution in Part Five.) Design a dynamic programming algorithm for the bigger-is-smarter elephant problem by comparing it with the longest-common-subsequence problem given in Section 19.1. To do this the LCS problem needs to be generalized to have weights on the letters.*

20 Reductions and NP-Completeness

A giraffe with its long neck is a very different beast than a mouse, which is different than a snake. However, Darwin and gang observed that the first two have some key similarities, both being social, nursing their young, and having hair. The third is completely different in these ways. Studying similarities and differences between things can reveal subtle and deep understandings of their underlining nature that would not have been noticed by studying them one at a time. Sometimes things that at first appear to be completely different, when viewed in another way, turn out to be the same except for superficial, cosmetic differences. This section will teach how to use reductions to discover these similarities between different optimization problems.

Reduction $P_1 \leq_{poly} P_2$: We say that we can *reduce* problem P_1 to problem P_2 if we can write a polynomial-time $(n^{\Theta(1)})$ algorithm for P_1 using a supposed algorithm for P_2 as a subroutine. (Note we may or may not actually have an algorithm for P_2.) The standard notation for this is $P_1 \leq_{poly} P_2$.

Why Reduce? A reduction lets us compare the time complexities and underlying structures of the two problems. Reduction is useful in providing algorithms for new problems (upper bounds), for giving evidence that there are no fast algorithms for certain problems (lower bounds), and for classifying problems according to their difficulty.

Upper Bounds: From the reduction $P_1 \leq_{poly} P_2$ alone, we cannot conclude that there is a polynomial-time algorithm for P_1. But it does tell us that if there is a polynomial-time algorithm for P_2, then there is one for P_1. This is useful in two ways. First, it allows us to construct algorithms for new problems from known algorithms for other problems. Moreover, it tells us that P_1 is *at least as easy as P_2*.

> Hot Dogs $\leq_{poly}$ **Linear Programming:** Section 15.4 describes how to solve the problem of making a cheap hot dog using an algorithm for linear programming.

Bipartite Matching $\leq_{poly}$ **Network Flows:** We will develop an algorithm for bipartite matching in Section 20.4 that uses the network flow algorithm.

Lower Bounds: The contrapositive of the last statement is that if there is not a polynomial-time algorithm for P_1, then there cannot be one for P_2 (otherwise there would be one for P_1.) This tells us that P_2 is *at least as hard as* P_1.

(Any Optimization Problem) $\leq_{poly}$ **CIR-SAT:** This small-looking statement, proved by Steve Cook in 1971, has become one of the foundations of theoretical computer science. There are many interesting optimization problems. Some people have worked hard on discovering fast algorithms for this one and others have done the same for that one. Cook's theorem shows that it is sufficient to focus on the optimization problem CIR-SAT, because if you can solve it quickly, then you can solve them all quickly. However, after many years of working hard, people have given up and strongly suspect that at least one optimization problem is hard. This gives strong evidence that CIR-SAT is hard. Cook's theorem is proved (and the problems defined) in Section 20.1.

CIR-SAT $\leq_{poly}$ **3-COL:** See Section 20.3. This states that the optimization problem 3-COL is as hard as CIR-SAT, already known to be hard problem. This gives evidence that 3-COL is also hard. Moreover, reductions are transitive, meaning that $P_1 \leq_{poly} P_2$ and $P_2 \leq_{poly} P_3$ automatically gives that $P_1 \leq_{poly} P_3$. Hence, together these last two statements give that (any optimization problem) $\leq_{poly}$ 3-COL.

3-COL $\leq_{poly}$ **Course Scheduling, 3-COL** $\leq_{poly}$ **Independent Set, 3-COL** $\leq_{poly}$ **3-SAT:** These give evidence that course scheduling, independent set, and 3-SAT are hard. See Sections 20.2 and 20.3.

(Halting Problem) $\leq_{poly}$ **(What Does This Turing Machine Do):** It can be proved that the *halting problem* (given a Turing machine M and an input I, does the M halt on I?) is undecidable (no algorithm can always answer it correctly in finite time). Given this, reductions can be used to prove that almost any problem asking what the computation of a given Turing machine does is also undecidable.

Reverse Reductions: Knowing $P_1 \leq_{poly} P_2$ and knowing that there is not a polynomial-time algorithm for P_2 does not tell us anything about the whether there is a polynomial-time algorithm for P_1. Though it does tell us that the algorithm for P_1 given in the reduction does not work, there well may be another, completely different algorithm for P_1. Similarly, knowing that there is a polynomial-time algorithm for P_1 does not tell us anything about whether there is one for P_2. To reach these two conclusions, you must prove the reverse reduction $P_2 \leq_{poly} P_1$.

Classifying Problems: Reductions are used to classify problems.

> **The Same Problem Except for Superficial Differences:** More than just being able to compare their time complexities, knowing $P_1 \leq_{poly} P_2$ and $P_2 \leq_{poly} P_1$ reveals that the two problems are somehow fundamentally the same problem, asking the same types of questions. Sometimes this similarity is quite superficial. They simply use different vocabulary. However, at other times this connection between the problems is quite surprising, providing a deeper understanding of each of the problems. One way in which we can make a reduction even more striking is by restricting the algorithm for the one to call the algorithm for the other only once. Then the mapping between them is even more direct.

> **NP-Completeness:** We have shown that the optimization problems CIR-SAT, 3-COL, course scheduling, independent set, and 3-SAT are all reducible to each other and in that sense are all fundamentally the same problem. In fact, there are thousands of very different problems that are equivalent to these. These problems are said to be *NP-complete*. We discuss this more in Section 20.2.

> **Halting-Problem Completeness:** Another important class defined in this way consists of all problems that are equivalent to the halting problem.

20.1 Satisfiability Is at Least as Hard as Any Optimization Problem

In Chapter 13 we saw that *optimization problems* involve searching through the exponential set of solutions for an instance to find one with optimal cost. Though there are quick (i.e., polynomial) algorithms for some of these problems, for most of them the best known algorithms require $2^{\Theta(n)}$ time on the worst case input instances, and it is strongly believed that there are no polynomial-time algorithms for them. The main reason for this belief is that many smart people have devoted many years of research to looking for fast algorithms and have not found them. This section uses reductions to prove that some of these optimization problems are universally hard, or *complete*, among the class of optimization problems, because if you could design an algorithm to solve such a problem quickly, then you could translate this algorithm into one that solves any optimization problem quickly. Conversely (and more likely), if there is even one optimization problem that cannot be solved quickly, then none of these complete problems can be either. Proving in this way that a problem that your boss wants you to solve is hard is useful, because you will know not to spend much time trying to design an all-purpose algorithm for it.

(Any Optimization Problem) $\leq_{poly}$ **CIR-SAT:** This reduction will prove the satisfiability problem is complete for the class of optimization problems, meaning that it is universally hard for this class.

The Circuit Satisfiability Problem: This famous computational problem, CIR-SAT, requires one to find a satisfying assignment for a given circuit. Section 17.4 gives a recursive backtracking algorithm for the satisfiability problem, but in the worst case its running time is $2^{\Theta(n)}$.

Circuit: A *circuit* can be either a useful notation for describing an algorithm in detail or a practical thing built in silicon in your computer.

Construction: It is built with *AND*, *OR*, and *NOT* gates. At the top are n wires labeled with the binary variables $x_1, x_2, \ldots, x_n$. To specify the circuit's input, each of these will take on either 1 or 0, *true* or *false*, 5 volts or 0 volts. Each *AND* gate has two wires coming into it, either from an input x_i or from the output of another gate. An *AND* gate outputs *true* if both of its inputs are *true*. Similarly, each *OR* gate outputs *true* if at least one of its inputs is *true*, and each *NOT* gate outputs *true* if its single input is

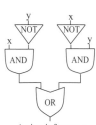

A circuit for $x \oplus y$

false. We will only consider circuits that have no cycles, so these *true* and *false* values percolate down to the output wires. There will be a single output wire if the circuit computes a *true–false* function of its input $x_1, x_2, \ldots, x_n$ and will have m output wires if it outputs an m-bit string, which can be used to encode some required information.

Binary Endoding: The function f that you want to compute may take as input some abstract object like a graph G and return another abstract object, like a path through this graph; however, whether the computation of f is done by a Java program, a Turing machine, or a circuit, these abstract objects first need to be encoded into strings of zeros and ones.

Compute Any Function: Given any function $f : \{0, 1\}^n \to \{0, 1\}^m$, a circuit can compute it with a most $O(nm \cdot 2^n)$ gates as follows. For any fixed input instance $\langle x_1, x_2, \ldots, x_n \rangle = \langle 1, 0, \ldots, 1 \rangle$, a circuit can say "the input is this fixed instance" simply by computing $[(x_1 = 1) \; AND \; NOT(x_2 = 1) \; AND \ldots AND \, (x_n = 1)]$. Then the circuit computes the ith bit of the function's output by outputting 1 if ["the input is this fixed instance" *OR* "this instance" *OR* ... *OR* "this instance"], where each instance is listed for which the ith bit of the function's output is 1.

Polynomial Size for Polynomial Time: More importantly, given any algorithm whose Turing machine's running time is $T(n)$ and given any fixed integer n, there is an easily constructed circuit with at most $\Theta(T(n)^2)$ gates that computes the output of the algorithm given any n-bit input instance. Change the definition of a Turing machine slightly so that each cell is big enough so that the cell currently being pointed to by the head can store not only its contents but also the current state of the machine. This cell's contents can be encoded with $\Theta(1)$ bits. Because the Turing machine uses only $T(n)$ time, it can use at most the first $T(n)$ cells of memory. For each of the $T(n)$ steps of the algorithm, the circuit will have a row of $\Theta(1) \cdot T(n)$ wires whose values encode the contents of memory of these $T(n)$ cells during this time step. The gates of the circuit between these rows of wires compute the next contents of memory from the current contents. Because the contents of cell i at time t depend only on the contents of cells $i - 1$, i, and $i + 1$ at time $t - 1$ and each of these is only a $\Theta(1)$ number of bits, this dependence can computed using a circuit with $\Theta(1)$ gates. This is repeated in a matrix of $T(n)$ time steps and $T(n)$ cells, for a total of $\Theta(T(n)^2)$ gates. At the bottom, the circuit computes the output of the function from the contents of memory of the Turing machine at time $T(n)$.

Circuit Satisfiability Specification: The CIR-SAT problem takes as input a circuit with a single *true–false* output and returns an assignment to the variables $x_1, x_2, \ldots, x_n$ for which the circuit gives *true*, if such an assignment exists.

Optimization Problems: This reduction will select a generic optimization problem and show that CIR-SAT is at least as hard as it is. To do this, we need to have a clear definition of what a generic optimization problem looks like.

Definition: Each such problem has a set of instances that might be given as input; each instance has a set of potential solutions, some of which are valid; and each solution has a cost. The goal, given an instance, is to find one of its valid solutions with optimal cost. An important feature of an optimization problem is that there are polynomial-time algorithms for the following:

Valid(I, S): Given an instance I and a potential solution S, there is an algorithm *Valid*(I, S) running in time $|I|^{O(1)}$ that determines if I is a valid instance for the optimization problem and that S is a valid solution for I.

Cost(S): Given a valid solution S, there is an algorithm *Cost*(S) running in time $|I|^{O(1)}$ that computes the cost of the solution S.

Example: Course Scheduling: Given the set of courses requested by each student and the set of time slots available, find a schedule that minimizes the number of conflicts.

I: The set of courses requested by each student and the set of time slots available

S: A schedule specifies at which time start each course will be taught.

Valid(I, S): An algorithm that returns whether the schedule S allocates each course requested in I to exactly one time slot provided in I.

Cost(*S*): A conflict occurs in the schedule when two courses requested by the same student are scheduled at the same time. Cost (*S*) is an algorithm that returns the number of conflicts in the schedule *S*.

Alg for the Optimization Problem: Given a fast algorithm $Alg_{CIR\text{-}SAT}$ for CIR-SAT and the descriptions $Valid(I, S)$ and $Cost(S)$ of an optimization problem *P* we will now design a fast algorithm Alg_P for the optimization problem and use it to prove that the problem CIR-SAT is at least as hard as the optimization problem, i.e. that $P \leq_{poly}$ CIR-SAT.

329

Binary Search for Cost: Given some instance I_P of the optimization problem, Alg_P's first task is to determine the cost c_{opt} of the optimal solution for *I*. Alg_P starts by determining whether or not there is a valid solution for *I* that has cost at least $c = 1$. If it does, Alg_P repeats this with $c = 2, 4, 8, 16, \ldots$. If it does not, Alg_P tries $c = 0, -1, -2, -4, \ldots$, until it finds c_1 and c_2 between which it knows the cost of an optimal solution lies. Then it does binary search to find c_{opt}. The last step is to find a solution for *I* that has this optimal cost.

Finding a Solution with Given Cost: Alg_P determines whether *I* has a solution *S* with cost at least *c* or finds a solution with cost c_{opt}, as follows. Alg_P will construct a circuit *C* and calls the algorithm $Alg_{CIR\text{-}SAT}$, which provides a satisfying assignment to *C*. Alg_P wants the satisfying assignment that $Alg_{CIR\text{-}SAT}$ provides to be the solution *S* that it needs. Hence, Alg_P designs *C* to be satisfied by the assignment *S* only if *S* is a solution *S* for *I* with a cost as required, i.e., $C(S) \equiv$ [$Valid(I, S)$ and $Cost(S) \geq c$]. Because there are polynomial-time algorithms for $Valid(I, S)$, for $Cost(S)$, and for $\geq$, the algorithm Alg_P can easily construct such a circuit $C(S)$. If such a solution *S* satisfying *C* exists, then $Alg_{CIR\text{-}SAT}$ kindly provides one.

This completes the reduction $P \leq_{poly}$ CIR-SAT of any Optimization problem to CIR-SAT.

EXERCISE 20.1.1 *For each of the following problems, define I, S, Valid(I, S), and Cost(S).*

1. **Graph coloring:** *Given a graph, color its nodes so that two nodes do not have the same color if they have an edge between them. Use as few colors as possible.*
2. **Independent set:** *Given a graph, find a largest subset of the nodes for which there are no edges between any pair in the set.*
3. **Airplane:** *Given the requirements of an airplane, design it, optimizing its performance.*
4. **Business:** *Given a description of a business, make a business plan to maximize its profits.*
5. **Factoring:** *Given an integer, factor it, e.g., $6 = 2 \times 3$.*
6. **Cryptography:** *Given an encrypted message, decode it.*

20.2 Steps to Prove NP-Completeness

In this section we define the class NP and give steps for proving that a computational problem is NP-complete.

Completeness for Nondeterministic Polynomial-Time Decision Problems:
The set of computational problems that are complete (universally hard) for optimization problems is extremely rich and varied. Studying them has become a fascinating field of research.

NP **Decision Problems:** Theoretical computer scientists generally only consider a subclass of the optimization problems, referred to as the class of *nondeterministic polynomial time* problems (NP).

One Level of Cost: Instead of worrying about whether one solution has a better cost than another, we will completely drop the notion of the cost of a solution. *S* will only be considered to be a *valid solution* for the instance *I* if it is a solution with a sufficiently good cost. This is not a big restriction, because if you want to consider solutions with different costs, you can always do binary search, as already done for the cost of the optimal solution.

Decision Problem: Given an instance to the problem, the goal is to determine either *yes* *I* does have a valid solution or *no* it does not.

Witness: A solution for an instance is often referred to as a *witness*, because, though it may take exponential time to find it, if it were provided by a (non-deterministic) fairy godmother, then it could be used in polynomial time to witness the fact that the answer for this instance is yes. In this respect, NP problems are asymmetrical in that there does not seem to be a witness that quickly proves that an instance does not have a solution.

Formal Definition: We say that such a computational problem P is in the class of nondeterministic polynomial-time problems (NP) if there is a polynomial-time algorithm $Valid(I, S)$ that specifies *Yes* when S is a (sufficiently good) solution for the instance I, and *No* if not. More formally, P can be defined as follows:

$$P(I) \equiv [\exists S, \ Valid(I, S)]$$

Examples:

Circuit Satisfiability (CIR-SAT): Circuit satisfiability could be defined as a decision problem: Given a circuit, determine whether there is an assignment that satisfies it.

Graph 3-Coloring (3-COL): Given a graph, determine whether its nodes can be colored with three colors so that two nodes do not have the same color if they have an edge between them.

Course Scheduling: Given the set of courses requested by each student, the set of time slots available, and an integer K, determine whether there is schedule with at most K conflicts.

Cook vs. Karp Reductions: Stephen Cook first proved that CIR-SAT is complete for the class of NP problems. His definition of a reduction $P_1 \leq_{poly} P_2$ is that one can write an algorithm Alg_1 for the problem P_1 using an algorithm Alg_2 for the problem P_2 as a subroutine. In general, this algorithm Alg_1 may call Alg_2 as many times as it likes and do anything it likes with the answers that it receives. Richard Karp later observed that when the problems P_1 and P_2 are sufficiently similar, the algorithm Alg_1 used in the reduction need only call Alg_1 once and answers *Yes* if and only if Alg_1 answers *Yes*. These two definitions of reductions are referred to as *Cook* and *Karp* reductions. Though we have defined Cook reductions because they are more natural, we will consider only Karp reductions from here on.

331

NP-Completeness: For the problem P to be NP-complete, it has to be hard, but not too hard. We say that a computational problem P is *NP-complete* if

> **Sufficiently Hard, $P' \leq_{poly} P$:** We say a problem P is *NP-Hard* if it is as hard as every other problem P' in the class NP. Intuitively, this means that if one did find a quick algorithm for P then this algorithm could be translated into quick algorithms for each NP problem P'. More formally, it means that every language in NP can be polynomially reduced to it using a Karp reduction.

$$\forall \text{ optimization problems } P', \ P' \leq_{poly} P.$$

> To prove this, it is sufficient to prove that our computational problem is at least as hard as some problem already known to be NP-complete. For example, because we now know that CIR-SAT is NP-complete, it is sufficient to prove that CIR-SAT $\leq_{poly} P$.

> **Not Too Hard, $P \in NP$:** On the other hand, for the problem P to be *complete* for the class NP, it has to be sufficiently easy that it is itself in the class. For example, the Halting problem is sufficiently hard to be NP-hard, but is far to hard to be in NP.

The Steps to Prove NP-Completeness: Proving that a problem P is NP-complete can be a bit of an art, but once you get the hang of it, it can be fun. I will now carefully lay out the steps needed. (After step 3, we will use P_{oracle} to denote the problem instead of P, because at that point we will be assuming that we have an oracle for it.)

Running Example: Course Scheduling is NP-Complete: The problem P that we will prove is NP-complete will be the course scheduling problem.

(0) $P \in$ NP: As said, in order for the problem P to be NP-complete, it needs to be sufficiently easy to be in NP. To prove this we effectively need to provide a non-deterministic polynomial time for it. This is accomplished by by providing polynomial-time algorithm *Valid*(I, H) that specifies whether S is a valid solution for instance I.

> **Course Scheduling:** It is not hard to determine in polynomial time whether the instance I and the solution S are properly defined and to check that within this schedule S, the number of times that a student wants to take two courses that are offered at the same time is at most K.

1) What to Reduce to It: An important and challenging step in proving that a problem is NP-complete is deciding which NP-complete problem to reduce to it. We will denote this problem with P_{alg} because later we will be designing an algorithm for it.

> **3-COL $\leq_{poly}$ Course Scheduling:** We will reduce 3-COL to course scheduling, that is, we will prove the reduction 3-COL $\leq_{poly}$ course scheduling. I will save the proof that 3-COL is NP-complete for our next example, because it is much harder.

> **Hint:** You want to choose a problem that is "similar" in nature to yours. In order to have more to choose from, it helps to know a large collection of problems that are NP-complete. There are entire books devoted to this. When in doubt, 3-SAT and 3-COL are good problems to use.

2) What is What: It is important to remember what everything is.

> **3-COL $\leq_{poly}$ Course Scheduling:**
> - P_{alg} = 3COL is the graph 3-coloring problem.
> - $I_{alg} = I_{graph}$, an instance of it, is an undirected graph.
> - $S_{alg} = S_{coloring}$, a potential solution, is a coloring of each of its nodes with either red, blue, or green. It is a valid solution if no edge has two nodes with the same color.
> - Alg_{alg} is an algorithm that takes the graph I_{graph} as input and determines whether it has a valid coloring.
> - P_{oracle} = course scheduling.
> - $I_{oracle} = I_{courses}$, an instance of it, is the set of courses requested by each student, the set of time slots available, and the integer K.
> - $S_{oracle} = S_{schedule}$, a potential solution, is a schedule assigning courses to time slots. It is a valid solution if it has at most K conflicts.
> - Alg_{oracle} is an algorithm that takes $I_{courses}$ as input and determines whether it has a valid schedule.
>
> Such instances may or may not be satisfiable and such potential solutions may or may not be valid.

Warning: Be especially careful about what is an instance and what is a solution for each of the two problems.

3) Direction of Reduction and Code: Another common source of mistakes is doing the reduction in the wrong direction. I recommend not memorizing this direction, but working it out each time. Our goal is to prove that the problem P sufficiently hard to be NP-complete. Hence, you must put P on the hard side of the inequality 3-COL $\leq_{poly} P$ with the problem, say 3-COL, chosen in step 1 on the easy side. At this point, turn your thinking around. Instead of proving P is relatively hard, we will prove that the problem 3-COL is relatively easy. To do this, we must designing a fast algorithm Alg_{alg} for it. Because this is are goal from here on, we will denote the problem 3-COL with P_{alg}. Our belief is that there is not a fast algorithm for this problem. Hence, to help us we will use a supposed fast algorithm Alg_{oracle} for P as a subroutine. Typically for reductions people assume that Alg_{oracle} is an *oracle* meaning that it solves its problem in one time step. Hence, from here on we will use P_{oracle} to denote the problem instead of P. The code for our algorithm for P_{alg} will be as follows.

algorithm $Alg_{alg}(I_{alg})$

⟨ **pre-cond** ⟩: I_{alg} is an instance of P_{alg}.
⟨ **post-cond** ⟩: Determine whether I_{alg} has a solution S_{alg}, and if so, return it.

begin
    $I_{oracle} = InstanceMap(I_{alg})$
    % I_{oracle} is an instance of P_{oracle}
    ⟨ans_{oracle}, S_{oracle}⟩ $= Alg_{oracle}(I_{oracle})$
    % If there is one, S_{oracle} is solution for I_{oracle}
    if($ans_{oracle} = Yes$) then
        $ans_{alg} = Yes$
        $S_{alg} = SolutionMap(S_{oracle})$
    else
        $ans_{alg} = No$
        $S_{alg} = nil$
    end if
    return(⟨ans_{alg}, S_{alg}⟩)
end algorithm

4) Look for Similarities: Though the problems P_{alg} and P_{oracle} may appear to be very different, the goal in this step is to look for underlying similarities. Compare how their solutions, S_{alg} and S_{oracle}, are formed out of their instances, I_{alg} and I_{oracle}. Generally, the instances can be thought of as sets of elements with a set of constraints between them. Can you view their solutions as subsets of these elements or as labelings of them? What allows a solution to form, and what constrains how it is formed? Can you talk about the two problems using the same language? For example, a subset of elements can be viewed as a labeling of the elements with zero and one. Similarly, a labeling of each element e with $\ell_e \in [1..L]$ can be viewed as a subset of the pairs $\langle e, \ell_e \rangle$.

3-COL $\leq_{poly}$ Course Scheduling: A solution $S_{coloring}$ is a coloring that assigns a color to each node. A solution $S_{schedule}$ is a schedule that assigns a time slot to each course. This similarity makes it clear that there is a similarity between the roles of the nodes of I_{graph} and of the courses of $I_{courses}$ and between the colors of $S_{coloring}$ and the time slots of $S_{schedule}$. Each coloring conflict arises from an edge between nodes, and each scheduling conflict arises from a student wanting two courses. This similarity makes it clear that there is a similarity between the roles of the edges of I_{graph} and of the course requests of $I_{courses}$.

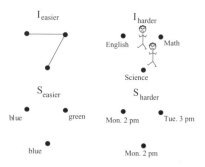

5) *InstanceMap*: You must define a polynomial-time algorithm *InstanceMap*(I_{alg}) that, given an instance I_{alg} of P_{alg}, constructs an instance I_{oracle} of P_{oracle} that has similar sorts of solutions. The main issue is that the constructed instance I_{oracle} has a solution if and only if the given instance I_{alg} has a solution, that is, *Yes* instances, get mapped to *Yes*, instances and *No* to *No*.

3-COL $\leq_{poly}$ Course Scheduling: Given a graph I_{graph} to be colored, we design an instance $I_{courses} = InstanceMap(I_{graph})$ to be scheduled. Using the similarities observed in step 4, our mapping we will have one course for each node of the graph, and one time slot for each of the three colors green, red, and blue. For each edge between nodes u and v in the graph, we will have a student who requests both course u and course v. The coloring problem does not allow any conflicts. Hence, we set $K = 0$.

Not Onto or 1-1: It is important that each instance I_{alg} be mapped to some instance I_{oracle}, but it is not important whether an instance P_{oracle} is mapped to more than one or none at all. In our example, we never mention instances to be scheduled that have more than three time slots or that allow $K > 0$ conflicts.

Warning: Be sure to do this mapping in the correct direction. The first step in designing an algorithm Alg_{alg} is to suppose that you have been given an input I_{alg} for it. Before your algorithm can call the algorithm Alg_{oracle} as a subroutine, your must construct an instance I_{oracle} to give to it.

Warning: Do not define the mapping only for the *Yes* instances or use a solution S_{alg} for I_{alg} for determining the instance I_{oracle} mapped to. The algorithm Alg_{alg} that you are designing is given an instance I_{alg}, but it does not know whether or not the instance has a solution. The whole point is to give an argument that finding a solution may take exponential time. It is safer, when defining the mapping *InstanceMap*(I_{alg}), not to even mention whether the instance I_{alg} has a solution or what that solution might be.

6) *SolutionMap:* You must also define a polynomial-time algorithm *SolutionMap* (S_{oracle}) mapping each valid solution S_{oracle} for the instance $I_{oracle} = InstanceMap(I_{alg})$ you just constructed to a valid solution S_{alg} for the instance I_{alg} that was given as input. Valid solutions can be subtle, and the instance I_{oracle} may have some solutions that you had not intended when you constructed it. One way to help avoid missing some is to throw a much wider net by considering all *potential* solutions. In this step, for each potential solution S_{oracle} for I_{oracle}, you must either give a reason why it is not a valid solution or map it to a solution $S_{alg} = SolutionMap(S_{oracle})$ for I_{alg}. It is fine if some of the solutions that you map happen not to be valid.

> **3-COL $\leq_{poly}$ Course Scheduling:** Given a schedule $S_{schedule}$ assigning course u to time slots c, we define $S_{coloring} = SolutionMap(S_{schedule})$ to be the coloring that colors node u with color c.

> **Warning:** When the instance I_{oracle} you constructed has solutions that you did not expect, there are two problems. First, the unknown algorithm Alg_{oracle} may give you one of these unexpected solutions. Second, there is a danger that I_{oracle} has solutions but your given instance I_{alg} does not. For example, if, in step 5, our I_{oracle} allowed more than three time slots or more than $K = 0$ conflicts, then the instance might have many unexpected solutions. In such cases, you may have to redo step 5, adding extra constraints to the instance I_{oracle} so that it no longer has these solutions.

7) Valid to Valid: In order to prove that the algorithm $Alg_{alg}(I_{alg})$ works, you must prove that if S_{oracle} is a valid solution for $I_{oracle} = InstanceMap(I_{alg})$, then $S_{alg} = SolutionMap(S_{oracle})$ is a valid solution for I_{alg}.

> **3-COL $\leq_{poly}$ Course Scheduling:** Supposing that the schedule is valid, we prove that the coloring is valid as follows. The instance to be scheduled is constructed so that, for each edge of the given graph, there is a student who requests the courses u and v associated with the nodes of this edge. Because the schedule is valid, there are $K = 0$ course conflicts, and hence these courses are all scheduled at different time slots. The constructed coloring therefore allocates different colors to these nodes.

8) *ReverseSolutionMap:* Though we do not need it for the code, for the proof you must define an algorithm *ReverseSolutionMap*(S'_{alg}) mapping in the reverse direction from each potential solution S'_{alg} for the instance I_{alg} to a potential solution S'_{oracle} for the instance I_{oracle}.

3-COL $\leq_{poly}$ Course Scheduling: Given a coloring $S'_{coloring}$ coloring node u with color c, we define $S'_{schedule} = ReverseSolutionMap(S'_{coloring})$ to be the schedule assigning course u to time slots c.

Warning: $ReverseSolutionMap(S'_{alg})$ does not need to be the inverse map of $SolutionMap(S_{oracle})$. You must define the mapping $ReverseSolutionMap(S_{alg})$ for every possible solution S'_{alg}, not just those mapped to by $SolutionMap(S_{oracle})$. Otherwise, there is the danger is that I_{alg} has solutions but your constructed instance I_{oracle} does not.

9) Reverse Valid to Valid: You must also prove the reverse direction: that if S'_{alg} is a valid solution for I_{alg}, then $S'_{oracle} = ReverseSolutionMap(S'_{alg})$ is a valid solution for $I_{oracle} = InstanceMap(I_{alg})$.

3-COL $\leq_{poly}$ Course Scheduling: Supposing that the coloring is valid, we prove that the schedule is valid as follows. The instance to be scheduled is constructed so that each student requests the courses u and v associated with nodes of some edge. Because the coloring is valid, these nodes have been allocated different colors and hence the courses are all scheduled in different time slots. Hence, there will be $K = 0$ course conflicts.

10) Working Algorithm: Given the above steps, it is now possible to prove that if the supposed algorithm Alg_{oracle} correctly solves P_{oracle}, then our algorithm Alg_{alg} correctly solves P_{alg}.

Yes to Yes: We start by proving that Alg_{alg} answers *Yes* when given an instance for which the answer is *Yes*. If I_{alg} is a *Yes* instance, then by the definition of the problem P_{alg}, it must have a valid solution. Let us denote by S'_{alg} one such valid solution. Then by step 9, it follows that $S'_{oracle} = ReverseSolutionMap(S'_{alg})$ is a valid solution for $I_{oracle} = InstanceMap(I_{alg})$. This witnesses the fact that I_{oracle} has a valid solution and hence I_{oracle} is an instance for which the answer is *Yes*. If Alg_{oracle} works correctly as supposed, then it returns *Yes* and a valid solution S_{oracle}. Our code for Alg_{alg} will then return the correct answer *Yes* and $S_{alg} = SolutionMap(S_{oracle})$, which by step 7 is a valid solution for I_{alg}.

No to No: We must now prove the reverse, that if the instance I_{alg} given to Alg_{alg} is a *No* instance, then Alg_{alg} answers *No*. The problem with *No* instances is that they have no witness to prove that they are *No* instances. Luckily, to prove something, it is sufficient to prove the contrapositive. Instead of proving $A \Rightarrow B$, where $A = $ "I_{alg} is a *No* instance" and $B = $ "Alg_{alg} answers *No*", we will prove that $\neg B \Rightarrow \neg A$, where $\neg B = $ "Alg_{alg} answers *Yes*" and $\neg A = $ "I_{alg} is a *Yes* instance". Convince yourself that this is equivalent.

If Alg_{alg} is given the instance I_{alg} and answers *Yes*, our code is such that Alg_{oracle} must have returned *Yes*. If Alg_{oracle} works correctly as supposed, the instance $I_{oracle} = InstanceMap(I_{alg})$ that it was given must be a *Yes* instance. Hence,

I_{oracle} must have a valid solution. Let us denote by S_{oracle} one such valid solution. Then by step 7, $S_{alg} = SolutionMap(S_{oracle})$ is a valid solution for I_{alg}, witnessing I_{alg} being a *Yes* instance. This is the required conclusion $\neg A$.

This completes the proof that if the supposed algorithm Alg_{oracle} correctly solves P_{oracle}, then our algorithm Alg_{alg} correctly solves P_{alg}.

11) Running Time: The remaining step is to prove that the constructed algorithm Alg_{alg} runs in polynomial-time ($|I_{alg}|^{\Theta(1)}$). Steps 5 and 6 require that both $InstanceMap(I_{alg})$ and $SolutionMap(S_{oracle})$ work in polynomial-time. Hence, if P_{oracle} can be solved quickly, then Alg_{alg} runs in polynomial-time. Typically, for reductions people assume that Alg_{oracle} is an *oracle*, meaning that it solves its problem in one time step. Exercise 20.2.5 explores the issue of running time further.

This concludes the proof that $P_{oracle} =$ course scheduling is NP-complete (assuming, of course, that $P_{alg} =$ 3-COL has already been proven to be NP-complete).

EXERCISE 20.2.1 *We began this section by proving (any optimization problem) $\leq_{poly}$ CIR-SAT. To make this proof more concrete, redo it, completing each of the above steps specifically for 3-COL $\leq_{poly}$ CIR-SAT. (Hint: The circuit $I_{oracle} = InstanceMap(I_{alg})$ should have a variable $x_{\langle u,c \rangle}$ for each pair $\langle u, c \rangle$.)*

EXERCISE 20.2.2 *3-SAT is a subset of the CIR-SAT problem in which the input circuit must be a big AND of clauses, each clause must be the OR of at most three literals, and each literal is either a variable or its negation. Prove that 3-SAT is NP-compete by proving that 3-COL $\leq_{poly}$ 3-SAT. (Hint: The answer is almost identical to that for Exercise 20.2.1.)*

EXERCISE 20.2.3 *Let $\overline{\text{CIR-SAT}}$ be the complement of the CIR-SAT problem, namely, the answer is Yes if and only if the input circuit is not satisfiable. Can you prove CIR-SAT $\leq_{poly} \overline{\text{CIR-SAT}}$ using Cook reductions? Can you prove it using Karp reductions?*

EXERCISE 20.2.4 *(See solution in Part Five.) Suppose problem P_1 is a restricted version of P_2, in that they are the same except P_1 is defined on a subset $\mathcal{I}_1 \subseteq \mathcal{I}_2$ of the instances that P_2 is defined on. For example, 3-SAT is a restricted version of CIR-SAT, because both determine whether a given circuit has a satisfying assignment; however, 3-SAT only considers special types of circuits with clauses of three literals. How hard is it to prove $P_1 \leq_{poly} P_2$? How hard is it to prove $P_2 \leq_{poly} P_1$?*

EXERCISE 20.2.5 *(See solution in Part Five.) Suppose that when proving $P_{alg} \leq_{poly} P_{oracle}$, the routines InstanceMap(I_{alg}) and SolutionMap(S_{oracle}) each run in $O(|I_{alg}|^3)$ time, and that the mapping InstanceMap(I_{alg}) constructs from the instance I_{alg} an* instance I_{oracle} that is much bigger, namely, $|I_{oracle}| = |I_{alg}|^2$. Given the following two running times of the algorithm Alg_{oracle}, determine the running time of the algorithm Alg_{alg}. (Careful!)

1. $Time(Alg_{oracle}) = \Theta(2^{n^{\frac{1}{3}}})$
2. $Time(Alg_{oracle}) = \Theta(n^c)$ for some constant c.

20.3 Example: 3-Coloring Is NP-Complete

We will now use the steps again to prove that 3-coloring is NP-complete.

0) In NP: The problem 3-COL is in NP because, given an instance graph I_{graph} and a solution coloring $S_{coloring}$, it is easy to have an algorithm $Valid(I_{graph}, S_{coloring})$ check that each node is colored with one of three colors and that the nodes of each edge have different colors.

1) What to Reduce to It: We will reduce CIR-SAT to 3-COL by proving CIR-SAT $\leq_{poly}$ 3-COL. In Section 20.1 we proved that (any optimization problem) $\leq_{poly}$ CIR-SAT and that 3-COL $\leq_{poly}$ course scheduling. By transitivity, this gives us that CIR-SAT, 3-COL, and course scheduling are each NP-complete problems.

2) What is What:
- P_{alg} is the circuit satisfiability problem (CIR-SAT).
- $I_{circuit}$, an instance of it, is a circuit.
- $S_{assignment}$, a potential solution, is an assignment to the circuit variables x_1, $x_2, \ldots, x_n$.
- P_{oracle} is the graph 3-coloring problem (3-COL).
- I_{graph}, an instance to it, is a graph.
- $S_{coloring}$, a potential solution, is an coloring of the nodes of the graph with three colors.

3) Direction of Reduction and Code: To prove 3-COL is at least as hard, we must prove that CIR-SAT is at least as easy, i.e., CIR-SAT $\leq_{poly}$ 3-COL. To do this, we must design an algorithm for CIR-SAT given an algorithm for 3-COL. The code will be identical to that in Section 20.2.

4) Look for Similarities: An assignment allocates *true or false* values to each variable, which in turn induces *true or false* values to the output of each gate. A coloring allocates one of three colors to each node. This similarity hints at mapping the variables and outputs of each gate to nodes in the graph and mapping *true* to one color and *false* to another. With these ideas in mind, Steven Rudich made a computer search for the smallest graph that behaves like an *OR* gate when colored with three colors. The graph found is shown in Figure 20.1. He calls it an *OR gadget*.

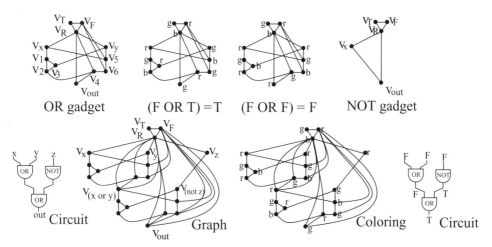

Figure 20.1: On the top, the first diagram is the *OR* gadget. The next two are colorings of this gadget demonstrating (*false or true*) = *true* and (*false or false*) = *false*. The top right diagram is the *NOT* gadget. On the bottom, the first diagram is the circuit given as an instance to SAT. The next is the graph that it is translated into. The next is a 3-coloring of this graph. The last is the assignment for the circuit obtained from the coloring.

Translating between Colors and True/False: The three nodes v_T, v_F, and v_R in the *OR* gadget are referred to as the *pallet*. Because of the edges between them, when the gadget is properly colored, these nodes need to be assigned different colors. We will call whatever color is assigned to the node v_T the color indicating *true*; that assigned to v_F, the color indicating *false*; and that assigned to v_R, the *remaining* color. For example, in all the colorings in Figure 20.1, green (g) indicates *true*, red (r) indicates *false*, and blue (b) is the remaining color.

Input and Output Values: The nodes v_x and v_y in the *OR* gadget act as the gadget's inputs, and the node v_{out} as its output. Because each of these nodes has an edge to node v_R, they cannot be colored with the remaining color. The node will be said to have the value *true*, if it is assigned the same color as v_T, and *false* if the same as v_F. The coloring in the second figure in Figure 20.1 sets $x = false$, $y = true$, and the output = *true*. The coloring in the third figure sets $x = false$, $y = false$, and the output = *false*.

Theorem 20.3.1: Rudich's *OR* gadget acts like an *OR* gate, in that it always can be and always must be colored so that the value of its output node v_{out} is the *OR* of the values of its two input nodes v_x and v_y. Similarly for the *NOT* gate.

Proof: There are four input instances to the gate to consider.

   (*false OR true*) = *true*: If node v_x is colored *false* and v_y is colored *true*, then because v_5 has an edge to each, it must be colored the remaining color. v_6, with edges to v_F and v_5, must be colored *true*. v_4, with edges to v_R and v_6, must be colored *false*. v_{out}, with edges to v_R and v_4, must be colored *true*. The coloring in the second diagram in Figure 20.1 proves that such a coloring is possible.

(*false OR false*) = *false*: If nodes v_x and v_y are both colored *false*, then neither nodes v_1 nor v_3 can be colored *false*. Because of the edge between them, one of them must be *true* and the other the remaining color. Because v_2 has an edge to each of them, it must be colored *false*. v_4, with edges to v_R and v_2, must be colored *true*. v_{out}, with edges to v_R and v_4, must be colored *false*. The coloring in the third diagram in Figure 20.1 proves that such a coloring is possible.

(*true OR true*) = *true*, and (*true OR false*) = *true*: See Exercise 20.3.1 for these cases and for the *NOT* gate.

5) *InstanceMap*, Translating the Circuit into a Graph: Our algorithm for CIR-SAT takes as input a circuit $I_{circuit}$ to be satisfied and, in order to receive help from the 3-COL algorithm, constructs from it a graph $I_{graph} = InstanceMap(I_{circuit})$ to be colored. See the first two diagrams on the bottom of Figure 20.1. The graph will have one pallet of nodes v_T, v_F, and v_R with which to define the *true* and the *false* color. For each variable x_i of the circuit, it will have one node labeled x_i. It will also have one node labeled x_{out}. For each *OR* gate and *NOT* gate in the circuit, the graph will have one copy of the *OR* gadget or the *NOT* gadget. The *AND* gates could be translated into a similar *AND* gadget or translated to $[x \ AND \ y] = [NOT(NOT(x) \ OR \ NOT(y))]$. All of these gadgets share the same three pallet nodes. If in the circuit the output of one gate is the input of another, then the corresponding nodes in the graph are the same. Finally, one extra edge is added to the graph from the v_F node to the v_{out} node.

6) *SolutionMap*, Translating a Coloring into an Assignment: When the supposed algorithm finds a coloring $S_{coloring}$ for the graph $I_{graph} = InstanceMap(I_{circuit})$, our algorithm must translate this coloring into an assignment $S_{assignment} = SolutionMap(S_{coloring})$ of the variables $x_1, x_2, \ldots, x_n$ for the circuit. See the last two diagrams on the bottom of Figure 20.1. The translation is accomplished by setting x_i to *true* if node v_{x_i} is colored the same color as node v_T, and *false* if the same as v_F. If node v_{x_i} has the same color as node v_R, then this is not a valid coloring (because there is an edge in the graph from node v_{x_i} to node v_R) and hence need not be considered.

> **Warning:** Suppose that the graph constructed had a separate node for each time that the circuit used the variable x_i. The statement "set x_i to *true* when the node v_{x_i} has some color" would then be ambiguous, because the different nodes representing x_i might be given different colors.

7) Valid to Valid: Here we must prove that if the supposed algorithm gives us a valid coloring $S_{coloring}$ for the graph $I_{graph} = InstanceMap(I_{circuit})$, then $S_{assignment} = SolutionMap(S_{coloring})$ is an assignment that satisfies the circuit. By the gadget theorem, each gadget in the graph must be colored in a way that acts like the corresponding gate. Hence, when we apply the assignment to the circuit, the output of each gate will have the value corresponding to the color of corresponding node. It is as if the coloring of the graph were performing the computation of the circuit. It follows that the output of the circuit will have the value corresponding to the color of node v_{out}. Because node v_{out} has an edge to v_R and an extra edge to v_F, v_{out} must be colored *true*. Hence, the assignment is one for which the output of the circuit is true.

8) *ReverseSolutionMap:* For the proof we must also define the reverse mapping from each assignment $S_{assignment}$ to a coloring $S_{coloring} = ReverseSolutionMap$ $(S_{assignment})$. Start by coloring the pallet nodes *true*, *false*, and the remaining color. Color each node v_{x_i} *true* or *false* according to the assignment. Then Theorem 20.3.1 states that no matter how the input nodes to a gadget are colored, the entire gadget can be colored with the output node having the color indicated by the output of the corresponding gate.

9) Reverse Valid to Valid: Now we prove that if the assignment $S_{assignment}$ satisfies the circuit, then the coloring $S_{coloring} = ReverseSolutionMap(S_{assignment})$ is valid. Theorem 20.3.1 ensured that each edge in each gadget has two different colors. The only edge remaining to consider is the extra edge. As the colors percolate down the graph, node v_{out} must have color corresponding to the output of the circuit, which must be the true color, because the assignment satisfies the circuit. This ensures that even the extra edge from v_F to v_{out} is colored with two different colors.

10) and 11): These steps are always the same. *InstanceMap*($I_{circuit}$) maps *Yes* circuit instances to *Yes* 3-COL instances and *No* to *No*. Hence, if the supposed algorithm 3-COL works correctly in polynomial-time, then our designed algorithm correctly solves CIR-SAT in polynomial-time. It follows that CIR-SAT $\leq_{poly}$ 3-COL. In conclusion, 3-coloring is NP-complete.

EXERCISE 20.3.1 *(a) Complete the proof of Theorem 20.3.1 by proving the cases (true OR true) = true and (true OR false) = true. (b) Prove a similar theorem for the NOT gadget. See the top right diagram in Figure 20.1.*

EXERCISE 20.3.2 *Verify that each edge in the graph $I_{graph} = InstanceMap(I_{circuit})$ is needed, by showing that if it were not there, then it would be possible for the graph to have a valid coloring even when the circuit is not satisfied.*

EXERCISE 20.3.3 *(See solution in Part Five.) Prove that independent set is NP-compete by proving that 3-COL $\leq$ poly Independent set. (Hint: A 3-coloring for the graph $G_{3\text{-}COL}$ can be thought of as a subset of the pairs $\langle u, c \rangle$ where u is a node of $G_{3\text{-}COL}$ and c is a color. An independent set of the graph G_{Ind} selects a subset of its nodes. Hence, a* *way to construct the graph G_{ind} in the instance $\langle G_{Ind}, N_{Ind} \rangle = InstanceMap(G_{3\text{-}COL})$ would be to have a node for each pair $\langle u, c \rangle$. Be careful when defining the edges for the graph $G_{Ind} = InstanceMap(G_{3\text{-}COL})$ so that each valid independent set of size n in the constructed graph corresponds to a valid 3-coloring of the original graph. If the constructed graph has unexpected independent sets, you may need to add more edges to it.)*

20.4 An Algorithm for Bipartite Matching Using the Network Flow Algorithm

Up to now we have been justifying our belief that certain computational problems are difficult by reducing them to other problems believed to be difficult. Here, we will give an example of the reverse, by proving that the problem of bipartite matching can be solved easily by reducing it to the network flow problem, which we already know is easy because we gave an polynomial-time algorithm for it in Chapter 15.

Bipartite Matching: Bipartite matching is a classic optimization problem. As always, we define the problem by giving a set of instances, a set of solutions for each instance, and a cost for each solution.

> **Instances:** An input instance to the problem is a bipartite graph. A bipartite graph is a graph whose nodes are partitioned into two sets U and V and all edges in the graph go between U and V. See the first diagram in Figure 20.2.

> **Solutions for an Instance:** Given an instance, a solution is a matching. A matching is a subset M of the edges such that no node appears more than once in M. See the last diagram in Figure 20.2.

> **Cost of a Solution:** The cost (or success) of a matching is the number of pairs matched. It is said to be a perfect matching if every node is matched.

> **Goal:** Given a bipartite graph, the goal of the problem is to find a matching that matches as many pairs as possible.

Network Flow: Network flow is another example of an optimization problem that involves searching for a best solution from some large set of solutions.

> **Instances:** An instance $\langle G, s, t \rangle$ consists of a directed graph G and specific nodes s and t. Each edge $\langle u, v \rangle$ is associated with a positive capacity $c_{\langle u,v \rangle}$.

> **Solutions for the Instance:** A solution for the instance is a *flow F*, which specifies a flow $F_{\langle u,v \rangle} \leq c_{\langle u,v \rangle}$ through each edges of the network with no leaking or additional flow at any node.

> **Measure of Success:** The cost (or success) of a flow is the amount of flow out of node s.

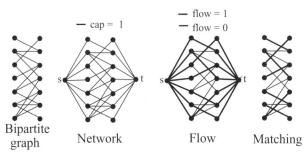

Figure 20.2: The first diagram is the bipartite graph given as an instance to bipartite matching. The next is the network that it is translated into. The next is a flow through this network. The last is the matching obtained from the flow.

Goal: Given an instance $\langle G, s, t \rangle$, the goal is to find an optimal solution, that is, a maximum flow.

Bipartite Matching $\leq_{poly}$ Network Flows: We go through the same steps as before.

3) Direction of Reduction and Code: We will now design an algorithm for bipartite matching given an algorithm for network flows.

4) Look for Similarities: A matching decides which edges to keep, and a flow decides which edges to put flow though. This similarity suggests keeping the edges that have flow through them.

5) *InstanceMap,* **Translating the Bipartite Graphs into a Network:** Our algorithm for bipartite matching takes as input a bipartite graph $G_{bipartite}$. The first step is to translate this into a network $G_{network} = InstanceMap(G_{bipartite})$. See the first two diagrams in Figure 20.2. The network will have the nodes U and V from the bipartite graph, and for each edge $\langle u, v \rangle$ in the bipartite graph, the network has a directed edge $\langle u, v \rangle$. In addition, the network will have a source node s with a directed edge from s to each node $u \in U$. It will also have a sink node t with a directed edge from each node $v \in V$ to t. Every edge out of s and every edge into t will have capacity one. The edges $\langle u, v \rangle$ across the bipartite graph could be given capacity one as well, but they could just as well be given capacity ∞.

6) *SolutionMap,* **Translating a Flow into a Matching:** When the network flow algorithm finds a flow S_{flow} through the network, our algorithm must translate this flow into a matching $S_{matching} = SolutionMap(S_{flow})$. See the last two diagrams in Figure 20.2.

SolutionMap: The translation puts the edge $\langle u, v \rangle$ in the matching if there is a flow of one through the corresponding edge in the network, and not if there is no flow in the edge.

Warning: Be careful to map every possible flow to a matching. The above mapping is ill defined when there is a flow of $\frac{1}{2}$ through an edge. This needs to be fixed and could be quite problematic.

Integer Flow: Luckily, Exercise 15.2.4 proves that if all the capacities in the given network are integers, then the algorithm always returns a solution in which the flow through each edge is an integer. Given that our capacities are all one, each edge will have a flow either of zero or of one. Hence, in our translation, it is well defined whether to include the edge $\langle u, v \rangle$ in the matching or not.

7) Valid to Valid: Here we must prove that if the flow S_{flow} is valid, than the matching $S_{matching}$ is also valid.

Each u Matched at Most Once: Consider a node $u \in U$. The flow into u can be at most one, because there is only one edge into it and it has capacity one. For the flow to be valid, the flow out of this node must equal that into it. Hence, it too can be at most one. Because each edge out of u either has flow zero or one, it follows that at most one edge out of u has flow. We can conclude that u is matched to at most one node $v \in V$.

Each v Matched at Most Once: See Exercise 20.4.1.

Cost to Cost: To be sure that the matching we obtain contains the maximum number of edges, it is important that the cost of the matching $S_{matching} = SolutionMap(S_{flow})$ equal the cost of the flow. The cost of the flow is the amount of flow out of node s, which equals the flow across the cut $\langle U, V \rangle$, which equals the number of edges $\langle u, v \rangle$ with flow of one, which equals the number of edges in the matching, which equals the cost of the matching.

8) *ReverseSolutionMap*: The reverse mapping from each matching $S_{matching}$ to a valid flow $S_{flow} = ReverseSolutionMap(S_{matching})$ is straightforward. If the edge $\langle u, v \rangle$ is in the matching, then put a flow of one from the source s, along the edge $\langle s, u \rangle$ to node u, across the corresponding edge $\langle u, v \rangle$, and then on through the edge $\langle v, t \rangle$ to t.

9) Reverse Valid to Valid: We must also prove that if the matching $S_{matching}$ is valid, then the flow $S_{flow} = ReverseSolutionMap(S_{matching})$ is also valid.

Flow in Equals Flow Out: Because the flow is a sum of paths, we can be assured that the flow in equals the flow out of every node except for the source and the sink. Because the matching is valid, each u and each v is matched at most once. Hence the flows through the edges $\langle s, u \rangle$, $\langle u, v \rangle$, and $\langle v, t \rangle$ will be at most their capacity one.

Cost to Cost: Again, we need to prove that the cost of the flow $S_{flow} =$ *ReverseSolutionMap*($S_{matching}$) is the same as the cost of the matching. See Exercise 20.4.2.

10) and 11): These steps are always the same. *InstanceMap*($G_{bipartite}$) maps bipartite graph instances to network flow instances G_{flow} with the same cost. Hence, because algorithm *Alg*$_{flow}$ correctly solves network flows quickly, our designed algorithm correctly solves bipartite matching quickly.

In conclusion, bipartite matching can be solved in the same time that network flow is solved.

EXERCISE 20.4.1 *Give a proof for the case where each v is matched at most once.*

EXERCISE 20.4.2 *Give a proof that the cost of the flow $S_{flow} = ReverseSolutionMap$ ($S_{matching}$) is the same as the cost of the matching*

EXERCISE 20.4.3 *Section 19.9 constructs three dynamic programming algorithms using reductions. For each of these, carry out the formal steps required for a reduction.*

EXERCISE 20.4.4 *There is a collection of software packages $S_1, \ldots, S_n$ that you are considering buying. These are partitioned into two groups. For those $i \in N \subseteq [n]$, the costs of buying it out ways the benefits and hence it effectively costs you a given amount $b_i \geq 0$ to buy it. For those $j \in P \subseteq [n]$, the benefits out way the costs of buying it and hence it effectively costs you a given amount $b_j \geq 0$ to not buy it. Some of these packages rely on each other; if S_i relies on S_j, then you will incur an additional cost of $a_{\langle i,j \rangle} \geq 0$ if you buy S_i but not S_j. Provide a polynomial-time algorithm to decide the subset $S \subseteq [n]$ of $S_2, \ldots, S_n$ that you should buy. The cost of your solution is $cost(S) = \sum_{i \in S \cap N} b_i + \sum_{j \in \overline{S} \cap P} b_j + \sum_{i \in S, j \in \overline{S}} a_{\langle i,j \rangle}$. (Hint: Do not design a new algorithm but do a reduction to min cut similar to that done for matching the boys and girls.)*

21 Randomized Algorithms

For some computational problems, allowing the algorithm to flip coins (i.e., use a random number generator) makes for a simpler, faster, easier-to-analyze algorithm. The following are the three main reasons.

Hiding the Worst Cases from the Adversary: The running time of a randomized algorithms is analyzed in a different way than that of a deterministic algorithm. At times, this way is fairer and more in line with how the algorithm actually performs in practice. Suppose, for example, that a deterministic algorithm quickly gives the correct answer on most input instances, yet is very slow or gives the wrong answer on a few instances. Its running time and its correctness are generally measured to be those on these worst case instances. A randomized algorithm might also sometimes be very slow or give the wrong answer. (See the discussion of quick sort, Section 9.1). However, we accept this, as long as on every input instance, the probability of doing so (over the choice of random coins) is small.

Probabilistic Tools: The field of probabilistic analysis offers many useful techniques and lemmas that can make the analysis of the algorithm simple and elegant.

Solution Has a Random Structure: When the solution that we are attempting to construct has a random structure, a good way to construct it is to simply flip coins to decide how to build each part. Sometimes we are then able to prove that with high probability the solution obtained this way has better properties than any solution we know how to construct deterministically. Moreover, if we can prove that the solution constructed randomly has extremely good properties with some very small but nonzero probability (for example, $prob = 10^{-100}$), then this proves the existence of such a solution even though we have no reasonably quick way of finding one. Another interesting situation is when the randomly constructed solution very likely has the desired properties, for example with probability 0.999999, but, there is no quick way of testing whether what we have produced has the desired properties.

This chapter considers these ideas further.

21.1 Using Randomness to Hide the Worst Cases

The standard way of measuring the running time and correctness of a deterministic algorithm is based on the worst case input instance chosen by some nasty adversary who has studied the algorithm in detail. This is not fair if the algorithm does very well on all but a small number of very strange and unlikely input instances. On the other hand, knowing that the algorithm works well on most instances is not always satisfactory, because for some applications it is just those hard instances that you want to solve. In such cases, it might be more comforting to use a randomized algorithm that guarantees that on every input instance, the correct answer will be obtained quickly with high probability.

A randomized algorithm is able to flip coins as it proceeds to decide what actions to take next. Equivalently, a randomized algorithm A can be thought of as a set of deterministic algorithms $A_1, A_2, A_3, \ldots$ where A_r is what algorithm A does when the outcome of the coin flips is $r = \langle heads, tails, heads, heads, \ldots, tails \rangle$. Each such deterministic algorithm A_r will have a small set of worst case input instances on which it either gives the wrong answer or runs too slow. The idea is that these algorithms $A_1, A_2, A_3, \ldots$ have different sets of worst case instances. This randomized algorithm is good if for each input instance, the fraction of the deterministic algorithms $A_1, A_2, A_3, \ldots$ for which it is not a worst case instance is at least p. Then when one of these A_r is chosen randomly, it solves this instance quickly with probability at least p.

I sometimes find it useful to consider the analysis of randomized algorithms as a game between an algorithm designer and an adversary who tries to construct input instances that will be bad for the algorithm. In the game, it is not always fair for the adversarial input chooser to know the algorithm first, because then she can choose the instance that is the worst case for this algorithm. Similarly, it is not always fair for the algorithm designer to know the input instance first or even which instances are likely, because then he can design the algorithm to work well on these. The way we analyze the running time of randomized algorithms compromises between these two. In this game, the algorithm designer, without knowing the input instance, must first fix what his algorithm will do given the outcome of the coins. Knowing this, but not knowing the outcomes of the coins, the instance chooser chooses the worst case instance. We then flip coins, run the algorithm, and see how well it does.

Three Models: The following are formal definitions of three models.

Deterministic Worst Case: In a worst case analysis, a deterministic algorithm A for a computational problem P must always give the correct answer quickly:

$$\forall I, \ [A(I) = P(I) \text{ and } Time(A, I) \leq T_{upper}(|I|)]$$

Las Vegas: The algorithm is said to be *Las Vegas* if it is always guaranteed to give the correct answer, but its running time depends on the outcomes of the random coin flips. The goal is to prove that on every input instance, the expected running time is small:

$$\forall I, \ [\forall r, \ A_r(I) = P(I) \text{ and } \text{Exp}_r[Time(A_r, I)] \leq T_{upper}(|I|)]$$

Monte Carlo: The algorithm is said to be *Monte Carlo* if the algorithm is guaranteed to stop quickly, but it can sometimes, depending on the outcomes of the random coin flips, give the wrong answer. The goal is to prove that on every input, the probability of it giving the wrong answer is small:

$$\forall I, \ [Pr_r[A_r(I) \neq P(I)] \leq p_{fails} \text{ and } \forall r, \ Time(A_r, I) \leq T_{upper}(|I|)]$$

The following examples demonstrate these ideas.

Quick Sort: Recall the quick sort algorithm from Section 9.1. The algorithm chooses a pivot element and partitions the list of numbers to be sorted into those that are smaller than the pivot and those that are larger than it. Then it recurses on each of these two parts. The running time varies from $\Theta(n \log n)$ to $\Theta(n^2)$, depending on the choices of pivots.

Deterministic Worst Case: A reasonable choice for the pivot is to always use the element that happens to be located in the middle of the array to be sorted. For all practical purposes, this would likely work well. It would work exceptionally well when the list is already sorted. However, there are some strange inputs, cooked up for the sole purpose of being nasty to this particular implementation of the algorithm, on which the algorithm runs in $\Theta(n^2)$ time. The adversary will provide such an input, giving a worst case time complexity of $\Theta(n^2)$.

Las Vegas: In practice, what is often done is to choose the pivot element randomly from the input elements. This makes it irrelevant in which order the adversary puts the elements in the input instance. The expected computation time is $\Theta(n \log n)$.

The Game Show Problem: The input I to the game show problem specifies which of N doors have prizes behind them. At least half the doors are promised to have prizes. An algorithm A is able to look behind the doors in any order that it likes, but nothing else. It solves the problem correctly when it finds a prize. The running time is the number of doors opened.

Deterministic Worst Case: Any deterministic algorithm fixes the order in which it looks behind the doors. Knowing this order, the adversary places no prizes behind the first $\frac{N}{2}$ doors looked behind.

Las Vegas: In contrast, a random algorithm will look behind doors in random order. It does not matter where the adversary puts the prizes; the probability that one is not found after t doors is $1/2^t$, and the expected time until a prize is found is $\text{Exp}[T] = \sum_t Pr[T = t] \cdot t = 2$.

Monte Carlo: If the promise is that either at least half the doors have prizes or none of them do and if the algorithm stops after 10 empty doors and claims that there are no prizes, then this algorithm is always fast, but gives the wrong answer with probability $1/2^{10}$.

Randomized Primality Testing: An integer x is said to be *composite* if it has factors other than one and itself. Otherwise, it is said to be *prime*. For example, $6 = 2 \times 3$ is composite and $2, 3, 5, 7, 11, 13, 17, \ldots$ are prime. See Chapter 23.1, Example 23.2, for explanations of why it takes $2^{\Theta(n)}$ time to factor an n-bit number.[1] Here I give an easy randomized algorithm, due to Rabin and Miller, for this problem.

> **Fermat's Little Theorem:** Don't worry about the math, but Fermat's little theorem says that if x is prime, then for every $a \in [1, x - 1]$, it is the case that $a^{x-1} \equiv_{(\bmod\ x)} 1$.
>
> If we want to test if x is prime, then we can pick random a's in the interval and see if the equality holds. If the equality does not hold for a value of a, then x is composite. If the equality does hold for many values of a, then we can say that x is probably prime, or a what we call a *pseudoprime*.

> **The Game Show Problem:** Finding an a for which $a^{x-1} \not\equiv_{(\bmod\ x)} 1$ is like finding a prize behind door a. See Exercise 21.1.1.

Randomized Counting: In many applications, one wants to count the number of occurrences of something. This problem can often be expressed as follows: Given the input instance x, count the number of y for which $f(x, y) = 1$. It is likely very difficult to determine the exact number. However, a good way to approximate this number is to randomly choose some large number of values y. For each, test whether $f(x, y) = 1$. Then the fraction of y for which $f(x, y) = 1$ can be approximated by [the number you found]/[the number you tried]. The number of y for which $f(x, y) = 1$ can be approximated by [the fraction you found]×[the total number of y].

For example, suppose you had some strange shape and you wanted to find its area. Then x would specify the shape, y would specify some point within a surrounding box, and $f(x, y) = 1$ if the point is within the shape. Then the number of y for which $f(x, y) = 1$ gives you the area of your shape.

EXERCISE 21.1.1 *Given an integer x, suppose that you have one door for each $a \in [1, x - 1]$. We will say that there is a prize behind this door if $a^{x-1} \not\equiv_{(\bmod\ x)} 1$. Fermat's little theorem says that if x is pseudoprime, then none of the doors have prizes behind*

---

[1] A major breakthrough by Agrawal et al. in 2002 was to find a polynomial-time deterministic algorithm for determining whether an n-bit number is prime.

them, and if it is composite, then at least half the doors have prizes. The algorithm attempts to determine which is the case by opening t randomly chosen doors for some integer t.

1. *If the algorithm finds a prize, what do you know about the integer? If it does not find a prize, what do you know?*
2. *If the algorithm must always give the correct answer, how many doors need to be opened, as a function of the number n of digits in the instance x?*
3. *If t doors are open and the input instance x is a pseudoprime, what is the probability that the algorithm gives the correct answer? If the instance is composite, what is this probability?*

EXERCISE 21.1.2 *Section 4.3 designed an iterative algorithm for separating n VLSI chips into those that are good and those that are bad by testing two chips at a time and learning either that they are the same or that they are different. To help, at least half of the chips are promised to be good. Now design (much easier) a randomized algorithm for this problem. Here are some hints.*

*   *Randomly select one of the chips. What is the probability that the chip is good?*
*   *How can you learn whether or not the selected chip is good?*
*   *If it is good, how can you easily partition the chips into good and bad chips?*
*   *If the chip is not good, what should your algorithm do?*
*   *When should the algorithm stop?*
*   *What is the expected running time of this algorithm?*

21.2 Solutions of Optimization Problems with a Random Structure

Optimization problems involve looking for the best solution for an instance. Sometimes good solutions have a random structure. In such cases, a good way to construct one is to simply flip coins to decide how to build each part. I give two examples. The first one, *max cut*, being NP-complete, likely requires exponential time to find the best solution. However, in $O(n)$ time, we can find a solution which is likely to be at least half as good as optimal. The second example, *expander graphs*, is even more extreme. Though there are deterministic algorithms for constructing graphs with fairly good expansion properties, a random graph almost for sure has much better expansion properties (with probability $p \geq 0.999999$). A complication, however, is that there is no polynomial-time algorithm that tests whether this randomly constructed graph has the desired properties. Pushing the limits further, it can be proved that the same random graph has extremely good properties with some very small but nonzero probability (e.g., $p \geq 10^{-100}$). Though we have no quick way to construct such a graph, this does proves that such a graph exists.

The Max Cut Problem: The input to the max cut problem is an undirected graph. The output is a partition of the nodes into two sets U and V such that the number of edges that cross over from one side to the other is as large as possible. This problem is NP-complete, and hence the best known algorithm for finding an optimal solution requires $2^{\Theta(n)}$ time. The following randomized algorithm runs in time $\Theta(n)$ and is expected to obtain a solution for which half the edges cross over. This algorithm is incredibly simple. It simply flips a coin for each node to decide whether to put it into U or into V. Each edge will cross over with probability $\frac{1}{2}$. Hence, the expected number of edges to cross over is $\frac{|E|}{2}$. The optimal solution cannot have more than all the edges cross over, so the randomized algorithm is expected to perform at least half as well as the optimal solution can do.

Expander Graphs: An n-node degree-d graph is said to be an *expander graph* if moving from a set of its nodes across its edges expands us out to an even larger set of nodes. More formally, for $0 < \alpha < 1$ and $1 < \beta < d$, a graph $G = \langle V, E \rangle$ is an $\langle \alpha, \beta \rangle$-expander if for every subset $S \subseteq V$ of its nodes, if $|S| \leq \alpha n$ then $|N(S)| \geq \beta |S|$. Here $N(S)$ is the neighborhood of S, that is, the set of all nodes with an edge from some node in S.

> **Nonoverlapping Sets of d Neighbors:** Because each node $v \in V$ has d neighbors $N(v)$, a set S has $d|S|$ edges leaving these nodes. However, if these sets $N(v)$ of neighbors overlap a lot, then the total number of neighbors $N(S) = \bigcup_{v \in S} N(v)$ of S might be very small. We can't expect $N(S)$ to be bigger than $d|S|$, but we do want it to have size at least $\beta|S|$ where $1 < \beta < d$. If S is too big, we can't expect it to expand further. Hence, we only require this expansion property for sets S of size at most αn. Because we do expect sets of size αn to expand to a neighborhood of size $\beta \alpha n$, we require that $\alpha \beta < 1$.

> **Connected with Short Paths:** If $\alpha \beta > \frac{1}{2}$, then every pair of nodes in G is connected with a path of length at most $\frac{2 \log(n/2)}{\log \beta}$.

> > **Proof:** Consider two nodes u and v. The node u has d neighbors, $N(u)$. These neighbors $N(u)$ must have at least $\beta|N(u)| = \beta d$ neighbors $N(N(u))$. These neighbors $N(N(u))$ must have at least $\beta^2 d$ neighbors. It follows that there are at least $\beta^{i-1}d$ nodes with distance i from u. The last time we are allowed to do this expands the neighbor set of size $|S| = \alpha n$ to $|N(S)| \geq \beta|S| = \beta \alpha n$. By the requirement that $\alpha \beta > \frac{1}{2}$, this new neighbor set has size greater than $\frac{n}{2}$ nodes. The distance of these nodes from u is at most $i = \log_\beta \frac{n}{2}$. This set might not contain v. However, starting from v there is another set of more than half the nodes that are distant $i = \log_\beta \frac{n}{2}$ from v. These two sets must over lap at some node w. Hence, there is a path from u to w to v of length at most $\frac{2 \log(n/2)}{\log \beta}$.

> **Uses:** Expander graphs are very useful both in practice and for proving theorems.

Fault-Tolerant Networks: As we have seen, every pair of nodes in an expander graph are connected. This is still true if a large number of nodes or edges fail. Hence, this is a good pattern for wiring a communications network.

Pseudorandom Generators: Taking a short random walk in an expander graph quickly gets you to a random node. This is useful for generating long random looking strings from a short seed string.

Concentrating and Recycling Random Bits: If we have a source that has some randomness in it (say n coin tosses with an unknown probability and with unknown dependences between the coins), we can use expander graphs to produce a string of m bits appearing to be the result of m fair and independent coins.

Error-Correcting Codes: Expander graphs are also useful in designing ways of encoding a message into a longer code so that if any reasonable fraction of the longer code is corrupted, the original message can still be recovered. The faulty bits are connected by short paths to correct bits.

If $\alpha\beta < 1$, Then Expander Graphs Exist: We will now prove that for any constants α and β for which $\alpha\beta < 1$ there exists an $\langle \alpha, \beta \rangle$-expander graph with n nodes and degree d for some sufficiently big constant d. For example, if $\alpha = \frac{1}{2}, \beta = \frac{3}{2}$, then $d = 5$ is sufficient. To make the analysis easier, we will consider directed graphs where each node u is connected to d nodes chosen independently at random. (If we ignore the directions of the edges, then each node has average degree $2d$ and neighborhood sets are only bigger.) We prove that the probability we do not get such an expander graph is strictly less than one. Hence, one must exist.

Event $E_{S,T}$: The graph G will not be a $\langle \alpha, \beta \rangle$-expander if there is some set S for which $|S| \leq \alpha n$ and $N(S) < \beta|S|$. Hence, for each pair of sets S and T, with $|S| \leq \alpha n$ and $|T| < \beta|S|$, let $E_{S,T}$ denote the bad event that $N(S) \subseteq T$. Let us bound the probability of $E_{S,T}$ when we choose G randomly. Each node in S needs d neighbors, for a total of $d|S|$ randomly chosen neighbors. The probability of a particular one of these landing in T is $|T|/n$. Because these edges are chosen independently, the probability of them all landing in T is $(|T|/n)^{d|S|}$.

Probability of Some Bad Event: The probability that G is not an expander is the probability that at least one of these bad events $E_{S,T}$ happens, which is at most the sum of the probabilities of these individual events:

$$\Pr[G \text{ not an expander}] = \Pr[\text{At least one of the events } E_{S,T} \text{ occurs}]$$

$$\leq \sum_{S,T} \Pr[E_{S,T}] = \sum_{(s \leq \alpha n)} \sum_{(S \mid |S|=s)} \sum_{(T \mid |T|=\beta s)} \Pr[E_{S,T}]$$

$$= \sum_{s \leq \alpha n} \binom{n}{s}\binom{n}{\beta s}\left(\frac{|T|}{n}\right)^{d|S|}$$

We now use the result that $\binom{n}{a} \leq \left(\frac{en}{a}\right)^a$:

$$\Pr[G \text{ not an expander}] \leq \sum_{s \leq \alpha n} \left(\frac{en}{s}\right)^s \left(\frac{en}{\beta s}\right)^{\beta s} \left(\frac{\beta s}{n}\right)^{ds} = \sum_{s \leq \alpha n} \left[\left(\frac{en}{s}\right)\left(\frac{en}{\beta s}\right)^{\beta}\left(\frac{\beta s}{n}\right)^d\right]^s$$

$$\leq \sum_{s \leq \alpha n} \left[\left(\frac{en}{\alpha n}\right)\left(\frac{en}{\beta \alpha n}\right)^{\beta}\left(\frac{\beta \alpha n}{n}\right)^d\right]^s = \sum_{s \leq \alpha n} \left[\frac{e^{\beta+1}}{\alpha} \cdot (\alpha\beta)^{d-\beta}\right]^s$$

353

The requirement is that $\alpha\beta < 1$. Hence, if d is sufficiently big ($d \geq \log\left(2e^{\beta+1}/\alpha\right) / \log\left(1/\alpha\beta\right) + \beta$), then the bracketed summand is at most $\frac{1}{2}$:

$$\Pr\left[G \text{ not an expander}\right] \leq \sum_{s \leq \alpha n} \left[\frac{1}{2}\right]^s < 1$$

It follows that $\Pr[G \text{ is an expander}] > 0$, meaning that there exists at least one such G that is an expander.

PART FOUR

Appendix

Existential and universal quantifiers provide an extremely useful language for making formal statements. You must understand them. A game between a prover and a verifier is a level of abstraction within which it is easy to understand and prove such statements.

The *Loves* Example: Suppose the relation (predicate) *Loves*(p_1, p_2) means that person p_1 loves person p_2. Then we have

Expression	Meaning
$\exists p_2$ *Loves*(*Sam*, p_2)	"Sam loves somebody."
$\forall p_2$ *Loves*(*Sam*, p_2)	"Sam loves everybody."
$\exists p_1 \forall p_2$ *Loves*(p_1, p_2)	"Somebody loves everybody."
$\forall p_1 \exists p_2$ *Loves*(p_1, p_2)	"Everybody loves somebody."
$\exists p_2 \forall p_1$ *Loves*(p_1, p_2)	"Theres one person who is loved by everybody."
$\exists p_1 \exists p_2$ (*Loves*(p_1, p_2) and ¬*Loves*(p_2, p_1))	"Somebody loves in vain."

Definition of Relation: A relation like *Loves*(p_1, p_2) states for every pair of objects (say $p_1 = Sam$ and $p_2 = Mary$) that the relation either holds between them or does not. Though we will use the word *relation*, *Loves*(p_1, p_2) is also considered to be a *predicate*. The difference is that a predicate takes only one argument and hence focuses on whether the property is *true* or *false* about the given tuple $\langle p_1, p_2 \rangle = \langle Sam, Mary \rangle$.

Representations: Relations (predicates) can be represented in a number of ways.

Functions: A relation can be viewed as a function mapping tuples of objects either to *true* or to *false*, for example, *Loves* : {$p_1 | p_1$ is a person } × {$p_2 | p_2$ is a person } ⇒ {*true, false*}.

Set of Tuples: Alternatively, it can be viewed as a set containing the tuples for which it is true, for example *Loves* = {⟨*Sam, Mary*⟩, ⟨*Sam, Ann*⟩, ⟨*Bob, Ann*⟩, . . .}. ⟨*Sam, Mary*⟩ ∈ *Loves* iff *Loves*(*Sam, Mary*) is true.

Directed Graph Representation: If the relation only has two arguments, it can be represented by a directed graph. The nodes consist of the objects in the domain. We place a directed edge ⟨p_1, p_2⟩ between pairs for which the relation is true. If the domains for the first and second objects are disjoint, then the graph is bipartite. Of course, the *Loves* relation could be defined to include *Loves*(*Bob, Bob*). See Figure 22.1.

Quantifiers: You will be using the following quantifiers and properties.

The Existential Quantifier: The quantifier ∃ means that there is at least one object in the domain with the property. This quantifier relates to the Boolean

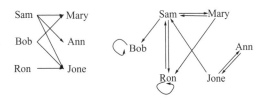

Figure 22.1: A directed graph representation of the *Loves* relation.

operator *OR*. For example, $\exists p_1$ *Loves*(*Sam, p_1*) $\equiv$ [*Loves*(*Sam, Mary*) *OR Loves*(*Sam, Ann*) *OR Loves*(*Sam, Bob*) *OR* ...].

The Universal Quantifier: The quantifier $\forall$ means that all of the objects in the domain have the property. It relates to the Boolean operator *AND*. For example, $\forall p_1$ *Loves*(*Sam, p_1*) $\equiv$ [*Loves*(*Sam, Mary*) *AND Loves*(*Sam, Ann*) *AND Loves*(*Sam, Bob*) *AND* ...].

Combining Quantifiers: Quantifiers can be combined. The order of operations is such that $\forall p_1 \exists p_2$ *Loves*(p_1, p_2) is understood to be bracketed as $\forall p_1[\exists p_1$ *Loves*(p_1, p_2)], i.e., "Every person has the property 'he loves some other person'." It relates to the following Boolean formula:

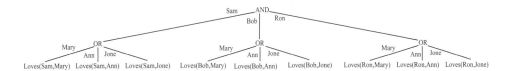

Order of Quantifiers: The order of the quantifiers matters. For example, if *b* is the class of boys and *g* is the class of girls, $\forall b \exists g$ *Loves*(*b, g*) and $\exists g \forall b$ *Loves*(*b, g*) mean different things. The second one states that the same girl is loved by every boy. For it to be true, there needs to be a Marilyn Monroe sort of girl that all the boys love. The first statement says that every boy loves some girl. A Marilyn Monroe sort of girl will make this statement true. However, it is also true in a monogamous situation in which every boy loves a different girl. Hence, the first statement can be true in more different ways than the second one. In fact, the second statement implies the first one, but not vice versa.

Definition of Free and Bound Variables: The statement $\exists p_2$ *Loves*(*Sam, p_2*) means "Sam loves someone." This is a statement about Sam. Similarly, the statement $\exists p_2$ *Loves*(p_1, p_2) means "p_1 loves someone." This is a statement about person p_1. Whether the statement is true depends on who p_1 is referring to. The statement is *not* about p_2. The variable p_2 is used as a local variable (similar to *for*($i = 1; i <= 10; i + +$)) to express "someone." It could be a brother or a friend or a dog. In this expression, we say that the variable p_2 is *bound*, while p_1 is *free*, because p_2 has a quantifier and p_1 does not.

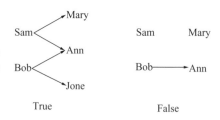

Figure 22.2: $\forall g \exists b \exists p$ $(Loves(b, g)$ and $Loves(b, p)$ and $g \neq p)$. On the left is an example of a situation in which the statement is true, and on the right is one in which it is false.

Defining Other Relations: You can define other relations by giving an expression with free variables. For example, you can define the unary relation *LovesSomeone* $(p_1) \equiv \exists p_2 \, Loves(p_1, p_2)$.

Building Expressions: Suppose you wanted to state that *every girl has been cheated on*, using the *Loves* relation. It may be helpful to break the problem into three steps.

> **Step 1. Assuming Other Relations:** Suppose you have the relation *Cheats(Sam, Mary)*, indicating that Sam cheats on Mary. How would you express the statement that every girl has been cheated on? The advantage of using this function is that we can focus on this one part of the statement. We are not claiming that every boy cheats. One boy may have broken every girl's heart.
>
> Given this, the answer is $\forall g \exists b \, Cheats(b, g)$.

> **Step 2. Constructing the Other Predicate:** Here we do not have a *Cheats* function. Hence, we must construct a sentence from the *loves* function stating that Sam cheats on Mary.
>
> Clearly, there must be someone else involved besides Mary, so let's start with $\exists p$. Now, in order for cheating to occur, who needs to love whom? (For simplicity's sake, let's assume that cheating means loving more than one person at the same time.) Certainly, Sam must love p. He must also love Mary. If he did not love her, then he would not be cheating on her. Must Mary love Sam? No. If Sam tells Mary he loves her dearly and then a moment later he tells Sue he loves *her* dearly, then he has cheated on Mary regardless of how Mary feels about him. Therefore, Mary does not have to love Sam. In conclusion, we might define *Cheats(Sam, Mary)* $\equiv \exists p \, (Loves(Sam, Mary)$ and $Loves(Sam, p))$. However, we have made a mistake here. In our example, the other person and Mary cannot be the same person. Hence, we must define the relation as *Cheats(Sam, Mary)* $\equiv \exists p \, (Loves(Sam, Mary)$ and $Loves(Sam, p)$ and $p \neq Mary)$.

> **Step 3. Combining the Parts:** Combining the two relations together gives you $\forall g \exists b \exists p \, (Loves(b, g)$ and $Loves(b, p)$ and $p \neq g)$. This statement expresses that every girl has been cheated on. See Figure 22.2.

The Domain of a Variable: Whenever you state $\exists g$ or $\forall g$, there must be an understood set of values that the variable g might take on. This set is called the *domain* of the variable. It may be explicitly given or implied, but it must be understood. Here the domain is "the" set of girls. You must make clear whether this means all girls in the room, all the girls currently in the world, or all girls that have ever existed. For example,

$$\forall x \exists y \; x \times y = 1$$

states that every value has a reciprocal. It is certainly not true of the domain of integers, because two does not have an integer reciprocal. It seems to be true of the domain of reals. Be careful, however: zero does not have a reciprocal. It would be better to write

$$\forall x \neq 0, \; \exists y \; x \times y = 1$$

or equivalently

$$\forall x \exists y \; (x \times y = 1 \; OR \; x = 0).$$

The Negation of a Statement: The negation of a statement is formed by putting a negation sign on the left-hand side. (Brackets sometimes help.) A negated statement, however, is best understood by moving the negation as deep (as far right) into the statement as possible. This is done as follows.

> **Negating *AND* and *OR*:** A negation on the outside of an *AND* or an *OR* statement can be moved deeper into the statement using De Morgan's law. Recall that the *AND* is replaced by an *OR* and the *OR* is replaced with an *AND*.

> > ¬(***Loves**(**S, M**) **AND Loves**(**S, A**)*) iff ¬***Loves**(**S, M**) **OR** ¬**Loves**(**S, A**)*: The negation of "Sam loves Mary and Ann" is "Either Sam does not love Mary or he does not love Ann." He can love one of the girls, but not both.
> > A common mistake is to make the negation ¬*Loves*(*Sam, Mary*) *AND* ¬*Loves*(*Sam, Ann*). However, this says that Sam loves neither Mary nor Ann.

> > ¬(***Loves**(**S, M**) **OR Loves**(**S,A**)*) iff ¬***Loves**(**S, M**) **AND** ¬**Loves**(**S, A**)*: The negation of "Sam either loves Mary or he loves Ann" is "Sam does not love Mary and he does not love Ann."

> **Negating Quantifiers:** Similarly, a negation can be moved past one or more quantifiers either to the right or to the left. However, you must then change these quantifiers from existential to universal and vice versa. Suppose d is the set of dogs. Then we have:

> > ¬(∃***d Loves**(**Sam, d**)*) iff ∀***d** ¬**Loves**(**Sam, d**)*: The negation of "There is a dog that Sam loves" is "There is no dog that Sam loves" or "All dogs are unloved by Sam." A common mistake is to state the negation as ∃*d* ¬*Loves*(*Sam, d*). However, this says that "There is a dog that is not loved by Sam."

> > ¬(∀***d Loves**(**Sam, d**)*) iff ∃***d** ¬**Loves**(**Sam, d**)*: The negation of "Sam loves every dog" is "There is a dog that Sam does not love."

$\neg(\exists b \forall d\, Loves(b, d))$ iff $\forall b \neg(\forall d\, Loves(b, d))$ iff $\forall b \exists d \neg Loves(b, d)$: The negation of "There is a boy who loves every dog" is "There are no boys who love every dog" or "For every boy, it is not the case that he loves every dog" or "For every boy, there is some dog that he does not love."

$\neg(\exists d_1 \exists d_2\, Loves(Sam, d_1)$ AND $Loves(Sam, d_2)$ AND $d_1 \neq d_2)$ iff
$\forall d_1 \forall d_2 \neg(Loves(Sam, d_1)$ AND $Loves(Sam, d_2)$ AND $d_1 \neq d_2)$ iff
$\forall d_1 \forall d_2 \neg Loves(Sam, d_1)$ OR $\neg Loves(Sam, d_2)$ OR $d_1 = d_2$: The negation of "There are two (distinct) dogs that Sam loves" is "Given any pair of (distinct) dogs, Sam does not love both" or "Given any pair of dogs, either Sam does not love the first or he does not love the second, or you gave me the same dog twice."

The Domain Does Not Change: The negation of $\exists x \geq 5,\ x + 2 = 4$ is $\forall x \geq 5,\ x + 2 \neq 4$. The negation does *not* begin $\exists x < 5$ .... Both the statement and its negation are about numbers greater than 5. Is there or is there not a number with the property such that $x + 2 = 4$?

Proving a Statement True: There are a number of seemingly different techniques for proving that an existential or universal statement is true. The core of all these techniques, however, is the same. Personally, I like to view the proof as a strategy for winning a game against an adversary.

Techniques for Proving $\exists d\, Loves(Sam, d)$:

Proof by Example or by Construction: The classic technique to prove that something with a given property exists is by example. You either directly provide an example, or you describe how to construct such an object. Then you prove that your example has the property. For the above statement, the proof would state "Let d be Fido" and then would prove that Sam loves Fido.

Proof by Adversarial Game: Suppose you claim to an adversary that there is a dog that Sam loves. What will the adversary say? Clearly, he challenges, "Oh, yeah? What dog?" You then meet the challenge by producing a specific dog d and proving that $Loves(Sam, d)$, that is, that Sam loves d. The statement is true if you have a strategy guaranteed to beat any adversary in this game.
- If the statement is true, then you can produce some dog d.
- If the statement is false, then you will not be able to.

Techniques for Proving $\forall d\, Loves(Sam, d)$:

Proof by Example Does Not Work: Proving that Sam loves Fido is interesting, but it does not prove that he loves all dogs.

Proof by Case Analysis: The laborious way of proving that Sam loves all dogs is to consider each dog, one at a time, and prove that Sam loves it.

This method is impossible if the domain of dogs is infinite.

Proof by Arbitrary Example: The classic technique to prove that every object from some domain has a given property is to let some symbol represent an arbitrary object from the domain and then to prove that that object has the property. Here the proof would begin "Let d be any arbitrary dog." Because we don't actually know which dog d is, we must either (1) prove $Loves(Sam, d)$ simply from the properties that d has *because* d is a dog or (2) go back to doing a case analysis, considering each dog d separately.

Proof by Adversarial Game: Suppose you claim to an adversary that Sam loves every dog. What will the adversary say? Clearly he challenges, "Oh, yeah? What about Fido?" You meet the challenge by proving that Sam loves Fido. In other words, the adversary provides a dog d'. You win if you can prove that $Loves(Sam, d')$.

The only difference between this game and the one for existential quantifiers is who provides the example. Interestingly, the game only has one round. The adversary is only given one opportunity to challenge you.

A proof of the statement $\forall d \, Loves(Sam, d)$ consists of a strategy for winning the game. Such a strategy takes an arbitrary dog d', provided by the adversary, and proves that "Sam loves d'." Again, because we don't actually know *which* dog d' is, we must either (1) prove that $Loves(Sam, d')$ simply from the properties that d' has because he is a dog or (2) go back to doing a case analysis, considering each dog d' separately.

- If the statement $\forall d \, Loves(Sam, d)$ is true, then you have a strategy. No matter how the adversary plays, no matter which dog d' he gives you, Sam loves it. Hence, you can win the game by proving that $Loves(Sam, d')$.
- If the statement is false, then there is a dog d' that Sam does not love. Any true adversary (not just a friend) will produce this dog, and you will lose the game. Hence, you cannot have a winning strategy.

Proof by Contradiction: A classic technique for proving the statement $\forall d \, Loves(Sam, d)$ is proof by contradiction. Except in the way that it is expressed, it is exactly the same as the proof by an adversary game.

By way of contradiction assume that the statement is false, that is, $\exists d \, \neg Loves(Sam, d)$ is true. Let d' be some such dog that Sam does not love. Then you must prove that in fact Sam does love d'. This contradicts the statement that Sam does not love d'. Hence, the initial assumption is false, and $\forall d \, Loves(Sam, d)$ is true.

Proof by Adversarial Game for More Complex Statements: The advantage to this technique is that it generalizes into a nice game for arbitrarily long statements.

The Steps of the Game:

> *Left to Right:* The game moves from left to right, providing an object for each quantifier.

> *Prover Provides ∃b:* You, as the prover, must provide any existential objects.

> *Adversary Provides ∀d:* The adversary provides any universal objects.

> *To Win, Prove the Relation Loves(b′, d′):* Once all the objects have been provided, you (the prover) must prove that the innermost relation is in fact true. If you can, then you win. Otherwise, you lose.

A Proof Is a Strategy: A proof of the statement consists of a strategy such that you win the game no matter how the adversary plays. For each possible move that the adversary takes, such a strategy must specify what move you will counter with.

Negations in Front: To prove a statement with a negation in the front of it, first put the statement into *standard* form with the negation moved to the right. Then prove the statement in the same way.

Examples:

> $\exists b \forall d \, Loves(b,d)$: To prove "There is a boy that loves every dog," you must produce a specific boy b'. Then the adversary, knowing your boy b', tries to prove that $\forall d \, Loves(b', d)$ is false. He does this by providing an arbitrary dog d' that he hopes b' does not love. You must prove "b' loves d'."

> $\neg(\exists b \forall d \, Loves(b,d))$ iff $\forall b \exists d \, \neg Loves(b, d)$: With the negation moved to the right, the first quantifier is universal. Hence, the adversary first produces a boy b'. Then, knowing the adversary's boy, you produce a dog d'. Finally, you prove that $\neg Loves(b', d')$.
>
> Your proof of the statement could be viewed as a function G that takes as input the boy b' given by the adversary and outputs the dog $d' = D(b')$ countered by you. Here, $d' = D(b')$ is an example of a dog that boy b' does not love. The proof must prove that $\forall b \neg Loves(b, D(b))$.

EXERCISE 22.0.1 *Let Loves(b, g) denote that boy b loves girl g. If Sam loves Mary and Mary does not love Sam back, then we say that Sam loves in vain.*

1. *Express the following statements using universal and existential quantifiers. Move any negations to the right.*
   (a) "Sam has loved in vain."
   (b) "There is a boy who has loved in vain."

(c) *"Every boy has loved in vain."*
(d) *"No boy has loved in vain."*

2. *For each of the above statements and each of the two relations below, prove either that the statement is true for the relation or that it is false:*

EXERCISE 22.0.2 *(See solution in Part Five.) For each, prove whether true or not when each variable is a real value. Be sure to play the correct game as to who is providing what value:*

1. $\forall x\, \exists y\; x + y = 5$.
2. $\exists y\, \forall x\; x + y = 5$.
3. $\forall x\, \exists y\; x \cdot y = 5$.
4. $\exists y\, \forall x\; x \cdot y = 5$.
5. $\forall x\, \exists y\; x \cdot y = 0$.
6. $\exists y\, \forall x\; x \cdot y = 0$.
7. $[\forall x\, \exists y\; P(x, y)] \Rightarrow [\exists y\, \forall x\; P(x, y)]$.
8. $[\forall x\, \exists y\; P(x, y)] \Leftarrow [\exists y\, \forall x\; P(x, y)]$.
9. $\forall a\, \exists y\, \forall x\; x \cdot (y + a) = 0$.
10. $\exists a\, \forall x\, \exists y\; [x = 0 \text{ or } x \cdot y = 5]$.

EXERCISE 22.0.3 *The game ping has two rounds. Player A goes first. Let m_1^A denote his first move. Player B goes next. Let m_1^B denote his move. Then player A goes m_2^A, and player B goes m_2^B. The relation $AWins(m_1^A, m_1^B, m_2^A, m_2^B)$ is true iff player A wins with these moves.*

1. *Use universal and existential quantifiers to express the fact that player A has a strategy with which he wins no matter what player B does. Use $m_1^A, m_1^B, m_2^A, m_2^B$ as variables.*
2. *What steps are required in the prover–adversary technique to prove this statement?*
3. *What is the negation of the above statement in standard form?*
4. *What steps are required in the prover–adversary technique to prove this negated statement?*

EXERCISE 22.0.4 *Why does $[\forall n_0,\ \exists n > n_0,\ P(n)]$ imply that there are an infinite number of values n for which the property P(n) is true?*

23 Time Complexity

It is important to classify algorithms based whether they solve a given computational problem and, if so, how quickly. Similarly, it is important to classify computational problems based whether they can be solved and, if so, how quickly.

23.1 The Time (and Space) Complexity of an Algorithm

Purpose:

Estimate Duration: To estimate how long an algorithm or program will run.

Estimate Input Size: To estimate the largest input that can reasonably be given to the program.

Compare Algorithms: To compare the efficiency of different algorithms for solving the same problem.

Parts of Code: To help you focus your attention on the parts of the code that are executed the largest number of times. This is the code you need to improve to reduce the running time.

Choose Algorithm: To choose an algorithm for an application:
- If the input size won't be larger than six, don't waste your time writing an extremely efficient algorithm.
- If the input size is a thousand, then be sure the program runs in polynomial, not exponential, time.
- If you are working on the Gnome project and the input size is a billion, then be sure the program runs in linear time.

Time and Space Complexities Are Functions, $T(n)$ **and** $S(n)$**:** The time complexity of an algorithm is not a single number, but is a function indicating how the running time depends on the size of the input. We often denote this by $T(n)$, giving the number of operations executed on the worst case input instance of size n. An example would be $T(n) = 3n^2 + 7n + 23$. Similarly, $S(n)$ gives the size of the rewritable memory the algorithm requires.

Ignoring Details, $\Theta(T(n))$ **and** $O(T(n))$**:** Generally, we ignore the low-order terms in the function $T(n)$ and the multiplicative constant in front. We also ignore the function for small values of n and focus on the *asymptotic* behavior as n becomes very large. Some of the reasons are the following.

> **Model-Dependent:** The multiplicative constant in front of the time depends on how fast the computer is and on the precise definition of "size" and "operation."

> **Too Much Work:** Counting every operation that the algorithm executes in precise detail is more work than it is worth.

> **Not Significant:** It is much more significant whether the time complexity is $T(n) = n^2$ or $T(n) = n^3$ than whether it is $T(n) = n^2$ or $T(n) = 3n^2$.

> **Only Large** n **Matter:** One might say that we only consider large input instances in our analysis, because the running time of an algorithm only becomes an issue when the input is large. However, the running time of some algorithms on small input instances is quite critical. In fact, the size n of a realistic input instance depends both on the problem and on the application. The choice was made to consider only large n in order to provide a clean and consistent mathematical definition.

See Chapter 25 on the Theta and BigOh notations.

Definition of Size: The formal definition of the size of an instance is the number of binary digits (*bits*) required to encode it. More practically, the size could be considered to be the number of *digits* or *characters* required to encode it. Intuitively, the size of an instance could be defined to be the area of paper needed to write down the instance, or the number of seconds it takes to communicate the instance along a narrow channel. These definitions are all within a multiplicative constant of each other.

> **An Integer:** Suppose that the input is the value $N = 8{,}398{,}346{,}386{,}236{,}876$. The number of bits required to encode it is $Size(N) = \log_2(N) = \log_2(8{,}398{,}346{,}386{,}236{,}876) = 53$, and the number of decimal digits is $Size(N) = \log_{10}(8{,}398{,}346{,}386{,}236{,}876) = 16$. Chapter 24 explains why these are within a multiplicative constant of each other. The one definition that you must *not* use is the *value*

of the integer, $Size(N) = N = 8{,}398{,}346{,}386{,}236{,}876$, because it is exponentially different than $Size(N) = \log_2(N) = 53$.

A Tuple: Suppose that the input is the tuple of b integers $I = \langle x_1, x_2, \ldots, x_b \rangle$. The number of bits required to encode it is $Size(I) = \log_2(x_1) + \log_2(x_2) + \cdots + \log_2(x_b) \approx \log_2(x_i) \cdot b$. A natural definition of the size of this tuple is the *number of integers* in it, $Size(I) = b$. With this definition, it is a much stronger statement to say that an algorithm requires only $Time(b)$ integer operations independent of how big the integers are.

A Graph: Suppose that the input is the graph $G = \langle V, E \rangle$ with $|V|$ nodes and $|E|$ edges. The number of bits required to encode it is $Size(G) = 2\,Size(node) \cdot |E| = 2\log_2(|V|) \cdot |E|$. Another reasonable definition of the size of G is the *number of edges*, $G(n) = |E|$. Often the time is given as a function of both $|V|$ and $|E|$. This is within a log factor of the other definitions, which for most applications is fine.

Definition of an Operation: The definition of an operation can be any reasonable operation on two bits, characters, nodes, or integers, depending on whether time is measured in bits, characters, nodes, or integers. An operation could also be defined to be any reasonable line of code or the number of seconds that the computation takes on your favorite computer.

Which Input: $T(n)$ is the number of operations required to execute the given algorithm on an input of size n. However, there are 2^n input instances with n bits. Here are three possibilities:

A Typical Input: The problem with considering a typical input instance this is that different applications will have very different typical inputs.

Average or Expected Case: The problem with taking the average over all input instances of size n is that it assumes that all instances are equally likely to occur.

Worst Case: The usual measure is to consider the instance of size n on which the given algorithm is the slowest, namely, $T(n) = \max_{I \in \{I \mid |I|=n\}} Time(I)$. This measure provides a nice clean mathematical definition and is the easiest to analyze. The only problem is that sometimes the algorithm does much better than the worst case, because the worst case is not a reasonable input. One such algorithm is quick sort (see Section 9.1).

Time Complexity of a Problem: The time complexity of a problem is the running time of the fastest algorithm that solves the problem.

EXAMPLE 23.1   **Polynomial Time vs Exponential Time**

Suppose program P_1 requires $T_1(n) = n^4$ operations and P_2 requires $T_2(n) = 2^n$. Suppose that your machine executes 10^6 operations per second. If $n = 1,000$, what is the running time of these programs?

Answer:

1. $T_1(n) = (1,000)^4 = 10^{12}$ operations, requiring 10^6 seconds, or 11.6 days.

2. $T_2(n) = 2^{(10^3)}$ operations. The number of years is $\frac{2^{(10^3)}}{10^6 \times 60 \times 60 \times 24 \times 365}$. This is too big for my calculator. The log of this number is $10^3 \times \log_{10}(2) - \log_{10} 10^6 - \log_{10}(60 \times 60 \times 24 \times 365) = 301.03 - 6 - 7.50 = 287.53$. Therefore, the number of years is $10^{287.53} = 3.40 \times 10^{287}$. Don't wait for it.

EXAMPLE 23.2   **Instance Size N vs Instance Value N**

Two simple algorithms, summation and factoring.

The Problems and Algorithms:

Summation: The task is to sum the N entries of an array, that is, $A(1) + A(2) + A(3) + \cdots + A(N)$.

Factoring: The task is to find divisors of an integer N. For example, on input $N = 5917$ we output that $N = 97 \times 61$. (This problem is central to cryptography.) The algorithm checks whether N is divisible by 2, by 3, by 4, ... by N.

Time: Both algorithms require $T = N$ operations (additions or divisions).

How Hard? The summation algorithm is considered to be very fast, while the factoring algorithm is considered to be very time-consuming. However, both algorithms take $T = N$ time to complete. The time complexity of these algorithms will explain why.

Typical Values of N: In practice, the N for factoring is much larger than that for summation. Even if you sum all the entries on the entire 8-G byte hard drive, then N is still only $N \approx 10^{10}$. On the other hand, the military wants to factor integers $N \approx 10^{100}$. However, the measure of complexity of an algorithm should not be based on how it happens to be used in practice.

Size of the Input: The input for summation contains is $n \approx 32N$ bits. The input for factoring contains is $n = \log_2 N$ bits. Therefore, with a few hundred bits you can write down a difficult factoring instance that is seemingly impossible to solve.

Time Complexity: The running time of summation is $T(n) = N = \frac{1}{32}n$, which is linear in its input size. The running time of factoring is $T(N) = N = 2^n$, which is exponential in its input size. This is why the summation algorithm is considered to be *feasible*, while the factoring algorithm is considered to be *infeasible*.

EXERCISE 23.1.1 *(See solution in Part Five.) For each of the two programs considered in Example 23.1, if you want it to complete in 24 hours, how big can your input be?*

EXERCISE 23.1.2 *In Example 23.1, for which input size, approximately, do the programs have the same running times?*

EXERCISE 23.1.3 *This problem compares the running times of the following two algorithms for multiplying:*

algorithm *KindergartenAdd(a, b)*

⟨ *pre-cond*⟩: *a and b are integers.*
⟨ *post-cond*⟩: *Outputs a × b.*

begin
    $c = 0$
    loop i = 1 ... a
        $c = c + b$
    end loop
    return(c)
end algorithm

algorithm *GradeSchoolAdd(a, b)*

⟨ *pre-cond*⟩: *a and b are integers.*
⟨ *post-cond*⟩: *Outputs a × b.*

begin
    Let $a_{s-1} \ldots a_3 a_2 a_1 a_0$ be the decimal digits of a, so that $a = \sum_{i=0}^{s-1} a_i \times 10^i$.
    Let $b_{t-1} \ldots b_3 b_2 b_1 b_0$ be the decimal digits of b, so that $b = \sum_{j=0}^{t-1} b_j \times 10^j$.
    $c = 0$
    loop i = 1 ... s
        loop j = 1 ... t
            $c = c + a_i b_j \times 10^{i+j}$.
        end loop
    end loop
    return(c)
end algorithm

For each of these algorithms, answer the following questions.

1. *Suppose that each addition to c requires time 10 seconds and every other operation (for example, multiplying two single digits such as 9 × 8 and shifting by zero) is free. What is the running time of each of these algorithms, either as a function of a and b or as a function of s and t? Give everything for this entire question exactly, i.e., not BigOh.*

2. *Let $a = 9{,}168{,}391$ and $b = 502$. (Without handing it in, trace the algorithm.) With 10 seconds per addition, how much time (seconds, minutes, etc.) does the computation require?*

3. *The formal size of an input instance is the number n of bits needed to write it down. What is n as a function of our instance $\langle a, b \rangle$?*

4. *Suppose your job is to choose the worst case instance $\langle a, b \rangle$ (i.e., the one that maximizes the running time), but you are limited in that you can only use n bits to represent your instance. Do you set a big and b small, a small and b big, or a and b the same size? Give the worst case a and b, or s and t, as a function of n.*

5. *The running time of an algorithm is formally defined to be a function $T(n)$ from n to the time required for the computation on the worst case instance of size n. Give $T(n)$ for each of these algorithms. Is this polynomial time?*

EXERCISE 23.1.4 *(See solution in Part Five.) Suppose that someone has developed an algorithm to solve a certain problem, which runs in time $T(n, k) \in \Theta(f(n, k))$, where n is the size of the input, and k is a parameter we are free to choose (we can choose it to depend on n). In each case determine the value of the parameter $k(n)$ to achieve the (asymptotically) best running time. Justify your answer. I recommend not trying much fancy math. Think of n as being some big fixed number. Try some value of k, say $k = 1$, $k = n^a$, or $k = 2^{an}$ for some constant a. Then note whether increasing or decreasing k increases or decreases f. Recall that "asymptotically" means that we only need the minimum to within a multiplicative constant.*

1. *You might want to first prove that $g + h = \Theta(\max(g, h))$.*
2. *$f(n, k) = \frac{n+k}{\log k}$. This is needed for the radix–counting sort in Section 5.4.*
3. *$f(n, k) = \frac{n^3}{k} + k \cdot n$.*
4. *$f(n, k) = \log^3 k + \frac{2^n}{k}$.*
5. *$f(n, k) = \frac{8^n n^2}{k} + k \cdot 2^n + k^2$.*

23.2 The Time Complexity of a Computational Problem

The Formal Definition of the Time Complexity of a Problem: As said, the time complexity of a problem is the running time of the fastest algorithm that solves the problem. We will now define this more carefully, using the existential and universal quantifiers that were defined in Chapter 22.

The Time Complexity of a Problem: The time complexity of a computational problem P is the minimum time needed by an algorithm to solve it.

Upper Bound: Problem P is said to be computable in time $T_{upper}(n)$ if there is an algorithm A that outputs the correct answer, namely $A(I) = P(I)$, within the bounded time, namely $Time(A, I) \leq T_{upper}(|I|)$, on every input instance I. The formal statement is

$$\exists A, \forall I, \; [A(I) = P(I) \text{ and } Time(A, I) \leq T_{upper}(|I|)]$$

$T_{upper}(n)$ is said to be only an *upper bound* on the complexity of the problem P, because there may be another algorithm that runs faster. For example, $P = Sorting$ is computable in $T_{upper}(n) = O(n^2)$ time. It is also computable in $T_{upper}(n) = O(n \log n)$.

Lower Bound of a Problem: A lower bound on the time needed to solve a problem states that no matter how smart you are, you cannot solve the problem faster than the stated time $T_{lower}(n)$, because such algorithm simply does not exist. There may be algorithms that give the correct answer or run sufficiently quickly on some input instances. But for every algorithm, there is at least one instance I for which either the algorithm gives the wrong answer, i.e., $A(I) \neq P(I)$, or it takes too much time, i.e., $Time(A, I) \geq T_{lower}(|I|)$. The formal statement is the negation (except for $\geq$ vs $>$) of that for the upper bound:

$$\forall A, \exists I, \; [A(I) \neq P(I) \text{ or } Time(A, I) \geq T_{lower}(|I|)]$$

For example, it should be clear that no algorithm can sort n values in only $T_{lower} = \sqrt{n}$ time, because in that much time the algorithm could not even look at all the values.

Proofs Using the Prover–Adversary Game: Recall the technique described in Chapter 22 for proving statements with existential and universal quantifiers.

Upper Bound: We can use the prover–adversary game to prove the upper bound statement $\exists A, \forall I, \; [A(I) = P(I) \text{ and } Time(A, I) \leq T_{upper}(|I|)]$ as follows: You, the prover, provide the algorithm A. Then the adversary provides an input I. Then you must prove that your A on input I gives the correct output in the allotted time. Note this is what we have been doing throughout the book: providing algorithms and proving that they work.

Lower Bound: A proof of the lower bound $\forall A, \exists I, [A(I) \neq P(I) \text{ or } Time$ $(A, I) \geq T_{lower}(|I|)]$ consists of a strategy that, when given an algorithm A by an adversary, you, the prover, study his algorithm and provide an input I. Then you prove either that his A on input I gives the wrong output or that it runs in more than the allotted time.

EXERCISE 23.2.1 *(See solution in Part Five.) Let Works(P, A, I) to true if algorithm A halts and correctly solves problem P on input instance I. Let $P = Halting$ be the halting problem that takes a Java program I as input and tells you whether or not it halts on the empty string. Let $P = Sorting$ be the sorting problem that takes a list of* *numbers I as input and sorts them. For each part, explain the meaning of what you are doing and why you don't do it another way.*

1. *Recall that a problem is* computable *if and only if there is an algorithm that halts and returns the correct solution on every valid input. Express in first-order logic that Sorting is computable.*
2. *Express in first-order logic that Halting is not computable.*
3. *Express in first-order logic that there are uncomputable problems.*
4. *Explain what the following means (not simply by saying the same in words), and either prove or disprove it:* $\forall I, \exists A,$ Works(Halting, A, I).
5. *Explain what the following means, and either prove or disprove it:* $\forall A, \exists P, \forall I,$ Works(P, A, I). *(Hint: An algorithm A on an input I can either halt and give the correct answer, halt and give the wrong answer, or run forever.)*

24 Logarithms and Exponentials

Logarithms $\log_2(n)$ and exponentials 2^n arise often when analyzing algorithms.

Uses: These are some of the places that you will see them.

Divide a Logarithmic Number of Times: Many algorithms repeatedly cut the input instance in half. A classic example is binary search (Section 1.4): You take something of size n and you cut it in half, then you cut one of these halves in half, and one of these in half, and so on. Even for a very large initial object, it does not take very long until you get a piece of size below 1. The number of divisions required is about $\log_2(n)$. Here the base 2 is because you are cutting them in half. If you were to cut them into thirds, then the number of times to cut would be about $\log_3(n)$.

A Logarithmic Number of Digits: Logarithms are also useful because writing down a given integer value n requires $\lceil \log_{10}(n+1) \rceil$ decimal digits. For example, suppose that $n = 1{,}000{,}000 = 10^6$. You would have to divide this number by 10 six times to get to 1. Hence, by definition, $\log_{10}(n) = 6$. This, however, is the number of zeros, not the number of digits. We forgot the leading digit 1. The formula $\lceil \log_{10}(n+1) \rceil = 7$ does the trick. For the value $n = 6{,}372{,}845$, the number of digits is given by $\log_{10}(6{,}372{,}846) = 6.804333$, rounded up to 7. Being in computer science, we store our values using bits. Similar arguments give that $\lceil \log_2(n+1) \rceil$ is the number of bits needed.

Height and Size of Binary Tree: A complete balanced binary tree of height h has 2^h leaves and $n = 2^{h+1} - 1$ nodes. Conversely, if it has n nodes, then its height is $h \approx \log_2 n$.

Exponential Search: Suppose a solution to your problem is represented by n digits. There are 10^n such strings of n digits. Doing a blind search through them all would take too much time.

Rules: There are lots of rules about logs and exponentials that one might learn. Personally, I like to confine them to the following:

$b^n = \overbrace{b \times b \times b \times \cdots \times b}^{n}$: This is the definition of exponentiation. b^n is n b's multiplied together.

$b^n \times b^m = b^{n+m}$: This is proved simply by counting the number of b's being multiplied:

$$\overbrace{(b \times b \times b \times \cdots \times b)}^{n} \times \overbrace{(b \times b \times b \times \cdots \times b)}^{m} = \overbrace{b \times b \times b \times \cdots \times b}^{n+m}.$$

$b^0 = 1$: One might guess that zero b's multiplied together is zero, but it needs to be one. One argument for this is as follows. $b^n = b^{0+n} = b^0 \times b^n$. For this to be true, b^0 must be one.

$b^{\frac{1}{2}} = \sqrt{n}$: By definition, $\sqrt{n}$ is the positive number that when multiplied by itself gives n. $b^{\frac{1}{2}}$ meets this definition because $b^{\frac{1}{2}} \times b^{\frac{1}{2}} = b^{\frac{1}{2}+\frac{1}{2}} = b^1 = b$.

$b^{-n} = 1/b^n$: The fact that this needs to be true can be argued in a similar way. $1 = b^{n+(-n)} = b^n \times b^{-n}$. For this to be true, b^{-n} must be $1/b^n$.

$(b^n)^m = b^{n \times m}$: Again we count the number of b's:

$$\overbrace{\overbrace{(b \times b \times b \times \cdots \times b)}^{n} \times \overbrace{(b \times b \times b \times \cdots \times b)}^{n} \times \cdots \times \overbrace{(b \times b \times b \times \cdots \times b)}^{n}}^{m}$$

$$= \overbrace{b \times b \times b \times \cdots \times b}^{n \times m}.$$

If $x = \log_b(n)$ then $n = b^x$: This is the definition of logarithms.

$\log_b(1) = 0$: This follows from $b^0 = 1$.

$\log_b(b^x) = x$ and $b^{\log_b(n)} = n$: Substituting $n = b^x$ into $x = \log_b(n)$ gives the first, and substituting $x = \log_b(n)$ into $n = b^x$ gives the second.

$\log_b(n \times m) = \log_b(n) + \log_b(m)$: The number of digits to write down the product of two integers is the number to write down each of them separately (up to rounding errors). We prove it by applying the definition of logarithms and the above rules: $b^{\log_b(n \times m)} = n \times m = b^{\log_b(n)} \times b^{\log_b(m)} = b^{\log_b(n)+\log_b(m)}$. It follows that $\log_b(n \times m) = \log_b(n) + \log_b(m)$.

$\log_b(n^d) = d \times \log_b(n)$: This is an extension of the above rule.

$\log_b(n) - \log_b(m) = \log_b(n) + \log_b(\frac{1}{m}) = \log_b(\frac{n}{m})$: This is another extension of the above rule.

$d^{c\log_2(n)} = n^{c\log_2(d)}$: This rule states that you can move things between the base and the exponent as long as you insert or remove a log. The proof is as follows.

$$d^{c \log_2(n)} = (2^{\log_2(d)})^{c \log_2(n)} = 2^{\log_2(d) \times c \log_2(n)} = 2^{\log_2(n) \times c \log_2(d)} = (2^{\log_2(n)})^{c \log_2(d)} = n^{c \log_2(d)}.$$

$\log_2(n) = 3.32\ldots \times \log_{10}(n)$: The number of bits needed to express the integer n is $3.32\ldots$ times the number of decimal digits needed. This can be seen as follows. Suppose $x = \log_2 n$. Then $n = 2^x$, giving $\log_{10} n = \log_{10}(2^x) = x \cdot \log_{10} 2$. Finally,

$$x = \frac{1}{\log_{10} 2} \log_{10}(n) = 3.32\ldots \log_{10} n$$

Which Base: We will write $\Theta(\log(n))$ without giving an explicit base. A high school student might use base 10 as the default, a scientist base $e = 2.718\ldots$, and a computer scientist base 2. My policy is to exclude the base when it does not matter. As seen above, $\log_{10}(n)$, $\log_2(n)$, and $\log_e(n)$ differ only by multiplicative constants. In general, we ignore multiplicative constants, and hence the base used is irrelevant. I only include the base when the base matters. For example, 2^n and 10^n differ by much more than a multiplicative constant.

The Ratio $\frac{\log a}{\log b}$: When computing the ratio between two logarithms, the base used does not matter, because changing the base will introduce the same constant on both the top and the bottom, which will cancel. Hence, when computing such a ratio, you can choose whichever base makes the calculation the easiest. For example, to compute $\frac{\log 16}{\log 8}$, the obvious base to use is 2, because $\frac{\log_2 16}{\log_2 8} = \frac{4}{3}$. On the other hand, to compute $\frac{\log 9}{\log 27}$, the obvious base to use is 3, because $\frac{\log_3 9}{\log_3 27} = \frac{2}{3}$.

EXERCISE 24.0.1 *(See solution in Part Five.) Simplify the following exponentials:* $a^3 \times a^5$, $3^a \times 5^a$, $3^a + 5^a$, $2^{6 \log_4 n + 7}$, $n^{3/\log_2 n}$.

25 Asymptotic Growth

Classes of Growth Rates: It is important to be able to classify functions $f(n)$ based on how quickly they grow: The following table outlines the few easy rules with which to classify functions with the basic form $f(n) = \Theta(b^{an} \cdot n^d \cdot \log^{en})$.

c	b^a	d	e	Class	Θ	Examples
> 0	> 1	Any	Any	**Exponentials**	$2^{\Theta(n)}$	$2^n, \frac{3^{0.001n}}{n^{100}}$
	$= 1$	> 0	Any	**Polynomials:**	$n^{\Theta(1)}$	$n^4, \frac{5n^{0.0001}}{\log^{100}(n)}$
		$= 2$	Any	• **Quadratic**	$\Theta(n^2)$	$5n^2, 2n^2 + 7n + 8$
		$= 1$	$= 1$	• **Sorting time**	$\Theta(n \log n)$	$5n \log n + 3n$
		$= 1$	$= 0$	• **Linear**	$\Theta(n)$	$5n + 3$
		$= 0$	> 0	**Polylogarithms:**	$\log^{\Theta(1)}(n)$	$5 \log^3(n)$
			$= 1$	• **Logarithms**	$\Theta(\log n)$	$5 \log(n)$
			$= 0$	**Constants**	$\Theta(1)$	$5, 5 + \sin n$
		< 0	Any	**Decreasing polynomials**	$\frac{1}{n^{\Theta(1)}}$	$\frac{1}{n^4}, \frac{5 \log^{100}(n)}{n^{0.0001}}$
	< 1	Any	Any	**Decreasing exponentials**	$\frac{1}{2^{\Theta(1)}}$	$\frac{1}{2^n}, \frac{n^{100}}{3^{0.001n}}$

Asymptotic Notation: When we want to bound the growth of a function while ignoring multiplicative constants, we use the following notation:

Name	Standard Notation	My Notation	Meaning
Theta	$f(n) = \Theta(g(n))$	$f(n) \in \Theta(g(n))$	$f(n) \approx c \cdot g(n)$
BigOh	$f(n) = O(g(n))$	$f(n) \leq O(g(n))$	$f(n) \leq c \cdot g(n)$
Omega	$f(n) = \Omega(g(n))$	$f(n) \geq \Omega(g(n))$	$f(n) \geq c \cdot g(n)$

Purpose:

Time Complexity: Generally, the functions that we will be classifying will be the time or space complexities of programs. On the other hand, these ideas can also be used to classify any function.

Function Growth: The purpose of classifying a function is to give an idea of how fast it grows without going into too much detail.

Asymptotic Growth Rate: When classifying animals, Darwin decided not to consider whether the animal sleeps during the day, but to consider whether it has hair. When classifying functions, complexity theorists decided to not consider its behavior for small values of n or even whether it is monotone increasing, but how quickly it grows when its input n grows really big. This is referred to as the *asymptotics* of the function. Here are some examples of different growth rates:

Function	Approximate value of $T(n)$ for $n=$				
$T(n)$	10	100	1,000	10,000	Animal
5	5	5	5	5	Virus
$\log_2 n$	3	6	9	13	Amoeba
$\sqrt{n}$	3	10	31	100	Bird
n	10	100	1,000	10,000	Human
$n \log n$	30	600	9,000	130,000	Giant
n^2	100	10,000	10^6	10^8	Elephant
n^3	1,000	10^6	10^9	10^{12}	Dinosaur
2^n	1,024	10^{30}	10^{300}	10^{3000}	The universe

Note: The universe contains approximately 10^{80} particles.

Exponential vs Polynomial: The table shows that an exponential function like $f(n) = 2^n$ grows extremely quickly. In fact, for sufficiently big n, this exponential 2^n grows much faster than any polynomial, even $n^{1,000,000}$. To take this to an extreme, the function $f(n) = 2^{0.001n}$ is also an exponential. It too grows much faster than $n^{1,000,000}$ for sufficiently large n.

Polynomial vs Logarithmic: The table also shows that a logarithmic function like $f(n) = \log_2 n$ grows, but very slowly. Hence, for sufficiently large n, it is bigger than any constant, but smaller than any polynomial.

EXERCISE 25.0.1 *Give a value of n for which $n^{1,000,000} < 10^n$.*
Give a value of n for which $n^{1,000} < 10^{0.001n}$.

EXERCISE 25.0.2 *Give a value of n for which $(\log_{10} n)^{1,000,000} < n$.*
Give a value of n for which $(\log_{10} n)^{1,000} < n^{0.001}$.

25.1 Steps to Classify a Function

Given a function $f(n)$, we will classify it according to its growth using the following steps.

1) Put $f(n)$ into Basic Form: Though there are strange functions out there, most functions $f(n)$ can be put into a basic form consisting of the sum of a number of terms, where each term has the basic form $c \cdot b^{an} \cdot n^d \cdot (\log n)^e$, where a, b, c, d, and e are real constants.

Examples:
- If $f(n) = 3 \cdot 2^{4n} \cdot n^7 \cdot (\log n)^5$, then $a = 4$, $b = 2$, $c = 3$, $d = 7$, and $e = 5$.
- Suppose $f(n) = n^2$. This has no exponential part b^{an}, but can be viewed as having $a = 0$, or $b = 1$, or $a^b = 1$. (Recall $x^0 = 1$ and $1^x = 1$.) The exponent on the polynomial n is $d = 2$. There is no logarithmic factor, so we have $e = 0$. Finally, the constant in front is $c = 1$.
- In $f(n) = 1/n^6 = n^{-6}$, it is also useful to see that $d = -6$.
- If $f(n) = n^2/\log n + 5$, then the function has two terms. In the first, $a^b = 1$, $c = 1$, $d = 2$, and $e = -1$. In the second, $a^b = 1$, $c = 5$, $d = 0$, and $e = 0$.

2) Get the Big-Picture Growth: We classify the set of all vertebrate animals into mammals, birds, reptiles, and so on. Similarly, we will classify functions into the major groups exponentials $2^{\Theta(n)}$, polynomials $n^{\Theta(1)}$, polylogarithms $\log^{\Theta(1)}(n)$, and constants $\Theta(1)$.

Exponentials $2^{\Theta(n)}$: If the function $f(n)$ is the sum of a bunch of things, one of which is $c \cdot b^{an} \cdot n^d \cdot (\log n)^e$, where $b^a > 1$, then $f(n)$ is considered to be an exponential.

Examples Included:
- $f(n) = 2^n$ and $f(n) = 3^{5n}$
- $f(n) = 2^n \cdot n^2 \log_2 n - 7n^8$ and $f(n) = \frac{2^n}{n^2}$

Examples Not Included:
- $f(n) = 1^n = 2^{0 \cdot n} = 1$, $f(n) = 2^{-1 \cdot n} = \left(\frac{1}{2}\right)^n$, and $f(n) = n^{1,000,000}$ (too small)
- $f(n) = n! \approx n^n = 2^{n \log_2 n}$ and $f(n) = 2^{n^2}$ (too big)

Definition of an Infeasible Algorithm: An algorithm is considered to be *infeasible* if it runs in exponential time. This is because such functions grow extremely quickly as n gets larger.

$(b^a)^n$: We require $b^a > 1$ because $b^{an} = (b^a)^n$, which grows as long as the base b^a is at least one.

The Notation $2^{\Theta(n)}$: We will see later that $\Theta(1)$ denotes any constant greater than zero. The notation $2^{\Theta(n)} = 2^{\Theta(1) \cdot n}$ is used to represent the class of exponentials, because $b^{an} = 2^{(a \log_2 b) \cdot n}$ and the constant $a \log_2 b = log_2(b^a)$ is greater than zero as long as b^a is greater than 1. Recall $\log_2 1 = 0$.

Bounded Between: By these rules, $f(n) = c \cdot b^{an} \cdot n^d \cdot (\log n)^e$ is exponential if $b^a > 1$, no matter what the constants c, d, e, and f are. Consider $f(n) = 2^n/n^{100}$. The rule states that it is an exponential because $b^a = 2^1 > 1$ and $d = -100$. We might question this, thinking that dividing by n^{100} would not let it grow faster enough to be considered to be an exponential. We see that it does grow fast enough by proving that it is bounded between the two exponential functions $2^{0.5n}$ and 2^n.

Polynomial $n^{\Theta(1)}$: If $f(n) = c \cdot b^{an} \cdot n^d \cdot (\log n)^e$ is such that $b^a = 1$, then we can ignore b^{an}, giving $f(n) = c \cdot n^d \cdot (\log n)^e$. If $d > 0$, then the function $f(n)$ is considered to be a polynomial.

Examples Included:
- $f(n) = 3n^2$ and $f(n) = 7n^2 - 8n \log n + 2n - 17$
- $f(n) = \sqrt{n} = n^{1/2}$ and $f(n) = n^{3.1}$
- $f(n) = n^2 \log_2 n$ and $f(n) = \frac{n^2}{\log_2 n}$
- $f(n) = 7n^3 \log^7 n - 8n^2 \log n + 2n - 17$

Examples Not Included:
- $f(n) = n^0 = 1$, $f(n) = n^{-1} = \frac{1}{n}$, and $f(n) = \log n$ (too small)
- $f(n) = n^{\log n}$ and $f(n) = 2^n$ (too big)

Definition of a Feasible Algorithm: An algorithm is considered to be *feasible* if it runs in polynomial time. (This is not actually true if $f(n) = n^{1,000,000}$.)

The Notation $n^{\Theta(1)}$: $\Theta(1)$ denotes any constant greater than zero, and hence $n^{\Theta(1)}$ represents any function $f(n) = n^d$ where $d > 0$.

Bounded Between: Though it would not be considered one in a mathematical study of polynomials, we also consider $f(n) = 3n^2 \log n$ to be a polynomial, because it is bounded between n^2 and n^3, which clearly are polynomials.

Polylogarithms $\log^{\Theta(1)}(n)$: Powers of logs like $(\log n)^3$ are referred to as *polylogarithms*. These are often written as $\log^3 n = (\log n)^3$. This is different than $\log(n^3) = 3 \log n$.

Example Included:
- $f(n) = 7(\log_2 n)^5$, $f(n) = 7 \log_2 n$, and $f(n) = 7\sqrt{\log_2 n}$
- $f(n) = 7(\log_2 n)^5 + 6(\log_2 n)^3 - 19 + 7(\log_2 n)^2/n$

Example Not Included:

- $f(n) = n$ (too big)

Constants $\Theta(1)$: A constant function is one whose output does not depend on its input, for example, $f(n) = 7$. One algorithm for which this function arises is popping an element off a stack that is stored as a linked list. This takes maybe seven operations, independent of the number n of elements in the stack.

The Notation $n^{\Theta(1)}$: We use the notation $\Theta(1)$ to replace any constant when we do not care what the actual constant is because determining whether it is 7, 9, or 8.829 may be more work and more detail than we need. On the other hand, in most applications being negative $[f(n) = -1]$ or zero $[f(n) = 0]$ would be quite a different matter. Hence, these are excluded.

Bounded Between: A function like $f(n) = 8 + \sin n$ changes continuously between 7 and 9, and $f(n) = 8 + \frac{1}{n}$ changes continuously on approaching 8. However, if we don't care whether it is 7, 9, or 8.829, why should we care if it is changing between them? Hence, both of these functions are included in $\Theta(1)$. On the other hand, the function $f(n) = \frac{1}{n}$ is not included, because the only constant that it is bounded below by is zero and the zero function is not included.

Examples Included:

- $f(n) = 7$ and $f(n) = 8.829$
- $f(n) = 8 + \sin n$, $f(n) = 8 + \frac{1}{n}$

Examples Not Included:

- $f(n) = -1$ and $f(n) = 0$ (fails $c > 0$)
- $f(n) = \sin n$ (fails $c > 0$)
- $f(n) = \frac{1}{n}$ (too small)
- $f(n) = \log_2 n$ (too big)

3) Determine $\Theta(f(n))$: We further classify mammals into humans, cats, dogs, and so on. Similarly, we further classify the polynomials $n^{\Theta(1)}$ into linear functions $\Theta(n)$, the time for sorting $\Theta(n \log n)$, quadratics $\Theta(n^2)$, and so on. These are classes that ignore the multiplicative constant.

Steps: One "takes the Theta" of a function $f(n)$ by dropping the low-order terms and then dropping the multiplicative constant c in front of the largest term.

Dropping Low-Order Terms: If $f(n)$ is a set of things added or subtracted together, then each of these things is called a *term*. We determine which of the terms grows fastest as n gets large. The slower-growing terms are referred to as *low-order terms*. We drop them because they are not significant.

Ordering Terms: The fastest-growing term is determined by first taking the term $c \cdot b^{an} \cdot n^d \cdot (\log n)^e$ with the largest b^a value. If the b^a's of terms are equal, then we take the term with the largest d value. If the d's are also equal, then we take the term with the largest e value.

Dropping the Multiplicative Constant: The running time of an algorithm might be $f(n) = 3n^2$ or $f(n) = 100n^2$. We say it is $\Theta(n^2)$ when we do not care what the multiplicative constant c is. The function $f(n) = c \cdot b^{an} \cdot n^d \cdot (\log n)^e$ is in the class of functions denoted $\Theta(b^{an} \cdot n^d \cdot (\log n)^e)$.

Examples of Functions:

- $f(n) = 3n^3 \log n - 1000n^2 + n - 29$ is in the class $\Theta(n^3 \log n)$.
- $f(n) = 7 \cdot 4^n \cdot n^2 / \log^3 n + 8 \cdot 2^n + 17 \cdot n^2 + 1000 \cdot n$ is in the class $\Theta(4^n \cdot n^2 / \log^3 n)$.
- $\frac{1}{n} + 18$ is in the class $\Theta(1)$. Since $\frac{1}{n}$ is a lower-order term than 18, it is dropped.
- $\frac{1}{n^2} + \frac{1}{n}$ is in the class $\Theta(\frac{1}{n})$, because $\frac{1}{n^2}$ is a smaller term.

Examples of Classes:

Linear Functions $\Theta(n)$: The classic linear function is $f(n) = c \cdot n + b$. The notation $\Theta(n)$ excludes any with $c \leq 0$ but includes any function that is bounded between two such functions.

What Can Be Done in $\Theta(n)$ Time: Given an input of n items, it takes $\Theta(n)$ time simply to look at the input. Looping over the items and doing a constant amount of work for each takes another $\Theta(n)$ time. Say we take $t_1(n) = 2n$ and $t_2(n) = 4n$ for a total of $6n$ time. Now if you do not want to do more than linear time, are you allowed to do any more work? Sure. You can do something that takes $t_3(n) = 3n$ time and something else that takes $t_4(n) = 5n$ time. You are even allowed to do a few things that take a constant amount of time, totaling say $t_5(n) = 13$. The entire algorithm then takes the sum of these, $t(n) = 14n + 13$ time. This is still considered to be linear time.

Examples Included:

- $f(n) = 7n$ and $f(n) = 8.829n$
- $f(n) = (8 + \sin n)n$ and $f(n) = 8n + \log^{10} n + \frac{1}{n} - 1{,}000{,}000$

Examples Not Included:

- $f(n) = -n$ and $f(n) = 0n$ (fails $c > 0$)
- $f(n) = \frac{n}{\log_2 n}$ (too small)
- $f(n) = n \log_2 n$ (too big)

Quadratic Functions $\Theta(n^2)$: Two nested loops from 1 to n take $\Theta(n^2)$ time if each inner iteration takes a constant amount of time. An $n \times n$ matrix requires $\Theta(n^2)$ space if each element takes constant space.

Time for Sorting, $\Theta(n \log n)$: Another running time that arises often in algorithms is $\Theta(n \log n)$. For example, this is the number of comparisons needed to sort n elements.

> *Not Linear:* The function $f(n) = n \log n$ grows slightly too quickly to be in the linear class of functions $\Theta(n)$. This is because $n \log n$ is $\log n$ times n, and $\log n$ is not constant.

> *A Polynomial:* The classes $\Theta(n)$, $\Theta(n \log n)$, and $\Theta(n^2)$ are subclasses of the class of polynomial functions $n^{\Theta(1)}$. For example, though the function $f(n) = n \log n$ is too big for $\Theta(n)$ and too small $\Theta(n^2)$, it is in $n^{\Theta(1)}$ because it is bounded between n^1 and n^2, both of which are in $n^{\Theta(1)}$.

Logarithms $\Theta(\log(n))$: See Chapter 24 for how logarithmic functions like $\log_2(n)$ arise and for some of their rules.

> *Which Base:* We write $\Theta(\log(n))$ without giving an explicit base. As shown in the list of rules about logarithms, $\log_{10}(n)$, $\log_2(n)$, and $\log_e(n)$ differ only by a multiplicative constant. Because we are ignoring multiplicative constants anyway, which base is used is irrelevant. The rules also indicate that $8 \log_2(n^5)$ also differs only by a multiplicative constant. All of these functions are include in $\Theta(\log(n))$.

EXERCISE 25.1.1 *Which grows faster, 3^{4n} or 4^{3n}?*

EXERCISE 25.1.2 *Does the notation $(\Theta(1))^n$ mean the same thing as $2^{\theta(n)}$?*

EXERCISE 25.1.3 *Prove that $2^{0.5n} \leq 2^n/n^{100} \leq 2^n$ for sufficiently big n.*

EXERCISE 25.1.4 *(See solution in Part Five.) Prove that $n^2 \leq 3n^2 \log n \leq n^3$ for sufficiently big n.*

EXERCISE 25.1.5 *(See solution in Part Five.) Sort the terms in $f(n) = 100n^{100} + 3^{4n} + \log^{1,000} n + 4^{3n} + 2^{0.001n}/n^{100}$.*

EXERCISE 25.1.6 *For each of the following functions, sort its terms by growth rate. Get the big picture growth by classifying it into $2^{\Theta(n)}$, $n^{\Theta(1)}$, $\log^{\Theta(1)}(n)$, $\Theta(1)$ or into a similar and appropriate class. Also give its Theta approximation.*

1. $f(n) = 5n^3 - 17n^2 + 4$
2. $f(n) = 5n^3 \log n + 8n^3$
3. $f(n) = 2^{2^{5n}}$
4. $f(n) = 7^{3 \log_2 n}$
5. $f(n) = \{ 1 \text{ if } n \text{ is odd, } 2 \text{ if } n \text{ is even} \}$
6. $f(n) = 2 \cdot 2^n \cdot n^2 \log_2 n - 7n^8 + 7\frac{3^n}{n^2}$

7. $f(n) = 100n^{100} + 3^{4n} + \log^{1,000}(n) + 4^{3n}$
8. $f(n) = 6\frac{n^4}{\log^3 n} + 8n^{100}2^{-5n} + 17$
9. $f(n) = \frac{1}{n^2} + \frac{5\log n}{n}$
10. $f(n) = 7\sqrt[5]{n} + 6\sqrt[3]{n}$
11. $f(n) = \frac{6n^{5.2}+7n^{7.5}}{2n^{3.1}+7n^{2.4}}$
12. $f(n) = -2n$
13. $f(n) = 5n^{\log^3 n}$

EXERCISE 25.1.7 *For each pair of classes of functions, how are they similar? How are they different? If possible, give a function that is included in the first of these but not included in the second. If possible, do the reverse, giving a function that is included in the second but not in the first.*

1. $\Theta(2^{2n})$ *and* $\Theta(2^{3n})$
2. $\Theta(2^n)$ *and* $3^{\Theta(n)}$

25.2 More about Asymptotic Notation

Other Useful Notations:

Name	Standard Notation	My Notation	Meaning
Theta	$f(n) = \Theta(g(n))$	$f(n) \in \Theta(g(n))$	$f(n) \approx c \cdot g(n)$
BigOh	$f(n) = O(g(n))$	$f(n) \leq O(g(n))$	$f(n) \leq c \cdot g(n)$
Omega	$f(n) = \Omega(g(n))$	$f(n) \geq \Omega(g(n))$	$f(n) \geq c \cdot g(n)$
Little Oh	$f(n) = o(g(n))$	$f(n) << o(g(n))$	$f(n) << g(n)$
Little Omega	$f(n) = \omega(g(n))$	$f(n) >> \omega(g(n))$	$f(n) >> g(n)$
Tilde	$f(n) = \tilde{\Theta}(g(n))$	$f(n) \in \tilde{\Theta}(g(n))$	$f(n) \approx \log^{\Theta(1)} \cdot g(n)$

Same: $7 \cdot n^3$ is within a constant of n^3. Hence, it is in $\Theta(n^3)$, $O(n^3)$, and $\Omega(n^3)$. However, because it is not much smaller than n^3, it is not in $o(n^3)$, and because it is not much bigger, it not in $\omega(n^3)$.

Smaller: $7 \cdot n^3$ is asymptotically much smaller than n^4. Hence, it is in $O(n^4)$ and in $o(n^4)$, but it is not in $\Theta(n^4)$, $\Omega(n^4)$, or $\omega(n^4)$.

Bigger: $7 \cdot n^3$ is asymptotically much bigger than n^2. Hence, it is in $\Omega(n^2)$ and in $\omega(n^2)$, but it is not in $\Theta(n^2)$, $O(n^2)$, or $o(n^2)$.

Log Factors: $7n^3 \log^2 n = \tilde{\Theta}(n^3)$ ignores the logarithmic factors.

Notation Considerations:

"$\in$" vs "=": I consider $\Theta(n)$ to be a class of functions, so I *ought* to use the set notation, $f(n) \in \Theta(g(n))$, to denote membership.

On the other hand, ignoring constant multiplicative factors, $f(n)$ has the same asymptotic growth as $g(n)$. Because of this, the notation $7n = \Theta(n)$ makes sense. This notation is standard.

Even the statements $3n^2 + 5n - 7 = n^{\Theta(1)}$ and $2^{3n} = 2^{\Theta(n)}$ make better sense when you think of the symbol Θ to mean "some constant." However, be sure to remember that $4^n \cdot n^2 = 2^{\Theta(n)}$ is also true.

"=" vs "≤": $7n = O(n^2)$ is also standard notation. This makes less sense to me. Because it means that $7n$ is at most some constant times n^2, a better notation would be $7n \le O(n^2)$. The standard notation is even more awkward, because $O(n) = O(n^2)$ should be true, but $O(n^2) = O(n)$ should be false. What sense does that make?

More Details: You can decide how much information about a function you want to reveal. If $f(n) = 5n^2 + 3n$, you could say

- $f(n) \in n^{\Theta(1)}$, i.e., a polynomial
- $f(n) \in \Theta(n^2)$, i.e., a quadratic
- $f(n) \in (5 + o(1))n^2 = 5n^2 + o(n^2)$, i.e., $5n^2$ plus some low-order terms.
- $f(n) \in 5n^2 + O(n)$, i.e., 5^2 plus at most some linear terms.

The Formal Definitions of Theta and BigOh:

$f(n) \in \Theta(g(n))$	iff	$\exists c_1, c_2 > 0\ \exists n_0\ \forall n \ge n_0,\ c_1 \cdot g(n) \le f(n) \le c_2 \cdot g(n)$
$f(n) \in O(g(n))$	iff	$\exists c > 0\quad\ \exists n_0\ \forall n \ge n_0,\ 0 \le f(n) \le c \cdot g(n)$
$f(n) \in \Omega(g(n))$	iff	$\exists c > 0\quad\ \exists n_0\ \forall n \ge n_0,\ c \cdot g(n) \le f(n)$
$f(n) \in n^{\Theta(1)}$	iff	$\exists c_1, c_2 > 0\ \exists n_0\ \forall n \ge n_0,\ n^{c_1} \le f(n) \le n^{c_2}$
$f(n) \in 2^{\Theta(n)}$	iff	$\exists c_1, c_2 > 0\ \exists n_0\ \forall n \ge n_0,\ 2^{c_1 n} \le f(n) \le 2^{c_2 n}$
$f(n) \notin \Theta(g(n))$	iff	$\forall c_1, c_2 > 0\ \forall n_0\ \exists n \ge n_0,\ [c_1 \cdot g(n) > f(n) \text{ or } f(n) > c_2 \cdot g(n)]$

Bounded Between: The statement $f(n) \in \Theta(g(n))$ means that the function $f(n)$ is bounded between $c_1 \cdot g(n)$ and $c_2 \cdot g(n)$. See Figure 25.1.

Requirements on c_1 and c_2: The only requirements on the constants are that c_1 be sufficiently small (e.g., 0.001) but positive and c_2 be sufficiently large (e.g., 1,000) to work, and that they be fixed (that is, do not depend on n). We allow unreasonably extreme values like $c_2 = 10^{100}$, to make the definition mathematically clean and not geared to a specific application.

Sufficiently Large n: Given fixed c_1 and c_2, the statement $c_1 g(n) \le f(n) \le c_2 g(n)$ should be true for all sufficiently large values of n, (i.e., $\forall n \ge n_0$).

Definition of Sufficiently Large n_0: Again to make the mathematics clean and not geared to a specific application, we will simply require that there exist some definition of sufficiently large n_0 that works. Exercise 25.0.2 gives an example in which n_0 needs to be unreasonably large.

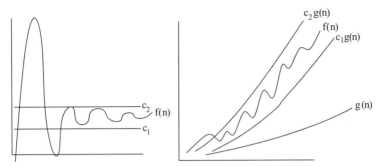

Figure 25.1: $f(n) \in \Theta(1)$ and $f(n) \in \Theta(g(n))$.

Proving $f(n) \in \Theta(g(n))$: Use the prover–adversary game.

- You as the prover provide c_1, c_2, and n_0.
- Some adversary gives you an n that is at least your n_0.
- You then prove that $c_1 g(n) \leq f(n) \leq c_2 g(n)$.

> **Example:** For example, $2n^2 + 100n = \Theta(n^2)$. Let $c_1 = 2$, $c_2 = 3$, and $n_0 = 100$. Then, for all $n \geq 100$, we have $c_1 g(n) = 2n^2 \leq 2n^2 + 100n = f(n)$ and $f(n) = 2n^2 + 100n \leq 2n^2 + n \cdot n = 3n^2 = c_2 g(n)$. The values of c_1, c_2, and n_0 are not unique. For example, $n_0 = 1$, $c_2 = 102$, and $n_0 = 1$ also work, because for all $n \geq 1$ we have $f(n) = 2n^2 + 100n \leq 2n^2 + 100n^2 = 102n^2 = c_2 g(n)$.

The Formal Definitions of Little Oh and Little Omega:

Class	$\lim_{n \to \infty} \frac{f(n)}{g(n)} =$	A practically equivalent definition
$f(n) = \Theta(g(n))$	Some constant	$f(n) = O(g(n))$ and $f(n) = \Omega(g(n))$
$f(n) = o(g(n))$	Zero	$f(n) = O(g(n))$, but $f(n) \neq \Omega(g(n))$
$f(n) = \omega(g(n))$	∞	$f(n) \neq O(g(n))$, but $f(n) = \Omega(g(n))$

Examples:

- $2n^2 + 100n = \Theta(n^2)$ and $\lim_{n \to \infty} \frac{2n^2 + 100n}{n^2} = 2$
- $2n + 100 = o(n^2)$ and $\lim_{n \to \infty} \frac{2n + 100}{n^2} = 0$
- $2n^3 + 100n = \omega(n^2)$ and $\lim_{n \to \infty} \frac{2n^3 + 100n}{n^2} = \infty$

EXERCISE 25.2.1 *As in Exercise 25.1.7, compare the classes $(5 + o(1))n^2$ and $5n^2 + O(n)$.*

EXERCISE 25.2.2 *(See solution in Part Five.) Formally prove or disprove the following:*

1. $14n^9 + 5{,}000n^7 + 23n^2 \log n \in O(n^9)$
2. $2n^2 - 100n \in \Theta(n^2)$
3. $14n^8 - 100n^6 \in O(n^7)$

4. $14n^8 + 100n^6 \in \Theta(n^9)$
5. $2^{n+1} \in O(2^n)$
6. $2^{2n} \in O(2^n)$

EXERCISE 25.2.3 *Prove that if $f_1(n) \in \Theta(g_1(n))$ and $f_2(n) \in \Theta(g_2(n))$, then $f_1(n) + f_2(n) \in \max(\Theta(g_1(n)), \Theta(g_2(n)))$.*

EXERCISE 25.2.4 *Prove that if $f_1(n), f_2(n) \in n^{\Theta(1)}$, then $f_1(n) \cdot f_2(n) \in n^{\Theta(1)}$.*

EXERCISE 25.2.5 *Let $f(n)$ be a function. As you know, $\Theta(f(n))$ drops low-order terms and the leading coefficient. Explain what each of the following does: $2^{\Theta(\log_2 f(n))}$ and $\log_2(\Theta(2^{f(n)}))$. For each, explain to what extent the function is approximated.*

EXERCISE 25.2.6 *Let x be a real value. As you know, $\lfloor x \rfloor$ rounds it down to the next integer. Explain what each of the following does: $2 \cdot \lfloor \frac{x}{2} \rfloor$, $\frac{1}{2} \cdot \lfloor 2 \cdot x \rfloor$, and $2^{\lfloor \log_2 x \rfloor}$.*

EXERCISE 25.2.7 *Suppose that $y = \Theta(\log x)$. Which of the following are true: $x = \Theta(2^y)$ and $x = 2^{\Theta(y)}$? Why?*

EXERCISE 25.2.8 *(See solution in Part Five.) It is impossible to algebraically solve the equation $x = 7y^3(\log_2 y)^{18}$ for y.*

1. *Approximate $7y^3(\log_2 y)^{18}$ and then solve for y. This approximates the value of y.*
2. *Get a better approximation as follows. Plug in your above approximation for y to express $(\log_2 y)^{18}$ in terms of x. Plug this into $x = 7y^3(\log_2 y)^{18}$. Now solve for y again. (You could repeat this step for better and better approximations.)*
3. *Observe how a similar technique was used in Exercises 25.0.1 and 25.0.2 to approximate a solution for $(\log_{10} n)^{1,000,000} = n$.*

26 Adding-Made-Easy Approximations

```
algorithm Eg(n)
    loop i = 1..n
        loop j = 1..i
            loop k = 1..j
                put "Hi"
            end loop
        end loop
    end loop
end algorithm
```

The inner loop requires time $\sum_{k=1}^{j} 1 = j$.
The next requires $\sum_{j=1}^{i} \sum_{k=1}^{j} 1 = \sum_{j=1}^{i} j = \Theta(i^2)$.
The total is $\sum_{i=1}^{n} \sum_{j=1}^{i} \sum_{k=1}^{j} 1 = \sum_{i=1}^{n} \Theta(i^2) = \Theta(n^3)$.

Sums arise often in the study of computer algorithms. For example, if the ith iteration of a loop takes time $f(i)$ and it loops n times, then the total time is $f(1) + f(2) + f(3) + \cdots + f(n)$. This we denote as $\sum_{i=1}^{n} f(i)$. It can be approximated by the integral $\int_{x=1}^{n} f(x) \, \delta x$, because the first is the area under the stairs of height $f(i)$ and the second under the curve $f(x)$. (In fact, both $\sum$ (from the Greek letter sigma) and $\int$ (from the old long S) are S for sum.) Note that, even though the individual terms are indexed by i (or x), the total is a function of n. The goal now is to approximate $\sum_{i=1}^{n} f(i)$ for various functions $f(i)$.

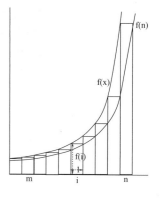

Beyond learning the classic techniques for computing $\sum_{i=1}^{n} 2^i$, $\sum_{i=1}^{n} i$, and $\sum_{i=1}^{n} \frac{1}{i}$, we do not study how to evaluate sums exactly, but only how to approximate them to within a constant factor. We develop easy rules that most computer scientists use but for some reason are not usually taught, partly because they are not always true. We have formally proven when they are true and when not. We call them collectively the *adding-made-easy technique*.

26.1 The Technique

The following table outlines the few easy rules with which you will be able to compute $\Theta(\sum_{i=1}^{n} f(i))$ for functions with the basic form $f(n) = \Theta(b^{an} \cdot n^d \cdot \log^e n)$. (We consider more general functions at the end of this section.)

b^a	d	e	Type of Sum	$\sum_{i=1}^{n} f(i)$	Examples	
> 1	Any	Any	Geometric Increase (dominated by last term)	$\Theta(f(n))$	$\sum_{i=0}^{n} 2^{2^i}$	$\approx 1 \cdot 2^{2^n}$
					$\sum_{i=0}^{n} b^i$	$= \Theta(b^n)$
					$\sum_{i=0}^{n} 2^i$	$= \Theta(2^n)$
$= 1$	> -1	Any	Arithmetic-like (half of terms approximately equal)	$\Theta(n \cdot f(n))$	$\sum_{i=1}^{n} i^d$	$= \Theta(n \cdot n^d) = \Theta(n^{d+1})$
					$\sum_{i=1}^{n} i^2$	$= \Theta(n \cdot n^2) = \Theta(n^3)$
					$\sum_{i=1}^{n} i$	$= \Theta(n \cdot n) = \Theta(n^2)$
					$\sum_{i=1}^{n} 1$	$= \Theta(n \cdot 1) = \Theta(n)$
					$\sum_{i=1}^{n} \frac{1}{i^{0.99}}$	$= \Theta(n \cdot \frac{1}{n^{0.99}}) = \Theta(n^{0.01})$
	$= -1$	$= 0$	Harmonic	$\Theta(\ln n)$	$\sum_{i=1}^{n} \frac{1}{i}$	$= \log_e(n) + \Theta(1)$
	< -1	Any	Bounded tail (dominated by first term)	$\Theta(1)$	$\sum_{i=1}^{n} \frac{1}{i^{1.001}}$	$= \Theta(1)$
					$\sum_{i=1}^{n} \frac{1}{i^2}$	$= \Theta(1)$
< 1	Any	Any			$\sum_{i=1}^{n} (\frac{1}{2})^i$	$= \Theta(1)$
					$\sum_{i=0}^{n} b^{-i}$	$= \Theta(1)$

Four Different Classes of Solutions: All of the sums that we will consider have one of four different classes of solutions. The intuition for each is quite straightforward.

Geometrically Increasing: If the terms grow very quickly, the total is dominated by the last and biggest term $f(n)$. Hence, one can approximate the sum by only considering the last term: $\sum_{i=1}^{n} f(i) = \Theta(f(n))$.

Examples: Consider the classic sum in which each of the n terms is twice the previous, $1 + 2 + 4 + 8 + 16 + \cdots + 2^n$. Either by examining areas within Figure 26.1.a or 26.1.b or using simple induction, one can prove that the total is always one less than twice the biggest term: $\sum_{i=0}^{n} 2^i = 2 \times 2^n - 1 = \Theta(2^n)$. More generally, $\sum_{i=0}^{n} b^i \approx \frac{b}{b-1} \cdot b^n$, which can be approximated by $\Theta(f(n)) = \Theta(b^n)$. (Similarly, $\int_{x=0}^{n} b^x \, \delta x = \frac{1}{\ln b} b^n$.) The same is true for even fastergrowing functions like $\sum_{i=0}^{n} 2^{2^i} \approx 1 \times 2^{2^n}$.

Basic-Form Exponentials: The same technique, $\sum_{i=1}^{n} f(i) = \Theta(f(n))$, works for all basic-form exponentials, i.e., for $f(n) = \Theta(b^{an} \cdot n^d \cdot \log^e n)$ with $b^a > 1$, we have that $\sum_{i=1}^{n} f(i) = \Theta(b^{an} \cdot n^d \cdot \log^e n)$.

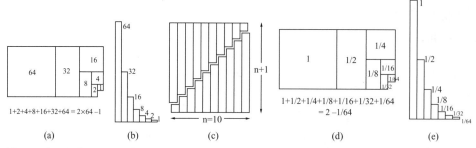

Figure 26.1: Examples of geometrically increasing, arithmetic-like, and bounded-tail function.

Arithmetic-like: If half of the terms are roughly the same size, then the total is roughly the number of terms times the last term, namely $\sum_{i=1}^{n} f(i) = \Theta(n \cdot f(n))$.

Examples:

> ***Constant:*** Clearly the sum of n ones is n, i.e., $\sum_{i=1}^{n} 1 = n$. This is $\Theta(n \cdot f(n))$.

> ***Linear:*** The classic example is the sum in which each of the n terms is only one bigger than the previous, $\sum_{i=1}^{n} i = 1 + 2 + 3 + 4 + 5 + \cdots + n = \frac{n(n+1)}{2}$. This can be approximated using $\Theta(n \cdot f(n)) = \Theta(n^2)$. See Figure 26.1.

> ***Polynomials:*** Both $\sum_{i=1}^{n} i^2 = \frac{1}{3}n^3 + \frac{1}{2}n^2 + \frac{1}{6}n$ and more generally $\sum_{i=1}^{n} i^d = \frac{1}{d+1}n^{d+1} + \Theta(n^d)$ can be approximated with $\Theta(n \cdot f(n)) = \Theta(n \cdot n^d) = \Theta(n^{d+1})$. (Similarly, $\int_{x=0}^{n} x^d \, \delta x = \frac{1}{d+1}n^{d+1}$.)

> ***Above Harmonic:*** $\sum_{i=1}^{n} \frac{1}{n^{0.999}} \approx 1{,}000 \ n^{0.001}$ can be approximated with $\Theta(n \cdot f(n)) = \Theta(n \cdot n^{-0.999}) = \Theta(n^{0.001})$.

Basic-Form Polynomials: The same technique, $\sum_{i=1}^{n} f(i) = \Theta(n \cdot f(n))$, works for all basic-form polynomials, constants, and slowly decreasing functions, i.e., for $f(n) = \Theta(n^d \cdot \log^e n)$ with $d > 1$ we have that $\sum_{i=1}^{n} f(i) = \Theta(n^{d+1} \cdot \log^e n)$.

Bounded Tail: If the terms shrink quickly, the total is dominated by the first and biggest term $f(1)$, which is assumed here to be $\Theta(1)$, i.e., $\sum_{i=1}^{n} f(i) = \Theta(1)$.

> **Examples:** The classic sum here is when each term is half of the previous, $1 + \frac{1}{2} + \frac{1}{4} + \frac{1}{8} + \frac{1}{16} + \cdots + \frac{1}{2^n}$. See Figure 26.1.d and 26.1.e. The total approaches but never reaches 2, so that $\sum_{i=0}^{n}(\frac{1}{2})^i = 2 - (\frac{1}{2})^n = \Theta(1)$. Similarly, $\sum_{i=1}^{n} \frac{1}{n^{1.001}} \approx 1{,}000 = \Theta(1)$ and $\sum_{i=1}^{n} \frac{1}{n^2} \approx \frac{\pi}{6} \approx 1.5497 = \Theta(1)$.

Basic-Form with Bounded Tail: The same technique, $\sum_{i=1}^{n} f(i) = \Theta(1)$, works for all basic-form polynomially or exponentially decreasing functions, i.e., for $f(n) = \Theta(b^{an} \cdot n^d \cdot \log^e n)$ with $b^a = 1$ and $d < 1$ or with $b^a < 1$.

The Harmonic Sum: The sum $\sum_{i=1}^{n} \frac{1}{i}$ is referred to as the *harmonic sum* because of its connection to music. It arises surprisingly often and it has an unexpected total:

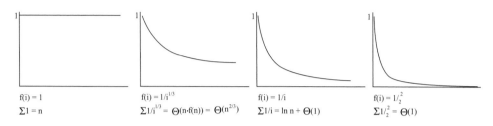

$f(i) = 1$
$\sum 1 = n$

$f(i) = 1/i^{1/3}$
$\sum 1/i^{1/3} = \Theta(n \cdot f(n)) = \Theta(n^{2/3})$

$f(i) = 1/i$
$\sum 1/i = \ln n + \Theta(1)$

$f(i) = 1/\frac{2}{i}$
$\sum 1/\frac{2}{i} = \Theta(1)$

On the Boundary: The boundary between those sums for which $\sum_{i=1}^{n} f(i) = \Theta(n \cdot f(n))$ and those for which $\sum_{i=1}^{n} f(i) = \Theta(1)$ occurs when these approximations meet, i.e., when $\Theta(n \cdot f(n)) = \Theta(1)$. This occurs at the harmonic function $f(n) = \frac{1}{n}$. Given that both approximations say the total is $\sum_{i=1}^{n} \frac{1}{i} = \Theta(1)$, it is reasonable to think that this is the answer, but it is not.

The Total: It turns out that the total is within 1 of the natural logarithm, $\sum_{i=1}^{n} \frac{1}{i} = \log_e n + \Theta(1)$. (Similarly, $\int_{x=1}^{n+1} \frac{1}{x} \delta x = \log_e n + \Theta(1)$.) See Figure 26.2.

More Examples:

Geometric Increasing:
- $\sum_{i=1}^{n} 8 \frac{2^i}{i^{100}} + i^3 = \Theta(\frac{2^n}{n^{100}})$
- $\sum_{i=1}^{n} 3^i \log i + 5^i + i^{100} = \Theta(3^n \log n)$
- $\sum_{i=1}^{n} 2^{i^2} + i^2 \log i = \Theta(2^{n^2})$
- $\sum_{i=1}^{n} 2^{2^i - i^2} = \Theta(2^{2^n - n^2})$

Arithmetic (Increasing):
- $\sum_{i=1}^{n} i^4 + 7i^3 + i^2 = \Theta(n^5)$
- $\sum_{i=1}^{n} i^{4.3} \log^3 i + i^3 \log^9 i = \Theta(n^{5.3} \log^3 n)$

Arithmetic (Decreasing):
- $\sum_{i=2}^{n} \frac{1}{\log i} = \Theta(\frac{n}{\log n})$
- $\sum_{i=1}^{n} \frac{\log^3 i}{i^{0.6}} = \Theta(n^{0.4} \log^3 n)$

Bounded Tail:
- $\sum_{i=1}^{n} \frac{\log^3 i}{i^{1.6} + 3i} = \Theta(1)$
- $\sum_{i=1}^{n} \frac{i^{100}}{2^i} = \Theta(1)$
- $\sum_{i=1}^{n} \frac{1}{2^{2^i}} = \Theta(1)$

Stranger Examples:
- A useful fact is $\sum_{i=m}^{n} f(i) = \sum_{i=1}^{n} f(i) - \sum_{i=1}^{m-1} f(i)$. Hence, $\sum_{i=m}^{n} \frac{1}{i} = \Theta(\log n) - \Theta(\log m) = \Theta(\log \frac{n}{m})$.

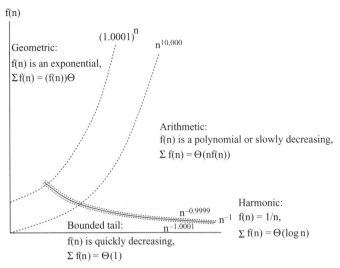

f(n)

Geometric:
f(n) is an exponential,
$\Sigma f(n) = (f(n))\Theta$

$(1.0001)^n$ $n^{10,000}$

Arithmetic:
f(n) is a polynomial or slowly decreasing,
$\Sigma f(n) = \Theta(nf(n))$

Harmonic:
$n^{-0.9999}$ n^{-1} f(n) = 1/n,
Bounded tail: $n^{-1.0001}$ $\Sigma f(n) = \Theta(\log n)$
f(n) is quickly decreasing,
$\Sigma f(n) = \Theta(1)$

Figure 26.2: Boundaries between geometric, arithmetic, harmonic, and bounded tail.

- If the sum is arithmetic, then the sum is the number of terms times the largest term. This gives $\sum_{i=m}^{m+n} i^2 = \Theta(n \cdot (m+n)^2)$.
- To solve $\sum_{i=1}^{5n^2+n} i^3 \log i$, let $N = 5n^2 + n$ denote the number of terms. Then $\sum_{j=1}^{N} i^3 \log i = \Theta(N \cdot f(N)) = \Theta(N^4 \log N)$. Substituting back in for N gives $\sum_{i=1}^{5n^2+n} i^3 \log i = \Theta((5n^2 + n)^4 \log(5n^2 + n)) = \Theta(n^8 \log n)$.
- Between terms, i changes, but n does not. Hence, n can be treated like a constant. For example, $\sum_{i=1}^{n} i \cdot n \cdot m = nm \cdot \sum_{i=1}^{n} i = nm \cdot \Theta(n^2) = \Theta(n^3 m)$.
- In $\sum_{i=\frac{n}{2}}^{n} \frac{1}{i^2}$, the terms are decreasing fast enough to be bounded by the first term. Here, however, the first term is not $\Theta(1)$, but is

$$\Theta\left(\frac{1}{(\frac{n}{2})^2}\right) = \Theta\left(\frac{1}{n^2}\right)$$

- When in doubt, start by determining the first term, the last term, and the number of terms. In $\sum_{i=1}^{\log_2 n} 2^{\log_2 n-i} \cdot i^2$, the first term is $f(1) = 2^{\log n-1} \cdot 1^2 = \Theta(n)$, and the last term is $f(\log n) = 2^{\log n-\log n} \cdot (\log n)^2 = \Theta(\log^2 n)$. The terms decrease geometrically in i. The total is then $\Theta(f(1)) = \Theta(n)$.
- $\sum_{i=1}^{n} \sum_{j=0}^{n} i^2 j^3 = \sum_{i=1}^{n} i^2 [\sum_{j=0}^{n} j^3] = \sum_{i=1}^{n} i^2 \Theta(n^4) = \Theta(n^4)[\sum_{i=1}^{n} i^2] = \Theta(n^4)\Theta(n^3) = \Theta(n^7)$.

EXERCISE 26.1.1 *Give the* Θ *approximation of the following sums. Indicate which rule you use, and show your work.*

1. $\sum_{i=0}^{n} 7i^3 - 300i^2 + 16$
2. $\sum_{i=0}^{n} i^8 + \frac{2^{3i}}{i^2}$
3. $\sum_{i=0}^{n} \frac{1}{i^{1.1}}$

4. $\sum_{i=0}^{n} \frac{1}{i^{0.9}}$

5. $\sum_{i=0}^{n} 7 \frac{i^{3.72}}{\log^2 i} - 300 i^2 \log^9 i$

6. $\sum_{i=1}^{n} \frac{\log^e i}{i}$

7. $\sum_{i=1}^{\log n} n \cdot i^2$

8. $\sum_{i=0}^{n} \sum_{j=0}^{m} \frac{j}{i}$

9. $\sum_{i=1}^{n} \sum_{j=1}^{i} j^i$

10. $\sum_{i=1}^{n} \sum_{j=1}^{i^2} ij \log(i)$

26.2 Some Proofs for the Adding-Made-Easy Technique

This section presents a few of the classic techniques for summing and sketches the proof of the adding-made-easy technique.

Simple Geometric Sums:

Theorem: When $b > 1$, $\sum_{i=1}^{n} b^i = \Theta(f(n))$ and when $b < 1$, $\sum_{i=1}^{n} f(i) = \Theta(1)$.

Proof:

$$S = 1 + b + b^2 + \cdots b^n$$
$$b \cdot S = b + b^2 + b^3 + \cdots b^{n+1}.$$

Subtracting those two equations gives

$$(1 - b) \cdot S = 1 - b^{n+1}$$
$$S = \frac{1 - b^{n+1}}{1 - b} \text{ or } \frac{b^{n+1} - 1}{b - 1}$$
$$= \Theta(\max(f(0), f(n)))$$

Ratio between Terms: To prove that a geometric sum is not more than a constant times the biggest term, we must compare each term $f(i)$ with this biggest term. One way to do this is to first compare each consecutive pairs of terms $f(i)$ and $f(i + 1)$.

Theorem: If for all sufficiently large i, the ratio between terms is bounded away from one, i.e., $\exists b > 1$, $\exists n_0$, $\forall i \geq n_0$, $f(i + 1)/f(i) \geq b$, then $\sum_{i=1}^{n} f(i) = \Theta(f(n))$.
Conversely, if $\exists b < 1$, $\exists n_0$, $\forall i \geq n_0$, $\frac{f(i+1)}{f(i)} \leq b$, then $\sum_{i=1}^{n} f(i) = \Theta(1)$.

Examples:

Typical: With $f(i) = 2^i/i$, the ratio between consecutive terms is
$$\frac{f(i + 1)}{f(i)} = \frac{2^{i+1}}{i + 1} \cdot \frac{i}{2^i} = 2 \cdot \frac{i}{i + 1} = 2 \cdot \frac{1}{1 + \frac{1}{i}}$$
which is at least 1.99 for sufficiently large i. Similarly for any $f(n) = \Theta(b^{an} \cdot n^d \cdot \log^e n)$ with $b^a > 1$.

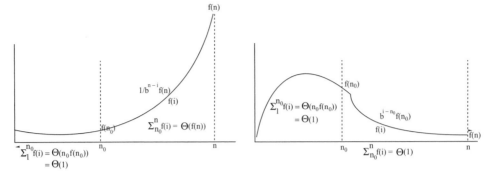

Figure 26.3: In both pictures, the total before n gets sufficiently large is some constant. On the left, the total for large n is bounded by an growing exponential, and on the right by a decreasing exponential.

Not Bounded Away: On the other hand, the arithmetic function $f(i) = i$ has a ratio between the terms of $\frac{i+1}{i} = 1 + \frac{1}{i}$. Though this is always bigger than one, it is not bounded away from one by any constant $b > 1$.

Proof: If $\forall i \geq n_0$, $f(i+1)/f(i) \geq b > 1$, then it follows either by unwinding or induction that

$$f(i) \leq \left(\frac{1}{b}\right)^1 f(i+1) \leq \left(\frac{1}{b}\right)^2 f(i+2) \leq \left(\frac{1}{b}\right)^3 f(i+3) \leq \cdots \leq \left(\frac{1}{b}\right)^{n-i} f(n)$$

See Figure 26.3. This gives that

$$\sum_{i=1}^{n} f(i) = \sum_{i=1}^{n_0} f(i) + \sum_{i=n_0}^{n} f(i) \leq \Theta(1) + \sum_{i=n_0}^{n} \left(\frac{1}{b}\right)^{n-i} f(n) \leq \Theta(1) + f(n) \cdot \sum_{j=0}^{n} \left(\frac{1}{b}\right)^j$$

which we have already proved is $\Theta(f(n))$.

A Simple Arithmetic Sum: We prove as follows that $\sum_{i=1}^{n} i = \Theta(n \cdot f(n)) = \Theta(n^2)$:

$$
\begin{aligned}
S &= 1 + 2 + 3 + \cdots + n-2 + n-1 + n \\
S &= n + n-1 + n-2 + \cdots + 3 + 2 + 1 \\
2S &= n+1 + n+1 + n+1 + \cdots + n+1 + n+1 + n+1 \\
&= n \cdot (n+1) \\
S &= \tfrac{1}{2} n \cdot (n+1)
\end{aligned}
$$

Arithmetic Sums: We will now justify the intuition that if half of the terms are roughly the same size, then the total is roughly the number of terms times the last term, namely $\sum_{i=1}^{n} f(i) = \Theta(n \cdot f(n))$.

Theorem: If for sufficiently large n, the function $f(n)$ is nondecreasing, and $f(\frac{n}{2}) = \Theta(f(n))$, then $\sum_{i=1}^{n} f(i) = \Theta(n \cdot f(n))$.

Examples:

Typical: The function $f(n) = n^d$ for $d \geq 0$ is non-decreasing and $f(\frac{n}{2}) = (\frac{n}{2})^d = \frac{1}{2^d} f(n)$. Similarly for $f(n) = \Theta(n^d \cdot \log^e n)$. We consider $-1 < d < 0$ later.

Without the Property: The function $f(n) = 2^n$ does not have this property, because $f(\frac{n}{2}) = 2^{n/2} = \frac{1}{2^{n/2}} f(n)$.

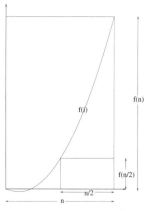

Proof: Because $f(i)$ is nondecreasing, half of the terms are at least the middle term $f(\frac{n}{2})$, and all of the terms are at most the biggest term $f(n)$. Hence, $\frac{n}{2} \cdot f(\frac{n}{2}) \leq \sum_{i=1}^{n} f(i) \leq n \cdot f(n)$. Because $f(\frac{n}{2}) = \Theta(f(n))$, these bounds match, giving $\sum_{i=1}^{n} f(i) = \Theta(n \cdot f(n))$.

The Harmonic Sum: The harmonic sum is a famous sum that arises surprisingly often. The total $\sum_{i=1}^{n} \frac{1}{i}$ is within 1 of $\log_e n$. However, we will not bound it quite so closely.

Theorem: $\sum_{i=1}^{n} \frac{1}{i} = \Theta(\log n)$.

Proof: One way of approximating the harmonic sum is to break it into $\log_2 n$ blocks with 2^k terms in the kth block, and then to prove that the total for each block is between $\frac{1}{2}$ and 1:

$$\sum_{i=1}^{n} \frac{1}{i} = \overbrace{\underbrace{\frac{1}{1}}_{\leq 1 \cdot 1 = 1}}^{\geq 1 \cdot \frac{1}{2} = \frac{1}{2}} + \overbrace{\underbrace{\frac{1}{2} + \frac{1}{3}}_{\leq 2 \cdot \frac{1}{2} = 1}}^{\geq 2 \cdot \frac{1}{4} = \frac{1}{2}} + \overbrace{\underbrace{\frac{1}{4} + \frac{1}{5} + \frac{1}{6} + \frac{1}{7}}_{\leq 4 \cdot \frac{1}{4} = 1}}^{\geq 4 \cdot \frac{1}{8} = \frac{1}{2}} + \overbrace{\underbrace{\frac{1}{8} + \cdots + \frac{1}{15}}_{\leq 8 \cdot \frac{1}{8} = 1}}^{\geq 8 \cdot \frac{1}{16} = \frac{1}{2}} + \cdots$$

From this, it follows that $\frac{1}{2} \cdot \log_2 n \leq \sum_{i=1}^{n} \frac{1}{i} \leq 1 \cdot \log_2 n$.

Close to Harmonic: We will now use a similar technique to prove the remaining two cases of the adding-made-easy technique.

Theorem: $\sum_{i=1}^{n} 1/i^{d'}$ is $\Theta(1)$ if $d' > 1$ and is $\Theta(n \cdot f(n))$ if $d' < 1$. (Similarly for $f(n) = \Theta(n^d \cdot \log^e n)$ with $d < -1$ or > -1.)

Proof: As we did with the harmonic sum, we break the sum $\sum_{i=1}^{n} f(n)$ into blocks where the kth block has the 2^k terms $\sum_{i=2^k}^{2^{k+1}-1} f(i)$. Because the terms are decreasing, the total for the block is at most $F(k) = 2^k \cdot f(2^k)$. The total overall is then at most

$$\sum_{k=0}^{\log_2 n} F(k) = \sum_{k=0}^{\log_2 n} 2^k \cdot f(2^k) = \sum_{k=0}^{\log_2 n} \frac{2^k}{(2^k)^{d'}} = \sum_{k=0}^{N} \frac{1}{2^{k \cdot (d'-1)}}.$$

If $d' > 1$, then this sum is exponentially decreasing and converges to $\Theta(1)$. If $d' < 1$, then this sum is exponentially increasing and diverges to $\Theta(F(N)) = \Theta(2^{\log_2 n} \cdot f(n)) = \Theta(n \cdot f(n)))$.

Functions without the Basic Form: (Warning: This topic may be a little hard.) Until now we have only considered functions with the basic form $f(n) = \Theta(b^{an} \cdot n^d \cdot \log^e n)$. We would like to generalize the adding-made-easy technique as follows:

	Geometric Increasing	Arithmetic	Harmonic	Bounded Tail
If	$f(n) \geq 2^{\Omega(n)}$	$f(n) = n^{\Theta(1)-1}$	$f(n) = \Theta(\frac{1}{n})$	$f(n) \leq n^{-1-\Omega(1)}$
then	$\sum_{i=1}^{n} f(i) = \Theta(f(n))$	$\sum_{i=1}^{n} f(i) = \Theta(n \cdot f(n))$	$\sum_{i=1}^{n} f(i) = \Theta(\log n)$	$\sum_{i=1}^{n} f(i) = \Theta(1)$

Example: Consider $f(n) = n^{8+\frac{1}{n}}$ or $f(n) = n^{-\frac{1}{n}}$. They are bounded between n^{d_1} and n^{d_2} for constants $d_2 \geq d_1 > 0 - 1$, and hence for both we have $f(n) \in n^{\Theta(1)-1}$. Adding made easy then gives that $\sum_{i=1}^{n} f(i) = \Theta(n \cdot f(n))$, so that $\sum_{i=1}^{n} i^{8+\frac{1}{i}} = \Theta(n^{9+\frac{1}{n}})$ and $\sum_{i=1}^{n} i^{-\frac{1}{i}} = \Theta(n^{1-\frac{1}{n}})$.

Counterexample: The goal here is to predict the sum $\sum_{i=1}^{n} f(i)$ from the value of the last term $f(n)$. We are unable to do this if the terms oscillate like those created with sines, cosines, floors, and ceilings. Exercise 26.2.4 proves that $f(n) = 2^{2^{\lceil \log_2 n \rceil}}$ and $f(n) = 2^{\lfloor \frac{1}{2} \cos(\pi \log_2 n)+1.5 \rfloor \cdot n}$ are counterexamples for the geometric case and that $f(n) = 2^{2^{\lfloor \log \log n \rfloor}}$ is one for the arithmetic case.

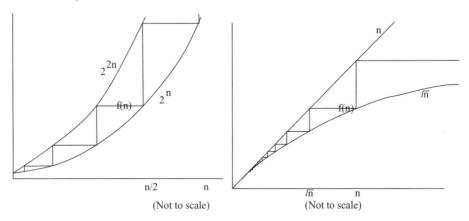

(Not to scale)   (Not to scale)

Simple Analytical Functions: We can prove that the adding-made-easy technique works for all functions $f(n)$ that can be expressed with n, real constants, plus, minus, times, divide, exponentiation, and logarithms. Such functions are said to be *simple analytical*.

Proof Sketch: I will only give a sketch of the proof here. For the geometric case, we must prove that if $f(n)$ is simple analytical and $f(n) \geq 2^{\Omega(n)}$, then $\exists b > 1$,

$\exists n_0, \; \forall n \geq n_0, \; f(n+1)/f(n) \geq b$. From this, the ratio-between-terms theorem above gives that $\sum_{i=1}^{n} f(i) = \Theta(f(n))$.

Because the function is growing exponentially, we know that generally it grows at least as fast as fast as b^n for some constant $b > 1$ and hence $f(n+1)/f(n) \geq b$, or equivalently $h(n) = \log f(n+1) - \log f(n) - \log b > 0$ for an infinite number of values for n.

A deep theorem about simple analytical functions is that they cannot oscillate forever and hence can change sign at most a finite number of places. It follows that there must be a last place n_0 at which the sign changes. We can conclude that $\forall n \geq n_0, \; h(n) > 0$ and hence $f(n+1)/f(n) \geq b$.

The geometrically decreasing case is the same except $f(n+1)/f(n) \leq b$. The arithmetic case is similar except that it proves that if $f(n)$ is simple analytical and $f(n) = n^{\Theta(1)-1}$, then $f(\frac{n}{2}) = \Theta(f(n))$.

EXERCISE 26.2.1 *(See solution in Part Five.) Zeno's classic paradox is that Achilles is traveling 1 km/hr and has 1 km to travel. First he must cover half his distance, then half of his remaining distance, then half of this remaining distance, ... He never arrives. By Bryan Magee states, "People have found it terribly disconcerting. There must be a fault in the logic, they have said. But no one has yet been fully successful in demonstrating what it is." Resolve this ancient paradox by adding up the time required for all steps.*

EXERCISE 26.2.2 *Prove that if $\exists b < 1, \; \exists n_0, \; \forall i \geq n_0, \; f(i+1)/f(i) \leq b$, then $\sum_{i=n_0}^{n} f(i) = \Theta(f(n_0)) = \Theta(1)$.*

EXERCISE 26.2.3 *A seeming paradox is how one could have a vessel that has finite volume and infinite surface area. This (theoretical) vessel could be filled with a small amount of paint but require an infinite amount of paint to paint. For $h \in [1, \infty)$, its cross section at h units from its top is a circle with radius $r = \frac{1}{h^c}$ for some constant c. Integrate (or add up) its cross-sectional circumference to compute its surface area, and integrate (or add up) its cross-sectional area to compute its volume. Give a value for c such that its surface area is infinite and its volume is finite.*

EXERCISE 26.2.4 *(See solution in Part Five.)*

1. *For $f(n) = 2^{2^{\lceil \log_2 n \rceil}}$, prove that $f(n) \geq 2^{\Omega(n)}$*
2. *and that $\sum_{i=1}^{n} f(i) \neq \Theta(f(n))$.*
3. *For $f(n) = 2^{2^{\lfloor \log\log n \rfloor}}$, prove that $f(n) = n^{\Theta(1)-1}$*
4. *and that $\sum_{i=1}^{n} f(i) \neq \Theta(n \cdot f(n))$.*
5. *Plot $f(n) = 2^{\lfloor \frac{1}{2} \cos(\pi \log_2 n) + 1.5 \rfloor \cdot n}$, and prove that it is also a counterexample for the geometric case.*

27 Recurrence Relations

A wise man told the king to give him one grain of rice one for the first square of a chessboard and for the each remaining square to give him twice the number for the previous square. Thirty-two days later, the king realized that there is not enough rice in all of world to reward him. The number of grains on the nth square is given by the recurrence relation $T(1) = 1$ and $T(n) = 2T(n-1)$.

The algebraic equation $x^2 = x + 2$ specifies the value of an unknown real that must be found. The differential equation $\frac{\delta f(x)}{\delta x} = f(x)$ specifies functions from reals to reals that must be found. Similarly, a recurrence relations like $T(n) = 2 \times T(n-1)$ specifies functions from integers to reals. One way to solve each of these is to guess a solution and check to see if it works. Here $T(n) = 2^n$ works, i.e., $2^n = 2 \times 2^{n-1}$. However, $T(n) = c \cdot 2^n$ also works for each value of c. Making the further requirement that $T(1) = 1$ narrows the solution set to only $T(n) = \frac{1}{2} \cdot 2^n = 2^{n-1}$.

27.1 The Technique

Timing of Recursive Programs: Recursive relations are used to determine the running time of recursive programs. (See Chapter 8.) For example, if a routine, when given an instance of size n, does $f(n)$ work itself and then recurses a times on subinstances of size $\frac{n}{b}$, then the running time is $T(n) = a \cdot T\left(\frac{n}{b}\right) + f(n)$.

See Section 8.6 to learn more about the *tree of stack frames*. Each stack frame consists of one execution of the routine on a single instance, ignoring subroutine calls. The top-level stack frame is called by the user on the required input instance. It recurses on a number of subinstances, creating the next level of stack frames. These in turn recurse again until the instance is sufficiently small that the stack frame returns without recursing. These final stack frames are referred to as *base cases*.

Let $T(n)$ denote the number of "Hi"s that the entire tree of stack frames, given the following code, prints on an instance of size n. The top level stack frame prints "Hi" $f(n)$ times. It then recurses a times on subinstances of size $\frac{n}{b}$. If $T(n)$ is the number of

"Hi"s for instances of size n, then it follows that $T\left(\frac{n}{b}\right)$ is the number for instances of size $\frac{n}{b}$. Repeating this a times will take time $a \cdot T\left(\frac{n}{b}\right)$. It follows that the total number satisfies the recursive relation $T(n) = a \cdot T\left(\frac{n}{b}\right) + f(n)$. The goal of this section is to determine which function $T(n)$ satisfies this relation.

If instead the routine recurses a times on instances of size $n - b$, then the related recurrence relation will be $T(n) = a \cdot T(n - b) + f(n)$.

algorithm $Eg(I_n)$

⟨ *pre-cond* ⟩: I_n is an instance of size n.
⟨ *post-cond* ⟩: Prints $T(n)$ "Hi"s.

begin
    $n = |I_n|$
    if($n \le 1$) then
        put "Hi"
    else
        loop $i = 1..f(n)$
            put "Hi"
        end loop
        loop $i = 1..a$
            $I_{\frac{n}{b}}$ = an input of size $\frac{n}{b}$
            $Eg(I_{\frac{n}{b}})$
        end loop
    end if
end algorithm

When the input has size zero or one, only one "Hi" is printed. In general, we will assume that recursive programs spend $\Theta(1)$ time for instances of size $\Theta(1)$. We express this as $T(1) = 1$, or more generally as $T(\Theta(1)) = \Theta(1)$.

Solving Recurrence Relations: Consider $T(n) = a \cdot T\left(\frac{n}{b}\right) + f(n)$, where $f(n) = \Theta(n^c \cdot \log^d n)$ or $f(n) = 0$.

$\frac{\log a}{\log b}$ vs c	d	Dominated by	$T(n)$	Example $\left(\frac{\log_3 9}{\log_3 3} = 2\right)$	Solution
$<$	Any	Top level	$\Theta(f(n))$	$T(n) = 9 \cdot T\left(\frac{n}{3}\right) + n^4$	$\Theta(n^4)$
$=$	> -1	All levels	$\Theta(f(n) \log n)$	$T(n) = 9 \cdot T\left(\frac{n}{3}\right) + n^2$	$\Theta(n^2 \log n)$
	< -1	Base cases	$\Theta\left(n^{\frac{\log a}{\log b}}\right)$	$T(n) = 9 \cdot T\left(\frac{n}{3}\right) + \frac{n^2}{\log^2 n}$	$\Theta(n^2)$
$>$	Any			$t(n) = 9 \cdot T\left(\frac{n}{3}\right)$	

Consider $T(n) = a \cdot T(n-b) + f(n)$, where $f(n) = \Theta(n^c \cdot \log^d n)$ or $f(n) = 0$.

a	$f(n)$	Dominated by	$T(n)$	Example	Solution
> 1	Any	Base cases	$\Theta(a^{\frac{n}{b}})$	$T(n) = 9 \cdot T(n-3) + n^4$	$\Theta(9^{\frac{n}{3}})$
$= 1$	≥ 1	All levels	$\Theta(n \cdot f(n))$	$T(n) = T(n-3) + n^4$	$\Theta(n^5)$
	$= 0$	Base cases	$\Theta(1)$	$T(n) = T(n-3)$	$\Theta(1)$

A Growing Number of Subinstances of Shrinking Size: Each instance having a subinstances means that the number of subinstances grows exponentially by a factor of a. On the other hand, the sizes of the subinstances shrink exponentially by a factor of b. The amount of work that the instance must do is the function f of this instance size. Whether the growing or the shrinking dominates this process depends upon the relationship between a, b, and $f(n)$.

Dominated By: When total work $T(n)$ done in the tree of stack frames is dominated by the work $f(n)$ done by the top stack frame, we say that the work is *dominated by the top level* of the recursion. The solution in this case will be $T(n) = \Theta(f(n))$. Conversely, we say that it is *dominated by the base cases* when the total is dominated by the sum of the work done by the base cases. Because each base case does only a constant amount of work, the solution will be $T(n) = \Theta(\# \text{ of base cases})$, which is $\Theta(n^{\log a / \log b})$, $\Theta(a^{\frac{n}{b}})$, or $\Theta(1)$ in the above examples. Finally, if the amounts of work at the different levels of recursion are sufficiently close to each other, then we say that the total work is *dominated by all the levels* and the total is the number of levels times this amount of work, namely $T(n) = \Theta(\log n \cdot f(n))$ or $\Theta(n \cdot f(n))$.

The Ratio $\frac{\log a}{\log b}$: See Chapter 24 for a discussion about logarithms. One trick that it gives us is that when computing the ratio between two logarithms, the base used does not matter, because changing the base will introduce the same constant both on the top and the bottom, which will cancel. Hence, when computing such a ratio, you can choose whichever base makes the calculation the easiest. For example, to compute $\frac{\log 16}{\log 8}$, the obvious base to use is 2, because $\frac{\log_2 16}{\log_2 8} = \frac{4}{3}$. This is useful in giving that $T(n) = 16 \cdot T(\frac{n}{8}) + f(n) = \Theta(n^{\log 16 / \log 8}) = \Theta(n^{4/3})$. On the other hand, to compute $\frac{\log 9}{\log 27}$, the obvious base to use is 3, because $\frac{\log_3 9}{\log_3 27} = \frac{2}{3}$, and hence we have $T(n) = 9 \cdot T(\frac{n}{27}) + f(n) = \Theta(n^{2/3})$. Another interesting fact given is that $\log 1 = 0$, which gives that $T(n) = 1 \cdot T(\frac{n}{2}) + f(n)$, $T(n) = \Theta(n^{\log 1 / \log 2}) = \Theta(n^0) = \Theta(1)$.

EXERCISE 27.1.1 *(See solution in Part Five.) Give solutions for the following examples:*

1. $T(n) = 2T(\frac{n}{2}) + n$
2. $T(n) = 2T(\frac{n}{2}) + 1$
3. $T(n) = 4T(\frac{n}{2}) + \Theta(\frac{n^3}{\log^3 n})$

4. $T(n) = 32T(\frac{n}{4}) + \Theta(\log n)$
5. $T(n) = 27T(\frac{n}{3}) + \Theta(n^3 \log^4 n)$
6. $T(n) = 8T(\frac{n}{4}) + \Theta((\frac{n}{\log n})^{1.5})$
7. $T(n) = 4T(\frac{n}{2}) + \Theta(\frac{n^2}{\log n})$

EXERCISE 27.1.2 *Give solutions for the following stranger examples:*

1. $T(n) = 4T(\frac{n}{2}) + \Theta(n^3 \log\log n)$
2. $T(n) = 4T(\frac{n}{2}) + \Theta(2^n)$
3. $T(n) = 4T(\frac{n}{2}) + \Theta(\log\log n)$
4. $T(n) = 4T(\frac{n}{2} - \sqrt{n} + \log n - 5) + \Theta(n^3)$

27.2 Some Proofs

I now present a few of the classic techniques for computing recurrence relations. As our example we will solve $T(n) = GT(n/0) + f(n)$, for $f(n) = n^c$.

Guess and Verify: To begin consider the example $T(n) = 4T\left(\frac{n}{2}\right) + n$ and $T(1) = 1$.

Plugging In: If we can guess $T(n) = 2n^2 - n$, the first way to verify that this is the solution is to simply plug it into the two equations and make sure that they are satisfied:

Left Side	Right Side
$T(n) = 2n^2 - n$	$4T(\frac{n}{2}) + n = 4\left[2\left(\frac{n}{2}\right)^2 - \left(\frac{n}{2}\right)\right] - n = 2n^2 - n$
$T(1) = 2n^2 - n = 1$	1

Proof by Induction: Similarly, we can use induction to prove that this is the solution for all n (at least for $n = 2^i$).

Base Case: Because $T(1) = 2(1)^2 - 1 = 1$, it is correct for $n = 2^0$.

Induction Step: Let $n = 2^i$. Assume that it is correct for $2^{i-1} = \frac{n}{2}$. Because $T(n) = 4T(\frac{n}{2}) + n = 4\left[2\left(\frac{n}{2}\right)^2 - \left(\frac{n}{2}\right)\right] + n = 2n^2 - n$, it is also true for n.

Calculate Coefficients: Suppose that instead we are only able to guess that the formula has the form $T(n) = an^2 + bn + c$ for some constants a, b, and c:

Left Side	Right Side
$T(n) = an^2 + bn + c$	$4T(\frac{n}{2}) + n = 4\left[a\left(\frac{n}{2}\right)^2 + b\left(\frac{n}{2}\right) + c\right] - n = an^2 + (2b+1)n + 4c$
$T(1) = a + b + c$	1

These left and right sides must be equal for all n. Both have a as the coefficient of n^2, which is good. To make the coefficient in front n be the same, we need that $b = 2b + 1$, which gives $b = -1$. To make the constant coefficient be the same, we need that $c = 4c$, which gives $c = 0$. To make $T(1) = a(1)^2 + b(1) + c = a(1)^2 - (1) + 0 = 1$, we need that $a = 2$. This gives us the solution $T(n) = 2n^2 - n$ that we had before.

Calculate Exponent: If we were to guess that $a \cdot T\left(\frac{n}{b}\right)$ is much bigger than $f(n)$, then $T(n) = a \cdot T\left(\frac{n}{b}\right) + f(n) \approx a \cdot T\left(\frac{n}{b}\right)$. Further we guess that $T(n) = n^\alpha$ for some constant α. Plugging this into $T(n) = a \cdot T\left(\frac{n}{b}\right)$ gives $n^\alpha = a \cdot \left(\frac{n}{b}\right)^\alpha$, or $b^\alpha = a$. Taking the log gives $\alpha \cdot \log b = \log a$, and solving gives $\alpha = \frac{\log a}{\log b}$. In conclusion, $T(n) = \Theta(n^{\log a / \log b}) = \Theta(n^{\log 4 / \log 2}) = \Theta(n^2)$.

Unwinding: A useful technique is to unwind a recursive relation for a few steps and to look for a pattern:

$$T(n) = f(n) + a \cdot T\left(\frac{n}{b}\right) = f(n) + a \cdot \left[f\left(\frac{n}{b}\right) + a \cdot T\left(\frac{n}{b^2}\right)\right]$$

$$= f(n) + af\left(\frac{n}{b}\right) + a^2 \cdot T\left(\frac{n}{b^2}\right) = f(n) + af\left(\frac{n}{b}\right) + a^2 \cdot \left[f\left(\frac{n}{b^2}\right) + a \cdot T\left(\frac{n}{b^3}\right)\right]$$

$$= f(n) + af\left(\frac{n}{b}\right) + a^2 f\left(\frac{n}{b^2}\right) + a^3 \cdot T\left(\frac{n}{b^3}\right) = \cdots$$

$$= \sum_{i=0}^{h-1} a^i \cdot f\left(\frac{n}{b^i}\right) + a^h \cdot T(1) = \Theta\left(\sum_{i=0}^{h} a^i \cdot f\left(\frac{n}{b^i}\right)\right).$$

Filling the Table: My recommended way to evaluate recursive relations is to fill out a table like that in Figure 27.1.

(a) **Number of Stack Frames at the ith Level:** Level 0 contains the one initial stack frame at the top of the tree of stack frame. It recursively calls a times. Hence, level 1 has a stack frames. Each of these recursively calls a times, giving a^2 stack frames at level 2. Each successive level, the number of stack frames goes up by a factor of a, giving a^i at level i.

(b) **Size of Instance at the ith Level:** The top stack frame at level 0 is given an instance of size n. It recurses on a subinstances of size $\frac{n}{b}$. Stack frames at level 1, given instances of size $\frac{n}{b}$, recurse on subinstance of size n/b^2. Each successive level decreases the instance size by a factor of b, giving size n/b^i at level i.

(c) **Time within One Stack Frame:** On an instance of size n, a single stack frame requires $f(n)$ time. Hence, a stack frame at the ith level, with an instance of size n/b^i, requires $f(n/b^i)$ time.

(d) **Number of Levels:** The recursive program stops recursing when the instance becomes sufficiently small, say of size 0 or 1. Let h denote the level at which this

Example	$T(n) = 4T(n/2) + n$	$T(n) = 9T(n/3) + n^2$	$T(n) = 2T(n/4) + n^2$
(a) No. of frames at the ith level	4^i	9^i	2^i
(b) Instance size at ith level	$\frac{n}{2^i}$	$\frac{n}{3^i}$	$\frac{n}{4^i}$
(c) Time within one stack frame	$f\left(\frac{n}{2^i}\right) = \left(\frac{n}{2^i}\right)$	$f\left(\frac{n}{3^i}\right) = \left(\frac{n}{3^i}\right)^2$	$f\left(\frac{n}{4^i}\right) = \left(\frac{n}{4^i}\right)^2$
(d) No. of levels	$\frac{n}{2^h} = 1$ $h = \frac{\log n}{\log 2} = \Theta(\log n)$	$\frac{n}{3^h} = 1$ $h = \frac{\log n}{\log 3} = \Theta(\log n)$	$\frac{n}{4^h} = 1$ $h = \frac{\log n}{\log 4} = \Theta(\log n)$
(e) No. of base case stack frames	$4^h = 4^{\frac{\log n}{\log 2}}$ $= n^{\frac{\log 4}{\log 2}} = n^2$	$9^h = 9^{\frac{\log n}{\log 3}}$ $= n^{\frac{\log 9}{\log 3}} = n^2$	$2^h = 2^{\frac{\log n}{\log 4}}$ $= n^{\frac{\log 2}{\log 4}} = n^{\frac{1}{2}}$
(f) $T(n)$ as a sum	$\sum_{i=0}^{h}$ (# at level) $\cdot$ (time each) $= \sum_{i=0}^{\Theta(\log n)} 4^i \cdot \left(\frac{n}{2^i}\right)$ $= n \cdot \sum_{i=0}^{\Theta(\log n)} 2^i$	$\sum_{i=0}^{h}$ (# at level) $\cdot$ (time each) $= \sum_{i=0}^{\Theta(\log n)} 9^i \cdot \left(\frac{n}{3^i}\right)^2$ $= n^2 \cdot \sum_{i=0}^{\Theta(\log n)} 1$	$\sum_{i=0}^{h}$ (# at level) $\cdot$ (time each) $= \sum_{i=0}^{\Theta(\log n)} 2^i \cdot \left(\frac{n}{4^i}\right)^2$ $= n^2 \cdot \sum_{i=0}^{\Theta(\log n)} \left(\frac{1}{8}\right)^i$
(g) Dominated by?	Geometric increase: base cases	Arithmetic sum: all levels	Geometric decrease: top level
(h) $\Theta(T(n))$	$T(n) = \Theta\left(n^{\log a / \log b}\right)$ $= \Theta\left(n^{\frac{\log 4}{\log 2}}\right) = \Theta(n^2)$	$T(n) = \Theta\left(f(n)\log n\right)$ $= \Theta(n^2 \log n)$	$T(n) = \Theta\left(f(n)\right)$ $= \Theta(n^2)$

Figure 27.1: Solving $T(n) = a \cdot T\left(\frac{n}{b}\right) + \Theta(n^c)$ by filling in the table.

occurs. We have seen that the instances at level h have size n/b^h. Setting $n/b^h = 1$ and solving for h gives $h = \frac{\log n}{\log b}$.

(e) Number of Base Case Stack Frames: The number of stack frames at level i is a^i. Hence, the number of base case stack frames is $a^h = a^{\log n/\log b}$. Though this looks ugly, Chapter 24 gives $a^{\log n/\log b} = (2^{\log a})^{\log n/\log b} = 2^{\log a \cdot \log n/\log b} = (2^{\log n})^{\log a/\log b} = n^{\log a/\log b}$. Given that $\frac{\log a}{\log b}$ is simply some constant, $n^{\log a/\log b}$ is a simple polynomial in n.

(f) $T(n)$ as a Sum: There are a^i stack frames at level i, and each requires $f(n/b^i)$ time, for a total of $a^i \cdot f(n/b^i)$ at the level. We obtain the total time $T(n)$ for the recursion by summing the times at all of these levels. This gives

$$T(n) = \left[\sum_{i=0}^{h-1} a^i \cdot f\left(\frac{n}{b^i}\right) \right] + a^h \cdot T(1) = \Theta\left(\sum_{i=0}^{h} a^i \cdot f\left(\frac{n}{b^i}\right) \right).$$

Plugging in $f(n) = n^c$ gives

$$T(n) = \Theta\left(\sum_{i=0}^{h} a^i \cdot \left(\frac{n}{b^i}\right)^c \right) = \Theta\left(n^c \cdot \sum_{i=0}^{h} \left(\frac{a}{b^c}\right)^i \right)$$

(g) Dominated By: The key things to remember about this sum are that it has $\Theta(\log n)$ terms, the top term being $a^0 f(n/b^0) = f(n)$ and the base case term being $a^n f(n/b^n) = a^{\log n/\log b} f(n) = n^{\log a/\log b} \Theta(n^{\log a/\log b})$. According to the adding-made-easy approximations given in Chapter 26, if either the top term or the base case term is sufficiently bigger then the other, then the total is dominated by this term. On the other hand, if they are roughly the same, then the total is approximately the number of terms times a typical term.

(h) Evaluating the Sum: If $\frac{\log a}{\log b} < c$, then $a/b^c < 1$, giving that the terms in $T(n) = \Theta(n^c \cdot \sum_{i=0}^{h} (\frac{a}{b^c})^i)$ decrease exponentially, giving $T(n) = \Theta(\text{top term}) = \Theta(f(n))$. Similarly, if $\frac{\log a}{\log b} > c$, then the terms increase exponentially, giving $T(n) = \Theta(\text{base case term}) = \Theta(n^{\log a/\log b})$. If $\frac{\log a}{\log b} = c$, then $\frac{a}{b^c} = 1$, giving $T(n) = \Theta(n^c \cdot \sum_{i=0}^{h} (\frac{a}{b^c})^i) = \Theta(n^c \cdot \sum_{i=0}^{h} 1) = \Theta(n^c \cdot h) = \Theta(f(n) \log n)$.

EXERCISE 27.2.1 *(See solution in Part Five.) Solve the famous Fibonacci recurrence relation $Fib(0) = 0$, $Fib(1) = 1$, and $Fib(n) = Fib(n-1) + Fib(n-2)$ by plugging in $Fib(n) = \alpha^n$ and solving for α.*

EXERCISE 27.2.2 *(See solution in Part Five.) Solve the following by unwinding them:*

1. $T(n) = T(n-1) + n$
2. $T(n) = 2 \cdot T(n-1) + 1$

Example	$T(n) = aT(n-b) + n^c$	$T(n) = T(n-b) + n^c$	$T(n) = T(n-b) + 0$
(a) No. of frames at the ith level	a^i		1
(b) Instance size at ith level		$n - i \cdot b$	
(c) Time within one stack frame		$f(n - i \cdot b) = (n - i \cdot b)^c$	$f(n - i \cdot b) = 0$ except for the base case, which has work $\Theta(1)$
(d) No. of levels		$n - h \cdot b = 0, h = \frac{n}{b}$	
		Having a base case of size zero makes the math the cleanest.	
(e) No of base case stack frames	$a^h = a^{\frac{1}{b}n}$	1	
(f) $T(n)$ as a sum	$\sum_{i=0}^{h}(\text{\# at level}) \cdot (\text{time each})$ $= \sum_{i=0}^{n/b} a^i \cdot (n - i \cdot b)^c$	$\sum_{i=0}^{h}(\text{\# at level}) \cdot (\text{time each})$ $= \sum_{i=0}^{n/b} 1 \cdot (n - i \cdot b)^c$	$\sum_{i=0}^{h}(\text{\# at level}) \cdot (\text{time each})$ $= \left(\sum_{i=0}^{n/b-1} 1 \cdot 0\right) + 1 \cdot \Theta(1)$ $= \Theta(1)$
(g) Dominated by	Geometric increase: base cases	Arithmetic sum: all levels	Geometric decrease: base cases
(h) $\Theta(T(n))$	$T(n) = \Theta(a^{n/b})$	$T(n) = \Theta\left(\frac{n}{b} \cdot n^c\right)$ $= \Theta(n^{c+1})$	$T(n) = \Theta(1)$

Figure 27.2: Solving $T(n) = a \cdot T(n - b) + \Theta(n^c)$ by filling in the table.

405

EXERCISE 27.2.3 *Does setting the size of the base case to 5 have any practical effect? How about setting the size to zero, i.e., $n/b^h = 0$?*

Why does this happen? If instead instances at the ith level had size $n - i$shape AB, would an instance size of 0, 1, or 2 be better? How many levels h are there?

EXERCISE 27.2.4 *(See solution in Part Five.) Section 27.2 solves $T(n) = aT(n/b) + f(n)$ for $f(n) = n^c$. If $f(n) = n^c \log^d n$ and $\frac{\log a}{\log b} = c$, then the math is harder. Compute the sum for $d > -1, d = -1, d < -1$. (Hint: Reverse the order of the terms.)*

EXERCISE 27.2.5 *Use the method in Figure 27.2 to compute each of the following recursive relations.*

1. $T(n) = nT(n-1) + 1$
2. $T(n) = 2T(\sqrt{n}) + n$
3. $T(n) = T(u \cdot n) + T(v \cdot n) + \Theta(n)$ *where* $u + v = 1$.

EXERCISE 27.2.6 *Running time:*

algorithm *Careful(n)*

⟨ *pre-cond*⟩: *n is an integer.*
⟨ *post-cond*⟩: *Q(n) "Hi"s are printed for some odd function Q*

begin
    if(n ≤ 1)
        PrintHi(1)
    else
        loop i = 1 . . . n
            PrintHi(i)
        end loop
        loop i = 1 . . . 8
            Careful($\frac{n}{2}$)
        end loop
    end if
end algorithm

algorithm *PrintHi(n)*

⟨ *pre-cond*⟩: *n is an integer.*
⟨ *post-cond*⟩: n^2 *"Hi"s are printed*

begin
    loop i = 1 . . . n^2
        Print("Hi")
    end loop
end algorithm

Recurrence Relations

1. *Give and solve the recurrence relation for the number of "Hi"s, $Q(n)$. Show your work. Give a sentence or two giving the intuition.*
2. *What is the running time (time complexity) of this algorithm as a function of the size of the input?*

407

28 A Formal Proof of Correctness

Though I mean is not to be too formal, it is useful to at least understand the required steps in a formal proof of correctness.

Specifications: Before we prove that an algorithm is correct, we need to know precisely what it is supposed to do.

Preconditions: Assertions that are promised be true about the input instance.

Postconditions: Assertions that must be true about the output.

Correctness: Consider some instance. If this instance meets the preconditions, then after the code has been run, the output must meet the postconditions:

$$\langle pre\text{-}cond \rangle \ \& \ code_{alg} \ \Rightarrow \ \langle post\text{-}cond \rangle$$

The correctness of an algorithm is only with respect to the stated specifications. It does not guarantee that it will work in situations that are not taken into account by this specification.

Breaking the Computation Path into Fragments: The method to prove that an algorithm is correct is as follows. Assertions are inserted into the code to act as checkpoints. Each assertion is a statement about the current state of the computation's data structures that is either true or false. If it is false, then something has gone wrong in the logic of the algorithm. These assertions break the path of the computation into fragments. For each such fragment, we prove that if the assertion at the beginning of the fragment is true and the fragment gets executed, then the assertion at the end of the fragment will be true. Combining all these fragments back together gives that if the first assertion is true and the entire computation is executed, then the last assertion will be true.

A Huge Number of Paths: There are likely an exponential number or even an infinite number of different paths that the computation might take, depending on the input instance and the tests that occur along the way. In contrast, there are not many different computation path fragments. Hence, it is much easier to prove the correctness of each fragment than of each path.

The following table outlines the computational path fragments that need to be tested for different code structures.

Single Line of Code:

$\langle$*pre-assignment-cond*$\rangle$: The variables x and y have meaningful values.

$z = x + y$

$\langle$*post-assignment-cond*$\rangle$: The variable z takes on the sum of the value of x and the value of y. The previous value of z is lost.

Blocks of Code:

$\langle$*assertion$_0$*$\rangle$
$code_1$
$\langle$*assertion$_1$*$\rangle$
$code_2$
$\langle$*assertion$_2$*$\rangle$

$\left. \begin{array}{l} [\langle assertion_0 \rangle \ \& \ code_1 \ \Rightarrow \ \langle assertion_1 \rangle] \\ [\langle assertion_1 \rangle \ \& \ code_2 \ \Rightarrow \ \langle assertion_2 \rangle] \end{array} \right\}$
$\Rightarrow [\langle assertion_0 \rangle \ \& \ code_{1\&2} \ \Rightarrow \ \langle assertion_2 \rangle]$

If Statements:

$\langle$*pre-if-cond*$\rangle$
if($\langle test \rangle$) then
$code_{true}$
else
$code_{false}$
end if
$\langle$*post-if-cond*$\rangle$

$\left. \begin{array}{l} [\langle pre\text{-}if\text{-}cond \rangle \ \& \ \langle test \rangle \ \& \ code_{true} \Rightarrow \langle post\text{-}if\text{-}cond \rangle] \\ [\langle pre\text{-}if\text{-}cond \rangle \ \& \ \neg \langle test \rangle \ \& \ code_{false} \Rightarrow \langle post\text{-}if\text{-}cond \rangle] \end{array} \right\}$
$\Rightarrow [\langle pre\text{-}if\text{-}cond \rangle \ \& \ code \Rightarrow \langle post\text{-}if\text{-}cond \rangle]$

Loops:

$\langle$*pre-loop-cond*$\rangle$
loop
$\langle$*loop-invar*$\rangle$
exit when $\langle$*exit-cond*$\rangle$
$code_{loop}$
end loop
$\langle$*post-loop-cond*$\rangle$

$\left. \begin{array}{l} [\langle pre\text{-}loop\text{-}cond \rangle \Rightarrow \langle loop\text{-}invar \rangle] \\ [\langle loop\text{-}invar' \rangle \ \& \ \neg \langle exit\text{-}cond \rangle \ \& \ code_{loop} \Rightarrow \langle loop\text{-}invar'' \rangle] \\ [\langle loop\text{-}invar \rangle \ \& \ \langle exit\text{-}cond \rangle \Rightarrow \langle post\text{-}loop\text{-}cond \rangle] \\ Termination \end{array} \right\}$
$\Rightarrow [\langle pre\text{-}loop\text{-}cond \rangle \ \& \ code \Rightarrow \langle post\text{-}loop\text{-}cond \rangle]$

Function Call:

$\langle$*pre-call-cond*$\rangle$
$output = Func(input)$
$\langle$*post-call-cond*$\rangle$

$\left. \begin{array}{l} [\langle pre\text{-}call\text{-}cond \rangle \Rightarrow \langle pre\text{-}cond \rangle_{Func}] \\ [\langle post\text{-}cond \rangle_{Func} \Rightarrow \langle post\text{-}call\text{-}cond \rangle] \end{array} \right\}$
$\Rightarrow [\langle pre\text{-}call\text{-}cond \rangle \ \& \ code \Rightarrow \langle post\text{-}call\text{-}cond \rangle]$

Exercise Solutions

Chapter 1. Iterative Algorithms: Measures of Progress and Loop Invariants

1.4.1 **Selection Sort:** If the input for selection sort is presented as an array of values, then sorting can happen in place. The first k entries of the array store the sorted sublist, while the remaining entries store the set of values that are on the side. Finding the smallest value from $A[k+1]\ldots A[n]$ simply involves scanning the list for it. Once it is found, moving it to the end of the sorted list involves only swapping it with the value at $A[k+1]$. The fact that the value $A[k+1]$ is moved to an arbitrary place in the right-hand side of the array is not a problem, because these values are considered to be an unsorted set anyway. The running time is computed as follows. We must select n times. Selecting from a sublist of size i takes $\Theta(i)$ time. Hence, the total time is $\Theta(n+(n-1)+\cdots+2+1) = \Theta(n^2)$ (see Chapter 26).

1.4.2 **Insertion Sort:** There are two steps involved in inserting an element into a sorted list. The most obvious step is to locate where it belongs. The second step to shift all the elements that are bigger than the new element one to the right to make room for it. You can find the location for the new element quickly using a binary search. However, it is easier to search and shift the larger elements simultaneously.

Linked List: Having the sorted elements stored in a linked list allows one to insert the new element in constant time. However, it then takes $\Theta(k)$ time to find where the new element goes.

Running Time: We must insert n times. Inserting into a sublist of size i takes $\Theta(i)$ time. Hence, the total time is $\Theta(1+2+3+\cdots+n) = \Theta(n^2)$.

Heap Sort: We will see in Section 10.4 that each of these steps can be done in $\Theta(\log n)$ time when the elements are stored in a data structure called a heap.

1.4.3 The algorithm repeatedly passes through the array, swapping adjacent pairs if needed. After k such passes, the largest k elements have bubbled up to where they belong. Hence, it requires at most n passes until all elements are in place. Each pass requires n comparisons.

1.5.1 There are a number of problems.

1. A loop invariant shall to be a picture of the current state and not say what the iteration does. The loop invariant should simply be $s = \sum_{j=1}^{i} j$.

2. The loop invariant is not established correctly. With $i = 1$, the loop invariant requires $s = \sum_{j=1}^{1} j = 1$, not $s = 0$. The choice $s = 0$ and $i = 0$ would be better.

3. The loop invariant is not maintained correctly. Let s' and i' be the values of s and i when at the top of the loop. Let s'' and i'' be the values after going around again. The loop invariant gives that $s' = \sum_{j=1}^{i'} j$. The code gives that $s'' = s' + i'$ and $i'' = i' + 1$. Together these give that $s'' = (\sum_{j=1}^{i'} j) + i'$. This is not $\sum_{j=1}^{i'+1} j$ as required, because i' is being added in twice. $i' + 1$ should be added in order to maintain the loop invariant.

4. The exit condition is not very well stated. An equivalent and easier-to-see exit condition would be "exit when $i > I$."

5. The exit condition, $i > I$, and the loop invariant, $s = \sum_{j=1}^{i} j$, together do not give the postcondition. Instead, they give that $s = \sum_{j=1}^{I+1} j$ is returned.

6. The algorithm as a whole happens to work. A quick fix is to change the loop invariant to $s = \sum_{j=1}^{i-1} j$.

Chapter 2. Examples Using More-of-the-Input Loop Invariant

2.2.1

Divide: Sorry, not provided.

Calculator:
algorithm *Calculator*()

⟨ **pre-cond**⟩**:** A stream of commands are entered.
⟨ **post-cond**⟩**:** The results are displayed on a screen.

begin
    allocate *accum,current* ∈ {0..$10^8 - 1$}
    allocate *screen* ∈ {*showA, showC*}
    accum = *current* = 0
    screen = *showC*
    loop
        ⟨**loop-invariant**⟩**:** The bounded memory of the machine remembers the current value of the accumulator and the current value being entered. It also has a Boolean variable that indicates whether the screen should display the current or the accumulator value.
        get(*c*)
        if($c \in \{0..9\}$) then
            current = $10 \times current + c \bmod 10^8$
            screen = *showC*
        else if($c =' +'$) then
            accum = $accum + current \bmod 10^8$
            current = 0
            screen = *showA*
        else if($c =' clr'$) then
            accum = 0

$$current = 0$$
$$screen = showC$$
        end if
        if($screen = showC$) then
            display($current$)
        else
            display($accum$)
        end if
    end loop
end algorithm

Longest Block of Ones:

algorithm *LongestBlockOfOnes(A, n)*

⟨ **pre-cond** ⟩**:** The input is A, a 0, 1 array of length n.

⟨ **post-cond** ⟩**:** The output is the location $A[k_1..k_2]$ of the longest block of ones and its length *leng*.

begin
    $i = 0$; $p_{max} = 1$; $q_{max} = 0$; $leng_{max} = 0$; $p_{current} = 1$; $leng_{current} = 0 \in \{0..n\}$
    loop
        ⟨**loop-invariant**⟩**:** $A[p_{max}, q_{max}]$ is a longest block of ones in $A[1..i]$ and
        $leng_{max} = q_{max} - p_{max}+1$ is its length.
        $A[p_{current}, i]$ is the longest block of ones in $A[1..i]$ ending in $A[i]$ and
        $leng_{current} = i - p_{current}+1$ is its length.
        exit when $i = n$
        if($A[i+1] = 1$) then
            $leng_{current} = leng_{current} + 1$
        else
            $p_{current} = i+2$
            $length_{current} = 0$
        end if
        if($leng_{max} < leng_{current}$) then
            $p_{max} = p_{current}$
            $q_{max} = i + 1$
            $length_{max} = length_{current}$
        end if
        $i = i+1$
    end loop
    return $A[p_{max}, q_{max}]$
end algorithm

2.3.1

(2): The loop invariant is:

a. The beginning $[0, a]$ of the cake has been partitioned into $|Q|$ disjoint pieces.

b. Each player $p_i \in Q$ has been allocated a piece $[a_i, b_i]$ worth at least $\frac{1}{n}$ to him.

c. The remaining $[a, 1]$ interval of the cake is worth at least $(n - |Q|)/n$ to each of the remaining players, i.e., to those in $P - Q$.

(3):

algorithm *Partition*(P)

⟨ ***pre-cond***⟩***:*** As above

⟨ ***post-cond***⟩***:*** As above

begin

    $a = 0$ and $Q = \emptyset$

    loop

        ⟨***loop-invariant***⟩***:*** As above.

        exit when $|Q| = n$

        loop $i \in P - Q$

            $c_i = Cut(p_i, a, \frac{1}{n})$

        end loop

        i_{min} = the $i \in P - Q$ that minimizes c_i

        $[a_{i_{min}}, b_{i_{min}}] = [a, c_{i_{min}}]$

        $a = c_{i_{min}}$

        $Q = Q + i_{min}$

    end loop

    return all parts $[a_i, b_i]$ for each $i \in P$

end algorithm

(1), (4)–(7): Sorry, the remaining solutions are not provided.

Chapter 3. Abstract Data Types

3.1.5 Instead of bounding the height given the number of nodes, it is easier to compute the reverse relation. Let $N(h)$ be the minimal number of nodes in an AVL tree of height h. In order for a tree to be of height h, it must have at least one subtree of height $h - 1$. In order for it to be an AVL tree, the other subtree can differ by at most one, so it must have height at least $h - 2$. It follows that the number of nodes in this tree is at least $N(h) = N(h-1) + N(h-2) + 1$. Except for the $+1$ of the root, this is that same as the famous Fibonacci numbers defined by $Fib(n) = Fib(n-1) + Fib(n-2)$. Exercise 27.2.1 goes on to prove that $Fib(n) = \Theta(\alpha^n)$, where $\alpha = \frac{1+\sqrt{5}}{2}$. If $N(h) = \Theta(\alpha^n)$, then $H(n) = \Theta(\log n)$.

3.2.4 The tests will be executed in the order that they are listed. If $next = nil$ is tested first and passes, then because there is an *OR* between the conditions, there is no need to test the second. However, if $next.info \geq key$ is the first test and *next* is nil, then using $next.info$ to retrieve the information in the node pointed to by *next* will cause a run-time error.

Chapter 4. Narrowing the Search Space: Binary Search

4.4.1 Doing binary search in $O(\log(n \times m))$ time is impossible. See the lower bound in question (Exercise 7.0.7). If you take $O(n \log m)$ time doing binary search in each row, then you are taking too much time. It can be done by examining $n + m - 1$ entries. Observe that the values in the matrix increase from $A[1, 1]$ to $A[n, m]$. Hence, the boundary between values that are less than or equal to x and those that are greater follows some monotonic path from $A[1, m]$ to $A[n, 1]$. The algorithm traces this path starting at $A[1, m]$. When it is at the point $A[i, j]$, the loop invariant is that we have stored the best answer from those outside the subrectangle $A[i..n, 1..j]$. Initially, this is true for $[i, j] = [1, m]$, because none of the matrix is excluded. Now suppose it is true for an arbitrary $[i, j]$. The algorithm then compares $A[i, j]$ with x. If it is better than our current best answer, then our current best is replaced. If $A[i, j] \leq x$, then because the values in the row $A[i, 1..j]$ are all smaller than or equal to $A[i, j]$, these are worse answers, and hence we can conclude that we now have the best answer from those outside the subrectangle $A[i+1..n, 1..j]$. We maintain the loop invariant by increasing i by one. On the other hand, if $A[i, j] > x$, then it is too big and so are all the elements in the column $A[i..n, j]$ which are even bigger. We can conclude that we have the best answer from those outside of the subrectangle $A[i..n, 1..j-1]$. We maintain the loop invariant by decreasing j by one. The exit condition is $|i..n| = 0$ or $|1..j| = 0$ (i.e., $i > n$ or $j < 1$). When this occurs, the subrectangle $A[i..n, 1..j]$ is empty. Hence, our best answer, which by the loop invariant is the best from those outside this subrectangle, must be the best overall. The measure of progress, $|i..n| + |1..j| - 1 = (n - i + 1) + (j) - 1$, is initially $n + m - 1$ and decrease by one each iteration. After $n + m - 1$ iterations, either the algorithm has already halted or the measure has reached zero, at which point the exit condition is definitely met.

Chapter 6. Euclid's GCD Algorithm

6.0.2

(2): The loop invariant $\ell \times r + s = x \times y$ is established trivially by setting $\ell = x$, $r = y$, and $s = 0$. Let ℓ', r', s' be the values when at the top of the loop, and assume that $\ell' \times r' + s' = x \times y$.

In the first step, if ℓ' is odd, then $\ell'' = \ell' - 1$ and $s'' = s' + r'$. This gives that $\ell'' \times r'' + s'' = (\ell' - 1) \times r' + (s' + r') = \ell' \times r' + s'$, which by the loop invariant is $x \times y$.

In the second step, $\ell''' = \ell''/2$ and $r''' = 2r''$. This gives that $\ell''' \times r''' + s''' = (\ell''/2) \times (2r'') + s'' = \ell'' \times r'' + s''$, which by the loop invariant is $x \times y$.

(4): The Ethiopians exit when $\ell = 1$. But this being odd, they must add r to s. We will iterate one more time and exit when $\ell = 0$. This exit condition gives $s = \ell \times r + s$, and the loop invariant gives $\ell \times r + s = x \times y$. Hence, in the end $s = x \times y$.

(1), (3), (5), and (6): Sorry, not provided.

Chapter 7. The Loop Invariant for Lower Bounds

7.0.2 The bound is $n \leq r^t$.

Each round, he selects one row; hence, there are r possible answers. After t rounds, there are r^t possible combinations of answers.

The only information that you know is which of these combinations he gave you. Which card you produce depends deterministically (no magic) on the combination of answers given to you. Hence, depending on his answers, there are at most r^t cards that you might output.

However, there are n cards, any of which may be the selected card. In conclusion, $n \leq r^t$.

The book has $n = 21$, $r = 3$, and $t = 2$. Because $21 = n \nleq r^t = 3^2 = 9$, the trick in the book does *not* work.

Two rounds is not enough. There need to be three rounds.

7.0.3 It is a trick question, because with a balance there are three, not two, outcomes and hence only $\log_3 n$ operations are needed. Divide the objects into three piles, two of equal size and the third as close as possible. Put the first two piles on the scale. If one is heavier, then it contains the heavier object; otherwise the third pile does. Recurse on this one pile.

7.0.6 In the lower bound for parity, any starting input I would have worked equally well. Here, however, there is only one input that will work, and that is I being the all-zero string. This ensures that, as before, changing the jth bit of I, for any $j \in J = [1, n]$, changes the answer from the AND being zero to the AND being one. This proves that any algorithm solving the problem requires time of at least n.

Chapter 8. Abstractions, Techniques, and Theory

8.5.2 R_a: One might complain that if my instance is $\langle n, m \rangle$, then my friend's instance cannot be $\langle n-1, 2m \rangle$, because $2m$ is not smaller then m. However, we can define the size of instance $\langle n, m \rangle$ to be simply n. According to this measure, my friend's instance is indeed smaller. Moreover, when the instance becomes of size zero or smaller, then $n \leq 0$ and the recursion stops. We prove that the depth of recursion is at most n as follows. On instance $\langle n, m \rangle$, the size starts at n and decreases by at least one every level of recursion, so after n levels the size is at most zero and the algorithm stops recursing further. For example, starting with $\langle 5, 2 \rangle$, it recurses on $\langle 4, 4 \rangle$, $\langle 3, 8 \rangle$, ..., $\langle 0, 64 \rangle$, and then halts.

R_b: One might claim that all is well because both friends get instances ($\langle n-1, m \rangle$ and $\langle n, m-1 \rangle$) that are smaller. However, for this to be true for both friends, the size must be something like $n + m$. However, according to this definition, the instance $\langle 5, -5 \rangle$ is small, but the algorithm does not halt. There is a path down this recursive tree that is infinite, namely $\langle n, m \rangle$, $\langle n, m-1 \rangle$, $\langle n, m-2 \rangle$, ... $\langle n, 1 \rangle$, $\langle n, 0 \rangle$, $\langle n, -1 \rangle$, $\langle n, -2 \rangle$....

R_c: Here the size of the instance $\langle n, m \rangle$ can be defined to be $n + m$. According to this measure, each friend is given a smaller instance. Moreover, if the size on the instance is zero, then either $n \leq 0$ or $m \leq 0$. Either way the program halts. The depth of recursion can be at most $n + m$ because this is the initial size and the size decreases by one each iteration.

R_d: Let the size of the instance $\langle n, m \rangle$ be $5n + 2m$. Then the first friend's instance $\langle n-1, m+2 \rangle$ has size $5(n-1) + 2(m+2) = 5n + 2m - 1$, which is one smaller. The second friend's instance $\langle n+1, m-3 \rangle$ has size $5(n+1) + 2(m-3) = 5n + 2m - 1$, which is also one smaller. Moreover, if the size on the instance is zero, then either $n \leq 0$ or $m \leq 0$. Either way the program halts. The depth of recursion can be at most $5n + 2m$ because this is the initial size and the size decreases by one each iteration.

R_e: I claim that there is a path down this recursion tree that is infinite. If my instance is $\langle n, m \rangle$, then my first friend has $\langle n-4, m+2 \rangle$, his first friend has $\langle n-8, m+4 \rangle$, his first friend has $\langle n-12, m+6 \rangle$, his second friend has $\langle n-6, m+3 \rangle$, and his second friend has $\langle n, m \rangle$ which is the same as my instance. This can be repeated infinitely often.

It is interesting that the last two examples can be generalized to the friend's instances of size $\langle n-a, m+b \rangle$ and $\langle n+c, m-d \rangle$. If $ad > bc$ then the program halts, else it does not.

8.6.2

$Fun(1) = X$

$Fun(2) = Y$

$Fun(3) = AYBXC$

$Fun(4) = A\ AYBXC\ B\ Y\ C$

$Fun(5) = A\ AAYBXCBYC\ B\ AYBX\ C$

$Fun(6) = A\ AAAYBXCBYCBAYBXC\ B\ AAYBXCBYC\ C$

8.7.2 To prove $S(0)$, let $n = 0$ in the inductive step. There are no values k where $0 \leq k < n$. Hence, no assumptions are being made. Hence, your proof proves $S(0)$ on its own.

Chapter 9. Some Simple Examples of Recursive Algorithms

9.1.1 Insertion sort and selection sort.

9.1.2 1. Given $\langle a_1, a_2, \ldots, a_n \rangle$, I remove the last character a_n. I give $\langle a_1, a_2, \ldots, a_{n-1} \rangle$ to my friend, and he returns the reversed tuple $\langle a_{n-1}, \ldots, a_1 \rangle$ to me. I add a_n to the front of the tuple, producing $\langle a_n, a_{n-1}, \ldots, a_1 \rangle$ as required. If my initial tuple has only zero (or one) element, then there is nothing to do.

algorithm $Reverse(\langle a_1, a_2, \ldots, a_n \rangle)$

⟨ **pre-cond** ⟩**:** An instance is a tuple.

⟨ **post-cond** ⟩**:** The output is the reverse tuple $\langle a_n, a_{n-1}, \ldots, a_1 \rangle$.

begin
    if($n = 0$ or $n = 1$) then
        return(instance unchanged)
    else
        return($\langle a_n, Reverse(\langle a_1, a_2, \ldots, a_{n-1} \rangle) \rangle$)
    end if
end algorithm

2. The iterative program has two (nonnested) loops. The first pushes each element on the stack, one at a time, starting with a_n. The loop invariant is that after i iterations what remains in the tuple is $\langle a_1, a_2, \ldots, a_{n-i-1}, a_{n-i} \rangle$ and the stack contains $\langle a_{n-i+1}, a_{n-i+2}, \ldots, a_n \rangle$ with a_{n-i+1} at the top. At the $i = 0$ iteration, the loop invariant is trivially true. The next iteration removes the last element a_{n-i} from the tuple and pushes it on the stack. This maintains the loop invariant while making progress. In the end, with $i = n$, $\langle a_1, a_2, \ldots, a_n \rangle$ is on the stack with a_1 at the top. The second loop pops each element off the stack and puts it at the beginning of the tuple. The loop invariant is that after i iterations, the stack again contains $\langle a_{i+1}, a_{i+2}, \ldots, a_n \rangle$ with a_{i+1} at the top, but now the tuple is $\langle a_i, a_{i-1}, \ldots, a_2, a_1 \rangle$. With $i = n$, the stack is empty and the tuple is $\langle a_n, a_{n-1}, \ldots, a_2, a_1 \rangle$.

3. Recursion is implemented on a computer, using a stack of stack frames. The first stack frame is given $\langle a_1, a_2, \ldots, a_n \rangle$, and it removes and remembers the last character a_n. Its friend is the second stack frame, which is given $\langle a_1, a_2, \ldots, a_{n-1} \rangle$. It removes and remembers its last character a_{n-1}. As we recurse deeper, the stack frames that have not yet completed are pushed on a stack. After i such stack frames, the loop invariant is that the the friend's friend's friend's ... friend is given the tuple

$\langle a_1, a_2, \ldots, a_{n-i-1}, a_{n-i} \rangle$ and the stack contains stack frames, each remembering one of the elements $a_{n-i+1}, a_{n-i+2}, \ldots, a_n$, with a_{n-i+1} at the top. Note this is the same loop invariant as the iterative program. The recursive base case is reached when $i = n$ and the stack frame is given the empty tuple. Then, one at a time, in reverse order the stack frames complete their computations by each adding its element to the beginning of the tuple. The loop invariant is that after i such returns, the stack of stack frames is remembering $a_{i+1}, a_{i+2}, \ldots, a_n$ with a_{i+1} at the top, and the current stack frame is returning the tuple $\langle a_i, a_{i-1}, \ldots, a_2, a_1 \rangle$. Again, note that this is the same loop invariant as the iterative algorithm. With $i = n$, the stack is empty and the first stack frame returns the tuple $\langle a_n, a_{n-1}, \ldots, a_2, a_1 \rangle$.

9.2.1

1). Given the integers a and b, the iterative algorithm creates two numbers $x = b$ and $y = a \bmod b$. It notes that $GCD(a, b) = GCD(x, y)$, and hence it can return $GCD(x, y)$ instead of $GCD(a, b)$. This algorithm is even easier when you have a friend. We simply give the subinstance $\langle x, y \rangle$ to the friend, and he computes $GCD(x, y)$ for us. For the iterative algorithm, we need to make sure we are making progress, and for the recursive algorithm, we need to make sure that we give the friend a smaller instance. Either way, we make sure that in some way $\langle x, y \rangle$ is smaller than $\langle a, b \rangle$. For the iterative algorithm, we need an exit condition that we are sure to eventually meet, and for the recursive algorithm, we need base cases such that every possible instance is handled. Either way, we consider the case when y or b is zero. The resulting code is

algorithm $GCD(a, b)$

$\langle$ **pre-cond** $\rangle$: a and b are integers.
$\langle$ **post-cond** $\rangle$: Returns $GCD(a, b)$.

begin
    if($b = 0$) then
        return(a)
    else
        return($GCD(b, a \bmod b)$)
    end if
end algorithm

2). We will need to understand this relationship $y = a \bmod b$ better. Here y is the remainder when you divide a by b. If we let $r = \lfloor \frac{a}{b} \rfloor$, then $a = r \cdot b + y$ or $y = a - r \cdot b$.

When we generalize the problem, the friend, in addition to g, also gives us u_{sub} and v_{sub} such that $u_{sub} \cdot x + v_{sub} \cdot y = g = GCD(x, y) = GCD(a, b)$. Plugging in $x = b$ and $y = a - r \cdot b$ gives $u_{sub} \cdot b + v_{sub} \cdot (a - r \cdot b) = g$, or $v_{sub} \cdot a + (u_{sub} - v_{sub} \cdot r) \cdot b = g$. Hence, if we set $u = v_{sub}$ and $v = u_{sub} - v_{sub} \cdot r$, then we get $u \cdot a + v \cdot b = g = GCD(a, b)$ as required. I simply provide these answers. For the base case with $b = 0$, we have $g = GCD(a, b) = a$. Hence, $u = 1$ and $v = 0$ gives that $u \cdot a + v \cdot b = g = GCD(a, b)$. The resulting code is

algorithm $GCD(a, b)$

$\langle$ **pre-cond** $\rangle$: a and b are integers.
$\langle$ **post-cond** $\rangle$: Returns integers g, u, and v such that $u \cdot a + v \cdot b = g = GCD(a, b)$.

```
begin
    if(b = 0) then
        return( ⟨a, 1, 0⟩ )
    else
        x = b
        r = ⌊a/b⌋
        y = a − r · b
        ⟨g, u_sub, v_sub⟩ = GCD(x, y)
        u = v_sub
        v = u_sub − v_sub · r
        return( ⟨g, u, v⟩ )
    end if
end algorithm
```

3). Our goal is to find two integers U and V such that $U \cdot a + V \cdot t = w$. Then you give the storekeeper U of the a coins and V of the b coins for a total worth of w dollars. If U or V is negative, this amounts to the storekeeper giving you coins as change.

To find U and V, let's start by calling the GCD algorithm on a and b. This returns integers g, u, and v such that $u \cdot a + v \cdot b = g = GCD(a, b)$.

If g divides evenly into w, then multiplying through by $\frac{w}{g}$ gives $(\frac{uw}{g}) \cdot a + (\frac{vw}{g}) \cdot b = g(\frac{w}{g}) = w$, and we are done.

By the definition of $g = GCD(a, b)$, we know g divides a and b, and hence it divides $U \cdot a + V \cdot b$ evenly. It follows that if g does not divide w evenly, then there is no integer solution to $U \cdot a + V \cdot b = w$.

4). Solution not provided.

Chapter 10. Recursion on Trees

10.3.1

algorithm *Smallest(tree, k)*

⟨ **pre-cond**⟩: *tree* is a binary search tree, and $k > 0$ is an integer.

⟨ **post-cond**⟩: Outputs the kth smallest element s and the number n of elements. If it this index is out of range, we output $s = NotPossible$.

```
begin
    if( tree = emptyTree ) then
        result( ⟨NotPossible, 0⟩ )
    else
        ⟨s_l, n_l⟩ = Smallest(leftSub(tree), k)
        % There are n_l + 1 nodes before the right subtree
        ⟨s_r, n_r⟩ = Smallest(rightSub(tree), k − (n_l + 1))
        n = n_l + 1 + n_r
        if( k ∈ [1..n_l] )then
            s = s_l
        elseif( k = n_l + 1 )then
            s = root(tree)
        elseif( k ∈ [n_l + 2..n] )then
            s = s_r
```

else then
$s = OutOfRange$
endif
result($\langle s, n \rangle$)
end if
end algorithm

10.4.1 1. Where in the heap can the value 1 go? It must be in one of the leaves. If 1 were not at a leaf, then the nodes below it would need a smaller number, of which there are none.
2. Which values can be stored in entry $A[2]$? It can contain any value in the range 7–14. It can't contain 15, because 15 must go in $A[1]$. We already know that $A[2]$ must be greater than each of the seven nodes in its subtree. Hence, it can't contain a value less than 7. For each of the other values, a heap can be constructed such that $A[2]$ has that value.
3. Where in the heap can the value 15 go? 15 must go in $A[1]$ (as we have mentioned).
4. Where in the heap can the value 6 go? 6 can go anywhere except $A[1]$, $A[2]$, or $A[3]$. $A[1]$ must contain 15, and $A[2]$ and $A[3]$ must be at least 7.

10.5.1

algorithm *Derivative(f, x)*

$\langle$ **pre-cond** $\rangle$: f is an equation and x is a variable
$\langle$ **post-cond** $\rangle$: The derivative of f with respect to x is returned.

begin
if($f = $ "x") then
result(1)
else if($f = $ a real value or a single variable other than "x") then
result(0)
end if

% if f is of the form (goph)
$g = Copy(leftSub(f))$ % Copy needed for "*" and "/".
$h = Copy(rightSub(f))$ % Three copies needed for "/".
$g' = Derivative(leftSub(f), x)$
$h' = Derivative(rightSub(f), x)$

if($f = g + h$) then
% See Figure 10.5.3.a
result($g' + h'$)
else if($f = g - h$) then
result($g' - h'$)
else if($f = g * h$) then
% See Figure 10.5.3.b
result($g' * h + g * h'$)
else if($f = g/h$) then
% See Figure 10.5.3.c
result($g' * h - g * h')/(h * h)$)
end if
end algorithm

10.5.3

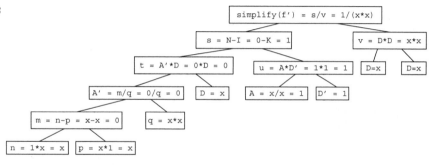

Chapter 11. Recursive Images

11.1.1 Falling Line: This construction consists of a single line with image $n-1$ raised, tilted, and shrunk:

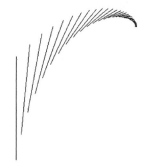

11.1.2 Binary Tilt: This image is the same as the birthday cake. The only differences are that the two places to recurse are tilted and one of them has be flipped upside down:

Chapter 12. Parsing with Context-Free Grammars

12.0.1

```
s = ( ( ( 1 ) * 2 + 3 ) * 5 * 6 + 7 )
    |-exp--------------------------|
    |-term-------------------------|
    |-fact-------------------------|
    ( |-exp----------------------| )
      |-term------------------| + t
      |-fact----------| * f * f   f
      ( |-exp-------| )   5   6   7
        |-t-----| + t
        |-f-| * f   f
        ( e )   2   3
          t
          f
          1
s = ( ( ( 1 ) * 2 + 3 ) * 5 * 6 + 7 )
```

Sorry, the solution for 2 and 3 are not included.

Chapter 14. Graph Search Algorithms

14.2.1 The node v can't be in $V_{k'}$ for $k' > k + 1$, because there is a path of length $k + 1$ to it, namely the path to u followed by the edge $\langle u, v, \rangle$. If v has not been found before, then we are just finding it. Its $d(v)$ is being set to $d(u) + 1 = k + 1$. By LI1, this must be its distance from s. Hence, v must be in V_{k+1}. If v has been found before, it is because a shortest path has already been found to it. If the edge $\langle u, v, \rangle$ is directed, then this previous path could have any length $k' \leq k + 1$. However, if this edge is undirected, then there is a catch. Suppose v is in $V_{k'}$. Then a possible path to u is that of length $k' + 1$ from s to v followed by the edge $\{u, v, \}$ backwards to u. because the shortest path to u is of length k, we have $k' + 1 \geq k$ or $k' \in \{k - 1, k, k + 1\}$.

14.2.2 The shortest-path algorithm given in this section is identical to the generic search algorithm in Section 14.1 except that a queue is used. Hence, the running time is $\Theta(|E|)$. The time is not less if you are searching for a path to a specific node t.

14.3.2 Despite differences in the algorithms, on a graph with edge weights one, breadth-first search and Dijkstra's algorithm are identical. Breadth-first search handles the first node in its queue, whereas Dijkstra's algorithm handles the node with the next smallest $d(v)$. However, breadth-first search's third loop invariant ensures that the nodes are found and added to the queue in the order of distance $d(v)$. Hence, handling the next in the queue amounts to handling the next smallest $d(v)$. Breadth-first search's first loop invariant states that the correct minimal distance $d(v)$ to v is obtained when the node v is first found, whereas with Dijkstra's algorithm we are not sure to have it until the node is handled. However, with edge weights one, when v is first found in Dijkstra's algorithm, $d(v)$ is set to the length of the overall shortest path and never changed again.

14.6.2 The shortest path to node v will not contain any nodes u that appear after it in the total order, because by the requirements of the total order there is no path from u to v. Hence, it is fine to handle v, committing to a shortest path to v, before considering u. Hence, it is fine to handle the nodes in the order given by the total order. The advantage of this algorithm is that you do not need to maintain a priority queue, as done in Dijkstra's algorithm. This decreases the time from $\Theta(|E| \log |V|)$ to $\Theta(|E|)$.

Chapter 15. Network Flows and Linear Programming

15.2.5 Given a network $\langle G, s, t \rangle$, run the max flow algorithm on it. In addition to returning a maximum flow, it also returns a minimum cut, which is used to witness the fact that there is no better flow.

15.5.1 1. The first does not have a matching. A witness is the fact that nodes 1, 3, and 5 are only connected to B and D. Hence, the three can't be matched to the two. In the language of Hall's theorem, let $A = \{1, 3, 5\}$; then $N(A) = \{B, D\}$. Because $|A| > |N(A)|$, Hall's theorem gives that there is no matching. The second does have a matching. A witness is the following matching:

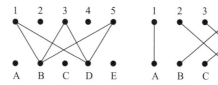

2. Consider an arbitrary $A \subseteq L$. Note that the set $B = \{M(u) \mid u \in A\}$ contains $|A|$ distinct nodes and that $B \subseteq N(A)$. Hence, $|A| \leq |N(A)|$.

3. Let $A = U \cap L$ be the set of nodes that are both on the left side of the bipartite graph and on the left side of the cut. Consider any node $v \in N(A)$. Because $v \in N(A)$, there is a node $u \in A \subset U$ such that $\langle u, v \rangle$ is an edge. If $v \in V$, then this edge (u, v) crosses the cut. But this edge has capacity ∞. In this case, the capacity of the cut is well over $|L|$. On the other hand, if $v \in U$, then the edge from v to t is across the cut. Now consider any node $u \in L - A \subset V$. The edge from s to u crosses the cut. This proves that the number of edges across the cut is at least $N(A) + (|L| - |A|)$, which by our assumption is at least $|A| + (|L| - |A|) = |L|$.

4. We have seen that there is a matching with $|L|$ edges iff the max flow in this graph has value $|L|$ iff the min cut in this graph has capacity $|L|$. The cut with s on one side by itself has $|L|$ edges going across the cut, namely those edges from s to L. By the last question, if $\forall A \subseteq L$, $|A| \leq |N(A)|$, then every cut has at least $|L|$ edges across it. Hence, the min cut must be $|L|$. Hence, the max flow has value $|L|$. Hence, there is a matching with $|L|$ edges. All the nodes in L must be matched.

5. By the last question, it is sufficient to prove that $\forall A \subseteq L$, $|A| \leq |N(A)|$ is true. Consider some set $A \subseteq L$. Because each every node in $A \subseteq L$ has degree at least k, we know that at least $k \cdot |A|$ edges leave A. All of the edges that leave A must enter its neighborhood set $N(A)$. Hence, the number that leave A is at most the number that enter $N(A)$. Because every node in $N(A) \subseteq R$ has degree at most k, we know that at most $k \cdot |N(A)|$ enter $N(A)$. It follows that $k \cdot |A| \leq \#$ leave $A \leq \#$ enter $N(A) \leq k \cdot |N(A)|$. Hence, $|A| \leq |N(A)|$, as is needed.

Chapter 16: Greedy Algorithms

16.2.2 In the following instance of the interval cover problem, the greedy criterion that selects the interval that covers the largest number of uncovered points would commit to the top interval. However, the optimal solution does not contain this interval, but contains the bottom two intervals.

16.3.2 Algorithms 1, 2, and 4 are suboptimal for the following counterexample instance:

(a) Room1 ——— ————————————   —————   ——————————
    Room2 ——————————— ———————————   (b) ——————————

Diagram (a) gives the events in the instance and the optimal schedule in two rooms. Diagram (b) gives the suboptimal schedule produced by these three algorithms. Note that the third algorithm, which schedules the next event in the room with the latest last-scheduled finishing time, gives the optimal schedule. We will now prove that it always gives an optimal solution.

As with all greedy algorithms, the loop invariant is that there is at least one optimal solution $optS_{LI}$ consistent with the choices made so far, that is, scheduling in the same rooms the same events whose schedule have been committed to so far and not scheduling the events rejected so far. Initially, no choices have been made, and hence trivially all optimal solutions are consistent with these choices. We prove that the loop invariant is maintained by modifying the schedule $optS_{LI}$ into another schedule $optS_{ours}$ and prove that this new schedule is valid, consistent with all previous and current choices, and optimal. There are three cases.

If our greedy algorithm did not schedule the next event i, then this event must conflict in each room with a previously scheduled event. Hence, $optS_{LI}$ cannot have this next event i scheduled either, because it too has scheduled these previous events. Hence, $optS_{LI}$ itself is already consistent with the most recent choice.

If our greedy algorithm did schedule the next event i in room j and $optS_{LI}$ does not schedule this event at all, then we modify the schedule $optS_{LI}$ into $optS_{ours}$ by adding i to room j and removing any events from j that conflict with it. Just as done with the one-room scheduling algorithm in Section 16.2.1, we can prove that only one event is removed and hence $optS_{ours}$ is valid, consistent, and optimal.

The remaining case occurs when our greedy algorithm scheduled the next event i in room j and $optS_{LI}$ schedules it in room j'. (See diagram (a).) We modify the schedule $optS_{LI}$ into $optS_{ours}$ as follows. (See diagram (b).) We cannot move the events whose schedule has already been committed to by the algorithm, because $optS_{ours}$ needs to remain consistent with these choices. (See the events in the *Commit* circle.) We need to move event i from room j' to room j so that it too is consistent with what the algorithm has done. But making this change may create conflicts. To fix these, we swap every event scheduled by $optS_{LI}$ in room j' with the finishing time of event i or later with every such job scheduled in room j. (See the events in the rectangle.)

We now prove that the resulting solution $optS_{ours}$ is valid, consistent, and optimal.

A Valid Solution: Our modified solution $optS_{ours}$ contains no conflicts, because $optS_{LI}$ contained none and we will prove now that no new conflicts were introduced. There are no new conflicts between the previously committed events (circle), because they did not change. There are no new conflicts between the later-committed events (rectangle), because they flipped rooms all together. Event i does not conflict with the previously committed events in room j, because the algorithm scheduled it there. The even later events that were in room j' don't either, because they are even later. The later events that were in room j won't conflict with the previously scheduled events in room j', because they did not conflict with those in room j and we know by the algorithm's choice of room j that the last-scheduled finishing time for j is later than that for room j'.

Consistent with Choices Made: $optS_{LI}$ was consistent with the previous choices. We moved event i from room j' to room j to make $optS_{ours}$ consistent with this most recent choice. We did not move any events in *Commit*.

Optimal: Schedule $optS_{ours}$ has the optimal number of events in it, because it has the same number of events as $optS_{LI}$.

Loop Invariant Has Been Maintained: In conclusion, we have constructed a valid optimal schedule $optS_{ours}$ that is consistent with the choices made by the algorithm. This proves that the loop invariant has been maintained.

The rest of the proof of correctness of this greedy algorithm is the same as that of all the others.

Chapter 17. Recursive Backtracking

17.5.1 Asking to provide the best word is not a "little question" for the bird. She would be doing most of the work for you. Asking the friend to provide the best place on the board to put the word is not a subinstance of the same problem as that of the given instance.

17.5.2 The simple brute force algorithm searches the dictionary for each permutation of each subset of the letters. The backtracking algorithm tries all of the possibilities for the first letter and then recurses. Each of these stack frames tries all of the remaining possibilities for the second letter, and so on. This can be pruned by observing that if the word constructed so far, e.g., 'xq', does not match the first letters of any word in the dictionary, then there is no need for this stack frame to recurse any further. (Another improvement on the running time ensures that the words are searched for in the dictionary in alphabetical order.)

17.5.3
1. $\langle 1, 5, 8, 6, 3, 7, 2, 4 \rangle$
2. $\langle 1, 6, 8, 3, 7, 4, 2, 5 \rangle$
3. $\langle 1, 7, 4, 6, 8, 2, 5, 3 \rangle$
4. $\langle 1, 7, 5, 8, 2, 4, 6, 3 \rangle$
5. $\langle 2, 4, 6, 8, 3, 1, 7, 5 \rangle$
6. $\langle 2, 5, 7, 1, 3, 8, 6, 4 \rangle$
7. $\langle 2, 5, 7, 4, 1, 8, 6, 3 \rangle$
8. $\langle 2, 6, 1, 7, 4, 8, 3, 5 \rangle$
9. $\langle 2, 6, 8, 3, 1, 4, 7, 5 \rangle$
10. $\langle 2, 7, 3, 6, 8, 5, 1, 4 \rangle$
11. $\langle 2, 7, 5, 8, 1, 4, 6, 3 \rangle$
12. $\langle 2, 8, 6, 1, 3, 5, 7, 4 \rangle$

17.5.4 We will prove that the running time is bounded between $\left(\frac{n}{2}\right)^{\frac{n}{6}}$ and n^n and hence is $n^{\Theta(n)} = 2^{\Theta(n \log n)}$. Without any pruning, there are n choices on each of n rows as to where to place the row's queen. This gives n^n different placements of the queens. Each of these solutions would correspond to a leaf of the tree of stack frames. This is clearly an upper bound on the number when there is pruning.

I will now give a lower bound on how many stack frames will be executed by this algorithm. Let j be one of the first $\frac{n}{6}$ rows. I claim that each time that a stack frame is placing a queen on this row, it has at least $\frac{n}{2}$ choices as to where to place it. The stack frame can place the queen on any of the n squares in the row as long as this square cannot be captured by one of the queens placed above it. If row i is above our row j, then the queen placed on row i can capture at most three squares of row j: one by moving on a diagonal to the left, one by moving straight down, and one by moving on a diagonal to the right. Because j is one of the first $\frac{n}{6}$ rows, there are at most this number of rows i above it, and hence at most $3 \times \frac{n}{6}$ of row j's squares can be captured. This leaves, as claimed, $\frac{n}{2}$ squares on which the stack frame can place the queen.

From the above claim, it follows that within the tree of stack frames, each stack frame within the tree's first $\frac{n}{6}$ levels branches out to at least $\frac{n}{2}$ children. Hence, at the $\left(\frac{n}{6}\right)$th level of the tree there are at least $\left(\frac{n}{2}\right)^{\frac{n}{6}}$ different stack frames. Many of these will terminate without finding a complete valid placement. However, this is a lower bound on the running time of the algorithm, because the algorithm recurses to each of them.

17.5.5 The line "$k_{min} = $ a k that maximizes $cost_k$."

Chapter 18. Dynamic Programming Algorithms

18.3.3

algorithm $PrintingNeatly(\langle M; l_1, \ldots, l_n \rangle)$

⟨ **pre-cond**⟩: $\langle l_1, \ldots, l_n \rangle$ are the lengths of the words, and M is the length of each line.
⟨ **post-cond**⟩: $optSol$ splits the text into lines in an optimal way, and $cost$ is its cost.

begin
    % Table: $optSol[i]$ would store an optimal way to print the first i words of the input, but actually we store only the bird's advice for the subinstance and the cost of its solution.
    $table[0..n]$ $birdAdvice, cost$

    % Base case: The only base case is for the best printing of the first zero words. Its solution is the empty printing with cost zero.
    % $optSol[0] = \emptyset$
    $cost[0] = 0$
    $birdAdvice[0] = \emptyset$

    % General cases: Loop over subinstances in the table.
    for $i = 1$ to n
        % Solve instance $\langle M; l_1, \ldots, l_i \rangle$ and fill in table entry $\langle i \rangle$.
        $K = $ maximum number k such that the words of length $l_{i-k+1}, \ldots, l_i$ fit on a single line.
        % Try each possible bird answers.
        for $k = 1$ to K
            % The bird-and-friend algorithm: The bird tells us to put k words on the last line. We ask the friend for an optimal printing of the first $i - k$ words. He gives us $optSol[i - k]$, which he had stored in the table. To this we add the bird's k words on a new last line. This gives us $optSol_k$, which is a best printing of the first i words from amongst those printings consistent with the bird's answer.
            % $optSol_k = \langle optSub[i - k], k \rangle$
            $cost_k = cost[i - k] + (M - k + 1 - \sum_{j=i-k+1}^{i} l_j)^3$
        end for
        % Having the best, $optSol_k$, for each bird's answer k, we keep the best of these best.
        $k_{min} = $ a k that minimizes $cost_k$
            $birdAdvice[i] = k_{min}$

% $optSol[i] = optSol_{k_{min}}$
% $cost[i] = cost_{k_{min}}$
    end for
    $optSol = PrintingNeatlyWithAdvice\,(\langle M; l_1, \ldots, l_n \rangle, birdAdvice)$
    return $\langle optSol, cost[n] \rangle$
end algorithm

Chapter 19. Examples of Dynamic Programs

19.1.1 (a): If $x_n = y_m$, then we must prove that there is at least one optimal solution that contains both of these last characters. Consider an optimal solution. It must end in this last character; otherwise it could be extended to contain it. It might not contain both of them, as in the case of $X = \langle \underline{A}, \underline{B}, B \rangle$, $Y = \langle \underline{A}, \underline{B} \rangle$, with optimal solution $Z = \langle A, B \rangle$. However, as in this case, we can just as well assume that the optimal solution takes both. If $x_n \neq y_m$, then the optimal solution cannot take both. Hence, it either does not take the last of X or does not take the last of Y. It might not take the last of either, but this is included in both the other two cases. See Section 17.3 for a further answer.

    (b) The loop over subinstances is then changed as follows.

% Solve instance $\langle \langle x_1, \ldots, x_i \rangle, \langle y_1, \ldots, y_j \rangle \rangle$ and fill in table entry $\langle i, j \rangle$.
if $x_i = y_j$ then
    $birdAdvice[i, j] = 3$
    % $optSol[i, j] = optSol[i - 1, j - 1] + x_i$
    $cost[i, j] = cost[i - 1, j - 1] + 1$
else
    % Try possible bird answers.
    % cases $k = 1, 2$
        % $optSol_1 = optSol[i - 1, j]$
        $cost_1 = cost[i - 1, j]$
        % $optSol_2 = optSol[i, j - 1]$
        $cost_2 = cost[i, j - 1]$
    % end cases
    % Having the best, $optSol_k$, for each bird's answer k,
        we keep the best of these best.
    $k_{max} = $ a $k \in [1, 2]$ that maximizes $cost_k$
    % $optSol[i, j] = optSol_{k_{max}}$
    $cost[i, j] = cost_{k_{max}}$
    $birdAdvice[i, j] = k_{max}$
end if

19.1.2 The running time is the number of subinstances times the number of possible bird answers, and the space is the number of subinstances. The number of subinstances is $\Theta(n^2)$, and the bird has $K = 3$ possible answers for you. Hence, the time and space requirements are both $\Theta(n^2)$.

19.4.2

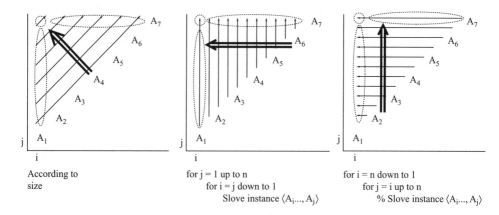

According to size

for j = 1 up to n
    for i = j down to 1
        Slove instance $\langle A_i..., A_j \rangle$

for i = n down to 1
    for j = i up to n
        % Slove instance $\langle A_j..., A_j \rangle$

19.5.1 1. An AVL tree of height h has left and right subtrees of heights either $\langle h-2, h-1 \rangle$, $\langle h-1, h-1 \rangle$, or $\langle h-1, h-2 \rangle$.

2. The bird tells me whether the subtree heights are $\langle h-2, h-1 \rangle$, $\langle h-1, h-1 \rangle$, or $\langle h-1, h-2 \rangle$. She also tells me which value a_k will be at the root. I can then ask the friends for the best left and right subtrees of the specified height.

3. In each of these three cases, the heights are within 1.

4. The complete set of subinstances is as following. Recall that in Chapter 10 we proved that the minimum height of an AVL tree with n nodes is $h = \log_2 n$ and that its maximum height is $h = 1.455 \log_2 n$. Hence, the complete set of subinstances is $S = \{\langle h; a_i, \ldots, a_j; p_i, \ldots, p_j \rangle \mid 1 \le i \le j \le n, \ h \in [\log_2(j-i+1)..1.455 \log_2(j-i+1)]\}$. The table is a three-dimensional $\Theta(n \times n \times \log n)$ box.

5. The table has size $\Theta(n \times n \times \log n)$. The bird can give $3 \cdot n$ different answers. Hence, the running time is $\Theta(n^3 \log n)$.

6. In the original problem, the height was not fixed. To solve this problem, we could simply run the previous algorithm for each h and take the best of the resulting AVL trees. However, after running the previous algorithm once, the table already contains the cost of the best AVL for each of the possible heights h. To find the best overall AVL tree, we need only compare those listed in the table.

19.7.1

algorithm *Parsing*$(\langle G, T_{start}, a_1, \ldots, a_n \rangle)$

$\langle$ **pre-cond**$\rangle$: G is a Chomsky normal form grammar, T_{start} is a nonterminal, and s is the string $\langle a_1, \ldots, a_n \rangle$ of terminal symbols.

$\langle$ **post-cond**$\rangle$: P, if possible, is a parsing that generates s starting from T_{start} using G.

begin

    % Table: *optSol*$[h, i, j]$ would store an optimal solution for $\langle G, T_h, a_i, \ldots, a_j \rangle$, namely a parsing for $a_i, \ldots, a_j$ starting with nonterminal T_h. Instead, we store only the bird's advice for the subinstance and the cost of its solution.
    table$[|V|, n, n]$ *birdAdvice, cost*

```
% The case s = ε is handled separately
if n = 0 then
    if T_start ⇒ ε is a rule then
        P = the parsing applies this one rule.
    else
        P = ∅
    end if
    return(P)
end if
```

```
% Base cases: The base cases are when the string to parse consists of only one
character a_i.
For i = 1 to n
    For each nonterminal T_h
        If there is a rule r_q = "A_q ⇒ b_q", where A_q is T_h and b_q is a_i, then
            birdAdvice[h, i, i] = ⟨q, ?⟩
            cost[h, i, i] = 1
        else
            birdAdvice[h, i, i] = ⟨?, ?⟩
            cost[h, i, i] = 0
        end if
    end loop
end loop
```

```
% General cases: Loop over subinstances in the table.
for size = 2 to n % length of substring ⟨a_i, ..., a_j⟩
    for i = 1 to n − size + 1
        j = i + size − 1
        For each nonterminal T_h, i.e., h ∈ [1..|V|]
            % Solve instance ⟨G, T_h, a_i, ..., a_j⟩, and fill in table entry ⟨h, i, j⟩.
            % Loop over possible bird answers.
            for each rule r_q = "A_q ⇒ B_q C_q" for which A_q is T_h
                for each split in the string k = i to j − 1
                    % Ask friend if you can generate ⟨a_i, ..., a_k⟩ from B_q.
                    % Ask another friend if you can generate ⟨a_{k+1}, ..., a_j⟩.
                    from C_q
                    cost_{⟨q, k⟩} = min(cost[B_q, i, k], cost[C_q, k + 1, j])
                end for
            end for
            % Take the best bird answer, i.e., one of cost one if s can be generated.
            ⟨q_{min}, k_{max}⟩ = a ⟨q, k⟩ that maximizes cost_{⟨q,k⟩}
            birdAdvice[h, i, j] = ⟨q_{min}, k_{max}⟩
            cost[h, i, j] = cost_{⟨q_{max}, k_{max}⟩}
        end for
    end for
end for
```

```
                % Constructing the solution P
                if(cost[1, 1, n] = 1) then        % i.e., if s can be generated from T_start
                        P = ParsingWithAdvice(⟨G, T_start, a_1, ..., a_n⟩, birdAdvice)
                else
                        P = ∅
                end if
                return(P)
        end algorithm
```

Time and space requirements: The running time is the number of subinstance times the number of possible bird answers, and the space is the number of subinstances. The number of subinstances indexing your table is $\Theta(|V|n^2)$, namely, $Table[h, i, j]$ for $h \in V$ and $1 \le i \le j \le n$. The number of answers that the bird might give you is at most $O(mn)$, namely, $\langle q, k \rangle$ for each of the m rules r_q and the split $k \in [1..n-1]$. This gives $time = O(|V|n^2 \cdot mn)$. If the grammar G is fixed, then the time is $\Theta(n^3)$.

A tighter analysis would note that the bird would only answer q for rules $r_q = $ "$A_q \Rightarrow B_q C_q$", for which the left-hand side A_q is the nonterminal T_h specified in the instance. Let m_{T_h} be the number of such rules. Then the loop over nonterminals T_h and the loop over rules r_q would not require $|V|m$ time, but $\sum_{T_h \in V} m_{T_h} = m$. This gives a total time of $\Theta(n^3 m)$.

19.8.2 Given an instance $E = \{e_1, e_2, ..., e_n\}$ of the elephant problem, we map this to an instance $\langle X, Y \rangle$ of the LCS problem as follows. Each elephant will be distinct. Let $X = \langle x_1, ..., x_n \rangle$ be the elephants sorted by weight w_i, and let $Y = \langle y_1, ..., y_m \rangle$ be the same sorted by smartness s_j. A solution to LCS is a subsequence $Z = \langle z_1, ..., z_l \rangle$ that is common to both X and Y. Note that Z is a subset of elephants $S \subseteq E$ for which bigger is smarter. This is because Z is sorted both with respect to weight and with respect to intelligence. The only difference between these problems is that the cost (or success) of a LCS solution is simply the length of Z, while for the elephant problem it is the sum of the values of the elephants. Hence, for this to work, the LCS problem needs to be generalized to have weights on the letters. But this would not change the dynamic programming algorithm at all.

Chapter 20. Reductions and NP-Completeness

20.2.4 The first is easy. $InstanceMap(I_1)$ simply maps each instance $I_1 \in S_1 \subseteq S_2$ of P_1 to itself, I_1, which is a valid instance of P_2. The second is much harder, because $InstanceMap(I_2)$ must map each instance $I_2 \in S_2$ of P_2 to some instance I_1 within the restricted set S_1.

20.2.5 The running time $Time(Alg_{oracle})$ is measured as a function of its own input size, namely $\Theta(2^{|I_{oracle}|^{\frac{1}{3}}})$. But because $|I_{oracle}| = |I_{alg}|^2$, this same time is $\Theta(2^{|I_{alg}|^{2/3}})$, in terms of Alg_{alg}'s input size. The extra $O(|I_{alg}|^3)$ time for the mappings is not substantial. Hence, Alg_{alg}'s total running time is $\Theta(2^{n^{2/3}})$.

Similarly, if Alg_{oracle} runs in polynomial time, namely $Time(Alg_{oracle}) = \Theta(|I_{oracle}|^c)$, then so does Alg_{alg}, namely $Time(Alg_{alg}) = \Theta(|I_{alg}|^{2c} + |I_{alg}|^3)$, but note that the polynomal is a different one.

20.3.3

Step 5: Given a graph G_{COL} that we want to color, we construct an instance $\langle G_{Ind}, N_{Ind} \rangle = InstanceMap(G_{COL})$ to give to the independent set oracle as follows. As said, G_{Ind} will have a node for each pair $\langle u, c \rangle$ where u is a node of G_{COL} and c is one of the three colors. For each node $u \in G_{COL}$, we put a triangle of edges around $\langle u, red \rangle$, $\langle u, blue \rangle$, and $\langle u, green \rangle$. For each edge $\langle u, v \rangle \in G_{COL}$, we put three parallel edges between $\langle u, c \rangle$ and $\langle v, c \rangle$, for each color c. The size of the required independent set will be the number of nodes, $N_{Ind} = |V_{COL}|$, in the graph G_{COL}.

Step 6: Given an independent-set solution S_{Ind} to G_{Ind} of size $|V_{COL}|$, we construct a coloring S_{COL} for G_{COL} by coloring u with color c if node $\langle u, c \rangle$ is in the independent set.

Step 7: We now show that if S_{Ind} is a valid independent set of size $|V_{COL}|$, then S_{COL} is a valid 3-coloring. First we show that it is impossible for a node to be given more than one color, because the edge between $\langle u, c \rangle$ and $\langle u, c' \rangle$ prevents both of these nodes being in the independent set. Because the independent set is of size $|V_{COL}|$ and no node u appears more than once, it follows that every node u appears exactly once. Hence, every node u is given a color. Finally, we show that the nodes in the edge $\langle u, v \rangle \in G_{COL}$ cannot both have the color c, because the edge between $\langle u, c \rangle$ and $\langle v, c \rangle$ prevents both of these nodes from being in the independent set.

Step 8: Given a coloring S_{COL} for G_{COL}, we construct an independent set S_{Ind} for G_{Ind} of size $|V_{COL}|$ by putting node $\langle u, c \rangle$ in the independent set if u is colored c.

Step 9: We now show that if S_{COL} is a valid 3-coloring, then S_{Ind} is a valid independent set. We need to show that for each edge in G_{Ind}, both nodes are not in S_{Ind}. There is an edge between $\langle u, c \rangle$ and $\langle u, c' \rangle$, but u cannot have both colors c and c'. There is an edge between $\langle u, c \rangle$ and $\langle v, c \rangle$, but u and v cannot both have color c.

Chapter 22. Existential and Universal Quantifiers

22.0.2 1. $\forall x \, \exists y \; x + y = 5$ is true. Let x have an arbitrary real value, and let $y = 5 - x$. Then $x + y = 5$.

2. $\exists y \, \forall x \; x + y = 5$ is false. Let y have an arbitrary real value, and let $x = 6 - y$. Then $x + y \neq 5$.

3. $\forall x \, \exists y \; x \cdot y = 5$ is false. Let $x = 0$. Then y must be $\frac{5}{0}$, which is impossible.

4. $\exists y \, \forall x \; x \cdot y = 5$ is false. Let y have an arbitrary real value, and let $x = \frac{6}{y}$ if $y \neq 0$ and $x = 0$ if $y = 0$. Then $x \cdot y \neq 5$.

5. $\forall x \, \exists y \; x \cdot y = 0$ is true. Let x have an arbitrary real value, and let $y = 0$. Then $x \cdot y = 0$.

6. $\exists y \, \forall x \; x \cdot y = 0$ is true. Let $y = 0$, and let x have an arbitrary real value. Then $x \cdot y = 0$.

7. $[\forall x \, \exists y \; P(x, y)] \Rightarrow [\exists y \, \forall x \; P(x, y)]$ is false. Let $P(x, y) = [x + y = 5]$. Then, as already seen, the first is true and the second is false.

8. $[\forall x \exists y \, P(x, y)] \Leftarrow [\exists y \forall x \, P(x, y)]$ is true. Assume the right side is true. Let y_0 be the y for which $[\forall x \, P(x, y)]$ is true. We prove the left side as follows. Let x have an arbitrary real value, and let $y = y_0$. Then $P(x, y_0)$ is true.

9. Sorry, not provided.

Chapter 23. Time Complexity

23.1.1 The number of operations is $T = 24 \times 60 \times 60 \times 10^6 = 8.64 \times 10^{10}$. We have $n_1 = T^{1/4} = 542$, $n_2 = \log_2 T = \frac{\log T}{\log 2} = 36$.

23.1.4 1. We first prove that $g + h = \Theta(\max(g, h))$ as follows. $\max(g, h) \leq g + h$, assuming that both g and h are positive and $g + h \leq 2\max(g, h)$.

2. One can set k to absolutely minimize $f(n, k)$ by setting f's derivative wrt k equal to zero and solving for k. Sometimes this is hard. Because $f(n, k) = \Theta(\max(\frac{n}{\log k}, \frac{k}{\log k}))$ and we do not care about the multiplicative constant, let us instead set k in order to minimize $\max(\frac{n}{\log k}, \frac{k}{\log k})$. Observe that if k is very small, then the first term, being very big, dominates. Hence, we can make the whole expression smaller by increasing k. Similarly, if k is big, the second term dominates the expression, and we can decrease it by decreasing k. So for the optimal solution the two terms should be roughly the same. In this case $\frac{n}{\log k} = \frac{k}{\log k}$ gives $n = k$ and $f(n, k) = \frac{n+k}{\log k} = \frac{n}{\log n}$. This is (asymptotically) the best result, because decreasing k increases the first term and increasing k increases the second.

3. Sorry, not included.

23.2.1 1. $\exists A, \forall I, Works(Sorting, A, I)$. We know that there at least one algorithm, e.g., $A = $ merge sort, that works for every input instance I.

2. $\forall A, \exists I, \neg Works(Halting, A, I)$ We know that contrary statement is true. Every algorithm fails to work for at least one input instance I.

3. $\exists P, \forall A, \exists I, \neg Works(P, A, I)$

4. It says that every input has some algorithm that happens to output the right answer. It is true. Consider an arbitrary instance I. If on instance I, *Halting* happens to say yes, then let A be the algorithm that simply halts and says yes. Otherwise, let A be the algorithm that simply halts and says no. Either way, A works for this instance I.

5. It says that every algorithm correctly solves some problem. This is not true, because some algorithms do not halt on some input instances. We prove the complement $\exists A, \forall P, \exists I, \neg Works(P, A, I)$ as follows. Let A be an algorithm that runs forever on some instance I'. Let P be an arbitrary problem. Let I be an instance I' on which A does not halt. Note that $Works(P, A, I)$ is not true.

Chapter 24. Logarithms and Exponentials

24.0.1 $a^3 \times a^5 = a^8$, $3^a \times 5^a = 15^a$, $3^a + 5^a = ?$, $2^{5\log_4 n + 7} = [4^{0.5}]^{6\log_4 n} \times 2^7 = [4^{\log_4 n}]^3 \cdot 128 = 128n^3$, $n^{3/\log_2 n} = [2^{\log_2 n}]^{3/\log_2 n} = 2^3 = 8$.

Chapter 25. Asymptotic Growth

25.1.4 Exercise 25.0.2 proves that $3\log n << n$ for sufficiently big n. Hence, $n^2 \leq 3n^2 \log n \leq n \cdot n^2 = n^3$.

25.1.5 $3^{4n} >> 4^{3n} >> \frac{2^{0.001n}}{n^{100}} >> 100n^{100} >> \log^{1,000} n$.

25.2.2

1. $14n^9 + 5,000n^7 + 23n^2 \log n \in O(n^9)$: Let $c = 15$ and $n_0 = 100$. For all $n \geq 100$, We have $f(n) = 14n^9 + 5,000n^7 + 23n^2 \leq 14n^9 + \frac{n^2}{2}n^7 + \frac{n^6}{2}n^2 \log n \leq 14n^9 + n^9 = c \cdot g(n)$.

2. $2n^2 - 100n \in \Theta(n^2)$: Let $c_1 = 1$, $c_2 = 2$, and $n_0 = 100$. For all $n \geq 100$, $c_1 g(n) = 1n^2 = 2n^2 - n \cdot n \leq 2n^2 - 100n = f(n) \leq 2n^2 = c_2 g(n)$.

3. $14n^8 - 100n^6 \notin O(n^7)$: Let c and n_0 be arbitrary values given to us by some adversary. We then let $n = \max(10, c, n_0)$. Then we demonstrate that $f(n)$ is too big. Because $n \geq 10$, we have $100n^6 \leq n^8$. This gives $f(n) = 14n^8 - 100n^6 \geq 14n^8 - 1n^8 > n \cdot n^7 \geq c \cdot n^7$.

4. $14n^8 + 100n^6 \notin \Theta(n^9)$: Let c_1, c_2, and n_0 be arbitrary values given to us by some adversary. Let us make $n = \max(15/c_1, 11, n_0)$. Then we demonstrate that $f(n)$ is too small: $c_1 g(n) = c_1 n^9 = n \cdot c_1 n^8 \geq \frac{15}{c_1} \cdot c_1 n^8 = 14n^8 + n^8 = 14n^8 + n^2 \cdot n^6 \geq 14n^8 + (11)^2 \cdot n^6 > 14n^8 + 100n^6 = f(n)$.

5. $2^{n+1} \in O(2^n)$: Let $c = 2$ and $n_0 = 0$. For all $n \geq 0$, $f(n) = 2^{n+1} \leq 2 \times 2^n = c \times g(n)$.

6. $2^{2n} \notin O(2^n)$: Let c and n_0 be arbitrary values. Let $n = \max(1 + \log_2 c, n_0)$. Then we have that $f(n) = 2^{2n} = 2^n \cdot 2^n > c \cdot g(n)$.

25.2.8

1. $x = 7y^3 (\log_2 y)^{18} \in y^{3+o(1)} = [y^3, y^{3+\epsilon}]$. Solving this gives $y = x^{1/(3+o(1))}$.

2. Substituting in $y = x^{1/3+o(1)}$ gives $x = 7y^3 (\log_2 y)^{18} = 7y^3 (\log_2 x^{1/(3+o(1))})^{18} = \Theta(y^3 (\log_2 x)^{18})$. Solving this gives $y = \Theta\left(x^{\frac{1}{3}}/(\log x)^6\right)$.

Chapter 26. Adding-Made-Easy Approximations

26.2.1 His first such step takes him half an hour, his second a quarter, his third an eighth, ... for a total of only $\sum_{i=1}^{\infty} \frac{1}{2^i} = \frac{1}{2} + \frac{1}{4} + \frac{1}{8} + \frac{1}{16} + \cdots = 1$ hour. Given that he travels one kilometer at one kilometer an hour, this is reasonable.

26.2.4

1. The function $f(n) = 2^{2^{\lceil \log_2 n \rceil}}$ is $2^{\Omega(n)}$, because it is bounded between 2^n and 2^{2n}. Let $n = 2^k$. Then $\lceil \log_2 n \rceil = k$ and $f(n) = 2^{2^k} = 2^n$, but for $n' = n + 1$ we have $\lceil \log n' \rceil = k + 1$ and $f(n') = 2^{2^{k+1}} = 2^{2n}$.

2. We show $\sum_{i=1}^{n} f(i) \neq \Theta(f(n))$ as follows. With $n = 2^k$, both functions are more or less constant from $f(\frac{n}{2})$ to $f(n)$. Because they behave like arithmetic functions within this range, the adding-made-easy techniques give that $\sum_{i=1}^{n} f(i) = \Theta(n \cdot f(n))$ and not $\Theta(f(n))$.

3. We show that $f(n) = 2^{2^{\lfloor \log \log n \rfloor}} \in n^{\Theta(1)-1}$ by bounding it between $\sqrt{n}$ and n. Let $n = 2^{2^k}$. Then $\lfloor \log \log n \rfloor = k$ and $f(n) = 2^{2^k} = n$, but for $n' = n - 1$ we have $\lfloor \log \log n' \rfloor = k - 1$ and $f(n') = 2^{2^{k-1}} = \sqrt{n}$.

4. We show that $\sum_{i=1}^{n} f(i) \notin \Theta(n \cdot f(n))$ as follows. Again let $n = 2^{2^k}$, so that $f(n) = n$, yet every previous term is most $\sqrt{n}$. The total of $\sum_{i=1}^{n} f(i)$ then is at most $(n-1) \cdot \sqrt{n} + n$. Because the last term $f(n)$ is so much bigger than the previous ones, the total is not $\Theta(n \cdot f(n))$, which is $\Theta(n^2)$.

5. The function $f(n) = 2^{[\frac{1}{2}\cos(\pi \log_2 n)+1.5]\cdot n}$ is a geometric counterexample squeezed between 2^n and 2^{2n}, just as $f(n) = 2^{2^{\lceil \log_2 n \rceil}}$ is:

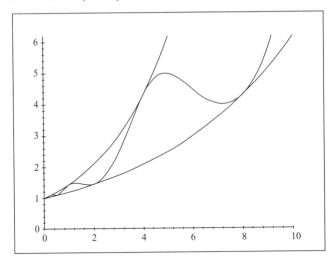

Chapter 27. Recurrence Relations

27.1.1 Examples:

$T(n)$	$\frac{\log a}{\log b}$	c	d vs -1	Dom.	Rule	Solution
$2T(\frac{n}{2}) + n$	$\frac{\log_2 2}{\log_2 2} = 1$	1	$0 >$	All	$\Theta(f(n)\log n)$	$\Theta(n\log n)$
$2T(\frac{n}{2}) + 1$	$\frac{\log_2 2}{\log_2 2} = 1$	0		Base	$\Theta(n^{\log a/\log b})$	$\Theta(n)$
$4T(\frac{n}{2}) + \Theta(n^3/\log^3 n)$	$\frac{\log_2 4}{\log_2 2} = 2$	3		Top	$\Theta(f(n))$	$\Theta(n^3/\log^3 n)$
$32T(\frac{n}{4}) + \Theta(\log n)$	$\frac{\log_2 32}{\log_2 4} = \frac{5}{2}$	0		Base	$\Theta(n^{\log a/\log b})$	$\Theta(n^{2.5})$
$27T(\frac{n}{3}) + \Theta(n^3 \log^4 n)$	$\frac{\log_3 27}{\log_3 3} = \frac{3}{1}$	3	$4 >$	All	$\Theta(f(n)\log(n))$	$\Theta(n^3 \log^5 n)$
$8T(\frac{n}{4}) + \Theta((n/\log n)^{1.5})$	$\frac{\log_2 8}{\log 4} = \frac{3}{2}$	$\frac{3}{2}$	$-1.5 <$	Base	$\Theta(n^{\log a/\log b})$	$\Theta(n^{1.5})$
$4T(\frac{n}{2}) + \Theta(n^2/\log n)$	$\frac{\log_2 4}{\log_2 2} = 2$	2	$-1 =$	Exercise 27.2.4 gives		

$$\Theta(n^c \cdot \log\log n) = \Theta(n^2 \log\log n)$$

27.2.1 Plugging $Fib(n) = \alpha^n$ into $Fib(n) = Fib(n-1) + Fib(n-2)$ gives that $\alpha^n = \alpha^{n-1} + \alpha^{n-2}$. Dividing through by α^{n-2} gives $\alpha^2 = \alpha + 1$. Solving this gives that either $\alpha = \frac{1+\sqrt{5}}{2}$ or $\alpha = \frac{1-\sqrt{5}}{2}$. Any linear combination of these two solutions will also be a valid solution, namely $Fib(n) = c_1 \cdot (\alpha_1)^n + c_2 \cdot (\alpha_2)^n$. Using the fact that $Fib(0) = 0$ and $Fib(1) = 1$ and solving for c_1 and c_2 gives that

$$Fib(n) = \frac{1}{\sqrt{5}}\left[\left[\frac{1+\sqrt{5}}{2}\right]^n - \left[\frac{1-\sqrt{5}}{2}\right]^n\right].$$

27.2.2 Unwinding:

1. $T(n) = T(n-1) + n$: Because $a = 1$ and $c > 1$, the table give $T(n) = \Theta(n \cdot f(n)) = \Theta(n^2)$. Unwinding gives $T(n) = n + T(n-1) = n + (n-1) + T(n-2) = n + (n-1) + (n-2) + T(n-3) = n + (n-1) + (n-2) + \cdots + (n-i+1) + T(n-i) = n + (n-1) + (n-2) + \cdots + 1 = \Theta(n^2)$.

2. $T(n) = 2 \cdot T(n-1) + 1$: Because $a = 2$, the table gives $T(n) = \Theta(a^{\frac{n}{b}}) = \Theta(2^n)$. Unwinding gives $T(n) = 1 + 2T(n-1) = 1 + 2 + 4T(n-2) = 1 + 2 + 4 + \cdots + 2^{i-1} + 2^i T(n-i) = 1 + 2 + 4 + \cdots + 2^{n-1} + 2^n = \Theta(2^n)$.

27.2.4 Suppose $f(n) = n^c \cdot \log^d n$ and $c = \frac{\log a}{\log b}$; then $T(n) = \Theta(\sum_{i=0}^{h} a^i f(n/b^i)) = \Theta(\sum_{i=0}^{h} a^i (n/b^i)^c \log^d(n/b^i)) = \Theta(n^c \cdot \sum_{i=0}^{h} (1)^i [\log(n/b^i)]^d)$. The expression n/b^i takes on the values $n, n/b, n/b^2, \ldots, 1$. Reversing this order gives $T(n) = \Theta(n^c \cdot \sum_{j=0}^{h} [\log(b^j)]^d) = \Theta(n^c \cdot \sum_{j=0}^{h} [j \log b]^d)$. Here $[\log b]^d$ is a constant that we can hide in the Theta. This gives $T(n) = \Theta(n^c \cdot \sum_{j=0}^{h} j^d)$. The adding-made-easy approximations state that this sum is arithmetic as long as $d > -1$. In this case, the total is $T(n) = \Theta(n^c \cdot h \cdot h^d) = \Theta(n^c \cdot \log^{d+1} n) = \Theta(f(n) \log n)$. If $d = -1$, then we get the harmonic sum $T(n) = \Theta(n^c \cdot \sum_{j=0}^{h} \frac{1}{j}) = \Theta(n^c \cdot \log h) = \Theta(n^c \log \log n)$. If $d < -1$, then the sum has a bounded tail, giving $T(n) = \Theta(n^c \cdot \Theta(1)) = \Theta(n^{\log a/\log b})$.

CONCLUSION

The overall goal of this entire text has been to teach skills in abstract thinking. I hope that it has been fruitful for you. Good luck at applying these skills to new problems that arise in other courses and in the workplace.

We say goodbye to our friends.

INDEX